The National Hockey League,
1917–1967

ALSO BY MARSHALL D. WRIGHT
AND FROM MCFARLAND

*The South Atlantic League, 1904–1963:
A Year-by-Year Statistical History* (2009)

*The Eastern League in Baseball:
A Statistical History, 1923–2005* (2007)

The Texas League in Baseball, 1888–1958 (2004)

The Southern Association in Baseball, 1885–1961 (2002)

*The National Association of Base Ball
Players, 1857–1870* (2000)

*The International League: Year-by-Year
Statistics, 1884–1953* (1998; softcover 2005)

*The American Association: Year-by-Year Statistics
for the Baseball Minor League, 1902–1952* (1997)

*Nineteenth Century Baseball: Year-by-Year
Statistics for the Major League Teams,
1871 through 1900* (1996; softcover 2004)

The National Hockey League, 1917–1967

A Year-by-Year Statistical History

MARSHALL D. WRIGHT

McFarland & Company, Inc., Publishers
Jefferson, North Carolina, and London

LIBRARY OF CONGRESS CATALOGUING-IN-PUBLICATION DATA

Wright, Marshall D.
　　The National Hockey League, 1917–1967 : a year-by-year statistical history / Marshall D. Wright.
　　　　p.　　cm.
　　Includes bibliographical references and index.

　　ISBN 978-0-7864-4444-1
　　softcover : 50# alkaline paper ∞

　　1. National Hockey League — History — 20th century.
2. Hockey teams — History — 20th century. I. Title.
GV847.8.N3W75　2010
796.962'64090904 — dc22　　　　　　　　　　2010026451

British Library cataloguing data are available

©2010 Marshall D. Wright. All rights reserved

No part of this book may be reproduced or transmitted in any form or by any means, electronic or mechanical, including photocopying or recording, or by any information storage and retrieval system, without permission in writing from the publisher.

On the cover: The Toronto Maple Leafs score against the Detroit Red Wings in the 1942 Stanley Cup Playoffs (Conn Smythe Fonds); "Original Six" patch from author's collection

Manufactured in the United States of America

McFarland & Company, Inc., Publishers
　Box 611, Jefferson, North Carolina 28640
　　www.mcfarlandpub.com

To Jay–
friend and teammate

Acknowledgments

Putting together a book is simply not a one-person job. To do the job right, many people need to be involved. I gratefully acknowledge all who helped along the way, especially the following.

First, I would like to thank my good friend Gary Austin — a fellow hockey enthusiast who I have known for over thirty years. Gary generously gave of his time, providing research on early Detroit hockey teams, ferreting out facts and confirming my suspicions about inconsistent data and provided the rare photo of the Original Six patch portrayed on the cover.

Also, I would like to acknowledge my friends and colleagues at B&N — especially Paul, Lisa and Carl. Our discussions through the years on many topics have always been invigorating, causing me to ponder the many facets of life. However, it was our discussions on hockey that rekindled my interest in the sport and made this book possible. Thank you all very much.

Next, my professional colleagues in SIHR need a special thank you — specifically the intrepid researchers who put together the magnificent *Total Hockey* tomes. Without both editions, that are each packed with stats and stories, a book like mine would not have been possible. Special mention should be given to the folks that supplied a significant portion of the articles cited: Bob Duff, Stan Fischler, Brian McFarlane and Eric Zweig. Thank you all. Also thanks to Marty Friedrich for providing info on games played data.

Finally, the biggest debt of gratitude goes to my family — my wife Jane, son Denny, father Robert, mother Joan and sister Karen. Each one of the above has never failed to encourage me to embark on these projects, knowing full well the commitment of time each one takes — and the time it takes away from my family.

As a last word, I would like to mention my friend Jay Alverson. We grew up together, discovered hockey at the same time, and enjoyed playing the game first in the driveway, later in the rink. Though he was taken from us too soon — memories of him remain fresh in my mind — and they always will.

Table of Contents

Acknowledgments vi

Introduction 1

Prelude: Professional Antecedents 5

1917–18 Exclusionary Tactics	9	
1918–19 Influenza	14	
1919–20 Joe Malone	19	
1920–21 Innovative Rival	24	
1921–22 Broadbent's Streak	29	
1922–23 Race to the Top	34	
1923–24 Trophy	39	
1924–25 Striking Southward	44	
1925–26 Georges Vezina	51	
1926–27 Sole Survivor	58	
1927–28 The Skipper Steps In	67	
1928–29 Shutout	76	
1929–30 Forward Pass	85	
1930–31 Howie Morenz	94	
1931–32 Palace	104	
1932–33 Tiebreaker	113	
1933–34 Cheap Shot	123	
1934–35 Penalty Shot	133	
1935–36 Sudden Death Overtime	143	
1936–37 Total Goal Series	152	
1937–38 All-American	162	
1938–39 Frank Brimsek	171	
1939–40 New York Rangers	180	
1940–41 Boston Bruins	189	
1941–42 The Hard Way	198	
1942–43 "The Puck Goes Inski"	207	
1943–44 Disparity	215	
1944–45 Maurice Richard	224	
1945–46 Nerves	232	
1946–47 Bill Durnan	240	
1947–48 Two Men Out	248	
1948–49 Individual Accolades	256	
1949–50 Linemates	264	
1950–51 A Moment in Time	273	
1951–52 Detroit Red Wings	282	
1952–53 Original Seven	290	
1953–54 Gordie Howe	299	
1954–55 Riot	308	
1955–56 Montreal Canadiens	317	
1956–57 Jacques Plante	326	
1957–58 Pioneer	334	

1958–59 Dynamic Duo	343	**1963–64** A League of Their Own	386
1959–60 The Drive for Five	351		
1960–61 Banana Blade	359	**1964–65** Unprotected	395
1961–62 Glenn Hall	368	**1965–66** Bobby Hull	404
1962–63 Toronto Maple Leafs	377	**1966–67** Chicago Blackhawks	413

Epilogue: The Great Expansion 423
Appendix: Year-by-Year Totals 427
Bibliography 429
Index 433

Introduction

In the 1970s, new types of sports statistical reference books began to be compiled, embracing major league baseball first, then football and finally basketball. These tomes, called the *Sports Encyclopedia: Baseball; ... Football;* and *... Basketball,* arranged their data in a new and pleasing format. Instead of mere alphabetical listings of players and their stats, these new reference tools arranged the stats by year and team, giving fans a chance to peruse the numbers — lingering over the statistical stories of the sport's strongest and weakest entries. As an ardent hockey fan, I eagerly awaited a potential *Sports Encyclopedia: Hockey* — covering the teams of the National Hockey League. This has been a wait that has yet to be fulfilled — until now.

Although the publishers of the Sports Encyclopedia series never produced a hockey version, other sources of similarly arranged data emerged over the years. First, in the early 1980s, Stan and Shirley Fischler wrote *The Hockey Encyclopedia* — a fine reference work, which combined an alphabetical sort of players and team statistical listings. However, the team stat pages were incomplete, as not all of a team's players were listed. In the 1990s, another excellent hockey tome was published — *Total Hockey.* Still, this massive work, complete as it was, did not contain team listings with stats. Later, as the 21st century dawned, several web sites popped up which addressed these concerns. These sites — such as Hockeydb, Hockey-Reference and Society of International Hockey Research (SIHR) — arranged all the pertinent data in a mostly pleasing manner. However — as thorough as they are — these websites can't duplicate the feel of a printed book, a volume which one can hold and enjoy. This is the primary reason I decided to create this particular kind of hockey reference book.

The National Hockey League has been around for nearly 100 years. Founded in the fall of 1917, the league has hosted dozens of teams and thousands of players. Encompassing all of them in a manageably sized book seemed overwhelming, so I decided to divide the story at a logical point. For many years, the NHL cruised along with the same six members—the so-called "Original Six." In 1967, this coterie of clubs was intruded upon by a wave of expansion, doubling the size of the circuit overnight. This event seems a logical dividing point, thus the present work will cover the first fifty years of the NHL.

The arrangement is by one chapter—for each of the first fifty years of the league. Prefacing each section, an essay discusses a particular event, player or theme salient to that particular season. Emphasis is placed on the many rule changes that affected the game on the ice, pioneers of the sport and great games and playoff series.

Following each essay, team and individual statistics are tabulated as follows. First, the standings are listed with the teams in point order. Then, the top ten scoring and goaltending leaders are listed in points and goals against average order, respectively. Also, top-five individual accomplishments are listed in the following scoring and goaltending categories: goals, assists, penalty minutes and shutouts.

Next follows the individual team listings for each particular season. The teams are arranged in standings order, noting wins, losses and ties; point total, placement (i.e., 1st, 2nd, etc.) and coach names. Then, each player is listed—in point order. For each player, the statistics noted are: position, games played, goals, assists, points and penalty minutes. In addition, since the NHL greatly emphasizes the playoffs, this same group of statistics is included for participating teams.

After the player listing, each club's goaltenders are listed in goals against average (GAA) order. Stats included are games played, minutes, goals allowed, shutouts and GAA. In addition, like the players, playoff stats for these categories are also included. For both players and goalies, league leaders are presented in bold type.

During each NHL season, several players played for more than one team. This is marked in the tables with a number in parentheses (1-2, 2-2, etc.) following the player's or goaltender's name, indicating if it was their first or second club. Occasionally, a traded player leads the league in a particular statistical category. In these cases, the number is marked with an asterisk and boldface type.

In the modern NHL, in addition to these basic numbers, many other statistics are compiled. For instance, for the players, power play and short-handed goals, shots on goal and shooting percentage are tabulated. For goaltenders, saves, save percentage, wins, losses and ties are compiled. However in the first 50 years of the NHL, only the basic stats were counted. So, logically, those are the only ones included in this book. However, to honor the work of intrepid hockey researchers, I have made a couple of exceptions.

Going back through the years, hockey historians have unearthed several statistical facts. Among them are individual goaltender's wins, losses and ties. Originally, these stats were not tracked for the simple reason that most goalies played in every game. Ergo, the netminder's record would mirror his team's record. As platooning became more prevalent, a goalie's won-loss-tie record became more important. As part of the same issue, researchers have determined goalie minutes. Since these seem like important parts of the puzzle, both won-loss-tie and minutes played are included in the goaltender statistics portion, the former listed in parentheses.

Originally, when a goaltender's GAA was compiled, it was done in a very basic way: goals allowed divided by games played. Since most goalies played complete games, this was a very logical way to compile the number. However, if a netminder played in only a portion of a game, the GAA could become badly skewed. Also, if the goaltender played in overtime contests — as was prevalent in the first quarter-century of the NHL — this was not originally reflected in the GAA. In addition, beginning in the 1950s, empty net goals began to be tabulated — a marker that was originally counted as a goal allowed. (These empty net goals are marked in parentheses in the tables.)

To level the ice surface, most hockey researchers have gone back and retroactively compiled early NHL GAAs using the modern formula: goals allowed times 60, divided by minutes played. In addition, empty net goals have been thrown out. I have also used these updated stats in this book. As a result of this tweaking, league GAA leaders have been shuffled from their original order, in some cases, resulting in a new league leader.

In the early days of the NHL, the battle for the sport's supreme glory, the Stanley Cup, was not exclusive to the league. Playing alongside the NHL in its first nine campaigns were two rival major leagues: the Pacific Coast Hockey Association (PCHA), and the Western Canada Hockey League (WCHL). The PCHA pitted its winner against the NHL's best through the spring of 1924, while the WCHL — later called the Western Hockey League — continued tilting with its eastern brethren through 1926. Early hockey reference sources lump all playoff stats, including those against the rival leagues, into one grouping. Later sources break these stats into separate listings — one for the NHL-only playoffs, and another for the playoffs with the other leagues. To give a better idea of the whole playoff picture, I have recombined the two groupings into one stat line. However, until 1926, the headings for the players and goaltenders are named "Postseason" rather than "Playoffs," indicating that the numbers reflect results from interleague action.

Following the end of the team listings is a game-by-game chronicle of the playoffs, by round. In the early years of the league, when the NHL contested other leagues for the Cup, those results are also included. Each round is listed "Series A, B," etc., with each season's highest letter being the league finals. This follows modern nomenclature, differing somewhat from the original records, which sometimes label each round as quarterfinals, semifinals and finals.

At the end of each chapter, I have included a team statistics table. Here are listed each club with the following numbers: games, goals, assists, scoring points (goals + assists), penalty minutes, goals allowed and shutouts. Also included in the same table is the "per game" average for goals, assists, penalty minutes and goals against — particularly interesting and useful numbers. Following this table are listed the individual trophy winners and all-star teams.

Also included is an appendix consisting of a table a year-by-year list of league totals. From this appendix, one can easily tell the most prolific, stingy and penalized years in the first 50 years of the NHL.

The statistical information in this book comes from the variety of sources listed above. In those sources, the statistics for the NHL have been well-chronicled. However, it doesn't mean they all agree. In some instances, some very basic facts, such as team goals, goals allowed and penalty minutes, don't match. In those cases, the most logical source was utilized. For the essay portions of the volume, I have relied on the many articles and books written about the NHL and its players through the years — most notably the work of the intrepid researchers of SIHR.

As this book was assembled, the real story of the NHL's first 50 years unfolded through its statistics. Scoring trends in the game — usually because of a significant rule change — directly affected seasons and careers. Cherished myths about certain records, and the stories behind them, were washed away by the numbers. In short, even for an ardent hockey fan like myself, looking at the overall picture changed my view of the game as it once was played.

To be truthful, this book is at least partially the result of a selfish interest of mine. I simply wanted a companion volume to my well-thumbed *Sports Encyclopedia* books from long ago. It took a while, but the journey and the result are satisfying, and I hope this book is just as enjoyable for the reader. Please, read on, and take a trip through the NHL of yesterday through its statistics and the stories behind the numbers.

Prelude: Professional Antecedents

Like baseball, the sport of ice hockey has its own murky beginning. References to the roots of hockey date back to the early 19th century, with one of the most reliable references coming from an Ontario army officer in the 1840s, who claimed to play "hockey on ice." It was called by different names at first, like "ice hurley" or "ice polo," the latter especially enjoying popularity in the 1880s in the Maritimes. This early manifestation of ice hockey modeled itself after lacrosse, with forward passing allowed up and down the ice. Completing the resemblance, offensive players sported lacrosse sticks.

Meanwhile, further west and about ten years earlier, a similar — yet different — game was emerging in the Montreal area. Called "hockey" this game was based on rugby, with no forward passing allowed. Started largely at McGill University, the new rules substituted a "puck"— a flat disk — for roller polo's ball, largely to keep the game on the ice and not into the spectators. This was the version of the game that eventually supplanted ice polo.

In 1886, an organization was formed to govern this version of the new sport. Called the Amateur Hockey Association of Canada, the Montreal-based group quickly codified the rules, setting stringent requirements for equipment and conduct on the ice. Some of the rules set down in the 1880s continue to be used today — such as the size of the puck (one inch thick, three inches wide). Others have evolved over time. For instance, in the early days of the AHAC, the goal consisted of a pair pipes only; no net was used.

In 1887 the AHAC formed a nascent league. Consisting of teams in the Montreal area, the group played a tournament in January, which was won by the Montreal Crystals. Over the next few years, teams from Quebec and Ottawa joined the mix. Until the turn of the century, this amateur league continued to showcase the best hockey in the land, in a series of compact, eight-game campaigns. The reason for the brevity was due to the whims of the weather — the days of artificial ice surfaces were yet to come.

During the final decade of the 19th century, hockey players had a new prize at the top of the championship pyramid. In 1893, government official Lord Stanley donated a silver cup to be given the best hockey club. Not exclusively the domain of the AHAC, the Stanley Cup, as it came to be known, could be handed out to any club that vanquished the current champion in a challenge series.

Although hockey has distinctive Canadian roots, nevertheless the sports first professional league emerged south of the border. In 1901-02, a three-team loop called the Western Pennsylvania Hockey League operated in Pittsburgh. Despite operating in the United States, the composition of the professional teams was Canadian, attracted to the south by the artificial ice plants in Pittsburgh, which allowed an earlier start of the season. Over the course of the 14-game campaign, the Keystones sported the best record (9–5), led by Art Sixsmith and Bert Morrison, who netted 22 goals between them. (Following the precedent of the amateur circuits, the WPHL used the point system to determine champions, with the victor in each contest receiving two points, and a tie gaining each participant one point. With some adjustment, this would become the system followed through the years to the present day.)

Over the next few years, other professional leagues emerged, this time featuring teams from Canada. First on the block was the International Professional Hockey League, which began play in 1904. Three years later, the Ontario Professional Hockey League (OPHL) came into existence, giving the city of Toronto its first pro club. Before the end of the decade, other pro leagues sprang up further west in Manitoba and Alberta. Although the life of most of these organizations was brief, they helped set the foundation of today's pro game.

In 1909, hockey leagues in eastern Canada faced with a new rival. Formed largely to satisfy the whims of wealthy men with Stanley Cup aspirations and located in the small Ontario towns of Renfrew and Cobalt, the new league enticed several members of the Eastern Canada Amateur Association to flesh out the organization. Called the National Hockey Association, the circuit consisted of the aforementioned Renfrew and Cobalt clubs, a team from Haileybury, and former ECAA members Ottawa, Montreal Wanderers and Shamrocks. At the last minute, another Montreal club was added to the mix. With a roster of French-Canadian players, the new club was called the Canadiens. Stung by the defections, the ECAA reformed as the Canada Hockey

Association and gamely placed teams in Ottawa and Montreal, going head-to-head with their rivals. However, just before the season began, the CHA was dealt a blow that was hard to overcome, as Cyclone Taylor — regarded as the sport's best player — signed a contract to play for the NHA's Renfrew club. Because of the competition, the CHA had no choice but fold, which it did on January 15, 1910.

Meanwhile, the NHA completed its first season while remaining intact, awarding the championship to the Montreal Wanderers (11–1). Renfrew, despite Taylor's presence, finished third with an 8–3 mark. Finishing dead last were the Canadiens (2–10), who enjoyed the presence (at least for half the season) of Newsy Lalonde, who netted 16 markers, then added 22 for his new team, Renfrew. Over the long run, though finishing last, the Canadiens proved to be the longest-living team from the NHA's inaugural season, as they just finished celebrating their 100th year of operation — a remarkable feat.

Over the next few years, the NHA solidified its position as the dominant pro hockey league in eastern Canada. Adding teams from Quebec City and Toronto, the league was able to increase its schedule to 24 games by the 1915-16 season. When Canada's involvement in World War I threatened to disrupt the game the following year, the league adapted. In 1916, several players joined the 228th Battalion, based in Toronto — so many so that the NHA allowed them to play as a team. When the unit was shipped overseas, the loop played gamely on with the remaining teams. However, the manner in which they did so caused an irreparable rift which led to the demise of the circuit.

When the 228th was sent to Europe, the NHA was left with an unwieldly five-team circuit. The owner of the other Toronto club, Eddie Livingstone, wanted the rest of the schedule played as a round-robin tournament. The other team owners had a different solution in mind. They dropped Livingstone's Blueshirt club, evening the number of teams and then played out the schedule. In addition, all of the Blueshirt players were divvied up among the remaining four members. On the surface, this looked like a mean and petty vendetta against one of their own. However, Livingstone was thoroughly disliked by the hockey rulers, dating back to an event two years earlier. In 1915, Livingstone gained controlling interest in two NHA teams, both in Toronto. Ordered to sell one of them, he instead disbanded the club (the Shamrocks), transferring all of the players to the Blueshirts.

Though after the 1916-17 season the NHA was only a four-team league, the other owners were glad to be rid of Livingstone. When he tried to bully his way back into the league, the other owners took the next logical step and simply shut him out.

1917-1918

Exclusionary Tactics

On November 17, 1917, the four remaining team owners in the National Hockey Association (league consisted of the Montreal Canadiens and Wanderers, the Ottawa Senators and Quebec Bulldogs, plus a new entry from Toronto) met in Montreal's Windsor Hotel. After emerging from behind closed doors, it soon became evident what had taken place: A new hockey league had been formed, signifying the end of the NHA, although the formal announcement wasn't made until nine days later. Left out was one key member of the old league—the recalcitrant owner of the Toronto Blueshirts, Eddie Livingstone.

Constantly arguing over every little point, Livingstone was not a friend of other hockey owners. As a matter of fact, most despised him. Thus, keeping Livingstone out of the new league was a deliberate act. Explaining the committee's action to reporter Elmer Ferguson, Canadiens owner George Kennedy stated: "We formed a new hockey league called the National Hockey League [NHL], and its just like the National Hockey Association with one exception. We haven't invited Eddie Livingston to be part of the new set-up."

Before the puck dropped on the inaugural season, the Quebec Bulldogs, citing financial problems, decided to sit out the season, leaving only four clubs to take the ice. The first game in the NHL was played on December 19, 1917, as the Montreal Wanderers outlasted the Toronto Arenas, 10–9. Alas for the Wanderers, the glory was short-lived. After three lopsided losses, (11–2, 6–3 and 9–2), the team's Westmount Arena burned to the ground, on January 2, causing the team to fold two days later. Although the Canadiens' also lost their home rink with the loss of Westmount, the team decided to continue. It was a sound decision, as the club triumphed (10–4, 20) over the first half of the schedule.

Over a brief eight-game second-half schedule, Montreal slipped to last, allowing Toronto (5–3, 10) to claim the half-season crown. Overall, Montreal and Toronto (13–9, 26) claimed the best record, both eight points to the better of Ottawa. In the post-season playoffs, pitting each half's victors against one another, Toronto dusted the Canadiens 7–3 in the first game before bowing in the second, 4–3. Thus, in the total-goal series, the Arenas came out on top, ten goals to seven.

The NHL's first scoring champion was Montreal's Joe Malone, on loan from the inactive Quebec club. In a scoring blitz, he netted 44 goals in only 20 games, a blistering 2.2 markers per game average, netting five in a game on three separate occasions. Assists were originally not tabulated, but modern research has determined who received helpers during the first campaign. Reg Noble (Toronto), Cy Denneny (Ottawa) and Harry Cameron (Toronto) finished tied with 10 assists each. Malone received four assists, giving him 48 points and the circuit's first scoring championship. In goal, Canadiens' Georges Vezina (3.93) finished with the lowest GAA, nearly a full tally below the runner-up. He also posted one of the league's two shutouts, matched by Ottawa's Clint Benedict. Malone's total goal total held up for many years and his goals-per-game average has never been equalled. Conversely, Vezina's 3.93 mark remains the highest winning GAA to date. Also of note, Montreal tough guy Joe Hall was penalized the most minutes (100).

After the season, Toronto faced Vancouver to decide the Stanley Cup. Playing in a rival big league, the Pacific Coast Hockey Association, Vancouver proved to be an even match for the Arenas on Toronto's home ice, where all the contests were held. The two clubs split the first two contests, before Toronto took the series lead with a 6–3 win in game three. Vancouver evened the score with an 8–1 trouncing, before the Arenas edged the Millionaires, 2–1, in the deciding fifth game to claim the Cup. (The seesaw nature of the series could be explained by the fact that the two leagues had different rules. The PCHA allowed forward passing, and had a seventh skater [rover] on the ice. Games 2 and 4, both Vancouver wins, were played using these rules.) In the overall playoffs, Toronto's Harry Mummery led all scorers with eight goals and 11 points, while teammate Ken Randall added a league-best seven assists. Arenas' netminder Hap Holmes (4.00) posted the lowest average.

Although the NHL was set up largely to dispense with the meddlings of one man, it was built on a firm enough foundation to withstand even the loss of one of its few core members. As for Livingstone, Montreal Wanderers owner Sam Lichtenhein, again to Ferguson, said it best: "He has his team, and we wish him well. The only problem is he's playing in a one-team league."

STANDINGS

TEAM	GP	W	L	T	PTS	GF	GA
MONTREAL (C)	22	13	9	0	26	115	84
TORONTO	22	13	9	0	26	108	109
OTTAWA	22	9	13	0	18	102	114
MONTREAL (W)*	6	1	5	0	2	17	35

*Wanderers disbanded January 4; two losses were claimed as forfeit wins by Montreal and Toronto.

LEADERS

PLAYER	TM	GP	G	A	PTS	PIM
Joe Malone	M(C)	20	44	4	48	30
Cy Denneny	OTT	20	36	10	46	80
Reg Noble	TOR	20	30	10	40	35
Newsy Lalonde	M(C)	14	23	7	30	51
Corbett Denneny	TOR	21	20	9	29	14
Harry Cameron	TOR	21	17	10	27	28
Didier Pitre	M(C)	20	17	6	23	29
Eddie Gerard	OTT	20	13	7	20	26
Three tied with					19	

GOALS
Malone, M(C)	44
Cy Denneny, OTT	36
Noble, TOR	30
Lalonde, M(C)	23
Co. Denneny, TOR	20

ASSISTS
Noble, TOR	10
Cameron, TOR	10
Cy Denneny, OTT	10
Co. Denneny, TOR	9
Meeking, TOR	9

GOALTENDER	TM	GP	MIN	GA	SH	GAA
Georges Vezina	M(C)	21	1282	84	1	3.93
Hap Holmes	TOR	16	965	76	0	4.73
Clint Benedict	OTT	22	1337	114	1	5.12

PENALTY MINUTES
Hall, M(C)	100
Randall, TOR	96
Cy Denneny, OTT	80
Crawford, O-T	66
Hyland, M(W)-O	65

SHUTOUTS
Benedict, OTT	1
Vezina, M(C)	1

MONTREAL 13-9-0   26   1st   George Kennedy
Canadiens

		REGULAR SEASON					POSTSEASON				
PLAYER	POS	GP	G	A	PTS	PIM	GP	G	A	PTS	PIM
Joe Malone	L	20	44	4	48	30	2	1	0	1	3
Newsy Lalonde	C	14	23	7	30	51	2	4	2	6	17
Didier Pitre	R	20	17	6	23	29	2	0	1	1	13
Bert Corbeau	D	20	8	8	16	41	2	1	1	2	11
Joe Hall	D	21	8	7	15	100	2	0	1	1	12
Jack McDonald (2-2)	L	8	9	1	10	12	2	1	0	1	0
Billy Coutu	D	20	2	2	4	49	2	0	0	0	3
Louis Berlinquette	F	20	2	1	3	12	2	0	0	0	0
Jack Laviolette	D	18	2	1	3	6	2	0	0	0	0
Billy Bell (2-2)	C	6	0	0	0	6					
Evariste Payer	C	1	0	0	0	0					
Georges Vezina	G	21	0	0	0	0	2	0	0	0	0

	REGULAR SEASON					POSTSEASON				
GOALTENDER	GP	MIN	GA	SH	GAA	GP	MIN	GA	SH	GAA
Georges Vezina (12-9-0)	21	1282	84	1	3.93	2	120	10	0	5.00

TORONTO 13-9-0 26 2nd Dick Carroll
Arenas

		REGULAR SEASON					POSTSEASON				
PLAYER	POS	GP	G	A	PTS	PIM	GP	G	A	PTS	PIM
Reg Noble	C	20	30	10	40	35	7	3	2	5	9
Corbett Denneny	C	21	20	9	29	14	7	3	1	4	6
Harry Cameron	D	21	17	10	27	28	7	4	3	7	0
Harry Meeking	L	21	10	9	19	28	7	4	2	6	6
Alf Skinner	R	20	13	5	18	28	7	8	3	11	9
Ken Randall	D	21	12	2	14	96	7	2	1	3	12
Harry Mummery	D	18	3	3	6	41	7	1	7	8	17
Rusty Crawford (2-2)	L	8	1	2	3	51	2	2	1	3	9
Jack Coughlin	R	5	2	0	2	3					
Jack Adams	C	8	0	0	0	31	2	0	0	0	6
Jack Marks (2-2)	D	5	0	0	0	0					
Hap Holmes	G	16	0	0	0	0	7	0	0	0	0
Arthur Brooks	G	4	0	0	0	0					
Sammy Hebert	G	2	0	0	0	0					

	REGULAR SEASON					POSTSEASON				
GOALTENDER	GP	MIN	GA	SH	GAA	GP	MIN	GA	SH	GAA
Hap Holmes (9-7-0)	16	965	76	0	4.73	7	420	28	0	4.00
Arthur Brooks (2-2-0)	4	220	23	0	6.27					
Sammy Hebert (1-0-0)	2	80	10	0	7.50					

OTTAWA 9-13-0 18 3rd Eddie Gerard
Senators

		REGULAR SEASON					POSTSEASON
PLAYER	POS	GP	G	A	PTS	PIM	no postseason play
Cy Denneny	L	20	36	10	46	80	
Eddie Gerard	D	20	13	7	20	26	
Jack Darragh	R	18	14	5	19	26	
Frank Nighbor	C	10	11	8	19	6	
Georges Boucher	D	21	9	8	17	46	
Hamby Shore	D	18	3	8	11	51	
Harry Hyland (2-2)	R	13	8	1	9	59	
Dave Ritchie (2-2)	D	14	4	1	5	18	
Rusty Crawford (1-2)	L	11	2	2	4	15	
Eddie Lowrey	F	12	2	1	3	3	
Morley Bruce	D	7	0	0	0	0	
Horace Merrill	D	3	0	0	0	3	
Clint Benedict	G	22	0	0	0	0	

	REGULAR SEASON					POSTSEASON
GOALTENDER	GP	MIN	GA	SH	GAA	no postseason play
Clint Benedict (9-13-0)	22	1337	114	1	5.12	

1917-1918

MONTREAL   1-3-0   2   —   Art Ross
Wanderers

		REGULAR SEASON					*POSTSEASON*
PLAYER	*POS*	*GP*	*G*	*A*	*PTS*	*PIM*	*no posteason play*
Harry Hyland (1–2)	R	4	6	1	7	6	
Dave Ritchie (1–2)	D	4	5	2	7	3	
Jack McDonald (1–2)	L	4	3	1	4	3	
Phil Stevens	C	4	1	0	1	3	
Art Ross	D	3	1	0	1	12	
Billy Bell (1–2)	C	2	1	0	1	0	
George O'Grady	D	4	0	0	0	0	
Gerry Geran	C	4	0	0	0	0	
Jack Marks (1–2)	D	1	0	0	0	0	
Raymond Skilton	D	1	0	0	0	0	
Ken Thompson	F	1	0	0	0	0	
Bert Lindsay	G	4	0	0	0	0	

		REGULAR SEASON					*POSTSEASON*
GOALTENDER		*GP*	*MIN*	*GA*	*SH*	*GAA*	*no posteason play*
Bert Lindsay	(1-3-0)	4	240	35	0	8.75	

TEAM TOTALS

								Per Game			
TEAM	*GP*	*G*	*A*	*P*	*PIM*	*GA*	*SH*	*G*	*A*	*PIM*	*GA*
Montreal (C)	21	**115**	37	152	336	84	1	**5.48**	1.76	16.00	**4.00**
Toronto	21	108	50	**158**	**355**	109	0	5.14	**2.38**	**16.90**	5.19
Ottawa	22	102	**51**	153	333	114	1	4.64	2.32	15.14	5.18
Montreal (W)	4	17	4	21	27	35	0	4.25	1.00	6.75	8.75
	68	342	142	484	1051	342	2	5.03	2.09	15.45	5.03

PLAYOFFS

SERIES "A"
Toronto 7, Montreal (C) 3
Montreal (C) 4, Toronto 3

TORONTO WINS
TOTAL GOAL SERIES, 10–7

STANLEY CUP (PCHA)
Toronto 5, Vancouver 3
Vancouver 6, Toronto 4
Toronto 6, Vancouver 3
Vancouver 8, Toronto 1
Toronto 2, Vancouver 1

TORONTO WINS
STANLEY CUP, 3–2

1918-1919
Influenza

As the National Hockey League was about to embark on its second season, a certain guarded optimism surrounded league members. True, one of the four failed to finish the opening season, but the three remaining active members decided to make a go of it in the fall of 1918, while the Quebec franchise continued to lay dormant. Little did the trio realize that optimism would turn to grief the following spring.

The NHL's second season began December 21, as Ottawa defeated Montreal 5-2. Despite the opening night loss, Montreal proved to be the team to beat over the first half of the split schedule, as the Canadiens (7-3, 14) finished four points up on runner-up Ottawa. Toronto, with only three wins, finished last, although one of the victories — an 11-3 pasting of the Canadiens — was certainly satisfying.

While the NHL meandered through its first month, a scourge was taking hold of North America. A particularly virulent form of influenza was affecting much of the general population, with often fatal results. From the army camps in the Northeast, the pandemic spread westward. By March 1919, it was firmly lodged in the Pacific Northwest. Here the epidemic would have a direct impact on the game itself.

On January 25, 1919, the second half of the NHL season got underway, as Ottawa's Clint Benedict blanked the Canadiens, 1-0. Over the second half of the campaign, Montreal — missing the services of Joe Malone, who played in only home games — faltered, allowing the Senators to pick up the slack. In the final eight games of the regular season, Ottawa went 7-1 (14), winning three of the contests in overtime. The Canadiens and Arenas finished far astern, with only five wins between them.

The NHL's top goal scorers both graced Montreal's roster as Newsy

Lalonde and Odie Cleghorn netted 22 apiece. Lalonde also added a circuit-best 10 helpers to capture the scoring title. In net, Ottawa's Clint Benedict posted the lowest goals against average (2.76) and most shutouts (2). Meanwhile, Montreal's tough guy, Joe Hall, accumulated the most penalty minutes (89).

In the playoffs, pitting both half-season winners, Montreal prevailed, dusting Ottawa four games to one in the best-of-seven format. Once completed, the Canadiens then journeyed west to contest the PCHA champion Seattle Metropolitans for the Stanley Cup. While en route, an ominous sign of trouble appeared: Hall became ill with influenza-like symptoms, requiring hospitalization, though he was released in time for the series.

On March 19, Seattle rudely dispatched their guests, 7–0, before Montreal returned the favor (4–2) three nights later. The Metropolitans planted another thrashing, 7–2, on the Canadiens on the 24th, before the clubs skated to a 0–0 overtime tie in game four.

During the fifth game, played on March 26, something was definitely amiss in the Montreal camp. Several of the players — including Hall and Jack McDonald — were quite ill, and played only intermittently. Somehow, McDonald rose to the occasion and scored the game-winner in overtime, evening the series at two games apiece with the 4–3 win. When it came time to play game six, the Seattle Department of Health stepped in and postponed the series. By this time, five Montreal players were seriously ill with influenza, with both McDonald and Hall in grave condition. Once stopped, the series never resumed, leaving the two combatants locked in a tie.

In the abbreviated series, Montreal's Lalonde led all scorers with 17 goals and 19 points, while teammate Didier Pitre amassed the most assists (6). Between the posts, goaler Georges Vezina allowed the fewest goals (3.38) while posting the lone shutout.

Through the spring of 1919, the influenza epidemic gradually waned, eventually petering out. The results were grim, as millions perished from coast to coast. For the Canadiens, the results were also tragic. Although McDonald would eventually recover from his illness, Hall never did. On April 5, the NHL's toughest player died in a Seattle hospital.

Although the professional hockey season ended tragically, a final act of sportsmanship gave cause for hope. Although Seattle arguably had a right to claim the Stanley Cup, based on their superior goal total for the series, the hosts never entered a plea. Simply put, PCHA president Frank Patrick did not exploit his fallen opponent in this matter, leaving the Cup unclaimed in 1919. This selfless act could not eliminate the harsh memory of Montreal's stark tragedy; nevertheless, it gave the hockey community a nugget of reassurance in carrying forward.

STANDINGS

TEAM	GP	W	L	T	PTS	GF	GA
OTTAWA	18	12	6	0	24	71	53
MONTREAL	18	10	8	0	20	88	78
TORONTO	18	5	13	0	10	64	92

LEADERS

PLAYER	TM	GP	G	A	PTS	PIM
Newsy Lalonde	MTL	17	22	10	32	40
Odie Cleghorn	MTL	17	22	6	28	22
Frank Nighbor	OTT	18	19	9	28	27
Cy Denneny	OTT	18	18	4	22	58
Didier Pitre	MTL	17	14	5	19	12
Alf Skinner	TOR	17	12	4	16	26
Harry Cameron	T-O	14	11	3	14	35
Jack Darragh	OTT	14	11	3	14	33
Reg Noble	TOR	17	10	5	15	35
Sprague Cleghorn	OTT	18	7	6	13	27

GOALS
Lalonde, MTL	22
O. Cleghorn, MTL	22
Nighbor, OTT	19
Cy Denneny, OTT	18
Pitre, MTL	14

ASSISTS
Lalonde, MTL	10
Nighbor, OTT	9
S. Cleghorn, OTT	6
Gerard, OTT	6
O. Cleghorn, MTL	6

GOALTENDER	TM	GP	MIN	GA	SH	GAA
Clint Benedict	OTT	18	1152	53	2	2.76
Georges Vezina	MTL	18	1117	78	1	4.19
Bert Lindsay	TOR	16	998	83	0	4.99

PENALTY MINUTES
Hall, MTL	89
Cy Denneny, OTT	58
Corbeau, MTL	51
Crawford, TOR	51
Lalonde, MTL	40

SHUTOUTS
Benedict, OTT	2
Vezina, MTL	1

OTTAWA 12-6-0 24 1st Alf Smith
Senators

		REGULAR SEASON					POSTSEASON				
PLAYER	POS	GP	G	A	PTS	PIM	GP	G	A	PTS	PIM
Frank Nighbor	C	18	19	9	28	27	2	0	2	2	3
Cy Denneny	L	18	18	4	22	58	5	3	2	5	0
Jack Darragh	R	14	11	3	14	33	5	2	0	2	3
Sprague Cleghorn	D	18	7	6	13	27	5	2	0	2	11
Eddie Gerard	D	18	4	6	10	17	5	3	0	3	3
Harry Broadbent	R	8	4	3	7	12	5	2	1	3	18
Harry Cameron (2-2)	D	7	5	1	6	26	5	4	0	4	6
Georges Boucher	D	17	3	2	5	29	5	2	0	2	9
Eddie Lowrey	D	10	0	1	1	3					
Clint Benedict	G	18	0	0	0	3	5	0	0	0	0
Skene Ronan	D	11	0	0	0	6					

		REGULAR SEASON				POSTSEASON				
GOALTENDER		GP	MIN	GA	SH	GAA	GP	MIN	GA	SH	GAA
Clint Benedict	(12-6-0)	18	1152	53	2	2.76	5	300	26	0	5.20

1918-1919

MONTREAL 10-8-0   20   2nd   George Kennedy
Canadiens

		REGULAR SEASON					POSTSEASON				
PLAYER	POS	GP	G	A	PTS	PIM	GP	G	A	PTS	PIM
Newsy Lalonde	C	17	22	10	32	40	10	17	2	19	9
Odie Cleghorn	C	17	22	6	28	22	10	9	0	9	9
Didier Pitre	L	17	14	5	19	12	10	2	6	8	3
Jack McDonald	L	18	8	4	12	9	10	1	2	3	6
Joe Malone	L	8	7	2	9	3	5	5	0	5	0
Joe Hall	F	17	7	1	8	89	10	0	0	0	17
Louis Berlinquette	L	18	5	3	8	9	10	1	3	4	11
Bert Corbeau	D	16	2	3	5	51	10	1	2	3	20
Billy Coutu	D	15	1	2	3	18	10	0	2	2	6
Georges Vezina	G	18	0	1	1	0	10	0	0	0	0
Frank Doherty	R	1	0	0	0	0					
Billy Bell	C	1	0	0	0	0					
Amos Arbour	F	1	0	0	0	0					

		REGULAR SEASON					POSTSEASON				
GOALTENDER		GP	MIN	GA	SH	GAA	GP	MIN	GA	SH	GAA
Georges Vezina	(10-8-0)	18	1117	78	1	4.19	10	656	37	1	3.38

TORONTO 5-13-0   10   3rd   Dick Carroll
Arenas

		REGULAR SEASON					POSTSEASON
PLAYER	POS	GP	G	A	PTS	PIM	no postseason play
Alf Skinner	R	17	12	4	16	26	
Reg Noble	C	17	10	5	15	35	
Ken Randall	D	14	8	6	14	27	
Rusty Crawford	F	18	7	4	11	51	
Corbett Denneny	C	16	8	3	11	15	
Harry Meeking	F	14	7	3	10	32	
Harry Cameron (1-2)	D	7	6	2	8	9	
Jack Adams	F	17	3	3	6	35	
Harry Mummery	D	13	2	0	2	30	
Dave Ritchie	D	4	0	0	0	9	
Paul Jacobs	D	1	0	0	0	0	
Bert Lindsay	G	16	0	0	0	0	
Hap Holmes	G	2	0	0	0	0	

		REGULAR SEASON					POSTSEASON
GOALTENDER		GP	MIN	GA	SH	GAA	no postseason play
Hap Holmes	(0-2-0)	2	120	9	0	4.50	
Bert Lindsay	(5-11-0)	16	998	83	0	4.99	

TEAM TOTALS

								Per Game			
TEAM	GP	G	A	P	PIM	GA	SH	G	A	PIM	GA
Ottawa	18	71	35	106	241	54	2	3.94	1.94	13.39	3.00
Montreal	18	88	37	125	302	78	1	4.89	2.06	16.77	4.33
Toronto	18	65	30	95	269	92	0	3.61	1.67	14.94	5.11
	54	224	102	326	812	224	3	4.15	1.89	15.03	4.15

PLAYOFFS

SERIES "A"
Montreal 8, Ottawa 4
Montreal 5, Ottawa 3
Montreal 6, Ottawa 0
Ottawa 6, Montreal 3
Montreal 4, Ottawa 2

MONTREAL, 4–1

STANLEY CUP (PCHA)
Seattle 7, Montreal 0
Montreal 4, Seattle 2
Seattle 7, Montreal 2
Montreal 0, Seattle 0 (OT)
Montreal 4, Seattle 3 (OT)

**MONTREAL 2, SEATTLE 2
STANLEY CUP NOT AWARDED**

1919-1920

Joe Malone

In its first few years, the NHL was a goal scorer's paradise. Many a sniper tallied marker after marker, as double-digit games became the norm. This trend would continue into the beginning of the 1920s, and one particular player was about to make hockey history.

In the NHL's first two seasons, a bevy of goal-scorers averaged at least one score a game, among them Montreal's Newsy Lalonde and Ottawa's Cy Denneny. However, they were outshined by a third who, ironically, accomplished many of his scoring feats while on loan, as his own team lay dormant.

Like other early NHL stars, Joe Malone — a native of Quebec City — cut his hockey teeth in the game's early pro leagues. In 1910-11, after a handful of games with his native Quebec OHA club, he joined the OPHL's (Ontario Professional Hockey League) Windsor franchise, scoring nine goals in 11 games. The following year, Malone rejoined the Bulldogs — now an NHA team — and remained with the club through the duration of the league. Highlights along the way included a 43-goal season for a first-place squad in 1912-13 and a 41-marker campaign in 1916-17. Malone led the 1912-13 squad to a Stanley Cup triumph, scoring nine goals in four games.

Although Malone's Quebec Bulldogs were one of the founding members of the NHL, the club opted to remain dark for the league's first two years. As a result, its players were loaned to other clubs, with Montreal becoming the lucky recipient of Malone's services. With his new team, Malone did not disappoint, as he led the way with 44 goals in 1917-18. The next season, he only played in eight games, netting seven markers. This drop in playing time was not due to injury or salary holdout. Said Malone, as noted by Bob Duff: "I had hooked on to a good job in Quebec City which promised a secure future, something hockey in those days couldn't." As a result, he participated only when Montreal was on home ice.

Before the 1919-20 season, Quebec announced it was returning to the fold, allowing Malone to return home. Over the campaign, he continued his assault on NHL netminders. On January 31, Malone scored seven goals in a 10–6 win over Toronto. Later, on March 20, he netted a half-dozen in a 10–4 drubbing of Ottawa. Overall, Malone scored 39 goals in 24 games — adding ten assists — to claim his second scoring title (49). Other individual feats included Frank Nighbor's (Ottawa) 15 assists and Cully Wilson's (Toronto) 86 penalty minutes. In net, in a dominant performance, Ottawa's Clint Benedict posted the lowest GAA (2.66) — more than three goals better than his closest pursuer — while earning the league's only five shutouts.

While Malone himself earned accolades, his team did not share the glory, as they won only four games all season. Instead, Ottawa (19–5, 38) took home team honors, winning each half of the schedule with ease, negating the need of a league playoff. Between the two, Montreal and Toronto ended near the .500 level.

As the winner of both portions, the Senators moved straight to the Stanley Cup finals, where they faced the PCHA's Seattle Metropolitans. In the first two contests of the series — all slated to be in Ottawa — the home team won 3–1 and 3–0. However, the visitors bounced back with 3–1 and 5–2 triumphs to knot the series. The latter game was held in Toronto because of warm-weather ice difficulties in Ottawa. Finally, again on Toronto's artificial ice, Ottawa prevailed in the deciding game, 6–1, to claim its first Cup. Frank Nighbor and Jack Darragh each amassed seven points in the postseason, with the former scoring a team-leading six goals. To go with his shutout, Benedict (2.20) also allowed the fewest scores.

Malone went on to enjoy another pair of decent 20-goal campaigns, before playing out the string with a pair of lackluster seasons in Montreal — the last with nary a tally to his name. At his retirement following the 1923-24 campaign, he was the second leading scorer (143) in NHL history, trailing only Cy Denneny, who had passed him that year.

Although later surpassed in total goals by other NHL stars, Joe Malone's legacy remains secure at the game, season and career level. In the nearly 90 years of the league, no other player has ever scored seven goals in a game. Also, his average of 2.2 goals per game in his first season with Montreal (1917-18) remains an all-time best. Finally, over his whole career, Malone averaged 1.13 goals per game. For those who played in over 100 NHL games, no one has ever scored at a higher rate.

1919-1920

STANDINGS

TEAM	GP	W	L	T	PTS	GF	GA
OTTAWA	24	19	5	0	38	121	64
MONTREAL	24	13	11	0	26	129	113
TORONTO	24	12	12	0	24	119	106
QUEBEC	24	4	20	0	8	91	177

LEADERS

PLAYER	TM	GP	G	A	PTS	PIM
Joe Malone	QUE	24	39	10	49	12
Newsy Lalonde	MTL	23	37	9	46	34
Frank Nighbor	OTT	23	26	15	41	18
Corbett Denneny	TOR	24	24	12	36	20
Jack Darragh	OTT	23	22	14	36	22
Reg Noble	TOR	24	24	9	33	52
Amos Arbour	MTL	22	21	5	26	13
Cully Wilson	TOR	23	20	6	26	86
Didier Pitre	MTL	22	14	12	26	6
Harry Broadbent	OTT	20	19	6	25	40

GOALS
Malone, QUE	39
Lalonde, MTL	37
Nighbor, OTT	26
Co. Denneny, TOR	24
Noble, TOR	24

ASSISTS
Nighbor, OTT	15
Darragh, OTT	14
Pitre, MON	12
Co. Denneny, TOR	12
Malone, QUE	10

GOALTENDER	TM	GP	MIN	GA	SH	GAA
Clint Benedict	OTT	24	1443	64	5	2.66
Ivan Mitchell	TOR	16	830	60	0	4.34
Georges Vezina	MTL	24	1456	113	0	4.66
Frank Brophy	QUE	21	1249	148	0	7.11

PENALTY MINUTES
Wilson, TOR	86
S. Cleghorn, OTT	85
Coutu, MTL	67
Courbeau, MTL	65
Boucher, OTT	55

SHUTOUTS
Benedict, OTT	5

OTTAWA 19-5-0 38 1st Pete Green
Senators

		REGULAR SEASON					POSTSEASON				
PLAYER	POS	GP	G	A	PTS	PIM	GP	G	A	PTS	PIM
Frank Nighbor	C	23	26	15	41	18	5	6	1	7	2
Jack Darragh	R	23	22	14	36	22	5	5	2	7	3
Harry Broadbent	F	20	19	6	25	40	4	0	0	0	3
Cy Denneny	L	24	16	6	22	31	5	0	2	2	3
Sprague Cleghorn	D	21	16	5	21	85	5	0	1	1	4
Georges Boucher	D	22	9	8	17	55	5	2	0	2	2
Eddie Gerard	D	21	9	7	16	19	5	2	1	3	3
Jack MacKell	D	23	2	1	3	33	5	0	0	0	0
Morley Bruce	D	21	1	1	2	2	5	0	0	0	0
Clint Benedict	G	24	0	0	0	2	5	0	0	0	0
Horace Merrill	D	5	0	0	0	0					

		REGULAR SEASON				POSTSEASON			
GOALTENDER		GP	MIN	GA	SH	GAA	GP	MIN	GA	SH	GAA
Clint Benedict	(19-5-0)	24	1443	64	5	2.66	5	300	11	1	2.20

MONTREAL Canadiens 13-11-0 26 2nd George Kennedy

REGULAR SEASON — *POSTSEASON: no postseason play*

PLAYER	POS	GP	G	A	PTS	PIM
Newsy Lalonde	C	23	37	9	46	34
Amos Arbour	L	22	21	5	26	13
Didier Pitre	R	22	14	12	26	6
Odie Cleghorn	F	21	20	4	24	30
Harry Cameron (2–2)	D	16	12	5	17	36
Bert Corbeau	D	23	11	6	17	65
Louis Berlinquette	L	24	8	9	17	36
Billy Coutu	D	20	4	0	4	67
Howard McNamara	D	10	1	0	1	4
Don Smith	F	12	1	0	1	6
Jack Coughlin (2–2)	R	3	0	0	0	0
Georges Vezina	G	24	0	0	0	0

REGULAR SEASON — *POSTSEASON: no postseason play*

GOALTENDER		GP	MIN	GA	SH	GAA
Georges Vezina	(13-11-0)	24	1456	113	0	4.66

TORONTO St. Pats 12-12-0 24 3rd Frank Heffernan / Harry Sproule

REGULAR SEASON — *POSTSEASON: no postseason play*

PLAYER	POS	GP	G	A	PTS	PIM
Corbett Denneny	L	24	24	12	36	20
Reg Noble	C	24	24	9	33	52
Cully Wilson	R	23	20	6	26	86
Ken Randall	D	22	10	8	18	42
Babe Dye	R	23	11	3	14	10
Goldie Prodgers	F	16	8	6	14	4
Mickey Roach	C	21	11	2	13	4
Joe Matte	D	17	8	3	11	19
Harry Cameron (1–2)	D	7	3	0	3	6
Frank Heffernan	D	19	0	1	1	10
Ivan Mitchell	G	16	0	0	0	0
Howie Lockhart (1–2)	G	7	0	0	0	0
Jake Forbes	G	5	0	0	0	0

REGULAR SEASON — *POSTSEASON: no postseason play*

GOALTENDER		GP	MIN	GA	SH	GAA
Jake Forbes	(2-3-0)	5	300	21	0	4.20
Ivan Mitchell	(6-7-0)	16	830	60	0	4.34
H. Lockhart (1–2)	(4-2-0)	7	310	25	0	4.84

QUEBEC Bulldogs 4-20-0 8 4th Mike Quinn

REGULAR SEASON — *POSTSEASON: no postseason play*

PLAYER	POS	GP	G	A	PTS	PIM
Joe Malone	C	24	39	10	49	12
George Carey	R	20	11	9	20	6
Tom McCarthy	F	12	12	6	18	0

		REGULAR SEASON					*POSTSEASON*
PLAYER	POS	GP	G	A	PTS	PIM	*no postseason play*
Harry Mummery	D/G	24	9	9	18	42	
Jack McDonald	L	24	6	7	13	4	
Ed Carpenter	D	24	8	4	12	24	
Dave Ritchie	D	23	6	3	9	18	
Tom Smith	F	10	0	1	1	11	
Jack Coughlin (1–2)	R	9	0	0	0	0	
Fred McLean	D	7	0	0	0	2	
Jack Marks	D	1	0	0	0	4	
George McNaughton	F	1	0	0	0	0	
Frank Brophy	G	21	0	0	0	0	
Howie Lockhart (2–2)	G	1	0	0	0	0	

		REGULAR SEASON					*POSTSEASON*
GOALTENDER		GP	MIN	GA	SH	GAA	*no post season play*
Frank Brophy	(3-**18**-0)	21	1249	**148**	0	7.11	
Harry Mummery	(1-1-0)	3	142	18	0	7.61	
H. Lockhart (2–2)	(0-1-0)	1	60	11	0	11.00	

TEAM TOTALS

									Per Game		
TEAM	GP	G	A	P	PIM	GA	SH	G	A	PIM	GA
Ottawa	24	121	63	184	307	64	5	5.04	**2.63**	**12.79**	**2.67**
Montreal	24	**129**	50	179	297	113	0	**5.38**	2.08	12.38	4.71
Toronto	24	119	50	169	253	106	0	4.96	2.08	10.54	4.42
Quebec	24	91	49	140	123	177	0	3.79	2.04	5.12	7.38
	96	460	212	672	980	460	5	4.79	2.21	10.21	4.79

PLAYOFFS

SERIES "A"
Ottawa won both halves;
no playoff held

STANLEY CUP (PCHA)
Ottawa 3, Seattle 2
Ottawa 3, Seattle 0
Seattle 3, Ottawa 1
Seattle 5, Ottawa 2
Ottawa 6, Seattle 1

**OTTAWA WINS
STANLEY CUP, 3–2**

1920-1921
Innovative Rival

Many of the features we take for granted in the NHL today, such as the blue lines, assists and flopping goaltenders, to name a few, were not part of the game when the league started play. These innovations gradually entered into the league's codebook as the years rolled by. But, as they were introduced, these were not fresh ideas concocted by NHL moguls. Instead, they came from the league's biggest rival.

As the old NHA got ready for its third year, what would become its biggest rival was emerging on the West Coast. The brainchild of Lester and Frank Patrick, the Pacific Coast Hockey Association started with three teams in the winter of 1911-12, located in Vancouver, Victoria and New Westminster — the latter a suburb of the former. Within three years, the PCHA had a team in Portland, OR, later adding American squads in Seattle and Spokane. Considered just as important as its eastern counterpart, the NHA, the PCHA began tilting with the NHA for Stanley Cup bragging rights in 1914. Three years later, the PCHA won its first Cup, as the Seattle Metropolitans took the heretofore Canadian trophy back to American soil.

To make the game flow more easily, the PCHA began to utilize new rules. For instance, to combat the constant offside calls — when a player precedes the puck carrier — the Patricks decided to divide the ice into three separate zones, delineated by blue stripes. In the middle zone, forward passing would be permitted. With the increasing in passing, a new statistic unfolded. From now on, players setting up goals with a pass would be credited with an "assist." In addition, to help thwart these fancy passing attacks, goaltenders were permitted to leave their feet to make a save.

Seeing the logic behind these changes, the new NHL began to fold them into their game plan. Midway through their first campaign, rules concerning goalie uprightness were relaxed, with blue lines and assists arriving the following year.

Before the 1920-21 campaign, the Quebec club announced its transfer to Hamilton, where it would be called the Tigers. As in its previous locale, success evaded the new club, and it finished last in both halves. Conversely, Ottawa (8–2, 16) won the first half, while Toronto (10–4, 20) came out on top in the second. Overall, the St. Pats (15–9, 30) finished with the most points, followed by Ottawa and Montreal.

Montreal's Newsy Lalonde (33-10-43) claimed the scoring prize, but was outgoaled by Toronto's Babe Dye (35). Dye actually scored two of his goals with loaner-club Hamilton, before he was recalled after a single game. Ottawa's Jack Darragh (15) amassed the most assists, while Billy Coutu (Hamilton) collected the most penalty minutes (95). Between the pipes, Ottawa's Clint Benedict (3.09, 2) earned his third straight GAA and shutout crown.

In the playoffs, Ottawa whitewashed Toronto, 5–0 and 2–0, in the total-goal series, earning its way to the Cup finals. Here, against the PCHA's Vancouver squad, the Senators faced a tougher tussle. Mirroring similar battles, this series too went the limit. Ottawa prevailed in the final game, 2–1. Jack Darragh and Georges Boucher led the way with five playoff goals each, while teammate Frank Nighbor collected a league-best four assists. Benedict, with his two shutouts, had the stingiest GAA (2.00).

One rule near and dear to the PCHA never found its way into the NHL. Through most of its history, the West Coast league utilized the "rover" position — a seventh player on the ice. This position — as the name implies — was free to wreak havoc all over the ice. Quite often, a team's best skater played this position — someone like Cyclone Taylor, who for many years plied his trade as a rover in the PCHA. However, come Stanley Cup time, this alternative method proved a problem. The solution was to alternate between the six- and seven-man games. Since each league was expert in its own version, quite often Stanley Cup series see-sawed back and forth, as it did in 1920-21. This time, the PCHA followed the lead of the NHL and abandoned seven-man hockey in 1922.

Although the PCHA folded its tents by the mid–1920s, its legacy is secure. Its innovative play — led by creative men like the Patricks — sparked a veritable revolution in the game, paving the way for the game as we know it today. So, it is no surprise that the PCHA is now considered by hockey historians a major league fully the equal of the NHL, which owes much to its West Coast brethren of yore.

STANDINGS

TEAM	GP	W	L	T	PTS	GF	GA
TORONTO	24	15	9	0	30	105	100
OTTAWA	24	14	10	0	28	97	75
MONTREAL	24	13	11	0	24	112	99
HAMILTON	24	6	18	0	12	92	132

LEADERS

PLAYER	TM	GP	G	A	PTS	PIM
Newsy Lalonde	MTL	24	33	10	43	36
Babe Dye	H-T	24	35	5	40	32
Cy Denneny	OTT	24	34	5	39	10
Joe Malone	HAM	20	28	9	37	6
Frank Nighbor	OTT	24	19	10	29	10
Reg Noble	TOR	24	19	8	27	54
Harry Cameron	TOR	24	18	9	27	35
Goldie Prodgers	HAM	23	18	9	27	8
Corbett Denneny	TOR	20	19	7	26	29
Jack Darragh	OTT	24	11	15	26	20

GOALS	
Dye, H-T	35
Cy Denneny, OTT	34
Lalonde, MTL	33
Malone, HAM	28
Three tied with	19

ASSISTS	
Darragh, OTT	15
Lalonde, MTL	10
Nighbor, OTT	10
Five tied with	9

GOALTENDER	TM	GP	MIN	GA	SH	GAA
Clint Benedict	OTT	24	1457	75	2	3.09
Jake Forbes	TOR	20	1221	78	0	3.83
Georges Vezina	MTL	24	1436	99	1	4.14
Howie Lockhart	HAM	24	1454	132	1	5.45

PENALTY MINUTES	
Coutu, HAM	95
Corbeau, MTL	86
Randall, TOR	74
Mummery, MTL	68
Noble, TOR	54

SHUTOUTS	
Benedict, OTT	2
Vezina, MTL	1
Lockhart, HAM	1

TORONTO 15-9-0 30 1st Dick Carroll
St. Pats

		REGULAR SEASON					POSTSEASON				
PLAYER	POS	GP	G	A	PTS	PIM	GP	G	A	PTS	PIM
Babe Dye (2-2)	R	23	*33	5	38	32	2	0	0	0	7
Reg Noble	C	24	19	8	27	54	2	0	0	0	0
Harry Cameron	D	24	18	9	27	35	2	0	0	0	2
Corbett Denneny	C	20	19	7	26	29	2	0	0	0	4
Ken Randall	D	22	6	5	11	74	2	0	0	0	11
Sprague Cleghorn	D	13	3	5	8	31	1	0	0	0	0
Cully Wilson (1-2)	R	8	2	3	5	22					
Rod Smylie	F	23	2	1	3	2	2	0	0	0	0
Billy Stuart	D	19	2	1	3	4	2	0	0	0	0
Mickey Roach (1-2)	C	9	1	1	2	2					
Jack McDonald (2-2)	L	6	0	0	0	2					
Jake Forbes	G	20	0	0	0	0	2	0	0	0	0
Ivan Mitchell	G	4	0	0	0	0					

1920–1921

GOALTENDER		REGULAR SEASON					POSTSEASON				
		GP	MIN	GA	SH	GAA	GP	MIN	GA	SH	GAA
Jake Forbes	(13-7-0)	20	1221	78	0	3.83	2	120	7	0	3.50
Ivan Mitchell	(2-2-0)	4	240	22	0	5.50					

OTTAWA 14-10-0 28 2nd Pete Green
Senators

PLAYER	POS	REGULAR SEASON					POSTSEASON				
		GP	G	A	PTS	PIM	GP	G	A	PTS	PIM
Cy Denneny	L	24	34	5	39	10	7	4	2	6	15
Frank Nighbor	C	24	19	10	29	10	7	1	4	5	2
Jack Darragh	R	24	11	15	26	20	7	5	0	5	14
Georges Boucher	D	23	11	8	19	53	7	5	0	5	19
Eddie Gerard	L	24	11	4	15	18	7	1	0	1	50
Harry Broadbent	R	9	4	1	5	10	6	2	2	4	4
Sprague Cleghorn	D	3	2	3	5	9	5	1	2	3	36
Morley Bruce	D	21	3	1	4	23	2	0	0	0	2
Jack MacKell	R	23	2	1	3	26	2	0	0	0	0
Leth Graham	L	14	0	0	0	0	1	0	0	0	0
Clint Benedict	G	24	0	0	0	0	7	0	0	0	0

GOALTENDER		REGULAR SEASON					POSTSEASON				
		GP	MIN	GA	SH	GAA	GP	MIN	GA	SH	GAA
Clint Benedict	(14-10-0)	24	1457	75	2	3.09	7	420	12	2	2.00

MONTREAL 13-11-0 24 3rd Leo Dandurand
Canadiens

PLAYER	POS	REGULAR SEASON					POSTSEASON
		GP	G	A	PTS	PIM	*no postseason play*
Newsy Lalonde	C	24	33	10	43	36	
Louis Berlinquette	L	24	12	9	21	24	
Harry Mummery	D	24	15	5	20	68	
Amos Arbour	L	22	14	3	17	40	
Didier Pitre	R	23	15	1	16	23	
Bert Corbeau	D	24	12	1	13	86	
Odie Cleghorn	R	21	5	4	9	8	
Cully Wilson (2-2)	R	9	6	1	7	40	
Dave Campbell	D	3	0	0	0	0	
Billy Bell	C	4	0	0	0	0	
Dave Ritchie	D	5	0	0	0	0	
Jack McDonald (1-2)	L	9	0	0	0	0	
Georges Vezina	G	24	0	0	0	0	

GOALTENDER		REGULAR SEASON					POSTSEASON
		GP	MIN	GA	SH	GAA	*no postseason play*
Georges Vezina	(13-11-0)	24	1436	99	1	4.14	

HAMILTON Tigers		6-18-0		12	4th		Percy Thompson	

		REGULAR SEASON					*POSTSEASON*
PLAYER	POS	GP	G	A	PTS	PIM	*no postseason play*
Joe Malone	C	20	28	9	37	6	
Goldie Prodgers	F	23	18	9	27	8	
Mickey Roach (2-2)	C	14	9	8	17	0	
Joe Matte	D	19	6	9	15	29	
Billy Coutu	D	24	8	4	12	95	
Tom McCarthy	R	22	10	1	11	10	
George Carey	R	20	6	1	7	8	
Ed Carpenter	D	20	2	1	3	17	
Moylan McDonnell	D	20	1	2	3	2	
Babe Dye (1-2)	R	*1	*2	0	2	0	
Leo Reise	D	6	2	0	2	8	
Eddie Lowrey	C	3	0	0	0	0	
Fred McLean	C	2	0	0	0	0	
Jack Coughlin	R	2	0	0	0	0	
Charles Pletsch	D	1	0	0	0	0	
Howie Lockhart	G	24	0	0	0	0	

		REGULAR SEASON				*POSTSEASON*
GOALTENDER		GP	MIN	GA	SH	GAA	*no postseason play*
Howie Lockhart	(6-18-0)	24	1454	132	1	5.45	

TEAM TOTALS

									Per Game		
TEAM	GP	G	A	P	PIM	GA	SH	G	A	PIM	GA
Toronto	24	105	45	150	287	100	0	4.38	1.88	11.96	4.17
Ottawa	24	97	48	145	170	75	2	4.04	2.00	7.08	3.13
Montreal	24	112	34	146	325	99	1	4.67	1.42	13.54	4.13
Hamilton	24	92	44	136	183	132	1	3.83	1.83	7.63	5.50
	96	406	171	577	965	406	4	4.23	1.78	10.05	4.23

PLAYOFFS

SERIES "A"
Ottawa 5, Toronto 0
Ottawa 2, Toronto 0

**OTTAWA WINS
TOTAL GOAL SERIES, 7-0**

STANLEY CUP (PCHA)
Vancouver 3, Ottawa 1
Ottawa 4, Vancouver 3
Ottawa 3, Vancouver 2
Vancouver 3, Ottawa 2
Ottawa 2, Vancouver 1

**OTTAWA WINS
STANLEY CUP, 3-2**

1921-1922

Broadbent's Streak

On the final day of 1921, Ottawa forward Harry Broadbent scored what seemed a routine goal in a 4–0 win over Hamilton — in the team's fifth game of the season. What made the goal special was that it started a streak, a string that would run through much of Ottawa's season.

The NHL's consecutive game goal scoring record had been set high right off the bat. During the league's first campaign, Montreal sniper Joe Malone netted a goal in 14 straight games, accumulating 35 total tallies during the run. Three years later, another Canadien nearly equaled the mark, as Newsy Lalonde tallied 24 goals in a 13-game scoring streak. However, before the end of the upcoming campaign, both marks would be shattered.

Before the 1921-22 campaign, several changes were implemented by the NHL. From now on, the league would not play a split schedule. Instead, the 24-game slate would be a seamless whole. Then, instead of half-season winners squaring off in a playoff, the top two teams would wrestle for bragging rights. Also, unlimited overtime was eliminated. Instead, if the two teams were tied after 20 extra minutes of skating, the contest went into the books as a tie game.

Following his goal on December 31, Broadbent continued to find the net. In January's eight games, he scored in every one. In February he continued the assault, netting markers in Ottawa's first seven games of the month. Finally, on February 25 — nearly two months after the streak began — he was thwarted in Toronto by the St. Pats in a 7–5 loss.

In perspective, Broadbent's goal scoring streak is remarkable. In Ottawa's 24-game season, he collected goals through most of the schedule, missing only the quartet of games on the front and back ends of the season. During the run, Broadbent didn't just keep the streak alive with a tally a game — he potted 27 markers in the sixteen contests.

Not surprisingly, Broadbent's individual success helped his team as well. During the 16 games, Ottawa went 11-3-2, forging a lead they never relinquished. Although the Senators lost the final four games of the season after the streak, the team (14-8-2, 30) still finished on top of Toronto by three points, and both were ahead of Montreal and Hamilton.

In addition to the 27 goals scored during his streak, Broadbent added five more in his team's other eight games to finish with a NHL leading 32 markers. In addition, he also collected 14 helpers, giving him a league-topping 46 points. Other leaders included Harry Cameron (Toronto), who garnered 17 assists and Montreal's Sprague Cleghorn, who amassed 80 penalty minutes. In goal, Ottawa's Clint Benedict continued his run of domination, earning GAA (3.34) and shutout (2) titles for the fourth straight year.

In the playoffs, Toronto surprised Ottawa in the first game, 5-4, then held the Senators to a 0-0 tie in the second to claim the total-goals series. For the Stanley Cup playoffs, a new wrinkle was added. Before the season, a new major league hockey outfit began play in the west. Called the Western Canada Hockey League (WCHL), the new loop consisted of four teams located in Alberta and Saskatoon. This complication necessitated a three-corner approach to claim the Cup. First, the PCHA champion (Vancouver) bested the WCHL playoff winner (Regina), five goals to two in the two game series. Then, the Maroons turned their attention to the NHL champion St. Patricks.

In the first game, Vancouver edged Toronto, 4-3, but the St. Pats evened the series with a 2-1 overtime triumph in game two. The Maroons then blanked their hosts, 3-0, before Toronto returned the favor, 6-0. In the deciding game, Toronto's Babe Dye exploded for four goals as the St. Patricks cruised to the Cup, 5-1. Overall, Dye paved the way with 11 postseason markers and 12 points, while teammates Harry Cameron (with four assists) and John Roach (1.84 GAA) also excelled.

Through the years, Broadbent's streak has stood up remarkably well. Though it has been approached at times, it has never been eclipsed. Assaulted by more recent snipers like Wayne Gretzky, Mario Lemieux and Alexander Ovechkin, only Lemieux's 12-game streak in the 1990s came close. As a result, Broadbent still stands alone atop the hill, his record untoppled for almost 90 years.

STANDINGS

TEAM	GP	W	L	T	PTS	GF	GA
OTTAWA	24	14	8	2	30	106	84
TORONTO	24	13	10	1	27	98	97
MONTREAL	24	12	11	1	25	88	94
HAMILTON	24	7	17	0	14	88	105

1921-1922 31

LEADERS

PLAYER	TM	GP	G	A	PTS	PIM
Harry Broadbent	OTT	24	32	14	46	28
Cy Denneny	OTT	22	27	12	39	20
Babe Dye	TOR	24	31	7	38	39
Harry Cameron	TOR	24	18	17	35	22
Joe Malone	HAM	24	24	7	31	4
Corbett Denneny	TOR	24	19	9	28	28
Reg Noble	TOR	24	17	11	28	19
Sprague Cleghorn	MTL	24	17	9	26	80
Georges Boucher	OTT	23	13	12	25	12
Odie Cleghorn	MTL	24	21	3	24	26

GOALS	
Broadbent, OTT	32
Dye, TOR	31
Cy Denneny, OTT	27
Malone, HAM	24
O. Cleghorn, MTL	21

ASSISTS	
Cameron, TOR	17
Reise, HAM	14
Broadbent, OTT	14
Cy Denneny, OTT	12
Boucher, OTT	12

GOALTENDER	TM	GP	MIN	GA	SH	GAA
Clint Benedict	OTT	24	1508	84	2	3.34
Georges Vezina	MTL	24	1468	94	0	3.84
John Roach	TOR	22	1340	91	0	4.07
Howie Lockhart	HAM	24	1409	103	0	4.39

PENALTY MINUTES	
S. Cleghorn, MTL	80
Mummery, HAM	40
Dye, TOR	39
Randall, TOR	32
Two tied with	28

SHUTOUTS	
Benedict, OTT	2

OTTAWA 14-8-2   30   1st   Pete Green
Senators

		REGULAR SEASON					POSTSEASON				
PLAYER	POS	GP	G	A	PTS	PIM	GP	G	A	PTS	PIM
Harry Broadbent	R	24	32	14	46	28	2	0	1	1	8
Cy Denneny	L	22	27	12	39	20	2	2	0	2	4
Georges Boucher	D	23	13	12	25	12	2	0	0	0	4
Frank Nighbor	C	20	8	10	18	4	2	2	1	3	4
Eddie Gerard (1-2)	L	21	7	11	18	16	2	0	0	0	8
Frank Boucher	C	24	8	2	10	4	1	0	0	0	0
King Clancy	D	24	4	6	10	21	2	0	0	0	2
Morley Bruce	D	22	4	1	5	2	1	0	0	0	0
Billy Bell (2-2)	C	17	1	2	3	4	1	0	0	0	0
Leth Graham	L	1	2	0	2	0					
Clint Benedict	G	24	0	0	0	0	2	0	0	0	0

		REGULAR SEASON					POSTSEASON				
GOALTENDER		GP	MIN	GA	SH	GAA	GP	MIN	GA	SH	GAA
Clint Benedict	(14-8-2)	24	1508	84	2	3.34	2	120	5	1	2.50

TORONTO 13-10-1   27   2nd   Eddie Powers
St. Patricks

		REGULAR SEASON					POSTSEASON				
PLAYER	POS	GP	G	A	PTS	PIM	GP	G	A	PTS	PIM
Babe Dye	R	24	31	7	38	39	7	11	1	12	5
Harry Cameron	D	24	18	17	35	22	6	0	4	4	22

32   The National Hockey League, 1917-1967

		REGULAR SEASON					POSTSEASON				
PLAYER	POS	GP	G	A	PTS	PIM	GP	G	A	PTS	PIM
Corbett Denneny	C	24	19	9	28	28	7	4	2	6	2
Reg Noble	C	24	17	11	28	19	7	0	1	1	21
Ken Randall	D	24	10	6	16	32	6	2	0	2	23
Billy Stuart	D	24	3	7	10	16	7	1	3	4	6
Rod Smylie	F	20	0	0	0	2	6	1	3	4	2
Ted Stackhouse	D	13	0	0	0	2	5	0	0	0	0
Lloyd Andrews	L	11	0	0	0	0	7	2	0	2	3
Paddy Nolan	D	2	0	0	0	0					
Stan Jackson	L	1	0	0	0	0					
Ivan Mitchell	G	2	0	0	0	0					
John Roach	G	22	0	0	0	0	7	0	0	0	0
Eddie Gerard (2-2)	L	1	0	0	0	0					

		REGULAR SEASON					POSTSEASON				
GOALTENDER		GP	MIN	GA	SH	GAA	GP	MIN	GA	SH	GAA
Ivan Mitchell	(2-0-0)	2	120	6	0	3.00					
John Roach	(11-10-1)	22	1340	91	0	4.07	7	425	13	2	1.84

MONTREAL   12-11-1   25   3rd   Leo Dandurand
Canadiens

		REGULAR SEASON					POSTSEASON
PLAYER	POS	GP	G	A	PTS	PIM	no postseason play
Sprague Cleghorn	D	24	17	9	26	80	
Odie Cleghorn	R	24	21	3	24	26	
Billy Boucher	R	24	17	5	22	18	
Louis Berlinquette	L	24	13	5	18	10	
Newsy Lalonde	C	20	9	5	14	20	
Bert Corbeau	D	22	3	7	10	26	
Billy Coutu	D	24	4	3	7	8	
Ed Bouchard	L	18	1	5	6	4	
Didier Pitre	R	23	2	4	6	12	
Billy Bell (1-2)	R	6	1	0	1	0	
Phil Stevens	F	4	0	0	0	0	
Jack McDonald	L	3	0	0	0	0	
Clement Piche		1	0	0	0	0	
Georges Vezina	G	24	0	0	0	0	

		REGULAR SEASON					POSTSEASON
GOALTENDER		GP	MIN	GA	SH	GAA	no postseason play
Georges Vezina	(12-11-1)	24	1468	94	0	3.84	

HAMILTON   7-17-0   14   4th   Percy Thompson
Tigers

		REGULAR SEASON					POSTSEASON
PLAYER	POS	GP	G	A	PTS	PIM	no postseason play
Joe Malone	C	24	24	7	31	4	
Leo Reise	D	24	9	14	23	11	
Goldie Prodgers	D	24	15	6	21	4	
Mickey Roach	C	24	14	6	20	7	
Cully Wilson	R	23	7	9	16	20	

1921–1922

PLAYER	POS	*REGULAR SEASON*					*POSTSEASON*
		GP	G	A	PTS	PIM	no postseason play
Amos Arbour	L	23	9	6	15	8	
Harry Mummery	D	21	4	2	6	40	
Joe Matte	D	21	3	3	6	6	
George Carey	R	23	3	2	5	6	
Howie Lockhart	G	24	0	0	0	0	

GOALTENDER		*REGULAR SEASON*					*POSTSEASON*
		GP	MIN	GA	SH	GAA	no postseason play
Harry Mummery	(1-0-0)	1	50	2	0	2.40	
Howie Lockhart	(6-17-0)	24	1409	103	0	4.39	

TEAM TOTALS

TEAM	GP	G	A	P	PIM	GA	SH	*Per Game*			
								G	A	PIM	GA
Ottawa	24	**106**	70	**176**	111	84	2	4.42	2.92	4.63	**3.50**
Toronto	24	98	57	155	160	97	0	4.08	2.38	6.67	4.04
Montreal	24	88	46	134	**204**	94	0	3.67	1.92	**8.50**	3.92
Hamilton	24	88	55	143	106	105	0	3.67	2.29	4.42	4.38
	96	380	228	608	581	380	2	3.96	2.38	6.05	3.96

PLAYOFFS

SERIES "A"
Toronto 5, Ottawa 4
Ottawa 0, Toronto 0

TORONTO WINS
TOTAL GOAL SERIES, 5–4

STANLEY CUP (PCHA)
Vancouver 3, Toronto 3
Toronto 2, Vancouver 1 (OT)
Vancouver 3, Toronto 0
Toronto 6, Vancouver 0
Toronto 5, Vancouver 1

TORONTO WINS
STANLEY CUP, 3–2

1922-1923

Race to the Top

In the first few years of the NHL, there had been several close finishes in the standings, some decided by a single victory. In each of these cases, the tussle was between two combatants. In the spring of 1923, another element was to be added, as a third team would be joining the race for the top.

In the first half of the 1919-20 campaign, both Ottawa and Montreal sported fancy records, but the Senators (9-3) managed to edge the Canadiens (8-4) by a single victory. The next year, Montreal (9-5) again was on the short end, as Toronto (10-4) edged them in the second half of the schedule. In 1921-22, Ottawa, Toronto and Montreal all finished over .500—with only five points separating the group. The following year would see the same gang pushing for the top.

Over the first month of the 1922-23 season, Montreal and Ottawa battled for bragging rights, while Toronto struggled. On January 20, the Senators (6-4-1) held a slim lead over the Canadiens (5-4-2), both with a comfortable lead over the St. Pats (4-6-1). Then, Toronto got hot, winning seven of its next ten games to pull nearly even with its foes. However, the Senators enjoyed a late four-game winning streak to salt away the top spot. By the time the schedule showed two games remaining, Ottawa (14-7-1, 29) had clinched first, with Montreal (11-9-2, 24) and Toronto (11-10-1, 23) left battling for the remaining playoff spot. As scheduling luck would have it, neither played the other. Instead, both the St. Pats and the Canadiens had contests against Ottawa and last-place Hamilton. All four of these were won by the contenders, leaving Montreal still one point up on Toronto and one behind Ottawa (14-9-1, 29) when the campaign ended.

Well behind the top trio, Hamilton (6-18) finished a bad last for the third straight year. The problem wasn't the offense, as the team scored 81 goals, only one behind league-leading Toronto. Simply put, the Tigers' defense was porous, allowing over four goals a game.

Individually, Toronto's Babe Dye won the goals (26) and scoring (37) championships, while Ed Bouchard (Hamilton-Montreal) earned the most assists (12) and Jack Adams (Toronto) was whistled for the most penalty minutes (64). In goal, Ottawa's Clint Benedict continued his domination of NHL skaters. For the fifth straight year, he earned top goalie honors—finishing with the lowest GAA (2.18) and most shutouts (4).

Although relegated to second by a slim margin for the third time in four years, the runner-up position the Canadiens earned in 1922-23 at least gave them a shot at the crown. Previously, in the split-season format, the second-place club got nothing. Now, in a full-campaign race, the second place club grabbed a coveted playoff slot. Alas, for Montreal, their luck ran out. Ottawa blanked them 2–0 in the first game, then held the Canadiens to a 2–1 win in the second, allowing the Senators to escape with a narrow win in the total goal series, three to two.

As in the previous year, the quest for the Stanley Cup was to be a two-tiered affair. First, the NHL champs would travel west to face the PCHA's Vancouver club, with the winner then journeying to Edmonton to play the WCHL's top club. On the West Coast, the Senators won the first game, 1–0, then the Maroons evened the series with a 4–1 victory of their own. Then, Ottawa put its foot on the throttle, outscoring their hosts by an eight to three margin in the final two games, claiming a spot in the Cup finals. A few days later, in Edmonton for the best-of-three series, the Senators squeaked by the Eskimos, 2–1, thanks to an overtime marker by Cy Denneny. Two days later, Ottawa completed the sweep, slipping by Edmonton, 1–0, earning their second Stanley Cup in three years.

In the postseason, Ottawa's Harry Broadbent scored the most goals (6) and points (7), while teammates Georges Boucher and Frank Nighbor each collected a pair of assists. In net, thanks to his three shutouts, Benedict posted a miniscule 1.00 goals against average.

In ensuing years, the NHL witnessed many close races—both for the top spot as well as for playoff positions. However, in its first 50 years, the race in 1922-23 was unique. At no other time would the top three clubs finish one win apart.

STANDINGS

TEAM	GP	W	L	T	PTS	GF	GA
OTTAWA	24	14	9	1	29	77	54
MONTREAL	24	13	9	2	28	73	61
TORONTO	24	13	10	1	27	82	88
HAMILTON	24	6	18	0	12	81	110

LEADERS

PLAYER	TM	GP	G	A	PTS	PIM
Babe Dye	TOR	22	26	11	37	19
Cy Denneny	OTT	24	23	11	34	28
Billy Boucher	MTL	24	24	7	31	52
Jack Adams	TOR	23	19	9	28	64
Mickey Roach	HAM	23	17	10	27	8
Odie Cleghorn	MTL	24	19	6	25	14
Georges Boucher	OTT	24	14	9	23	58
Reg Noble	TOR	24	12	11	23	47
Cully Wilson	HAM	23	16	5	21	46
Aurel Joliat	MTL	24	12	9	21	37

GOALS
Dye, TOR	26
B. Boucher, MTL	24
Cy Denneny, OTT	23
Adams, TOR	19
O. Cleghorn, MTL	19

ASSISTS
Bouchard, M-H	12
Dye, TOR	11
Cy Denneny, OTT	11
Noble, TOR	11
Roach, HAM	10

GOALTENDER	TM	GP	MIN	GA	SH	GAA
Clint Benedict	OTT	24	1486	54	4	2.18
Georges Vezina	MTL	24	1488	61	2	2.46
John Roach	TOR	24	1469	88	1	3.59
Jake Forbes	HAM	24	1469	110	0	4.49

PENALTY MINUTES
Adams, TOR	64
G. Boucher, OTT	58
B. Boucher, MTL	51
Randall, TOR	51
Noble, TOR	47

SHUTOUTS
Benedict, OTT	4
Vezina, MTL	2
Roach, TOR	1

OTTAWA Senators   14-9-1   29   1st   Pete Green

		REGULAR SEASON					POSTSEASON				
PLAYER	POS	GP	G	A	PTS	PIM	GP	G	A	PTS	PIM
Cy Denneny	L	24	23	11	34	28	8	3	1	4	10
Georges Boucher	D	24	14	9	23	58	8	2	2	4	8
Frank Nighbor	C	22	11	7	18	14	8	1	2	3	10
Harry Broadbent	R	24	14	1	15	34	8	6	1	7	14
Jack Darragh	R	24	6	9	15	10	2	1	0	1	2
Eddie Gerard	L	23	6	8	14	24	8	1	0	1	4
King Clancy	D	24	3	1	4	20	8	1	0	1	2
Lionel Hitchman	D	3	0	1	1	12	7	1	0	1	4
Harry Helman	R	24	0	0	0	5	4	0	0	0	0
Clint Benedict	G	24	0	0	0	2	8	0	0	0	0

		REGULAR SEASON					POSTSEASON				
GOALTENDER		GP	MIN	GA	SH	GAA	GP	MIN	GA	SH	GAA
Clint Benedict	(14-9-1)	24	1486	54	4	2.18	8	480	10	3	1.00

MONTREAL Canadiens   13-9-2   28   2nd   Leo Dandurand

		REGULAR SEASON					POSTSEASON				
PLAYER	POS	GP	G	A	PTS	PIM	GP	G	A	PTS	PIM
Billy Boucher	R	24	24	7	31	52	2	1	0	1	2

1922–1923

		REGULAR SEASON					POSTSEASON				
PLAYER	POS	GP	G	A	PTS	PIM	GP	G	A	PTS	PIM
Odie Cleghorn	R	24	19	6	25	14	2	0	0	0	2
Aurel Joliat	L	24	12	9	21	37	2	1	0	1	11
Sprague Cleghorn	D	24	9	8	17	34	1	0	0	0	0
Billy Coutu	D	24	5	2	7	37	1	0	0	0	12
Louis Berlinquette	L	24	2	4	6	4	2	0	1	1	0
Didier Pitre	R	22	1	2	3	0	2	0	0	0	0
Joe Malone	C	20	1	0	1	2	2	0	0	0	0
Billy Bell	R	19	0	0	0	0	2	0	0	0	0
Ed Bouchard (1–2)	L	*2	0	0	0	0					
Georges Vezina	G	24	0	0	0	0	2	0	0	0	0

		REGULAR SEASON					POSTSEASON				
GOALTENDER		GP	MIN	GA	SH	GAA	GP	MIN	GA	SH	GAA
Georges Vezina	(13-9-2)	24	1488	61	2	2.46	2	120	3	0	2.00

TORONTO   13-10-1   27   3rd   Charles Querrie
St. Pats   Jack Adams

		REGULAR SEASON					POSTSEASON
PLAYER	POS	GP	G	A	PTS	PIM	no postseason play
Babe Dye	R	22	26	11	37	19	
Jack Adams	C	23	19	9	28	64	
Reg Noble	C	24	12	11	23	47	
Harry Cameron	D	22	9	7	16	27	
Billy Stuart	D	23	7	3	10	16	
Lloyd Andrews	L	23	5	4	9	10	
Ken Randall	D	24	3	5	8	51	
Corbett Denneny	C	1	1	0	1	0	
Gerry Denoird	C	17	0	1	1	0	
Ganton Scott	R	17	0	0	0	0	
Rod Smylie	F	2	0	0	0	0	
John Roach	G	24	0	0	0	0	

		REGULAR SEASON					POSTSEASON
GOALTENDER		GP	MIN	GA	SH	GAA	no postseason play
John Roach	(13-10-1)	24	1469	88	1	3.59	

HAMILTON   6-18-0   12   4th   Art Ross
Tigers

		REGULAR SEASON					POSTSEASON
PLAYER	POS	GP	G	A	PTS	PIM	no postseason play
Mickey Roach	C	23	17	10	27	8	
Cully Wilson	R	23	16	5	21	46	
Ed Bouchard (2–2)	L	*22	5	12	17	40	
Goldie Prodgers	D	23	13	3	16	13	
Bert Corbeau	D	21	10	4	14	42	
Leo Reise	D	24	6	6	12	35	
Amos Arbour	L	23	6	3	9	12	
Billy Burch	C	10	6	3	9	4	
George Carey	R	5	1	0	1	0	
Leth Graham	L	5	1	0	1	0	

PLAYER	POS	*REGULAR SEASON*					*POSTSEASON*
		GP	G	A	PTS	PIM	*no postseason play*
Harry Mummery	D	7	0	0	0	4	
Jake Forbes	G	24	0	0	0	0	

GOALTENDER		*REGULAR SEASON*					*POSTSEASON*
		GP	MIN	GA	SH	GAA	*no postseason play*
Jake Forbes	(6-18-0)	24	1469	110	0	4.49	

TEAM TOTALS

TEAM	GP	G	A	P	PIM	GA	SH	*Per Game*			
								G	A	PIM	GA
Ottawa	24	77	47	124	205	54	4	3.21	1.96	8.54	**2.25**
Montreal	24	73	38	111	184	61	2	3.04	1.58	7.67	2.54
Toronto	24	**82**	51	**133**	**234**	88	1	**3.42**	**2.13**	**9.75**	3.67
Hamilton	24	81	46	127	204	110	0	3.38	1.92	8.50	4.58
	96	313	182	495	827	313	7	3.26	1.89	8.61	3.26

PLAYOFFS

SERIES "A"
Ottawa 2, Montreal 0
Montreal 2, Ottawa 1

OTTAWA WINS
TOTAL GOAL SERIES, 3-2

STANLEY CUP (WCHL)
Ottawa 2, Edmonton 1 (OT)
Ottawa 1, Edmonton 0

OTTAWA WINS
STANLEY CUP, 2-0

SEMIFINALS (PCHA)
Ottawa 1, Vancouver 0
Vancouver 4, Ottawa 1
Ottawa 3, Vancouver 2
Ottawa 5, Vancouver 1

OTTAWA, 3-1

1923-1924
Trophy

After modern NHL seasons, much hardware is handed out. Awards — named after historic officials and legendary hockey persona — are given to honor individual excellence in many categories, including scoring, defense and goaltending. In the opening years of the league, leaders of excellence were not honored in this manner, but in 1923, this was about to change.

With the same roster of teams as the year before, the NHL embarked on its seventh season in the winter of 1923. As before, Ottawa rolled along. Playing in a new artificial-ice arena, the Senators cruised to their accustomed large lead. Both the Canadiens and St. Pats won frequently enough to stay within shouting distance, while even Hamilton kept the pace for a while.

Midway through the campaign the league moguls met, in February 1924. On the agenda was an idea to honor the league's best player with a trophy. As stated by Brian McFarlane in *50 years of Hockey*: "it was announced a special trophy called the Dr. Hart trophy would be awarded to the player judged most useful to his team during the season." Later shortened to the Hart Trophy, the hardware was donated by Dr. David Hart to honor his son Cecil Hart, who would later serve as a Montreal coach.

At the end of the season, Ottawa (16-8-32) took its accustomed place as the leader of the pack, eight points better than Montreal. Toronto ended third, but had to hold off a resurgent Hamilton squad, the latter finishing with its best record to date. Ottawa's Cy Denneny (22-2-24) won the scoring title by a single point over teammate Georges Boucher. Although outpointed in the end, Boucher (10) did collect the most assists, while Toronto's Reg Noble (79) was whistled for the most penalties. In net, Montreal's Georges Vezina (1.97) ended Clint Benedict's record five straight GAA titles, slipping by the Ottawa netminder by a scant margin. Both goalies shared the league shutout lead with three each.

The first recipient of the Hart Trophy — as voted upon by league officials — was Ottawa's Frank Nighbor, who finished one slim vote ahead of Montreal's Sprague Cleghorn. Nighbor, a founding member of the NHL, was one of the league's best two-way players. Not only a scoring threat — he led the league in assists in 1918-19 — he was also a huge defensive presence on the ice, frequently thwarting his opponents with his patented "poke check." Nighbor went on to win another assist crown before retiring in 1930 at the age of 37. Seventeen years later, he took his rightful place alongside other immortals in the hockey Hall of Fame.

As in 1923, the battle for the Stanley Cup in 1924 involved all three major hockey leagues. First, before the interleague festivities began, Montreal upset the Senators, besting them 1–0 and 4–1 in the total goal series. Next, with all the games scheduled in the home city of the NHL champions, the Canadiens defeated the PCHA's Vancouver club, 3–2 and 2–1. In the finals, against the Calgary Tigers of the WCHL, Montreal walloped the westerners, 6–1 in the opening game. With a mid–March thaw affecting their natural ice surface, the Canadiens were forced to play the rest of the series in Ottawa's new home. Once there, the outcome was not to be in doubt for long, as Montreal blanked the Tigers, 3–0, to claim the Cup.

Individually, Montreal's talented newcomer Howie Morenz tallied seven markers and nine points to lead all postseason scorers. The league's best regular season netminder, Georges Vezina, continued his stellar play in the après-season portion of the campaign, allowing only a goal a game while posting two shutouts.

In subsequent seasons, the Hart continued to be awarded, becoming in reality hockey's MVP award. As the years rolled on, the NHL would add other trophies alongside the Hart. These new awards would honor players for a variety of accomplishments: great goaltending; great defense; great rookies; and even great playoff performances. Like the Hart, most of these new trophies were named after a member of hockey's community, linking a current star to a historic figure in the sport — in short, honoring today, while remembering yesterday.

STANDINGS

TEAM	GP	W	L	T	PTS	GF	GA
OTTAWA	24	16	8	0	32	74	54
MONTREAL	24	13	11	0	24	59	48
TORONTO	24	10	14	0	20	59	85
HAMILTON	24	9	15	0	18	63	68

LEADERS

PLAYER	TM	GP	G	A	PTS	PIM	GOALS	
Cy Denneny	OTT	22	22	2	24	10	Cy Denneny, OTT	22
Georges Boucher	OTT	21	13	10	23	38	Bi. Boucher, MTL	16

1923–1924

PLAYER	TM	GP	G	A	PTS	PIM
Billy Boucher	MTL	23	16	6	22	48
Billy Burch	HAM	24	16	6	22	6
Aurel Joliat	MTL	24	15	5	20	27
Babe Dye	TOR	19	16	3	19	23
Jack Adams	TOR	22	14	4	18	51
Reg Noble	TOR	21	12	5	17	79
Frank Nighbor	OTT	20	11	6	17	16
Two tied with					16	

GOALTENDER	TM	GP	MIN	GA	SH	GAA
Georges Vezina	MTL	24	1459	48	3	1.97
Clint Benedict	OTT	22	1356	45	3	1.99
Jake Forbes	HAM	24	1483	68	1	2.75
John Roach	TOR	23	1380	80	1	3.48

GOALS
Billy Burch, HAM	16
Dye, TOR	16
Joliat, MTL	15

ASSISTS
G. Boucher, OTT	10
Clancy, TOR	8
Four tied with	6

PENALTY MINUTES
Noble, TOR	79
Corbeau, TOR	55
Adams, TOR	51
Bi. Boucher, MTL	48
S. Cleghorn, MTL	45

SHUTOUTS
Benedict, OTT	3
Vezina, MTL	3
Roach, TOR	1
Forbes, HAM	1

OTTAWA Senators   16-8-0   32   1st   Pete Green

		REGULAR SEASON					POSTSEASON				
PLAYER	POS	GP	G	A	PTS	PIM	GP	G	A	PTS	PIM
Cy Denneny	L	22	22	2	24	10	2	2	0	2	2
Georges Boucher	D	21	13	10	23	38	2	0	1	1	4
Frank Nighbor	C	20	11	6	17	16	2	0	1	1	0
King Clancy	D	24	8	8	16	26	2	0	0	0	4
Harry Broadbent	R	22	9	4	13	44	2	0	0	0	2
Earl Campbell	D	18	5	3	8	8	1	0	0	0	6
Lionel Hitchman	D	24	2	6	8	24	2	0	0	0	4
Jack Darragh	R	18	2	0	2	2	2	0	0	0	2
Rod Smylie	F	13	1	1	2	8					
Harry Helman	R	19	1	0	1	2					
Leth Graham	L	3	0	0	0	0					
Frank Finnigan	R	2	0	0	0	0	2	0	0	0	2
Clint Benedict	G	22	0	0	0	0	2	0	0	0	0
Sammy Hebert	G	2	0	0	0	0					

		REGULAR SEASON					POSTSEASON				
GOALTENDER		GP	MIN	GA	SH	GAA	GP	MIN	GA	SH	GAA
Clint Benedict	(16-6-0)	22	1356	45	3	1.99	2	120	5	0	2.50
Sammy Hebert	(0-2-0)	2	120	9	0	4.50					

MONTREAL Canadiens   13-11-0   26   2nd   Leo Dandurand

		REGULAR SEASON					POSTSEASON				
PLAYER	POS	GP	G	A	PTS	PIM	GP	G	A	PTS	PIM
Billy Boucher	R	23	16	6	22	48	5	6	2	8	14

42   The National Hockey League, 1917–1967

PLAYER	POS	REGULAR SEASON					POSTSEASON				
		GP	G	A	PTS	PIM	GP	G	A	PTS	PIM
Aurel Joliat	L	24	15	5	20	27	6	4	2	6	6
Howie Morenz	C	24	13	3	16	20	6	7	2	9	10
Sprague Cleghorn	D	23	8	4	12	45	6	2	2	4	2
Odie Cleghorn	R	22	3	3	6	14	6	0	1	1	0
Billy Coutu	D	16	3	1	4	18	6	0	0	0	0
Sylvio Mantha	D	24	1	3	4	11	6	0	0	0	0
Billy Cameron	R	18	0	0	0	2	6	0	0	0	0
Bobby Boucher	C	12	0	0	0	0	3	0	0	0	0
Billy Bell	R	10	0	0	0	0	5	0	0	0	0
Joe Malone	C	10	0	0	0	0					
Charles Fortier		1	0	0	0	0					
Georges Vezina	G	24	0	0	0	0	6	0	0	0	0

GOALTENDER		REGULAR SEASON					POSTSEASON				
		GP	MIN	GA	SH	GAA	GP	MIN	GA	SH	GAA
Georges Vezina	(13-11-0)	24	1459	48	3	1.97	6	360	6	2	1.00

TORONTO 10-14-0   20   3rd   Eddie Powers
St. Pats

PLAYER	POS	REGULAR SEASON					POSTSEASON
		GP	G	A	PTS	PIM	no postseason play
Babe Dye	R	19	16	3	19	23	
Jack Adams	C	22	14	4	18	51	
Reg Noble	C	21	12	5	17	79	
Bert Corbeau	D	24	8	6	14	55	
Billy Stuart	D	24	4	3	7	16	
Amos Arbour	L	21	1	3	4	4	
Lloyd Andrews	L	12	2	1	3	0	
Stan Jackson	L	21	1	1	2	6	
Al Holway	D	6	1	0	1	0	
Wilf Loughlin	D	14	0	0	0	2	
George Carey	R	4	0	0	0	0	
Ganton Scott (1–2)	R	8	0	0	0	0	
Chris Speyer	D	3	0	0	0	0	
John Roach	G	23	0	0	0	0	
Howie Lockhart	G	1	0	0	0	0	

GOALTENDER		REGULAR SEASON					POSTSEASON
		GP	MIN	GA	SH	GAA	no postseason play
John Roach	(10-13-0)	23	1380	80	1	3.48	
Howie Lockhart	(0-1-0)	1	60	5	0	5.00	

HAMILTON 9-15-0   18   4th   Percy LeSueur
Tigers

PLAYER	POS	REGULAR SEASON					POSTSEASON
		GP	G	A	PTS	PIM	no postseason play
Billy Burch	C	24	16	6	22	6	
Red Green	L	23	11	2	13	31	
Goldie Prodgers	D	23	9	1	10	6	
Shorty Green	R	22	7	2	9	19	

		REGULAR SEASON					*POSTSEASON*
PLAYER	POS	GP	G	A	PTS	PIM	*no postseason play*
Ken Randall	R	24	7	1	8	18	
Mickey Roach	C	21	5	3	8	0	
Ed Bouchard	L	20	5	0	5	2	
Jesse Spring	D	20	3	2	5	8	
Corbett Denneny	C	23	0	1	1	6	
Leo Reise	D	4	0	0	0	0	
Ganton Scott (2–2)	R	4	0	0	0	0	
Charles Fraser	D	1	0	0	0	0	
Jake Forbes	G	24	0	0	0	0	

		REGULAR SEASON					*POSTSEASON*
GOALTENDER		GP	MIN	GA	SH	GAA	*no postseason play*
Jake Forbes	(9-15-0)	24	1483	68	1	2.75	

TEAM TOTALS

								Per Game			
TEAM	GP	G	A	P	PIM	GA	SH	G	A	PIM	GA
Ottawa	24	74	40	114	168	54	3	3.08	1.66	7.00	2.25
Montreal	24	59	25	84	170	48	3	2.46	1.04	7.08	2.00
Toronto	24	59	26	85	236	85	1	2.46	1.08	9.83	3.54
Hamilton	24	63	18	81	96	68	1	2.63	0.75	4.00	2.83
	96	255	109	364	670	255	8	2.66	1.14	6.98	2.66

PLAYOFFS

SERIES "A"
Montreal 1, Ottawa 0
Montreal 4, Ottawa 2

**MONTREAL WINS
TOTAL GOAL SERIES, 5–2**

STANLEY CUP (WCHL)
Montreal 6, Calgary 1
Montreal 3, Calgary 0

**MONTREAL WINS
STANLEY CUP, 2–0**

SEMIFINALS (PCHA)
Montreal 3, Vancouver 2
Montreal 2, Vancouver 1

MONTREAL WINS, 2–0

INDIVIDUAL TROPHY WINNERS

HART TROPHY (Most Valuable Player): Frank Nighbor, OTT

1924-1925
Striking Southward

At the same owner's meeting in February 1924, where plans to issue the NHL's first trophy were finalized, another key issue was voted upon: expansion. After much discussion, two new franchises were handed out — both to begin play in 1924-25. Entertaining offers from New York, Pittsburgh, Philadelphia and Boston, NHL directors decided to grant the latter's request. Then, holding off the other American suitors, a second expansion franchise was awarded to Montreal — this one to serve its English-speaking populace. However, as momentous as these changes would be, they were nearly upstaged by another event that would strike at the end of the upcoming season.

For many seasons, the Canadian-born NHL had been content to remain in the country of its naissance. However, the fact that the teams routinely played before five-figure audiences was not lost on league magnates. Seeing this as a good thing, the NHL decided more was better. As most of the suitable Canadian locales already had clubs, the only logical direction to expand was south — to the United States.

Adding the Boston Bruins and Montreal Maroons to the mix, the NHL also decided to expand its schedule in 1924-25, upping the ante to 30 games. To the surprise of all, the Hamilton Tigers — long the league's punching bag — bolted out of the gate and took an early lead. Fending off the usual leaders — Toronto, Montreal and Ottawa — the Tigers (19-10-1, 39) ended the campaign in first, one solitary point ahead of Toronto. Montreal and Ottawa finished strong, both ending within four points of the top. The newcomers did not fare as well, combining for only 15 wins between them.

Individually, Toronto's Babe Dye connected for the most goals (38) and amassed the most points (46), while two skaters — Hamilton's Red Green and

Ottawa's Cy Denneny — received the most helpers (15). Senators toughman Georges Boucher was penalized the most minutes (95).

Between the pipes, Montreal's Georges Vezina (1.81) set a new GAA record. Also, Ottawa newcomer Alec Connell set a record of his own, posting seven shutouts.

Accounting for its expanded roster, the NHL decided to increase the number of playoff qualifying teams. As the plan was drawn up, the second- and third-place clubs would square off, with the first-place team receiving a bye. However, in the spring of 1925, this new format didn't go according to plan.

After the regular season, several of the Hamilton contingent — led by Red Green — noted that their contracts were based on the previous year's 24-game schedule. Since the team had already played 30 games with playoffs to come, they reasoned that they were entitled to more money — $200 per man to be exact, and the Tigers were going to strike unless the team ponied up the extra dough. Stung by the betrayal, league president Frank Calder had no choice but to suspend and fine the recalcitrants.

With the first place club on the sidelines, second-place Toronto and third-place Montreal squared off for the NHL championship. In the first contest, the Canadiens edged the St. Pats 3–2, then Vezina blanked Toronto 2–0, allowing Montreal to claim the total goal series, five to two.

Before the season, one of the NHL's western rivals — the PCHA — had folded its tents, leaving only the WCHL as a fellow Cup contender. Following its victory over Toronto, Montreal journeyed to Victoria to face the champion Cougars. On home ice, Victoria — one of two PCHA teams absorbed by the WCHL — dominated the visitors, skating to 5–2 and 3–1 wins. The Canadiens pulled out a 4–2 win in game three, but the Cougars shut them down three days later, 6–1, to give the West Coast its first Stanley Cup in eight years.

For the second straight year, Canadien sniper Howie Morenz led all post-season NHLers — this time with seven goals and eight points. Because of Montreal's surprising loss in Victoria, Toronto's John Roach (2.50) posted the lowest postseason GAA, though Vezina still claimed the lone shutout.

Despite the moribund records of its two newest franchises, both played before appreciative, paying audiences. Thus the NHL decided that expansion was a good thing. So, in the next couple of years, several more clubs joined the circuit — all of them from the United States. Although the league was healthy and growing, the NHL was still spinning away from its Canadian origins. Not helping was the situation in Hamilton. Fed up with the strike, the embarrassed league allowed the team to be sold lock, stock and barrel to

American interests. To date, the NHL has not returned to the Ontario city — leaving one of the league's early locale's bereft of a club.

STANDINGS

TEAM	GP	W	L	T	PTS	GF	GA
HAMILTON	30	19	10	1	39	90	60
TORONTO	30	19	11	0	38	91	84
MONTREAL (C)	30	17	11	2	36	93	56
OTTAWA	30	17	12	1	35	82	66
MONTREAL (M)	30	9	19	2	20	45	65
BOSTON	30	6	24	0	12	49	119

LEADERS

PLAYER	TM	GP	G	A	PTS	PIM
Babe Dye	TOR	29	38	8	46	41
Cy Denneny	OTT	29	27	15	42	16
Aurel Joliat	M(C)	25	30	11	41	85
Howie Morenz	M(C)	30	28	11	39	46
Red Green	HAM	30	19	15	34	81
Jack Adams	TOR	27	21	10	31	67
Billy Boucher	M(C)	30	17	13	30	92
Billy Burch	HAM	27	20	7	27	10
Jimmy Herbert	BOS	30	17	7	24	55
Reg Smith	OTT	30	10	13	23	81

GOALS
Dye, TOR — 38
A. Joliat, M(C) — 30
Morenz, M(C) — 28
Cy Denneny, OTT — 27
Adams, TOR — 21

ASSISTS
R. Green, HAM — 15
Cy Denneny, OTT — 15
B. Boucher, M(C) — 13
R. Smith, OTT — 13
Day, TOR — 12

GOALTENDER	TM	GP	MIN	GA	SH	GAA
Georges Vezina	M(C)	30	1860	56	5	1.81
Jake Forbes	HAM	30	1833	60	6	1.96
Clint Benedict	M(M)	30	1843	65	2	2.12
Alec Connell	OTT	30	1852	66	7	2.14
John Roach	TOR	30	1800	84	1	2.80
Charles Stewart	BOS	21	1266	65	2	3.08

PENALTY MINUTES
G. Boucher, OTT — 95
B. Boucher, M(C) — 92
S. Cleghorn, M(C) — 89
A. Joliat, M(C) — 85
Two tied with — 81

SHUTOUTS
Connell, OTT — 7
Forbes, HAM — 6
Vezina, M(C) — 5
Benedict, M(M) — 2
Stewart, BOS — 2

HAMILTON 19-10-1 39 1st Jimmy Gardner
Tigers

		REGULAR SEASON					POSTSEASON
PLAYER	POS	GP	G	A	PTS	PIM	*no postseason play*
Red Green	L	30	19	15	34	81	
Billy Burch	C	27	20	7	27	10	
Shorty Green	R	28	18	1	19	75	
Alex McKinnon	R	30	8	2	10	45	
Mickey Roach	C	30	6	4	10	4	
Ken Randall	R	30	8	0	8	49	

1924-1925

PLAYER	POS	REGULAR SEASON					POSTSEASON
		GP	G	A	PTS	PIM	no postseason play
Charlie Langlois	R	30	6	1	7	59	
Ed Bouchard	D	29	2	2	4	14	
Jesse Spring	D	29	2	0	2	11	
Charlie Cotch (1-2)	L	4	1	0	1	0	
Goldie Prodgers	F	1	0	0	0	0	
Jake Forbes	G	30	0	0	0	2	

GOALTENDER		REGULAR SEASON					POSTSEASON
		GP	MIN	GA	SH	GAA	no postseason play
Jake Forbes	(19-10-1)	30	1833	60	6	1.96	

TORONTO   19-11-0   38   2nd   Eddie Powers
St. Pats

PLAYER	POS	REGULAR SEASON					POSTSEASON				
		GP	G	A	PTS	PIM	GP	G	A	PTS	PIM
Babe Dye	R	29	38	8	46	41	2	0	0	0	0
Jack Adams	C	27	21	10	31	67	2	1	0	1	7
Hap Day	D	26	10	12	22	33	2	0	0	0	0
Bert McCaffrey	R	30	10	6	16	12	2	1	0	1	6
Bert Corbeau	D	30	4	6	10	74	2	0	0	0	6
Al Holway	D	25	2	2	4	20	2	0	0	0	0
Mike Neville	C	13	1	2	3	4	2	0	0	0	0
Reg Reid	L	27	1	0	1	2	2	0	0	0	0
Lloyd Andrews	L	7	1	0	1	0					
Alvin Fisher	R	9	1	0	1	4					
Reg Noble (1-2)	C	3	1	0	1	8					
Rod Smylie	F	11	1	0	1	0	1	0	0	0	0
Billy Stuart (1-2)	D	4	0	1	1	2					
Charlie Cotch (2-2)	L	7	0	0	0	0					
Stan Jackson (1-2)	L	3	0	0	0	7					
Chris Speyer	D	2	0	0	0	0					
John Roach	G	30	0	0	0	0	2	0	0	0	0

GOALTENDER		REGULAR SEASON					POSTSEASON				
		GP	MIN	GA	SH	GAA	GP	MIN	GA	SH	GAA
John Roach	(19-11-0)	30	1800	84	1	2.80	2	120	5	0	2.50

MONTREAL   17-11-2   36   3rd   Leo Dandurand
Canadiens

PLAYER	POS	REGULAR SEASON					POSTSEASON				
		GP	G	A	PTS	PIM	GP	G	A	PTS	PIM
Aurel Joliat	L	25	30	11	41	85	5	3	0	3	21
Howie Morenz	C	30	28	11	39	46	6	7	1	8	10
Billy Boucher	R	30	17	13	30	92	6	2	1	3	17
Sprague Cleghorn	D	27	8	10	18	89	6	1	2	3	4
Odie Cleghorn	R	30	3	3	6	14	5	0	1	1	0
Billy Coutu	D	28	3	2	5	56	6	1	0	1	10
Johnny Matz	C	30	2	3	5	0	5	0	0	0	2
Sylvio Mantha	D	30	2	3	5	18	6	0	1	1	2
Fern Headley (2-2)	D	17	0	1	1	6	5	0	0	0	0

		REGULAR SEASON					*POSTSEASON*				
PLAYER	*POS*	*GP*	*G*	*A*	*PTS*	*PIM*	*GP*	*G*	*A*	*PTS*	*PIM*
Rene Joliat	R	1	0	0	0	0					
Roland Lafleur	L	1	0	0	0	0					
Dave Ritchie	D	5	0	0	0	0	1	0	0	0	0
Georges Vezina	G	30	0	0	0	0	6	0	0	0	0

		REGULAR SEASON					*POSTSEASON*				
GOALTENDER		*GP*	*MIN*	*GA*	*SH*	*GAA*	*GP*	*MIN*	*GA*	*SH*	*GAA*
Georges Vezina	(17-11-2)	30	1860	56	5	**1.81**	6	360	18	1	3.00

OTTAWA 17-12-1 35 4th Pete Green
Senators

		REGULAR SEASON					*POSTSEASON*
PLAYER	*POS*	*GP*	*G*	*A*	*PTS*	*PIM*	*no postseason play*
Cy Denney	L	29	27	**15**	42	16	
Reg Smith	C	30	10	13	23	81	
Georges Boucher	D	28	15	5	20	**95**	
King Clancy	D	29	14	5	19	61	
Ed Gorman	D	30	11	4	15	49	
Frank Nighbor	C	26	5	5	10	18	
Earl Campbell	D	29	0	0	0	0	
Frank Finnigan	R	29	0	0	0	22	
Lionel Hitchman (1–2)	D	12	0	0	0	2	
Alex Smith	D	7	0	0	0	2	
Leth Graham	L	3	0	0	0	0	
Harry Helman	R	1	0	0	0	0	
Alec Connell	G	30	0	0	0	0	

		REGULAR SEASON					*POSTSEASON*
GOALTENDER		*GP*	*MIN*	*GA*	*SH*	*GAA*	*no postseason play*
Alec Connell	(17-12-1)	30	1852	66	7	2.14	

MONTREAL 9-19-2 20 5th Eddie Gerard
Maroons

		REGULAR SEASON					*POSTSEASON*
PLAYER	*POS*	*GP*	*G*	*A*	*PTS*	*PIM*	*no postseason play*
Harry Broadbent	R	30	14	6	20	75	
Reg Noble (2–2)	C	27	8	11	19	56	
Sam Rothschild	L	28	5	4	9	5	
Dunc Munro	D	27	5	1	6	16	
Louis Berlinquette	L	29	4	2	6	22	
Francis Cain	D	28	4	0	4	27	
Charles Dinsmore	C	30	2	1	3	26	
Ganton Scott	R	28	1	1	2	0	
Alf Skinner (2–2)	R	19	1	1	2	16	
Gerry Munro	D	30	1	0	1	37	
Fred Lowrey	R	27	0	1	1	6	
George Carroll (1–2)	D	5	0	0	0	2	
Ernie Parkes	R	17	0	0	0	2	
Clint Benedict	G	30	0	0	0	2	

1924-1925 49

		REGULAR SEASON					POSTSEASON
GOALTENDER		GP	MIN	GA	SH	GAA	no postseason play
Clint Benedict	(9-19-2)	30	1843	65	2	2.12	
Dunc Munro		1	2	0	0	0.00	

BOSTON 6-24-0 12 6th Art Ross
Bruins

		REGULAR SEASON					POSTSEASON
PLAYER	POS	GP	G	A	PTS	PIM	no postseason play
Jimmy Herbert	C	30	17	7	24	55	
Carson Cooper	R	12	5	3	8	4	
Stan Jackson (2-2)	L	24	5	2	7	30	
Billy Stuart (2-2)	D	25	5	3	8	30	
George Redding	L	27	3	2	5	10	
Fred Harris	L	6	3	1	4	8	
Lionel Hitchman (2-2)	D	19	3	1	4	22	
Herb Mitchell	L	18	3	0	3	22	
Fern Headley (2-2)	D	13	1	2	3	4	
Bernie Morris	C	6	1	0	1	0	
Bobby Benson	D	8	0	1	1	4	
Norm Shay	D	18	1	2	3	14	
Lloyd Cook	D	4	1	0	1	0	
Bobby Rowe	R	4	1	0	1	0	
George Carroll (2-2)	D	11	0	0	0	9	
Jack Ingram	C	1	0	0	0	0	
Werner Schnarr	C	25	0	0	0	0	
Alf Skinner (1-2)	R	10	0	0	0	15	
Emory Sparrow	R	8	0	0	0	4	
Charles Stewart	G	21	0	0	0	0	
Norm Fowler	G	7	0	0	0	0	
Howie Lockhart	G	2	0	0	0	0	

		REGULAR SEASON					POSTSEASON
GOALTENDER		GP	MIN	GA	SH	GAA	no postseason play
Charles Stewart	(5-16-0)	21	1266	65	2	3.08	
Norm Fowler	(1-6-0)	7	420	43	0	6.14	
Howie Lockhart	(0-2-0)	2	120	11	0	5.50	

TEAM TOTALS

								Per Game			
TEAM	GP	G	A	P	PIM	GA	SH	G	A	PIM	GA
Hamilton	30	90	32	122	348	60	6	3.00	1.07	11.60	2.00
Toronto	30	91	47	138	272	84	1	3.03	1.57	9.07	2.80
Montreal (C)	30	93	57	150	391	56	5	**3.10**	**1.90**	**13.03**	**1.87**
Ottawa	30	82	47	129	344	66	7	2.73	1.57	11.46	2.20
Montreal (M)	30	45	28	73	276	65	2	1.50	0.93	9.20	2.17
Boston	30	49	24	73	226	119	2	1.63	0.80	7.53	3.97
	180	450	235	685	1857	450	23	2.50	1.31	10.31	2.50

PLAYOFFS

SERIES "A"
Montreal (C) 3, Toronto 2
Montreal (C) 2, Toronto 0

MONTREAL (C) WINS
TOTAL GOAL SERIES, 5-2

STANLEY CUP (WCHL)
Victoria 5, Montreal (C) 2
Victoria 3, Montreal (C) 1
Montreal (C) 4, Victoria 2
Victoria 6, Montreal (C) 1

VICTORIA (WCHL) WINS
STANLEY CUP, 3-1

Note: First-place Hamilton did not participate in playoffs due to player strike.

INDIVIDUAL TROPHY WINNERS

HART TROPHY (Most Valuable Player): Billy Burch, HAM
LADY BYNG TROPHY (Gentlemanly Conduct): Frank Nighbor, OTT

1925-1926
Georges Vezina

On the night of November 28, 1925, the Montreal Canadiens opened the new season. In goal, a fixture for many years, was their veteran netminder, Georges Vezina. Although one of hockey's top backstops for over a decade, it seemed to his teammates and onlookers that something was amiss. After the first period, Vezina collapsed in the locker room. Determined to go on, he skated out to start the second period, then was stricken again and had to be helped off the ice. Spitting up blood, Vezina was taken to the hospital. Once there, the cause was found, and the resulting prognosis was not good.

Born in Chicoutimi, Quebec, in 1887, Georges Vezina entered pro hockey playing for the Canadiens in 1910 in the second year of the club's existence. In his rookie season in the NHA, he won the GAA title with a mark of 3.80. Over the next few campaigns, Vezina continued as Montreal's lead goaltender, leading the league in GAA in 1913-14, then pushing the Canadiens to a Stanley Cup two years later. After the NHA morphed into the NHL, he led the new league with a 3.93 mark in its first campaign. In later seasons, Vezina was overshadowed by Ottawa's Clint Benedict, finally edging the Senator goalie (1.97 to 1.99) in 1923-24, all while leading his Canadiens to Cup victory once again. Often called the "Chicoutimi Cucumber" for his coolness under fire, he won his second consecutive title the following year (1.81), setting a new league mark. Although now 38, there was no reason to conclude that Vezina could not keep up the pace in 1925.

Before the season started, the NHL added one member to its roster — the Pittsburgh Pirates — sending the league back to the sport's professional roots. In addition, the ill-fated Hamilton squad was sold to New York interests, which called the team the Americans. Over the course of the now 36-game schedule, Ottawa (24-8-2, 50) won the regular season hands down, besting the other playoff teams — the Maroons and Pirates — by more than a half-dozen points.

Behind the frontrunners, Boston narrowly missed a playoff berth, while the rest of the pack (Toronto, New York and the Canadiens) finished well behind. For last place Montreal, they had a good excuse — they were missing their star netminder. Diagnosed with tuberculosis, Vezina missed the whole season. His replacement, Herb Rheaume, was not equal to the task, finishing near the bottom of the leaderboard as the only NHL regular netminder not to post a shutout.

Taking Vezina's place as the league's best goalie was Alec Connell, who set new benchmarks of GAA (1.12) and shutout (15) excellence. Offensively, Maroon forward Nels Stewart scored the most goals (34) and collected the most points (42), while Frank Nighbor (Ottawa) garnered the most helpers (13). In addition, Toronto's Bert Corbeau (121) spent the most time in the penalty box.

In the first two-tiered playoff in NHL history, the Maroons knocked off Pittsburgh, six goals to four in a two-game series, then tied Ottawa 1–1 in the opening contest of the finals. In a shocking upset, Montreal upended the frontrunners 1–0 in the second game to claim the total goal series.

Out west, the Western Canada Hockey League had been renamed the Western Hockey League, as the circuit now sported an American (Portland) member. In the tussle for the Cup, the Maroons overmatched Victoria, as Clint Benedict shut out the Cougars, 3–0, 3–0 and 2–0. Only in the third game did Victoria manage to squeak out a 3–2 win. In the postseason, Stewart built on his regular season domination, paving the way in goals (6), assists (3) and points (9). In net, Benedict allowed only a paltry goal per game to go along with his four shutouts.

Earlier, during the regular campaign, Vezina visited his mates before a game. In an emotional reunion, he promised he would do his best to return to action. Alas, such was not to be. On March 27, 1926 — the same day the Montreal Maroons clinched the NHL championship — Georges Vezina passed away at the age of 39. Nineteen years later, he took his place in hockey's Hall of Fame as one of its original 12 inductees.

To honor their great goaltender, the Canadiens donated a trophy to the NHL in his name. Beginning the following year, the Vezina Trophy was handed out to the goalie posting the lowest GAA each season. Now given to the most valuable netminder, the Vezina remains today the supreme award for goaltending prowess, giving today's stars a direct link to gallant goalie from long ago.

STANDINGS

TEAM	GP	W	L	T	PTS	GF	GA
OTTAWA	36	24	8	4	52	77	42
MONTREAL (M)	36	20	11	5	45	91	73
PITTSBURGH	36	19	16	1	39	82	70
BOSTON	36	17	15	4	38	92	85
NEW YORK (A)	36	12	20	4	28	68	89
TORONTO	36	12	21	3	27	92	114
MONTREAL (C)	36	11	24	1	23	79	108

LEADERS

PLAYER	TM	GP	G	A	PTS	PIM
Nels Stewart	M(M)	36	34	8	42	119
Cy Denneny	OTT	36	24	12	36	18
Carson Cooper	BOS	36	28	3	31	10
Jimmy Herbert	BOS	36	26	5	31	47
Howie Morenz	M(C)	31	23	3	26	39
Jack Adams	TOR	36	21	5	26	52
Aurel Joliat	M(C)	35	17	9	26	52
Billy Burch	N(A)	36	22	3	25	33
Reg Smith	OTT	28	16	9	25	53
Frank Nighbor	OTT	35	12	13	25	40

GOALS
Stewart, M(M)	34
Cooper, BOS	28
Herbert, BOS	26
Denneny, OTT	24
Morenz, M(C)	23

ASSISTS
Nighbor, OTT	13
Denneny, OTT	12
Joliat, M(C)	9
Smith, OTT	9
Noble, M(M)	9

GOALTENDER	TM	GP	MIN	GA	SH	GAA
Alec Connell	OTT	36	2251	42	15	1.12
Roy Worters	PIT	35	2145	68	7	1.90
Clint Benedict	M(M)	36	2288	73	6	1.91
Charles Stewart	BOS	35	2173	80	6	2.21
Jake Forbes	N(A)	36	2241	86	2	2.30
Herb Rheaume	M(C)	31	1889	92	0	2.92
John Roach	TOR	36	2231	114	2	3.07

PENALTY MINUTES
Corbeau, TOR	121
Stewart, M(M)	119
Boucher, M(C)	112
Broadbent, M(M)	112
Suebert, M(M)	108

SHUTOUTS
Connell, OTT	15
Worters, PIT	7
Benedict, M(M)	6
Stewart, BOS	6
Two tied with	2

OTTAWA Senators   24-8-4   52   1st   Pete Green

		REGULAR SEASON					POSTSEASON				
PLAYER	POS	GP	G	A	PTS	PIM	GP	G	A	PTS	PIM
Cy Denneny	L	36	24	12	36	18	2	0	0	0	4
Reg Smith	R	28	16	9	25	53	2	0	0	0	14
Frank Nighbor	C	35	12	13	25	40	2	0	0	0	2
Georges Boucher	D	36	8	4	12	64	2	0	0	0	10
King Clancy	D	35	8	4	12	80	2	1	0	1	8
Hec Kilrea	L	35	5	0	5	12	2	0	0	0	0
Ed Gorman	D	23	2	1	3	12	2	0	0	0	2
Frank Finnigan	R	36	2	0	2	24	2	0	0	0	0

		REGULAR SEASON				*POSTSEASON*				
PLAYER	*POS*	*GP*	*G*	*A*	*PTS*	*PIM*	*GP*	*G*	*A*	*PTS*	*PIM*
Alex Smith	D	36	0	0	0	36	2	0	0	0	14
Jack Duggan	L	27	0	0	0	0	2	0	0	0	0
Leth Graham	L	1	0	0	0	0					
Alec Connell	G	36	0	0	0	0	2	0	0	0	0

		REGULAR SEASON				*POSTSEASON*				
GOALTENDER		*GP*	*MIN*	*GA*	*SH*	*GAA*	*GP*	*MIN*	*GA*	*SH*	*GAA*
Alec Connell	(24-8-4)	36	2251	42	15	**1.12**	2	120	2	0	**1.00**

MONTREAL 20-11-5 45 2nd Eddie Gerard
Maroons

		REGULAR SEASON				*POSTSEASON*				
PLAYER	*POS*	*GP*	*G*	*A*	*PTS*	*PIM*	*GP*	*G*	*A*	*PTS*	*PIM*
Nels Stewart	C	36	34	8	42	119	8	6	3	9	24
Al Siebert	L	35	16	8	24	108	8	2	2	4	6
Reg Noble	C	33	9	9	18	96	8	1	1	2	10
Harry Broadbent	R	36	12	5	17	112	8	3	1	4	**34**
Dunc Munro	D	33	4	6	10	55	6	1	0	1	6
Chapman Kitchen	D	30	5	2	7	16					
Charles Dinsmore	C	33	3	1	4	18	8	1	0	1	8
Merlyn Phillips	C	12	3	1	4	6	8	4	1	5	4
Sam Rothschild	L	33	2	1	3	8	8	0	0	0	0
Frank Carson	R	16	2	1	3	6	8	0	0	0	0
Fred Lowrey (1-2)	R	10	1	0	1	2					
Al Holway (2-2)	D	17	0	0	0	6	6	0	0	0	2
George Horne	R	13	0	0	0	2					
Bernie Brophy	L	10	0	0	0	0					
Francis Cain (1-2)	D	10	0	0	0	0					
Clint Benedict	G	36	0	0	0	0	8	0	0	0	0

		REGULAR SEASON				*POSTSEASON*				
GOALTENDER		*GP*	*MIN*	*GA*	*SH*	*GAA*	*GP*	*MIN*	*GA*	*SH*	*GAA*
Clint Benedict	(20-11-5)	36	2288	73	6	1.91	8	480	8	4	**1.00**

PITTSBURGH 19-16-1 39 3rd Odie Cleghorn
Pirates

		REGULAR SEASON				*POSTSEASON*				
PLAYER	*POS*	*GP*	*G*	*A*	*PTS*	*PIM*	*GP*	*G*	*A*	*PTS*	*PIM*
Hib Milks	L	36	14	5	19	17	2	0	0	0	0
Francis McCurry	L	36	13	4	17	32	2	0	2	2	4
Harold Darragh	L	35	10	7	17	6	2	0	1	1	0
Lionel Conacher	D	33	9	4	13	64	2	0	0	0	0
Rodger Smith	D	36	9	1	10	22	2	1	0	1	0
Tex White	R	35	7	1	8	22					
Harold Cotton	L	33	7	1	8	22	2	1	0	1	0
Herb Drury	D	33	6	2	8	40	2	1	0	1	0
Jesse Spring	D	32	5	0	5	23	2	0	2	2	2
Odie Cleghorn	R	17	2	1	3	4	1	0	0	0	0
Louis Berlinquette	L	30	0	0	0	8	2	0	0	0	0
Fred Lowrey (2-2)	R	16	0	0	0	2	2	0	0	0	6

1925-1926

PLAYER	POS	REGULAR SEASON					POSTSEASON				
		GP	G	A	PTS	PIM	GP	G	A	PTS	PIM
Alf Skinner	R	7	0	0	0	2					
Roy Worters	G	35	0	0	0	0	2	0	0	0	0

GOALTENDER		REGULAR SEASON					POSTSEASON				
		GP	MIN	GA	SH	GAA	GP	MIN	GA	SH	GAA
Roy Worters	(18-16-1)	35	2145	68	7	1.90	2	120	6	0	3.00
Odie Cleghorn	(1-0-0)	1	60	2	0	2.00					

BOSTON   17-15-4   38   4th   Art Ross
Bruins

PLAYER	POS	REGULAR SEASON					POSTSEASON
		GP	G	A	PTS	PIM	no postseason play
Carson Cooper	R	36	28	3	31	10	
Jimmy Herbert	C	36	26	5	31	47	
Lionel Hitchman	D	36	7	4	11	70	
Sprague Cleghorn	D	28	6	5	11	49	
Hago Harrington	L	26	7	2	9	6	
Billy Stuart	D	33	6	1	7	41	
Gerry Geran	C	33	5	1	6	6	
Stan Jackson	L	26	3	3	6	30	
Herb Mitchell	L	26	3	0	3	14	
Norm Shay	D	13	1	0	1	2	
Charlie Cahill	R	31	0	1	1	4	
Phil Stevens	R	17	0	0	0	0	
George Redding	L	8	0	0	0	0	
John Brackenborough	L	7	0	0	0	0	
Charles Larose	L	6	0	0	0	0	
Joe Matte (1-2)	D	3	0	0	0	0	
Fred Bergdinon	R	2	0	0	0	0	
Werner Schnarr	C	1	0	0	0	0	
Charles Stewart	G	35	0	0	0	0	
Moe Roberts	G	2	0	0	0	0	

GOALTENDER		REGULAR SEASON					POSTSEASON
		GP	MIN	GA	SH	GAA	no postseason play
Charles Stewart	(16-14-4)	35	2173	80	6	2.21	
Moe Roberts	(1-1-0)	2	90	5	0	3.33	

NEW YORK   12-20-4   28   5th   Tommy Gorman
Americans

PLAYER	POS	REGULAR SEASON					POSTSEASON
		GP	G	A	PTS	PIM	no postseason play
Billy Burch	C	36	22	3	25	33	
Red Green	L	35	13	4	17	42	
Charlie Langlois	D	36	9	1	10	76	
Shorty Green	R	32	6	4	10	40	
Alex McKinnon	R	35	5	3	8	34	
Ken Randall	R	34	4	2	6	94	
Ed Bouchard	L	34	3	1	4	10	
Joe Simpson	D	32	2	2	4	2	

56   The National Hockey League, 1917–1967

		REGULAR SEASON				POSTSEASON
PLAYER	POS	GP	G	A	PTS	PIM	no postseason play
Mickey Roach	C	25	3	0	3	4
Earl Campbell	D	29	1	0	1	6
Billy Cameron	R	21	0	0	0	0
John Morrison	L	18	0	0	0	0
Bob Hall	C	8	0	0	0	0
Rene Boileau	C	7	0	0	0	0
Jake Forbes	G	36	0	0	0	0
Joe Ironstone	G	1	0	0	0	0

		REGULAR SEASON				POSTSEASON
GOALTENDER		GP	MIN	GA	SH	GAA	no postseason play
Jake Forbes	(12-20-4)	36	2241	86	2	2.30
Joe Ironstone		1	40	3	0	4.50

TORONTO   12-21-3   27   6th   Eddie Powers
St. Pats

		REGULAR SEASON				POSTSEASON
PLAYER	POS	GP	G	A	PTS	PIM	no postseason play
Jack Adams	C	36	21	5	26	52
Babe Dye	R	31	18	5	23	26
Bert McCaffrey	R	36	14	7	21	42
Pete Bellefeuille	R	36	14	2	16	22
Hap Day	D	36	14	2	16	26
Bert Corbeau	D	36	5	5	10	121
Mike Neville	C	33	3	3	6	8
Norm Shay	D	22	3	1	4	18
Francis Cain (2–2)	D	23	0	0	0	8
Al Holway (2–2)	D	12	0	0	0	0
Reg Reid	L	12	0	0	0	2
Rod Smylie	R	5	0	0	0	0
Gerry Munro	D	4	0	0	0	0
Gordon Spence	L	3	0	0	0	0
John Roach	G	36	0	0	0	0

		REGULAR SEASON				POSTSEASON
GOALTENDER		GP	MIN	GA	SH	GAA	no postseason play
John Roach	(12-**21**-3)	36	2231	114	2	3.07

MONTREAL   11-24-1   23   7th   Cecil Hart
Canadiens

		REGULAR SEASON				POSTSEASON
PLAYER	POS	GP	G	A	PTS	PIM	no postseason play
Howie Morenz	C	31	23	3	26	39
Aurel Joliat	L	35	17	9	26	52
Al Leduc	D	32	10	3	13	62
Billy Boucher	R	34	8	5	13	112
Alfred Lepine	C	27	9	1	10	18
Hec Lepine	C	33	5	2	7	2
Billy Coutu	D	33	2	4	6	95
Sylvio Mantha	D	34	2	1	3	66

1925-1926

PLAYER	POS	REGULAR SEASON					POSTSEASON
		GP	G	A	PTS	PIM	no postseason play
Wildor Larochelle	R	33	2	1	3	10	
Bill Holmes	C	9	1	0	1	2	
Rollie Paulhus	D	33	0	0	0	0	
Joe Matte (2-2)	D	6	0	0	0	0	
John McKinnon	D	2	0	0	0	0	
Dave Ritchie	D	2	0	0	0	0	
Roger Cormier	R	1	0	0	0	0	
Herb Rheaume	G	31	0	0	0	0	
Al Lacroix	G	5	0	0	0	0	
Georges Vezina	G	1	0	0	0	0	

GOALTENDER		REGULAR SEASON					POSTSEASON
		GP	MIN	GA	SH	GAA	no postseason play
Georges Vezina		1	20	0	0	0.00	
Herb Rheaume	(10-20-1)	31	1889	92	0	2.92	
Al Lacroix	(1-4-0)	5	280	16	0	3.43	

TEAM TOTALS

TEAM	GP	G	A	P	PIM	GA	SH	Per Game G	A	PIM	GA
Ottawa	36	77	43	120	339	42	15	2.13	1.19	9.41	1.17
Montreal (M)	36	91	42	133	554	73	6	2.53	1.17	15.38	2.03
Pittsburgh	36	82	26	108	264	70	7	2.28	0.72	7.33	1.94
Boston	36	92	25	117	279	85	6	2.56	0.69	7.75	2.36
New York (A)	36	68	20	88	341	89	2	1.88	0.55	9.47	2.47
Toronto	36	92	30	122	325	114	2	2.56	0.83	9.02	3.17
Montreal (C)	36	79	29	108	458	108	0	2.19	0.81	12.72	3.00
	252	581	215	796	2560	581	38	2.31	0.85	10.16	2.31

PLAYOFFS

SERIES "A"
Montreal (M) 3, Pittsburgh 1
Montreal (M) 3, Pittsburgh 3

MONTREAL (M) WINS
TOTAL GOAL SERIES, 6-4

SERIES "B"
Montreal (M) 1, Ottawa 1
Montreal (M) 1, Ottawa 0

MONTREAL (M) WINS
TOTAL GOAL SERIES, 2-1

STANLEY CUP (WHL)
Montreal (M) 3, Victoria 0
Montreal (M) 3, Victoria 0
Victoria 3, Montreal (M) 2
Montreal (M) 2, Victoria 0

MONTREAL (M) WINS
STANLEY CUP, 3-1

INDIVIDUAL TROPHY WINNERS

HART TROPHY (Most Valuable Player): Nels Stewart, M(M)
LADY BYNG TROPHY (Gentlemanly Conduct): Frank Nighbor, OTT

1926-1927
Sole Survivor

At the midpoint of the 1920s, the western rival of the NHL — the Western Hockey League — was in trouble. Although showcasing the same major league hockey as the easterners, the WHL, which was located in a swath from Canada's Prairie Provinces to the West Coast, played in smaller venues, which generated significantly less income. Most of the region's biggest cities could simply not compete in size with the large American markets into which the NHL was expanding. Though the picture looked bleak for the WHL and players and its owners, the league's president, Lester Patrick, had a plan.

While the WHL was foundering, the NHL was planning its next round of expansion, prepping to add three more teams. Naturally, these new clubs would need talented personnel in order to ice a competitive product. This was where Patrick stepped in. After getting the support of five WHL owners, he stated, as noted by Eric Zweig, "My plan was to merge the five rosters into three strong teams and sell the teams intact for $100,000 each."

In the end, the idea did not unfold completely as scheduled, but the basic tenets were followed. One of the NHL expansion clubs — Chicago — snapped up the Portland Rosebuds, while Detroit's new club grabbed the Victoria Cougars. The NHL's third new team — the New York Rangers — did not buy a WHL club of their own, but did nab several stars, including the fabulous Cook brothers. Existing NHL clubs — like the Boston Bruins who landed Eddie Shore — gobbled up the rest.

Now a ten-team league, the NHL decided to bisect itself for the 1926-27 season. Populating the Canadian Division would be the four Canadian teams (Ottawa, Montreal Canadiens and Maroons and the renamed Toronto

Maple Leafs) as well as the New York Americans. The five remaining teams (New York Rangers, Boston, Pittsburgh, Chicago and Detroit) would constitute the American Division. The league also expanded the schedule, raising to 44 the number of league games.

On the ice, Ottawa (30-10-4, 64) continued to dominate the NHL regular season, outlasting the Canadiens by six points to win the Canadian Division race. Right at .500, the Maroons latched on to the final playoff rung, well ahead of both the Americans and Leafs. In the American, the first-year Rangers — behind the prowess of WHL refugee Bill Cook — claimed top honors (25-13-6, 56). The final two playoff berths were snagged by Chicago and Boston, while Detroit and Pittsburgh brought up the rear.

Top individual scoring honors fell to the Ranger's Bill Cook, who potted the most goals (33) and earned the most points (37), narrowly edging Chicago's Dick Irvin, although the latter set a new assist record (18). The Maroon's Nels Stewart also pushed an NHL record higher, as he was whistled for 133 penalty minutes. In goal, the Maroons' Clint Benedict (1.42) led a cluster of sub–1.50 GAA netminders, one of which (Canadiens' George Hainsworth) shut out league opponents the most times (14).

In the Canadian Division playoffs, the Canadiens edged the Maroons two goals to one in the total goal series, while Boston bruised Chicago, 10 goals to five, in the American. In the Division finals, Ottawa ousted Montreal by five goals to one margin, while Boston supplanted New York as the top team of the American, three tallies to one.

With the WHL now in the rear-view mirror, the battle for the Stanley Cup was now an exclusive NHL affair, pitting the division winners Ottawa and Boston against one another. In the best of three series, the Senators knocked off the Bruins with a pair of 3–1 wins, although two other games in the series ended in ties. Ottawa's Cy Denneny led all playoff scorers with five goals, although Boston's Harry Oliver and Percy Galbraith each collected more points (6), the latter with the most assists (3). Between the posts, Ottawa's Alec Connell posted a sparkling 0.60 GAA, while earning two shutouts.

Although the WHL was dismantled, its legacy continued with its former players, teams and president finding niches in the NHL. Individually, one aforementioned WHL alum — Bill Cook — was a prolific scorer for many years to come. Also, one WHL team nickname was carried forward by Detroit, which called itself the Cougars after the Victoria team it had purchased. Finally, in a fitting tribute, the New York Rangers hired the architect of the WHL–NHL merger, Lester Patrick, to run their hockey program — a program which he competently led for many years to come.

STANDINGS

TEAM	GP	W	L	T	PTS	GF	GA
CANADIAN							
OTTAWA	44	30	10	4	64	86	69
MONTREAL (C)	44	28	14	2	58	106	67
MONTREAL (M)	44	20	20	4	44	71	68
NEW YORK (A)	44	17	25	2	36	83	91
TORONTO	44	15	24	5	35	78	94
AMERICAN							
NEW YORK (R)	44	25	13	6	56	96	72
BOSTON	44	21	20	3	45	91	89
CHICAGO	44	19	22	3	41	115	116
PITTSBURGH	44	15	26	3	33	78	108
DETROIT	44	12	28	4	28	75	105

LEADERS

PLAYER	TM	GP	G	A	PTS	PIM
Bill Cook	N(R)	44	**33**	4	37	58
Dick Irvin	CHI	43	18	**18**	36	34
Howie Morenz	M(C)	44	25	7	32	49
Frank Fredrickson	D-B	41	18	13	31	46
Babe Dye	CHI	41	25	5	30	14
Ace Bailey	TOR	42	15	13	28	82
Frank Boucher	N(R)	44	13	15	28	17
Billy Burch	N(A)	43	19	8	27	4
Harry Oliver	BOS	42	18	6	24	17
Duke Keats	B-D	42	16	8	24	52

GOALS	
Bill Cook, N(R)	33
Morenz, M(C)	25
Dye, CHI	25
Burch, N(A)	19
Three tied with	18

ASSISTS	
Irvin, CHI	18
Boucher, N(R)	15
Fredrickson, D-B	13
Bailey, TOR	13
Clancy, OTT	10

GOALTENDER	TM	GP	MIN	GA	SH	GAA
Clint Benedict	M(M)	43	2748	65	13	**1.42**
Lorne Chabot	N(R)	36	2307	56	10	1.46
George Hainsworth	M(C)	44	2732	67	**14**	1.47
Alec Connell	OTT	44	2782	69	13	1.49
Hal Winkler	N-B	31	1959	56	6	1.72
Jake Forbes	N(A)	44	2715	91	8	2.01
John Roach	TOR	44	2764	94	4	2.04
Hap Holmes	DET	41	2685	100	6	2.23
Charles Stewart	BOS	21	1303	49	2	2.26
Roy Worters	PIT	44	2711	108	4	2.39

PENALTY MINUTES	
Stewart, M(M)	133
Shore, BOS	130
Smith, OTT	125
Siebert, M(M)	116
Boucher, OTT	115

SHUTOUTS	
Hainsworth, M(C)	14
Benedict, M(M)	13
Connell, OTT	13
Chabot, N(R)	10
Forbes, N(A)	8

OTTAWA 30-10-4 64 1st (C) David Gill
Senators

		REGULAR SEASON					POSTSEASON			
PLAYER	POS	GP	G	A	PTS	PIM	GP	G	A	PTS	PIM
Cy Denneny	L	42	17	6	23	16	6	5	0	5	0
King Clancy	D	43	9	10	19	78	6	1	1	2	14
Hec Kilrea	L	42	11	7	18	48	6	1	1	2	4

1926–1927

		REGULAR SEASON					POSTSEASON				
PLAYER	POS	GP	G	A	PTS	PIM	GP	G	A	PTS	PIM
Frank Finnigan	R	36	15	1	16	52	6	3	0	3	0
Reg Smith	R	43	9	6	15	125	6	1	0	1	16
Frank Nighbor	C	38	6	6	12	26	6	1	1	2	0
Georges Boucher	D	40	8	3	11	115	6	0	0	0	43
Jack Adams	C	40	5	1	6	66	6	0	0	0	0
Alex Smith	D	42	4	1	5	58	6	0	0	0	8
Ed Gorman	D	41	1	0	1	17	6	0	0	0	0
Milt Halliday	L	38	1	0	1	2	6	0	0	0	0
Stan Jackson	L	8	0	0	0	2					
Alec Connell	G	44	0	0	0	2	6	0	0	0	0

		REGULAR SEASON				POSTSEASON				
GOALTENDER		GP	MIN	GA	SH	GAA	GP	MIN	GA	SH	GAA
Alec Connell	(30-10-4)	44	2782	69	13	1.49	6	400	4	2	0.60

MONTREAL 28-14-2 58 2nd (C) Cecil Hart
Canadiens

		REGULAR SEASON					POSTSEASON				
PLAYER	POS	GP	G	A	PTS	PIM	GP	G	A	PTS	PIM
Howie Morenz	C	44	25	7	32	49	4	1	0	1	4
Aurel Joliat	L	43	14	4	18	79	4	1	0	1	10
Alfred Lepine	C	44	16	1	17	20	4	0	0	0	4
Art Gagne	R	44	14	3	17	42	4	0	0	0	0
Sylvio Mantha	D	43	10	5	15	77	4	1	0	1	0
Carson Cooper (2–2)	R	14	9	3	12	16	3	0	0	0	0
Herb Gardiner	D	44	6	6	12	26	4	0	0	0	10
Al Leduc	D	43	5	2	7	62	4	0	0	0	2
Wilfred Hart (2–2)	L	40	3	3	6	8	4	0	0	0	0
Billy Boucher (1–2)	R	21	4	0	4	14					
Wildor Larochelle	R	41	0	1	1	6	4	0	0	0	0
Art Gauthier	C	13	0	0	0	0	1	0	0	0	0
Amby Moran	D	12	0	0	0	10					
Pete Palangio	L	6	0	0	0	0	4	0	0	0	0
Leo Lafrance	L	4	0	0	0	0					
George Hainsworth	G	44	0	0	0	0	4	0	0	0	0

	REGULAR SEASON					POSTSEASON				
GOALTENDER	GP	MIN	GA	SH	GAA	GP	MIN	GA	SH	GAA
George Hainsworth (28-14-2)	44	2732	67	14	1.47	4	252	6	1	1.43

MONTREAL 20-20-4 44 3rd (C) Eddie Gerard
Maroons

		REGULAR SEASON					POSTSEASON				
PLAYER	POS	GP	G	A	PTS	PIM	GP	G	A	PTS	PIM
Nels Stewart	C	43	17	4	21	**133**	2	0	0	0	4
Merlyn Phillips	C	43	15	1	16	45	2	0	0	0	0
Harry Broadbent	R	42	9	5	14	88	2	0	0	0	0
Russ Oatman (2–2)	L	25	8	4	12	30	2	0	0	0	0
Dunc Munro	D	43	6	5	11	42	2	0	0	0	4
Al Siebert	F	42	5	3	8	116	2	1	0	1	2

		REGULAR SEASON					POSTSEASON				
PLAYER	POS	GP	G	A	PTS	PIM	GP	G	A	PTS	PIM
Mervyn Dutton	D	44	4	4	8	108	2	0	0	0	4
Reg Noble	C	43	3	3	6	112	2	0	0	0	2
Frank Carson	R	44	2	3	5	12	2	0	0	0	2
Sam Rothschild	L	22	1	1	2	8	2	0	0	0	0
Charles Dinsmore	C	28	1	0	1	6					
James Donnelly	D	34	0	1	1	14	2	0	0	0	0
Hap Emms	L	8	0	0	0	0					
Al Holway	D	13	0	0	0	2					
George Horne	R	2	0	0	0	0					
Clint Benedict	G	43	0	0	0	0	2	0	0	0	0
James Walsh	G	1	0	0	0	0					

		REGULAR SEASON					POSTSEASON				
GOALTENDER		GP	MIN	GA	SH	GAA	GP	MIN	GA	SH	GAA
Clint Benedict	(20-19-4)	43	2748	65	13	**1.42**	2	132	2	0	0.91
James Walsh	(0-1-0)	1	60	3	0	3.00					

NEW YORK 17-25-2 36 4th (C) Newsy Lalonde
Americans

		REGULAR SEASON					POSTSEASON
PLAYER	POS	GP	G	A	PTS	PIM	no postseason play
Billy Burch	C	43	19	8	27	40	
Lionel Conacher	D	30	8	9	17	81	
Red Green	L	43	10	4	14	53	
Leo Reise	D	40	7	6	13	24	
Mickey Roach	C	44	11	0	11	14	
Norm Himes	C	42	9	2	11	14	
Laurie Scott	L	39	6	2	8	22	
Joe Simpson	D	43	4	2	6	39	
Alex McKinnon	R	42	2	1	3	29	
Ed Bouchard	L	38	2	1	3	12	
Shorty Green	R	21	2	1	3	17	
Charlie Langlois	D	9	2	0	2	8	
Bob Connors	L	6	1	0	1	0	
Clarence Boucher	D	11	0	1	1	4	
Newsy Lalonde	C	1	0	0	0	2	
Ken Randall	R	3	0	0	0	0	
Bill Holmes	C	1	0	0	0	0	
Jake Forbes	G	44	0	0	0	0	

		REGULAR SEASON					POSTSEASON
GOALTENDER		GP	MIN	GA	SH	GAA	no postseason play
Jake Forbes	(17-25-2)	44	2715	91	8	2.01	

TORONTO 15-24-5 35 5th (C) Conn Smythe
Maple Leafs

		REGULAR SEASON					POSTSEASON
PLAYER	POS	GP	G	A	PTS	PIM	no postseason play
Ace Bailey	R	42	15	13	28	82	
Bill Carson	C	40	16	6	22	41	

1926–1927 63

PLAYER	POS	REGULAR SEASON					POSTSEASON
		GP	G	A	PTS	PIM	*no postseason play*
Hap Day	D	44	11	5	16	50	
Butch Keeling	L	30	11	2	13	29	
Bert McCaffrey	R	43	5	5	10	43	
Bill Brydge	D	41	6	3	9	76	
Corbett Denneny	C	29	7	1	8	24	
George Patterson	L	17	4	2	6	17	
Bert Corbeau	D	41	1	2	3	88	
Haldor Halderson (2–2)	D	25	1	2	3	36	
Lloyd Gross	L	6	1	1	2	0	
Danny Cox	L	14	0	1	1	4	
Leo Bourgeault (1–2)	D	22	0	0	0	44	
Pete Bellefeuille	R	13	0	0	0	12	
Carl Voss	C	12	0	0	0	0	
Al Pudas	R	4	0	0	0	0	
Jesse Spring	D	2	0	0	0	0	
John Roach	G	44	0	0	0	0	

GOALTENDER		REGULAR SEASON					POSTSEASON
		GP	MIN	GA	SH	GAA	*no postseason play*
John Roach	(15-24-5)	44	2764	94	4	2.04	

NEW YORK 25-13-6 56 1st (A) Lester Patrick
Rangers

PLAYER	POS	REGULAR SEASON					POSTSEASON				
		GP	G	A	PTS	PIM	GP	G	A	PTS	PIM
Bill Cook	R	44	33	4	37	58	2	1	0	1	6
Frank Boucher	C	44	13	15	28	17	2	0	0	0	4
Bun Cook	L	44	14	9	23	42	2	0	0	0	6
Clarence Abel	D	44	8	4	12	78	2	0	1	1	8
Paul Thompson	L	43	7	3	10	12	2	0	0	0	0
Murray Murdoch	L	44	6	4	10	12	2	0	0	0	0
Stan Brown	D	24	6	2	8	14	2	0	0	0	0
Bill Boyd	R	41	4	1	5	40					
Ivan Johnson	D	27	3	2	5	66	2	0	0	0	8
Leo Bourgeault (2–2)	D	20	2	1	3	28	2	0	0	0	4
Reg Mackey	D	34	0	0	0	16	1	0	0	0	0
Ollie Reinikka	C	16	0	0	0	0					
Lester Patrick	D	1	0	0	0	2					
Lorne Chabot	G	36	0	0	0	0	2	0	0	0	0
Hal Winkler (1–2)	G	8	0	0	0	0					

GOALTENDER		REGULAR SEASON					POSTSEASON				
		GP	MIN	GA	SH	GAA	GP	MIN	GA	SH	GAA
Lorne Chabot	(22-9-5)	36	2307	56	10	1.46	2	120	3	1	1.50
Hal Winkler (1–2)	(3-4-1)	8	514	16	2	1.87					

BOSTON 21-20-3 45 2nd (A) Art Ross
Bruins

PLAYER	POS	REGULAR SEASON					POSTSEASON				
		GP	G	A	PTS	PIM	GP	G	A	PTS	PIM
Harry Oliver	R	42	18	6	24	17	8	4	2	6	4

		REGULAR SEASON				*POSTSEASON*				
PLAYER	*POS*	*GP*	*G*	*A*	*PTS*	*PIM*	*GP*	*G*	*A*	*PTS*	*PIM*
Jimmy Herbert	C	34	15	7	22	51	8	3	0	3	8
Frank Fredrickson (2–2)	C	28	14	7	21	33	8	2	2	4	22
Eddie Shore	D	40	12	6	18	130	8	1	1	2	40
Percy Galbraith	L	42	9	8	17	26	8	3	3	6	2
Duke Keats (1–2)	C	17	4	7	11	20					
Lionel Hitchman	D	41	3	6	9	70	8	1	0	1	31
Sprague Cleghorn	D	44	7	1	8	84	8	1	0	1	8
Billy Stuart	D	43	3	1	4	20	8	0	0	0	6
Archie Briden (1–2)	L	16	2	2	4	8					
Billy Boucher (2–2)	R	14	2	0	2	12	8	0	0	0	2
Billy Coutu	D	40	1	1	2	35	7	1	0	1	4
Harry Meeking (2–2)	L	23	1	0	1	2	7	0	0	0	0
Carson Cooper (1–2)	R	10	0	0	0	0					
Charlie Cahill	R	1	0	0	0	0					
Hal Winkler (2–2)	G	23	0	0	0	0	8	0	0	0	0
Charles Stewart	G	21	0	0	0	0					

		REGULAR SEASON				*POSTSEASON*			
GOALTENDER		*GP*	*MIN*	*GA*	*SH*	*GAA*	*GP*	*MIN*	*GA*	*SH*	*GAA*
Hal Winkler (2–2) (12-9-2)		23	1445	40	4	1.66	8	520	13	2	2.00
Charles Stewart (9-11-1)		21	1303	49	2	2.26					

CHICAGO 19-22-3 41 3rd (A) Pete Muldoon
Blackhawks

		REGULAR SEASON				*POSTSEASON*				
PLAYER	*POS*	*GP*	*G*	*A*	*PTS*	*PIM*	*GP*	*G*	*A*	*PTS*	*PIM*
Dick Irvin	C	43	18	18	36	34	2	2	0	2	4
Babe Dye	R	41	25	5	30	14	2	0	0	0	2
George Hay	L	35	14	8	22	12	2	1	2	3	2
Dunc MacKay	C	34	14	8	22	23	2	0	0	0	0
Gord Fraser	D	44	14	6	20	89	2	1	0	1	6
Charley McVeigh	C	43	12	4	16	23	2	0	0	0	0
Cully Wilson	R	39	8	4	12	40	2	1	0	1	6
Bob Trapp	D	44	4	2	6	92	2	0	0	0	4
Eddie Rodden	C	19	3	3	6	0	2	0	1	1	0
Duke Dukowski	D	28	3	2	5	16	2	0	0	0	0
Percy Traub	D	42	0	2	2	93	2	0	0	0	6
Ken Doraty	F	18	0	0	0	0					
Art Townsend	D	5	0	0	0	0					
Jim Riley (1–2)	L	3	0	0	0	0					
Gord McFarlane	R	2	0	0	0	0					
Hugh Lehman	G	44	0	0	0	0					

		REGULAR SEASON				*POSTSEASON*			
GOALTENDER		*GP*	*MIN*	*GA*	*SH*	*GAA*	*GP*	*MIN*	*GA*	*SH*	*GAA*
Hugh Lehman (19-22-3)		44	2797	116	5	2.49	2	120	10	0	5.00

1926-1927

PITTSBURGH 15-26-3 33 4th (A) Odie Cleghorn
Pirates

		REGULAR SEASON					POSTSEASON
PLAYER	POS	GP	G	A	PTS	PIM	no postseason play
Hib Milks	C	44	16	6	22	18	
Ty Arbour	L	41	7	8	18	10	
Harold Darragh	L	42	12	3	15	4	
John McKinnon	D	44	13	0	13	21	
Tex White	R	43	5	4	9	21	
Herb Drury	D	42	5	1	6	48	
Charlie Langlois (2-2)	R	36	5	1	6	36	
Francis McCurry	L	33	3	3	6	23	
Harold Cotton	L	37	5	0	5	17	
Rodger Smith	D	36	4	0	4	6	
Mickey McGuire	L	32	3	0	3	6	
Odie Cleghorn	R	3	0	0	0	0	
Lionel Conacher	D	9	0	0	0	12	
Roy Worters	G	44	0	0	0	0	

		REGULAR SEASON					POSTSEASON
GOALTENDER		GP	MIN	GA	SH	GAA	no postseason play
Roy Worters	(15-26-3)	44	2711	108	4	2.39	

DETROIT 12-28-4 28 5th (A) Art Duncan
Cougars

		REGULAR SEASON					POSTSEASON
PLAYER	POS	GP	G	A	PTS	PIM	no postseason play
Johnny Sheppard	L	43	13	8	21	60	
Frank Foyston	C	41	10	5	15	16	
Duke Keats (2-2)	C	25	12	1	13	32	
Clem Loughlin	D	34	7	3	10	40	
Fred Gordon	R	38	5	5	10	28	
Frank Fredrickson (1-2)	C	16	4	6	10	12	
Jack Walker	F	37	3	4	7	6	
Pete Bellefeuille (2-2)	R	18	6	0	6	14	
Jack Arbour	D	37	4	1	5	46	
Art Duncan	D	34	3	2	5	26	
Russ Oatman (1-2)	L	14	3	0	3	12	
Archie Briden (2-2)	L	26	3	0	3	28	
Haldor Halderson (1-2)	D	19	2	0	2	29	
Chapman Kitchen	D	17	0	2	2	42	
Jim Riley (2-2)	L	6	0	2	2	14	
Harry Meeking (1-2)	L	6	0	0	0	4	
Wilfred Hart (1-2)	L	2	0	0	0	0	
Hap Holmes	G	41	0	0	0	0	
Herb Stuart	G	3	0	0	0	0	

		REGULAR SEASON					POSTSEASON
GOALTENDER		GP	MIN	GA	SH	GAA	no postseason play
Herb Stuart	(1-2-0)	3	180	5	0	1.67	
Hap Holmes	(11-26-4)	41	2685	100	6	2.23	

TEAM TOTALS

TEAM	GP	G	A	P	PIM	GA	SH	Per Game G	A	PIM	GA
Canadian											
Ottawa	44	86	41	127	605	69	13	1.95	0.93	13.75	1.57
Montreal (C)	44	106	35	141	409	67	14	2.41	0.80	9.30	**1.52**
Montreal (M)	44	71	34	105	**716**	68	13	1.61	0.77	**16.27**	1.55
New York (A)	44	83	37	120	359	91	8	1.89	0.84	8.15	2.07
Toronto	44	78	43	121	545	94	4	1.77	0.97	12.39	2.14
American											
New York (R)	44	96	45	141	385	72	12	2.18	1.02	8.75	1.64
Boston	44	91	52	143	508	89	6	2.07	1.18	11.55	2.02
Chicago	44	**115**	**62**	**177**	436	116	5	**2.61**	**1.41**	9.90	2.64
Pittsburgh	44	78	26	104	222	108	4	1.77	0.59	5.05	2.45
Detroit	44	75	39	114	409	105	6	1.70	0.88	9.29	2.39
	440	879	414	1293	4594	879	85	2.00	0.94	10.44	2.00

PLAYOFFS

SERIES "A"
Montreal (C) 1, Montreal (M) 1
Montreal (C) 1, Montreal (M) 0 (OT)

MONTREAL (C) WINS
TOTAL GOAL SERIES, 2-1

SERIES "C"
Ottawa 4, Montreal (C) 0
Ottawa 1, Montreal (C) 1

OTTAWA WINS
TOTAL GOAL SERIES, 5-1

SERIES "E"
Ottawa 0, Boston 0
Ottawa 3, Boston 1
Ottawa 1, Boston 1
Ottawa 3, Boston 1

OTTAWA WINS
STANLEY CUP, 2-0

SERIES "B"
Boston 6, Chicago 1
Boston 4, Chicago 4

BOSTON WINS
TOTAL GOAL SERIES, 10-5

SERIES "D"
Boston 0, New York (R) 0
Boston 3, New York (R) 1

BOSTON WINS
TOTAL GOAL SERIES, 3-1

INDIVIDUAL TROPHY WINNERS

HART TROPHY (Most Valuable Player): Herb Gardiner, M(C)
LADY BYNG TROPHY (Gentlemanly Conduct): Billy Burch, N(A)
VEZINA TROPHY (Best Goaltender): George Hainsworth, M(C)

1927-1928
The Skipper Steps In

Midway through their playoff game on April 7, 1928, Lester Patrick's New York Rangers were in a pickle. Four minutes into the second stanza, in a 0–0 tie, Ranger goaltender Lorne Chabot was felled by a shot from the stick of Maroon forward Nels Stewart. As Chabot was being carted off to the hospital, Patrick was scrambling to find a replacement — a necessity in this era when teams suited up only one goalie each. In attendance at the contest were two candidates — Ottawa's Alec Connell and minor leaguer Hugh McCormick. However, as was his right, Maroon coach Eddie Gerard failed to sign off on either. Frustrated, Patrick turned to what he felt was his only option.

Patrick had been a stalwart in hockey circles for over two decades. First a pro in Eastern Canada, he, along with his brother Frank, helped found the Pacific Coast Hockey Association in 1911, centered in Vancouver. Over the next several seasons, as a player and a coach, he starred in the West Coast circuit, finally retiring as an active player in 1922, then after a comeback, for good in 1926.

A rule in effect during Patrick's career stated that penalized goaltenders had to serve their own penalties. In those cases, a player on the ice had to drop back to defend the cage — a practice that he had done on a few occasions. In this pivotal 1928 game, Patrick's expertise was about to be fully tested.

Earlier, with the same roster of clubs as the previous season, the NHL embarked on its eleventh season. Over the course of the campaign, the Montreal Canadiens (26-11-4, 59) kicked Ottawa out of its accustomed first-place position, knocking the Senators down to third. The Maroons finished between the two, claiming the Canadian Division's other playoff spot. Toronto and the New York Americans finished out of contention. In the American Division, Boston (20-13-11, 51) clambered on top, followed closely by the

Rangers and Pittsburgh. Detroit just missed the final playoff rung, while Chicago ended far behind.

Individually, Howie Morenz (Canadiens) swept scoring honors, accumulating the most goals (33), assists (18) and points (51), with the latter setting a new NHL record. At the other end of the spectrum, Boston's Eddie Shore racked up 165 penalty minutes. In net, Canadien goalie George Hainsworth let in barely more than a goal a game (1.05) to take GAA honors, while Alec Connell (Ottawa) and Hal Winkler (Boston), with 15 each, were at the top of the list of a half-dozen goalies with double-digit totals in shutouts.

In the opening round of the playoffs, the Maroons outgoaled the Senators, three to one, while the Rangers polished off the Pirates, six goals to four. In the semifinals, the Maroons outlasted their Montreal brethren with an overtime goal in game two, while the Rangers easily bested the Bruins, five goals to two. In the finals, the Maroons claimed a victory in the first game, 2–0, setting up the epic struggle on April 7.

When play resumed in the second period of game two, hockey fans were surprised to see the skipper himself skating to the Ranger goal, wearing Chabot's gear. Robert Styer in *The Hockey Encyclopedia* described what happened next: "The Rangers determinedly defended their gallant general-manager and at the end of the second period there was no score. Thirty seconds after the third period started, Cook scored and with six minutes left to play Stewart tied it up. At 7:05 in overtime, Frank Boucher threaded his way through the Maroon defense, drew out Clint Benedict and scored. Lester Patrick made 18 saves and as the tears rolled down his cheeks his joyous Rangers raised him to their shoulders and carried him to the dressing room." With sheer determination, and emotional adrenaline, Patrick had led his team to an improbable victory in probably the longest 45 minutes of his life.

In subsequent days, with substitute Joe Miller in net, the Rangers capped an impressive Cup run with a 2–1 win in the decisive fifth game, to take Lord Stanley's hardware home in only their second year of existence. Game two hero Frank Boucher led all playoff scorers with seven goals, three assists and 10 points. Despite playing for the losers, Maroon backstop Clint Benedict allowed a goal a game (1.00), while posting four shutouts.

As the NHL meandered through the next decade and beyond, other playoff teams pressed into service emergency netminders after starters went down with injury. However, in each of these cases the emergency backup would come from the ranks of fellow professionals from the NHL or the minors. Never again would the skipper have to don the "tools of ignorance" as the silver-haired Lester Patrick did that April night in 1928 — when he carried his Rangers to victory on his 44-year-old back.

1927-1928

STANDINGS

TEAM	GP	W	L	T	PTS	GF	GA
CANADIAN							
MONTREAL (C)	44	26	11	7	59	116	48
MONTREAL (M)	44	24	14	6	54	96	77
OTTAWA	44	20	14	10	50	78	57
TORONTO	44	18	18	8	44	89	88
NEW YORK (A)	44	11	27	6	28	63	128
AMERICAN							
BOSTON	44	20	13	11	51	77	70
NEW YORK (R)	44	19	16	9	47	94	79
PITTSBURGH	44	19	17	8	46	67	76
DETROIT	44	19	19	6	44	88	79
CHICAGO	44	7	34	3	17	68	134

LEADERS

PLAYER	TM	GP	G	A	PTS	PIM
Howie Morenz	M(C)	43	33	18	51	66
Aurel Joliat	M(C)	44	28	11	39	105
Frank Boucher	N(R)	44	23	12	35	15
George Hay	DET	42	22	13	35	20
Nels Stewart	M(M)	41	27	7	34	104
Art Gagne	M(C)	44	20	10	30	75
Bun Cook	N(R)	44	14	14	28	45
Bill Carson	TOR	32	20	6	26	36
Frank Finnigan	OTT	38	20	5	25	34
Two tied with					24	

GOALS	
Morenz, M(C)	33
Joliat, M(C)	28
Stewart, M(M)	27
Boucher, N(R)	23
Hay, DET	22

ASSISTS	
Morenz, M(C)	18
Bun Cook, N(R)	14
Hay, DET	13
Boucher, N(R)	12
Two tied with	11

GOALTENDER	TM	GP	MIN	GA	SH	GAA
George Hainsworth	M(C)	44	2730	48	13	**1.05**
Alec Connell	OTT	44	2760	57	15	1.24
Hal Winkler	BOS	44	**2780**	70	15	1.51
Roy Worters	PIT	44	2740	76	11	1.66
Clint Benedict	M(M)	44	2690	76	7	1.70
Hap Holmes	DET	44	2740	79	11	1.73
Lorne Chabot	N(R)	44	2730	79	11	1.74
John Roach	TOR	43	2690	88	4	1.96
Joe Miller	N(A)	28	1721	77	5	2.68
Chuck Gardiner	CHI	40	2420	**114**	3	2.83

PENALTY MINUTES	
Shore, BOS	165
Johnson, N(R)	146
Boucher, N(A)	129
Siebert, M(M)	109
Joliat, M(C)	105

SHUTOUTS	
Winkler, BOS	15
Connell, OTT	15
Hainsworth, M(C)	13
Three tied with	11

MONTREAL   26-11-7   59   1st (C)   Cecil Hart
Canadiens

		REGULAR SEASON					POSTSEASON				
PLAYER	POS	GP	G	A	PTS	PIM	GP	G	A	PTS	PIM
Howie Morenz	C	43	33	18	51	66	2	0	0	0	12
Aurel Joliat	L	44	28	11	39	105	2	0	0	0	4
Art Gagne	R	44	20	10	30	75	2	1	1	2	4
Sylvio Mantha	D	43	4	11	15	61	2	0	0	0	6

70   The National Hockey League, 1917–1967

PLAYER	POS	REGULAR SEASON					POSTSEASON				
		GP	G	A	PTS	PIM	GP	G	A	PTS	PIM
Albert Leduc	D	42	8	5	13	73	2	1	0	1	5
Leo Gaudreault	L	32	6	2	8	24					
Herb Gardiner	D	44	4	3	7	26	2	0	1	1	4
Al Lepine	C	20	4	1	5	6	1	0	0	0	0
Wilfred Hart	L	44	3	2	5	4	2	0	0	0	0
Wildor Larochelle	R	40	3	1	4	30	2	0	0	0	0
Leo Lafrance (1–2)	L	15	1	0	1	2					
George Patterson (2–2)	R	16	0	1	1	0					
Charlie Langlois (2–2)	R	32	0	0	0	14	2	0	0	0	0
Marty Burke (1–2)	D	11	0	0	0	10					
George Hainsworth	G	44	0	0	0	0	2	0	0	0	0

GOALTENDER		REGULAR SEASON					POSTSEASON				
		GP	MIN	GA	SH	GAA	GP	MIN	GA	SH	GAA
George Hainsworth	(26-11-7)	44	2730	48	13	1.05	2	128	3	0	1.41

MONTREAL   24-14-6   54   2nd (C)   Eddie Gerard
Maroons

PLAYER	POS	REGULAR SEASON					POSTSEASON				
		GP	G	A	PTS	PIM	GP	G	A	PTS	PIM
Nels Stewart	C	41	27	7	34	104	9	2	2	4	13
Reg Smith	C	34	14	5	19	72	9	2	1	3	23
Al Siebert	L	39	8	9	17	109	9	2	0	2	26
Joe Lamb	R	21	8	5	13	39	8	1	0	1	32
Mervyn Dutton	D	42	7	6	13	94	9	1	0	1	27
Jimmy Ward	R	42	10	2	12	44	9	1	1	2	6
Merlyn Phillips	C	40	7	5	12	33	9	2	1	3	9
Russ Oatman	L	43	7	4	11	36	9	1	0	1	18
Dunc Munro	D	43	5	2	7	35	9	0	2	2	8
Bill Touhey	L	29	2	0	2	2					
Fred Brown	L	19	1	0	1	0	9	0	0	0	0
Frank Carson	R	21	0	1	1	10	9	0	0	0	0
Hap Emms	L	10	0	1	1	10					
James Walsh	G	1	0	0	0	0					
Clint Benedict	G	44	0	0	0	0	9	0	0	0	0

GOALTENDER		REGULAR SEASON					POSTSEASON				
		GP	MIN	GA	SH	GAA	GP	MIN	GA	SH	GAA
James Walsh		1	40	1	0	1.50					
Clint Benedict	(24-14-6)	44	2690	76	7	1.70	9	555	8	4	**1.00**

OTTAWA   20-14-10   50   3rd (C)   David Gill
Senators

PLAYER	POS	REGULAR SEASON					POSTSEASON				
		GP	G	A	PTS	PIM	GP	G	A	PTS	PIM
Frank Finnigan	R	38	20	5	25	34	2	0	1	1	6
Hec Kilrea	L	43	19	4	23	66	2	1	0	1	0
King Clancy	D	39	8	7	15	73	2	0	0	0	6
Alex Smith	D	44	9	4	13	90	2	0	0	0	4
Frank Nighbor	C	42	8	5	13	46	2	0	0	0	2

1927–1928

PLAYER	POS	REGULAR SEASON					POSTSEASON				
		GP	G	A	PTS	PIM	GP	G	A	PTS	PIM
Georges Boucher	D	43	7	5	12	78	2	0	0	0	4
Harry Broadbent	R	43	3	2	5	62	2	0	0	0	0
Cy Denneny	L	43	3	0	3	12	2	0	0	0	0
Len Grosvenor	C	43	1	2	3	18	2	0	0	0	2
Al Shields	D	7	0	1	1	2	2	0	0	0	0
Sammy Godin	R	24	0	0	0	0					
Milt Halliday	L	13	0	0	0	2					
Gene Chouinard	D	8	0	0	0	0					
Alec Connell	G	44	0	0	0	0	2	0	0	0	0

GOALTENDER		REGULAR SEASON					POSTSEASON				
		GP	MIN	GA	SH	GAA	GP	MIN	GA	SH	GAA
Alec Connell	(20-14-10)	44	2760	57	15	1.24	2	120	3	0	1.50

TORONTO 18-18-8 44 4th (C) Conn Smythe
Maple Leafs

PLAYER	POS	REGULAR SEASON					POSTSEASON
		GP	G	A	PTS	PIM	no postseason play
Bill Carson	C	32	20	6	26	36	
Hap Day	D	27	9	8	17	48	
Butch Keeling	L	43	10	6	16	52	
Danny Cox	L	41	9	6	15	27	
Ace Bailey	R	43	9	3	12	72	
Art Duncan	D	43	7	5	12	97	
Gerry Lowrey	L	25	6	5	11	29	
Eddie Rodden (2–2)	C	25	3	6	9	36	
Jimmy Herbert (2–2)	C	31	7	1	8	40	
Art Smith	D	15	5	3	8	22	
Bert McCaffrey (1–2)	R	9	1	1	2	9	
Beattie Ramsay	D	43	0	2	2	10	
George Patterson (1–2)	L	12	1	0	1	14	
Ed Gorman	D	19	0	1	1	30	
Joe Primeau	C	2	0	0	0	0	
John Roach	G	43	0	0	0	0	
Joe Ironstone	G	1	0	0	0	0	

GOALTENDER		REGULAR SEASON					POSTSEASON
		GP	MIN	GA	SH	GAA	no postseason play
Joe Ironstone	(0-0-1)	1	70	0	1	0.00	
John Roach	(18-18-7)	43	2690	88	4	1.96	

NEW YORK 11-27-6 28 5th (C) Shorty Green
Americans

PLAYER	POS	REGULAR SEASON					POSTSEASON
		GP	G	A	PTS	PIM	no postseason play
Norm Himes	C	44	14	5	19	22	
Lionel Conacher	D	35	11	6	17	82	
Billy Burch	C	32	10	2	12	34	
Leo Reise	D	43	8	1	9	62	
Red Green	L	40	6	1	7	67	

		REGULAR SEASON					*POSTSEASON*
PLAYER	*POS*	*GP*	*G*	*A*	*PTS*	*PIM*	no postseason play
Billy Boucher	R	43	5	2	7	58	
Alex McKinnon	R	43	3	3	6	71	
Clarence Boucher	D	36	2	1	3	129	
Joe Simpson	D	24	2	0	2	32	
Ed Bouchard	D	39	1	0	1	27	
Marty Barry	C	9	1	0	1	2	
Sam Rothschild (1–2)	L	5	0	0	0	4	
Jake Forbes	G	16	0	0	0	0	
Joe Miller (1–2)	G	28	0	0	0	0	

		REGULAR SEASON					*POSTSEASON*
GOALTENDER		*GP*	*MIN*	*GA*	*SH*	*GAA*	no postseason play
Norm Himes		1	19	0	0	0.00	
Joe Miller (1–2)	(8-16-4)	28	1721	77	5	2.68	
Jake Forbes	(3-11-2)	16	980	51	2	3.12	

BOSTON 20-13-11   51   1st (A)   Art Ross
Bruins

		REGULAR SEASON					*POSTSEASON*				
PLAYER	*POS*	*GP*	*G*	*A*	*PTS*	*PIM*	*GP*	*G*	*A*	*PTS*	*PIM*
Harry Oliver	R	43	13	5	18	20	2	2	0	2	4
Eddie Shore	D	43	11	6	17	**165**	2	0	0	0	8
Frank Fredrickson	C	41	10	4	14	83	2	0	1	1	4
Norm Gainor	C	42	8	4	12	35	2	0	0	0	6
Jimmy Herbert (1–2)	C	12	8	3	11	22					
Percy Galbraith	L	42	6	5	11	26	2	0	1	1	6
Harry Connor	L	42	9	1	10	36	2	0	0	0	0
Lionel Hitchman	D	44	5	3	8	87	2	0	0	0	2
Dit Clapper	R	40	4	1	5	20	2	0	0	0	2
Fred Gordon	R	43	3	2	5	40	2	0	0	0	0
Sprague Cleghorn	D	37	2	2	4	14	2	0	0	0	0
Hago Harrington	L	22	1	0	1	7	2	0	0	0	0
Patrick Clark	D	5	0	0	0	0					
Marty Lauder	D	3	0	0	0	2					
Hal Winkler	G	44	0	0	0	0	2	0	0	0	0

		REGULAR SEASON					*POSTSEASON*				
GOALTENDER		*GP*	*MIN*	*GA*	*SH*	*GAA*	*GP*	*MIN*	*GA*	*SH*	*GAA*
Hal Winkler	(20-13-**11**)	44	2780	70	**15**	1.51	2	120	5	0	2.50

NEW YORK 19-16-9   47   2nd (A)   Lester Patrick
Rangers

		REGULAR SEASON					*POSTSEASON*				
PLAYER	*POS*	*GP*	*G*	*A*	*PTS*	*PIM*	*GP*	*G*	*A*	*PTS*	*PIM*
Frank Boucher	C	44	23	12	35	15	9	7	3	10	2
Bun Cook	L	44	14	14	28	45	9	2	1	3	10
Bill Cook	R	43	18	6	24	42	9	2	3	5	26
Ivan Johnson	D	42	10	6	16	146	9	1	1	2	**46**
Murray Murdoch	L	44	7	3	10	14	9	2	1	3	12
Paul Thompson	L	42	4	4	8	22	8	0	0	0	30

1927–1928 73

		REGULAR SEASON					*POSTSEASON*				
PLAYER	*POS*	*GP*	*G*	*A*	*PTS*	*PIM*	*GP*	*G*	*A*	*PTS*	*PIM*
Alex Gray	R	43	7	0	7	30	9	1	0	1	0
Leo Bourgeault	D	37	7	0	7	7	9	0	0	0	8
Bill Boyd	R	43	4	0	4	11	9	0	0	0	4
Clarence Abel	D	23	0	1	1	28	9	1	0	1	14
Laurie Scott	C	23	0	1	1	6					
Francis Callighen	D	36	0	0	0	32	9	0	0	0	0
Lorne Chabot	G	44	0	0	0	0	6	0	0	0	0
Joe Miller (2–2)	G						3	0	0	0	0
Lester Patrick	G						1	0	0	0	0

		REGULAR SEASON					*POSTSEASON*				
GOALTENDER		*GP*	*MIN*	*GA*	*SH*	*GAA*	*GP*	*MIN*	*GA*	*SH*	*GAA*
Lorne Chabot	(19-16-9)	44	2730	79	11	1.74	6	321	8	1	1.50
Joe Miller (2–2)							3	180	3	1	1.00
Lester Patrick							1	45	1	0	0.75

PITTSBURGH 19-17-8 46 3rd (A) Odie Cleghorn
Pirates

		REGULAR SEASON					*POSTSEASON*				
PLAYER	*POS*	*GP*	*G*	*A*	*PTS*	*PIM*	*GP*	*G*	*A*	*PTS*	*PIM*
Hib Milks	C	44	18	3	21	32	2	0	0	0	2
Harold Darragh	L	44	13	2	15	16	2	0	1	1	0
Harold Cotton	L	42	9	3	12	40	2	1	1	2	2
Herb Drury	R	44	6	4	10	44	2	0	1	1	0
Bert McCaffrey (2–2)	R	35	6	3	9	14					
Francis McCurry	L	44	5	3	8	60	2	0	0	0	0
Tex White	R	44	5	1	6	54	2	0	0	0	2
John McKinnon	D	43	3	3	6	71	2	0	0	0	4
Marty Burke (2–2)	D	35	2	1	3	51	2	1	0	1	2
Rodger Smith	D	43	1	0	1	30	2	2	0	2	0
Sam Rothschild (2–2)	L	12	0	0	0	0					
Charlie Langlois (1–2)	D	8	0	0	0	8					
Ty Arbour	L	7	0	0	0	0					
Mickey McGuire	L	4	0	0	0	0					
Odie Cleghorn	R	2	0	0	0	4					
Roy Worters	G	44	0	0	0	0	2	0	0	0	0

		REGULAR SEASON					*POSTSEASON*				
GOALTENDER		*GP*	*MIN*	*GA*	*SH*	*GAA*	*GP*	*MIN*	*GA*	*SH*	*GAA*
Roy Worters	(19-17-8)	44	2740	76	11	1.66	2	120	6	0	3.00

DETROIT 19-19-6 44 4th (A) Jack Adams
Cougars

		REGULAR SEASON					*POSTSEASON*
PLAYER	*POS*	*GP*	*G*	*A*	*PTS*	*PIM*	*no postseason play*
George Hay	L	42	22	13	35	20	
Johnny Sheppard	L	44	10	10	20	40	
Carson Cooper	R	43	15	2	17	32	
Larry Aurie	R	44	13	3	16	43	

		REGULAR SEASON					*POSTSEASON*
PLAYER	*POS*	*GP*	*G*	*A*	*PTS*	*PIM*	*no postseason play*
Reg Noble	D	44	6	8	14	63	
Frank Foyston	C	23	7	2	9	16	
Jack Walker	F	43	2	4	6	12	
Percy Traub	D	44	3	1	4	78	
Gord Fraser (2–2)	D	30	3	1	4	50	
Pete Palangio	L	14	3	0	3	8	
Clem Loughlin	D	43	1	2	3	21	
Stan Brown	D	24	2	0	2	4	
Frank Sheppard	C	8	1	1	2	0	
Duke Keats (1–2)	C	5	0	2	2	6	
Hap Holmes	G	44	0	0	0	0	

		REGULAR SEASON					*POSTSEASON*
GOALTENDER		*GP*	*MIN*	*GA*	*SH*	*GAA*	*no postseason play*
Hap Holmes	(19-19-6)	44	2740	79	11	1.73	

CHICAGO   7-34-3   17   5th (A)   Barney Stanley
Blackhawks   Hugh Lehman

		REGULAR SEASON					*POSTSEASON*				
PLAYER	*POS*	*GP*	*G*	*A*	*PTS*	*PIM*	*GP*	*G*	*A*	*PTS*	*PIM*
Duke Keats (2–2)	C	32	14	8	22	55					
Dunc MacKay	C	36	17	4	21	23					
Charley McVeigh	L	43	6	7	13	10					
Cy Wentworth	D	43	5	5	10	31					
Ty Arbour (2–2)	L	32	5	5	10	32					
Dick Irvin	C	12	5	4	9	14					
Corbett Denneny	C	18	5	0	5	12					
Allison McCalmon	R	23	2	0	2	8					
Cecil Browne	L	13	2	0	2	4					
Amby Moran	D	23	1	1	2	14					
Ralph Taylor	D	22	1	1	2	39					
Earl Miller	L	21	1	1	2	32					
Gord Fraser (1–2)	D	11	1	1	2	10					
Bob Trapp	D	38	0	2	2	37					
Eddie Rodden (1–2)	C	9	0	2	2	6					
Teddy Graham	D	19	1	0	1	8					
Leo Lafrance (2–2)	L	14	1	0	1	4					
Nick Wasnie	R	14	1	0	1	22					
Val Hoffinger	L	18	0	1	1	18					
Babe Dye	R	10	0	0	0	0					
Bobby Burns	L	1	0	0	0	0					
Barney Stanley	R	1	0	0	0	0					
Chuck Gardiner	G	40	0	0	0	0					
Hugh Lehman	G	4	0	0	0	0					

		REGULAR SEASON					*POSTSEASON*
GOALTENDER		*GP*	*MIN*	*GA*	*SH*	*GAA*	*no postseason play*
Chuck Gardiner	(6-**32**-2)	40	2420	**114**	3	2.83	
Hugh Lehman	(1-2-1)	4	250	20	1	4.80	

1927-1928

TEAM TOTALS

TEAM	GP	G	A	P	PIM	GA	SH	Per Game G	A	PIM	GA
Canadian											
Montreal (C)	44	114	65	179	496	48	13	2.59	1.47	11.27	**1.09**
Montreal (M)	44	96	47	143	588	77	7	2.18	1.07	13.36	1.73
Ottawa	44	78	35	113	483	57	15	1.77	0.80	10.98	1.30
Toronto	44	87	53	140	522	88	5	1.98	1.20	11.86	2.00
New York (A)	44	63	21	84	**590**	128	7	1.43	0.47	**13.40**	2.91
American											
Boston	44	80	36	116	557	70	15	1.82	0.81	12.66	1.59
New York (R)	44	94	47	141	398	79	11	2.14	1.07	9.05	1.80
Pittsburgh	44	68	23	91	424	76	11	1.55	0.52	9.64	1.73
Detroit	44	88	49	137	393	79	11	2.00	1.11	8.93	1.80
Chicago	44	68	42	110	379	**134**	4	1.55	0.95	8.61	3.05
	440	836	418	1254	4830	836	99	1.90	0.95	10.98	1.90

PLAYOFFS

SERIES "A"
Montreal (M) 1, Ottawa 0
Montreal (M) 2, Ottawa 1

**MONTREAL (M) WINS
TOTAL GOAL SERIES, 3-1**

SERIES "C"
Montreal (M) 2, Montreal (C) 2
Montreal (M) 1, Montreal (C) 0 (OT)

**MONTREAL (M) WINS
TOTAL GOAL SERIES, 3-2**

SERIES "E"
Montreal (M) 2, New York (R) 0
New York (R) 2, Montreal (M) 1 (OT)
Montreal (M) 2, New York (R) 0
New York (R) 1, Montreal (M) 0
New York (R) 2, Montreal 1

**NEW YORK (R) WINS
STANLEY CUP, 3-2**

SERIES "B"
New York (R) 4, Pittsburgh 0
Pittsburgh 4, New York (R) 2

**NEW YORK (R) WINS
TOTAL GOAL SERIES, 6-4**

SERIES "D"
New York (R) 1, Boston 1
New York (R) 4, Boston 1

**NEW YORK (R) WINS
TOTAL GOAL SERIES, 5-2**

INDIVIDUAL TROPHY WINNERS

HART TROPHY (Most Valuable Player): Howie Morenz, M(C)
LADY BYNG TROPHY (Gentlemanly Conduct): Frank Boucher, N(R)
VEZINA TROPHY (Best Goaltender): George Hainsworth, M(C)

1928-1929
Shutout

As the decade of the 1920s wound down, the high-scoring days of the early NHL were but a memory. By the time the league entered its second decade, stingy defense featuring strong goaltending was the name of the game, while scoring took a back seat. For instance, in the previous season (1927-28), 99 shutouts were registered by NHL netminders. As high as this total was, the mark was about to be obliterated.

In the first year of the NHL (1917-18), teams averaged over five goals a game apiece. As team defenses clamped down the totals dropped year-by-year. By 1923-24, teams were scoring only a little over 2.5 goals per contest. Despite rule changes that opened up forward passing in the defensive and neutral zones, goal scoring continued to plummet, dropping to below two goals a game in 1927-28. Low as this was, the bottom had yet to be reached.

Continuing this trend, opening night of the 1928-29 season saw only nine goals scored by the ten competing teams. Over the full season, league scorers managed to muster less than 1.5 goals per game. The clubs were "led" by the Bruins who netted two goals per game, while on the back end, the punchless Blackhawks had a particularly frustrating campaign, scoring only 33 markers in their 44 games (0.75). However, this paucity on the scoring sheets would lead to goaltending marvels never before seen in league annals.

In the overall standings, the Canadiens (22-7-15, 59) won the Canadian Division, while Boston (26-13-5, 57) took top honors in the American. The New York Americans and Toronto snagged the two other Canadian playoff slots, while the Rangers and Detroit claimed the American Division's final two postseason berths. The Maroons, Ottawa, Pittsburgh and Chicago finished out of contention.

Virtually every NHL goaltender during the 1928-29 season enjoyed a solid season. Every starting netminder had a GAA under 1.85, with most coming in under 1.50. In addition, eight of the starting ten had at least 10 shutouts each. However, in this stellar array of goaltending performances, one effort stood above the rest.

Canadiens' goalie George Hainsworth had a season for the ages in 1928-29. Over the campaign, he allowed only 43 goals in 44 games — giving him an eye-popping 0.92 GAA. In addition, he posted 22 shutouts — including four in a row in late February and early March. (Not every one of the 22 shutouts was a win — five were 0-0 ties.) Only once did he allow as many as five goals to an opponent.

Taking a back seat to the netminders, Toronto's Ace Bailey won the scoring title with a modest total of 32 points, courtesy of his league best 22 goals. In addition, Frank Boucher added the most helpers (16) and Maroon enforcer Mervyn Dutton spent the most time in the sin bin (139).

In the playoffs, a new wrinkle was added. Beginning this year, the two division winners would square off in a best-of-five series, while the two second place clubs and two third place teams would battle in total goal series. Then, the winners of the second and third place series would face one another to determine an opponent for the victorious first place combatant.

In the battle of division winners, Boston came out on top, three games to none, shutting out Hainsworth's Canadiens twice. The other two matchups were won by Toronto and the Rangers, with the latter series witnessing only one tally — the lone marker coming well into the second overtime period of the second game. In the semifinals, the Rangers prevailed again with an overtime marker in game two. In the finals, the Bruins waltzed to victory, scoring 2-0 and 2-1 victories to claim the Cup. Toronto's Andy Blair and the Rangers' Butch Keeling led playoff scorers with three goals and points apiece. Bruins goaler Tiny Thompson posted a sparkling 0.60 GAA with three shutouts, though he was tied in the latter mark by John Roach (Rangers).

The very next year, the NHL unveiled a new rule, causing tears of joy to course down the faces of long frustrated league skaters. The new rule changes ensured that Hainsworth's record 0.96 GAA and 22 shutouts would remain safe — neither has been approached since. Never again has the league witnessed such a goalie-dominated season — a campaign where more than a quarter of all the games resulted in a shutout

STANDINGS

TEAM	GP	W	L	T	PTS	GF	GA
CANADIAN							
MONTREAL (C)	44	22	7	15	59	71	43
NEW YORK (A)	44	19	13	12	50	53	53

TEAM	GP	W	L	T	PTS	GF	GA
TORONTO	44	21	18	5	47	85	69
OTTAWA	44	14	17	13	41	54	67
MONTREAL (M)	44	15	20	9	39	67	65
AMERICAN							
BOSTON	44	26	13	5	57	89	52
NEW YORK (R)	44	21	13	10	52	72	65
DETROIT	44	19	16	9	47	72	63
PITTSBURGH	44	9	27	8	26	46	80
CHICAGO	44	7	29	8	22	33	85

LEADERS

PLAYER	TM	GP	G	A	PTS	PIM
Ace Bailey	TOR	44	22	10	32	78
Nels Stewart	M(M)	44	21	8	29	74
Carson Cooper	DET	44	18	9	27	14
Howie Morenz	M(C)	42	17	10	27	47
Andrew Blair	TOR	44	12	15	27	41
Frank Boucher	N(R)	44	10	16	26	8
Harry Oliver	BOS	43	17	6	23	24
Bill Cook	N(R)	43	15	8	23	41
Jimmy Ward	M(M)	44	14	8	22	46
Seven tied with			19			

GOALS
Bailey, TOR		22
Stewart, M(M)		21
Cooper, DET		18
Oliver, BOS		17
Morenz, M(C)		17

ASSISTS
Boucher, N(R)		16
Blair, TOR		15
Lowrey, T-P		12
Bailey, TOR		10
Morenz, M(C)		10

GOALTENDER	TM	GP	MIN	GA	SH	GAA
George Hainsworth	M(C)	44	2800	43	22	0.92
Tiny Thompson	BOS	44	2710	52	12	1.15
Roy Worters	N(A)	38	2390	46	13	1.15
Clarence Dolson	DET	44	2750	63	10	1.37
John Roach	N(R)	44	2760	65	13	1.41
Alec Connell	OTT	44	2820	67	7	1.43
Clint Benedict	M(M)	37	2300	57	11	1.49
Lorne Chabot	TOR	43	2458	66	12	1.61
Joe Miller	PIT	44	2780	80	11	1.73
Chuck Gardiner	CHI	44	2758	85	5	1.85

PENALTY MINUTES
Dutton, M(M)		139
Conacher, N(A)		122
R. Smith, M(M)		120
Shore, BOS		96
A. Smith, OTT		96

SHUTOUTS
Hainsworth, M(C)		22
Worters, N(A)		13
Roach, N(R)		13
Thompson, BOS		12
Chabot, TOR		12

MONTREAL Canadiens   22-7-15   59   1st (C)   Cecil Hart

		REGULAR SEASON					POSTSEASON				
PLAYER	POS	GP	G	A	PTS	PIM	GP	G	A	PTS	PIM
Howie Morenz	C	42	17	10	27	47	3	0	0	0	6
Aurel Joliat	L	44	12	5	17	59	3	1	1	2	10
Sylvio Mantha	D	44	9	4	13	56	3	0	0	0	0
Al Leduc	D	43	9	2	11	79	3	1	0	1	4
Art Gagne	R	44	7	3	10	52	3	0	0	0	12
George Patterson	C	44	4	5	9	34	3	0	0	0	2
Alfred Lepine	C	44	6	1	7	48	3	0	0	0	2

1928–1929 79

PLAYER	POS	REGULAR SEASON					POSTSEASON				
		GP	G	A	PTS	PIM	GP	G	A	PTS	PIM
Armand Mondou	L	32	3	4	7	6	3	0	0	0	2
Marty Burke	D	44	4	2	6	68	3	0	0	0	8
Wildor Larochelle	R	2	0	0	0	0					
Pete Palangio	L	2	0	0	0	0					
Herb Gardiner (2–2)	D	8	0	0	0	0	3	0	0	0	0
Leo Gaudreault	L	11	0	0	0	4					
Art Lesieur (2–2)	D	15	0	0	0	0					
Gerry Carson (1–2)	D	30	0	0	0	4					
Georges Mantha	L	31	0	0	0	8	3	0	0	0	0
George Hainsworth	G	44	0	0	0	0	3	0	0	0	0

GOALTENDER	REGULAR SEASON					POSTSEASON				
	GP	MIN	GA	SH	GAA	GP	MIN	GA	SH	GAA
George Hainsworth (22-7-15)	44	2800	43	22	0.92	3	180	5	0	1.66

NEW YORK 19-13-12 50 2nd (C) Tommy Gorman
Americans

PLAYER	POS	REGULAR SEASON					POSTSEASON				
		GP	G	A	PTS	PIM	GP	G	A	PTS	PIM
Billy Burch	C	44	11	5	16	45	2	0	0	0	0
Norm Himes	C	44	10	0	10	25	2	0	0	0	0
Johnny Sheppard	L	43	5	4	9	38	2	0	0	0	0
Harry Connor	L	43	6	2	8	83	2	0	0	0	6
Charley McVeigh	C	44	6	2	8	16	2	0	0	0	2
Lionel Conacher	D	44	5	2	7	132	2	0	0	0	10
Leo Reise	D	44	4	1	5	32	2	0	0	0	0
Joe Simpson	D	43	3	2	5	29	2	0	0	0	0
Harry Broadbent	R	44	1	4	5	59	2	0	0	0	2
Tex White (2–2)	R	13	1	1	2	8	2	0	0	0	2
Babe Dye	R	42	1	0	1	17	1	0	0	0	0
Jesse Spring (1–2)	D	23	0	0	0	0					
Ed Bouchard (1–2)	L	6	0	0	0	2					
Roy Worters	G	38	0	0	0	0	2	0	0	0	0
James Walsh (1–2)	G	4	0	0	0	0					
Jake Forbes	G	1	0	0	0	0					

GOALTENDER		REGULAR SEASON					POSTSEASON				
		GP	MIN	GA	SH	GAA	GP	MIN	GA	SH	GAA
James Walsh (1–2)	(2-0-2)	4	260	1	3	0.23					
Roy Worters	(16-12-10)	38	2390	46	13	1.15	2	150	1	0	0.40
Norm Himes	(0-1-0)	1	60	3	0	3.00					
Jake Forbes	(1-0-0)	1	60	3	0	3.00					

TORONTO 21-18-5 47 3rd (C) Conn Smythe
Maple Leafs

PLAYER	POS	REGULAR SEASON					POSTSEASON				
		GP	G	A	PTS	PIM	GP	G	A	PTS	PIM
Ace Bailey	L	44	22	10	32	78	4	1	2	3	4
Andy Blair	C	44	12	15	27	41	4	3	0	3	2
Danny Cox	L	42	12	7	19	14	4	0	1	1	4

80 The National Hockey League, 1917–1967

		REGULAR SEASON					POSTSEASON				
PLAYER	POS	GP	G	A	PTS	PIM	GP	G	A	PTS	PIM
Bill Carson (1–2)	C	24	7	6	13	45					
George Horne	R	39	9	3	12	32	4	0	0	0	2
Hap Day	D	44	6	6	12	85	4	1	0	1	4
Gerry Lowrey (1–2)	L	28	3	9	12	24					
Art Duncan	D	39	4	4	8	53	4	0	0	0	0
Eric Pettinger (2–2)	L	25	3	3	6	24	4	1	0	1	8
Art Smith	D	43	5	0	5	91	4	1	1	2	8
Harold Cotton (2–2)	L	11	1	2	3	8					
Jack Arbour	D	10	1	0	1	10					
Joe Primeau	C	6	0	1	1	2					
Carl Voss	C	2	0	0	0	0					
Benny Grant	G	3	0	0	0	0					
Alex Gray	R	7	0	0	0	2					
Red Horner	D	22	0	0	0	30	4	1	0	1	2
Lorne Chabot	G	43	0	0	0	2	4	0	0	0	0

		REGULAR SEASON					POSTSEASON				
GOALTENDER		GP	MIN	GA	SH	GAA	GP	MIN	GA	SH	GAA
Lorne Chabot	(20-18-5)	43	2458	66	12	1.61	4	242	5	0	1.24
Benny Grant	(1-0-0)	3	110	3	0	1.64					

OTTAWA 14-17-13   41   4th (C)   David Gill
Senators

		REGULAR SEASON					POSTSEASON
PLAYER	POS	GP	G	A	PTS	PIM	no postseason play
Frank Finnigan	R	44	15	4	19	71	
King Clancy	D	44	13	2	15	89	
Bill Tuohey	L	44	9	3	12	28	
Hec Kilrea	R	38	5	7	12	36	
Alex Smith	D	44	1	7	8	96	
Len Grosvenor	C	42	3	2	5	16	
Frank Nighbor	C	30	1	4	5	22	
Georges Boucher (1–2)	D	29	3	1	4	60	
Sammy Godin	R	23	2	1	3	21	
Fred Elliott	R	43	2	0	2	6	
Al Shields	D	42	0	1	1	10	
Joe Lamb (2–2)	R	6	0	0	0	8	
Milt Halliday	L	16	0	0	0	0	
Alec Connell	G	44	0	0	0	0	

		REGULAR SEASON					POSTSEASON
GOALTENDER		GP	MIN	GA	SH	GAA	no postseason play
Alec Connell	(14-17-13)	44	2820	67	7	1.43	

MONTREAL 15-20-9   39   5th (C)   Eddie Gerard
Maroons

		REGULAR SEASON					POSTSEASON				
PLAYER	POS	GP	G	A	PTS	PIM	GP	G	A	PTS	PIM
Nels Stewart	C	44	21	8	29	74					
Jimmy Ward	R	44	14	8	22	46					

1928-1929

PLAYER	POS	REGULAR SEASON					POSTSEASON
		GP	G	A	PTS	PIM	no postseason play
Reg Smith	C	41	10	9	19	120	
Merlyn Phillips	C	42	6	5	11	41	
Al Siebert	L	39	3	5	8	52	
Dave Trottier	W	37	2	4	6	69	
Joe Lamb (1–2)	R	30	4	1	5	34	
Mervyn Dutton	D	44	1	3	4	**139**	
Earl Robinson	R	33	2	1	3	2	
Henry Hicks	D	44	2	0	2	27	
Georges Boucher (2–2)	D	12	1	1	2	10	
Russ Oatman (1–2)	L	11	1	0	1	12	
Lorne Northcutt	L	6	0	0	0	0	
Cliff McBride	R	1	0	0	0	0	
Dunc Munro	D	1	0	0	0	0	
James Walsh (2–2)	G	7	0	0	0	0	
Clint Benedict	G	37	0	0	0	0	

GOALTENDER		REGULAR SEASON					POSTSEASON
		GP	MIN	GA	SH	GAA	no postseason play
James Walsh (2–2) (1-4-2)		7	450	8	1	1.07	
Clint Benedict (14-16-7)		37	2300	57	11	1.49	

BOSTON 26-13-5 57 1st (A) Cy Denneny
Bruins

PLAYER	POS	REGULAR SEASON					POSTSEASON				
		GP	G	A	PTS	PIM	GP	G	A	PTS	PIM
Harry Oliver	R	43	17	6	23	24	5	1	1	2	8
Norm Gainor	C	39	14	5	19	30	5	2	0	2	4
Eddie Shore	D	39	12	7	19	96	5	1	1	2	28
Cooney Weiland	C	40	11	7	18	16	5	2	0	2	2
Dit Clapper	D	40	9	2	11	48	5	1	0	1	0
Dunc MacKay (2–2)	C	30	8	2	10	18	3	0	0	0	2
George Owen	D	26	5	4	9	48	5	0	0	0	0
Bill Carson (2–2)	C	19	4	2	6	10	5	2	0	2	8
Fr. Frederickson (1–2)	C	12	3	1	4	24					
Percy Galbraith	L	38	2	1	3	44	5	0	0	0	2
Cy Denneny	L	23	1	2	3	2	3	0	0	0	0
Myles Lane (2–2)	D	5	1	0	1	2	5	0	0	0	0
Lloyd Klein	R	14	1	0	1	5	1	0	0	0	0
Lionel Hitchman	D	37	1	0	1	64	5	0	1	1	22
Eric Pettinger (1–2)	L	17	0	0	0	17					
Eddie Rodden	C	20	0	0	0	10	1	0	0	0	0
Red Green	L	25	0	0	0	16	1	0	0	0	0
Tiny Thompson	G	44	0	0	0	0	5	0	0	0	0

GOALTENDER	REGULAR SEASON					POSTSEASON				
	GP	MIN	GA	SH	GAA	GP	MIN	GA	SH	GAA
Tiny Thompson (**26-13-5**)	44	2710	52	12	1.15	5	300	3	**3**	**0.60**

NEW YORK 21-13-10 52 2nd (A) Lester Patrick
Rangers

		REGULAR SEASON				POSTSEASON				
PLAYER	POS	GP	G	A	PTS	PIM	GP	G	A	PTS	PIM
Frank Boucher	C	44	10	16	26	8	6	1	0	1	0
Bill Cook	R	43	15	8	23	41	6	0	0	0	6
Bun Cook	L	43	13	5	18	70	6	1	0	1	12
Paul Thompson	L	44	10	7	17	38	6	0	2	2	6
Murray Murdoch	L	44	8	6	14	18	6	0	0	0	2
Butch Keeling	L	43	6	3	9	35	6	3	0	3	2
Leo Bourgeault	D	44	2	3	5	59	6	0	0	0	0
Clarence Abel	D	33	3	1	4	41	6	0	0	0	8
Melville Vail	D	18	3	0	3	16	6	0	0	0	2
Russ Oatman (2–2)	L	27	1	1	2	10	4	0	0	0	0
Myles Lane (1–2)	D	24	1	0	1	22					
Bill Boyd	R	11	0	0	0	5	1	0	0	0	0
Gerry Carson (2–2)	D	10	0	0	0	5	4	0	0	0	0
Ivan Johnson	D	9	0	0	0	14	6	0	0	0	26
John Roach	G	44	0	0	0	0	6	0	0	0	0
Leroy Goldsworthy	R	1	0	0	0	0					
Ralph Taylor (2–2)	D	1	0	0	0	0					

		REGULAR SEASON				POSTSEASON			
GOALTENDER		GP	MIN	GA	SH	GAA	GP	MIN	GA	SH	GAA
John Roach	(21-13-10)	44	2760	65	13	1.41	6	392	5	3	0.77

DETROIT 19-16-9 47 3rd (A) Jack Adams
Cougars

		REGULAR SEASON				POSTSEASON				
PLAYER	POS	GP	G	A	PTS	PIM	GP	G	A	PTS	PIM
Carson Cooper	R	44	18	9	27	14	2	0	0	0	2
George Hay	L	42	11	8	19	14	2	1	0	1	0
Bob Connors	L	41	13	3	16	68	2	0	0	0	10
Herbie Lewis	L	37	9	5	14	33					
Jimmy Herbert	C	40	9	5	14	34	1	0	0	0	2
Reg Noble	D	44	6	4	10	52	2	0	0	0	2
Bernie Brophy	L	37	2	4	6	23	2	0	0	0	2
Bill Brydge	D	31	2	2	4	59	2	0	0	0	4
Larry Aurie	R	35	1	1	2	26	2	1	0	1	2
Pete Bellefeuille	R	1	1	0	1	0					
Frank Daley	L	5	0	0	0	0	2	0	0	0	0
Farrand Gillie	F	1	0	0	0	0					
Gord Fraser	D	13	0	0	0	12					
Percy Traub	D	44	0	0	0	46	1	0	0	0	0
Clarence Dolson	G	44	0	0	0	0	2	0	0	0	0

		REGULAR SEASON				POSTSEASON			
GOALTENDER		GP	MIN	GA	SH	GAA	GP	MIN	GA	SH	GAA
Clarence Dolson	(19-16-9)	44	2750	63	10	1.37	2	120	7	0	3.50

1928-1929

PITTSBURGH Pirates   9-27-8   26   4th (A)   Odie Cleghorn

PLAYER	POS	GP	G	A	PTS	PIM		
		REGULAR SEASON					*POSTSEASON*	
Harold Darragh	R	43	9	3	12	6	no postseason play	
Hib Milks	L	44	9	3	12	22		
Fr. Frederickson (2–2)	C	31	3	7	10	28		
Herb Drury	D	44	5	4	9	49		
Tex White (1–2)	R	32	4	4	8	18		
Rodger Smith	D	44	4	2	6	49		
Harold Cotton (1–2)	L	32	3	2	5	38		
Gerry Lowrey (2–2)	L	16	2	3	5	6		
Al Holway	D	44	4	0	4	20		
Dunc MacKay (1–2)	C	10	1	0	1	2		
John McKinnon	D	39	1	0	1	44		
Bert McCaffrey	D	42	1	0	1	34		
Francis McCurry	L	35	0	1	1	4		
Jesse Spring (2–2)	D	9	0	0	0	2		
Ed Bouchard (2–2)	L	11	0	0	0	2		
Joe Miller	G	44	0	0	0	0		

GOALTENDER		GP	MIN	GA	SH	GAA	
		REGULAR SEASON					*POSTSEASON*
Joe Miller	(9-27-8)	44	2780	80	11	1.73	no postseason play

CHICAGO Blackhawks   7-29-8   22   5th (A)   Herb Gardiner

PLAYER	POS	GP	G	A	PTS	PIM		
		REGULAR SEASON					*POSTSEASON*	
Vic Ripley	C	39	11	2	13	31	no postseason play	
Johnny Gottselig	L	44	5	3	8	26		
Dick Irvin	C	36	6	1	7	30		
Ty Arbour	L	44	3	4	7	32		
Harold March	R	35	3	3	6	6		
Rosie Couture	R	43	1	3	4	22		
Cy Wentworth	D	44	2	1	3	44		
Earl Miller	L	17	1	1	2	24		
Alex McKinnon	R	44	1	1	2	51		
Duke Keats	C	3	0	1	1	0		
Clem Loughlin	D	24	0	1	1	16		
Art Lesieur (1–2)	D	2	0	0	0	0		
Herb Gardiner (1–2)	D	5	0	0	0	0		
Bobby Burns	L	6	0	0	0	6		
Val Hoffinger	D	10	0	0	0	12		
Ralph Taylor	D	38	0	0	0	56		
Chuck Gardiner	G	44	0	0	0	2		

GOALTENDER		GP	MIN	GA	SH	GAA	
		REGULAR SEASON					*POSTSEASON*
Chuck Gardiner	(7-29-8)	44	2758	85	5	1.85	no postseason play

TEAM TOTALS

TEAM	GP	G	A	P	PIM	GA	SH	Per Game G	A	PIM	GA
Canadian											
Montreal (C)	44	71	36	107	465	43	22	1.61	0.81	10.57	**0.98**
New York (A)	44	53	23	76	486	53	13	1.20	0.52	11.05	1.20
Toronto	44	85	**66**	151	541	69	12	1.93	**1.50**	12.30	1.57
Ottawa	44	54	32	86	461	67	7	1.23	0.73	10.48	1.52
Montreal (M)	44	67	45	112	**638**	65	12	1.52	1.02	**14.50**	1.48
American											
Boston	44	**89**	39	128	472	52	12	**2.02**	0.89	10.73	1.18
New York (R)	44	72	50	122	384	65	13	1.64	1.14	8.68	1.48
Detroit	44	72	41	113	381	63	10	1.64	0.93	8.66	1.43
Pittsburgh	44	46	29	75	324	80	11	1.05	0.64	7.36	1.82
Chicago	44	33	21	54	363	85	5	0.75	0.48	8.25	1.93
	440	642	382	1024	4515	642	117	1.46	0.87	10.26	1.46

PLAYOFFS

SERIES "A"
Boston 1, Montreal (C) 0
Boston 1, Montreal (C) 0
Boston 3, Montreal (C) 2

BOSTON, 3-0

SERIES "C"
Toronto 3, Detroit 1
Toronto 4, Detroit 1

TORONTO WINS
TOTAL GOAL SERIES, 7-2

SERIES "E"
Boston 2, New York (R) 0
Boston 2, New York (R) 1

BOSTON WINS
STANLEY CUP, 2-0

SERIES "B"
New York (R) 0, New York (A) 0
New York (R) 1, New York (A) 0 (OT)

NEW YORK (R) WINS
TOTAL GOAL SERIES, 1-0

SERIES "D"
New York (R) 1, Toronto 0
New York (R) 2, Toronto 1 (OT)

NEW YORK (R), 2-0

INDIVIDUAL TROPHY WINNERS

HART TROPHY (Most Valuable Player): Roy Worters, N(A)
LADY BYNG TROPHY (Gentlemanly Conduct): Frank Boucher, N(R)
VEZINA TROPHY (Best Goaltender): George Hainsworth, M(C)

1929-1930

Forward Pass

Before the 1929-30 season, the NHL passed a new rule which opened up the ice. Beginning that year, the league was about to permit forward passing in the attacking zone, as well as in the center and defensive portions of the ice. However, in adding this new dimension, league directors overlooked one tiny loophole — a loophole, which was about to be exploited to the maximum.

In the first years of the NHL, forward passing was not allowed, continuing a practice dating back to the 19th century. As originally set up, ice hockey used rugby as a model — a game in which no forward passing is allowed. As offensive output dwindled during the 1920s, league magnates decided that more scoring was a good thing, so beginning in 1927-28, forward passing was permitted in the defensive two thirds of the ice. Still, scoring dropped, so the next logical step was made — adding forward passing to the attacking area. This addendum was about to accomplish its intended goal.

Right out of the gate in 1929-30, NHL nets were being filled at a rate not seen in many years. For instance, in the second game of the campaign, previous year's tailender Pittsburgh, reached double digits, pumping in 10 goals in a victory over Toronto. By mid–December, the league clubs, as a whole, were scoring nearly 3.5 goals per contest — more than double the rate from 1928-29. For example, in its first dozen games, Chicago netted 44 markers — one more than its total from the entire previous year.

When the forward pass was allowed in the offensive zone, league rule makers made no stipulations regarding placement of players — both passer and receiver — when the forward thrust was made. In short, there was no rule stating the player couldn't wait in the offensive end for the puck — even in the goaltender's lap if he so chose, a practice which happened many times in the opening third of the campaign. Recognizing the imbalance, NHL governors met on December 16 to iron out the problem. What emerged was a refinement which read: "No attacking player allowed to precede the play when entering the opposing defensive zone." Roughly translated, this ruling, which went into effect on December 21, started the offside rule.

Over the rest of the campaign, scoring leveled off at 2.75 goals per game — lower than the meteoric start, but still much higher than recent years. The biggest beneficiary of this was Boston's Cooney Weiland (43-30-73) who obliterated the single-season scoring record. Also raising the bar was the Rangers' Frank Boucher, who assisted on 36 goals. In addition, Ottawa's Joe Lamb was penalized the most minutes (119). In net, George Hainsworth (2.15) more than doubled his GAA from 1928-29, yet still captured the title and Toronto's Lorne Chabot posted the most shutouts (6) — 16 less than last year's winner.

Riding Weiland's prowess, the Bruins (38-5-1, 77) romped to the American Division flag with the NHL's best mark to date. Chicago and the Rangers captured the two other playoff berths — both more than 30 points behind the division winner. Detroit and Pittsburgh — the latter with only five wins — brought up the rear. In the Canadian, the Maroons (23-16-5, 51) and the Canadiens both finished with 51 points, but the former had two more wins, thus giving them the division. Ottawa nabbed the third playoff slot, well ahead of Toronto and the Americans.

In the series between the two first place clubs, Boston came out on top, three games to one. In the two auxiliary series, the Rangers beat Ottawa six goals to three, while the Canadiens edged the Blackhawks, three goals to two. In the semifinals, Montreal grabbed a quick lead with a 2–1 overtime win against New York, then iced the series with a 2–0 blanking in the second game. In the finals, the shutout string continued as Hainsworth shut down the vaunted Bruins, 3–0. Two nights later, the Canadiens completed the upset, knocking off Boston 4–3 and capturing Lord Stanley's Cup.

Despite being on the losing end, two Boston forwards captured playoff scoring honors: Dit Clapper for most goals (4) and Weiland for most assists (5) and points (6). Hainsworth — courtesy of a league best three shutouts — posted the lowest playoff GAA —0.75.

One can only imagine what today's NHL would look like without the offside rule, with stars like Ovechkin and Malkin camped on the doorstep, waiting for the puck. It's probably a good thing that the league added the offside codicil in December of 1929, balancing the ice once again. Though league scorers were probably quite happy without it, goalies were happy to have the crease to themselves once again.

1929–1930

STANDINGS

TEAM	GP	W	L	T	PTS	GF	GA
CANADIAN							
MONTREAL (M)	44	23	16	5	51	141	109
MONTREAL (C)	44	21	14	9	51	141	114
OTTAWA	44	21	15	8	50	138	120
TORONTO	44	17	21	6	40	116	124
NEW YORK (A)	44	14	25	5	33	110	161
AMERICAN							
BOSTON	44	38	5	1	77	179	98
CHICAGO	44	21	18	5	47	117	111
NEW YORK (R)	44	17	17	10	44	136	143
DETROIT	44	14	24	6	34	118	133
PITTSBURGH	44	5	36	3	13	102	185

LEADERS

PLAYER	TM	GP	G	A	PTS	PIM
Cooney Weiland	BOS	44	43	30	73	27
Frank Boucher	N(R)	42	26	36	62	16
Dit Clapper	BOS	44	41	20	61	48
Bill Cook	N(R)	44	29	30	59	56
Hec Kilrea	OTT	44	36	22	58	72
Nels Stewart	M(M)	44	39	16	55	81
Howie Morenz	M(C)	44	40	10	50	72
Norm Himes	N(A)	44	28	22	50	15
Joe Lamb	OTT	44	29	20	49	119
Norm Gainor	BOS	42	18	31	49	39

GOALS	
Weiland, BOS	43
Clapper, BOS	41
Morenz, M(C)	40
Stewart, M(M)	39
Kilrea, OTT	36

ASSISTS	
Boucher, N(R)	36
Gainor, BOS	31
Bill Cook, N(R)	30
Weiland, BOS	30
Clancy, OTT	23

GOALTENDER	TM	GP	MIN	GA	SH	GAA
George Hainsworth	M(C)	42	3008	108	4	2.15
Tiny Thompson	BOS	44	2680	98	3	2.19
James Walsh	M(M)	30	1897	74	2	2.34
Chuck Gardiner	CHI	44	2750	111	3	2.42
Alec Connell	OTT	44	2780	118	3	2.55
Lorne Chabot	TOR	42	2620	113	6	2.59
Bill Beveridge	DET	39	2410	109	2	2.71
John Roach	N(R)	44	2770	143	1	3.10
Roy Worters	N-M	37	2330	137	2	3.53
Joe Miller	PIT	43	2630	179	0	4.08

PENALTY MINUTES	
Lamb, OTT	119
S. Mantha, M(C)	108
Shore, BOS	105
Dutton, M(M)	98
Rockburn, DET	97

SHUTOUTS	
Chabot, TOR	6
Hainsworth, M(C)	4
Thompson, BOS	3
Gardiner, CHI	3
Connell, OTT	3

MONTREAL Maroons   23-16-5   51   1st (C)   Dunc Munro

		REGULAR SEASON					POSTSEASON				
PLAYER	POS	GP	G	A	PTS	PIM	GP	G	A	PTS	PIM
Nels Stewart	C	44	39	16	55	81	4	1	1	2	2
Al Siebert	R	39	14	19	33	94	3	0	0	0	0
Reg Smith	R	42	21	9	30	83	4	1	1	2	14

88   The National Hockey League, 1917–1967

PLAYER	POS	REGULAR SEASON					POSTSEASON				
		GP	G	A	PTS	PIM	GP	G	A	PTS	PIM
Dave Trottier	L	41	17	10	27	73	4	0	2	2	8
Merlyn Phillips	C	44	13	10	23	48	4	0	0	0	2
Jimmy Ward	R	44	10	7	17	54	4	0	1	1	12
Mervyn Dutton	D	43	3	13	16	98	4	0	0	0	2
Lorne Northcutt	D	43	10	1	11	6	4	0	0	0	4
Dunc Munro	D	40	7	2	9	10	4	2	0	2	4
Archie Wilcox	R	42	3	5	8	38	4	1	0	1	2
Georges Boucher	D	37	2	6	8	50	3	0	0	0	2
Earl Robinson	R	31	1	2	3	10	4	0	0	0	0
Bill Phillips	C	27	1	1	2	6	4	0	0	0	2
Charles Dinsmore	C	9	0	0	0	0	4	0	0	0	0
James Walsh	G	30	0	0	0	0	4	0	0	0	0
Clint Benedict	G	14	0	0	0	0					
Abbie Cox	G	1	0	0	0	0					

GOALTENDER		REGULAR SEASON					POSTSEASON				
		GP	MIN	GA	SH	GAA	GP	MIN	GA	SH	GAA
Abbie Cox	(1-0-0)	1	60	2	0	2.00					
James Walsh	(16-10-4)	30	1897	74	2	2.34	4	312	11	1	2.12
Clint Benedict	(6-6-1)	14	752	33	0	2.63					

MONTREAL   21-14-9   51   2nd (C)   Cecil Hart
Canadiens

PLAYER	POS	REGULAR SEASON					POSTSEASON				
		GP	G	A	PTS	PIM	GP	G	A	PTS	PIM
Howie Morenz	C	44	40	10	50	72	6	3	0	3	10
Alfred Lepine	C	44	24	9	33	47	6	2	2	4	6
Aurel Joliat	L	42	19	12	31	40	6	0	2	2	6
Wildor Larochelle	R	44	14	11	25	28	6	1	0	1	12
Sylvio Mantha	D	44	13	11	24	108	6	2	1	3	18
Nick Wasnie	R	44	12	11	23	64	6	2	2	4	12
Al Leduc	D	44	6	8	14	90	6	1	3	4	8
Marty Burke	D	44	2	11	13	71	6	0	1	1	6
Armand Mondou	L	44	3	5	8	24	6	1	1	2	6
Georges Mantha	D	44	5	2	7	16	6	0	0	0	8
Bert McCaffrey (2–2)	R	28	1	3	4	26	6	1	1	2	6
Gerry Carson	D	35	1	0	1	8	6	0	0	0	0
Gus Rivers	R	19	1	0	1	2	6	1	0	1	2
Gord Fraser (1–2)	D	10	0	0	0	4					
George Hainsworth	G	42	0	0	0	0	6	0	0	0	0
Mickey Murray	G	1									
Roy Worters (2–2)	G	1									

GOALTENDER		REGULAR SEASON					POSTSEASON				
		GP	MIN	GA	SH	GAA	GP	MIN	GA	SH	GAA
Roy Worters (2–2)	(1-0-0)	1	60	2	0	2.00					
George Hainsworth	(20-13-9)	42	**3008**	108	4	2.15	6	481	6	**3**	**0.75**
Mickey Murray	(0-1-0)	1	60	4	0	4.00					

1929-1930

OTTAWA 21-15-8 50 3rd (C) Newsy Lalonde
Senators

PLAYER	POS	REGULAR SEASON					POSTSEASON				
		GP	G	A	PTS	PIM	GP	G	A	PTS	PIM
Hec Kilrea	L	44	36	22	58	72	2	0	0	0	4
Joe Lamb	R	44	29	20	49	**119**	2	0	0	0	11
King Clancy	D	44	17	23	40	63	2	0	1	1	2
Frank Finnigan	R	43	21	15	36	46	1	0	0	0	4
Bill Touhey	L	44	10	3	13	24	2	1	0	1	0
Art Gagne (2-2)	R	33	6	4	10	32	2	1	0	1	4
Al Shields	D	44	6	3	9	32	2	0	0	0	0
Alex Smith	D	43	2	6	8	90	2	0	0	0	4
Wally Kilrea	C	38	4	2	6	4	2	0	0	0	0
Danny Cox (2-2)	L	24	3	2	5	20	2	0	0	0	0
Harold Starr	D	28	2	1	3	12	2	1	0	1	0
Harry Connor (1-2)	L	25	1	2	3	22					
Len Grosvenor	C	15	0	3	3	19					
Syd Howe	C	12	1	1	2	0	2	0	0	0	0
Bill Hutton (2-2)	D	18	0	1	1	0	2	0	0	0	0
Frank Nighbor (1-2)	C	19	0	0	0	0					
Alec Connell	G	44	0	0	0	0	2	0	0	0	0

GOALTENDER		REGULAR SEASON					POSTSEASON				
		GP	MIN	GA	SH	GAA	GP	MIN	GA	SH	GAA
Alec Connell	(21-15-8)	44	2780	118	3	2.55	2	120	6	0	3.00

TORONTO 17-21-6 40 4th (C) Conn Smythe
Maple Leafs

PLAYER	POS	REGULAR SEASON					POSTSEASON
		GP	G	A	PTS	PIM	no postseason play
Ace Bailey	R	43	22	21	43	69	
Harold Cotton	L	41	21	17	38	47	
Charlie Conacher	R	38	20	9	29	48	
Joe Primeau	C	43	5	21	26	22	
Andy Blair	C	42	11	10	21	27	
Hap Day	D	43	7	14	21	77	
Harvey Jackson	L	31	12	6	18	29	
Eric Pettinger	L	43	4	9	13	40	
Art Duncan	D	38	4	5	9	49	
Red Horner	D	33	2	7	9	96	
Art Smith	D	43	3	3	6	75	
Danny Cox (1-2)	L	18	1	4	5	18	
Frank Nighbor (2-2)	C	22	2	0	2	2	
Gord Brydson	R	8	2	0	2	8	
Cliff McBride	R	1	0	0	0	0	
Lorne Chabot	G	42	0	0	0	0	
Benny Grant (1-2)	G	2	0	0	0	0	

GOALTENDER		REGULAR SEASON					POSTSEASON
		GP	MIN	GA	SH	GAA	no postseason play
Lorne Chabot	(16-20-6)	42	2620	113	6	2.59	
Benny Grant (1-2)	(1-1-0)	2	130	11	0	5.08	

NEW YORK Americans

14-25-5   33   5th (C)   Lionel Conacher

REGULAR SEASON / POSTSEASON

PLAYER	POS	GP	G	A	PTS	PIM
Norm Himes	C	44	28	22	50	15
Johnny Sheppard	L	43	14	15	29	32
Charley McVeigh	C	40	14	14	28	32
Joe Simpson	D	44	8	13	21	41
George Patterson	R	39	13	4	17	24
Bill Boyd	R	43	7	6	13	16
George Massecar	L	43	7	3	10	18
Billy Burch	C	35	7	3	10	22
Lionel Conacher	D	40	4	6	10	73
Bill Holmes	C	42	5	4	9	33
Bill Brydge	D	41	2	6	8	64
Roy Burmeister	L	40	1	1	2	0
Jesse Spring	D	29	0	0	0	0
Leo Reise (1–2)	D	24	0	0	0	0
Jake Forbes	G	1	0	0	0	0
Benny Grant (2–2)	G	7	0	0	0	0
Roy Worters (1–2)	G	36	0	0	0	0

no postseason play

GOALTENDER		GP	MIN	GA	SH	GAA
Jake Forbes	(0-0-1)	1	70	1	0	0.86
Benny Grant (2–2)	(3-4-0)	7	420	25	0	3.57
Roy Worters (1–2)	(11-21-4)	36	2270	135	2	3.57

no postseason play

BOSTON Bruins

38-5-1   77   1st (A)   Art Ross

PLAYER	POS	GP	G	A	PTS	PIM	GP	G	A	PTS	PIM
Cooney Weiland	C	44	43	30	73	27	6	1	5	6	2
Dit Clapper	R	44	41	20	61	48	6	4	0	4	4
Norm Gainor	C	42	18	31	49	39	3	0	0	0	0
Marty Barry	C	44	18	15	33	34	6	3	3	6	14
Eddie Shore	D	42	12	19	31	105	6	1	0	1	26
Harry Oliver	R	40	16	5	21	12	6	2	1	3	6
Percy Galbraith	L	44	7	9	16	38	6	1	3	4	8
George Owen	D	42	9	4	13	31	6	0	2	2	6
Bill Carson	C	44	7	4	11	24	6	1	0	1	6
Dunc MacKay	C	37	4	5	9	13	6	0	0	0	4
Lionel Hitchman	D	39	2	7	9	58	6	1	0	1	14
Bill Hutton (1–2)	D	16	2	0	2	2					
Art Gagne (1–2)	R	6	0	1	1	6					
Harry Connor (2–2)	L	13	0	0	0	4	6	0	0	0	0
Bob Taylor	R	8	0	0	0	6					
Myles Lane	D	3	0	0	0	0	6	0	0	0	0
Tiny Thompson	G	44	0	0	0	0	6	0	0	0	0

GOALTENDER		GP	MIN	GA	SH	GAA	GP	MIN	GA	SH	GAA
Tiny Thompson	(**38-5-1**)	44	2680	98	3	2.19	6	432	12	0	1.67

1929–1930 91

CHICAGO Blackhawks		21-18-5		47	2nd (A)	Tom Shaughnessy Bill Tobin				
		REGULAR SEASON					*POSTSEASON*			
PLAYER	*POS*	*GP*	*G*	*A*	*PTS*	*PIM*	*GP*	*G*	*A*	*PTS*	*PIM*
Tommy Cook	C	41	14	16	30	16	2	0	1	1	4
Johnny Gottselig	L	39	21	4	25	28	2	0	0	0	4
Art Somers	C	44	11	13	24	74	2	0	0	0	2
Ty Arbour	L	42	10	8	18	26	2	1	0	1	0
Duke Dukowski	D	44	7	10	17	42	2	0	0	0	6
Earl Miller	L	28	11	5	16	50	2	1	0	1	6
Rosie Couture	R	43	8	8	16	63	2	0	0	0	2
Vic Ripley	C	40	8	8	16	33	2	0	0	0	2
Frank Ingram	R	37	6	10	16	28	2	0	0	0	0
Harold March	R	43	8	7	15	48					
Stew Adams	L	24	4	6	10	16	2	0	0	0	6
Cy Wentworth	D	37	3	4	7	28					
Clarence Abel	D	38	3	3	6	42	2	0	0	0	10
Teddy Graham	D	26	1	2	3	23	2	0	0	0	8
Helge Bostrom	D	20	0	1	1	8	2	0	0	0	0
Ralph Taylor (1–2)	D	17	1	0	1	42					
Bobby Burns	L	12	1	0	1	2					
Chuck Gardiner	G	44	0	0	0	0	2	0	0	0	0

		REGULAR SEASON					*POSTSEASON*			
GOALTENDER		*GP*	*MIN*	*GA*	*SH*	*GAA*	*GP*	*MIN*	*GA*	*SH*	*GAA*
Chuck Gardiner	(21-18-5)	44	2750	111	3	2.42	2	172	3	0	1.05

NEW YORK Rangers		17-17-10		44	3rd (A)	Lester Patrick				
		REGULAR SEASON					*POSTSEASON*			
PLAYER	*POS*	*GP*	*G*	*A*	*PTS*	*PIM*	*GP*	*G*	*A*	*PTS*	*PIM*
Frank Boucher	C	42	26	36	62	16	3	1	1	2	0
Bill Cook	R	44	29	30	59	56	4	0	1	1	11
Bun Cook	L	43	24	18	42	55	4	2	0	2	2
Butch Keeling	L	43	19	7	26	34	4	0	3	3	8
Murray Murdoch	L	44	13	13	26	22	4	3	0	3	6
Paul Thompson	L	44	7	12	19	39	4	0	0	0	2
Leo Bourgeault	D	44	7	6	13	54	3	1	1	2	6
Ivan Johnson	D	30	3	3	6	82	4	0	0	0	14
Leroy Goldsworthy	R	44	4	1	5	16	4	0	0	0	2
Leo Quenneville	L	25	0	3	3	10	3	0	0	0	0
Ralph Taylor (2–2)	D	22	2	0	2	32	4	0	0	0	10
Melville Vail	D	32	1	1	2	2	4	0	0	0	0
Obs Heximer	L	19	1	0	1	4					
Leo Reise (1–2)	D	14	0	1	1	8	4	0	0	0	16
Harry Foster	D	31	0	0	0	10					
Bill Regan	D	10	0	0	0	4	4	0	0	0	0
John Roach	G	44	0	0	0	0	4	0	0	0	0

		REGULAR SEASON					*POSTSEASON*			
GOALTENDER		*GP*	*MIN*	*GA*	*SH*	*GAA*	*GP*	*MIN*	*GA*	*SH*	*GAA*
John Roach	(17-17-**10**)	44	2770	143	1	3.10	4	309	7	0	1.36

DETROIT   14-24-6   34   4th (A)   Jack Adams
Cougars

PLAYER	POS	GP	G	A	PTS	PIM
		REGULAR SEASON				
Carson Cooper	R	44	18	18	36	14
Ebbie Goodfellow	C	44	17	17	34	54
George Hay	L	44	18	15	33	8
Herb Lewis	L	44	20	11	31	36
Larry Aurie	R	43	14	5	19	28
Stan McCabe	L	25	7	3	10	23
Reg Noble	C	43	6	4	10	72
Bob Connors	L	31	3	7	10	42
Pete Bellefeuille	R	24	5	2	7	10
Henry Hicks	D	30	3	2	5	35
Harvey Rockburn	D	36	4	0	4	97
Jimmy Herbert	C	23	1	3	4	4
Bernie Brophy	L	15	2	0	2	2
James Hughes	D	40	0	1	1	48
Joe Matte	D	12	0	1	1	0
Bill Beveridge	G	39	0	0	0	0
Clarence Dolson	G	5	0	0	0	0

POSTSEASON — no postseason play

GOALTENDER		GP	MIN	GA	SH	GAA
		REGULAR SEASON				
Bill Beveridge	(14-20-5)	39	2410	109	2	2.71
Clarence Dolson	(0-4-1)	5	320	24	0	4.50

POSTSEASON — no postseason play

PITTSBURGH   5-36-3   13   5th (A)   Frank Fredrickson
Pirates

PLAYER	POS	GP	G	A	PTS	PIM
		REGULAR SEASON				
Harold Darragh	L	42	15	17	32	6
Gerry Lowrey	L	44	16	14	30	30
Hib Milks	L	41	13	11	24	36
Jim Jarvis	L	44	11	8	19	32
John McKinnon	D	41	10	7	17	42
Frank Fredrickson	C	9	4	7	11	20
Gord Fraser (2–2)	D	30	6	4	10	37
Tex White	R	29	8	1	9	16
Cliff Barton	R	39	4	2	6	4
Archie Briden	L	29	4	3	7	20
Bert McCaffrey (1–2)	R	15	3	4	7	12
Ren Manners	C	33	3	2	5	14
Rodger Smith	D	42	2	1	3	65
Herb Drury	D	27	2	0	2	12
Jesse Spring	D	22	1	0	1	18
Joe Miller	G	43	0	0	0	0
Andrew Spooner	G	1	0	0	0	0

POSTSEASON — no postseason play

GOALTENDER		GP	MIN	GA	SH	GAA
		REGULAR SEASON				
Joe Miller	(5-**35**-3)	43	2630	179	0	4.08
Andrew Spooner	(0-1-0)	1	60	6	0	6.00

POSTSEASON — no postseason play

TEAM TOTALS

TEAM	GP	G	A	P	PIM	GA	SH	Per Game G	A	PIM	GA
Canadian											
Montreal (M)	44	141	101	242	**651**	109	2	3.20	2.30	**14.80**	2.48
Montreal (C)	44	141	93	234	600	114	4	3.20	2.11	13.64	2.59
Ottawa	44	138	108	246	536	120	3	3.14	2.45	12.18	2.70
Toronto	44	116	126	242	613	124	6	2.64	2.86	13.93	2.82
New York (A)	44	110	97	207	372	161	2	2.50	2.20	8.45	3.66
American											
Boston	44	**179**	150	329	449	98	3	4.07	**3.41**	10.20	**2.23**
Chicago	44	117	105	222	573	111	3	2.66	2.37	13.02	2.52
New York (R)	44	136	131	267	445	143	1	3.09	2.97	10.02	3.25
Detroit	44	118	89	207	474	133	2	2.68	2.02	10.77	3.02
Pittsburgh	44	102	81	183	384	185	0	2.32	1.84	8.73	4.20
	440	1298	1081	2379	5097	1298	26	2.95	2.46	11.58	2.95

PLAYOFFS

SERIES "A"
Boston 2, Montreal (M) 1 (OT)
Boston 4, Montreal (M) 2
Montreal (M) 1, Boston 0 (OT)
Boston 5, Montreal (M) 1

BOSTON, 3-1

SERIES "B"
Montreal (C) 1, Chicago 0
Montreal (C) 2, Chicago 2

**MONTREAL (C) WINS
TOTAL GOAL SERIES, 3-2**

SERIES "C"
New York (R) 1, Ottawa 1
New York (R) 5, Ottawa 2

**NEW YORK (R) WINS
TOTAL GOAL SERIES, 6-3**

SERIES "D"
Montreal (C) 2, New York (R) 1 (OT)
Montreal (C) 2, New York (R) 0

MONTREAL (C), 2-0

SERIES "E"
Montreal (C) 3, Boston 0
Montreal (C) 4, Boston 3

**MONTREAL (C) WINS
STANLEY CUP, 2-0**

INDIVIDUAL TROPHY WINNERS

HART TROPHY (Most Valuable Player): Nels Stewart, M(M)
LADY BYNG TROPHY (Gentlemanly Conduct): Frank Boucher, N(R)
VEZINA TROPHY (Best Goaltender): Tiny Thompson, BOS

1930-1931
Howie Morenz

In the opening years of the NHL, many stars graced the roster of the Montreal Canadiens. Serving on all ends of the ice, these players led the club to a handful of Cups in the first dozen years of the circuit. In 1930-31, one of these greats was about to enjoy his greatest season, leading his team to the promised land once again. Alas — as happened several years before with their great goaltender Georges Vezina — this player's career also would not end well.

On opening night in 1923, a highly-touted rookie suited up for the first time for the Canadiens. Already the possessor of several regular season and playoff scoring titles for the Stratford Midgets, 21-year-old Howie Morenz scored his first goal on December 26. In his first campaign, he netted a respectable 13 goals and finished tied for tenth in the scoring race. Capping his campaign, Morenz scored four postseason goals in as many games to lead Montreal to the Cup. Over the next several campaigns, he never scored less than 23 goals, breaking through for his first scoring championship in 1927-28, with a record-breaking 33-18-51 total. Two years later, Morenz crested the 40-goal plateau, leading his Canadiens to their second Cup sparked by his presence. Continuing the same trend, the NHL was about to find out that he still had plenty of juice left in the tank.

Before the 1930-31 campaign, the NHL made its first franchise shift in many years, as the Pittsburgh Pirates moved across the state and became the Philadelphia Quakers. Winners of only 14 games in the past two years, the Pirates were a victim of the Great Depression, which hamstrung the steel industry — the city's life blood. In the City of Brotherly Love, the Quakers — clad in black and orange — put no fear into the NHL, as the club won only four of 44 games, the league's worst showing to date. Contrarily, Boston (28-

10-6, 62) cruised to its second straight American Division title, well ahead of playoff brethren Chicago and the Rangers, as well as fourth-place Detroit.

In the Canadian Division, thanks to another banner year from Morenz, the Canadiens (26-10-8, 60) marched to the forefront, seven points to the better of Toronto and 14 up on the Maroons. The hard-luck Americans had the same point total as the latter, but with two fewer wins, were regulated to fourth — but still well ahead of Ottawa.

In winning his second scoring title, Morenz (28-23-51) equaled his career best mark set three years before. In a tribute to his balanced game, he did not lead in either goals or assists, the first time an NHL scoring leader had failed to cop either crown. Instead, a pair of Leafs — Charlie Conacher (31) and Joe Primeau (32) finished with the most markers and helpers. Detroit toughguy Harvey Rockburn (118), compiled the most penalty minutes, while goaltenders Roy Worters (Americans) and Chuck Gardiner (Chicago) had the lowest GAA (1.61) and most shutouts (12), respectively.

In the first-place series of the playoffs, Montreal and Boston staged a memorable battle — a battle that wasn't decided until overtime of the fifth and deciding game, when the Canadiens' Wildor Larochelle slid in the winner. In the second and third place series, the Rangers mauled the Maroons and Chicago edged Toronto in overtime to come out on top. Then, the Blackhawks — who had been a league doormat only two years before, blanked the Rangers in two games to reach the finals.

In the battle for the Cup, the stubborn Blackhawks refused to buckle. After losing the first game, 2-1, Chicago bounced back with a pair of extra-session victories — 2-1 and 3-2, to take the series lead. Faced with elimination, Morenz's Canadiens took command — besting the Hawks with 4-2 and 2-0 wins to wrap up their second straight Cup. In the playoffs, Morenz and teammate Aurel Joliat collected the most assists (4), while fellow Canadien Johnny Gagnon scored the most goals (6) and garnered the most points (8). In net, George Hainsworth (1.75, 2) once again proved his mettle.

In succeeding years, Morenz continued to fill NHL nets. Eventually, he was traded to Chicago, then the Rangers, before rejoining the Canadiens in 1936. Midway through the campaign, tragedy would strike. In a January 1937 game, Morenz's skate hit a rut near the boards and he crashed awkwardly, severely breaking his leg. While in the hospital, complications would arise causing a blood clot — which sadly claimed his life in early March. Morenz was only 34 years old.

Although gone at a too-early age, Morenz's legacy lived on. When he left the game, he was the NHL's career goal scoring leader (270) — although a mark which would soon be eclipsed. Furthermore, when the Hockey Hall of Fame was formed in 1945, Morenz would be voted one of its 12 inaugural members. In 1950, he was selected as Canada's greatest hockey player of the first half-century — truly a great honor bestowed on one of the game's finest athletes.

STANDINGS

TEAM	GP	W	L	T	PTS	GF	GA
CANADIAN							
MONTREAL (C)	44	26	10	8	60	129	89
TORONTO	44	22	13	9	53	118	99
MONTREAL (M)	44	20	18	6	46	105	106
NEW YORK (A)	44	18	16	10	46	76	74
OTTAWA	44	10	30	4	24	91	142
AMERICAN							
BOSTON	44	28	10	6	62	143	90
CHICAGO	44	24	17	3	51	108	78
NEW YORK (R)	44	19	16	9	47	106	87
DETROIT	44	16	21	7	39	102	105
PHILADELPHIA	44	4	36	4	12	76	184

LEADERS

PLAYER	TM	GP	G	A	PTS	PIM		GOALS	
Howie Morenz	M(C)	39	28	23	**51**	49		Conacher, TOR	31
Ebbie Goodfellow	DET	44	25	23	48	32		Bill Cook, N(R)	30
Charlie Conacher	TOR	37	**31**	12	43	78		Morenz, M(C)	28
Bill Cook	N(R)	43	30	12	42	39		Three tied with	25
Ace Bailey	TOR	40	23	19	42	46			
Joe Primeau	TOR	38	9	**32**	41	18			
Nels Stewart	M(M)	42	25	14	39	75		*ASSISTS*	
Frank Boucher	N(R)	44	12	27	39	20		Primeau, TOR	32
Cooney Weiland	BOS	44	25	13	38	14		Boucher, N(R)	27
Two tied with					35			Morenz, M(C)	23
								Goodfellow, DET	23
								Joliat, M(C)	22

GOALTENDER	TM	GP	MIN	GA	SH	GAA		PENALTY MINUTES	
Roy Worters	N(A)	44	2760	74	8	**1.61**		Rockburn, DET	118
Chuck Gardiner	CHI	44	2710	78	**12**	1.77		Shore, BOS	108
John Roach	N(R)	44	2760	87	7	1.89		Coulson, PHI	103
George Hainsworth	M(C)	44	2740	89	8	1.95		Shields, PHI	98
Tiny Thompson	BOS	44	2730	90	3	1.98		Lamb, OTT	91
Lorne Chabot	TOR	37	2300	80	6	2.09			
Clarence Dolson	DET	44	2750	105	6	2.29		*SHUTOUTS*	
Dave Kerr	M(M)	29	1769	70	1	2.37		Gardiner, CHI	12
Alec Connell	OTT	36	2190	110	3	3.01		Worters, N(A)	8
Wilf Cude	PHI	29	1750	**127**	0	4.38		Hainsworth, M(C)	8
								Roach, N (R)	7
								Two tied with	6

1930–1931

MONTREAL 26-10-8 60 1st (C) Cecil Hart
Canadiens

		REGULAR SEASON					POSTSEASON				
PLAYER	POS	GP	G	A	PTS	PIM	GP	G	A	PTS	PIM
Howie Morenz	C	39	28	23	51	49	10	1	4	5	10
Aurel Joliat	L	43	13	22	35	73	10	0	4	4	12
Johnny Gagnon	R	41	18	7	25	43	10	6	2	8	8
Al Lepine	C	44	17	7	24	63	10	4	2	6	6
Georges Mantha	D	44	11	6	17	25	10	5	1	6	4
Al Leduc	D	44	8	6	14	82	7	0	2	2	9
Wildor Larochelle	R	40	8	5	13	35	10	1	2	3	8
Nick Wasnie	R	44	9	2	11	26	10	4	1	5	8
Sylvio Mantha	D	44	4	7	11	75	10	2	1	3	26
Armand Mondou	L	40	5	4	9	10	8	0	0	0	0
Marty Burke	D	44	2	5	7	91	10	1	2	3	10
Gus Rivers	R	44	2	5	7	6	10	1	0	1	0
Bert McCaffrey	R	22	2	1	3	10					
Art Lesieur	D	21	2	0	2	14	10	0	0	0	4
Jean Pusie	D	6	0	0	0	0	3	0	0	0	0
George Hainsworth	G	44	0	0	0	0	10	0	0	0	0

		REGULAR SEASON				POSTSEASON			
GOALTENDER		GP	MIN	GA	SH	GAA	GP	MIN	GA	SH	GAA
George Hainsworth (26-10-8)		44	2740	89	8	1.95	10	722	21	2	1.75

TORONTO 22-13-9 53 2nd (C) Conn Smythe
Maple Leafs Art Duncan

		REGULAR SEASON					POSTSEASON				
PLAYER	POS	GP	G	A	PTS	PIM	GP	G	A	PTS	PIM
Charlie Conacher	R	37	31	12	43	78	2	0	1	1	0
Ace Bailey	R	40	23	19	42	46	2	1	1	2	0
Joe Primeau	C	38	9	32	41	18	2	0	0	0	0
Harvey Jackson	L	43	18	13	31	81	2	0	0	0	0
Harold Cotton	L	43	12	17	29	45	2	0	0	0	2
King Clancy	D	44	7	14	21	63	2	1	0	1	0
Andy Blair	C	44	11	8	19	32	2	1	0	1	0
Hap Day	D	44	1	13	14	56	2	0	3	3	7
Red Horner	D	42	1	11	12	71	2	0	0	0	4
Bob Gracie	C	8	4	2	6	4	2	0	0	0	0
Rolly Huard	C	1	1	0	1	0					
Alex Levinsky	D	8	0	1	1	2	2	0	0	0	0
Roger Jenkins (1–2)	D	21	0	0	0	12					
Babe Dye	R	6	0	0	0	0					
Art Duncan	D	2	0	0	0	0	1	0	0	0	0
Herb Hamel	R	2	0	0	0	4					
Lorne Chabot	G	37	0	0	0	0	2	0	0	0	0
Benny Grant	G	7	0	0	0	0					

		REGULAR SEASON					POSTSEASON				
GOALTENDER		GP	MIN	GA	SH	GAA	GP	MIN	GA	SH	GAA
Lorne Chabot	(21-8-8)	37	2300	80	6	2.09	2	139	4	0	1.73
Benny Grant	(1-5-1)	7	430	19	2	2.65					

MONTREAL 20-18-6   46   3rd (C)   Dunc Munro
Maroons   George Boucher

		REGULAR SEASON					POSTSEASON				
PLAYER	POS	GP	G	A	PTS	PIM	GP	G	A	PTS	PIM
Nels Stewart	C	42	25	14	39	75	2	1	0	1	6
Al Siebert	R	43	16	12	28	76	2	0	0	0	6
Reg Smith	R	39	12	14	26	68					
Jimmy Ward	R	41	14	8	22	52	2	0	0	0	2
Dave Trottier	L	43	9	8	17	58	2	0	0	0	6
Lorne Northcutt	D	22	7	3	10	15	2	0	1	1	0
Merlyn Phillips	C	43	6	1	7	38	1	0	0	0	2
Lionel Conacher	D	36	4	3	7	57	2	0	0	0	2
John Gallagher	D	35	4	2	6	35	2	0	0	0	0
Jack McVicar	D	40	2	4	6	35	2	0	0	0	2
Archie Wilcox	R	39	2	2	4	42	2	0	0	0	2
Earl Roche	L	42	2	0	2	18	2	0	0	0	0
Al Huggins	L	20	1	1	2	2					
Paul Haynes	C	19	1	0	1	0					
Des Roche	R	19	0	1	1	6					
Dunc Munro	D	4	0	1	1	0					
Georges Boucher	D	30	0	0	0	25					
Glenn Brydson	R	14	0	0	0	4	2	0	0	0	0
Dave Kerr	G	29	0	0	0	0	2	0	0	0	0
James Walsh	G	16	0	0	0	0					

		REGULAR SEASON					POSTSEASON				
GOALTENDER		GP	MIN	GA	SH	GAA	GP	MIN	GA	SH	GAA
James Walsh	(7-7-2)	16	961	36	2	2.25					
Dave Kerr	(13-11-4)	29	1769	70	1	2.37	2	120	8	0	4.00

NEW YORK 18-16-10   46   4th (C)   Eddie Gerard
Americans

		REGULAR SEASON					POSTSEASON
PLAYER	POS	GP	G	A	PTS	PIM	no postseason play
Norm Himes	C	44	15	9	24	18	
Billy Burch	C	44	14	8	22	35	
Charley McVeigh	C	44	5	11	16	23	
George Patterson	R	44	8	6	14	67	
Frank Carson	R	44	6	7	13	36	
Johnny Sheppard	L	42	5	8	13	16	
Al Hughes	C	42	5	7	12	14	
Mervyn Dutton	D	44	1	11	12	71	
George Massecar	L	43	4	7	11	16	
Hap Emms	L	44	5	4	9	56	
Bill Brydge	D	43	2	5	7	70	
Vern Ayres	D	26	2	1	3	54	
Joe Simpson	D	42	2	0	2	13	
Duke Dukowski (2-2)	D	12	1	1	2	12	
Mike Neville	C	19	1	0	1	2	
Roy Burmeister	L	11	0	0	0	0	
Ellie Pringle	D	6	0	0	0	0	

1930–1931

PLAYER	POS	REGULAR SEASON GP	G	A	PTS	PIM	POSTSEASON
Eddie Convey	L	2	0	0	0	0	no postseason play
Yip Radley	D	1	0	0	0	0	
Roy Worters	G	44	0	0	0	0	

GOALTENDER		REGULAR SEASON GP	MIN	GA	SH	GAA	POSTSEASON
Roy Worters	(18-16-10)	44	2760	74	8	1.61	no postseason play

OTTAWA 10-30-4   24   5th (C)   Newsy Lalonde
Senators

PLAYER	POS	REGULAR SEASON GP	G	A	PTS	PIM	POSTSEASON
Art Gagne	R	44	19	11	30	50	no postseason play
Bill Touhey	L	44	15	15	30	8	
Joe Lamb	R	44	11	14	25	91	
Hec Kilrea	L	44	14	8	22	44	
Danny Cox	L	44	9	12	21	12	
Frank Finnigan	R	44	9	8	17	40	
Alex Smith	D	37	5	6	11	73	
Len Grosvenor	C	33	5	4	9	25	
Art Smith	D	43	2	4	6	61	
Leo Bourgeault (2–2)	D	28	0	4	4	28	
Harold Starr	D	35	2	1	3	48	
Ray Kinsella	L	14	0	0	0	0	
Eric Pettinger	L	13	0	0	0	2	
Harry Connor	L	11	0	0	0	4	
Alec Connell	G	36	0	0	0	0	
Bill Beveridge	G	9	0	0	0	0	

GOALTENDER		REGULAR SEASON GP	MIN	GA	SH	GAA	POSTSEASON
Alec Connell	(10-**22**-4)	36	2190	110	3	3.01	no postseason play
Bill Beveridge	(0-8-0)	9	520	32	0	3.69	

BOSTON 28-10-6   62   1st (A)   Art Ross
Bruins

PLAYER	POS	REGULAR SEASON GP	G	A	PTS	PIM	POSTSEASON GP	G	A	PTS	PIM
Cooney Weiland	C	44	25	13	38	14	5	6	3	9	2
Marty Barry	C	44	20	11	31	26	5	1	1	2	4
Eddie Shore	D	44	15	16	31	105	5	2	1	3	24
Dit Clapper	R	43	22	8	30	50	5	2	4	6	4
Harry Oliver	R	44	16	14	30	18	5	0	0	0	2
George Owen	D	38	12	13	25	33	5	2	3	5	13
John Beattie	L	32	10	11	21	25	4	0	0	0	0
Art Chapman	C	44	7	7	14	22	5	0	1	1	7
Norm Gainor	C	35	8	3	11	14	5	0	1	1	2
Henry Harris	R	32	2	4	6	20					
Harold Darragh (2–2)	L	25	2	4	6	4	5	0	1	1	2

		REGULAR SEASON				*POSTSEASON*				
PLAYER	*POS*	*GP*	*G*	*A*	*PTS*	*PIM*	*GP*	*G*	*A*	*PTS*	*PIM*
Percy Galbraith	L	43	2	3	5	28	5	0	0	0	6
Jack Pratt	C	32	2	0	2	36	4	0	0	0	0
Lionel Hitchman	D	41	0	2	2	40	5	0	0	0	0
Ron Lyons (2–2)	L	14	0	0	0	19	5	0	0	0	0
Bill Hutton (1–2)	D	9	0	0	0	2					
Paul Runge	C	1	0	0	0	0					
Tiny Thompson	G	44	0	0	0	0	5	0	0	0	0

		REGULAR SEASON				*POSTSEASON*			
GOALTENDER		*GP*	*MIN*	*GA*	*SH*	*GAA*	*GP*	*MIN*	*GA*	*SH*	*GAA*
Tiny Thompson	(28-10-6)	44	2730	90	3	1.98	5	343	13	0	2.27

CHICAGO 24-17-3   51   2nd (A)   Dick Irvin
Blackhawks

		REGULAR SEASON				*POSTSEASON*				
PLAYER	*POS*	*GP*	*G*	*A*	*PTS*	*PIM*	*GP*	*G*	*A*	*PTS*	*PIM*
Johnny Gottselig	L	42	20	12	32	14	9	3	3	6	2
Tommy Cook	C	44	15	14	29	34	9	1	3	4	11
Frank Ingram	R	43	17	4	21	37	9	0	1	1	2
Rosie Couture	R	44	8	11	19	30	9	0	3	3	2
Stew Adams	L	37	5	16	18	18	9	3	3	6	8
Harold March	R	44	11	6	17	36	9	3	1	4	11
Vic Desjardins	C	38	3	12	15	11	9	0	0	0	0
Vic Ripley	C	37	8	4	12	9	9	2	1	3	4
Elwin Romnes	C	30	5	7	12	8	9	1	1	2	2
Art Somers	C	33	3	6	9	33	9	0	0	0	0
Cy Wentworth	D	44	4	4	8	12	9	1	1	2	14
Earl Miller	L	19	3	4	7	8	1	0	0	0	0
Teddy Graham	D	42	0	7	7	38	9	0	0	0	12
Ty Arbour	L	41	3	3	6	12	9	1	0	1	6
Helge Bostrom	D	42	2	2	4	32	9	0	0	0	16
Duke Dukowski (1–2)	D	25	1	3	4	28					
Clarence Abel	D	43	0	1	1	45	9	0	0	0	8
Roger Jenkins (2–2)	D	10	0	1	1	2	3	0	0	0	0
Eddie Vokes	L	5	0	0	0	0					
Chuck Gardiner	G	44	0	0	0	0	9	0	0	0	0

		REGULAR SEASON				*POSTSEASON*			
GOALTENDER		*GP*	*MIN*	*GA*	*SH*	*GAA*	*GP*	*MIN*	*GA*	*SH*	*GAA*
Chuck Gardiner	(24-17-3)	44	2710	78	**12**	1.77	9	638	14	**2**	1.73

NEW YORK   19-16-9   47   3rd (A)   Lester Patrick
Rangers

		REGULAR SEASON				*POSTSEASON*				
PLAYER	*POS*	*GP*	*G*	*A*	*PTS*	*PIM*	*GP*	*G*	*A*	*PTS*	*PIM*
Bill Cook	R	43	30	12	42	39	4	3	0	3	4
Frank Boucher	C	44	12	27	39	20	4	0	2	2	0
Bun Cook	L	44	18	17	35	72	4	0	0	0	2
Butch Keeling	L	44	13	9	22	35	4	1	1	2	0

1930–1931

		REGULAR SEASON					*POSTSEASON*				
PLAYER	*POS*	*GP*	*G*	*A*	*PTS*	*PIM*	*GP*	*G*	*A*	*PTS*	*PIM*
Murray Murdoch	L	44	7	7	14	8	4	0	2	2	0
Paul Thompson	L	44	7	7	14	36	4	3	0	3	2
Joe Jerwa	D	33	4	7	11	72	4	0	0	0	4
Cecil Dillon	R	25	7	3	10	8	4	0	1	1	2
Ivan Johnson	D	44	2	6	8	77	4	1	0	1	17
Frank Waite	C	17	1	3	4	4					
Henry Maracle	L	11	1	3	4	4	4	0	0	0	0
Bill Regan	D	42	2	1	3	49	4	0	0	0	2
Eddie Rodden	C	24	0	3	3	8					
Gene Carrigan	C	33	2	0	2	13					
Leo Bourgeault (1–2)	D	10	0	1	1	12					
Frank Peters	D	43	0	0	0	59	4	0	0	0	2
Ernie Kenny	D	6	0	0	0	0					
Sam McAdam	C	5	0	0	0	0					
John Roach	G	44	0	0	0	0	4	0	0	0	0

		REGULAR SEASON					*POSTSEASON*				
GOALTENDER		*GP*	*MIN*	*GA*	*SH*	*GAA*	*GP*	*MIN*	*GA*	*SH*	*GAA*
John Roach	(19-16-9)	44	2760	87	7	1.89	4	240	4	1	1.00

DETROIT 16-21-7 39 4th (A) Jack Adams
Falcons

		REGULAR SEASON					*POSTSEASON*				
PLAYER	*POS*	*GP*	*G*	*A*	*PTS*	*PIM*	*GP*	*G*	*A*	*PTS*	*PIM*
Ebbie Goodfellow	C	44	25	23	48	32					
Carson Cooper	R	44	14	14	28	10					
Herb Lewis	L	43	15	6	21	38					
Larry Aurie	R	42	12	6	18	23					
George Hay	L	44	8	10	18	24					
John Sorrell	L	39	9	7	16	10					
Tommy Filmore	R	39	6	2	8	10					
Bert McInenly	D	44	3	5	8	48					
Reg Noble	C	44	2	5	7	42					
Stew Evans	D	43	1	4	5	14					
Stan McCabe	L	44	2	1	3	22					
Frank Fredrickson	C	24	1	2	3	6					
Henry Hicks	D	22	2	0	2	10					
John Newman	C	8	1	1	2	0					
Leroy Goldsworthy	R	12	1	0	1	2					
Jimmy Creighton	C	11	1	0	1	2					
Harvey Rockburn	D	42	0	1	1	118					
Frank Steele	R	1	0	0	0	0					
Clarence Dolson	G	44	0	0	0	0					

		REGULAR SEASON					*POSTSEASON*
GOALTENDER		*GP*	*MIN*	*GA*	*SH*	*GAA*	*no postseason play*
Clarence Dolson	(16-21-7)	44	2750	105	6	2.29	

PHILADELPHIA Quakers 4-36-4 12 5th (A) Cooper Smeaton

REGULAR SEASON

POSTSEASON
no postseason play

PLAYER	POS	GP	G	A	PTS	PIM
Gerry Lowrey	L	43	13	14	27	27
Hib Milks	L	44	17	6	23	42
Wally Kilrea	C	44	8	12	20	22
Syd Howe	C	44	9	11	20	20
Cliff Barton	R	43	6	7	13	18
Jim Jarvis	L	44	5	7	12	30
Al Shields	D	43	7	3	10	98
Ron Lyons (1-2)	L	22	2	4	6	8
Allison McCalmon	R	16	3	0	3	6
Tex White	R	9	3	0	3	2
John McKinnon	D	39	1	1	2	46
Bill Hutton (2-2)	D	21	1	1	2	4
Harold Darragh (1-2)	L	10	1	1	2	2
Herb Drury	D	24	0	2	2	10
D'Arcy Coulson	D	31	0	0	0	103
Stan Crossett	D	21	0	0	0	10
Rodger Smith	D	9	0	0	0	0
Gord Fraser	D	5	0	0	0	22
Ren Manners	C	4	0	0	0	0
Aubrey Shores	D	1	0	0	0	0
Aubrey Webster	R	1	0	0	0	0
Wilf Cude	G	29	0	0	0	0
Joe Miller	G	15	0	0	0	0
Jake Forbes	G	2	0	0	0	0

REGULAR SEASON

POSTSEASON
no postseason play

GOALTENDER		GP	MIN	GA	SH	GAA
Jake Forbes	(0-2-0)	2	120	7	0	3.50
Joe Miller	(2-12-1)	15	850	50	0	3.53
Wilf Cude	(2-22-3)	29	1750	127	0	4.38

TEAM TOTALS

TEAM	GP	G	A	P	PIM	GA	SH	Per Game G	A	PIM	GA
Canadian											
Montreal (C)	44	129	100	229	602	89	8	2.93	2.27	**13.68**	2.02
Toronto	44	118	**142**	**260**	540	99	8	2.68	**3.23**	12.27	2.25
Montreal (M)	44	105	74	179	568	106	3	2.39	1.68	12.91	2.41
New York (A)	44	76	85	161	495	74	8	1.72	1.93	11.25	**1.68**
Ottawa	44	91	87	178	486	142	3	2.07	1.98	11.04	3.23
American											
Boston	44	**143**	109	252	403	90	3	**3.25**	2.48	9.15	2.05
Chicago	44	108	114	222	416	78	12	2.45	2.59	9.45	1.77
New York	44	106	106	212	514	87	7	2.41	2.41	11.70	1.98
Detroit	44	103	87	190	429	105	6	2.34	1.98	9.75	2.39
Philadelphia	44	76	69	145	477	184	0	1.72	1.57	10.84	4.18
	440	1054	973	2027	4930	1054	58	2.40	2.21	11.20	2.40

PLAYOFFS

SERIES "A"
Boston 5, Montreal (C) 4 (OT)
Montreal (C) 1, Boston 0
Montreal (C) 4, Boston 3 (OT)
Boston 3, Montreal (C) 1
Montreal (C) 3, Boston 2 (OT)

MONTREAL (C), 3-2

SERIES "C"
New York (R) 5, Montreal (M) 1
New York (R) 3, Montreal (M) 0

NEW YORK (R) WINS
TOTAL GOAL SERIES, 8-1

SERIES "E"
Montreal (C) 3, Chicago 1
Chicago 2, Montreal (C) 1 (OT)
Chicago 3, Montreal (C) 2 (OT)
Montreal (C) 4, Chicago 2
Montreal (C) 2, Chicago 0

MONTREAL (C) WINS
STANLEY CUP, 3-2

SERIES "B"
Chicago 2, Toronto 2
Chicago 2, Toronto 1 (OT)

CHICAGO WINS
TOTAL GOAL SERIES, 4-3

SERIES "D"
Chicago 2, New York (R) 0
Chicago 1, New York (R) 0

CHICAGO WINS
TOTAL GOAL SERIES, 3-0

ALL-STAR TEAMS

First Team
G — Chuck Gardiner, CHI
D — King Clancy, TOR
D — Eddie Shore, BOS
C — Howie Morenz, M(C)
R — Bill Cook, N(R)
L — Aurel Joliat, M(C)

Second Team
G — Tiny Thompson, BOS
D — Ivan Johnson, N(R)
D — Sylvio Mantha, M(C)
C — Frank Boucher, N(R)
R — Dit Clapper, BOS
L — Bun Cook, N(R)

INDIVIDUAL TROPHY WINNERS

HART TROPHY (Most Valuable Player): Howie Morenz, M(C)
LADY BYNG TROPHY (Gentlemanly Conduct): Frank Boucher, N(R)
VEZINA TROPHY (Best Goaltender): Roy Worters, N(A)

1931-1932
Palace

As professional hockey evolved through the first quarter of the 20th century, the venues in which games were played changed as well. Having started off in small, unheated arenas, by the late 1920s, many of the league members played in huge amphitheaters, seating upwards of 10,000 fans. Before the 1931-32 season, another NHL club was set to unveil a new home — a home that was erected amidst myriad challenges.

The first truly large NHL arena was built in Montreal in 1924 to serve as the home of the Maroons, then later the Canadiens. Three years later, the Detroit club began a long stay in their new home — the Olympia. In 1928, the Bruins' Boston Garden opened, followed by Chicago Stadium the next season. Two years later, plans were underway for a new ice palace — this time in the city of one of the NHL's founding members.

After taking over the reins of the Toronto club in 1927, hockey executive Conn Smythe sought a new look for the club. He redesigned their uniforms, scrapping the old green and blue and replacing it with a snappy blue and white color scheme. At the same time, Smythe gave the club a new name — the Maple Leafs. To complete the transformation, he unveiled plans for a new stadium — to be called Maple Leaf Gardens. Construction was set to begin in the spring of 1931, an ambitious six-months before its scheduled christening.

Actual construction began in early April, when the existing buildings on the property were razed. As the project continued through the summer, the ambitious pace began to take its toll. With the country deep in the Great Depression, funds were tight and it looked for a while that construction would grind to a halt. However, in a clever bit of negotiating, Smythe and his assistant Frank Selke made a deal with the trade unions — a deal which included shares in the building itself—in exchange for labor. Buoyed by this unusual arrangement, construction continued on pace.

On November 12, 1931, Maple Leaf Gardens opened up on schedule. Featuring many amenities, including a full-throated pipe organ, the Gardens was truly an ice palace. Although the team lost the opener, 3–1, to the Blackhawks, the Leafs went on to enjoy a solid campaign, finishing second in the Canadian Division, only four points behind the Canadiens (25-16-7, 57) in the increased 48-game schedule. The Maroons claimed the final playoff spot by five points over the Americans in the four-team division (Ottawa had been granted a leave of absence). In the American, the Rangers (23-17-8, 54) rose to the top, fending off Chicago and Detroit, while the Bruins slid to the cellar. Like the Canadian, this division also featured only four teams, as the Philadelphia club also didn't answer the bell.

Individually, three Toronto linemates captured scoring glory, as Harvey Jackson notched the most points (53), Charlie Conacher the most goals (34) and Joe Primeau the most helpers (37). In addition, the Rangers' Bill Cook also scored 34 goals, while Mervyn Dutton (Americans) served the most time in the box (107). In goal, Chuck Gardiner (Chicago) allowed the fewest goals (2.03), while John Roach (Rangers) and Tiny Thompson (Bruins) blanked the most opponents (9).

In the first-place playoff set, the Rangers put an end to a possible Canadiens three-peat, knocking off the defending Cup holders, three games to one. In the runner-up series, Chicago blanked the Leafs in the first contest, 1–0, then was buried 6–1, allowing Toronto to capture the total goals series. In the other opening round matchup, the Maroons defeated Detroit, three goals to one. In the semifinals, the Leafs and Maroons skated to a 1–1 draw, before Toronto squeaked out a 4–3 overtime victory to move into the finals.

In the battle for the Cup, the Leafs capped their first season in their new digs in style. In what was later called the "Tennis Series," Toronto subdued the Rangers: 6–4, 6–2 and 6–4—grabbing the championship for the first time in many years. A pair of opponents, Conacher and the Rangers' Bun Cook, each scored the most goals (6), while a similar duo—Primeau and Frank Boucher—each garnered six assists, with the latter also collecting the most points (9). In net, the Maroons' James Walsh posted the lowest GAA (1.16) and claimed—along with Roach—the only playoff shutouts.

Maple Leaf Gardens continued to serve as a home to the Leafs for many years to come. By the time the author visited this shrine—many years later— several of its features, like the organ, were gone. Still, one could see it was a grand old place, with many photos of its heroes gracing its corridors, serving as reminders of past glories when Toronto's ice palace was new.

STANDINGS

TEAM	GP	W	L	T	PTS	GF	GA
CANADIAN							
MONTREAL (C)	48	25	16	7	57	128	110
TORONTO	48	23	18	7	53	155	126
MONTREAL (M)	48	19	22	7	45	144	139
NEW YORK (A)	48	16	24	8	40	93	133
AMERICAN							
NEW YORK (R)	48	23	17	8	54	135	112
CHICAGO	48	18	19	11	47	84	110
DETROIT	48	18	20	10	46	94	108
BOSTON	48	15	21	12	42	122	117

LEADERS

PLAYER	TM	GP	G	A	PTS	PIM
Harvey Jackson	TOR	48	28	25	**53**	63
Joe Primeau	TOR	46	13	37	50	25
Howie Morenz	M(C)	48	24	25	49	46
Charlie Conacher	TOR	44	**34**	14	48	66
Bill Cook	N(R)	48	**34**	14	48	33
Dave Trottier	M(M)	48	26	18	44	94
Reg Smith	M(M)	43	11	33	44	49
Al Siebert	M(M)	48	21	18	39	64
Dit Clapper	BOS	48	17	22	39	21
Aurel Joliat	M(C)	48	15	24	39	46

GOALS	
Conacher, TOR	34
Bill Cook, N(R)	34
Jackson, TOR	28
Trottier, M(M)	26
Morenz, M(C)	24

ASSISTS	
Primeau, TOR	37
Smith, M(M)	33
Jackson, TOR	25
Morenz, M(C)	25
Joliat, M(C)	24

GOALTENDER	TM	GP	MIN	GA	SH	GAA
Chuck Gardiner	CHI	48	2989	101	4	**2.03**
Alec Connell	DET	48	3050	108	6	2.12
George Hainsworth	M(C)	48	2998	110	6	2.20
John Roach	N(R)	48	3020	112	9	2.23
Tiny Thompson	BOS	43	2698	103	9	2.29
Lorne Chabot	TOR	44	2698	106	4	2.36
Roy Worters	N(A)	40	2459	110	5	2.68
James Walsh	M(M)	27	1670	77	2	2.77
Norm Smith	M(M)	21	1267	62	0	2.94

PENALTY MINUTES	
Dutton, N(A)	107
Johnson, N(R)	106
Horner, TOR	97
Trottier, M(M)	94
Seibert, N(R)	88

SHUTOUTS	
Roach, N(R)	9
Thompson, BOS	9
Hainsworth, M(C)	6
Connell, DET	6
Worters, N(A)	5

MONTREAL
Canadiens 25-16-7   57   1st (C)   Cecil Hart

			REGULAR SEASON				POSTSEASON				
PLAYER	POS	GP	G	A	PTS	PIM	GP	G	A	PTS	PIM
Howie Morenz	C	48	24	25	49	46	4	1	0	1	4
Aurel Joliat	L	48	15	24	39	46	4	2	0	2	4
Johnny Gagnon	R	48	19	18	37	40	4	1	1	2	4
Alfred Lepine	C	48	19	11	30	42	3	1	0	1	4
Wildor Larochelle	R	48	18	8	26	16	4	2	1	3	4

1931–1932 107

PLAYER	POS	REGULAR SEASON					POSTSEASON				
		GP	G	A	PTS	PIM	GP	G	A	PTS	PIM
Armand Mondou	L	47	6	12	18	22	4	1	2	3	2
Nick Wasnie	R	48	10	2	12	16	4	0	0	0	0
Sylvio Mantha	D	47	5	5	10	62	4	0	1	1	8
Marty Burke	D	48	3	6	9	50	4	0	0	0	12
Al Leduc	D	41	5	3	8	60	4	1	1	2	2
Georges Mantha	D	48	1	7	8	8	4	0	1	1	8
Art Lesieur	D	24	1	2	3	12	4	0	0	0	0
Dunc Munro	D	48	1	1	2	14	4	0	0	0	2
Art Alexandre	L	10	0	2	2	8	4	0	0	0	0
Gus Rivers	R	25	1	0	1	4					
Jean Pusie	D	1	0	0	0	0					
George Hainsworth	G	48	0	0	0	2	4	0	0	0	0

GOALTENDER		REGULAR SEASON					POSTSEASON				
		GP	MIN	GA	SH	GAA	GP	MIN	GA	SH	GAA
George Hainsworth	(25-16-7)	48	2998	110	6	2.20	4	300	13	0	2.60

TORONTO 23-18-7   53   2nd (C)   Art Duncan
Maple Leafs   Dick Irvin

PLAYER	POS	REGULAR SEASON					POSTSEASON				
		GP	G	A	PTS	PIM	GP	G	A	PTS	PIM
Harvey Jackson	L	48	28	25	53	63	7	5	2	7	13
Joe Primeau	C	46	13	37	50	25	7	0	6	6	2
Charlie Conacher	R	44	34	14	48	66	7	6	2	8	6
Andy Blair	C	48	9	14	23	35	7	2	2	4	6
Bob Gracie	C	48	13	8	21	29	7	3	1	4	0
Frank Finnigan	R	47	8	13	21	45	7	2	3	5	8
King Clancy	D	48	10	9	19	61	7	2	1	3	14
Harold Cotton	L	48	5	13	18	41	7	2	2	4	8
Red Horner	D	42	7	9	16	97	7	2	2	4	20
Hap Day	D	47	7	8	15	33	7	3	3	6	6
Harold Darragh	L	48	5	10	15	6	7	0	1	1	2
Ace Bailey	R	41	8	5	13	62	7	1	0	1	4
Alex Levinsky	D	47	5	5	10	29	7	0	0	0	6
Earl Miller (1–2)	L	15	3	3	6	10	7	0	0	0	0
Fred Robertson	D	8	0	0	0	23	7	0	0	0	0
Syd Howe	C	3	0	0	0	0					
Lorne Chabot	G	44	0	0	0	2	7	0	0	0	0
Benny Grant	G	5	0	0	0	0					

GOALTENDER		REGULAR SEASON					POSTSEASON				
		GP	MIN	GA	SH	GAA	GP	MIN	GA	SH	GAA
Lorne Chabot	(22-16-6)	44	2698	106	4	2.36	7	438	15	0	2.05
Benny Grant	(1-2-1)	5	320	18	1	3.38					
Red Horner		1	1	1	0	60.00					
Alex Levinsky		1	1	1	0	60.00					

MONTREAL 19-22-7 45 3rd (C) Sprague Cleghorn
Maroons

		REGULAR SEASON					POSTSEASON				
PLAYER	POS	GP	G	A	PTS	PIM	GP	G	A	PTS	PIM
Dave Trottier	L	48	26	18	44	94	4	1	0	1	0
Reg Smith	R	43	11	33	44	49	4	2	1	3	2
Al Siebert	R	48	21	18	39	64	4	0	1	1	4
Jimmy Ward	R	48	19	19	38	39	4	2	1	3	0
Nels Stewart	C	38	22	11	33	61	4	0	1	1	2
Lorne Northcutt	D	48	19	6	25	33	4	1	2	3	4
Glenn Brydson	R	47	12	13	25	44	4	0	0	0	4
Lionel Conacher	D	45	7	9	16	60	4	0	0	0	2
Archie Wilcox	R	48	3	3	6	37	4	0	0	0	4
Harold Starr	D	47	1	2	3	47	4	0	0	0	0
Earl Robinson	R	26	0	3	3	2					
Merlyn Phillips	C	46	1	1	2	11	4	0	0	0	2
John Gallagher	D	19	1	0	1	18					
Jack McVicar	D	48	0	0	0	28	4	0	0	0	0
Lorne Duguid	L	13	0	0	0	6					
Paul Haynes	C	12	1	0	1	0	4	0	0	0	0
James Walsh	G	27	0	0	0	0	4	0	0	0	0
Norm Smith	G	21	0	0	0	0					

		REGULAR SEASON					POSTSEASON				
GOALTENDER		GP	MIN	GA	SH	GAA	GP	MIN	GA	SH	GAA
James Walsh	(14-10-3)	27	1670	77	2	2.77	4	258	5	**1**	**1.16**
Norm Smith	(5-12-4)	21	1267	62	0	2.94					

NEW YORK 16-24-8 40 4th (C) Eddie Gerard
Americans

		REGULAR SEASON					POSTSEASON
PLAYER	POS	GP	G	A	PTS	PIM	no postseason play
Norm Himes	C	48	7	21	28	9	
Charley McVeigh	C	48	12	15	27	16	
Joe Lamb	R	48	14	11	25	71	
Billy Burch	C	48	7	15	22	20	
Bert McInenly (2–2)	D	30	12	6	18	44	
Tommy Filmore (2–2)	R	31	8	6	14	12	
Wally Kilrea	C	48	3	8	11	18	
Bill Brydge	D	48	2	8	10	77	
Jackie Keating	L	22	5	3	8	6	
Mervyn Dutton	D	47	3	5	8	**107**	
George Patterson	R	20	6	0	6	26	
Vern Ayres	D	45	2	4	6	82	
Al Shields	D	48	4	1	5	45	
Roy Burmeister	L	16	3	2	5	2	
Al Hughes	C	18	1	1	2	8	
George Massecar	L	14	1	1	2	12	
Eddie Convey	L	21	1	0	1	21	
Hap Emms (1–2)	L	13	1	0	1	11	
Johnny Sheppard	L	5	1	0	1	2	

1931–1932 109

		REGULAR SEASON					*POSTSEASON*
PLAYER	*POS*	*GP*	*G*	*A*	*PTS*	*PIM*	*no postseason play*
Ed Jeremiah	D	9	0	1	1	0	
Len Grosvenor	C	12	0	0	0	0	
Hub Wilson	L	2	0	0	0	0	
Roy Worters	G	40	0	0	0	0	
Jake Forbes	G	6	0	0	0	0	
Dave Kerr	G	1	0	0	0	0	
Moe Roberts	G	1	0	0	0	0	

		REGULAR SEASON					*POSTSEASON*
GOALTENDER		*GP*	*MIN*	*GA*	*SH*	*GAA*	*no postseason play*
Moe Roberts	(1-0-0)	1	60	1	0	1.00	
Jake Forbes	(3-3-0)	6	360	16	0	2.67	
Roy Worters	(12-20-8)	40	2459	110	5	2.68	
Dave Kerr	(0-1-0)	1	60	6	0	6.00	

NEW YORK Rangers 23-17-8 54 1st (A) Lester Patrick

		REGULAR SEASON					*POSTSEASON*				
PLAYER	*POS*	*GP*	*G*	*A*	*PTS*	*PIM*	*GP*	*G*	*A*	*PTS*	*PIM*
Bill Cook	R	48	34	14	48	33	7	3	3	6	2
Cecil Dillon	R	48	23	15	38	22	7	2	1	3	4
Frank Boucher	C	48	12	23	35	18	7	3	6	9	0
Bun Cook	L	45	14	20	34	43	7	6	2	8	12
Art Somers	C	48	11	15	26	45	7	0	1	1	8
Murray Murdoch	L	48	5	16	21	32	7	0	2	2	2
Butch Keeling	L	48	17	3	20	38	7	2	1	3	12
Ivan Johnson	D	47	3	10	13	106	7	2	0	2	24
Norm Gainor	C	46	3	9	12	9	7	0	0	0	2
Earl Seibert	D	46	4	6	10	88	7	1	2	3	14
Doug Brennan	D	38	4	3	7	40	7	1	0	1	10
Vic Desjardins	C	48	3	3	6	16	7	0	0	0	0
Ott Heller	D	21	2	2	4	9	7	3	1	4	8
Hib Milks	L	48	0	4	4	12	7	0	0	0	0
John Roach	G	48	0	0	0	0	7	0	0	0	0

		REGULAR SEASON					*POSTSEASON*				
GOALTENDER		*GP*	*MIN*	*GA*	*SH*	*GAA*	*GP*	*MIN*	*GA*	*SH*	*GAA*
John Roach	(23-17-8)	48	3020	112	9	2.23	7	480	27	1	3.38

CHICAGO Blackhawks 18-19-11 47 2nd (A) Dick Irvin / Bill Tobin

		REGULAR SEASON					*POSTSEASON*				
PLAYER	*POS*	*GP*	*G*	*A*	*PTS*	*PIM*	*GP*	*G*	*A*	*PTS*	*PIM*
Johnny Gottselig	L	44	13	15	28	28	2	0	0	0	2
Tommy Cook	C	48	12	13	25	36	2	0	0	0	2
Harold March	R	48	12	10	22	59	2	0	0	0	2
Paul Thompson	L	48	8	14	22	34	2	0	0	0	2
Vic Ripley	C	46	12	6	18	47	2	0	0	0	0
Rosie Couture	R	48	9	9	18	8	2	0	0	0	2
Cy Wentworth	D	48	3	10	13	30	2	0	0	0	0

		REGULAR SEASON					POSTSEASON				
PLAYER	POS	GP	G	A	PTS	PIM	GP	G	A	PTS	PIM
Gerry Lowrey	L	48	8	3	11	32	2	1	0	1	2
Clarence Abel	D	48	3	3	6	34	2	0	0	0	2
Georges Boucher	D	43	1	5	6	50	2	0	1	1	0
Lou Holmes	C	41	1	4	5	6	2	0	0	0	2
Stew Adams	L	26	0	5	5	26					
Frank Ingram	R	21	1	2	3	4					
Teddy Graham	D	48	0	3	3	40	2	0	0	0	2
Elwin Romnes	C	18	1	0	1	6	2	0	0	0	0
Art Coulter	D	14	0	1	1	23	2	1	0	1	0
Pat Shea	D	10	0	1	1	0					
Helge Bostrom	D	14	0	0	0	4	2	0	0	0	0
Earl Miller (2–2)	L	9	0	0	0	0					
Chuck Gardiner	G	48	0	0	0	0	2	0	0	0	0
Wilf Cude (2–2)	G	1	0	0	0	0					

	REGULAR SEASON					POSTSEASON				
GOALTENDER	GP	MIN	GA	SH	GAA	GP	MIN	GA	SH	GAA
Chuck Gardiner (18-19-**11**)	48	2989	101	4	**2.03**	2	120	6	0	3.00
Wilf Cude (2–2)	1	41	9	0	13.17					

DETROIT 18-20-10 46 3rd (A) Jack Adams
Falcons

		REGULAR SEASON					POSTSEASON				
PLAYER	POS	GP	G	A	PTS	PIM	GP	G	A	PTS	PIM
Ebbie Goodfellow	C	48	14	16	30	56	2	0	0	0	0
Frank Carson	R	31	10	14	24	31	2	0	0	0	2
Larry Aurie	R	48	12	8	20	18	2	0	0	0	0
Herb Lewis	L	48	5	14	19	21	2	0	0	0	0
Hec Kilrea	L	47	13	3	16	28	2	0	0	0	0
Alex Smith	D	48	6	8	14	47	2	0	0	0	4
Hap Emms (2–2)	L	20	5	9	14	27	2	0	0	0	2
John Sorrell	L	48	8	5	13	22	2	1	0	1	0
Doug Young	D	47	10	2	12	45	2	0	0	0	2
Danny Cox	L	47	4	6	10	23	2	0	0	0	2
Carson Cooper	R	48	3	5	8	11	2	0	0	0	0
Reg Noble	C	48	3	3	6	72	2	0	0	0	0
Art Gagne	R	13	1	1	2	0					
Bert McInenly (1–2)	D	17	0	1	1	16					
Tommy Filmore (1–2)	R	9	0	0	0	2					
Alec Connell	G	48	0	0	0	0	2	0	0	0	0

	REGULAR SEASON					POSTSEASON				
GOALTENDER	GP	MIN	GA	SH	GAA	GP	MIN	GA	SH	GAA
Alec Connell (18-20-10)	48	3050	108	6	2.12	2	120	3	0	1.50

BOSTON 15-21-12 42 4th (A) Art Ross
Bruins

		REGULAR SEASON					POSTSEASON
PLAYER	POS	GP	G	A	PTS	PIM	no postseason play
Dit Clapper	R	48	17	22	39	21	

1931-1932

PLAYER	POS	REGULAR SEASON					POSTSEASON
		GP	G	A	PTS	PIM	no postseason play
Marty Barry	C	48	21	17	38	22	
Cooney Weiland	C	46	14	12	26	20	
Art Chapman	C	48	11	14	25	18	
George Owen	D	42	12	10	22	29	
Eddie Shore	D	45	9	13	22	80	
Harry Oliver	R	44	13	7	20	22	
Bill Touhey	L	26	5	4	9	12	
Frank Jerwa	L	24	4	5	9	14	
Bud Cook	C	28	4	4	8	14	
Lionel Hitchman	D	48	4	3	7	36	
Eddie Burke	R	16	3	0	3	12	
Percy Galbraith	L	47	2	1	3	28	
Irwin Boyd	R	29	2	1	3	10	
Harry Foster	D	34	1	2	3	12	
Lloyd Klein	L	5	1	0	1	0	
Paul Runge	C	14	0	1	1	8	
Joe Jerwa	D	11	0	0	0	8	
Ed Jeremiah (2-2)	D	6	0	0	0	0	
Jack Pratt	C	5	0	0	0	6	
Max Sutherland	L	2	0	0	0	0	
John Beattie	L	1	0	0	0	0	
Tiny Thompson	G	43	0	0	0	0	
Percy Jackson	G	4	0	0	0	0	
Wilf Cude (1-2)	G	2	0	0	0	0	

GOALTENDER		REGULAR SEASON					POSTSEASON
		GP	MIN	GA	SH	GAA	no postseason play
Percy Jackson	(1-1-1)	4	232	8	0	2.07	
Tiny Thompson	(13-19-11)	43	2698	103	9	2.29	
Wilf Cude (1-2)	(1-1-0)	2	120	6	0	3.00	

TEAM TOTALS

TEAM	GP	G	A	P	PIM	GA	SH	Per Game			
								G	A	PIM	GA
Canadian											
Montreal (C)	48	128	126	254	450	110	6	2.67	2.63	9.38	2.29
Toronto	48	**155**	**173**	**328**	**625**	126	5	**3.23**	**3.60**	**13.02**	2.63
Montreal (M)	48	144	136	280	593	139	2	3.00	2.83	12.35	2.90
New York (A)	48	93	108	201	596	133	5	1.94	2.25	12.42	2.77
American											
New York (R)	48	135	143	278	511	112	9	2.81	2.98	10.64	2.33
Chicago	48	84	104	188	464	110	4	1.75	2.17	9.67	2.29
Detroit	48	94	95	189	415	**108**	6	1.96	1.98	8.65	**2.25**
Boston	48	123	116	239	373	117	**10**	2.56	2.42	7.77	2.44
	384	955	1001	1956	4027	955	47	2.49	2.61	10.49	2.49

PLAYOFFS

SERIES "A"
Montreal (C) 4, New York (R) 3
New York (R) 4, Montreal (C) 3 (OT)
New York (R) 1, Montreal (C) 0
New York (R) 5, Montreal (C) 2

NEW YORK (R), 3-1

SERIES "C"
Montreal (M) 1, Detroit 1
Montreal (M) 2, Detroit 0

MONTREAL (M) WINS
TOTAL GOAL SERIES, 3-1

SERIES "E"
Toronto 6, New York (R) 4
Toronto 6, New York (R) 2
Toronto 6, New York (R) 4

TORONTO WINS
STANLEY CUP, 3-0

SERIES "B"
Chicago 1, Toronto 0
Toronto 6, Chicago 1

TORONTO WINS
TOTAL GOAL SERIES, 6-2

SERIES "D"
Toronto 1, Montreal (M) 1
Toronto 4, Montreal (M) 3 (OT)

TORONTO WINS
TOTAL GOAL SERIES, 4-3

ALL-STAR TEAMS

First Team
G — Chuck Gardiner, CHI
D — Ivan Johnson, N(R)
D — Eddie Shore, BOS
C — Howie Morenz, M(C)
R — Bill Cook, N(R)
L — Harvey Jackson, TOR

Second Team
G — Roy Worters, N(A)
D — King Clancy, TOR
D — Sylvio Mantha, M(C)
C — Lorne Northcutt, M(M)
R — Charlie Conacher, TOR
L — Aurel Joliat, M(C)

INDIVIDUAL TROPHY WINNERS

HART TROPHY (Most Valuable Player): Howie Morenz, M(C)
LADY BYNG TROPHY (Gentlemanly Conduct): Joe Primeau, TOR
VEZINA TROPHY (Best Goaltender): Chuck Gardiner, CHI

1932-1933
Tiebreaker

At the conclusion of the 1932-33 season, two division rivals finished deadlocked. The teams were so even that using the usual tiebreakers failed to resolve the issue. As a result, the NHL had to peer deep into the rulebook to determine the division winner. However, before the cessation of games in the spring, the aforementioned equality would be upstaged by a different kind of tie — a tie that would also take a good deal of effort to unravel.

In the first few years of the league, because of the relatively few games in the schedule, ties in the point standings were fairly commonplace. Also, because points were awarded for wins (2) and ties (1), two teams could finish with the same point total, but with an unequal number of wins. For instance, in 1929-30, both the Maroons and Canadiens finished atop the Canadian Division standings with 51 points. To break the tie, the league rules stated the team with the most wins — in this case the Maroons — received the prize. However, in 1932-33, that particular tiebreaker would prove useless and another layer would be needed.

In the NHL's American Division, Boston — rebounding from its fourth-place finish the year before — got out to a fast start, posting a 10-6-4 record by the beginning of January. Surprisingly, one of their closest pursuers was Detroit, a perennial also-ran. By the end of January, the newly rechristened Red Wings caught the Bruins, with each team sporting a 15-10-4 record. A month later, with Boston slumping, the Wings took the lead by four points — 48 to 44. Then, the Bruins rattled off a seven-game unbeaten streak — highlighted by a 10–0 thrashing of the Canadiens. With three games left, Detroit trailed by a pair of points. Responding to the challenge, the Red Wings won their final trio to finish with a 25-15-8 mark. Boston, after a pair of ties, needed a win in its last game on March 21 to catch Detroit. They too responded to the pressure, beating the Rangers 3–2 and lifting their record to 25-15-8 — exactly the same as Detroit's.

With the two teams tied with the most wins and ties, another tiebreaker was needed to snap the deadlock. Fortunately, the NHL had a contingency in place. In case of a W-L-T tie, the team with the most goals scored was declared the winner. In this category, Boston, helped by the double-digit outburst against Montreal, came out on top — 124 to 111.

The other American Division playoff berth was captured by the Rangers, who bested Chicago by ten points. In the Canadian, Toronto (24-18-6, 54) and the two Montreal clubs qualified for the postseason. The Americans lost a tiebreaker with the Canadiens, while Ottawa returned to the league, only to finish a bad last. Individually, Bill Cook (Rangers) won the scoring title 28-22-50, scoring the most goals to boot. His teammate, Frank Boucher, added the most assists (28), while Toronto's Red Horner piled up the most penalty minutes (144). Between the pipes, Boston's Tiny Thompson allowed the fewest goals (1.76) and blanked the most foes (11).

Up until now, the NHL had witnessed only a handful of playoff games that were not settled after one period of overtime. Previously, the longest game had been the contest between the Canadiens and Rangers in the spring of 1930, which ended in the 69th minute of overtime. This record was about to be shattered in the first-place series between Boston and Toronto. In the first four games — three which also were decided in OT — each team had won a pair, setting up a deciding fifth game. Brian McFarlane in *50 Years of Hockey* best described the action: "The game was still scoreless after sixty minutes. It remained scoreless after the first overtime. Then came a second, third, a fourth and even a fifth overtime.... At 4:46 of the sixth overtime period, Andy Blair of the Leafs intercepted a pass from Eddie Shore and fed the puck to little Ken Doraty, who raced in to score. Time of the goal was 164:46."

The rest of the playoff action in 1933 was mundane in comparison. Detroit knocked off the Maroons, while the Rangers dispatched the Canadiens. Next, New York defeated the Wings to reach the finals. Facing a bone-weary Toronto squad less than then 24 hours after its marathon win, the Rangers rolled to 5–1 win, setting the stage for a three-games-to-one Cup victory. In addition, all of the playoff leaders graced the roster of the Rangers as Cecil Dillon scored the most goals (8) and points (10), Art Somers and Murray Murdoch added the most helpers (4) and Andy Aitkenhead posted the best GAA (1.63)

In later years, the NHL occasionally had to break ties in this fashion, giving the nod to the most prolific scoring squad. As for the lengthy overtime contest, the duration of the 164-minute game would be eclipsed as well — an event not long in coming.

1932–1933

STANDINGS

TEAM	GP	W	L	T	PTS	GF	GA
CANADIAN							
TORONTO	48	24	18	6	54	119	111
MONTREAL (M)	48	22	20	6	50	134	119
MONTREAL (C)	48	18	25	5	41	92	115
NEW YORK (A)	48	15	22	11	41	91	118
OTTAWA	48	11	27	10	32	89	131
AMERICAN							
BOSTON	48	25	15	8	58	124	88
DETROIT	48	25	15	8	58	111	93
NEW YORK (R)	48	23	17	8	54	135	107
CHICAGO	48	16	20	12	44	88	101

LEADERS

PLAYER	TM	GP	G	A	PTS	PIM
Bill Cook	N(R)	48	28	22	50	51
Busher Jackson	TOR	48	27	17	44	43
Lorne Northcutt	M(M)	47	22	21	43	30
Reg Smith	M(M)	48	20	21	41	66
Paul Haynes	M(M)	47	16	25	41	18
Auriel Joliat	M(C)	48	18	21	39	53
Bun Cook	N(R)	48	22	15	37	35
Four tied with					35	

GOALS
Bill Cook, N(R)	28
Jackson, TOR	27
Barry, BOS	24
Bun Cook, N(R)	22
Northcutt, M(M)	22

ASSISTS
Boucher, N(R)	28
Shore, BOS	27
Haynes, M(M)	25
Himes, N(A)	25
Gagnon, M(C)	23

GOALTENDER	TM	GP	MIN	GA	SH	GAA
Tiny Thompson	BOS	48	3000	88	11	1.76
John Roach	DET	48	2970	93	10	1.88
Chuck Gardiner	CHI	48	3010	101	5	2.01
Andy Aitkenhead	N(R)	48	2970	107	3	2.16
Lorne Chabot	TOR	48	2946	111	5	2.26
Dave Kerr	M(M)	25	1520	58	4	2.29
George Hainsworth	M(C)	48	2980	115	8	2.32
Roy Worters	N(A)	47	2970	116	5	2.34
James Walsh	M(M)	22	1303	56	2	2.58
Bill Beveridge	OTT	35	2195	95	5	2.60

PENALTY MINUTES
Horner, TOR	144
Johnson, N(R)	127
Shields, OTT	119
Shore, BOS	102
Ayres, N(A)	97

SHUTOUTS
Thompson, BOS	11
Roach, DET	10
Hainsworth, M(C)	8
Four tied with	5

TORONTO 24-18-6 54 1st (C) Dick Irvin
Maple Leafs

		REGULAR SEASON					POSTSEASON				
PLAYER	POS	GP	G	A	PTS	PIM	GP	G	A	PTS	PIM
Harvey Jackson	L	48	27	17	44	43	9	3	1	4	2
Charlie Conacher	C	40	14	19	33	64	9	1	1	2	10
Joe Primeau	R	48	11	21	32	4	8	0	1	1	4
King Clancy	D	48	13	12	25	79	9	0	3	3	14
Bob Gracie	F	48	9	13	22	27	9	0	1	1	0

		REGULAR SEASON				*POSTSEASON*				
PLAYER	*POS*	*GP*	*G*	*A*	*PTS*	*PIM*	*GP*	*G*	*A*	*PTS*	*PIM*
Harold Cotton	F	48	10	11	21	29	9	0	3	3	6
Hap Day	D	47	6	14	20	46	9	0	1	1	**21**
Ace Bailey	F	47	10	8	18	52	8	0	1	1	4
Ken Doraty	F	38	5	11	16	16	9	5	0	5	2
Alex Levinsky	D	48	5	11	16	61	9	1	0	1	14
Andy Blair	F	43	6	9	15	38	9	0	2	2	4
Bill Thoms	F	29	3	9	12	15	9	1	1	2	4
Red Horner	D	48	3	8	11	**144**	9	1	0	1	10
Harold Darragh	F	9	1	2	3	0					
Stew Adams	F	19	0	2	2	0					
Charlie Sands	C	3	0	3	3	0	9	2	2	4	2
Lorne Chabot	G	48	0	0	0	2	9	0	0	0	0

		REGULAR SEASON				*POSTSEASON*			
GOALTENDER		*GP*	*MIN*	*GA*	*SH*	*GAA*	*GP*	*MIN*	*GA*	*SH*	*GAA*
Lorne Chabot	(24-18-6)	48	2946	111	5	2.26	9	686	18	2	1.57
Charlie Conacher		2	4	0	0	0.00					

MONTREAL   22-20-6   50   2nd (C)   Eddie Gerard
Maroons

		REGULAR SEASON				*POSTSEASON*				
PLAYER	*POS*	*GP*	*G*	*A*	*PTS*	*PIM*	*GP*	*G*	*A*	*PTS*	*PIM*
Lorne Northcott	L	47	22	21	43	30	2	0	0	0	4
Reg Smith	C	48	20	21	41	66	2	2	0	2	2
Paul Haynes	C	47	16	25	41	18	2	0	0	0	2
Jimmy Ward	R	48	16	17	33	52	2	0	0	0	0
Dave Trottier	L	48	16	15	31	38	2	0	0	0	6
Glenn Brydson	R	48	11	17	28	26	2	0	0	0	0
Lionel Conacher	D	47	7	21	28	61	2	0	1	1	0
Earl Robinson	F	44	15	9	24	6	2	0	0	0	0
Cy Wentworth	D	47	4	10	14	48	2	0	1	1	0
Lorne Duguid	F	48	4	7	11	38	2	0	0	0	4
Wally Kilrea (2–2)	F	19	1	7	8	2	2	0	0	0	0
Hugh Plaxton	F	15	1	2	3	4					
Archie Wilcox	D	47	0	3	3	37	2	0	0	0	0
John Gallagher (1–2)	F	6	1	0	1	0					
Stan McCabe	D	1	0	0	0	0					
Merlyn Phillips (1–2)	F	2	0	0	0	0					
Earl Roche (1–3)	L	5	0	0	0	0					
Des Roche (1–2)	R	5	0	0	0	0					
Andy Bellemer	D	15	0	0	0	0					
Reg Noble (2–2)	D	20	0	0	0	16	2	0	0	0	0
Dave Kerr	G	25	0	0	0	0	2	0	0	0	0
James Walsh	G	22	0	0	0	0					

		REGULAR SEASON				*POSTSEASON*			
GOALTENDER		*GP*	*MIN*	*GA*	*SH*	*GAA*	*GP*	*MIN*	*GA*	*SH*	*GAA*
Dave Kerr	(14-8-3)	25	1520	58	4	2.29	2	120	8	0	4.00
Flat Walsh	(8-11-3)	22	1303	56	2	2.58					
Hugh Plaxton	(0-1-0)	1	57	5	0	5.26					

MONTREAL Canadiens

18-25-5   41   3rd (C)   Newsy Lalonde

PLAYER	POS	REGULAR SEASON					POSTSEASON				
		GP	G	A	PTS	PIM	GP	G	A	PTS	PIM
Auriel Joliat	L	48	18	21	39	53	2	2	1	3	2
Howie Morenz	C	46	14	21	35	32	2	0	3	3	2
Johnny Gagnon	R	48	12	23	35	64	2	0	2	2	0
Alfred Lepine	C	46	8	8	16	45	2	0	0	0	2
Wildor Larochelle	R	47	11	4	15	27	2	1	0	1	0
Sylvio Mantha	D	48	4	7	11	50	2	0	1	1	2
Georges Mantha	L	43	3	6	9	10					
Al Leduc	D	48	5	3	8	62	2	1	0	1	2
Art Giroux	F	40	5	2	7	14	2	0	0	0	0
Gerry Carson	D	48	5	2	7	53	2	0	0	0	2
Marty Burke (1-2)	L	29	2	5	7	36					
Leo Gaudreault	F	24	2	2	4	2					
Armand Mondou	F	24	1	3	4	15					
Wilfred Hart	F	18	0	3	3	0	2	0	1	1	0
Leo Bourgeault (2-2)	D	15	1	1	2	9	2	0	0	0	0
Hago Harrington	F	24	1	1	2	2	2	1	0	1	2
Art Alexandre	F	1	0	0	0	0					
Len Grosvenor	F	4	0	0	0	0	2	0	0	0	0
Harold Starr (2-2)	F	15	0	0	0	6	2	0	0	0	2
George Hainsworth	G	48	0	0	0	0	2	0	0	0	0
Leo Murray	C	6	0	0	0	2					
Walt McCartney	L	2	0	0	0	0					

GOALTENDER		REGULAR SEASON					POSTSEASON				
		GP	MIN	GA	SH	GAA	GP	MIN	GA	SH	GAA
George Hainsworth	(18-25-5)	48	2980	115	8	2.32	2	120	8	0	4.00

NEW YORK Americans

15-22-11   41   4th (C)   Joe Simpson

REGULAR SEASON

POSTSEASON
no postseason play

PLAYER	POS	GP	G	A	PTS	PIM
Norm Himes	C	48	9	25	34	12
Johnny Sheppard	L	46	17	9	26	32
Nick Wasnie	F	48	11	12	23	36
Pat Patterson	F	48	12	7	19	26
Charley McVeigh	R	40	7	12	19	10
Bill Brydge	D	48	4	15	19	60
Walt Jackson	F	35	10	2	12	6
Ron Martin	F	47	5	7	12	6
Duke Dukowski	D	48	4	7	11	43
Merlyn Phillips (2-2)	F	26	1	7	8	10
Wilf Starr	F	27	4	3	7	8
Tommy Filmore	F	33	1	4	5	9
Lloyd Klein	L	15	2	2	4	4
Vern Ayres	D	48	0	3	3	97
Eddie Burke	F	15	2	0	2	4
Bill Regan	D	15	1	1	2	14
Gord Kuhn	R	12	1	1	2	4

		REGULAR SEASON					*POSTSEASON*
PLAYER	*POS*	*GP*	*G*	*A*	*PTS*	*PIM*	*no postseason play*
Jack Keating	F	13	0	2	2	11	
Mervyn Dutton	D	43	0	2	2	74	
Eddie Convey	F	13	0	1	1	12	
Joe Thorsteinson	F	4	0	0	0	0	
Roy Worters	G	47	0	0	0	0	
Jake Forbes	G	1	0	0	0	0	

		REGULAR SEASON					*POSTSEASON*
GOALTENDER		*GP*	*MIN*	*GA*	*SH*	*GAA*	*no postseason play*
Jake Forbes	(0-0-1)	1	70	2	0	1.71	
Roy Worters	(15-22-10)	47	2970	**116**	5	2.34	

OTTAWA 11-27-10 32 5th (C) Cy Denneny
Senators

		REGULAR SEASON					*POSTSEASON*
PLAYER	*POS*	*GP*	*G*	*A*	*PTS*	*PIM*	*no postseason play*
Cooney Weiland	C	**48**	16	11	27	4	
Syd Howe	R	**48**	12	12	24	17	
Hec Kilrea	L	**48**	14	8	22	26	
Bill Tuohey	F	47	12	7	19	12	
Frank Finnigan	F	44	4	14	18	37	
Gus Forslund	F	**48**	4	9	13	2	
Danny Cox	F	47	4	7	11	8	
Al Shields	D	**48**	4	7	11	119	
Earl Roche (3–3)	F	20	4	5	9	6	
Wally Kilrea (1–2)	F	32	4	5	9	14	
Des Roche (2–2)	F	16	3	6	9	6	
Bert McInenly	D	30	2	2	4	8	
Hib Milks	L	18	0	3	3	0	
Alex Smith (1–2)	D	34	2	0	2	42	
Leo Bourgeault (1–2)	D	35	1	1	2	13	
Harvey Rockburn	D	16	0	1	1	39	
Gerry Lowrey	F	6	0	0	0	0	
Norm Gainor	C	2	0	0	0	0	
Harold Starr (1–2)	D	31	0	0	0	30	
Marty Burke (2–2)	D	16	0	0	0	10	
Bert Burry	D	4	0	0	0	0	
Bill Beveridge	G	35	0	0	0	0	
Alec Connell	G	15	0	0	0	0	

		REGULAR SEASON					*POSTSEASON*
GOALTENDER		*GP*	*MIN*	*GA*	*SH*	*GAA*	*no postseason play*
Alec Connell	(4-8-2)	15	845	36	1	2.55	
Bill Beveridge	(7-19-8)	35	2195	95	5	2.60	

BOSTON 25-15-8 58 1st (A) Art Ross
Bruins

		REGULAR SEASON					*POSTSEASON*				
PLAYER	*POS*	*GP*	*G*	*A*	*PTS*	*PIM*	*GP*	*G*	*A*	*PTS*	*PIM*
Marty Barry	C	48	24	13	37	40	5	2	2	4	6

1932-1933 119

		REGULAR SEASON					*POSTSEASON*				
PLAYER	*POS*	*GP*	*G*	*A*	*PTS*	*PIM*	*GP*	*G*	*A*	*PTS*	*PIM*
Nels Stewart	C	47	18	18	36	62	5	2	0	2	4
Eddie Shore	D	48	8	27	35	102	5	0	1	1	14
Dit Clapper	R	48	14	14	28	42	5	1	1	2	2
John Beattie	L	48	8	12	20	12	5	0	0	0	2
Joe Lamb	F	42	11	8	19	68	5	0	1	1	6
Harry Oliver	R	47	11	7	18	10	5	0	0	0	0
Obs Heximer	F	48	7	5	12	24	5	0	0	0	2
Alex Smith (2-2)	D	15	5	4	9	30	5	0	2	2	6
Art Chapman	F	46	3	6	9	19	5	0	0	0	2
George Owen	D	42	6	2	8	10	5	0	0	0	6
Frank Jerwa	F	34	3	4	7	23					
Vic Ripley (2-2)	F	23	2	5	7	27	5	1	0	1	0
Billy Burch (1-2)	C	3	1	4	4	4					
Percy Galbraith	L	47	1	2	3	28	5	0	0	0	0
Lionel Hitchman	D	45	0	1	1	34	5	1	0	1	0
Earl Roche (3-3)	L	3	0	0	0	0					
Tiny Thompson	G	48	0	0	0	0	5	0	0	0	0

		REGULAR SEASON					*POSTSEASON*				
GOALTENDER		*GP*	*MIN*	*GA*	*SH*	*GAA*	*GP*	*MIN*	*GA*	*SH*	*GAA*
Tiny Thompson	(**25**-15-8)	48	3000	88	**11**	**1.76**	5	438	9	0	**1.23**

DETROIT 25-15-8 58 2nd (A) Jack Adams
Red Wings

		REGULAR SEASON					*POSTSEASON*				
PLAYER	*POS*	*GP*	*G*	*A*	*PTS*	*PIM*	*GP*	*G*	*A*	*PTS*	*PIM*
Herb Lewis	L	48	20	14	34	20	4	1	0	1	0
Frank Carson	F	47	12	13	25	35	4	0	1	1	0
John Sorrell	L	47	14	10	24	11	4	2	2	4	4
Larry Aurie	R	47	12	11	23	25	4	1	0	1	4
Hap Emms	F	41	9	13	22	63	4	0	0	0	8
Ebbie Goodfellow	F	40	12	8	20	47	4	1	0	1	11
Carl Voss (2-2)	C	38	6	14	20	6	4	1	1	2	0
Eddie Wiseman	F	47	8	8	16	16	2	0	0	0	0
Doug Young	D	48	5	6	11	59	4	1	1	2	0
John Gallagher (2-2)	F	35	3	6	9	48	4	1	1	2	4
Leroy Goldsworthy	D	26	3	6	9	6	2	0	0	0	0
Stew Evans	D	48	2	6	8	74	4	0	0	0	6
George Hay	F	34	1	6	7	6	4	0	1	1	0
Walt Buswell	D	46	2	4	6	16	4	0	0	0	4
Ron Moffatt	F	24	1	1	2	6	4	0	0	0	0
Gus Marker	F	15	1	1	2	8					
Bob Davis	F	3	0	0	0	0					
Jack Riley	C	1	0	0	0	0					
Emil Hanson	D	7	0	0	0	6					
Reg Noble (1-2)	D	5	0	0	0	0					
John Roach	G	48	0	0	0	0	4	0	0	0	0

		REGULAR SEASON					*POSTSEASON*				
GOALTENDER		*GP*	*MIN*	*GA*	*SH*	*GAA*	*GP*	*MIN*	*GA*	*SH*	*GAA*
John Roach	(**25**-15-8)	48	2970	93	10	1.88	4	240	8	1	2.00

NEW YORK 23-17-8 54 3rd (A) Lester Patrick
Rangers

		REGULAR SEASON				POSTSEASON				
PLAYER	POS	GP	G	A	PTS	PIM	GP	G	A	PTS	PIM
Bill Cook	R	48	28	22	50	51	8	3	2	5	4
Bun Cook	L	48	22	15	37	35	8	2	0	2	4
Frank Boucher	C	46	7	28	35	4	8	2	2	4	6
Cecil Dillon	R	48	21	10	31	12	8	8	2	10	6
Art Somers	F	48	7	15	22	28	8	1	4	5	8
Al Siebert	D	42	9	10	19	38	8	1	0	1	12
Ivan Johnson	D	48	8	9	17	127	8	1	0	1	14
Murray Murdoch	C	48	5	11	16	16	8	3	4	7	2
Oscar Asmundson	F	48	5	10	15	20	8	0	2	2	4
Butch Keeling	L	47	8	6	14	22	8	0	2	2	8
Ott Heller	D	40	5	7	12	31	8	3	0	3	10
Doug Brennan	D	48	5	4	9	94	8	0	0	0	11
Earl Seibert	D	45	2	3	5	92	8	1	0	1	14
Carl Voss (1–2)	C	10	2	1	3	4					
Gord Pettinger	F	35	1	2	3	18	8	0	0	0	0
Andy Aitkenhead	G	48	0	0	0	0	8	0	0	0	0

	REGULAR SEASON					POSTSEASON			
GOALTENDER	GP	MIN	GA	SH	GAA	GP	MIN	GA	SH	GAA
Andy Aitkenhead (23-17-8)	48	2970	107	3	2.16	8	488	13	2	1.63

CHICAGO 16-20-12 44 4th (A) Emil Iverson
Blackhawks Tommy Gorman

		REGULAR SEASON				POSTSEASON
PLAYER	POS	GP	G	A	PTS	PIM	*no postseason play*
Paul Thompson	L	48	13	20	33	27
Tommy Cook	F	47	12	14	26	30
Johnny Gottsleig	F	42	11	11	22	6
Elwin Romnes	C	47	10	12	22	2
Harold March	R	48	9	11	20	38
Rosie Couture	F	46	10	7	17	26
Don McFadyen	F	48	5	9	14	20
Roger Jenkins	F	45	3	10	13	42
Teddy Graham	D	47	3	8	11	57
Bill MacKenzie	D	35	4	4	8	13
Vic Ripley (1–2)	L	15	2	4	6	6
Art Coulter	D	46	3	2	5	53
Clarence Abel	D	45	0	4	4	63
Billy Burch (2–2)	F	24	2	0	2	2
Helge Bostrom	D	20	1	0	1	14
Lou Holmes	F	18	0	0	0	0
Art Wiebe	D	3	0	0	0	0
Chuck Gardiner	G	48	0	0	0	0

	REGULAR SEASON					POSTSEASON
GOALTENDER	GP	MIN	GA	SH	GAA	*no postseason play*
Chuck Gardiner (16-20-12)	48	3010	101	5	2.01

TEAM TOTALS

TEAM	GP	G	A	P	PIM	GA	SH	Per Game G	A	PIM	GA
Canadian											
Toronto	48	119	164	283	**622**	111	5	2.48	3.41	**12.96**	2.31
Montreal (M)	48	**134**	**175**	**309**	442	119	6	**2.79**	**3.64**	9.20	2.48
Montreal (C)	48	92	111	203	482	115	8	1.92	2.31	10.04	2.40
New York (A)	48	91	119	210	478	118	5	1.90	2.48	9.96	2.46
Ottawa	48	89	95	184	398	131	6	1.85	1.98	8.29	2.73
American											
Boston	48	124	129	253	517	**88**	11	2.58	2.69	10.77	**1.83**
Detroit	48	111	127	238	458	93	10	2.31	2.64	9.54	1.94
New York (R)	48	135	153	288	599	107	3	2.81	3.19	12.48	2.23
Chicago	48	88	116	204	399	101	5	1.83	2.42	8.31	2.10
	432	983	1189	2172	4395	983	59	2.28	2.75	10.17	2.28

PLAYOFFS

SERIES "A"
Boston 2, Toronto 1 (OT)
Toronto 1, Boston 0 (OT)
Boston 2, Toronto 1 (OT)
Toronto 5, Boston 3
Toronto 1, Boston 0 (6 OT)

TORONTO, 3–2

SERIES "B"
Detroit 2, Montreal (M) 0
Detroit 3, Montreal (M) 2

DETROIT WINS
TOTAL GOAL SERIES, 5–2

SERIES "C"
New York (R) 5, Montreal (C) 2
New York (R) 3, Montreal (C) 3

NEW YORK (R) WINS
TOTAL GOAL SERIES, 8–5

SERIES "D"
New York (R) 2, Detroit 0
New York (R) 4, Detroit 3

NEW YORK (R) WINS
TOTAL GOAL SERIES, 6–3

SERIES "E"
New York (R) 5, Toronto 1
New York (R) 3, Toronto 1
Toronto 3, New York (R) 2
New York (R) 1, Toronto 0 (OT)

NEW YORK (R) WINS
STANLEY CUP, 3–1

ALL-STAR TEAMS

First Team
G — John Roach, DET
D — Ivan Johnson, N(R)
D — Eddie Shore, BOS
C — Frank Boucher, N(R)
R — Bill Cook, N(R)
L — Lorne Northcutt, M(M)

Second Team
G — Chuck Gardiner, CHI
D — King Clancy, TOR
D — Lionel Conacher, M(M)
C — Howie Morenz, M(C)
R — Charlie Conacher, TOR
L — Harvey Jackson, TOR

INDIVIDUAL TROPHY WINNERS
HART TROPHY (Most Valuable Player): Eddie Shore, BOS
LADY BYNG TROPHY (Gentlemanly Conduct): Frank Boucher, N(R)
VEZINA TROPHY (Best Goaltender): Tiny Thompson, BOS

1933-1934
Cheap Shot

In a league which stressed tough and manly play, Boston's Eddie Shore more than held his own. A rugged defensemen from his rookie year, he regularly finished NHL seasons with triple-digit penalty minutes, leading the circuit with a then-record 165 in 1927-28. However, in 1933-34, Shore would step over the line.

As a sport, hockey is a fast-moving, physical game. Hits are dished out on a regular basis, with the donor usually getting hit back by his docent during some portion of the match. However, in some cases, despite a code of behavior in which physical retribution was usually returned in kind, retaliation is given to an innocent party by mistake. A very grave example of mistaken identity was about to engulf the NHL.

As the nine-team NHL neared the halfway point of the 1933-34 season, Shore's Boston Bruins faced the Toronto Maple Leafs on the night of December 12 in Boston Garden. Midway through the contest, with Toronto nursing a one-goal lead, Shore was upended by Toronto defenseman King Clancy. Infuriated that no infraction had been ruled, Shore pounced on the nearest Leaf—which happened to be talented forward Ace Bailey, a former scoring champ. With Bailey unaware of his presence, Shore leveled a cheap shot at his Toronto foe, sending him crashing to the ice. As Bailey lay motionless, Leaf enforcer Red Horner in turn smacked Shore down. Blood was everywhere, and only cooler heads prevented a full-fledged riot.

In the immediate aftermath, the Boston team doctor saw right away that Bailey was gravely hurt. After first wanting to summon a priest for last rites, instead the injured Leaf was turned over to Boston's medical community. Over a period of several weeks, as reported in headlines of in American and Canadian newspapers, Boston's finest physicians worked diligently to save the player's life. After many days, the corner was turned and Bailey was moved off the critical list.

With this dramatic event unfolding, the rest of the NHL season was in many ways a mere afterthought. In a bold statement, Toronto (26-13-9, 61), even without their star, claimed the Canadian Division's top prize, followed by the two playoff-bound Montreal clubs, all well ahead of the Americans and Ottawa. In the other division, Detroit (24-14-10, 58) repeated as champion, followed by Chicago and the Rangers. Boston—not responding to the Bailey incident as well as the Leafs—finished last.

Toronto forwards Charlie Conacher (32) and Joe Primeau (32) finished with the most goals and assists, respectively, with the former winning the overall scoring title as well (52). Bailey's defender Red Horner (146) accumulated the most penalty minutes. Goaltender Wilf Cude, who spent time with both Detroit and the Canadiens, had the lowest GAA (1.47), while Chicago's Chuck Gardiner whitewashed the most foes (10).

In the playoffs, Detroit won the first-place series in five games, besting the Leafs 1–0 in the deciding game. The other two series were close as well, with Chicago and Maroons squeaking out one-goal victories. In the semifinals, the Blackhawks buried Montreal, six goals to two. In the finals, the Hawks completed their Cup run with a four wins over Detroit, with two of their victories coming in overtime. Despite being on the short end, two Wings led all playoff scorers: Larry Aurie, with seven assists and 10 points, and Herb Lewis with five goals. In net, Gardiner guarded the cage with style, allowing only 1.33 goals per game, while shutting out his opponents twice.

Earlier, the Leafs staged a tribute night for their injured player, Ace Bailey. On the night of February 14 at Maple Leaf Gardens, a picked all-star squad from the other eight teams faced the Leafs. Ironically, since Shore was still one of the stars of the NHL, he was picked as member of the all-stars. Brian McFarlane in *50 Years of Hockey* described what happened next: "Bailey, clad in a knee-length brown overcoat, his head bare and wearing dark glasses, walked slowly to center ice. The players on the two teams were lined up on the blue line, and when Bailey reached the face-off circle, Shore skated over to greet him with outstretched hand. Bailey did not hesitate; he grasped Shore's hand firmly, and the two embraced each other."

Although this act of forgiveness ended the incident, the long-term outcome hardly seemed fair. In subsequent years, Shore resumed his career, finally retiring six years later—five years before his election to the Hall of Fame. On the other side, with one cheap shot Bailey's career was over at the age of 32, as he never played again. Thankfully, hockey eventually evened the score, finally allowing Bailey his rightful place in hockey's hallowed halls alongside his one-time attacker.

STANDINGS

TEAM	GP	W	L	T	PTS	GF	GA
CANADIAN							
TORONTO	48	26	13	9	61	174	119
MONTREAL (C)	48	22	20	6	50	99	101
MONTREAL (M)	48	19	18	11	49	117	122
NEW YORK (A)	48	15	23	10	40	104	132
OTTAWA	48	13	29	6	32	115	143
AMERICAN							
DETROIT	48	24	14	10	58	113	98
CHICAGO	48	20	17	11	51	88	83
NEW YORK (R)	48	21	19	8	50	120	113
BOSTON	48	18	25	5	41	111	130

LEADERS

PLAYER	TM	GP	G	A	PTS	PIM
Charlie Conacher	TOR	42	**32**	20	**52**	38
Joe Primeau	TOR	45	14	**32**	46	8
Frank Boucher	N(R)	48	14	30	44	4
Marty Barry	BOS	48	27	12	39	12
Nels Stewart	BOS	48	22	17	39	68
Cecil Dillon	N(R)	48	13	26	39	10
Harvey Jackson	TOR	38	20	18	38	38
Aurel Joliat	M(C)	48	22	15	37	27
Reg Smith	M(M)	47	18	19	37	58
Paul Thompson	CHI	48	20	16	36	17

GOALS	
C. Conacher, TOR	32
Barry, BOS	27
Stewart, BOS	22
Joliat, M(C)	22
Sorrell, DET	21

ASSISTS	
Primeau, TOR	32
Boucher, N(R)	30
Dillon, N(R)	26
Romnes, CHI	21
C. Conacher, TOR	20

GOALTENDER	TM	GP	MIN	GA	SH	GAA
Wilf Cude	D-M	30	1920	47	4	**1.47**
Chuck Gardiner	CHI	48	3050	83	**10**	1.63
Roy Worters	N(A)	36	2240	75	4	2.01
Lorne Chabot	M(C)	47	2928	101	8	2.07
Andy Aitkenhead	N(R)	48	2990	113	7	2.27
George Hainsworth	TOR	48	3010	119	3	2.37
Dave Kerr	M(M)	48	**3060**	122	6	2.39
John Roach	DET	19	1030	45	1	2.62
Tiny Thompson	BOS	48	2980	130	5	2.62
Bill Beveridge	OTT	48	3000	**143**	3	2.86

PENALTY MINUTES	
Horner, TOR	146
L. Conacher, CHI	87
Johnson, N(R)	86
Stewart, BOS	68
Seibert, N(R)	66

SHUTOUTS	
Gardiner, CHI	10
Chabot, M(C)	8
Aitkenhead, N(R)	7
Kerr, M(M)	6
Thompson, BOS	5

TORONTO 26-13-9 61 1st (C) Dick Irvin
Maple Leafs

			REGULAR SEASON				POSTSEASON			
PLAYER	POS	GP	G	A	PTS	PIM	GP	G	A	PTS	PIM
Charlie Conacher	R	42	**32**	20	**52**	38	5	3	2	5	0

		REGULAR SEASON					POSTSEASON				
PLAYER	POS	GP	G	A	PTS	PIM	GP	G	A	PTS	PIM
Joe Primeau	C	45	14	32	46	8	5	2	4	6	6
Harvey Jackson	L	38	20	18	38	38	5	1	0	1	8
King Clancy	D	46	11	17	28	62	3	0	0	0	8
Bill Thoms	C	47	8	18	26	24	5	0	2	2	0
Andy Blair	L	42	14	9	23	35	5	0	2	2	16
Hec Kilrea	L	43	10	13	23	15	5	2	0	2	2
Harold Cotton	L	47	8	14	22	46	5	0	2	2	0
Red Horner	D	40	11	10	21	146	5	1	0	1	6
Frank Boll	L	42	12	8	20	21	5	0	0	0	9
Hap Day	D	48	9	10	19	35	5	0	0	0	6
Ken Doraty	F	34	9	10	19	6	5	2	2	4	0
Charlie Sands	C	45	8	8	16	2	5	1	0	1	0
Alex Levinsky	D	47	5	11	16	38	5	0	0	0	6
Ace Bailey	R	13	2	3	5	11					
Jack Shill	C	7	0	1	1	0	2	0	0	0	0
Bill Hollett (1–2)	D	4	0	0	0	4					
Fred Robertson (1–2)	D	2	0	0	0	0					
George Hainsworth	G	48	0	0	0	0	5	0	0	0	0

		REGULAR SEASON					POSTSEASON				
GOALTENDER		GP	MIN	GA	SH	GAA	GP	MIN	GA	SH	GAA
George Hainsworth	(26-13-9)	48	3010	119	3	2.37	5	301	11	0	2.19

MONTREAL Canadiens 22-20-6 50 2nd (C) Newsy Lalonde

		REGULAR SEASON					POSTSEASON				
PLAYER	POS	GP	G	A	PTS	PIM	GP	G	A	PTS	PIM
Aurel Joliat	L	48	22	15	37	27	2	0	1	1	0
Wildor Larochelle	R	48	16	11	27	27	2	1	1	2	0
Johnny Gagnon	R	48	9	15	24	25	2	1	0	1	2
Howie Morenz	C	39	8	13	21	21	2	1	1	2	0
Alfred Lepine	C	48	10	8	18	44	2	0	0	0	0
Jack Riley	C	48	6	11	17	4	2	0	1	1	0
Georges Mantha	D	44	6	9	15	12					
Sylvio Mantha	D	48	4	6	10	24	2	0	0	0	2
Armand Mondou	L	48	5	3	8	4	1	0	1	1	0
Leo Bourgeault	D	48	4	3	7	10	2	0	0	0	0
Gerry Carson	D	48	5	1	6	51	2	0	0	0	2
Marty Burke	D	45	1	4	5	28	2	0	1	1	2
Sammy Godin	R	36	2	2	4	15					
Jack Portland	D	31	0	2	2	10	2	0	0	0	0
Paul Raymond	R	29	1	0	1	2	2	0	0	0	0
Adie LaFrance	L	3	0	0	0	2	2	0	0	0	0
Lorne Chabot	G	47	0	0	0	2	2	0	0	0	0
Wilf Cude (2–2)	G	1									

		REGULAR SEASON					POSTSEASON				
GOALTENDER		GP	MIN	GA	SH	GAA	GP	MIN	GA	SH	GAA
Wilf Cude (2–2)	(1-0-0)	1	60	0	1	*0.00					
Lorne Chabot	(21-20-6)	47	2928	101	8	2.07	2	131	4	0	1.83

1933-1934

MONTREAL Maroons 19-18-11   49   3rd (C)   Eddie Gerard

PLAYER	POS	REGULAR SEASON					POSTSEASON				
		GP	G	A	PTS	PIM	GP	G	A	PTS	PIM
Reg Smith	R	47	18	19	37	58	4	0	1	1	6
Lorne Northcutt	D	47	20	13	33	27	4	2	0	2	0
Earl Robinson	R	47	12	16	28	14	4	2	0	2	0
Dave Trottier	L	48	9	17	26	47	4	0	0	0	6
Jimmy Ward	R	48	14	9	23	46	4	0	0	0	0
Russ Blinco	C	31	14	9	23	2	4	0	1	1	0
Paul Haynes	C	44	5	4	9	18	4	0	1	1	2
Glenn Brydson	R	37	4	5	9	19	1	0	0	0	0
Herb Cain	L	30	4	5	9	14	4	0	0	0	0
Bill MacKenzie	D	47	4	3	7	20	4	0	0	0	0
Cy Wentworth	D	18	2	5	7	31	4	0	2	2	2
Stew Evans (2-2)	D	27	4	2	6	35	4	0	0	0	4
Wally Kilrea	C	45	3	1	4	7	4	0	0	0	0
Irv Frew	D	30	2	1	3	41	4	0	0	0	6
Teddy Graham (1-2)	D	19	2	1	3	10					
Lorne Duguid	L	5	0	1	1	0					
Vern Ayres	D	17	0	0	0	19					
Archie Wilcox (1-2)	R	10	0	0	0	2					
Stan McCabe	L	8	0	0	0	4					
Paul Runge	C	4	0	0	0	0					
Harold Starr	D						3	0	0	0	0
Dave Kerr	G	48	0	0	0	0	4	0	0	0	0

GOALTENDER		REGULAR SEASON					POSTSEASON				
		GP	MIN	GA	SH	GAA	GP	MIN	GA	SH	GAA
Dave Kerr	(19-18-11)	48	3060	122	6	2.39	4	240	7	1	1.75

NEW YORK Americans 15-23-10   40   4th (C)   Joe Simpson

PLAYER	POS	REGULAR SEASON					POSTSEASON
		GP	G	A	PTS	PIM	no postseason play
Eddie Burke	R	46	20	10	30	24	
Charley McVeigh	C	48	15	12	27	4	
Norm Himes	C	48	9	16	25	10	
Lloyd Klein	L	48	13	9	22	34	
Maitland Conn	L	48	4	17	21	12	
Bill Brydge	D	48	6	7	13	44	
Ron Martin	R	47	8	9	17	30	
Walt Jackson	L	47	6	9	15	12	
Lloyd Gross (1-3)	L	21	7	3	10	10	
Bob Gracie (2-2)	C	24	4	6	10	10	
Art Chapman (2-2)	C	25	3	7	10	8	
Mervyn Dutton	D	48	2	8	10	65	
John Doran	D	39	1	4	5	40	
Hal Picketts	R	48	3	1	4	32	
George Patterson (1-2)	R	13	3	0	3	6	
Allan Murray	D	39	1	1	2	20	

		REGULAR SEASON					*POSTSEASON*
PLAYER	POS	GP	G	A	PTS	PIM	*no postseason play*
Duke Dukowski (1–3)	D	9	0	1	1	11	
Chris Speyer	D	9	0	0	0	0	
Roy Worters	G	36	0	0	0	0	
Moe Roberts	G	6	0	0	0	0	
Benny Grant	G	5	0	0	0	0	
Alec Connell	G	1	0	0	0	0	
Abbie Cox (1–2)	G	1	0	0	0	0	
Percy Jackson	G	1	0	0	0	0	

		REGULAR SEASON					*POSTSEASON*
GOALTENDER		GP	MIN	GA	SH	GAA	*no postseason play*
Roy Worters	(12-13-10)	36	2240	75	4	2.01	
Alec Connell	(1-0-0)	1	40	2	0	3.00	
Benny Grant	(1-4-0)	5	320	18	1	3.38	
Moe Roberts	(1-4-0)	6	336	25	0	4.46	
Abbie Cox (1–2)	(0-1-0)	1	24	3	0	7.50	
Percy Jackson	(0-1-0)	1	60	9	0	9.00	

OTTAWA 13-29-6   32   5th (C)   Georges Boucher
Senators

		REGULAR SEASON					*POSTSEASON*
PLAYER	POS	GP	G	A	PTS	PIM	*no postseason play*
Earl Roche	L	45	13	16	29	22	
Gerry Shannon	L	48	11	15	26	26	
Max Kaminsky	C	38	9	17	26	14	
Des Roche	R	46	14	10	24	22	
Carl Voss (2–2)	C	40	7	16	23	10	
Syd Howe	C	42	13	7	20	18	
Bill Touhey	L	46	12	8	20	21	
Frank Finnigan	R	48	10	10	20	10	
Nick Wasnie	R	37	11	6	17	10	
Bill Hollett (2–2)	D	30	7	4	11	21	
Al Shields	D	47	4	7	11	44	
Al Leduc (1–2)	D	32	1	3	4	34	
Ted Saunders	R	18	1	3	4	4	
Danny Cox (1–2)	L	29	0	4	4	0	
Jeff Kalbfleisch	D	22	0	4	4	20	
Cooney Weiland (1–2)	C	*9	2	0	2	4	
Ralph Bowman	D	16	0	2	2	64	
Bud Cook	C	18	1	0	1	8	
Percy Galbraith (1–2)	L	2	0	0	0	0	
Bert McInenly (1–2)	D	2	0	0	0	0	
Bill Beveridge	G	48	0	0	0	0	

		REGULAR SEASON					*POSTSEASON*
GOALTENDER		GP	MIN	GA	SH	GAA	*no postseason play*
Bill Beveridge	(13-**29**-6)	48	3000	**143**	3	2.86	

1933-1934

DETROIT Red Wings		24-14-10		58		1st (A)	Jack Adams			
		REGULAR SEASON					*POSTSEASON*			
PLAYER	POS	GP	G	A	PTS	PIM	GP	G	A	PTS	PIM
Larry Aurie	R	48	16	19	35	36	9	3	7	**10**	2
John Sorrell	L	47	21	10	31	8	8	0	2	2	0
Herb Lewis	L	43	16	15	31	15	9	5	2	7	2
Cooney Weiland (2-2)	C	*39	11	19	30	6	9	2	2	4	4
Ebbie Goodfellow	C	48	13	13	26	45	9	4	3	7	12
Frank Carson	R	47	10	9	19	36	6	0	1	1	5
Gord Pettinger	C	48	3	14	17	14	7	1	0	1	2
Hap Emms	L	45	7	7	14	51	8	0	0	0	2
Eddie Wiseman	R	48	5	9	14	13	7	0	1	1	4
Doug Young	D	47	4	0	4	36	9	0	0	0	10
Wilf Starr	C	28	2	2	4	17	7	0	2	2	2
Walt Buswell	D	47	1	2	3	8	9	0	1	1	2
Lloyd Gross (3-3)	L	13	1	1	2	2	1	0	0	0	0
Carl Voss (1-2)	C	8	0	2	2	2					
Teddy Graham (2-2)	D	28	1	0	1	29	9	3	1	4	8
Fred Robertson (2-2)	D	24	1	0	1	12					
Gus Marker	R	7	1	0	1	2	4	0	0	0	2
Burr Williams	D	1	0	1	1	12	7	0	0	0	8
Stew Evans (1-2)	D	17	0	0	0	20					
Harry Foster	D	6	0	0	0	2					
Ron Moffatt	L	5	0	0	0	2	3	0	0	0	0
John Gallagher	D	1	0	0	0	0					
George Hay	L	1	0	0	0	0					
Gene Carrigan	C						4	0	0	0	0
Wilf Cude (1-2)	G	29	0	0	0	0	9	0	0	0	0
John Roach	G	19	0	0	0	0					
Abbie Cox (2-2)	G	2	0	0	0	0					

		REGULAR SEASON					*POSTSEASON*			
GOALTENDER		GP	MIN	GA	SH	GAA	GP	MIN	GA	SH	GAA
Wilf Cude (1-2)	(15-6-8)	29	1860	47	4	***1.52**	9	593	21	1	2.00
John Roach	(9-8-1)	19	1030	45	1	2.62					
Abbie Cox	(0-0-1)	2	109	5	0	2.75					
Doug Young		1	21	1	0	2.86					

CHICAGO Blackhawks		20-17-11		51		2nd (A)	Tommy Gorman			
		REGULAR SEASON					*POSTSEASON*			
PLAYER	POS	GP	G	A	PTS	PIM	GP	G	A	PTS	PIM
Paul Thompson	L	48	20	16	36	17	8	4	3	7	6
Johnny Gottselig	L	48	16	14	30	4	8	4	3	7	4
Elwin Romnes	C	47	8	21	29	6	8	2	7	9	0
Lionel Conacher	D	48	10	13	23	87	8	2	0	2	4
Harold March	R	48	4	13	17	26	8	2	2	4	6
Tommy Cook	C	37	5	9	14	15	8	1	0	1	0
Rosie Couture	R	48	5	8	13	21	8	1	2	3	4
Jack Leswick	C	37	1	7	8	16					
Art Coulter	D	46	5	2	7	39	8	1	0	1	10

		REGULAR SEASON				*POSTSEASON*				
PLAYER	*POS*	*GP*	*G*	*A*	*PTS*	*PIM*	*GP*	*G*	*A*	*PTS*	*PIM*
Johnny Sheppard (2–2)	L	38	3	4	7	4	8	0	0	0	0
Leroy Goldsworthy	R	27	3	3	6	0	7	0	0	0	0
Roger Jenkins	D	48	2	2	4	37	8	0	0	0	0
Don McFadyen	C	46	1	3	4	20	8	2	2	4	5
Louis Trudel	L	31	1	3	4	13	7	0	0	0	0
Bill Kendall	R	21	3	0	3	0	2	0	0	0	0
Clarence Abel	D	46	2	1	3	28	8	0	0	0	8
Duke Dukowski (2–3)	D	5	0	0	0	2					
Tom Coulter	D	2	0	0	0	0					
Chuck Gardiner	G	48	0	0	0	0	8	0	0	0	0

	REGULAR SEASON					*POSTSEASON*			
GOALTENDER	*GP*	*MIN*	*GA*	*SH*	*GAA*	*GP*	*MIN*	*GA*	*SH*	*GAA*
Chuck Gardiner (20-17-**11**)	48	3050	83	**10**	1.63	8	542	12	**2**	**1.33**

NEW YORK 21-19-8 50 3rd (A) Lester Patrick
Rangers

		REGULAR SEASON				*POSTSEASON*				
PLAYER	*POS*	*GP*	*G*	*A*	*PTS*	*PIM*	*GP*	*G*	*A*	*PTS*	*PIM*
Frank Boucher	C	48	14	30	44	4	2	0	0	0	0
Cecil Dillon	R	48	13	26	39	10	2	0	1	1	2
Bun Cook	L	48	18	15	33	36	2	0	0	0	2
Murray Murdoch	L	48	17	10	27	29	2	0	0	0	0
Bill Cook	R	48	13	13	26	21	2	0	0	0	2
Earl Seibert	D	48	13	10	23	66	2	0	0	0	4
Butch Keeling	L	48	15	5	20	20	2	0	0	0	0
Vic Ripley (1–2)	C	34	5	12	17	10	2	1	0	1	4
Ivan Johnson	D	48	2	6	8	86	2	0	0	0	4
Oscar Asmundson	C	46	2	6	8	8	1	0	0	0	0
Ott Heller	D	48	2	5	7	29	2	0	0	0	0
Duke Dukowski (3–3)	D	29	0	6	6	18	2	0	0	0	0
Danny Cox (2–2)	L	13	5	0	5	2	2	0	0	0	0
Art Somers	C	8	1	2	3	5	2	0	0	0	0
Jean Pusie	D	19	0	2	2	17					
Al Siebert (1–2)	R	13	0	1	1	18					
Lorne Carr	R	14	0	0	0	0					
Al Leduc (2–2)	D	10	0	0	0	6					
Andy Aitkenhead	G	48	0	0	0	0	2	0	0	0	0

	REGULAR SEASON					*POSTSEASON*			
GOALTENDER	*GP*	*MIN*	*GA*	*SH*	*GAA*	*GP*	*MIN*	*GA*	*SH*	*GAA*
Andy Aitkenhead (21-19-8)	48	2990	113	7	2.27	2	120	2	1	**1.00**

BOSTON 18-25-5 41 4th (A) Art Ross
Bruins

		REGULAR SEASON				*POSTSEASON*
PLAYER	*POS*	*GP*	*G*	*A*	*PTS*	*PIM*
Marty Barry	C	48	27	12	39	12
Nels Stewart	C	48	22	17	39	68
John Beattie	L	48	9	13	22	26

no postseason play

1933-1934

		REGULAR SEASON					POSTSEASON
PLAYER	POS	GP	G	A	PTS	PIM	no postseason play
Joe Lamb	R	48	10	15	25	47	
Dit Clapper	R	48	10	12	22	6	
Harry Oliver	R	48	5	9	14	6	
Eddie Shore	D	30	2	10	12	57	
Al Siebert (2-2)	R	32	5	6	11	31	
Alex Smith	D	45	4	6	10	32	
Bob Gracie (1-2)	C	24	2	6	8	8	
Art Chapman (1-2)	C	21	2	5	7	7	
Peggy O'Neil	R	23	2	2	4	15	
Don Smilie	L	12	2	2	4	4	
Myles Lane	D	25	2	1	3	17	
Vic Ripley (1-2)	C	14	2	1	3	6	
Percy Galbraith (2-2)	L	42	0	2	2	6	
Lionel Hitchman	D	27	1	0	1	4	
Lloyd Gross (2-3)	L	6	1	0	1	6	
Archie Wilcox (2-2)	R	14	0	1	1	2	
George Patterson (2-2)	R	10	0	1	1	2	
Bob Davie	D	9	0	0	0	6	
Bert McInenly (2-2)	D	7	0	0	0	4	
Walt Harnott	L	6	0	0	0	2	
Frank Jerwa	L	5	0	0	0	2	
Johnny Sheppard (1-2)	L	4	0	0	0	0	
Tommy Filmore	R	3	0	0	0	0	
Joe Jerwa	R	2	0	0	0	2	
Tiny Thompson	G	48	0	0	0	0	

	REGULAR SEASON					POSTSEASON
GOALTENDER	GP	MIN	GA	SH	GAA	no postseason play
Tiny Thompson (18-25-5)	48	2980	130	5	2.62	

TEAM TOTALS

								Per Game			
TEAM	GP	G	A	P	PIM	GA	SH	G	A	PIM	GA
Canadian											
Toronto	48	173	202	375	529	119	3	3.60	4.21	11.02	2.48
Montreal (C)	48	99	103	202	308	101	9	2.06	2.14	6.42	2.10
Montreal (M)	48	117	111	228	414	122	6	2.44	2.31	8.63	2.54
New York (A)	48	105	120	225	365	132	5	2.19	2.50	7.60	2.75
Ottawa	48	116	132	248	344	143	3	2.42	2.75	7.17	2.98
American											
Detroit	48	113	123	236	368	98	5	2.35	2.56	7.67	2.04
Chicago	48	89	119	208	337	83	10	1.85	2.48	7.02	**1.73**
New York (R)	48	120	149	269	401	113	7	2.50	3.10	8.35	2.35
Boston	48	108	121	229	385	130	5	2.25	2.52	8.02	2.71
	432	1043	1180	2223	3451	1041	51	2.41	2.73	7.99	2.41

PLAYOFFS

SERIES "A"
Detroit 2, Toronto 1 (OT)
Detroit 6, Toronto 3
Toronto 3, Detroit 1
Toronto 5, Detroit 1
Detroit 1, Toronto 0

DETROIT, 3–2

SERIES "B"
Chicago 3, Montreal (C) 2
Chicago 1, Montreal (C) 1

CHICAGO WINS
TOTAL GOAL SERIES, 4–3

SERIES "C"
Montreal (M) 0, New York (R) 0
Montreal (M) 2, New York (R) 1

MONTREAL (M) WINS
TOTAL GOAL SERIES, 2–1

SERIES "D"
Chicago 3, Montreal (M) 0
Chicago 3, Montreal (M) 2

CHICAGO WINS
TOTAL GOAL SERIES, 6–2

SERIES "E"
Chicago 2, Detroit 1 (OT)
Chicago 4, Detroit 1
Detroit 5, Chicago 2
Chicago 1, Detroit 0 (OT)

CHICAGO WINS
STANLEY CUP, 3–1

ALL-STAR TEAMS

First Team
G — Chuck Gardiner, CHI
D — King Clancy, TOR
D — Lionel Conacher, CHI
C — Frank Boucher, N(R)
R — Charlie Conacher, TOR
L — Harvey Jackson, TOR

Second Team
G — Roy Worters, N(A)
D — Ivan Johnson, N(R)
D — Eddie Shore, BOS
C — Joe Primeau, TOR
R — Bill Cook, N(R)
L — Aurel Joliat, M(C)

INDIVIDUAL TROPHY WINNERS

HART TROPHY (Most Valuable Player): Aurel Joliat, M(C)
LADY BYNG TROPHY (Gentlemanly Conduct): Frank Boucher, N(R)
VEZINA TROPHY (Best Goaltender): Chuck Gardiner, CHI

1934-1935
Penalty Shot

Midway through the Canadiens-Toronto game on November 10, 1934, the referee stopped play. As the players on both sides watched, he placed the puck in a circle some three-dozen feet from Leaf goalie George Hainsworth. He then motioned Montreal's Armand Mondou into the circle. The NHL's newest rule change was about to be tested.

From nearly the beginning of the pro game, the rules of ice hockey had punished offenders with a time out. In the first years of the NHL, minor penalties called for three minutes in the penalty box, with major penalties garnering more time. Infractions included stick work — that is hitting or chopping at an opponent with ones stick, roughing another player with excessive body work, or even fighting — an event which could lead to a game suspension.

Slipping through the cracks were the cases where a sure scoring opportunity was prevented because of an infraction — such as a breakaway skater being hauled down from behind when he had a clear shot at the net. Usually a tripping case would warrant only a minor penalty — a penalty well worth the effort to the offender, since it prevented a solo dash to the net. To balance the scales, NHL rulemakers instituted a new rule before the 1934-35 season. In short, as stated in the NHL Guide: "A penalty shot [shall be] awarded when a player is tripped and thus prevented from having a clear shot on goal." As originally set down, the offended player could shoot the stationary puck from anywhere inside a 10-foot circle centered 38 feet from the net. Thus, on this November night in 1934, Mondou took the first penalty shot in NHL history. With only Hainsworth between him and the cage, Mondou aimed, fired — and anticlimactically — missed.

Earlier, before the season started, the NHL underwent a significant realignment. In financial trouble for several years, the charter Ottawa Senators finally gave up the ghost, transferring to far-away St. Louis — then on the fringes of major league sports. The new team — which was to be called the Eagles — was ironically placed in the Canadian Division, although the Missouri city was many hundreds of miles from Canadian soil.

Following in the steps of their Canadian predecessors, the St. Louis Eagles finished dead last in the Canadian Division, with only 11 wins. At the top, Toronto (30-14-4, 64) ruled the roost, well ahead of the Maroons, Canadiens and Americans — although the former duo did earn playoff positions. The American Division witnessed a complete reversal, as the previous year's doormat, Boston (26-16-6, 58), captured first, while the reigning champion, Detroit, slid into the cellar. Sandwiched in between, Chicago and the Rangers qualified for the postseason.

Toronto's Charlie Conacher (36-21-57) won his second straight goals and points titles, while Art Chapman (Americans) amassed the most assists (34). In addition, Leaf tough guy Red Horner (125) was whistled for the most penalties. In the cage, Chicago's Lorne Chabot (1.80) edged Maroons netminder Alec Connell for the GAA title, but the latter still earned the most shutouts (9).

In the playoffs, Toronto ruled the first-place series, besting Boston, three games to one, as Hainsworth posted a pair of shutouts. In the second-place series, Maroons' forward Lorne Northcutt scored the only goal of the series in overtime of the second game, leading Montreal past Chicago. In the other matchup, the Rangers edged the Canadiens, six goals to five. The semifinals witnessed another close battle, as the Maroons slid by the Rangers, five markers to four, setting up the first all-Canadian final in nine years.

In the finals, the Maroons made quick work of the Leafs, beating them in three straight — 3–2, 3–1 and 4–1— as Montreal's English-speaking team claimed its second Cup. Individually, Chicago's Lorne Chabot allowed only one goal in 124 minutes to claim the lowest GAA (0.48) in league history to date. On the scoring side, three players (Toronto's Charlie Conacher and Harvey Jackson, as well as Northcutt) each garnered five points, with the latter and former collecting the most goals and assists (4).

Over the years, the rules governing penalty shots were altered, eventually allowing a player a moving run at the net. Today — although somewhat diluted by the plethora of "shootout" contests currently en vogue — it remains one of the most exciting events in professional sports. As for the St. Louis Eagles, they quietly folded after their only campaign. Still, they are remembered for an NHL first. Three days after Mondou missed the NHL's first free attempt, Eagles' defenseman Ralph Bowman made his shot count, giving him and his team the honor of the league's first successful penalty shot.

STANDINGS

TEAM	GP	W	L	T	PTS	GF	GA
CANADIAN							
TORONTO	48	30	14	4	64	157	111
MONTREAL (M)	48	24	19	5	53	123	92
MONTREAL (C)	48	19	23	6	44	110	145
NEW YORK (A)	48	12	27	9	33	100	142
ST. LOUIS	48	11	31	6	28	86	144
AMERICAN							
BOSTON	48	26	16	6	58	129	112
CHICAGO	48	26	17	5	57	118	88
NEW YORK (R)	48	22	20	6	50	137	139
DETROIT	48	19	22	7	45	127	114

LEADERS

PLAYER	TM	GP	G	A	PTS	PIM
Charlie Conacher	TOR	47	36	21	57	24
Syd Howe	S-D	50	22	25	47	34
Larry Aurie	DET	48	17	29	46	24
Frank Boucher	N(R)	48	13	32	45	2
Harvey Jackson	TOR	42	22	22	44	27
Herb Lewis	DET	47	16	27	43	26
Art Chapman	N(A)	47	9	34	43	4
Marty Barry	BOS	48	20	20	40	33
David Schriner	N(A)	48	18	22	40	6
Two tied with					39	

GOALS		
C. Conacher, TOR		36
Dillon, N(R)		25
Jackson, TOR		22
Howe, S-D		22
Three tied with		21

ASSISTS		
Chapman, N(A)		34
Boucher, N(R)		32
Aurie, DET		29
Lewis, DET		27
Two tied with		26

GOALTENDER	TM	GP	MIN	GA	SH	GAA
Lorne Chabot	CHI	48	2940	88	8	1.80
Alec Connell	M(M)	48	2970	92	9	1.86
Norm Smith	DET	25	1550	52	2	2.01
George Hainsworth	TOR	48	2957	111	8	2.25
Tiny Thompson	BOS	48	2970	112	8	2.26
Dave Kerr	N(R)	37	2290	94	4	2.46
John Roach	DET	23	1460	62	4	2.55
Roy Worters	N(A)	48	3000	142	3	2.84
Bill Beveridge	STL	48	2990	144	3	2.89
Wilf Cude	M(C)	48	2960	145	1	2.94

PENALTY MINUTES		
Horner, TOR		125
Frew, STL		89
Seibert, N(R)		86
Siebert, BOS		80
Bowman, S-D		72

SHUTOUTS		
Connell, M(M)		9
Chabot, CHI		8
Hainsworth, TOR		8
Thompson, BOS		8
Two tied with		4

TORONTO 30-14-4 64 1st (C) Dick Irvin
Maple Leafs

			REGULAR SEASON				POSTSEASON				
PLAYER	POS	GP	G	A	PTS	PIM	GP	G	A	PTS	PIM
Charlie Conacher	R	47	36	21	57	24	7	1	4	5	6
Harvey Jackson	L	42	22	22	44	27	7	3	2	5	2
Joe Primeau	C	37	10	20	30	16	7	0	3	3	0
Bill Hollett	D	48	10	16	26	38	7	0	0	0	6

		REGULAR SEASON					POSTSEASON				
PLAYER	POS	GP	G	A	PTS	PIM	GP	G	A	PTS	PIM
Andy Blair	C	45	6	14	20	22	2	0	0	0	2
Harold Cotton	L	47	11	14	25	36	7	0	0	0	17
Hec Kilrea	L	46	11	13	24	16	6	0	0	0	4
Bill Thoms	C	47	9	13	22	15	7	2	0	2	0
King Clancy	D	47	5	16	21	53	7	1	0	1	8
Regis Kelly	R	47	11	8	19	14	7	2	0	2	4
Frank Boll	L	47	14	4	18	4	6	0	0	0	0
Red Horner	D	46	4	8	12	**125**	7	0	1	1	4
Hap Day	D	45	2	4	6	38	7	0	0	0	4
Ken Doraty	F	11	1	4	5	0	1	0	0	0	0
Nick Metz	L	18	2	2	4	4	6	1	1	2	0
Art Jackson	C	20	1	3	4	4	1	0	0	0	2
Frank Finnigan (2–2)	R	11	2	0	2	2	7	1	2	3	2
Bob Davidson	L	5	0	0	0	0					
George Hainsworth	G	48	0	0	0	0	7	0	0	0	0

		REGULAR SEASON				POSTSEASON				
GOALTENDER		GP	MIN	GA	SH	GAA	GP	MIN	GA	SH	GAA
George Hainsworth	(**30**-14-4)	48	2957	111	8	2.25	7	460	12	**2**	1.57

MONTREAL Maroons 24-19-5 53 2nd (C) Tommy Gorman

		REGULAR SEASON					POSTSEASON				
PLAYER	POS	GP	G	A	PTS	PIM	GP	G	A	PTS	PIM
Earl Robinson	R	48	17	18	35	23	7	2	2	4	0
Herb Cain	L	44	20	7	27	13	7	1	0	1	2
Russ Blinco	C	48	13	14	27	4	7	2	2	4	2
Reg Smith	R	46	5	22	27	41	6	0	0	0	14
Lorne Northcutt	D	47	9	14	23	44	7	4	1	5	0
Dave Trottier	L	34	10	9	19	22	7	1	3	4	4
Bob Gracie (2–2)	C	32	10	8	18	11	7	0	2	2	2
Gus Marker	R	44	11	4	15	18	7	1	1	2	4
Jimmy Ward	R	41	9	6	15	24	7	1	1	2	0
Cy Wentworth	D	48	4	9	13	28	7	3	2	5	0
Stew Evans	D	46	5	7	12	54	7	0	0	0	8
Al Shields	D	42	4	8	12	45	7	0	1	1	6
Lionel Conacher	D	38	2	6	8	44	7	0	0	0	14
Norm Gainor	C	35	0	4	4	2					
Bill Miller	C	22	3	0	3	2	7	0	0	0	0
Paul Haynes (1–2)	C	11	1	2	3	0					
Sammy McManus	L	25	0	1	1	8	1	0	0	0	0
Toe Blake	L	8	0	0	0	0	1	0	0	0	0
Bill MacKenzie (2–2)	D	5	0	0	0	0					
Aubrey Webster	R	4	0	0	0	0					
Alec Connell	G	48	0	0	0	0	7	0	0	0	0

		REGULAR SEASON				POSTSEASON				
GOALTENDER		GP	MIN	GA	SH	GAA	GP	MIN	GA	SH	GAA
Alec Connell	(24-19-5)	48	2970	92	**9**	1.86	7	429	8	**2**	1.12

1934-1935

MONTREAL Canadiens   19-23-6   44   3rd (C)   Newsy Lalonde / Leo Dandurand

PLAYER	POS	REGULAR SEASON					POSTSEASON				
		GP	G	A	PTS	PIM	GP	G	A	PTS	PIM
Alfred Lepine	C	48	12	19	31	16	2	0	0	0	2
L. Goldsworthy (2-2)	R	33	20	9	29	13	2	1	0	1	0
Aurel Joliat	L	48	17	12	29	18	2	1	0	1	0
Wildor Larochelle	R	48	9	19	28	12	2	0	0	0	0
Armand Mondou	L	46	9	15	24	6	2	0	1	1	0
Georges Mantha	D	42	12	10	22	14	2	0	0	0	4
Jack Riley	C	47	4	11	15	4	2	0	2	2	0
Sylvio Mantha	D	47	3	11	14	36	2	0	0	0	2
Jack McGill	L	44	9	1	10	34	2	2	0	2	0
Nels Crutchfield	C	41	5	5	10	20	2	0	1	1	22
Roger Jenkins	D	45	4	6	10	63	2	1	0	1	2
Johnny Gagnon (2-2)	R	23	1	5	6	2	2	0	1	1	2
Tony Savage (2-2)	D	41	1	5	6	4	2	0	0	0	0
Joe Lamb (1-2)	R	7	3	2	5	4					
Gerry Carson	D	48	0	5	5	56	2	0	0	0	4
Paul Raymond	R	20	1	1	2	0					
Norm Collings	L	1	0	1	1	0					
Des Roche (2-3)	R	5	0	1	1	0					
Jack Portland (1-2)	D	5	0	0	0	2					
Leo Bourgeault	D	4	0	0	0	0					
Polly Drouin	L	4	0	0	0	0					
Al Leduc	D	4	0	0	0	4					
Paul Runge	C	3	0	0	0	2					
Bob McCulley	D	1	0	0	0	0					
Wilf Cude	G	48	0	0	0	0	2	0	0	0	0

GOALTENDER		REGULAR SEASON					POSTSEASON				
		GP	MIN	GA	SH	GAA	GP	MIN	GA	SH	GAA
Wilf Cude	(19-23-6)	48	2960	145	1	2.94	2	120	6	0	3.00

NEW YORK Americans   12-27-9   33   4th (C)   Joe Simpson

PLAYER	POS	REGULAR SEASON					POSTSEASON
		GP	G	A	PTS	PIM	no postseason play
Art Chapman	C	47	9	34	43	4	
David Schriner	L	48	18	22	40	6	
Lorne Carr	R	48	17	14	31	14	
Charley McVeigh	C	47	7	11	18	4	
Norm Himes	C	40	5	13	18	2	
Harry Oliver	R	47	7	9	16	4	
Maitland Conn	L	48	5	11	16	10	
Eddie Burke	R	29	4	10	14	15	
Alex Smith	D	48	3	8	11	46	
Lloyd Klein	L	29	7	3	10	9	
Mervyn Dutton	D	48	3	7	10	46	
Bill Brydge	D	47	2	6	8	29	
Obs Heximer	L	17	5	2	7	0	

		REGULAR SEASON					*POSTSEASON*
PLAYER	*POS*	*GP*	*G*	*A*	*PTS*	*PIM*	no postseason play
Fred Hergert	C	19	2	4	6	2	
Hap Emms (2–2)	L	28	2	2	4	19	
Bob Gracie (1–2)	C	14	2	1	3	4	
Allan Murray	D	43	2	1	3	36	
Walt Jackson	L	1	0	0	0	0	
Roy Worters	G	48	0	0	0	0	

		REGULAR SEASON					*POSTSEASON*
GOALTENDER		*GP*	*MIN*	*GA*	*SH*	*GAA*	no postseason play
Roy Worters	(12-27-9)	48	3000	142	3	2.84	

ST. LOUIS   11-31-6   28   5th (C)   Eddie Gerard
Eagles   Georges Boucher

		REGULAR SEASON					*POSTSEASON*
PLAYER	*POS*	*GP*	*G*	*A*	*PTS*	*PIM*	no postseason play
Carl Voss	C	48	13	18	31	14	
Glenn Brydson	R	48	11	18	29	45	
Syd Howe (1–2)	C	*36	14	13	27	23	
Joe Lamb (2–2)	R	31	11	12	23	19	
Pete Kelly	R	25	3	10	13	14	
Bill Cowley	C	41	5	7	12	10	
O. Asmundson (2–2)	C	11	4	7	11	2	
Frank Jerwa	L	16	4	7	11	14	
Frank Finnigan (1–2)	R	34	5	5	10	10	
Earl Roche (1–2)	L	19	3	3	6	2	
Vic Ripley (2–2)	C	31	1	5	6	10	
Nick Wasnie	R	13	3	1	4	2	
Vern Ayres	D	47	2	2	4	60	
Ralph Bowman (1–2)	D	31	2	2	4	51	
Gerry Shannon (1–2)	L	25	2	2	4	11	
Cliff Purpur	R	25	1	2	3	8	
Francis Blake	D	8	1	1	2	2	
Eddie Finnigan	L	12	1	1	2	2	
Irv Frew	D	48	0	2	2	89	
G. Patterson (2–2)	R	21	0	1	1	2	
Gene Carrigan	C	4	0	1	1	0	
Teddy Graham	D	13	0	0	0	2	
Max Kaminsky	C	12	0	0	0	0	
Burr Williams (1–2)	D	9	0	0	0	6	
Archie Wilcox	R	8	0	0	0	0	
Des Roche (1–3)	R	7	0	0	0	0	
Bud Cook	C	4	0	0	0	0	
Jeff Kalbfleisch	D	3	0	0	0	6	
Bill Beveridge	G	48	0	0	0	0	

		REGULAR SEASON					*POSTSEASON*
GOALTENDER		*GP*	*MIN*	*GA*	*SH*	*GAA*	no postseason play
Bill Beveridge	(11-**31**-6)	48	2990	144	3	2.89	

1934–1935

BOSTON 26-16-6   58   1st (A)   Frank Patrick
Bruins

		REGULAR SEASON					POSTSEASON			
PLAYER	POS	GP	G	A	PTS	PIM	GP	G	A	PTS	PIM
Marty Barry	C	48	20	20	40	33	4	0	0	0	2
Nels Stewart	C	47	21	18	39	45	4	0	1	1	0
Dit Clapper	R	48	21	16	37	21	3	1	0	1	0
Eddie Shore	D	48	7	26	33	32	4	0	1	1	2
Charlie Sands	C	41	15	12	27	0	4	0	0	0	0
Max Kaminsky (2–2)	C	38	12	15	27	4	4	0	0	0	0
John Beattie	L	48	9	18	27	27	4	1	0	1	2
Al Siebert	R	48	6	18	24	80	4	0	0	0	6
Peggy O'Neil	R	48	2	11	13	35	4	0	0	0	9
Jack Shill	C	45	4	4	8	22	2	0	0	0	0
Paul Haynes (2–2)	C	37	4	3	7	8	3	0	0	0	0
Bert McInenly	D	33	2	1	3	24	4	0	0	0	2
Johnny Gagnon (1–2)	R	24	1	1	2	9					
Gerry Shannon (2–2)	L	17	1	1	2	4	4	0	0	0	2
Jack Portland (2–2)	D	15	1	1	2	2					
Hap Emms (1–2)	L	11	1	1	2	8					
Art Giroux	R	10	1	0	1	0					
Jean Pusie	D	4	1	0	1	0	4	0	0	0	0
Bob Davie	D	30	0	1	1	17	3	0	0	0	0
Tony Savage (1–2)	D	8	0	0	0	2					
Burr Williams (2–2)	D	7	0	0	0	6					
Frank Jerwa	L	5	0	0	0	0					
Alex Motter	C	3	0	0	0	0	4	0	0	0	0
Tiny Thompson	G	48	0	0	0	0	4	0	0	0	0

	REGULAR SEASON					POSTSEASON				
GOALTENDER	GP	MIN	GA	SH	GAA	GP	MIN	GA	SH	GAA
Tiny Thompson (26-16-6)	48	2970	112	8	2.26	4	275	7	1	1.53

CHICAGO 26-17-5   57   2nd (A)   Clem Loughlin
Blackhawks

		REGULAR SEASON					POSTSEASON			
PLAYER	POS	GP	G	A	PTS	PIM	GP	G	A	PTS	PIM
Paul Thompson	L	48	16	23	39	20	2	0	0	0	0
Johnny Gottselig	L	48	19	18	37	16	2	0	0	0	0
Howie Morenz	C	48	8	26	34	21	2	0	0	0	0
Tommy Cook	C	48	13	18	31	33	2	0	0	0	2
Harold March	R	48	13	17	30	48	2	0	0	0	0
Elwin Romnes	C	35	10	14	24	8	2	0	0	0	0
Louis Trudel	L	47	11	11	22	28	2	0	0	0	0
Rosie Couture	R	27	7	9	16	14	2	0	0	0	5
Art Coulter	D	48	4	8	12	68	2	0	0	0	5
Bill Kendall	R	47	6	4	10	16	2	0	0	0	0
Alex Levinsky (2–2)	D	23	3	4	7	16	2	0	0	0	0
Don McFadyen	C	37	2	5	7	4	2	0	0	0	0
Norm Locking	L	35	2	5	7	19					
Marty Burke	D	47	2	2	4	29	2	0	0	0	2
Art Wiebe	D	42	2	1	3	27	2	0	0	0	2

		REGULAR SEASON				*POSTSEASON*				
PLAYER	*POS*	*GP*	*G*	*A*	*PTS*	*PIM*	*GP*	*G*	*A*	*PTS*	*PIM*
L. Goldsworthy (1–2)	R	7	0	0	0	2					
Ernie Kenny	D	4	0	0	0	18					
Lorne Chabot	G	48	0	0	0	0	2	0	0	0	0

		REGULAR SEASON				*POSTSEASON*			
GOALTENDER		*GP*	*MIN*	*GA*	*SH*	*GAA*	*GP*	*MIN*	*GA*	*SH*	*GAA*
Lorne Chabot	(26-17-5)	48	2940	88	8	**1.80**	2	124	1	1	**0.48**

NEW YORK 22-20-6 50 3rd (A) Lester Patrick
Rangers

		REGULAR SEASON				*POSTSEASON*				
PLAYER	*POS*	*GP*	*G*	*A*	*PTS*	*PIM*	*GP*	*G*	*A*	*PTS*	*PIM*
Frank Boucher	C	48	13	32	45	2	4	0	3	3	0
Bill Cook	R	48	21	15	36	23	4	1	2	3	7
Cecil Dillon	R	48	25	9	34	4	4	2	1	3	0
Bun Cook	L	48	13	21	34	26	4	2	0	2	0
Murray Murdoch	L	48	14	15	29	14	4	0	2	2	4
Earl Seibert	D	48	6	19	25	86	4	0	0	0	6
Lynn Patrick	C	48	9	13	22	17	4	2	2	4	0
Bert Connelly	L	47	10	11	21	23	4	1	0	1	0
Butch Keeling	L	47	15	4	19	14	4	2	1	3	0
Charlie Mason	R	46	5	9	14	14	4	0	1	1	0
Ott Heller	D	47	3	11	14	31	4	0	1	1	4
Ivan Johnson	D	29	2	3	5	34	4	0	0	0	2
Art Somers	C	41	0	5	5	4	2	0	0	0	2
Alex Levinsky (1–2)	D	20	0	4	4	6					
Harold Starr (2–2)	D	33	1	1	2	31	4	0	0	0	2
Vic Ripley (1–2)	C	4	0	2	2	0					
Bill MacKenzie (2–2)	D	15	1	0	1	10	3	0	0	0	0
Dave Kerr	G	37	0	0	0	0	4	0	0	0	0
Andy Aitkenhead	G	10	0	0	0	0					
Percy Jackson	G	1	0	0	0	0					

		REGULAR SEASON				*POSTSEASON*			
GOALTENDER		*GP*	*MIN*	*GA*	*SH*	*GAA*	*GP*	*MIN*	*GA*	*SH*	*GAA*
Dave Kerr	(19-12-6)	37	2290	94	4	2.46	4	240	10	0	2.50
Andy Aitkenhead	(3-7-0)	10	610	37	1	3.64					
Percy Jackson	(0-1-0)	1	60	8	0	8.00					

DETROIT 19-22-7 45 4th (A) Jack Adams
Red Wings

		REGULAR SEASON				*POSTSEASON*
PLAYER	*POS*	*GP*	*G*	*A*	*PTS*	*PIM*	*no postseason play*
Larry Aurie	R	48	17	29	46	24	
Herb Lewis	L	47	16	27	43	26	
Cooney Weiland	C	48	13	25	38	10	
John Sorrell	L	47	20	16	36	12	
Ebbie Goodfellow	C	48	12	24	36	44	
Eddie Wiseman	R	39	11	13	24	14	

		REGULAR SEASON					POSTSEASON
PLAYER	POS	GP	G	A	PTS	PIM	no postseason play
Syd Howe (2–2)	C	*14	8	12	20	11	
Doug Young	D	48	4	6	10	37	
Tom Anderson	L	27	5	2	7	16	
Lorne Duguid	L	34	3	3	6	9	
Earl Roche (2–2)	L	13	3	3	6	0	
Irwin Boyd	R	42	2	3	5	14	
Gord Pettinger	C	13	2	3	5	2	
Walt Buswell	D	47	1	3	4	32	
Ralph Bowman (2–2)	D	13	1	3	4	21	
Des Roche (3–3)	R	15	3	0	3	10	
Bucko McDonald	D	15	1	2	3	8	
Harry Foster	D	12	2	0	2	8	
Wilf Starr (1–2)	C	24	1	1	2	0	
Teddy Graham (2–2)	D	24	0	2	2	26	
Lloyd Gross	L	6	1	0	1	2	
Ron Moffatt	L	8	0	0	0	0	
G. Patterson (2–2)	R	7	0	0	0	0	
Oscar Asmundson (2–2)	C	3	0	0	0	0	
Wally Kilrea	C	3	0	0	0	0	
Norm Smith	G	25	0	0	0	0	
John Roach	G	23	0	0	0	0	

		REGULAR SEASON					POSTSEASON
GOALTENDER		GP	MIN	GA	SH	GAA	no postseason play
Norm Smith	(12-11-2)	25	1550	52	2	2.01	
John Roach	(7-11-5)	23	1460	62	4	2.55	

TEAM TOTALS

								Per Game			
TEAM	GP	G	A	P	PIM	GA	SH	G	A	PIM	GA
Canadian											
Toronto	48	157	182	339	444	111	8	**3.27**	**3.79**	9.25	2.31
Montreal (M)	48	123	139	262	380	92	9	2.56	2.90	7.92	1.92
Montreal (C)	48	110	138	248	314	145	1	2.29	3.14	6.54	3.02
New York (A)	48	100	158	258	250	142	3	2.08	3.29	5.20	2.96
St. Louis	48	86	120	206	385	144	3	1.79	2.50	8.02	3.00
American											
Boston	48	129	167	296	368	112	8	2.69	3.48	7.67	2.33
Chicago	48	118	165	283	375	**88**	8	2.46	3.44	7.81	**1.83**
New York (R)	48	138	174	312	334	139	5	2.88	3.63	6.96	2.90
Detroit	48	126	177	303	305	114	6	2.63	3.69	6.35	2.38
	432	1087	1420	2507	3155	1087	51	2.52	3.28	7.30	2.52

PLAYOFFS

SERIES "A"
Boston 1, Toronto 0 (OT)
Toronto 2, Boston 0
Toronto 3, Boston 0
Toronto 2, Boston 1

TORONTO, 3-1

SERIES "C"
New York (R) 2, Montreal (C) 1
New York (R) 4, Montreal (C) 4
**NEW YORK (R) WINS
TOTAL GOAL SERIES, 6-5**

SERIES "E"
Montreal (M) 3, Toronto 2 (OT)
Montreal (M) 3, Toronto 1
Montreal (M) 4, Toronto 1

**MONTREAL (M) WINS
STANLEY CUP, 3-0**

SERIES "B"
Montreal (M) 0, Chicago 0
Montreal (M) 1, Chicago 0 (OT)

**MONTREAL (M) WINS
TOTAL GOAL SERIES, 1-0**

SERIES "D"
Montreal (M) 2, New York (R) 1
Montreal (M) 3, New York (R) 3
**MONTREAL (M) WINS
TOTAL GOAL SERIES, 5-4**

ALL-STAR TEAMS

First Team
G — Lorne Chabot, CHI
D — Eddie Shore, BOS
D — Earl Seibert, N(R)
C — Frank Boucher, N(R)
R — Charlie Conacher, TOR
L — Harvey Jackson, TOR

Second Team
G — Tiny Thompson, BOS
D — Art Coulter, CHI
D — Cy Wentworth, M(M)
C — Cooney Weiland, DET
R — Dit Clapper, BOS
L — Aurel Joliat, M(C)

INDIVIDUAL TROPHY WINNERS

HART TROPHY (Most Valuable Player): Eddie Shore, BOS
LADY BYNG TROPHY (Gentlemanly Conduct): Frank Boucher, N(R)
VEZINA TROPHY (Best Goaltender): Lorne Chabot, CHI

1935-1936

Sudden Death Overtime

During the 1933 playoffs, two evenly-matched teams battled well into the night, before one club scored in the sixth overtime period. At the time, this match set a record for NHL longevity — a record that many thought would last through the ages. Little did the pundits realize that it was about to be broken.

In the early days of the NHL, regular season tie games were resolved by skating an extra period — first 20 minutes, later changed to 10. During these extra sessions, all goals counted. For instance, during a game on March 11, 1934, the Maroons scored four times in the allotted 10 minutes, beating the Rangers, 7–3. In the playoffs, overtime was handled differently. Here, where a clear winner was needed, the first goal scored determined the winner. The term coined to describe this practice was "sudden death."

In the history of the Stanley Cup playoffs, sudden death scores had been a part of the lore, even predating the formation of the NHL. In 1901, the Winnipeg Victorias scored an overtime goal to wrest the Cup from the Montreal Shamrocks, 2–1. Thirteen years later, the NHA's Toronto Blueshirts accomplished the same against the PCHA's Victoria club. As the NHA evolved into the NHL, playoff overtime games became more common. By the 1930s, virtually every series saw at least one. However, no one as yet had seen a game that would open the 1936 postseason action.

Before the playoff action unfolded, the eight-team NHL (now bereft of the St. Louis Eagles) skated through its 19th season. Coming out on top in the Canadian Division, the Montreal Maroons (22-16-10, 54) edged the Leafs by a pair of points. The Division's other playoff bound team was the Americans — the first time in many years the New York club had qualified for the postseason. Dropping into the basement, with only 11 wins, were the Canadiens with one of their worst seasons to date.

In the American Division, the Red Wings (24-16-8, 56) returned to the top after a year's absence. Six points behind them, the other three teams were clustered at 50 points apiece. Of the trio, Boston (22) and Chicago (21) had more wins than the Rangers (19), so they qualified for the playoffs, leaving New York out of the mix in the league's first three-way tie.

Leading their club back into the playoffs, two New York Americans — David Schriner, with 45 points, and Art Chapman, with 28 assists — finished atop the NHL leaderboard. Other scoring stars included a pair of Leafs — Charlie Conacher and Bill Thoms — who netted 23 markers each. Their teammate, Red Horner, kept his tough-guy reputation intact, collecting 167 minutes in penalties. In addition, Boston Netminder Tiny Thompson posted the lowest GAA, while blanking the most foes (1.68, 10).

In the first game of the first place series, played in Montreal on March 24, the Red Wings faced the Maroons. In goal that night for the home team was Lorne Chabot — his Red Wing opponent was Norm Smith. Both netminders were sharp, with neither making any mistakes through regulation. One overtime period went by, then another, followed by a third. As the marathon continued, many of the 9,000 remained in the building as the fourth and fifth extra sessions slid by. Lubricated by shots of brandy by their coach between periods, the Red Wings finally struck. Late in the sixth overtime, Detroit youngster Modere Bruneteau beat Chabot at 116:30, beating the three-year-old longevity record by more than 10 minutes. Legend has it that the puck just dangled in the twine behind the Toronto netminder, too tired to fall to the ice. The time was 2:25 A.M. on the morning of March 25.

After his 92-save masterpiece, Smith shut out the Maroons in the next game as well, before wrapping up the series with a 2–1 win. In the second place series, Toronto bested Boston, eight goals to six, while the Americans surprised the Blackhawks, seven scores to five, in their third-place matchup. In the semifinals — now a best of three affair — Toronto beat the stubborn Americans, scoring a 3–1 win in the third game. In the finals, the Red Wings broke out of their scoring slump, netting 12 markers in the first two contests on their way to a three games to one Cup triumph.

Coming as no surprise, Smith dominated other playoff goalies, posting a 1.00 GAA with two shutouts — although the aforementioned first was nearly three full games in length. In a losing effort, Toronto's Frank Boll collected the most points (10) and goals (7), while fellow Leaf Thoms had the most assists (5).

Over the years, other marathon-length games have been played by NHL playoff participants. However, as of yet, none have come within 10 minutes of this 1936 masterpiece; to this day it remains the longest game in NHL history.

STANDINGS

TEAM	GP	W	L	T	PTS	GF	GA
CANADIAN							
MONTREAL (M)	48	22	16	10	54	114	106
TORONTO	48	23	19	6	52	126	106
NEW YORK (A)	48	16	25	7	39	109	122
MONTREAL (C)	48	11	26	11	33	82	123
AMERICAN							
DETROIT	48	24	16	8	56	124	103
BOSTON	48	22	20	6	50	92	83
CHICAGO	48	21	19	8	50	93	92
NEW YORK (R)	48	19	17	12	50	91	96

LEADERS

PLAYER	TM	GP	G	A	PTS	PIM
Dave Schriner	N(A)	48	19	26	**45**	8
Marty Barry	DET	48	21	19	40	16
Paul Thompson	CHI	45	17	23	40	19
Bill Thoms	TOR	48	**23**	15	38	29
Charlie Conacher	TOR	44	**23**	15	38	74
Reg Smith	M(M)	47	19	19	38	75
Elwin Romnes	CHI	48	13	25	38	6
Art Chapman	N(A)	48	10	**28**	38	14
Herb Lewis	DET	45	14	23	37	25
Lorne Northcutt	M(M)	48	15	21	36	41

GOALS	
C. Conacher, TOR	23
Thoms, TOR	23
Barry, DET	21
Smith, M(M)	19
Schriner, N(A)	19

ASSISTS	
Chapman, N(A)	28
Schriner, N(A)	26
Romnes, CHI	25
Lewis, DET	23
Thompson, CHI	23

GOALTENDER	TM	GP	MIN	GA	SH	GAA
Tiny Thompson	BOS	48	2930	82	**10**	**1.68**
Mike Karakas	CHI	48	2990	92	9	1.85
Dave Kerr	N(R)	47	2980	95	8	1.91
Norm Smith	DET	48	**3030**	103	6	2.04
George Hainsworth	TOR	48	3000	106	8	2.12
Bill Beveridge	M(M)	32	1970	71	1	2.16
Roy Worters	N(A)	48	3000	**122**	6	2.44
Wilf Cude	M(C)	47	2940	**122**	6	2.49

PENALTY MINUTES	
Horner, TOR	167
Shields, M(M)	81
Smith, M(M)	75
Conacher, TOR	74
Three tied with	69

SHUTOUTS	
Thompson, BOS	10
Karakas, CHI	9
Hainsworth, TOR	8
Kerr, N(R)	8
Three tied with	6

MONTREAL 22-16-10 54 1st (C) Tommy Gorman
Maroons

		REGULAR SEASON					POSTSEASON				
PLAYER	POS	GP	G	A	PTS	PIM	GP	G	A	PTS	PIM
Reg Smith	R	47	19	19	38	75	3	0	0	0	2
Lorne Northcutt	D	48	15	21	36	41	3	0	0	0	0
Jimmy Ward	R	48	12	19	31	30	3	0	0	0	6
Bob Gracie	C	48	11	14	25	31	3	0	1	1	0
Russ Blinco	C	46	13	10	23	10	3	0	0	0	0

		REGULAR SEASON					*POSTSEASON*				
PLAYER	*POS*	*GP*	*G*	*A*	*PTS*	*PIM*	*GP*	*G*	*A*	*PTS*	*PIM*
Dave Trottier	L	46	10	10	20	25	3	0	0	0	4
Earl Robinson	R	39	6	14	20	27	3	0	0	0	0
Gus Marker	R	48	7	12	19	10	3	1	0	1	2
Herb Cain	L	48	5	13	18	16	3	0	1	1	0
Lionel Conacher	D	46	7	7	14	65	3	0	0	0	0
Cy Wentworth	D	48	4	5	9	24	3	0	0	0	0
Al Shields	D	45	2	7	9	81	3	0	0	0	6
Stew Evans	D	48	3	5	8	57	3	0	0	0	0
Joe Lamb	R	35	0	3	3	12	3	0	0	0	2
Bill Miller (1–2)	C	8	0	0	0	0					
Bill Beveridge	G	32	0	0	0	0					
Lorne Chabot	G	16	0	0	0	0	3	0	0	0	0

		REGULAR SEASON				*POSTSEASON*			
GOALTENDER		*GP*	*MIN*	*GA*	*SH*	*GAA*	*GP*	*MIN*	*GA*	*SH*	*GAA*
Lorne Chabot	(8-3-5)	16	1010	35	2	2.08	3	297	6	0	1.21
Bill Beveridge	(14-13-5)	32	1970	71	1	2.16					

TORONTO 23-19-6 52 2nd (C) Dick Irvin
Maple Leafs

		REGULAR SEASON					*POSTSEASON*				
PLAYER	*POS*	*GP*	*G*	*A*	*PTS*	*PIM*	*GP*	*G*	*A*	*PTS*	*PIM*
Bill Thoms	C	48	23	15	38	29	9	3	5	8	0
Charlie Conacher	R	44	23	15	38	74	9	3	2	5	12
Frank Boll	L	44	15	13	28	14	9	7	3	**10**	2
Harvey Jackson	L	47	11	11	22	19	9	3	2	5	4
Nick Metz	L	38	14	6	20	14					
Art Jackson	C	48	5	15	20	14	8	0	3	3	2
Regis Kelly	R	42	11	8	19	24	9	2	3	5	4
Joe Primeau	C	45	4	13	17	10	9	3	4	7	0
King Clancy	D	47	5	10	15	61	9	2	2	4	10
Hap Day	D	44	1	13	14	41	9	0	0	0	8
Red Horner	D	43	2	9	11	**167**	9	1	2	3	22
Andy Blair	C	45	5	4	9	60	9	0	0	0	2
Bob Davidson	L	35	4	4	8	32	9	1	3	4	2
Frank Finnigan	R	48	2	6	8	10	9	0	3	3	0
Bill Hollett (1–2)	D	11	1	4	5	8					
Jack Markle	R	8	0	1	1	0					
Jack Shill	C	3	0	1	1	0	9	0	3	3	8
Reg Hamilton	D	7	0	0	0	0					
Francis Blake	D	1	0	0	0	2					
George Hainsworth	G	48	0	0	0	0	9	0	0	0	0
Norm Mann	R						1	0	0	0	0

		REGULAR SEASON					*POSTSEASON*				
GOALTENDER		*GP*	*MIN*	*GA*	*SH*	*GAA*	*GP*	*MIN*	*GA*	*SH*	*GAA*
George Hainsworth	(23-19-6)	48	3000	106	8	2.12	9	541	27	0	2.99

1935-1936

NEW YORK Americans 16-25-7   39   3rd (C)   Mervyn Dutton

PLAYER	POS	REGULAR SEASON					POSTSEASON				
		GP	G	A	PTS	PIM	GP	G	A	PTS	PIM
David Schriner	L	48	19	26	45	8	5	3	1	4	2
Art Chapman	C	48	10	28	38	14	5	0	3	3	0
Nels Stewart	C	48	14	15	29	16	5	1	2	3	4
Eddie Wiseman (2-2)	R	44	12	16	28	15	4	2	1	3	0
Harry Oliver	R	45	9	16	25	12	5	1	2	3	0
Joe Jerwa	D	47	9	12	21	65	5	2	3	5	2
Lorne Carr	R	44	8	10	18	4	5	1	1	2	0
Harold Cotton	L	45	7	9	16	27	5	0	1	1	9
Mervyn Dutton	D	46	5	8	13	69	3	0	0	0	0
Lloyd Klein	L	42	4	8	12	14	5	0	0	0	2
Carl Voss	C	46	3	9	12	10	5	0	0	0	0
John Doran	D	25	4	2	6	44	3	0	0	0	0
Hap Emms	L	32	1	5	6	12					
Tom Anderson	L	24	3	2	5	20	5	0	0	0	0
Allan Murray	D	48	1	0	1	33	5	0	0	0	2
Bill Brydge	D	21	0	0	0	27					
Jeff Kalbfleisch	D	4	0	0	0	2	5	0	0	0	2
Tony Hemmerling	L	3	0	0	0	0					
Fred Hergert	C	1	0	0	0	0					
Roy Worters	G	48	0	0	0	0	5	0	0	0	0

GOALTENDER		REGULAR SEASON					POSTSEASON				
		GP	MIN	GA	SH	GAA	GP	MIN	GA	SH	GAA
Roy Worters	(16-25-7)	48	3000	122	6	2.44	5	300	11	2	2.20

MONTREAL Canadiens 11-26-11   33   4th (C)   Sylvio Mantha

PLAYER	POS	REGULAR SEASON					POSTSEASON
		GP	G	A	PTS	PIM	*no postseason play*
Leroy Goldsworthy	R	47	15	11	26	8	
Paul Haynes	C	48	5	19	24	24	
Aurel Joliat	L	48	15	8	23	16	
Jack McGill	L	46	13	7	20	28	
Armand Mondou	L	36	7	11	18	10	
Johnny Gagnon	R	48	7	9	16	42	
Alfred Lepine	C	32	6	10	16	4	
Joffre Desilets	R	38	7	6	13	0	
Georges Mantha	D	35	1	12	13	14	
Polly Drouin	L	30	1	8	9	19	
Sylvio Mantha	D	42	2	4	6	25	
Bill Miller (2-2)	C	17	1	2	3	2	
Toe Blake	L	11	1	2	3	28	
Walt Buswell	D	44	0	2	2	34	
Jean Pusie	D	31	0	2	2	11	
Irv Frew	D	18	0	2	2	16	
W. Larochelle (1-2)	R	13	0	2	2	6	
Paul Runge (1-2)	C	12	0	2	2	4	
Art Lesieur	D	38	1	0	1	24	

148 The National Hockey League, 1917–1967

		REGULAR SEASON				*POSTSEASON*
PLAYER	*POS*	*GP*	*G*	*A*	*PTS*	*PIM*	*no postseason play*
Rosie Couture	R	10	0	1	1	0
Jean Bourcier	L	9	0	1	1	0
Conrad Bourcier	C	6	0	0	0	0
Red Goupile	D	4	0	0	0	0
Gus Leroux	D	2	0	0	0	0
Max Bennett	R	1	0	0	0	0
Rod Lorrain	R	1	0	0	0	2
Wilf Cude	G	47	0	0	0	0
Abbie Cox	G	1	0	0	0	0

		REGULAR SEASON				*POSTSEASON*
GOALTENDER		*GP*	*MIN*	*GA*	*SH*	*GAA*	*no postseason play*
Abbie Cox	(0-0-1)	1	70	1	0	0.86
Wilf Cude	(11-26-10)	47	2940	**122**	6	2.49

DETROIT 24-16-8 56 1st (A) Jack Adams
Red Wings

		REGULAR SEASON					*POSTSEASON*			
PLAYER	*POS*	*GP*	*G*	*A*	*PTS*	*PIM*	*GP*	*G*	*A*	*PTS*	*PIM*
Marty Barry	C	**48**	21	19	40	16	7	2	4	6	6
Herb Lewis	L	45	14	23	37	25	7	2	3	5	0
Larry Aurie	R	44	16	18	34	17	7	1	2	3	2
Syd Howe	C	**48**	16	14	30	26	7	3	3	6	2
John Sorrell	L	**48**	13	15	28	8	7	3	4	7	0
Hec Kilrea	L	**48**	6	17	23	37	7	0	3	3	2
Ebbie Goodfellow	D	**48**	5	18	23	69	7	1	0	1	4
Doug Young	D	47	5	12	17	54	7	0	2	2	0
Gord Pettinger	C	30	8	7	15	6	7	2	2	4	0
Pete Kelly	R	46	6	8	14	30	7	1	1	2	2
Wally Kilrea	C	**48**	4	10	14	10	7	2	2	4	2
Bucko McDonald	D	47	4	6	10	32	7	3	0	3	10
Ralph Bowman	D	**48**	3	2	5	44	7	2	1	3	2
Modere Bruneteau	R	24	2	0	2	2	7	2	2	4	4
Art Giroux	R	4	0	2	2	0					
Wilf Starr	C	9	1	0	1	0					
Lorne Duguid (1–2)	L	5	0	0	0	0					
Rolly Roulston	L	1	0	0	0	0					
John Sherf	L	1	0	0	0	0					
Eddie Wiseman (1–2)	R	1	0	0	0	0					
Norm Smith	G	**48**	0	0	0	0	7	0	0	0	0

		REGULAR SEASON					*POSTSEASON*			
GOALTENDER		*GP*	*MIN*	*GA*	*SH*	*GAA*	*GP*	*MIN*	*GA*	*SH*	*GAA*
Norm Smith	(24-16-8)	**48**	**3030**	103	6	2.04	7	538	12	**2**	**1.00**

BOSTON 22-20-6 50 2nd (A) Frank Patrick
Bruins

		REGULAR SEASON					*POSTSEASON*			
PLAYER	*POS*	*GP*	*G*	*A*	*PTS*	*PIM*	*GP*	*G*	*A*	*PTS*	*PIM*
John Beattie	L	**48**	14	18	32	27	2	0	0	0	2

1935–1936 149

PLAYER	POS	REGULAR SEASON					POSTSEASON				
		GP	G	A	PTS	PIM	GP	G	A	PTS	PIM
Cooney Weiland	C	48	14	13	27	15	2	1	0	1	2
Dit Clapper	R	44	12	13	25	14	2	0	1	1	0
Al Siebert	R	45	12	9	21	66	2	0	1	1	0
Bill Cowley	C	48	11	10	21	17	2	2	1	3	2
Eddie Shore	D	45	3	16	19	61	2	1	1	2	12
Peggy O'Neil	R	48	2	11	13	49	2	1	1	2	4
Paul Runge (2–2)	C	33	8	2	10	14	2	0	0	0	2
Charlie Sands	C	40	6	4	10	8	2	0	0	0	0
Roger Jenkins	D	40	2	6	8	51	2	0	1	1	2
Teddy Graham	D	48	4	1	5	37	2	0	0	0	0
Lorne Duguid (2–2)	L	29	1	4	5	2	2	1	0	1	2
Alex Motter	C	23	1	4	5	4	2	0	0	0	0
Max Kaminsky	C	36	1	2	3	20					
Bill Hollett	D	6	1	2	3	2					
Gerry Shannon	L	23	0	1	1	6					
Bob Blake	L	12	0	0	0	0					
Phil Besler	R	8	0	0	0	0					
Jack Riley	C	8	0	0	0	0					
Eddie Finnigan	L	3	0	0	0	0					
Bert McInenly	D	3	0	0	0	0					
Bob Davie	D	2	0	0	0	2					
Walt Jackson	L	2	0	0	0	0					
Jack Portland	D	2	0	0	0	0					
Woody Dumart	L	1	0	0	0	0					
Ray Getliffe	L	1	0	0	0	2	2	0	0	0	0
Tiny Thompson	G	48	0	0	0	0	2	0	0	0	0
Percy Jackson	G	1	0	0	0	0					

GOALTENDER		REGULAR SEASON					POSTSEASON				
		GP	MIN	GA	SH	GAA	GP	MIN	GA	SH	GAA
Percy Jackson		1	40	1	0	1.50					
Tiny Thompson (22–20–6)		48	2930	82	10	1.68	2	12	8	0	4.00

CHICAGO 21-19-8 50 3rd (A) Clem Loughlin
Blackhawks

PLAYER	POS	REGULAR SEASON					POSTSEASON				
		GP	G	A	PTS	PIM	GP	G	A	PTS	PIM
Paul Thompson	L	45	17	23	40	19	2	0	3	3	0
Elwin Romnes	C	48	13	25	38	6	2	1	2	3	0
Harold March	R	48	16	19	35	42	2	2	3	5	0
Johnny Gottselig	L	40	14	15	29	4	2	0	2	2	0
Don McFadyen	C	48	4	16	20	33	1	0	0	0	0
Howie Morenz (1–2)	C	23	4	11	15	20					
Tommy Cook	C	47	4	8	12	20	1	0	0	0	0
Glenn Brydson (2–2)	R	22	6	4	10	32	2	0	0	0	4
Earl Seibert (2–2)	D	15	3	6	9	19	2	2	0	2	0
Alex Levinsky	D	48	1	7	8	69	2	0	1	1	0
Louis Trudel	L	47	3	4	7	27	2	0	0	0	2
Eddie Oulette	C	43	3	2	5	11	1	0	0	0	0
W. Larochelle (2–2)	R	27	2	1	3	8	2	0	0	0	0

		REGULAR SEASON					*POSTSEASON*				
PLAYER	*POS*	*GP*	*G*	*A*	*PTS*	*PIM*	*GP*	*G*	*A*	*PTS*	*PIM*
Bill Kendall	R	22	2	1	3	0	2	0	0	0	0
Marty Burke	D	40	0	3	3	49	2	0	0	0	2
Art Coulter (1–2)	D	25	0	2	2	18					
Art Wiebe	D	46	1	0	1	25	2	0	0	0	0
Norm Locking	L	13	0	1	1	7					
Mike Karakas	G	48	0	0	0	0	2	0	0	0	0

		REGULAR SEASON					*POSTSEASON*				
GOALTENDER		*GP*	*MIN*	*GA*	*SH*	*GAA*	*GP*	*MIN*	*GA*	*SH*	*GAA*
Mike Karakas	(21-19-8)	48	2990	92	9	1.85	2	120	7	0	3.50

NEW YORK Rangers   19-17-12   50   4th (A)   Lester Patrick

		REGULAR SEASON					*POSTSEASON*
PLAYER	*POS*	*GP*	*G*	*A*	*PTS*	*PIM*	*no postseason play*
Cecil Dillon	R	48	18	14	32	12	
Frank Boucher	C	48	11	18	29	2	
Lynn Patrick	C	48	11	14	25	29	
Butch Keeling	L	46	13	5	18	22	
Bill Cook	R	44	7	10	17	16	
Glenn Brydson (1–2)	R	30	4	12	16	7	
Ott Heller	D	43	2	11	13	40	
Murray Murdoch	L	48	2	9	11	9	
Bun Cook	L	26	4	5	9	12	
Ivan Johnson	D	47	5	3	8	58	
Alex Shibicky	R	18	4	2	6	6	
Howie Morenz (2–2)	C	19	2	4	6	6	
Charlie Mason	R	28	1	5	6	30	
Art Coulter (2–2)	D	23	1	5	6	26	
Earl Seibert (1–2)	D	17	2	3	5	6	
Mac Colville	R	18	1	4	5	6	
Bert Connelly	L	25	2	2	4	10	
Vern Ayres	D	28	0	4	4	38	
Babe Pratt	D	17	1	1	2	16	
Phil Watson	R	24	0	2	2	24	
Harold Starr	D	16	0	0	0	12	
Neil Colville	C	1	0	0	0	0	
Joe Cooper	D	1	0	0	0	0	
Dave Kerr	G	47	0	0	0	0	
Bert Gardiner	G	1	0	0	0	0	

		REGULAR SEASON					*POSTSEASON*
GOALTENDER		*GP*	*MIN*	*GA*	*SH*	*GAA*	*no postseason play*
Bert Gardiner	(1-0-0)	1	60	1	0	1.00	
Dave Kerr	(18-17-**12**)	47	2980	95	8	1.91	

TEAM TOTALS

								Per Game			
TEAM	*GP*	*G*	*A*	*P*	*PIM*	*GA*	*SH*	*G*	*A*	*PIM*	*GA*
Canadian											
Montreal (M)	48	114	159	273	504	106	3	2.38	3.31	10.50	2.21

								Per Game		
TEAM	GP	G	A	P	PIM	GA	SH	G	A	PIM	GA
Toronto	48	**126**	148	274	**579**	106	8	**2.63**	3.08	**12.06**	2.21
New York (A)	48	109	166	275	392	122	3	2.27	3.46	8.17	2.54
Montreal (C)	48	82	121	203	317	123	6	1.71	2.52	6.60	2.56
American											
Detroit	48	124	**171**	295	384	103	6	2.58	**3.56**	8.00	2.15
Boston	48	92	116	208	397	**83**	10	1.92	2.42	8.27	**1.73**
Chicago	48	93	148	241	411	92	9	1.94	3.08	8.56	1.92
New York (R)	48	91	133	224	381	96	8	1.90	2.77	7.94	2.00
	384	831	1162	1993	3365	831	53	2.16	3.03	8.76	2.16

PLAYOFFS

SERIES "A"
Detroit 1, Montreal (M) 0 (OT)
Detroit 3, Montreal (M) 0
Detroit 2, Montreal (M) 1

DETROIT, 3-0

SERIES "C"
New York (A) 3, Chicago 0
Chicago 5, New York (A) 4

NEW YORK (A) WINS
TOTAL GOAL SERIES, 7-5

SERIES "E"
Detroit 3, Toronto 1
Detroit 9, Toronto 4
Toronto 4, Detroit 3 (OT)
Detroit 3, Toronto 2

DETROIT WINS
STANLEY CUP, 3-1

SERIES "B"
Boston 3, Toronto 0
Toronto 8, Boston 3

TORONTO WINS
TOTAL GOAL SERIES, 8-6

SERIES "D"
Toronto 3, New York (A) 1
New York (A) 1, Toronto 0
Toronto 3, New York (A) 1

TORONTO, 2-1

ALL-STAR TEAMS

First Team
G — Tiny Thompson, BOS
D — Eddie Shore, BOS
D — Al Siebert, M(C)
C — Reg Smith, M(M)
R — Charlie Conacher, TOR
L — David Schriner, N(A)

Second Team
G — Wilf Cude, M(C)
D — Ebbie Goodfellow, DET
D — Earl Seibert, N(R)-C
C — Bill Thoms, TOR
R — Cecil Dillon, N(R)
L — Paul Thompson, CHI

INDIVIDUAL TROPHY WINNERS

HART TROPHY (Most Valuable Player): Eddie Shore, BOS
LADY BYNG TROPHY (Gentlemanly Conduct): Elwin Romnes, CHI
VEZINA TROPHY (Best Goaltender): Tiny Thompson, BOS

1936-1937
Total Goal Series

In the opening rounds of the 1936 playoffs, in the Toronto-Boston series, as well as the set played by the Americans and Blackhawks, each of the participants won one of the two games. Despite this seeming deadlock, each series featured a clear winner, as these series were determined by which team scored the most goals, not by the club that won the most games. However, these "total goal" series, long a tradition in hockey circles, were about to come to an end in the NHL.

Reaching back to the dawn of organized hockey, total goal series were often used to determine a winner between two clubs — even in the final battle for the Stanley Cup. Later, as the pro leagues coalesced, "best of" series came into vogue — where the victor was the club which won the most games of a predetermined set of games, usually best of five. As the NHL developed, both types of series were used — "total goals" for the opening rounds and "best of" for the finals.

On the surface, it would seem that the "best of" series was a superior way to determine a champion. Simply put, the team that beat its opponent the most times should receive the glory. However, the "total goals" series had its advantages as well. First, since the name of the game in hockey is to score goals — shouldn't the team that connects the most be rewarded for its efforts? Also, a "total goal" series is a scheduler's dream. Beforehand, one would know exactly how long the series would last — two games — no more, no less. With a "best of" series — for instance, best of five games — three, four or even five games could be held, and no one could know the number of games necessary beforehand. Nevertheless, the NHL ruled that beginning in 1937, all playoff series would be "best of" affairs.

During the 1936-37 regular season, the Montreal Canadiens (24-18-6,

54) rose from the depths of a moribund season to capture first place in the Canadian Division by a single point over the Maroons. Toronto claimed the Division's final berth, well ahead of the last-place Americans. In the American Division, Detroit (25-14-9, 59) repeated its first-place showing, as Boston and the Rangers slid into the other playoff slots. The Blackhawks — with 27 losses — thumped into the cellar.

Individually, two players — Larry Aurie (Detroit) and Nels Stewart (Bruins/Americans) — scored a league best 23 goals each. For Stewart, one of the markers was particularly sweet, as it allowed him to pass the great Howie Morenz (270) to become the league's career leader to date. Other notable scoring efforts were put forth by David Schriner (Americans) who collected the most points (46) and by first-year player Syl Apps (Detroit) who amassed the most helpers (29). In the penalty box, Toronto's Red Horner (124) served the most time for the third year running. In net, Detroit's Norm Smith finished with the lowest GAA (2.05) and most shutouts (6), although he was tied in the latter category by Boston's Tiny Thompson.

In a bruising battle, Detroit outlasted the Canadiens in the first-place series, three games to two, edging Montreal 2–1 in the deciding game. In the second- and third-place series — now best-of-three affairs — the Rangers and Maroons prevailed. In the semifinals — also a best-of-three grouping — the Rangers' netminder posted consecutive shutouts as New York blanked the Maroons, 1–0 and 4–0. In the best-of-five finals, the upstart Rangers took a two games to one lead over the favored Wings, before goalie Norm Smith posted a pair of shutouts himself—1–0 and 3–0—allowing Detroit to capture its second straight Cup.

Despite being on the short end, Ranger's goaler Dave Kerr still led all playoff netminders with a 1.08 GAA and four shutouts. Scoring honors were grabbed by a pair of Wings — Marty Barry and Herb Lewis. Both scored four goals, while the former collected league-topping seven assists and 11 points.

As the NHL marched through the years, the "best of" series continued to be the playoff format of choice, as the "total goal" series were dropped permanently. However, in an interesting sidebar, the format still does exist today in professional sports, as "total goal" series are still used by Major League Soccer in its opening rounds. Still, for the NHL it made its decision long ago, when it decided the most important feature of a playoff game was which team won and which lost — rather than how many goals were scored in accomplishing the objective.

STANDINGS

TEAM	GP	W	L	T	PTS	GF	GA
CANADIAN							
MONTREAL (C)	48	24	18	6	54	115	111
MONTREAL (M)	48	22	17	9	53	126	110
TORONTO	48	22	21	5	49	119	115
NEW YORK (A)	48	15	29	4	34	122	161
AMERICAN							
DETROIT	48	25	14	9	59	128	102
BOSTON	48	23	18	7	53	120	110
NEW YORK (R)	48	19	20	9	47	117	106
CHICAGO	48	14	27	7	35	99	131

LEADERS

PLAYER	TM	GP	G	A	PTS	PIM
David Schriner	N(A)	48	21	25	**46**	17
Syl Apps	TOR	48	16	**29**	45	10
Marty Barry	DET	47	17	27	44	6
Larry Aurie	DET	45	**23**	20	43	20
Harvey Jackson	TOR	46	21	19	40	12
Johnny Gagnon	M(C)	48	20	16	36	38
Bob Gracie	M(M)	47	11	25	36	18
Nels Stewart	B-N(A)	43	**23**	12	35	37
Paul Thompson	CHI	47	17	18	35	28
Bill Cowley	BOS	46	13	22	35	4

GOALS	
Stewart, B-N(A)	23
Aurie, DET	23
Keeling, N(R)	22
Jackson, TOR	21
Schriner, N(A)	21

ASSISTS	
Apps, TOR	29
Barry, DET	27
Gracie, M(M)	25
Schriner, N(A)	25
Chapman, N(A)	23

GOALTENDER	TM	GP	MIN	GA	SH	GAA
Norm Smith	DET	48	2980	102	6	**2.05**
Dave Kerr	N(R)	48	**3020**	106	4	2.11
Wilf Cude	M(C)	44	2730	99	5	2.18
Bill Beveridge	M(M)	21	1290	47	1	2.19
Alec Connell	M(M)	27	1710	63	2	2.21
Tiny Thompson	BOS	48	2970	110	6	2.22
Turk Broda	TOR	45	2770	106	3	2.30
Mike Karakas	CHI	48	2978	**131**	5	2.64
Roy Worters	N(A)	23	1430	69	2	2.90
Alfie Moore	N(A)	18	1110	64	1	3.46

PENALTY MINUTES	
Horner, TOR	124
Shields, N(A)-B	94
Conacher, M(M)	64
Portland, BOS	58
Jerwa, B-N(A)	57

SHUTOUTS	
Thompson, BOS	6
Smith, DET	6
Cude, M(C)	5
Karakas, CHI	5
Kerr, N(R)	4

MONTREAL 24-18-6 54 1st (C) Cecil Hart
Canadiens

		REGULAR SEASON					POSTSEASON				
PLAYER	POS	GP	G	A	PTS	PIM	GP	G	A	PTS	PIM
Johnny Gagnon	R	48	20	16	36	38	5	2	1	3	9
Aurel Joliat	L	47	17	15	32	30	5	0	3	3	2
Al Siebert	D	44	8	20	28	38	5	1	2	3	2
Georges Mantha	D	47	13	14	27	17	5	0	0	0	0
Paul Haynes	C	47	8	18	26	24	5	2	3	5	0

1936–1937

	REGULAR SEASON					POSTSEASON				
PLAYER	POS	GP	G	A	PTS	PIM	GP	G	A	PTS	PIM
Toe Blake	L	43	10	12	22	12	5	1	0	1	0
Howie Morenz	C	30	4	16	20	12					
Joffre Desilets	R	48	7	12	19	17	5	1	0	1	0
Alfred Lepine	C	34	7	8	15	15	5	0	1	1	0
George Brown	C	27	4	6	10	10	4	0	0	0	0
Rod Lorrain	R	47	3	6	9	8	5	0	0	0	0
Jack McGill	L	44	5	2	7	9	1	0	0	0	0
Bill MacKenzie (2–2)	D	39	4	3	7	22	5	1	0	1	0
Bill Miller	C	48	3	1	4	12	5	0	0	0	0
Walt Buswell	D	44	0	4	4	30	5	0	0	0	2
Armand Mondou	L	7	1	1	2	0	5	0	0	0	0
Paul Runge (1–2)	C	4	1	0	1	2					
Wilf Cude	G	44	0	0	0	0					
Roger Jenkins (1–3)	D	10	0	0	0	8					
Polly Drouin	L	4	0	0	0	0					
Red Goupile	D	4	0	0	0	0					
George Hainsworth (2–2)	G	4	0	0	0	0					

	REGULAR SEASON					POSTSEASON				
GOALTENDER		GP	MIN	GA	SH	GAA	GP	MIN	GA	SH	GAA
Wilf Cude	(22-17-5)	44	2730	99	5	2.18	5	352	13	0	2.22
George Hainsworth (2–2)	(2-1-1)	4	270	12	0	2.67					

MONTREAL Maroons 22-17-9 53 2nd (C) Tommy Gorman

	REGULAR SEASON					POSTSEASON				
PLAYER	POS	GP	G	A	PTS	PIM	GP	G	A	PTS	PIM
Bob Gracie	C	47	11	25	36	18	5	1	2	3	2
Earl Robinson	R	47	16	18	34	19	5	1	2	3	0
Herb Cain	L	42	13	17	30	18	5	1	1	2	0
Lorne Northcutt	D	46	15	14	29	18	5	1	1	2	2
Jimmy Ward	R	40	14	14	28	34					
Lionel Conacher	D	47	6	19	25	64	5	0	1	1	2
Dave Trottier	L	43	12	11	23	33	5	1	0	1	5
Gus Marker	R	47	10	12	22	22	5	0	1	1	0
Russ Blinco	C	48	6	12	18	2	5	1	0	1	2
Gerry Shannon	L	31	9	7	16	13	5	0	1	1	0
Paul Runge (2–2)	C	30	4	10	14	6	5	0	0	0	4
Stew Evans	D	47	6	7	13	54	5	0	0	0	0
Cy Wentworth	D	43	3	4	7	29	5	1	0	1	0
Gerry Carson	D	42	1	3	4	28	5	0	0	0	4
Carl Voss	C	20	0	2	2	4	5	1	0	1	0
Yip Radley	D	17	0	1	1	13					
Bill MacKenzie (1–2)	D	10	0	1	1	6					
Max Kaminsky	C	6	0	0	0	0					
Roger Jenkins (2–3)	D	1	0	0	0	0					
Alec Connell	G	27	0	0	0	0					
Bill Beveridge	G	21	0	0	0	0	5	0	0	0	0

		REGULAR SEASON					POSTSEASON				
GOALTENDER		GP	MIN	GA	SH	GAA	GP	MIN	GA	SH	GAA
Bill Beveridge	(12-6-3)	21	1290	47	1	2.19	5	300	11	0	2.20
Alec Connell	(10-11-6)	27	1710	63	2	2.21					

TORONTO 22-21-5   49   3rd (C)   Dick Irvin
Maple Leafs

		REGULAR SEASON					POSTSEASON				
PLAYER	POS	GP	G	A	PTS	PIM	GP	G	A	PTS	PIM
Syl Apps	C	48	16	29	45	10	2	0	1	1	0
Harvey Jackson	L	46	21	19	40	12	2	1	0	1	2
Gordie Drillon	R	41	16	17	33	2	2	0	0	0	0
Nick Metz	L	48	9	11	20	19	2	0	0	0	0
Bill Thoms	C	48	10	9	19	14	2	0	0	0	0
Jimmy Fowler	D	48	7	11	18	22	2	0	0	0	0
Bob Davidson	L	46	8	7	15	43	2	0	0	0	5
Red Horner	D	48	3	9	12	**124**	2	0	0	0	7
Reg Hamilton	D	39	3	7	10	32	2	0	1	1	2
Frank Boll	L	25	6	3	9	12	2	0	0	0	0
Frank Finnigan	R	48	2	7	9	4	2	0	0	0	0
Jack Shill	C	32	4	4	8	26	2	0	0	0	0
Charlie Conacher	R	15	3	5	8	13	2	0	0	0	5
Hap Day	D	48	3	4	7	20	2	0	0	0	0
Bill Kendall (2-2)	R	15	2	4	6	4					
Regis Kelly (1-2)	R	16	2	0	2	8					
Art Jackson	C	14	2	0	2	2					
Jim Jarvis	L	24	1	0	1	0					
King Clancy	D	6	1	0	1	4					
George Parsons	L	5	0	0	0	0					
Jack Howard	D	2	0	0	0	0					
Turk Broda	G	45	0	0	0	0	2	0	0	0	0
George Hainsworth (1-2)	G	3	0	0	0	0					

		REGULAR SEASON					POSTSEASON				
GOALTENDER		GP	MIN	GA	SH	GAA	GP	MIN	GA	SH	GAA
Turk Broda	(22-19-4)	45	2770	106	3	2.30	2	133	5	0	2.26
George Hainsworth (1-2)	(0-2-1)	3	190	9	0	2.84					

NEW YORK 15-29-4   34   4th (C)   Mervyn Dutton
Americans

		REGULAR SEASON					POSTSEASON
PLAYER	POS	GP	G	A	PTS	PIM	no postseason play
David Schriner	L	**48**	21	25	**46**	17	
Lorne Carr	R	**48**	18	16	34	22	
Eddie Wiseman	R	44	14	19	33	12	
Art Chapman	C	43	8	23	31	36	
Nels Stewart (2-2)	C	32	*20	10	30	31	
Tom Anderson	L	45	10	15	25	24	
Joe Jerwa (2-2)	D	20	6	8	14	27	
Hap Emms	L	46	4	8	12	48	

1936–1937

PLAYER	POS	REGULAR SEASON					POSTSEASON
		GP	G	A	PTS	PIM	no postseason play
Joe Lamb	R	48	3	9	12	53	
Les Cunningham	C	23	1	8	9	19	
Tony Hemmerling	L	19	3	3	6	4	
Roger Jenkins (3–3)	D	26	1	4	5	6	
Al Shields (1–2)	D	27	3	0	3	79	
Teddy Graham (2–2)	D	31	2	1	3	30	
Harry Oliver	R	20	2	1	3	2	
Lloyd Klein	L	14	2	1	3	2	
Harold Cotton	L	29	2	0	2	23	
Lloyd Jackson	C	14	1	1	2	0	
Allan Murray	D	40	0	2	2	22	
Pete Leswick	R	1	1	0	1	0	
John Doran	D	21	0	1	1	10	
John Gallagher (2–2)	D	9	0	0	0	8	
Jeff Kalbfleisch (1–2)	D	6	0	0	0	4	
Wilf Field	D	2	0	0	0	0	
Oscar Asmundson	C	1	0	0	0	0	
Frank Beisler	D	1	0	0	0	0	
Gord Reid	D	1	0	0	0	2	
Roy Worters	G	23	0	0	0	0	
Alfie Moore	G	18	0	0	0	0	
Lorne Chabot	G	6	0	0	0	0	
Alex Wood	G	1	0	0	0	0	

GOALTENDER		REGULAR SEASON					POSTSEASON
		GP	MIN	GA	SH	GAA	no postseason play
Alex Wood	(0-1-0)	1	70	3	0	2.57	
Roy Worters	(6-14-3)	23	1430	69	2	2.90	
Alfie Moore	(7-11-0)	18	1110	64	1	3.46	
Lorne Chabot	(2-3-1)	6	270	25	0	4.05	

DETROIT
Red Wings

25-14-9   59   1st (A)   Jack Adams

PLAYER	POS	REGULAR SEASON					POSTSEASON				
		GP	G	A	PTS	PIM	GP	G	A	PTS	PIM
Marty Barry	C	48	17	27	44	6	10	4	7	11	2
Larry Aurie	R	45	23	20	43	20					
Herb Lewis	L	45	14	18	32	14	10	4	3	7	4
Syd Howe	C	45	17	10	27	10	10	2	5	7	0
Ebbie Goodfellow	D	48	9	16	25	43	9	2	2	4	12
John Sorrell	L	18	8	16	24	4	10	2	4	6	2
Gord Pettinger	C	48	7	15	22	13	10	0	2	2	2
Wally Kilrea	C	47	8	13	21	6	10	0	2	2	4
Modere Bruneteau	R	42	9	7	16	18	10	2	0	2	6
Hec Kilrea	L	48	6	9	15	20	10	3	1	4	2
Pete Kelly	R	47	5	4	9	12	8	2	0	2	0
Bucko McDonald	D	47	3	5	8	20	10	0	0	0	2
Rolly Roulston	L	21	0	5	5	10					
Howie Mackie	R	13	1	0	1	4	8	0	0	0	0
John Gallagher (1–2)	D	11	1	0	1	4	10	1	0	1	17

		REGULAR SEASON					POSTSEASON				
PLAYER	POS	GP	G	A	PTS	PIM	GP	G	A	PTS	PIM
Ralph Bowman	D	37	0	1	1	24	10	0	1	1	4
Jimmy Orlando	D	9	0	1	1	8					
Doug Young	D	11	0	0	0	6					
Don Deacon	L	4	0	0	0	2					
Burr Williams	D	2	0	0	0	4					
John Sherf	L	1	0	0	0	0	5	0	1	1	2
Norm Smith	G	48	0	0	0	0	5	0	0	0	0
Earl Robertson	G						6	0	0	0	0
Jim Franks	G						1	0	0	0	0

		REGULAR SEASON					POSTSEASON				
GOALTENDER		GP	MIN	GA	SH	GAA	GP	MIN	GA	SH	GAA
Norm Smith	(25-14-9)	48	2980	102	6	**2.05**	5	282	6	1	1.28
Earl Robertson							6	340	8	2	1.41
Jim Franks							1	30	2	0	4.00

BOSTON 23-18-7   53   2nd (A)   Art Ross
Bruins

		REGULAR SEASON					POSTSEASON				
PLAYER	POS	GP	G	A	PTS	PIM	GP	G	A	PTS	PIM
Bill Cowley	C	46	13	22	35	4	3	0	3	3	0
Ray Getliffe	L	48	16	15	31	28	3	2	1	3	2
Dit Clapper	R	48	17	8	25	25	3	2	0	2	5
Charlie Sands	C	47	18	5	23	6	3	1	2	3	0
Reg Smith	R	44	8	10	18	36	3	0	0	0	0
John Beattie	L	48	8	7	15	10	3	1	0	1	0
Cooney Weiland	C	48	6	9	15	6	3	0	0	0	0
Leroy Goldsworthy	R	47	8	6	14	8	3	0	0	0	0
Bill Hollett	D	48	3	7	10	22	3	0	0	0	2
Milt Schmidt	C	26	2	8	10	15	3	0	0	0	0
Bun Cook	L	40	4	5	9	8					
Woody Dumart	L	17	4	4	8	2	3	0	0	0	0
Joe Jerwa (1–2)	D	26	3	5	8	30					
Jack Portland	D	46	2	4	6	58	3	0	0	0	4
Nels Stewart (1–2)	C	11	*3	2	5	6					
Eddie Shore	D	20	3	1	4	12					
Al Shields (2–2)	D	18	0	4	4	15	3	0	0	0	2
Peggy O'Neil	R	21	0	2	2	6					
Bobby Bauer	R	1	1	0	1	0	1	0	0	0	0
Lorne Duguid	L	1	1	0	1	2					
Sylvio Mantha	D	4	0	0	0	2					
Teddy Graham (1–2)	D	1	0	0	0	0					
Jeff Kalbfleisch (2–2)	D	1	0	0	0	0					
Sammy McManus	L	1	0	0	0	0					
Tiny Thompson	G	48	0	0	0	0	3	0	0	0	0

		REGULAR SEASON					POSTSEASON				
GOALTENDER		GP	MIN	GA	SH	GAA	GP	MIN	GA	SH	GAA
Tiny Thompson	(23-18-7)	48	2970	110	6	2.22	3	180	8	1	2.67

1936–1937

NEW YORK Rangers   19-20-9   47   3rd (A)   Lester Patrick

		REGULAR SEASON					POSTSEASON				
PLAYER	POS	GP	G	A	PTS	PIM	GP	G	A	PTS	PIM
Cecil Dillon	R	48	20	11	31	13	9	0	3	3	0
Phil Watson	R	48	11	17	28	22	9	0	2	2	9
Neil Colville	C	45	10	18	28	33	9	3	3	6	0
Butch Keeling	L	48	22	4	26	18	9	3	2	5	2
Lynn Patrick	C	45	8	16	24	23	9	3	0	3	2
Alex Shibicky	R	47	14	8	22	30	9	1	4	5	0
Frank Boucher	C	44	7	13	20	5	9	2	3	5	0
Mac Colville	R	46	7	12	19	10	9	1	2	3	2
Ott Heller	D	48	5	12	17	42	9	0	0	0	11
Babe Pratt	D	47	8	7	15	23	9	3	1	4	11
Murray Murdoch	L	48	0	14	14	16	9	1	1	2	0
Art Coulter	D	47	1	5	6	27	9	0	3	3	15
Bill Cook	R	21	1	4	5	6					
Joe Cooper	D	48	0	3	3	42	9	1	1	2	12
Eddie Wares	D	2	2	0	2	0					
Clint Smith	C	2	1	0	1	0					
Bryan Hextall	R	3	0	1	1	0					
Ivan Johnson	D	35	0	0	0	2	9	0	1	1	4
Joe Krol	L	1	0	0	0	0					
Dave Kerr	G	48	0	0	0	0	9	0	0	0	0

		REGULAR SEASON					POSTSEASON			
GOALTENDER		GP	MIN	GA	SH	GAA	GP	MIN	GA	SH	GAA
Dave Kerr	(19-20-9)	48	3020	106	4	2.11	9	553	10	4	**1.08**

CHICAGO Blackhawks   14-27-7   35   4th (A)   Clem Loughlin

		REGULAR SEASON					POSTSEASON
PLAYER	POS	GP	G	A	PTS	PIM	*no postseason play*
Paul Thompson	L	47	17	18	35	28	
Johnny Gottselig	L	47	9	21	30	10	
Wildor Larochelle	R	43	9	10	19	6	
Louis Trudel	L	45	6	12	18	11	
Elwin Romnes	C	28	4	14	18	2	
Regis Kelly (2–2)	R	29	13	4	17	0	
Harold March	R	37	11	6	17	31	
Pete Palangio	L	30	8	9	17	16	
Earl Seibert	D	43	9	6	15	46	
Glenn Brydson	R	34	7	7	14	20	
Alex Levinsky	D	18	0	8	8	32	
Marty Burke	D	41	1	3	4	28	
Hal Jackson	D	38	1	3	4	6	
Bill Kendall (1–2)	R	17	3	0	3	6	
Ernest Klingbeil	D	5	1	2	3	2	
Andy Blair	C	44	0	3	3	33	
Art Wiebe	D	43	0	2	2	6	
Tommy Cook	C	15	0	2	2	0	
Ben LaPrarie	D	7	0	0	0	0	

		REGULAR SEASON					*POSTSEASON*
PLAYER	POS	GP	G	A	PTS	PIM	*no postseason play*
Milt Brink	C	5	0	0	0	0	
Paul Schaefer	D	5	0	0	0	6	
Al Suomi	L	5	0	0	0	0	
Mike Karakas	G	48	0	0	0	2	

		REGULAR SEASON				*POSTSEASON*
GOALTENDER		GP	MIN	GA	SH	GAA	*no postseason play*
Mike Karakas	(14-27-7)	48	2978	131	5	2.64	

TEAM TOTALS

								Per Game			
TEAM	GP	G	A	P	PIM	GA	SH	G	A	PIM	GA
Canadian											
Montreal (C)	48	115	154	269	298	111	5	2.40	3.21	6.21	2.31
Montreal (M)	48	126	**177**	**303**	379	110	3	2.63	**3.69**	7.80	2.29
Toronto	48	119	146	265	371	115	3	2.48	3.04	7.73	2.40
New York (A)	48	122	155	277	**481**	161	4	2.54	3.23	**10.02**	3.35
American											
Detroit	48	**128**	167	295	244	**102**	6	**2.67**	3.48	5.08	**2.13**
Boston	48	120	124	244	303	110	6	2.50	2.58	6.31	2.29
New York (R)	48	117	145	262	312	106	4	2.44	3.03	6.50	2.21
Chicago	48	99	130	229	291	131	5	2.06	2.71	6.06	2.73
	384	946	1198	2141	2679	946	36	2.46	3.12	6.98	2.46

PLAYOFFS

SERIES "A"
Detroit 4, Montreal (C) 0
Detroit 5, Montreal (C) 1
Montreal 3, Detroit 1
Montreal 3, Detroit 1
Detroit 2, Montreal 1 (OT)

DETROIT, 3–2

SERIES "B"
Montreal (M) 4, Boston 1
Boston 4, Montreal (M) 0
Montreal 4, Boston 1

MONTREAL (M), 2–1

SERIES "C"
New York (R) 3, Toronto 0
New York (R) 2, Toronto 1 (OT)

NEW YORK (R), 2–0

SERIES "D"
New York (R) 1, Montreal (M) 0
New York (R) 4, Montreal (M) 0

NEW YORK (R), 2–0

SERIES "E"
New York (R) 5, Detroit 1
Detroit 4, New York (R) 2
New York (R) 1, Detroit 0
Detroit 1, New York (R) 0
Detroit 3, New York (R) 0

**DETROIT WINS
STANLEY CUP, 3–2**

ALL-STAR TEAMS

First Team
G — Norm Smith, DET
D — Ebbie Goodfellow, DET
D — Al Siebert, M(C)
C — Marty Barry, DET
R — Larry Aurie, DET
L — Harvey Jackson, TOR

Second Team
G — Wilf Cude, M(C)
D — Lionel Conacher, M(M)
D — Earl Seibert, CHI
C — Art Chapman, N(A)
R — Cecil Dillon, N(R)
L — David Schriner, N(A)

INDIVIDUAL TROPHY WINNERS

HART TROPHY (Most Valuable Player): Al Siebert M(C)
LADY BYNG TROPHY (Gentlemanly Conduct): Marty Barry, DET
VEZINA TROPHY (Best Goaltender): Norm Smith, DET
CALDER MEMORIAL TROPHY (Best Rookie): Syl Apps, TOR

1937-1938
All-American

The sport of ice hockey is unquestionably a Canadian product — invented in that country, nurtured and developed by its citizens — from the onset of amateur leagues, through the development of most of the first pro leagues. Even later, when the NHL's center gravitated to the United States in the late 1920s, Canadian influence continued. Simply put, even with most of the league's cities operating in the United States — under American ownership — the game itself was still played almost entirely by Canadian players. However, beginning in the mid–1930s, one team owner wanted to put a different stamp on his club.

Major Frederic McLaughlin, the original owner of the Chicago Blackhawks, wanted to make a change in his team's personnel. He was tired of the Canadian-centric nature of the sport and he wanted to prove to one and all that American hockey players were just as talented. So, he began assembling an all-American team. First, McLaughlin began with the goaltender — Mike Karakas — who hailed from Minnesota. Later, he added Alex Levinsky (New York), Elwin Romnes (Minnesota), and Louis Trudel (Massachusetts). During the 1936-37 season, the Hawks had enough Americans to ice an all–American team at least for one contest. In this particular matchup against the Bruins, the American contingent didn't fare well, losing 6–2. Over the full season, the Blackhawks did not prosper, as they limped home with a 14-27-7 mark — last in the division. Undeterred, McLaughlin added what he though to be the final missing piece. Beginning in the upcoming season, Chicago would be coached by Bill Stewart — also an American.

Over the course of the 1937-38 campaign, the Blackhawks did not perform well, loitering near the bottom of the standings. After a modest three-game winning streak near the end of the schedule, the club then proceeded to drop its last three games, finishing with the same win total (14) as the previous year's last-place club. Lucky for them, the Wings were two points worse, allowing Chicago to sneak into the playoffs.

Meanwhile, Boston (30-11-7, 67) and the Rangers enjoyed solid seasons in the American Division, while the Maple Leafs (24-15-9, 57), Americans and Canadiens ruled the roost in the Canadian. The Maroons, with only 12 wins, finished with the worst record in the league.

Two Leafs — Gordie Drillon with 26 goals and 52 points, and Syl Apps, with 29 helpers — captured league-scoring honors. Art Coulter (Rangers) served the most time in the penalty box (90). Guarding the net, Boston's Tiny Thompson allowed the fewest goals (1.80), while the Rangers' Dave Kerr posted the most shutouts (8).

As the playoffs began, critics thought little of the chances of the "Americanized" Blackhawks. After the first game — a 6-4 loss to the Canadiens — the pundits seemed correct. However, much to the astonishment of all, Chicago bounced back with a 4-0 shutout behind Karakas, then finished off the surprised Canadiens with a 3-2 overtime win. In the other opening rounds, the Americans ousted the favored Rangers, two games to one, while Toronto edged Boston by the same count — with all four wins in both series coming in overtime. In the semifinals, the Americans beat the Hawks in the first game, before Chicago took control — winning the final two (1-0 and 3-2) to stake their claim in the finals.

During the last win against the Americans, Karakas was struck by a shot, which injured his foot, so he was unable to answer the bell in game one against the Leafs. Chicago scrambled to find a replacement. Utilizing the services of Alfie Moore — a career minor-leaguer — the Blackhawks rose to the occasion, beating the favored Leafs 3-1. After a technicality ruled Moore ineligible for game two, another sub (Paul Goodman) was rushed in without success, as the Leafs buried him, 5-1. However, by game three, Karakas was sufficiently healed to join his seven fellow Americans and that proved to be the difference, as the Hawks breezed to the Cup with 2-1 and 4-1 wins, capping their unlikely run.

Individually, Drillon scored the most goals (7) and collected the most points (8) although he was tied in the latter category by Chicago's Johnny Gottselig. Two other Hawks — Roger Jenkins (6 assists) and Karakas (1.71, 2) rounded out the other playoff leaders.

As the NHL continued, despite the success of Chicago's American contingent, teams would consist of almost entirely Canadian players. Only in recent years have a significant portion of roster spots been apportioned to players hailing outside the Dominion. Still, this Blackhawk squad holds a special place in NHL history. Of all the league teams competing for the Cup, for almost 60 years no other winner would have as many Americans on its team as the Blackhawks of 1938.

STANDINGS

TEAM	GP	W	L	T	PTS	GF	GA
CANADIAN							
TORONTO	48	24	15	9	57	151	127
NEW YORK (A)	48	19	18	11	49	110	111
MONTREAL (C)	48	18	17	13	49	123	128
MONTREAL (M)	48	12	30	6	30	101	149
AMERICAN							
BOSTON	48	30	11	7	67	142	89
NEW YORK (R)	48	27	15	6	60	149	96
CHICAGO	48	14	25	9	37	97	139
DETROIT	48	12	25	11	35	99	133

LEADERS

PLAYER	TM	GP	G	A	PTS	PIM
Gordie Drillon	TOR	48	**26**	26	**52**	4
Syl Apps	TOR	47	21	**29**	50	9
Paul Thompson	CHI	48	22	22	44	14
Georges Mantha	M(C)	47	23	19	42	12
Cecil Dillon	N(R)	48	21	18	39	6
Bill Cowley	BOS	48	17	22	39	8
David Schriner	N(A)	48	21	17	38	22
Bill Thoms	TOR	48	14	24	38	14
Clint Smith	N(R)	48	14	23	37	0
Two tied with					36	

GOALS
Drillon, TOR 26
Mantha, M(C) 23
Thompson, CHI 22
Three tied with 21

ASSISTS
Apps, TOR 29
Chapman, N(A) 27
Drillon, TOR 26
Watson, N(R) 25
Thoms, TOR 24

GOALTENDER	TM	GP	MIN	GA	SH	GAA
Tiny Thompson	BOS	48	2970	89	7	**1.80**
Dave Kerr	N(R)	48	2960	96	8	1.95
Earl Robertson	N(A)	48	**3000**	111	6	2.22
Wilf Cude	M(C)	47	2990	126	3	2.53
Turk Broda	TOR	48	2980	127	6	2.56
Norm Smith	DET	47	2930	130	3	2.66
Mike Karakas	CHI	48	2980	139	1	2.80
Bill Beveridge	M(M)	48	2980	**149**	2	3.00

PENALTY MINUTES
Coulter, N(R) 90
Horner, TOR 82
Heller, N(R) 68
Shields, M(M) 67
Evans, M(M) 59

SHUTOUTS
Kerr, N(R) 8
Thompson, BOS 7
Robertson, N(A) 6
Broda, TOR 6
Two tied with 3

TORONTO 24-15-9 57 1st (C) Dick Irvin
Maple Leafs

		REGULAR SEASON					*POSTSEASON*			
PLAYER	POS	GP	G	A	PTS	PIM	GP	G	A	PTS	PIM
Gordie Drillon	R	48	26	26	**52**	4	7	7	1	**8**	2

1937-1938

PLAYER	POS	REGULAR SEASON					POSTSEASON				
		GP	G	A	PTS	PIM	GP	G	A	PTS	PIM
Syl Apps	C	47	21	29	50	9	7	1	4	5	0
Bill Thoms	C	48	14	24	38	14	7	0	1	1	0
Harvey Jackson	L	48	17	17	34	18	6	1	0	1	8
Frank Boll	L	44	14	11	25	18	7	0	0	0	2
Red Horner	D	47	4	20	24	82	7	0	1	1	14
Nick Metz	L	48	15	7	22	12	7	0	2	2	0
Jimmy Fowler	D	48	10	12	22	8	7	0	2	2	0
Bob Davidson	L	48	3	17	20	52	4	0	2	2	7
Regis Kelly	R	43	9	10	19	25	7	2	2	4	2
Charlie Conacher	R	19	7	9	16	6					
Murph Chamberlain	C	43	4	12	16	51	5	0	0	0	2
George Parsons	L	30	5	6	11	6	7	3	2	5	11
Reg Hamilton	D	45	1	4	5	43	7	0	1	1	2
Rudolph Kampman	D	32	1	2	3	56	7	0	1	1	6
Turk Broda	G	48	0	0	0	0	7	0	0	0	0
Murray Armstrong	C	9	0	0	0	0	3	0	0	0	0
Chuck Corrigan	R	3	0	0	0	0					

GOALTENDER		REGULAR SEASON					POSTSEASON				
		GP	MIN	GA	SH	GAA	GP	MIN	GA	SH	GAA
Turk Broda	(24-15-9)	48	2980	127	6	2.56	7	452	13	1	1.73

NEW YORK Americans   19-18-11   49   2nd (C)   Mervyn Dutton

PLAYER	POS	REGULAR SEASON					POSTSEASON				
		GP	G	A	PTS	PIM	GP	G	A	PTS	PIM
David Schriner	L	48	21	17	38	22	6	1	0	1	0
Nels Stewart	C	48	19	17	36	29	6	2	3	5	2
Eddie Wiseman	R	48	18	14	32	32	6	0	4	4	10
Art Chapman	C	45	2	27	29	8	6	0	1	1	0
Tom Anderson	L	45	4	21	25	22	6	1	4	5	2
Lorne Carr	R	48	16	7	23	12	6	3	1	4	2
Reg Smith	R	47	10	10	20	23	6	0	3	3	0
Joe Jerwa	D	48	3	14	17	53	6	0	0	0	8
John Sorrell (2-2)	L	17	8	2	10	9	6	4	0	4	2
John Gallagher	D	46	3	6	9	18	6	0	2	2	6
John Beattie (3-3)	L	19	3	4	7	5	6	2	2	4	2
Jack Shill (1-2)	C	22	1	3	4	10					
Hap Emms	L	20	1	3	4	6					
Hap Day	D	43	0	3	3	14	6	0	0	0	0
Joe Lamb (1-2)	R	25	1	0	1	20					
Allan Murray	D	47	0	1	1	34	6	0	0	0	6
Lloyd Klein (1-2)	L	3	0	1	1	0					
Earl Robertson	G	48	0	0	0	0	6	0	0	0	0
Ivan Johnson	D	31	0	0	0	10	6	0	0	0	2
Charlie Mason	R	2	0	0	0	0					

GOALTENDER		REGULAR SEASON					POSTSEASON				
		GP	MIN	GA	SH	GAA	GP	MIN	GA	SH	GAA
Earl Robertson	(19-18-11)	48	3000	111	6	2.22	6	475	12	0	2.00

MONTREAL 18-17-13 49 3rd (C) Cecil Hart
Canadiens

		REGULAR SEASON				POSTSEASON				
PLAYER	POS	GP	G	A	PTS	PIM	GP	G	A	PTS	PIM
Georges Mantha	D	47	23	19	42	12	3	1	0	1	0
Paul Haynes	C	48	13	22	35	25	3	0	4	4	5
Toe Blake	L	43	17	16	33	33	3	3	1	4	2
Rod Lorrain	R	48	13	19	32	14	3	0	0	0	0
Johnny Gagnon	R	47	13	17	30	9	3	1	3	4	2
Polly Drouin	L	31	7	13	20	8	1	0	0	0	0
Al Siebert	D	37	8	11	19	56	3	1	1	2	0
Alfred Lepine	C	47	5	14	19	24	3	0	0	0	0
Walt Buswell	D	48	2	15	17	24	3	0	0	0	0
Aurel Joliat	L	44	6	7	13	24					
Joffre Desilets	R	32	6	7	13	6	2	0	0	0	7
Red Goupile	D	47	4	5	9	44	3	2	0	2	4
Don Wilson	C	18	2	7	9	0	3	0	0	0	0
George Brown	C	34	1	7	8	14	3	0	0	0	2
Armand Mondou	L	7	2	4	6	0					
Marty Burke (2–2)	D	38	0	5	5	31					
Gus Mancuso	R	17	1	1	2	4					
Armand Raymond	D	11	0	2	2	4	3	0	0	0	2
Wilf Cude	G	47	0	0	0	0	3	0	0	0	0
Bill MacKenzie (1–2)	D	11	0	0	0	4					
Tony Demers	R	6	0	0	0	0					
Oscar Asmundson	C	2	0	0	0	0					
Paul Gauthier	G	1	0	0	0	0					
Bill Summerhill	R						1	0	0	0	0

		REGULAR SEASON					POSTSEASON
GOALTENDER		GP	MIN	GA	SH	GAA	no postseason play
Paul Gauthier	(0-0-1)	1	70	2	0	1.71	
Wilf Cude	(18-17-**12**)	47	2990	126	3	2.53	

MONTREAL 12-30-6 30 4th (C) King Clancy
Maroons   Tommy Gorman

		REGULAR SEASON				POSTSEASON
PLAYER	POS	GP	G	A	PTS	PIM	no postseason play
Bob Gracie	C	48	12	19	31	32	
Herb Cain	L	47	11	19	30	10	
Jimmy Ward	R	48	11	15	26	34	
Gus Marker	R	48	9	15	24	35	
Lorne Northcutt	D	46	11	12	23	50	
Russ Blinco	C	47	10	9	19	4	
Dave Trottier	L	47	9	10	19	42	
Stew Evans	D	48	5	11	16	59	
Al Shields	D	48	5	7	12	67	
Paul Runge	C	39	5	7	12	21	
Earl Robinson	R	39	4	7	11	13	
Cy Wentworth	D	48	4	5	9	32	
Tommy Cook	C	21	2	4	6	0	

1937–1938

PLAYER	POS	REGULAR SEASON					POSTSEASON
		GP	G	A	PTS	PIM	no postseason play
Des Smith	D	40	3	1	4	47	
Gerry Shannon	L	36	0	3	3	20	
Bill Beveridge	G	48	0	0	0	0	
Moe Croghan	D	16	0	0	0	0	
Carl Voss (1–2)	C	3	0	0	0	0	

GOALTENDER		REGULAR SEASON					POSTSEASON
		GP	MIN	GA	SH	GAA	no postseason play
Bill Beveridge	(12-**30**-6)	48	2980	**149**	2	3.00	

BOSTON 30-11-7   67   1st (A)   Art Ross
Bruins

PLAYER	POS	REGULAR SEASON					POSTSEASON				
		GP	G	A	PTS	PIM	GP	G	A	PTS	PIM
Bill Cowley	C	48	17	22	39	8	3	2	0	2	0
Bobby Bauer	R	48	20	14	34	9	3	0	0	0	2
Charlie Sands	C	46	17	12	29	12	3	1	1	2	0
Woody Dumart	L	48	13	14	27	6	3	0	0	0	0
Milt Schmidt	C	44	13	14	27	15	3	0	0	0	0
Ray Getliffe	L	36	11	13	24	16	3	0	1	1	2
Cooney Weiland	C	48	11	12	23	16	3	0	0	0	0
Leroy Goldsworthy	R	46	9	10	19	14	3	0	0	0	2
Gord Pettinger (2–2)	C	35	7	10	17	10	3	0	0	0	0
Eddie Shore	D	48	3	14	17	42	3	0	1	1	6
Dit Clapper	R	46	6	9	15	24	3	0	0	0	12
Bill Hollett	D	48	4	10	14	54	3	0	1	1	0
Art Jackson	C	48	9	3	12	24	3	0	0	0	0
Jack Portland	D	48	0	5	5	26	3	0	0	0	4
Mel Hill	R	6	2	0	2	2	1	0	0	0	0
Red Hamill	L	6	0	1	1	2					
Tiny Thompson	G	48	0	0	0	0	3	0	0	0	0
John Beattie (1–3)	L	14	0	0	0	0					
Jack Crawford	D	2	0	0	0	0					

GOALTENDER		REGULAR SEASON					POSTSEASON				
		GP	MIN	GA	SH	GAA	GP	MIN	GA	SH	GAA
Tiny Thompson	(**30**-11-7)	48	2970	89	7	**1.80**	3	212	6	0	**1.70**

NEW YORK 27-15-6   60   2nd (A)   Lester Patrick
Rangers

PLAYER	POS	REGULAR SEASON					POSTSEASON				
		GP	G	A	PTS	PIM	GP	G	A	PTS	PIM
Cecil Dillon	R	48	21	18	39	6	3	1	0	1	0
Clint Smith	C	48	14	23	37	0	3	2	0	2	0
Neil Colville	C	45	17	19	36	11	3	0	1	1	0
Alex Shibicky	R	48	17	18	35	26	3	2	0	2	2
Lynn Patrick	C	48	15	19	34	24	3	0	1	1	2
Phil Watson	R	48	7	25	32	52	3	0	2	2	0
Mac Colville	R	48	14	14	28	18	3	0	2	2	0
Bryan Hextall	R	48	17	4	21	6	3	2	0	2	0

		REGULAR SEASON					POSTSEASON				
PLAYER	POS	GP	G	A	PTS	PIM	GP	G	A	PTS	PIM
Babe Pratt	D	47	5	14	19	56	2	0	0	0	2
Butch Keeling	L	38	8	9	17	12	3	0	1	1	2
Ott Heller	D	48	2	14	16	68	3	0	1	1	2
Art Coulter	D	43	5	10	15	90					
Bobby Kirk	R	39	4	8	12	14					
Joe Cooper	D	46	3	2	5	56	3	0	0	0	4
Muzz Patrick	D	1	0	2	2	0	3	0	0	0	2
Frank Boucher	C	18	0	1	1	2					
Dutch Hiller	L	8	0	1	1	2	1	0	0	0	0
Dave Kerr	G	48	0	0	0	0	3	0	0	0	0
Larry Molyneaux	D	2	0	0	0	2	3	0	0	0	8

		REGULAR SEASON					POSTSEASON				
GOALTENDER		GP	MIN	GA	SH	GAA	GP	MIN	GA	SH	GAA
Dave Kerr	(27-15-6)	48	2960	96	8	1.95	3	262	8	0	1.83

CHICAGO 14-25-9   37   3rd (A)   Bill Stewart
Blackhawks

		REGULAR SEASON					POSTSEASON				
PLAYER	POS	GP	G	A	PTS	PIM	GP	G	A	PTS	PIM
Paul Thompson	L	48	22	22	44	14	10	4	3	7	6
Johnny Gottselig	L	48	13	19	32	22	10	5	3	8	4
Elwin Romnes	C	44	10	22	32	4	10	2	4	6	2
Harold March	R	41	11	17	28	16	9	2	4	6	12
Louis Trudel	L	42	6	16	22	15	10	0	3	3	2
Earl Seibert	D	48	8	13	21	38	10	5	2	7	12
Cully Dahlstrom	C	48	10	9	19	11	10	3	1	4	2
Carl Voss (2–2)	C	34	3	8	11	0	10	3	2	5	0
Roger Jenkins	D	37	1	8	9	26	10	0	6	6	8
Jack Shill (2–2)	C	23	4	3	7	8	10	1	3	4	15
Alex Levinsky	D	48	3	2	5	18	10	1	0	1	0
Glenn Brydson	R	19	1	3	4	6					
Pete Palangio	L	19	2	1	3	4	3	0	0	0	0
Bill MacKenzie (2–2)	D	35	1	2	3	20	9	0	1	1	11
Bert Connelly	L	15	1	2	3	4	10	0	0	0	0
Art Wiebe	D	43	0	3	3	24	10	0	1	1	2
Virgil Johnson	D	25	0	2	2	2	10	0	0	0	0
Ivan Nicholson	L	2	1	0	1	0					
Bill Kendall	R	9	0	1	1	2					
Mike Karakas	G	48	0	0	0	0	8	0	0	0	0
Marty Burke (1–2)	D	12	0	0	0	8					
Ossie Hanson	C	8	0	0	0	0					
Vic Heyliger	C	7	0	0	0	0					
Hal Jackson	D	3	0	0	0	0	1	0	0	0	2
Tony Ahlin	L	1	0	0	0	0					
Paul Goodman	G						1	0	0	0	0
Alfie Moore	G						1	0	0	0	0

1937–1938

GOALTENDER		REGULAR SEASON					POSTSEASON				
		GP	MIN	GA	SH	GAA	GP	MIN	GA	SH	GAA
Mike Karakas	(14-25-9)	48	2980	139	1	2.80	8	525	15	2	1.71
Alfie Moore							1	60	1	0	1.00
Paul Goodman							1	60	5	0	5.00

DETROIT 12-25-11   35   4th (A)   Jack Adams
Red Wings

PLAYER	POS	REGULAR SEASON					POSTSEASON
		GP	G	A	PTS	PIM	no postseason play
Herb Lewis	L	42	13	18	31	12	
Marty Barry	C	48	9	20	29	34	
Syd Howe	C	48	8	19	27	14	
Carl Liscombe	L	41	14	10	24	30	
Alex Motter	C	32	5	17	22	6	
Larry Aurie	R	47	10	9	19	19	
Hec Kilrea	L	48	9	9	18	10	
Eddie Wares	D	21	9	7	16	2	
Bucko McDonald	D	47	3	7	10	14	
John Sorrell (1–2)	L	23	3	7	10	0	
Modere Bruneteau	R	24	3	6	9	16	
Doug Young	D	48	3	5	8	24	
Ronnie Hudson	C	32	5	2	7	2	
Ebbie Goodfellow	C	30	0	7	7	13	
Joe Lamb (2–2)	R	14	3	1	4	6	
Gord Pettinger (1–2)	C	12	1	3	4	4	
John Beattie (2–3)	L	11	1	2	3	0	
Ralph Bowman	D	45	0	2	2	26	
Clare Drouillard	C	10	0	1	1	0	
Pete Kelly	R	9	0	1	1	2	
Pete Bessone	D	6	0	1	1	6	
Ken Doraty	F	2	0	1	1	2	
Rolly Roulston	L	2	0	1	1	0	
Norm Smith	G	47	0	0	0	0	
John Doran	D	7	0	0	0	10	
Howie Mackie	R	7	0	0	0	0	
Jimmy Orlando	D	6	0	0	0	4	
John Sherf	L	6	0	0	0	2	
Wally Kilrea	C	5	0	0	0	4	
Jim Franks	G	1	0	0	0	0	

GOALTENDER		REGULAR SEASON					POSTSEASON
		GP	MIN	GA	SH	GAA	no postseason play
Norm Smith	(11-25-11)	47	2930	130	3	2.66	
Jim Franks	(1-0-0)	1	60	3	0	3.00	

TEAM TOTALS

TEAM	GP	G	A	P	PIM	GA	SH	Per Game			
								G	A	PIM	GA
Canadian											
Toronto	48	**151**	**206**	357	404	127	6	**3.15**	**4.29**	8.42	2.65
New York (A)	48	110	150	260	327	111	6	2.29	3.13	6.81	2.31

170　　The National Hockey League, 1917–1967

								Per Game		
TEAM	GP	G	A	P	PIM	GA	SH	G	A	PIM	GA
Montreal (C)	48	123	191	314	340	128	3	2.56	3.98	7.08	2.67
Montreal (M)	48	101	144	245	470	149	2	2.10	3.00	9.79	3.10
American											
Boston	48	142	163	305	284	89	7	2.96	3.40	5.92	1.85
New York (R)	48	149	201	350	435	96	8	3.10	4.19	9.06	2.00
Chicago	48	97	153	250	238	139	1	2.02	3.19	4.96	2.90
Detroit	48	99	156	255	258	133	3	2.06	3.25	5.38	2.77
	384	972	1364	2336	2756	972	36	2.53	3.55	7.18	2.53

PLAYOFFS

SERIES "A"
Toronto 1, Boston 0 (OT)
Toronto 2, Boston 1
Toronto 3, Boston 2 (OT)

TORONTO, 3–0

SERIES "B"
New York (A) 2, New York (R) 1 (OT)
New York (R) 4, New York (A) 3
New York (A) 3, New York (R) 2 (OT)

NEW YORK (A), 2–1

SERIES "C"
Montreal (C) 6, Chicago 4
Chicago 4, Montreal (C) 0
Chicago 3, Montreal (C) 2 (OT)

CHICAGO, 2–1

SERIES "D"
New York (A) 3, Chicago 1
Chicago 1, New York (A) 0 (OT)
Chicago 3, New York (A) 2

CHICAGO, 2–1

SERIES "E"
Chicago 3, Toronto 1
Toronto 5, Chicago 1
Chicago 2, Toronto 1
Chicago 4, Toronto 1

**CHICAGO WINS
STANLEY CUP, 3–1**

ALL-STAR TEAMS

First Team
G — Tiny Thompson, BOS
D — Eddie Shore, BOS
D — Al Siebert, M(C)
C — Bill Cowley, BOS
R — Cecil Dillon, N(R)
R — Gordie Drillon, TOR
L — Paul Thompson, CHI

Second Team
G — Dave Kerr, N(R)
D — Art Coulter, N(R)
D — Earl Seibert, CHI
C — Syl Apps, TOR

L — Toe Blake, M(C)

INDIVIDUAL TROPHY WINNERS

HART TROPHY (Most Valuable Player): Eddie Shore, BOS
LADY BYNG TROPHY (Gentlemanly Conduct): Gordie Drillon, TOR
VEZINA TROPHY (Best Goaltender): Tiny Thompson, BOS
CALDER MEMORIAL TROPHY (Best Rookie): Cully Dahlstrom, CHI

1938-1939

Frank Brimsek

By the end of the 1930s, Cecil "Tiny" Thompson had been a mainstay in the Bruins net for more than a decade. Over that period, he led the league in shutouts and GAA four times each — for the latter most recently in the previous campaign. Thompson also led his team to several first-place finishes and a Stanley Cup (1929). Yet, midway through the upcoming campaign he would be discarded, sent to another team. The reason — the Bruins felt there was someone better waiting in the wings.

Frank Brimsek, a native of Minnesota, cut his hockey teeth for the Pittsburgh Yellowjackets of the Eastern Hockey League in 1935-36, winning the most games (20) and posting the most shutouts (8). Two years later, now in Providence (AHL) one notch below the majors, he led the Reds to the Calder Cup, earning the league's lowest GAA (1.75) along the way. Brimsek had certainly proven he was ready for the next step — a fact certainly noticed by NHL executives.

Before the 1938-39 campaign got underway, a familiar friend was lost. During the summer of 1938, Montreal's Maroons announced they were folding, leaving the league with only seven members. As a result, the circuit removed the divisional headings, allowing the septet to play as one group. Also the playoff structure changed accordingly. After the campaign, the first and second place teams would meet in a best-of-seven matchup, while the third and fourth, as well as the fifth and sixth place teams would meet in a best-of-three qualifier. The survivors of the latter two series would then play another best-of-three grouping to decide who would face the winner of the 1-2 matchup in a best-of-seven finals for the Cup.

Early in the 1938-39 campaign, Boston's Thompson went down with an injury. Quick as a wink, the Bruins replaced him with Brimsek, who they had signed as a free agent before the season. In what seemed to be a huge gamble, Thompson was then dealt to Detroit, leaving the netminding chores solely on Brimsek's shoulders. The Bruins roll of the dice paid off in a big way. Within two weeks, Brimsek posted three shutouts in a row — then allowed two goals to the Canadiens on December 13 — before blanking another consecutive trio before the end of the month. This stellar goalie work gave a him nickname which he would carry throughout his career — Mr. Zero.

With this hot rookie between the pipes, the Bruins (36-10-2, 74) waltzed to the regular season championship by sixteen points over the Rangers. Toronto, the Americans, Detroit and Montreal also qualified for the playoffs, leaving the defending champion Blackhawks on the outside looking in. Individually, for the whole season, Brimsek served up 10 blankings to go with a 1.56 GAA — both league highs. On the scoring front, Montreal's Toe Blake (47) collected the most points, Boston's Roy Conacher (26) netted the most markers and fellow Bruin Bill Cowley (34) added the most assists. Toronto tough guy Red Horner (85) spent the most time in the sin bin.

In the playoffs, another Bruin earned himself a colorful nickname. In the first contest of the first round series between the Bruins and Rangers, Mel Hill scored the game-winner in overtime. Two nights later, he repeated the feat. Eventually, the Rangers climbed back into the series, setting up a decisive game seven in Boston. Tied 1–1 after regulation, the game was won 48 minutes into the extra session by Mr. Hill once again, earning him the nickname "Sudden Death."

In the other playoff series, Toronto ousted the Americans, while the Wings outlasted the Canadiens. In the semis, Toronto eliminated Detroit in overtime, sending the Leafs into the finals. In the first game, the Bruins prevailed, 2–1. An overtime win by the Leafs briefly evened the count, then Brimsek took over, allowing only two goals in the final three contests to lead Boston to its first Cup in ten years. In the playoff run, Brimsek posted the best GAA (1.25) while his teammate Cowley set a record for most assists (11). Although on the losing end, Toronto's Gordie Drillon scored the most playoff goals (7).

Over the next several seasons, Brimsek continued to lead the Bruins into battle, although he never again quite attained the high levels he reached in his rookie campaign. After nine years in Boston, which included other GAA and shutout titles as well as another Cup, he was traded to Chicago, where he played the final year of his pro career.

Sixteen years following his retirement, Brimsek was elected to the Hall of Fame, joining the netminder he had replaced many years before — Tiny Thompson. This was a fitting tribute for "Mr. Zero," certainly one of the best goalies to ever have played the game.

1938–1939

STANDINGS

TEAM	GP	W	L	T	PTS	GF	GA
BOSTON	48	36	10	2	74	156	76
NEW YORK (R)	48	26	16	6	58	149	105
TORONTO	48	19	20	9	47	114	107
NEW YORK (A)	48	17	21	10	44	119	157
DETROIT	48	18	24	6	42	107	128
MONTREAL	48	15	24	9	39	115	146
CHICAGO	48	12	28	8	32	91	132

LEADERS

PLAYER	TM	GP	G	A	PTS	PIM
Toe Blake	MTL	48	24	23	47	10
David Schriner	N(A)	48	13	31	44	20
Bill Cowley	BOS	34	8	34	42	2
Clint Smith	N(R)	48	21	20	41	2
Marty Barry	DET	48	13	28	41	4
Syl Apps	TOR	44	15	25	40	4
Tom Anderson	N(A)	47	13	27	40	14
Johnny Gottselig	CHI	48	16	23	39	15
Paul Haynes	MTL	47	5	33	38	27
Four tied with					37	

GOALS	
Conacher, BOS	26
Blake, MTL	24
Shibicky, N(R)	24
Smith, N(R)	21
Hextall, N(R)	20

ASSISTS	
Cowley, BOS	34
Haynes, MTL	33
Schriner, N(A)	31
Bary, DET	28
Anderson, N(A)	27

GOALTENDER	TM	GP	MIN	GA	SH	GAA
Frank Brimsek	BOS	43	2610	68	10	1.56
Dave Kerr	N(R)	48	2970	105	6	2.12
Turk Broda	TOR	48	2990	107	8	2.15
Tiny Thompson	B-D	44	2707	109	4	2.42
Mike Karakas	CHI	48	2988	132	5	2.65
Claude Bourque	MTL	25	1560	69	2	2.65
Earl Robertson	N(A)	46	2850	136	3	2.86
Wilf Cude	MTL	23	1440	77	2	3.21

PENALTY MINUTES	
Horner, TOR	85
M. Patrick, N(R)	64
Coulter, N(R)	58
Evans, MTL	58
Seibert, CHI	57

SHUTOUTS	
Brimsek, BOS	10
Broda, TOR	8
Kerr, N(R)	6
Karakas, CHI	5
Thompson, B-D	4

BOSTON 36-10-2 74 1st Art Ross
Bruins

		REGULAR SEASON					POSTSEASON				
PLAYER	POS	GP	G	A	PTS	PIM	GP	G	A	PTS	PIM
Bill Cowley	C	34	8	34	42	2	12	3	11	14	2
Roy Conacher	L	47	26	11	37	12	12	6	4	10	12
Milt Schmidt	C	41	15	17	32	13	12	3	3	6	2
Bobby Bauer	R	48	13	18	31	4	12	3	2	5	0
Woody Dumart	L	46	14	15	29	2	12	1	3	4	6
Bill Hollett	D	44	10	17	27	35	12	1	3	4	2
Dit Clapper	R	42	13	13	26	22	12	0	1	1	6
Gord Pettinger	C	48	11	14	25	8	12	1	1	2	7

		REGULAR SEASON				POSTSEASON				
PLAYER	POS	GP	G	A	PTS	PIM	GP	G	A	PTS	PIM
Ray Getliffe	L	43	10	12	22	11	11	1	1	2	2
Mel Hill	R	46	10	10	20	16	12	6	3	9	12
Eddie Shore	D	44	4	14	18	47	12	0	4	4	19
Cooney Weiland	C	45	7	9	16	9	12	0	0	0	0
Charlie Sands	C	37	7	5	12	10	1	0	0	0	0
Jack Crawford	D	48	4	8	12	12	12	1	1	2	9
Jack Portland	D	48	4	5	9	46	12	0	0	0	11
Red Hamill	L	6	0	1	1	0	12	0	0	0	8
Frank Brimsek	G	43	0	0	0	0	12	0	0	0	0
Pat McReavy	C	6	0	0	0	0					
Tiny Thompson (1–2)	G	5	0	0	0	0					
Harry Frost	R	4	0	0	0	0	1	0	0	0	0
Terry Reardon	C	4	0	0	0	0					
Jack Shewchuk	D	3	0	0	0	2					

		REGULAR SEASON				POSTSEASON				
GOALTENDER		GP	MIN	GA	SH	GAA	GP	MIN	GA	SH	GAA
Tiny Thompson (1–2)	(3-1-1)	5	310	8	0	1.55					
Frank Brimsek	(33-9-1)	43	2610	68	10	1.56	12	863	18	1	1.25

NEW YORK 26-16-6   58   2nd   Lester Patrick
Rangers

		REGULAR SEASON				POSTSEASON				
PLAYER	POS	GP	G	A	PTS	PIM	GP	G	A	PTS	PIM
Clint Smith	C	48	21	20	41	2	7	1	2	3	0
Neil Colville	C	47	18	19	37	12	7	0	2	2	2
Phil Watson	R	48	15	22	37	42	7	1	1	2	7
Bryan Hextall	R	48	20	15	35	18	7	0	1	1	4
Alex Shibicky	R	48	24	9	33	24	7	3	1	4	2
Dutch Hiller	L	48	10	19	29	22	7	1	0	1	9
Lynn Patrick	C	35	8	21	29	25	7	1	1	2	0
Mac Colville	R	48	7	21	28	24	7	1	2	3	4
Cecil Dillon	R	48	12	15	27	6	1	0	0	0	0
Ott Heller	D	48	0	23	23	42	7	0	1	1	10
Babe Pratt	D	48	2	19	21	20	7	1	2	3	9
George Allen	L	19	6	6	12	10	7	0	0	0	4
Art Coulter	D	44	4	8	12	58	7	1	1	2	6
Muzz Patrick	D	48	1	10	11	64	7	1	0	1	17
Joe Krol	L	1	1	1	2	0					
Larry Molyneaux	D	43	0	1	1	18	7	0	0	0	0
Bill Carse	C	1	0	1	1	0	6	1	1	2	0
Dave Kerr	G	48	0	0	0	0	1	0	0	0	0
Bert Gardiner	G						6	0	0	0	0

		REGULAR SEASON				POSTSEASON				
GOALTENDER		GP	MIN	GA	SH	GAA	GP	MIN	GA	SH	GAA
Dave Kerr	(26-16-6)	48	2970	105	6	2.12	1	119	2	0	1.01
Bert Gardiner							6	433	12	0	1.66

1938-1939   175

TORONTO 19-20-9 47 3rd Dick Irvin
Maple Leafs

		REGULAR SEASON					POSTSEASON				
PLAYER	POS	GP	G	A	PTS	PIM	GP	G	A	PTS	PIM
Syl Apps	C	44	15	25	40	4	10	2	6	8	2
Gordie Drillon	R	40	18	16	34	15	10	7	6	13	4
Harvey Jackson	L	41	10	17	27	12	7	0	1	1	2
Murph Chamberlain	C	48	10	16	26	32	10	2	5	7	4
Elwin Romnes (2-2)	C	36	7	16	23	0	10	1	4	5	0
Regis Kelly	R	48	11	11	22	12	9	1	0	1	0
Nick Metz	L	47	11	10	21	15	10	3	3	6	6
Gus Marker	R	29	9	6	15	11	10	2	2	4	0
George Parsons	L	43	7	7	14	14					
Red Horner	D	48	4	10	14	85	10	1	2	3	26
Bob Davidson	L	47	4	10	14	29	10	1	1	2	6
Rudolph Kampman	D	41	2	8	10	52	10	1	1	2	20
Jimmy Fowler	D	39	1	6	7	9	9	0	1	1	2
Reg Hamilton	D	48	0	7	7	54	10	0	2	2	4
Bucko McDonald (2-2)	D	33	3	3	6	20	10	0	0	0	4
Bill Thoms	C	12	1	4	5	4					
Jack Church	D	3	0	2	2	2	1	0	0	0	0
Pete Langelle	C	2	1	0	1	0	11	1	2	3	2
Murray Armstrong	C	3	0	1	1	0					
Turk Broda	G	48	0	0	0	0	10	0	0	0	0
Norm Mann	R	16	0	0	0	2					
Frank Boll	L	11	0	0	0	0					
Red Heron	C	6	0	0	0	0	2	0	0	0	0
Don Metz	L						2	0	0	0	0

		REGULAR SEASON					POSTSEASON				
GOALTENDER		GP	MIN	GA	SH	GAA	GP	MIN	GA	SH	GAA
Turk Broda	(19-20-9)	48	2990	107	8	2.15	10	617	20	2	1.94

NEW YORK 17-21-10 44 4th Mervyn Dutton
Americans

		REGULAR SEASON					POSTSEASON				
PLAYER	POS	GP	G	A	PTS	PIM	GP	G	A	PTS	PIM
David Schriner	L	48	13	31	44	20	2	0	0	0	30
Tom Anderson	L	47	13	27	40	14	2	0	0	0	0
Lorne Carr	R	46	19	18	37	16	2	0	0	0	0
Nels Stewart	C	46	16	19	35	43	2	0	0	0	0
Eddie Wiseman	R	47	12	21	33	8	2	0	0	0	0
Art Jackson	C	48	12	13	25	15	2	0	0	0	2
John Sorrell	L	48	13	9	22	10	2	0	0	0	0
Art Chapman	C	45	3	19	22	2	2	0	0	0	0
Reg Smith	R	48	8	11	19	18	2	0	0	0	14
Joe Jerwa	D	47	4	12	16	52	2	0	0	0	2
Leory Goldsworthy	R	48	3	11	14	10	2	0	0	0	0
John Gallagher	D	43	1	5	6	22	2	0	0	0	0
Wilf Field	D	47	1	3	4	37	2	0	0	0	2
Roger Jenkins (2-2)	D	27	1	1	2	4					
Earl Robertson	G	46	0	0	0	0					

		REGULAR SEASON					POSTSEASON				
PLAYER	POS	GP	G	A	PTS	PIM	GP	G	A	PTS	PIM
Allan Murray	D	18	0	0	0	8					
John Beattie	L	17	0	0	0	5					
Alfie Moore	G	2	0	0	0	0	2	0	0	0	0
Jack Tomson	D						2	0	0	0	0

		REGULAR SEASON				POSTSEASON				
GOALTENDER		GP	MIN	GA	SH	GAA	GP	MIN	GA	SH	GAA
Earl Robertson	(17-18-**10**)	46	2850	**136**	3	2.86					
Alfie Moore	(0-2-0)	2	120	14	0	7.00	2	120	6	0	3.00
Roger Jenkins	(0-1-0)	1	30	7	0	14.00					

DETROIT 18-24-6 42 5th Jack Adams
Red Wings

		REGULAR SEASON					POSTSEASON				
PLAYER	POS	GP	G	A	PTS	PIM	GP	G	A	PTS	PIM
Marty Barry	C	**48**	13	28	41	4	6	3	1	4	0
Syd Howe	C	**48**	16	20	36	11	6	3	1	4	4
Carl Liscombe	L	41	8	18	26	13	6	0	0	0	2
Charlie Conacher	R	40	8	15	23	39	5	2	5	7	2
Gus Giesebrecht	C	28	10	10	20	2	6	0	2	2	0
Hec Kilrea	L	**48**	8	9	17	8	6	1	2	3	0
Ebbie Goodfellow	C	**48**	8	8	16	36	6	0	0	0	8
Eddie Wares	D	28	8	8	16	10	6	1	0	1	8
Herb Lewis	L	42	6	10	16	8	6	1	2	3	0
Alex Motter	C	44	5	11	16	17	4	0	1	1	0
Pete Kelly	R	32	4	9	13	4	4	0	0	0	0
Modere Bruneteau	R	20	3	7	10	0	6	0	0	0	0
Doug Young	D	42	1	5	6	16	6	0	2	2	4
Ralph Bowman	D	43	2	3	5	26	5	0	0	0	0
Don Deacon	L	8	1	3	4	2	2	2	1	3	0
Sid Abel	C	15	1	1	2	0	6	1	1	2	2
Dave Trottier	L	11	1	1	2	16					
Don Grosso	C	1	1	1	2	0	3	1	2	3	7
Connie Brown	C	2	1	0	1	0					
Larry Aurie	R	1	1	0	1	0					
Jack Keating	L	1	1	0	1	2					
Jack Stewart	D	32	0	1	1	18					
Alvin Jones	D	11	0	1	1	6	6	0	1	1	10
Charlie Mason (2-2)	R	6	0	1	1	0					
Phil Besler (1-2)	R	5	0	1	1	2					
Tiny Thompson (2-2)	G	39	0	0	0	0	6	0	0	0	0
Bucko McDonald (1-2)	D	14	0	0	0	2					
Eddie Bush	D	8	0	0	0	0					
Harvie Teno	G	5	0	0	0	0					
Norm Smith	G	5	0	0	0	0					
Bill Thomson	C	4	0	0	0	0					
John Sherf	L	3	0	0	0	0	3	0	0	0	0
Ken Kilrea	L	1	0	0	0	0	3	1	1	2	4

1938–1939 177

		REGULAR SEASON					POSTSEASON				
GOALTENDER		GP	MIN	GA	SH	GAA	GP	MIN	GA	SH	GAA
T. Thompson (2–2)	(16-17-6)	39	2397	101	4	2.53	6	374	15	1	2.41
Harvie Teno	(2-3-0)	5	300	15	0	3.00					
Norm Smith	(0-4-0)	4	240	12	0	3.00					

MONTREAL Canadiens   15-24-9   39   6th   Cecil Hart / Jules Dugal

		REGULAR SEASON					POSTSEASON			
PLAYER	POS	GP	G	A	PTS	PIM	GP	G	A	PTS	PIM
Toe Blake	L	48	24	23	47	10	3	1	1	2	2
Paul Haynes	C	47	5	33	38	27	3	0	0	0	4
Johnny Gagnon	R	45	12	22	34	23	3	0	2	2	10
Herb Cain	L	45	13	14	27	26	3	0	0	0	2
Louis Trudel	L	31	8	13	21	2	3	1	0	1	0
Rod Lorrain	R	38	10	9	19	0	3	0	3	3	0
Polly Drouin	L	28	7	11	18	2	3	0	1	1	5
Al Siebert	R	44	9	7	16	36	3	0	0	0	0
Bill Summerhill	R	43	6	10	16	28	2	0	0	0	2
Georges Mantha	D	25	5	5	10	6	3	0	0	0	0
Walt Buswell	D	46	3	7	10	10	3	2	0	2	2
Armand Mondou	L	34	3	7	10	2	3	1	0	1	2
George Brown	C	18	1	9	10	10					
Stew Evans	D	43	2	7	9	58	3	0	0	0	2
Jimmy Ward	R	36	4	3	7	0	1	0	0	0	0
Des Smith	D	16	3	3	6	8	3	0	0	0	4
Cy Wentworth	D	45	0	3	3	12	3	0	0	0	4
Red Goupille	D	18	0	2	2	24					
Paul Raymond	R	11	0	2	2	4	3	0	0	0	2
Marcel Tremblay	R	10	0	2	2	0					
Bob Gracie (1–2)	C	7	0	1	1	4					
Claude Bourque	G	25	0	0	0	0	3	0	0	0	0
Wilf Cude	G	23	0	0	0	0					
Don Wilson	C	4	0	0	0	0					
Gus Mancuso	R	2	0	0	0	0					

		REGULAR SEASON					POSTSEASON				
GOALTENDER		GP	MIN	GA	SH	GAA	GP	MIN	GA	SH	GAA
Claude Bourque	(7-13-5)	25	1560	69	2	2.65	3	188	8	0	2.55
Wilf Cude	(8-11-4)	23	1440	77	2	3.21					

CHICAGO Blackhawks   12-28-8   32   7th   Bill Stewart / Paul Thompson

		REGULAR SEASON					POSTSEASON
PLAYER	POS	GP	G	A	PTS	PIM	*no postseason play*
Johnny Gottselig	L	48	16	23	39	15	
Joffre Desilets	R	48	11	13	24	28	
Harold March	R	46	10	11	21	29	
Cully Dahlstrom	C	48	6	14	20	2	
Bill Thoms (2–2)	C	36	6	11	17	16	

		REGULAR SEASON					*POSTSEASON*
PLAYER	POS	GP	G	A	PTS	PIM	*no postseason play*
Earl Robinson	R	47	9	6	15	13	
Paul Thompson	L	33	5	10	15	33	
Earl Seibert	D	48	4	11	15	57	
Russ Blinco	C	48	3	12	15	2	
Lorne Northcutt	D	46	5	7	12	9	
Bob Gracie (2-2)	C	31	4	6	10	27	
Joe Cooper	D	17	3	3	6	10	
Jack Shill	C	28	2	4	6	4	
Alex Levinsky	D	30	1	3	4	36	
Phil Besler (1-2)	R	17	1	3	4	16	
Charlie Mason (2-2)	R	13	1	3	4	0	
Elwin Romnes (1-2)	C	12	0	4	4	0	
Art Wiebe	D	47	1	2	3	24	
Roger Jenkins (1-2)	D	14	1	1	2	2	
Bill MacKenzie	D	47	1	0	1	36	
Ab DeMarco	C	2	1	0	1	0	
Mike Karakas	G	48	0	0	0	2	

		REGULAR SEASON				*POSTSEASON*
GOALTENDER		GP	MIN	GA	SH	GAA	*no postseason play*
Mike Karakas	(12-**28**-8)	48	2988	132	5	2.65	

TEAM TOTALS

								Per Game			
TEAM	GP	G	A	P	PIM	GA	SH	G	A	PIM	GA
Boston	48	**156**	203	359	251	76	**10**	**3.25**	4.23	5.23	**1.58**
New York (R)	48	149	**230**	**379**	**393**	105	6	3.10	**4.79**	**8.19**	2.19
Toronto	48	114	175	289	370	107	8	2.38	3.65	7.71	2.23
New York (A)	48	119	200	319	276	157	3	2.48	4.17	5.75	3.27
Detroit	48	107	172	278	240	128	4	2.23	3.58	5.00	2.67
Montreal	48	115	193	308	294	146	4	2.40	4.02	6.13	3.04
Chicago	48	91	147	238	367	132	5	1.90	3.06	7.65	2.75
	336	851	1320	2170	2191	851	40	2.53	3.92	6.52	2.53

PLAYOFFS

SERIES "A"
Boston 2, New York (R) 1 (OT)
Boston 3, New York (R) 2 (OT)
Boston 4, New York (R) 1
New York (R) 2, Boston 1
New York (R) 2, Boston 1 (OT)
New York (R) 3, Boston 1
Boston 2, New York (R) 1 (OT)

BOSTON, 4-3

SERIES "B"
Toronto 4, New York (A) 0
Toronto 2, New York (A) 0

TORONTO, 2-0

1938-1939

SERIES "C"
Montreal 2, Detroit 0
Detroit 7, Montreal 3
Detroit 1, Montreal 0 (OT)

DETROIT, 2-1

SERIES "E"
Boston 2, Toronto 1
Toronto 3, Boston 2 (OT)
Boston 3, Toronto 1
Boston 2, Toronto 0
Boston 3, Toronto 1

**BOSTON WINS
STANLEY CUP, 4-1**

SERIES "D"
Toronto 4, Detroit 1
Detroit 3, Toronto 1
Toronto 5, Detroit 4 (OT

TORONTO, 2-1

ALL-STAR TEAMS

First Team
G — Frank Brimsek, BOS
D — Dit Clapper, BOS
D — Eddie Shore, BOS
C — Syl Apps, TOR
R — Gordie Drillon, TOR
L — Toe Blake, MTL

Second Team
G — Earl Robertson, N(A)
D — Art Coulter, N(R)
D — Earl Seibert, CHI
C — Neil Colville, N(R)
R — Bobby Bauer, BOS
L — Johnny Gottselig, CHI

INDIVIDUAL TROPHY WINNERS

HART TROPHY (Most Valuable Player): Toe Blake, MTL
LADY BYNG TROPHY (Gentlemanly Conduct): Clint Smith, N(R)
VEZINA TROPHY (Best Goaltender): Frank Brimsek, BOS
CALDER MEMORIAL TROPHY (Best Rookie): Frank Brimsek, BOS

1939-1940

New York Rangers

As the 1930s turned the corner into the 1940s, one NHL club was about to enjoy one of its finest seasons. Spurred in part by the skipper, this squad would reach the pinnacle of achievement. Alas for them, it would be the last time they reached such heights for more than a generation.

Born in the second wave of American expansion, the New York Rangers played their first game in the fall of 1926, beating the defending Cup holders — the Montreal Maroons —1–0. Assembled and coached by the legendary Lester Patrick, the Rangers soon became the darling of the Big Apple. Led by a cluster of stars, whom Patrick had signed out of the defunct Western Hockey League — most importantly Bill and Bun Cook, as well as Frank Boucher — the Rangers skated to their first division title in their very first campaign. In their second go-round, the club won the Cup, in part due to the heroics of their skipper himself, who actually donned the "tools of ignorance" when the starting goalie went down in the playoffs.

During the early 1930s, the Rangers earned their second Cup the hard way. While tilting with Toronto for the prize, the team found itself under the handicap of playing on the road for most of the series, as the circus had been booked into Madison Square Garden for a series of early April dates. As a result, the Rangers and the Leafs played three of the four games of the finals in Toronto. Despite this handicap, New York prevailed, three games to one. Again, four years later, upon reaching the finals, New York was forced to play on the road for most of the games. This time the result wasn't as favorable, as the Rangers lost to the Wings, three games to two. Unfortunately for the team, this would not be the last time this scenario would play out.

The 1939-40 Rangers blasted out of the gate with a remarkable streak. After losing their third game, on November 19, the team did not lose again for almost two months. In that span the Rangers won 14, while tying five. After the streak-breaking loss on January 14 the club reeled off five more wins in a row, forging a 20-4-7 mark by January 28, seven points better than the Bruins. Then, the Rangers cooled off while Boston won seven of nine to take over first. Down the stretch, both teams remained hot, but the Bruins (31-12-5, 67) held on to defeat New York by three points. The other playoff teams (Toronto, Chicago, Detroit and the Americans) finished well behind, while Montreal brought up the rear.

Although ceding the overall point and assist total to the Bruins' Milt Schmidt (22-30-52), the Rangers held their own in individual scoring feats, as Bryan Hextall (24) scored the most goals. Other contributing Rangers included Neil Coville (19-19-38) and Phil Watson (7-28-35). Also helping out were a couple of familiar names — full-timers Lynn and Muzz Patrick — both sons of the boss. Despite this scoring prowess, the Rangers achieved their success with a strong defense and good goaltending. Overall, the team allowed over twenty fewer goals than their nearest rival, thanks mostly to the efforts of Dave Kerr (1.54, 8) who posted the most shutouts as well. Tough guy Art Coulter (68) kept the Rangers' foes honest, although Toronto's Red Horner (87) reigned supreme in the penalty box.

In the playoffs, the Rangers faced the Bruins in the opening, best-of-seven, round. Here, after trailing two games to one, New York won the next three —1–0, 1–0, 4–1— sending the first-place team packing. In the other series, Toronto bested Chicago, while Detroit outlasted the Americans. In the semifinals, the Leafs swept the Wings, setting up a New York–Toronto final. However, once again the circus intervened. After the Rangers won the first two contests at home, the team was forced to play out the series on the road. After Toronto evened the series, the Rangers skated to a pair of overtime wins — 2–1 and 3–2 — to claim their third Cup. In an especially proud moment for the coach, Muzz Patrick scored one of the extra-session winners. Overall, Watson (3-6-9) claimed the most playoff assists and points, while Gordie Drillon (Toronto) scored the most goals (5). As he did during the regular campaign, Kerr (1.55, 3) was the top goalie in the playoffs.

As the NHL moved on through the decades, the years were not kind to the Rangers. The team bottomed out during the World War II era, then rebounded somewhat during the 1950s, qualifying for the playoffs a handful of times. More lean years followed in the 1960s, before the club enjoyed some success in the 1970s, reaching the finals in the last year of the decade. However, ultimate Cup success waited until the mid–1990s, when another Rangers squad would make another spirited playoff run to capture the prize — the team's first in over 50 years, the longest such drought in NHL history.

STANDINGS

TEAM	GP	W	L	T	PTS	GF	GA
BOSTON	48	31	12	5	67	170	98
NEW YORK (R)	48	27	11	10	64	136	77
TORONTO	48	25	17	6	56	134	110
CHICAGO	48	23	19	6	52	112	120
DETROIT	48	16	26	6	38	90	126
NEW YORK (A)	48	15	29	4	34	106	140
MONTREAL	48	10	33	5	25	90	167

LEADERS

PLAYER	TM	GP	G	A	PTS	PIM
Milt Schmidt	BOS	48	22	**30**	52	37
Woody Dumart	BOS	48	22	21	43	16
Bobby Bauer	BOS	48	17	26	43	2
Gordie Drillon	TOR	43	21	19	40	13
Bill Cowley	BOS	48	13	27	40	24
Bryan Hextall	N(R)	48	**24**	15	39	52
Neil Colville	N(R)	48	19	19	38	22
Syd Howe	DET	46	14	23	37	17
Toe Blake	MTL	48	17	19	36	48
Murray Armstrong	N(A)	47	16	20	36	12

GOALS	
Hextall, N(R)	24
Schmidt, BOS	22
Dumart, BOS	22
Drillon, TOR	21
Cain, BOS	21

ASSISTS	
Schmidt, BOS	30
Watson, N(R)	28
Cowley, BOS	27
Bauer, BOS	26
Howe, DET	23

GOALTENDER	TM	GP	MIN	GA	SH	GAA
Dave Kerr	N(R)	48	**3000**	77	8	**1.54**
Paul Goodman	CHI	31	1920	62	4	1.94
Frank Brimsek	BOS	48	2950	98	6	1.99
Turk Broda	TOR	47	2900	108	4	2.23
Tiny Thompson	DET	46	2830	120	3	2.54
Earl Robertson	N(A)	48	2960	**140**	6	2.84
Claude Bourque	M-D	37	2270	122	3	3.22
Mike Karakas	C-M	22	1360	76	0	3.35

PENALTY MINUTES	
Horner, TOR	87
Coulter, N(R)	68
Chamberlain, TOR	63
Church, TOR	62
Pratt, N(R)	61

SHUTOUTS	
Kerr, N(R)	8
Robertson, N(A)	6
Brimsek, BOS	6
Goodman, CHI	4
Broda, TOR	4

BOSTON 31-12-5 67 1st Cooney Weiland
Bruins

		REGULAR SEASON					POSTSEASON				
PLAYER	POS	GP	G	A	PTS	PIM	GP	G	A	PTS	PIM
Milt Schmidt	C	48	22	**30**	52	37	6	0	0	0	0
Woody Dumart	L	48	22	21	43	16	6	1	0	1	0
Bobby Bauer	R	48	17	26	43	2	6	1	0	1	2
Bill Cowley	C	48	13	27	40	24	6	0	1	1	7
Herb Cain	L	48	21	10	31	30	6	1	3	4	2
Roy Conacher	L	31	18	12	30	9	6	2	1	3	0
Dit Clapper	R	44	10	18	28	25	5	0	2	2	2
Bill Hollett	D	44	10	18	28	18	5	1	2	3	2

1939-1940

		REGULAR SEASON					POSTSEASON				
PLAYER	POS	GP	G	A	PTS	PIM	GP	G	A	PTS	PIM
Art Jackson	C	46	7	18	25	6	5	1	2	3	0
Mel Hill	R	38	9	11	20	19	3	0	0	0	0
Red Hamill	L	30	10	8	18	16	5	0	1	1	5
Gord Pettinger	C	24	2	6	8	2					
Eddie Wiseman (2-2)	R	*18	2	6	8	0	6	2	1	3	2
Jack Shewchuk	D	47	2	4	6	55	6	0	0	0	0
Jack Crawford	D	35	1	4	5	26	6	0	0	0	0
Jack Portland (1-2)	D	28	0	5	5	16					
Des Smith (2-2)	D	20	2	2	4	23	6	0	0	0	0
Eddie Shore (1-2)	D	4	2	1	3	4					
Frank Brimsek	G	48	0	0	0	0	6	0	0	0	0
Pat McReavy	C	2	0	0	0	2					
Terry Reardon	C						1	0	1	1	0

		REGULAR SEASON					POSTSEASON				
GOALTENDER		GP	MIN	GA	SH	GAA	GP	MIN	GA	SH	GAA
Frank Brimsek	(31-12-5)	48	2950	98	6	1.99	6	360	15	0	2.50

NEW YORK 27-11-10 64 2nd Frank Boucher
Rangers

		REGULAR SEASON					POSTSEASON				
PLAYER	POS	GP	G	A	PTS	PIM	GP	G	A	PTS	PIM
Bryan Hextall	R	48	24	15	39	52	12	4	3	7	11
Neil Colville	C	48	19	19	38	22	12	2	7	9	18
Phil Watson	R	48	7	28	35	42	12	3	6	9	16
Alex Shibicky	R	44	11	21	32	33	11	2	5	7	4
Dutch Hiller	L	48	13	18	31	57	12	2	4	6	2
Kilby MacDonald	L	44	15	13	28	19	12	0	2	2	4
Lynn Patrick	C	48	12	16	28	34	12	2	2	4	4
Clint Smith	C	41	8	16	24	2	11	1	3	4	2
Mac Colville	R	47	7	14	21	12	12	3	2	5	6
Ott Heller	D	47	5	14	19	26	12	0	3	3	12
Alf Pike	L	47	8	9	17	38	12	3	1	4	6
Babe Pratt	D	48	4	13	17	61	12	3	1	4	18
Art Coulter	D	48	1	9	10	68	12	1	0	1	21
Muzz Patrick	D	46	2	4	6	44	12	3	0	3	13
Dave Kerr	G	48	0	0	0	0	12	0	0	0	0
Cliff Barton	R	3	0	0	0	0					
John Polich	R	1	0	0	0	0					
Stan Smith	C	1	0	0	0	0	1	0	0	0	0

		REGULAR SEASON					POSTSEASON				
GOALTENDER		GP	MIN	GA	SH	GAA	GP	MIN	GA	SH	GAA
Dave Kerr	(27-11-10)	48	3000	77	8	1.54	12	770	20	3	1.56

TORONTO 25-17-6 51 3rd Dick Irvin
Maple Leafs

		REGULAR SEASON					POSTSEASON				
PLAYER	POS	GP	G	A	PTS	PIM	GP	G	A	PTS	PIM
Gordie Drillon	R	43	21	19	40	13	10	3	1	4	0

		REGULAR SEASON				POSTSEASON				
PLAYER	POS	GP	G	A	PTS	PIM	GP	G	A	PTS	PIM
Syl Apps	C	27	13	17	30	5	10	5	2	7	2
David Schriner	L	39	11	15	26	10	9	1	3	4	4
Bob Davidson	L	48	8	18	26	56	10	0	3	3	16
Red Heron	C	42	11	12	23	12	9	2	0	2	2
Murph Chamberlain	C	40	5	17	22	63	3	0	0	0	0
Pete Langelle	C	39	7	14	21	2	10	0	3	3	0
Regis Kelly	R	34	11	9	20	15	6	0	1	1	0
Gus Marker	R	42	10	9	19	15	10	1	3	4	23
Rudolph Kampman	D	39	6	9	15	59	10	0	0	0	0
Lex Chisholm	C	28	6	8	14	11					
Nick Metz	L	31	6	5	11	2	9	1	3	4	9
Hank Goldup	L	21	6	4	10	2	10	5	1	6	4
Billy Taylor	C	29	4	6	10	9	2	1	0	1	0
Red Horner	D	31	1	9	10	87	9	0	2	2	55
Wally Stanowski	D	27	2	7	9	11	10	1	0	1	2
Bucko McDonald	D	34	2	5	7	13	1	0	0	0	0
Jack Church	D	31	1	4	5	62	10	1	1	2	6
Reg Hamilton	D	23	2	2	4	23	10	0	0	0	0
Don Metz	L	10	1	1	2	4	2	0	0	0	0
Turk Broda	G	47	0	0	0	0	10	0	0	0	0
Phil Stein	G	1	0	0	0	0					

		REGULAR SEASON					POSTSEASON				
GOALTENDER		GP	MIN	GA	SH	GAA	GP	MIN	GA	SH	GAA
Phil Stein	(0-0-1)	1	70	2	0	1.71					
Turk Broda	(25-17-5)	47	2900	108	4	2.23	10	657	19	1	1.74

CHICAGO 23-19-6 52 4th Paul Thompson
Blackhawks

		REGULAR SEASON					POSTSEASON				
PLAYER	POS	GP	G	A	PTS	PIM	GP	G	A	PTS	PIM
Cully Dahlstrom	C	45	11	19	30	15	2	0	0	0	0
Bill Carse	C	48	10	13	23	10	2	1	0	1	0
Johnny Gottselig	L	39	8	15	23	7	2	0	1	1	0
Harold March	R	45	9	14	23	49	2	1	0	1	2
George Allen	L	48	10	12	22	26	2	0	0	0	0
Bill Thoms	C	48	9	13	22	2	1	0	0	0	0
Phil Hergesheimer	R	42	9	11	20	6	1	0	0	0	0
Doug Bentley	L	39	12	7	19	12	2	0	0	0	0
Les Cunningham	C	37	6	11	17	2	1	0	0	0	0
Joffre Desilets	R	26	6	7	13	6					
John Chad	R	22	8	3	11	11	2	0	0	0	0
Joe Cooper	D	44	4	7	11	59	2	0	0	0	0
Earl Seibert	D	36	3	7	10	35	2	0	1	1	8
Bob Carse	L	22	3	5	8	11	2	0	0	0	0
Ab DeMarco	C	17	0	5	5	17	2	0	0	0	0
Jack Portland (2-2)	D	16	1	4	5	20	2	0	0	0	2
Des Smith (1-2)	D	24	1	4	5	27					
Art Wiebe	D	47	2	2	4	20	2	1	0	1	2
Bill MacKenzie	D	19	0	1	1	14					

		REGULAR SEASON					POSTSEASON				
PLAYER	POS	GP	G	A	PTS	PIM	GP	G	A	PTS	PIM
Paul Goodman	G	31	0	0	0	0	2	0	0	0	0
Mike Karakas (1–2)	G	17	0	0	0	0					

		REGULAR SEASON					POSTSEASON				
GOALTENDER		GP	MIN	GA	SH	GAA	GP	MIN	GA	SH	GAA
Paul Goodman	(16-10-5)	31	1920	62	4	1.94	2	127	5	0	2.36
Mike Karakas (1–2)	(7-9-1)	17	1050	58	0	3.31					

DETROIT Red Wings   16-26-6   38   5th   Jack Adams

		REGULAR SEASON					POSTSEASON				
PLAYER	POS	GP	G	A	PTS	PIM	GP	G	A	PTS	PIM
Syd Howe	C	46	14	23	37	17	5	2	2	4	2
Ebbie Goodfellow	D	43	11	17	28	31	5	0	2	2	9
Modere Bruneteau	R	48	10	14	24	10	5	3	2	5	0
Alex Motter	C	37	7	12	19	28	5	1	1	2	15
Ken Kilrea	L	40	10	8	18	4	5	1	1	2	0
Cecil Dillon	R	44	7	10	17	12	5	1	0	1	0
Connie Brown	C	36	8	3	11	2	5	2	1	3	0
Gus Giesebrecht	C	30	4	7	11	2					
Carl Liscombe	L	25	2	7	9	4					
Eddie Wares	D	33	2	6	8	19	5	0	0	0	0
Byron McDonald	L	37	1	6	7	2	5	0	2	2	10
Don Deacon	L	18	5	1	6	2					
Joe Fisher	R	34	2	4	6	2	5	1	1	2	0
Sid Abel	C	24	1	5	6	4	5	0	3	3	21
Don Grosso	C	29	2	3	5	11	5	0	0	0	0
Jimmy Orlando	D	48	1	3	4	54	5	0	0	0	15
Jack Keating	L	10	2	0	2	2					
Ralph Bowman	D	11	0	2	2	4					
Jack Stewart	D	48	1	0	1	40	5	0	0	0	4
Tiny Thompson	G	46	0	0	0	0	5	0	0	0	0
Hec Kilrea	L	12	0	0	0	0					
Alvin Jones	D	2	0	0	0	0					
Ronnie Hudson	C	1	0	0	0	0					
Bert Peer	R	1	0	0	0	0					
Claude Bourque (2–2)	G	1	0	0	0	0					
Alfie Moore	G	1	0	0	0	0					

		REGULAR SEASON					POSTSEASON				
GOALTENDER		GP	MIN	GA	SH	GAA	GP	MIN	GA	SH	GAA
Tiny Thompson	(16-24-6)	46	2830	120	3	2.54	5	300	12	0	2.40
Claude Bourque (2–2)	(0-1-0)	1	60	3	0	3.00					
Alfie Moore	(0-1-0)	1	60	3	0	3.00					

NEW YORK 15-29-4 34 6th Mervyn Dutton
Americans

REGULAR SEASON / POSTSEASON

PLAYER	POS	GP	G	A	PTS	PIM	GP	G	A	PTS	PIM
Murray Armstrong	C	47	16	20	36	12	3	0	0	0	0
Tom Anderson	L	48	12	19	31	22	3	1	3	4	0
Charlie Conacher	R	47	10	18	28	41	3	1	1	2	8
Lorne Carr	R	48	8	17	25	17	3	0	0	0	0
John Sorrell	L	48	8	16	24	4	3	0	3	3	2
Harvey Jackson	L	43	12	8	20	10	3	0	1	1	2
Eddie Wiseman (1–2)	R	*31	5	13	18	8					
Reg Smith	R	47	7	8	15	41	3	3	1	4	2
Frank Boll	L	47	5	10	15	18	1	0	0	0	0
Nels Stewart	C	35	6	7	13	6	3	0	0	0	0
Art Chapman	C	26	4	6	10	2	3	1	0	1	0
Johnny Gagnon (2–2)	R	24	4	3	7	0	1	1	0	1	0
Pat Egan	D	10	4	3	7	6	2	0	0	0	4
Eddie Shore (2–2)	D	10	2	3	5	9	3	0	2	2	2
Allan Murray	D	36	1	4	5	10	3	0	0	0	2
Wilf Field	D	45	1	3	4	28	3	0	0	0	0
Jack Tomson	D	12	1	1	2	0					
Elwin Romnes	C	15	0	1	1	0					
Earl Robertson	G	48	0	0	0	0	3	0	0	0	0
Chuck Shannon	D	4	0	0	0	2					
Frank Beisler	D	1	0	0	0	0					

REGULAR SEASON / POSTSEASON

GOALTENDER		GP	MIN	GA	SH	GAA	GP	MIN	GA	SH	GAA
Earl Robertson	(15-**29**-4)	48	2960	**140**	6	2.84	3	180	9	0	3.00

MONTREAL 10-33-5 25 7th Alfred Lepine
Canadiens

REGULAR SEASON

POSTSEASON — no postseason play

PLAYER	POS	GP	G	A	PTS	PIM
Toe Blake	L	48	17	19	36	48
Charlie Sands	C	47	9	20	29	10
Ray Getliffe	L	46	11	12	23	29
Georges Mantha	D	42	9	11	20	6
Louis Trudel	L	47	12	7	19	24
Polly Drouin	L	42	4	11	15	51
Marty Barry	C	30	4	10	14	2
Doug Young	D	47	3	9	12	22
Red Goupile	D	48	2	10	12	48
Paul Haynes	C	23	2	8	10	8
Johnny Gagnon (1–2)	R	10	4	5	9	0
Rod Lorrain	R	41	1	5	6	6
Bill Summerhill	R	13	3	2	5	24
Tony Demers	R	14	2	3	5	2
Earl Robinson	R	11	1	4	5	4
Armand Mondou	L	21	2	2	4	0
Bill Meronek	C	7	2	2	4	0
Walt Buswell	D	46	1	3	4	10

		REGULAR SEASON					*POSTSEASON*
PLAYER	POS	GP	G	A	PTS	PIM	*no postseason play*
Cy Wentworth	D	32	1	3	4	6	
John Doran	D	6	0	3	3	6	
Armand Raymond	D	11	0	1	1	10	
Claude Bourque (1–2)	G	36	0	0	0	0	
Gordie Poirier	C	10	0	0	0	0	
Rhys Thompson	D	7	0	0	0	16	
Wilf Cude	G	7	0	0	0	0	
Mike Karakas (2–2)	G	5	0	0	0	0	
Gus Mancuso	R	2	0	0	0	0	

		REGULAR SEASON				*POSTSEASON*
GOALTENDER		GP	MIN	GA	SH	GAA	*no postseason play*
C. Bourque (1–2)	(9-24-3)	36	2210	120	3	3.26	
Wilf Cude	(1-5-1)	7	415	24	0	3.47	
Mike Karakas (2–2)	(0-4-1)	5	310	18	0	3.48	
Charlie Sands		1	25	5	0	12.00	

TEAM TOTALS

								Per Game			
TEAM	GP	G	A	P	PIM	GA	SH	G	A	PIM	GA
Boston	48	170	227	397	330	98	6	**3.54**	4.73	6.88	2.04
New York (R)	48	136	209	345	**520**	77	8	2.83	4.35	**10.83**	**1.60**
Toronto	48	134	190	324	485	110	4	2.79	3.96	10.10	2.29
Chicago	48	112	160	272	351	120	4	2.33	3.33	7.31	2.50
Detroit	48	90	131	221	250	126	3	1.88	2.73	5.21	2.63
New York (A)	48	106	160	266	236	140	6	2.21	3.33	4.92	2.92
Montreal	48	90	150	240	338	167	3	1.88	3.13	7.04	3.48
	336	838	1227	2065	2510	838	34	2.49	3.65	7.47	2.49

PLAYOFFS

SERIES "A"
New York (R) 4, Boston 0
Boston 4, New York (R) 2
Boston 4, New York (R) 3
New York (R) 1, Boston 0
New York (R) 1, Boston 0
New York (R) 4, Boston 1

NEW YORK (R), 4–2

SERIES "C"
Detroit 2, New York (A) 1 (OT)
New York (A) 5, Detroit 4
Detroit 3, New York (A) 1

TORONTO, 2–0
DETROIT, 2–1

SERIES "B"
Toronto 3, Chicago 2 (OT)
Toronto 2, Chicago 1

TORONTO, 2–0

SERIES "D"
Toronto 2, Detroit 1
Toronto 3, Detroit 1

SERIES "E"
New York (R) 2, Toronto 1 (OT)
New York (R) 6, Toronto 2
Toronto 2, New York (R) 1
Toronto 3, New York (R) 0
New York (R) 2, Toronto 1 (OT)
New York (R) 3, Toronto 2 (OT)

NEW YORK (R) WINS STANLEY CUP, 4-2

ALL-STAR TEAMS

First Team
G — Dave Kerr, N(R)
D — Dit Clapper, BOS
D — Ebbie Goodfellow, DET
C — Milt Schmidt, BOS
R — Bryan Hextall, N(R)
L — Toe Blake, MTL

Second Team
G — Frank Brimsek, BOS
D — Art Coulter, N(R)
D — Earl Seibert, CHI
C — Neil Colville, N(R)
R — Bobby Bauer, BOS
L — Woody Dumart, BOS

INDIVIDUAL TROPHY WINNERS

HART TROPHY (Most Valuable Player): Ebbie Goodfellow, DET
LADY BYNG TROPHY (Gentlemanly Conduct): Bobby Bauer, BOS
VEZINA TROPHY (Best Goaltender): Dave Kerr, N(R)
CALDER MEMORIAL TROPHY (Best Rookie): Kilby MacDonald, N(R)

1940-1941

Boston Bruins

From the late 1920s through the earliest years of the 1940s, one American-based NHL team had enjoyed more success than most — the Boston Bruins. Coming off three straight first-place finishes, the team was determined to continue their winning ways. As the league was about to find out, this version of the Bruin juggernaut would do so in style.

The Bruins entered the NHL in the fall of 1924 as the league's first team based in the United States. Following a moribund last-place, six-win club in the inaugural season, the team rose to fourth the next year, then second in 1926-27. Completing their rise, the Bruins next rattled off four first place finishes in a row, led by a stellar 38-5-1 club in 1929-30 — a team which set a winning percentage mark (.875) that has never been equaled. The team's biggest star during this run was their netminder — Cecil "Tiny" Thompson — who led the NHL in GAA and shutouts several times. Despite this regular season success, Cup triumphs largely eluded Boston, as the team only won once (1928-29) during the string.

After a series of up and down seasons, which included a set of alternating firsts and lasts, the Bruins began another string of regular season championships in 1937-38. Following the first triumph, the team seamlessly switched goalies early in the next campaign, adding Frank "Mr. Zero" Brimsek into the mix. With their new backstop, the team won another crown, which was also the prelude to the team's second Stanley Cup. The following year, with another first-place team, the Bruins' Kraut Line — Milt Schmidt, Woody Dumart and Bobby Bauer — became the first NHL single-team trio to finish in the top three slots of the scoring race.

As the 1940-41 campaign began, Boston looked nothing like a championship caliber club. Meandering through the first few weeks of the schedule, the club lost consistently, slipping below the .500 mark (6-7-3) after a 3–1 loss to the Canadiens on December 21. Turning things around abruptly, the Bruins went on a streak like none seen to date. After that setback in late December, the team refused to lose, as it played its next 23 games (15-0-8) without a loss. Following a 2–0 blanking at the hand of the Rangers, the Bruins closed out the season with an eight-game unbeaten streak, to finish the season with a 27-8-13, 67 point record — three better than Toronto. The other clubs (Detroit, the Rangers, Chicago, Montreal and the Americans) all finished well behind, though all but the latter qualified for the playoffs. Analyzing Boston's last two-thirds of the campaign illustrated a stunning fact. Over the team's final 32 contests, the Bruins went 21-1-10 — a feat unparalleled in the league to date.

Individually, the 1940-41 Bruins were led by scoring champion Bill Cowley (17-45-62), who also collected the most assists, and was helped by Eddie Wiseman (16-24-40) and Bobby Bauer (17-22-39). Goalie Frank Brimsek (2.01, 6) paved the way with the most shutouts, although he was squeezed out of the GAA title by Toronto's Turk Broda (2.00). Other notable efforts on other teams were put forth by the Rangers' Bryan Hextall (26) for most goals and by Detroit's Jimmy Orlando (99) for most penalty minutes.

In the opening round of the playoffs, the Bruins and Leafs staged a memorable series. After Toronto took a three games to two lead, Boston responded with a pair of 2–1 wins to advance. In the other pairings, Chicago bested Montreal, while the Wings did in the Rangers. Then Detroit advanced to the finals, beating the Hawks in two straight — 3–1 and 2–1 — with the latter win coming in overtime. In the finals, the Bruins made quick work of Detroit, defeating the Red Wings 3–2, 2–1, 4–2 and 3–1 to capture their second Cup in three years — the first Cup win in NHL history to be decided with four straight triumphs.

Boston's Eddie Wiseman (6) scored the most playoff goals, while teammate Milt Schmidt (11) garnered the most points. In addition, Detroit's Syd Howe (7) collected the most assists. In net, Brimsek (2.04) edged Broda (2.05), reversing their regular season roles, although both were beaten by the Rangers' Dave Kerr (1.88), who posted the lowest GAA, albeit in only three games.

After their second quartet of first-place finishes in 15 years, the Bruins did not reach such heights for many years. Through the 1940s and 1950s, the team continued to ice playoff-caliber clubs on many occasions, though they never finished first. In the 1960s, the Bruins hit rock-bottom, finishing last for five consecutive seasons before a new messiah led them back to the promised land.

1940-1941

STANDINGS

TEAM	GP	W	L	T	PTS	GF	GA
BOSTON	48	27	8	13	67	168	102
TORONTO	48	28	14	6	62	145	99
DETROIT	48	21	16	11	53	112	102
NEW YORK (R)	48	21	19	8	50	143	125
CHICAGO	48	16	25	7	39	112	139
MONTREAL	48	16	26	6	38	121	147
NEW YORK (A)	48	8	29	11	27	99	186

LEADERS

PLAYER	TM	GP	G	A	PTS	PIM
Bill Cowley	BOS	46	17	45	62	16
Bryan Hextall	N(R)	48	26	18	44	16
Gordie Drillon	TOR	42	23	21	44	2
Syl Apps	TOR	41	20	24	44	6
Lynn Patrick	N(R)	48	20	24	44	12
Syd Howe	DET	48	20	24	44	8
Neil Colville	N(R)	48	14	28	42	28
Eddie Wiseman	BOS	48	16	24	40	10
Bobby Bauer	BOS	48	17	22	39	2
Three tied with					38	

GOALS	
Hextall, N(R)	26
Conacher, BOS	24
Schriner, TOR	24
Drillon, TOR	23
Three tied with	20

ASSISTS	
Cowley, BOS	45
N. Colville, N(R)	28
Taylor, TOR	26
Schmidt, BOS	25
Watson, N(R)	25

GOALTENDER	TM	GP	MIN	GA	SH	GAA
Turk Broda	TOR	48	2970	99	5	2.00
Frank Brimsek	BOS	48	3040	102	6	2.01
Johnny Mowers	DET	48	3040	102	4	2.01
Dave Kerr	N(R)	48	3010	125	2	2.49
Paul Goodman	CHI	21	1320	55	2	2.50
Bert Gardiner	MTL	42	2600	119	2	2.75
Sam LoPresti	CHI	27	1670	84	1	3.02
Earl Robertson	N(A)	36	2260	142	1	3.77

PENALTY MINUTES	
Orlando, DET	99
Goupile, MTL	81
Chamberlain, MTL	75
Cooper, CHI	66
Smith, BOS	61

SHUTOUTS	
Brimsek, BOS	6
Broda, TOR	5
Mowers, DET	4
Three tied with	2

BOSTON 27-8-13 67 1st Cooney Weiland
Bruins

		REGULAR SEASON					POSTSEASON				
PLAYER	POS	GP	G	A	PTS	PIM	GP	G	A	PTS	PIM
Bill Cowley	C	46	17	45	62	16	2	0	0	0	0
Eddie Wiseman	R	48	16	24	40	10	11	6	2	8	0
Bobby Bauer	R	48	17	22	39	2	11	2	2	4	0
Roy Conacher	L	41	24	14	38	7	11	1	5	6	0
Milt Schmidt	C	45	13	25	38	23	11	5	6	11	9
Woody Dumart	L	40	18	15	33	2	11	1	3	4	9
Art Jackson	C	48	17	15	32	10	11	1	3	4	16
Dit Clapper	R	48	8	18	26	24	11	0	5	5	4
Bill Hollett	D	41	9	15	24	23	11	3	4	7	8

		REGULAR SEASON				POSTSEASON				
PLAYER	POS	GP	G	A	PTS	PIM	GP	G	A	PTS	PIM
Herb Cain	L	41	8	10	18	6	11	3	2	5	5
Des Smith	D	48	6	8	14	61	11	0	2	2	12
Terry Reardon	C	34	6	5	11	19	11	2	4	6	6
Jack Crawford	D	45	2	8	10	27	11	0	2	2	7
Mel Hill	R	41	5	4	9	4	8	1	1	2	0
Jack Shewchuk	D	20	2	2	4	8					
Gordie Bruce	L	8	0	1	1	2	2	0	0	0	0
Red Hamill	L	8	0	1	1	0					
Pat McReavy	C	7	0	1	1	2	11	2	2	4	5
Frank Brimsek	G	48	0	0	0	0	11	0	0	0	0

		REGULAR SEASON				POSTSEASON				
GOALTENDER		GP	MIN	GA	SH	GAA	GP	MIN	GA	SH	GAA
Frank Brimsek	(27-8-13)	48	3040	102	6	2.01	11	678	23	1	2.04

TORONTO 28-14-6 62 2nd Hap Day
Maple Leafs

		REGULAR SEASON				POSTSEASON				
PLAYER	POS	GP	G	A	PTS	PIM	GP	G	A	PTS	PIM
Gordie Drillon	R	42	23	21	44	2	7	3	2	5	2
Syl Apps	C	41	20	24	44	6	7	3	2	5	2
David Schriner	L	48	24	14	38	6	7	2	1	3	4
Nick Metz	L	47	14	21	35	10	7	3	4	7	0
Billy Taylor	C	47	9	26	35	15	7	0	3	3	5
Wally Stanowski	D	47	7	14	21	35	7	0	3	3	2
Pete Langelle	C	47	4	15	19	0	7	1	1	2	0
Bucko McDonald	D	31	6	11	17	12	7	2	0	2	2
Hank Goldup	L	26	10	5	15	9	7	0	0	0	0
Reg Hamilton	D	45	3	12	15	59	7	1	2	3	13
Red Heron	C	35	9	5	14	12	7	0	2	2	0
Don Metz	L	31	4	10	14	6	7	1	1	2	2
Gus Marker	R	27	4	5	9	10	7	0	0	0	5
Bob Davidson	L	37	3	6	9	39	7	0	2	2	7
Rudolph Kampman	D	39	1	4	5	53	7	0	0	0	0
Lex Chisholm	C	26	4	0	4	8	3	1	0	1	0
Norm Mann	R	15	0	3	3	2	1	0	0	0	0
Jack Church	D	11	0	1	1	22	5	0	0	0	8
Turk Broda	G	48	0	0	0	0	7	0	0	0	0

		REGULAR SEASON				POSTSEASON				
GOALTENDER		GP	MIN	GA	SH	GAA	GP	MIN	GA	SH	GAA
Turk Broda	(28-14-6)	48	2970	99	5	**2.00**	7	438	15	0	2.05

DETROIT 21-16-11 53 3rd Jack Adams
Red Wings

		REGULAR SEASON				POSTSEASON				
PLAYER	POS	GP	G	A	PTS	PIM	GP	G	A	PTS	PIM
Syd Howe	C	48	20	24	44	8	9	1	7	8	0
Sid Abel	C	47	11	22	33	29	9	2	2	4	2
Modere Bruneteau	R	45	11	17	28	12	9	2	1	3	2

1940–1941

PLAYER	POS	REGULAR SEASON GP	G	A	PTS	PIM	POSTSEASON GP	G	A	PTS	PIM
Eddie Wares	D	42	10	16	26	34	9	0	0	0	0
Alex Motter	C	48	13	12	25	18	9	1	3	4	4
Gus Giesebrecht	C	43	7	18	25	7	9	2	1	3	0
Ebbie Goodfellow	C	47	5	17	22	35	3	0	1	1	9
Carl Liscombe	L	33	10	10	20	0	8	4	3	7	12
Don Grosso	C	45	8	7	15	14	9	1	4	5	0
Joe Fisher	R	27	5	8	13	11	5	1	0	1	6
Jimmy Orlando	D	48	1	10	11	99	9	0	2	2	31
Jack Stewart	D	47	2	6	8	56	9	1	2	3	8
Bill Jennings	R	12	1	5	6	2	9	2	2	4	0
Joe Carveth	R	19	2	1	3	2					
Les Douglas	C	18	1	2	3	2					
Art Herchenratter	L	10	1	2	3	2					
Connie Brown	C	3	1	2	3	0	9	0	2	2	0
Ken Kilrea	L	15	2	0	2	0	5	0	0	0	0
Eddie Bruneteau	R	11	1	1	2	2	3	0	0	0	0
Bob Whitelaw	D	23	0	2	2	2	8	0	0	0	0
Archie Wilder	L	18	0	2	2	2					
Johnny Mowers	G	48	0	0	0	0	9	0	0	0	0
Dick Behling	D	3	0	0	0	0					
Hal Jackson	D	1	0	0	0	0					

GOALTENDER	REGULAR SEASON GP	MIN	GA	SH	GAA	POSTSEASON GP	MIN	GA	SH	GAA
Johnny Mowers (21-16-11)	48	3040	102	4	2.01	9	561	20	0	2.14

NEW YORK Rangers 21-19-8 50 4th Frank Boucher

PLAYER	POS	REGULAR SEASON GP	G	A	PTS	PIM	POSTSEASON GP	G	A	PTS	PIM
Bryan Hextall	R	48	26	18	44	16	3	0	1	1	0
Lynn Patrick	C	48	20	24	44	12	3	1	0	1	14
Neil Colville	C	48	14	28	42	28	3	1	1	2	0
Phil Watson	R	40	11	25	36	49	3	0	2	2	9
Mac Colville	R	47	14	17	31	18	3	1	1	2	2
Clint Smith	C	48	14	11	25	0	3	0	0	0	0
Alex Shibicky	R	41	10	14	24	14	3	1	0	1	2
Babe Pratt	D	47	3	17	20	52	3	1	1	2	6
Alf Pike	L	48	6	13	19	23	3	0	1	1	2
Art Coulter	D	35	5	14	19	42	3	0	0	0	0
Dutch Hiller	L	44	8	10	18	20	3	0	0	0	0
Ott Heller	D	48	2	16	18	42	3	0	1	1	4
Kilby MacDonald	L	47	5	6	11	12	3	1	0	1	0
Muzz Patrick	D	47	2	8	10	21	3	0	0	0	2
Stan Smith	C	8	2	1	3	0					
Herb Foster	L	5	1	0	1	5					
John Polich	R	2	0	1	1	0					
Bill Allum	D	1	0	1	1	0					
Dave Kerr	G	48	0	0	0	0	3	0	0	0	0
Bill Juzda	D	5	0	0	0	2					

194   The National Hockey League, 1917–1967

		REGULAR SEASON				POSTSEASON			
GOALTENDER		GP	MIN	GA	SH	GAA	GP	MIN	GA	SH	GAA
Dave Kerr	(21-19-8)	48	3010	125	2	2.49	3	192	6	0	**1.88**

CHICAGO 16-25-7 39 5th Paul Thompson
Blackhawks

		REGULAR SEASON				POSTSEASON			
PLAYER	POS	GP	G	A	PTS	PIM	GP	G	A	PTS	PIM
Bill Thoms	C	48	13	19	32	4					
George Allen	L	44	14	17	31	22	5	2	2	4	10
Doug Bentley	L	47	8	20	28	12	5	1	1	2	0
Cully Dahlstrom	C	40	11	14	25	6	5	3	3	6	2
John Chad	R	45	7	18	25	16	5	0	0	0	2
Phil Hergesheimer	R	48	8	16	24	9	5	0	0	0	2
Bill Carse	C	32	5	15	20	12	2	0	0	0	0
Earl Seibert	D	46	3	17	20	52	5	0	0	0	12
Bob Carse	L	43	9	9	18	9	5	0	0	0	2
Harold March	R	44	8	9	17	16	4	2	3	5	0
Max Bentley	C	36	7	10	17	6	4	1	3	4	2
Joe Cooper	D	45	5	5	10	66	5	1	0	1	8
Regis Kelly	R	21	5	3	8	7					
Art Wiebe	D	45	3	2	5	28	4	0	0	0	0
Johnny Gottselig	L	5	1	4	5	5					
John Mariucci	D	23	0	5	5	33	5	0	2	2	16
Joe Papike	R	9	2	2	4	2	5	0	2	2	0
Dave MacKay	D	29	3	0	3	26	5	0	1	1	2
Sam LoPresti	G	27	0	0	0	0	5	0	0	0	0
Paul Goodman	G	21	0	0	0	0					
Jack Portland (1-2)	D	5	0	0	0	4					

		REGULAR SEASON				POSTSEASON			
GOALTENDER		GP	MIN	GA	SH	GAA	GP	MIN	GA	SH	GAA
Paul Goodman	(7-10-4)	21	1320	55	2	2.50					
Sam LoPresti	(9-15-3)	27	1670	84	1	3.02	5	343	12	0	2.10

MONTREAL 16-26-6 38 6th Dick Irvin
Canadiens

		REGULAR SEASON				POSTSEASON			
PLAYER	POS	GP	G	A	PTS	PIM	GP	G	A	PTS	PIM
John Quilty	C	48	18	16	34	31	3	0	2	2	0
Joe Benoit	R	45	16	16	32	32	3	4	0	4	2
Toe Blake	L	48	12	20	32	49	3	0	3	3	5
Ray Getliffe	L	39	15	10	25	25	3	1	1	2	0
Murph Chamberlain	C	45	10	15	25	75	3	0	2	2	11
Tony Demers	R	46	13	10	23	17	2	0	0	0	0
Elmer Lach	C	43	7	14	21	16	3	1	0	1	0
Jack Adams	L	42	6	12	18	11	3	0	0	0	0
Charlie Sands	C	43	5	13	18	4	2	1	0	1	0
Polly Drouin	L	21	4	7	11	0	1	0	0	0	0
Ken Reardon	D	34	2	8	10	41	3	0	0	0	4
Red Goupile	D	48	3	6	9	81	2	0	0	0	0
Jack Portland (2-2)	D	42	2	7	9	34	3	0	1	1	2

		REGULAR SEASON					*POSTSEASON*				
PLAYER	POS	GP	G	A	PTS	PIM	GP	G	A	PTS	PIM
Tony Graboski	L	34	4	3	7	12	3	0	0	0	6
Louis Trudel	L	16	2	3	5	2					
Alex Singbush	D	32	0	5	5	15	3	0	0	0	4
Stu Smith	L	3	2	1	3	2	1	0	0	0	0
Peggy O'Neil	R	12	0	3	3	0	3	0	0	0	0
Georges Mantha	D	6	0	1	1	0					
Bert Gardiner	G	42	0	0	0	0	3	0	0	0	0
Paul Haynes	C	7	0	0	0	12					
Paul Bibeault	G	4	0	0	0	0					
Doug Young	D	3	0	0	0	4					
Wilf Cude	G	3	0	0	0	0					

		REGULAR SEASON					*POSTSEASON*				
GOALTENDER		GP	MIN	GA	SH	GAA	GP	MIN	GA	SH	GAA
Bert Gardiner	(13-**23**-6)	42	2600	119	2	2.75	3	214	8	0	2.00
Paul Bibeault	(1-2-0)	4	210	15	0	4.29					
Wilf Cude	(2-1-0)	3	180	13	0	4.33					

NEW YORK 8-29-11 27 7th Mervyn Dutton
Americans

		REGULAR SEASON					*POSTSEASON*
PLAYER	POS	GP	G	A	PTS	PIM	*no postseason play*
Lorne Carr	R	**48**	13	19	32	10	
Frank Boll	L	47	12	14	26	16	
Harvey Jackson	L	46	8	18	26	4	
Murray Armstrong	C	**48**	10	14	24	6	
Charlie Conacher	R	46	7	16	23	32	
Norm Larson	R	**48**	9	9	18	6	
Tom Anderson	L	35	3	12	15	8	
Pat Egan	D	39	4	9	13	51	
Wilf Field	D	36	5	6	11	31	
Ralph Wycherly	L	26	4	5	9	4	
Reg Smith	R	41	2	7	9	4	
Pete Kelly	R	11	3	5	8	2	
John Sorrell	L	30	2	6	8	2	
Bill Benson	C	22	3	4	7	4	
Fred Hunt	R	15	2	5	7	0	
Peter Slobodian	D	41	3	2	5	54	
Peanuts O'Flaherty	R	10	4	0	4	0	
Chuck Corrigan	R	16	2	2	4	2	
Fred Thurier	C	3	2	1	3	0	
Andy Branigan	D	6	1	0	1	5	
Squee Allen	R	6	0	1	1	0	
Earl Robertson	G	36	0	0	0	0	
Charlie Rayner	G	12	0	0	0	0	
Jack Tomson	D	3	0	0	0	0	

		REGULAR SEASON					POSTSEASON
GOALTENDER		GP	MIN	GA	SH	GAA	no postseason play
Andy Branigan		1	7	0	0	0.00	
Charlie Rayner	(2-7-3)	12	773	44	0	3.42	
Earl Robertson	(6-22-8)	36	2260	142	1	3.77	

TEAM TOTALS

								Per Game			
TEAM	GP	G	A	P	PIM	GA	SH	G	A	PIM	GA
Boston	48	168	233	401	246	102	6	3.50	4.85	5.13	2.13
Toronto	48	145	197	342	306	99	5	3.02	4.10	6.38	2.06
Detroit	48	112	184	296	337	102	4	2.33	3.83	7.02	2.13
New York (R)	48	143	224	367	356	125	2	2.98	4.67	7.42	2.60
Chicago	48	112	185	297	335	139	3	2.33	3.85	6.98	2.90
Montreal	48	121	170	291	435	147	2	2.52	3.54	9.06	3.06
New York (A)	48	99	155	254	231	186	1	2.06	3.23	4.81	3.88
	336	900	1348	2248	2246	900	23	2.68	4.01	6.68	2.68

PLAYOFFS

SERIES "A"
Boston 3, Toronto 0
Toronto 5, Boston 3
Toronto 7, Boston 2
Boston 2, Toronto 1
Toronto 2, Boston 1 (OT)
Boston 2, Toronto 1
Boston 2, Toronto 1

BOSTON, 4-3

SERIES "B"
Detroit 2, New York (R) 1 (OT)
New York (R) 3, Detroit 1
Detroit 3, New York (R) 2

DETROIT, 2-1

SERIES "C"
Chicago 2, Montreal 1
Montreal 4, Chicago 3 (OT)
Chicago 3, Montreal 2

CHICAGO, 2-1

SERIES "D"
Detroit 3, Chicago 1
Detroit 2, Chicago 1 (OT)

DETROIT, 2-0

SERIES "E"
Boston 3, Detroit 2
Boston 2, Detroit 1
Boston 4, Detroit 2
Boston 3, Detroit 1

**BOSTON WINS
STANLEY CUP, 4-0**

ALL-STAR TEAMS

First Team
G — Turk Broda, TOR
D — Dit Clapper, BOS
D — Wally Stanowski, TOR
C — Bill Cowley, BOS
R — Bryan Hextall, N(R)
L — David Schriner, TOR

Second Team
G — Frank Brimsek, BOS
D — Ott Heller, N(R)
D — Earl Seibert, CHI
C — Syl Apps, TOR
R — Bobby Bauer, BOS
L — Woody Dumart, BOS

INDIVIDUAL TROPHY WINNERS

HART TROPHY (Most Valuable Player): Bill Cowley, BOS
LADY BYNG TROPHY (Gentlemanly Conduct): Bobby Bauer, BOS
VEZINA TROPHY (Best Goaltender): Turk Broda, TOR
CALDER MEMORIAL TROPHY (Best Rookie): John Quilty, MON

1941-1942
The Hard Way

Since the NHL had instituted a best-of-seven playoff format in 1939, one team had managed to sweep the Cup Finals — the 1941 Bruins. In the 1942, finals the victor also would win four straight. However, unlike the '41 Bruins, this club would do it the hard way.

Before the start of the 1941-42 season, the NHL made one small change. In order to foster a sense of competition, the New York Americans were re-christened the Brooklyn Americans. The idea was to create an interborough rivalry between the Americans and the Rangers, the hockey equivalent of baseball's Giants-Dodgers testy exchanges. Sadly, it did not have the desired effect. For instance, although dubbed "Brooklyn," the Americans still shared the same ice as the Rangers. Also, the Americans were still a woeful club, not a true rival to first-division Rangers in any real sense.

Over the course of the campaign, the Rangers (29-17-2, 60) took home the bunting, finishing three points up on the Leafs and four on the Bruins. Chicago, Detroit and Montreal also finished as playoff qualifiers, while Brooklyn — new moniker notwithstanding — ended last.

The first-place Rangers claimed all of the scoring hardware, as Bryan Hextall earned the most points (56), Lynn Patrick potted the most markers (32) and Phil Watson amassed the most assists (37). Although 25 points behind the leaders, Brooklyn did have its own claim to fame, as Pat Egan finished as the league's toughest player and had the most minutes in the penalty box (124). Between the posts, Boston's Frank Brimsek (2.35) allowed the fewest goals, while Toronto's Turk Broda (6) shut out the most opponents.

In the opening playoff series between the first and second place clubs, Toronto jumped out to a quick lead, winning 3–1 and 4–2. The Rangers won two of the next three games, before Toronto completed the upset with a 3–

2 triumph in the sixth game. Meanwhile, the fifth place Red Wings knocked out the Canadiens in a three game set, while the third place Bruins duplicated the feat against the Blackhawks. Continuing their hot run, the Wings then surprised the Bruins 6–4 and 3–1 to reach the finals.

On the surface, the finals seemed a mismatch. On the one side were the Toronto Maple Leafs, the proud owners of a 57-point season. Facing them were the fifth-place Red Wings, a club that finished six games under .500. Much to the surprise of all, Detroit snatched the first game of the series, 3–2, on Toronto's home ice. Three nights later, the Wings repeated, this time by a 4–2 score. In Detroit for the third game, the Red Wings skated to an easy 5–2 victory, climbing to within one win of the Cup.

Frustrated by Detroit's "dump in" system that throttled Toronto's high-octane offense, Toronto's coach Hap Day unveiled some drastic changes for the fourth game. He benched two of his best players, Gordie Drillon and Bucko McDonald — standouts in the New York series, but clueless against Detroit — replacing them with Bob Goldham and Don Metz. As it turned out, this move would pay huge dividends — but not right away.

When Detroit took a 2–0 lead midway through the fourth game, most thought the series over. But the Leafs battled back. Tying the score by the end of the second stanza, Toronto watched while the Wings retook the lead early in the third. With time running out on their season, Syl Apps scored the tying goal, then helped on the winner as the Leafs squeezed out a 4–3 win. Two nights later, Toronto blasted its way back into the series, as Metz scored a hat trick in a 9–3 blowout. The stunned Red Wings had little to offer in game six, as Johnny Bower posted a 3–0 shutout, pulling the two teams even at three wins apiece.

Over 16,000 fans greeted the two teams on April 18 in Toronto for the deciding game of this epic series. The game was scoreless until the second, when the Wings took a 1–0 lead, but then Toronto's David Schriner took over. First, he scored the equalizer, and later the go-ahead marker in the third. After an insurance tally, the Leafs held on for a 3–1 triumph, capping their remarkable comeback.

The leading playoff scorers — with 14 points apiece — were Toronto's Apps and Detroit's Don Grosso. In addition, the former led the way in assists (9) while the latter scored the most goals (8). In net, Chicago's Sam LoPresti (1.60) posted the lowest GAA.

Although rare, four wins a row to end a best-of-seven series had happened a few years before, when Newark accomplished the feat over Columbus in baseball's Junior World Series. In years to come, the NHL witnessed similar turnarounds. However, none of these events can take away from the thrill the

Leafs experienced in the spring of 1942, when they won four straight, and each while facing elimination.

STANDINGS

TEAM	GP	W	L	T	PTS	GF	GA
NEW YORK	48	29	17	2	60	177	143
TORONTO	48	27	18	3	57	158	136
BOSTON	48	25	17	6	56	160	118
CHICAGO	48	22	23	3	47	145	155
DETROIT	48	19	25	4	42	140	147
MONTREAL	48	18	27	3	39	134	173
BROOKLYN	48	16	29	3	35	133	175

LEADERS

PLAYER	TM	GP	G	A	PTS	PIM
Bryan Hextall	NY	48	24	32	**56**	30
Lynn Patrick	NY	47	**32**	22	54	18
Don Grosso	DET	48	23	30	53	13
Phil Watson	NY	48	15	37	52	58
Sid Abel	DET	48	18	31	49	45
Toe Blake	MTL	48	17	28	45	19
Bill Thoms	CHI	47	15	30	45	4
Gordie Drillon	TOR	48	23	18	41	6
Syl Apps	TOR	38	18	23	41	0
Tom Anderson	BRK	48	12	29	41	54

GOALS	
Patrick, NY	32
Conacher, BOS	24
Hextall, NY	24
Drillon, TOR	23
Grosso, DET	23

ASSISTS	
Watson, NY	37
Hextall, NY	32
Abel, DET	31
Grosso, DET	30
Thoms, CHI	30

GOALTENDER	TM	GP	MIN	GA	SH	GAA
Frank Brimsek	BOS	47	2930	115	3	**2.35**
Turk Broda	TOR	48	**2960**	136	6	2.76
Jim Henry	NY	48	**2960**	143	1	2.90
Johnny Mowers	DET	47	2880	144	5	3.00
Sam LoPresti	CHI	47	2860	**152**	3	3.19
Paul Bibeault	MTL	38	2380	131	1	3.30
Charlie Rayner	BRK	36	2230	129	1	3.47

PENALTY MINUTES	
Egan, BRK	124
Orlando, DET	111
Stewart, DET	93
Reardon, MTL	93
Smith, BOS	70

SHUTOUTS	
Broda, TOR	6
Mowers, DET	5
Brimsek, BOS	3
LoPresti, CHI	3
Three tied with	1

NEW YORK Rangers   29-17-2   60   1st   Frank Boucher

		REGULAR SEASON					POSTSEASON				
PLAYER	POS	GP	G	A	PTS	PIM	GP	G	A	PTS	PIM
Bryan Hextall	R	48	24	32	**56**	30	6	1	1	2	4
Lynn Patrick	C	47	**32**	22	54	18	6	1	0	1	0
Phil Watson	R	48	15	37	52	58	6	1	4	5	8
Alex Shibicky	R	45	20	14	34	16	6	3	2	5	2
Clint Smith	C	47	10	24	34	4	5	0	0	0	0

1941–1942 201

PLAYER	POS	REGULAR SEASON					POSTSEASON				
		GP	G	A	PTS	PIM	GP	G	A	PTS	PIM
Grant Warwick	R	44	16	17	33	36	6	0	1	1	2
Neil Colville	C	48	8	25	33	37	6	0	5	5	6
Mac Colville	R	46	14	16	30	26	6	3	1	4	0
Babe Pratt	D	47	4	24	28	55	6	1	3	4	24
Alf Pike	L	34	8	19	27	16	6	1	0	1	4
Alan Kuntz	L	31	10	11	21	10	6	1	0	1	2
Art Coulter	D	47	1	16	17	31	6	0	1	4	4
Bill Juzda	D	45	4	8	12	29	6	0	1	1	4
Ott Heller	D	35	6	5	11	22	6	0	0	0	0
Hub Macey	L	9	3	5	8	0	1	0	0	0	0
Norm Tustin	L	18	2	4	6	0					
Norm Burns	C	11	0	4	4	2					
Jim Henry	G	48	0	0	0	0	6	0	0	0	0

GOALTENDER		REGULAR SEASON					POSTSEASON				
		GP	MIN	GA	SH	GAA	GP	MIN	GA	SH	GAA
Jim Henry	(29-17-2)	48	2960	143	1	2.90	6	360	13	1	2.17

TORONTO 27-18-3 57 2nd Hap Day
Maple Leafs

PLAYER	POS	REGULAR SEASON					POSTSEASON				
		GP	G	A	PTS	PIM	GP	G	A	PTS	PIM
Gordie Drillon	R	48	23	18	41	6	9	2	3	5	2
Syl Apps	C	38	18	23	41	0	13	5	9	14	2
Billy Taylor	C	48	12	26	38	20	13	2	8	10	4
David Schriner	L	47	20	16	36	21	13	6	3	9	10
Lorne Carr	R	47	16	17	33	4	13	3	2	5	6
Pete Langelle	C	48	10	22	32	9	13	3	3	6	2
Hank Goldup	L	44	12	18	30	13	9	0	0	0	2
Bob Davidson	L	37	6	20	26	39	13	1	2	3	20
John McCreedy	R	47	15	8	23	14	13	4	3	7	6
Bucko McDonald	D	48	2	19	21	24	9	0	1	1	2
Nick Metz	L	30	11	9	20	20	13	4	4	8	12
Rudolph Kampman	D	38	4	7	11	67	13	0	2	2	12
Bob Goldham	D	19	4	7	11	25	13	2	2	4	31
Wally Stanowski	D	24	1	7	8	10	13	2	8	10	2
Don Metz	L	25	2	3	5	8	4	4	3	7	0
Ernie Dickens	D	10	2	2	4	6	13	0	0	0	4
Reg Hamilton	D	22	0	4	4	27					
Jack Church (1–2)	D	27	0	3	3	30					
Turk Broda	G	48	0	0	0	0	13	0	0	0	0
Gaye Stewart	L						1	0	0	0	0

GOALTENDER		REGULAR SEASON					POSTSEASON				
		GP	MIN	GA	SH	GAA	GP	MIN	GA	SH	GAA
Turk Broda	(27-18-3)	48	2960	136	6	2.76	13	780	31	1	2.38

BOSTON Bruins 25-17-6 56 3rd Art Ross

		REGULAR SEASON					POSTSEASON				
PLAYER	POS	GP	G	A	PTS	PIM	GP	G	A	PTS	PIM
Roy Conacher	L	43	24	13	37	12	5	2	1	3	0
Milt Schmidt	C	36	14	21	35	34					
Bobby Bauer	R	36	13	22	35	11					
Eddie Wiseman	R	45	12	22	34	8	5	0	1	1	0
Bill Hollett	D	48	19	14	33	21	5	0	1	1	2
Woody Dumart	L	35	14	15	29	8					
Bill Cowley	C	28	4	23	27	6	5	0	3	3	5
Art Jackson	C	47	6	18	24	25	5	0	1	1	0
Jack McGill	C	13	8	11	19	2	5	4	1	5	6
Herb Cain	L	34	8	10	18	2	5	1	0	1	0
Dutch Hiller (2–2)	L	43	7	10	17	19	5	0	1	1	0
Dit Clapper	R	32	3	12	15	31					
Des Smith	D	48	7	7	14	70	5	1	2	3	2
Harvey Jackson	L	26	5	7	12	18	5	0	1	1	0
Gordie Bruce	L	15	4	8	12	11	5	2	3	5	4
Jack Crawford	D	43	2	9	11	37	5	0	1	1	4
Red Hamill (1–2)	L	9	6	3	9	2					
Lloyd Gronsdahl	R	10	1	2	3	0					
Jack Shewchuk	D	22	2	0	2	14	5	0	1	1	7
Frank Mario	C	9	1	1	2	0					
Clare Martin	D	13	0	1	1	4	5	0	0	0	0
Pat McReavy (1–2)	C	6	0	1	1	0					
Frank Brimsek	G	47	0	0	0	0	5	0	0	0	0
P. Hergesheimer (2–2)	R	3	0	0	0	2					
Cliff Thompson	D	3	0	0	0	2					
Nick Damore	G	1	0	0	0	0					

		REGULAR SEASON					POSTSEASON				
GOALTENDER		GP	MIN	GA	SH	GAA	GP	MIN	GA	SH	GAA
Frank Brimsek	(24-17-6)	47	2930	115	3	**2.35**	5	307	16	0	3.13
Nick Damore	(1-0-0)	1	60	3	0	3.00					

CHICAGO Blackhawks 22-23-3 47 4th Paul Thompson

		REGULAR SEASON					POSTSEASON				
PLAYER	POS	GP	G	A	PTS	PIM	GP	G	A	PTS	PIM
Bill Thoms	C	47	15	30	45	4	3	0	1	1	0
Harold March	R	48	6	26	32	22	3	0	2	2	4
Max Bentley	C	39	13	17	30	2	3	2	0	2	0
Alex Kaleta	L	48	7	21	28	12	3	1	2	3	0
Red Hamill (2–2)	L	34	18	9	27	21	3	0	1	1	0
Bill Carse	C	43	13	14	27	16	3	1	1	2	0
Cully Dahlstrom	C	33	13	14	27	6	3	0	0	0	0
Doug Bentley	L	38	12	14	26	11	3	0	1	1	4
Bob Carse	L	33	7	16	23	10	3	0	2	2	0
Earl Seibert	D	46	7	14	21	52	3	0	0	0	0
George Allen	L	43	7	13	20	31	3	1	1	2	0
Joe Cooper	D	47	6	14	20	58	3	0	2	2	2

1941–1942 203

		REGULAR SEASON				*POSTSEASON*				
PLAYER	*POS*	*GP*	*G*	*A*	*PTS*	*PIM*	*GP*	*G*	*A*	*PTS*	*PIM*
Bill Mosienko	R	12	6	8	14	4	3	2	0	2	0
P. Hergesheimer (1–2)	R	23	3	11	14	2					
John Mariucci	D	47	5	8	13	44	3	0	0	0	0
Art Wiebe	D	43	2	4	6	20	3	0	0	0	0
George Johnston	R	2	2	0	2	0					
Ken Stewart	D	6	1	1	2	2					
Aud Tuten	D	5	1	1	2	10					
Joe Papike	R	9	1	0	1	0					
Sam LoPresti	G	47	0	0	0	0	3	0	0	0	0
Cliff Purpur	R	8	0	0	0	0					
Bill Mitchell	D	1	0	0	0	4					
Bill Dickie	G	1	0	0	0	0					

		REGULAR SEASON				*POSTSEASON*				
GOALTENDER		*GP*	*MIN*	*GA*	*SH*	*GAA*	*GP*	*MIN*	*GA*	*SH*	*GAA*
Bill Dickie	(1-0-0)	1	60	3	0	3.00					
Sam LoPresti	(21-23-3)	47	2860	**152**	3	3.19	3	187	5	**1**	**1.60**

DETROIT 19-25-4 42 5th Jack Adams
Red Wings

		REGULAR SEASON				*POSTSEASON*				
PLAYER	*POS*	*GP*	*G*	*A*	*PTS*	*PIM*	*GP*	*G*	*A*	*PTS*	*PIM*
Don Grosso	C	**48**	23	30	53	13	12	**8**	6	**14**	29
Sid Abel	C	**48**	18	31	49	45	12	4	2	6	8
Eddie Wares	D	43	9	29	38	31	12	1	3	4	22
Syd Howe	C	**48**	16	19	35	6	12	3	5	8	0
Modere Bruneteau	R	**48**	14	19	33	8	12	5	1	6	6
Carl Liscombe	L	47	13	17	30	14	12	6	6	12	2
Gus Giesebrecht	C	34	6	16	22	2	2	0	0	0	0
Joe Carveth	R	29	6	11	17	2	9	4	0	4	0
Adam Brown	L	28	6	9	15	15	10	0	2	2	4
Ken Kilrea	L	21	3	12	15	4					
Pat McReavy (2–2)	C	34	5	8	13	0	11	1	1	2	4
Jack Stewart	D	44	4	7	11	93	12	0	1	1	12
Eddie Bush	D	18	4	6	10	50	11	1	6	7	23
Gerry Brown	L	13	4	4	8	0	12	2	1	3	4
Jimmy Orlando	D	**48**	1	7	8	111	12	0	4	4	**45**
Alex Motter	C	19	2	4	6	20	12	1	3	4	20
Ebbie Goodfellow	C	9	2	2	4	2					
Alvin Jones	D	21	2	1	3	8					
Bill Jennings	R	16	2	1	3	6					
Connie Brown	C	9	0	3	3	4					
Johnny Mowers	G	47	0	1	1	0	12	0	0	0	0
Doug McCaig	D	9	0	1	1	6	2	0	0	0	6
Bob Whitelaw	D	9	0	0	0	0					
Dutch Hiller (1–2)	L	7	0	0	0	0					
Joe Fisher	R	3	0	0	0	0	1	0	0	0	0
Joe Turner	G	1	0	0	0	0					

GOALTENDER		REGULAR SEASON					POSTSEASON				
		GP	MIN	GA	SH	GAA	GP	MIN	GA	SH	GAA
Joe Turner	(0-0-1)	1	70	3	0	2.57					
Johnny Mowers	(19-25-3)	47	2880	144	5	3.00	12	720	**38**	0	3.17

MONTREAL 18-27-3 39 6th Dick Irvin
Canadiens

PLAYER	POS	REGULAR SEASON				POSTSEASON				
		GP	G	A	PTS	PIM	GP	G	A	PTS	PIM
Toe Blake	L	48	17	28	45	19	3	0	3	3	2
Joe Benoit	R	46	20	16	36	27	3	1	0	1	5
Terry Reardon	C	33	17	17	34	14	3	2	2	4	2
Charlie Sands	C	38	11	16	27	6	3	0	1	1	2
Ray Getliffe	L	45	11	15	26	35	3	0	0	0	0
Herb O'Connor	C	36	9	16	25	4	3	0	1	1	0
John Quilty	C	**48**	12	12	24	44	3	0	1	1	0
Pete Morin	L	31	10	12	22	7	1	0	0	0	0
Gerry Heffernan	R	40	5	15	20	15	2	2	1	3	0
Ken Reardon	D	41	3	12	15	93	3	0	0	0	4
Jack Portland	D	46	2	9	11	53	3	0	0	0	0
M. Chamberlain (1–2)	C	26	6	3	9	30					
Tony Demers	R	7	3	4	7	4					
Bunny Dame	L	34	2	5	7	4					
Tony Graboski	L	23	2	5	7	8					
Red Goupile	D	47	1	5	6	51	3	0	0	0	2
Emile Bouchard	D	44	0	6	6	38	3	1	1	2	0
Red Heron (2–2)	C	12	1	1	2	12	3	0	0	0	0
Jimmy Haggarty	L	5	1	1	2	0	3	2	1	3	0
Rod Lorrain	R	4	1	0	1	0					
Peggy O'Neil	R	4	0	1	1	4					
Connie Tudin	C	4	0	1	1	4					
Elmer Lach	C	1	0	1	1	0					
Stu Smith	L	1	0	1	1	0					
Paul Bibeault	G	38	0	0	0	0	3	0	0	0	0
Bert Gardiner	G	10	0	0	0	0					
Leo Lamoureux	D	1	0	0	0	0					

GOALTENDER		REGULAR SEASON					POSTSEASON				
		GP	MIN	GA	SH	GAA	GP	MIN	GA	SH	GAA
Paul Bibeault	(17-19-2)	38	2380	131	1	3.30	3	180	8	**1**	2.67
Bert Gardiner	(1-8-1)	10	620	42	0	4.06					

BROOKLYN 16-29-3 35 7th Mervyn Dutton
Americans

PLAYER	POS	REGULAR SEASON				POSTSEASON
		GP	G	A	PTS	PIM
							no postseason play
Tom Anderson	L	48	12	29	41	54
Mel Hill	R	47	14	23	37	10
Bill Benson	C	45	8	21	29	31
Pat Egan	D	48	8	20	28	**124**
Murray Armstrong	C	45	6	22	28	15

1941–1942

PLAYER	POS	REGULAR SEASON					POSTSEASON
		GP	G	A	PTS	PIM	no postseason play
Frank Boll	L	48	11	15	26	23	
Norm Larson	R	40	16	9	25	6	
Harry Watson	L	47	10	8	18	6	
Kenny Mosdell	C	41	7	9	16	16	
Wilf Field	D	41	6	9	15	23	
M. Chamberlain (2–2)	C	11	6	9	15	16	
Fred Thurier	C	27	7	7	14	4	
Joe Krol	L	24	9	3	12	8	
Bill Summerhill	R	16	5	5	10	18	
Gus Marker	R	17	2	5	7	2	
Nick Knott	D	14	3	1	4	9	
Jack Church (2–2)	D	15	1	3	4	10	
Peanuts O'Flaherty	R	11	1	1	2	0	
Andy Branigan	D	21	0	2	2	26	
Ralph Wycherly	L	2	0	2	2	2	
Regis Kelly	R	8	1	0	1	0	
Red Heron (1–2)	C	11	0	1	1	2	
Pete Kelly	R	7	0	1	1	4	
Hazen McAndrew	D	7	0	1	1	6	
Charlie Rayner	G	36	0	0	0	0	
Earl Robertson	G	12	0	0	0	0	

GOALTENDER		REGULAR SEASON					POSTSEASON
		GP	MIN	GA	SH	GAA	no postseason play
Charlie Rayner	(13-21-2)	36	2230	129	1	3.47	
Earl Robertson	(3-8-1)	12	750	46	0	3.68	

TEAM TOTALS

TEAM	GP	G	A	P	PIM	GA	SH	Per Game			
								G	A	PIM	GA
New York	48	177	283	460	400	143	1	**3.69**	**5.90**	8.33	2.98
Toronto	48	158	229	387	341	136	6	3.29	4.77	7.10	2.83
Boston	48	160	230	390	349	**118**	3	3.33	4.79	7.27	**2.46**
Chicago	48	145	235	380	365	155	3	3.02	4.90	7.60	3.23
Detroit	48	140	237	377	440	147	5	2.92	4.94	9.17	3.06
Montreal	48	134	202	336	**504**	173	1	2.79	4.21	10.50	3.60
Brooklyn	48	133	206	339	425	175	1	2.77	4.29	8.85	3.65
	336	1047	1622	2669	2824	1047	20	3.11	4.82	8.40	3.11

PLAYOFFS

SERIES "A"
Toronto 3, New York 1
Toronto 4, New York 2
New York 3, Toronto 0
Toronto 2, New York 1
New York 3, Toronto 1
Toronto 3, New York 2

TORONTO, 4–2

SERIES "B"
Boston 2, Chicago 1 (OT)
Chicago 4, Boston 0
Boston 3, Chicago 2

BOSTON, 2–1

SERIES "C"
Detroit 2, Montreal 1
Montreal 5, Detroit 0
Detroit 6, Montreal 2

DETROIT, 2-1

SERIES "E"
Detroit 3, Toronto 2
Detroit 4, Toronto 2
Detroit 5, Toronto 2
Toronto 4, Detroit 3
Toronto 9, Detroit 3
Toronto 3, Detroit 0
Toronto 3, Detroit 1

**TORONTO WINS
STANLEY CUP, 4-3**

SERIES "D"
Detroit 6, Boston 4
Detroit 3, Boston 1

DETROIT, 2-0

ALL-STAR TEAMS

First Team
G — Frank Brimsek, BOS
D — Tom Anderson, BRK
D — Earl Seibert, CHI
C — Syl Apps, TOR
R — Bryan Hextall, NY
L — Lynn Patrick, NY

Second Team
G — Turk Broda, TOR
D — Pat Egan, BRK
D — Bucko McDonald, TOR
C — Phil Watson, NY
R — Gordie Drillon, TOR
L — Sid Abel, DET

INDIVIDUAL TROPHY WINNERS

HART TROPHY (Most Valuable Player): Tom Anderson, BRK
LADY BYNG TROPHY (Gentlemanly Conduct): Syl Apps, DET
VEZINA TROPHY (Best Goaltender): Frank Brimsek, BOS
CALDER MEMORIAL TROPHY (Best Rookie): Grant Warwick, NY

1942-1943
"The Puck Goes Inski"

By the onset of the 1942-43 season, the NHL was beginning to feel the effect of the war raging in Europe and the Pacific, as nearly 100 Canadian and American players answered the call of duty. Particularly hard hit were the defending regular season champs, the New York Rangers. Although the club's top trio (Bryan Hextall, Lynn Patrick and Phil Watson) were to return intact, much of the supporting cast would be gone—including their goalie, Jim Henry. Replacing him would not be easy.

Before the season, the Brooklyn Americans, also hard-hit by war-time losses, were disbanded by the NHL, reducing the league to the "Original Six." To maintain balance, the circuit added two games to the schedule, raising each team's slate of contests to 50.

Before the season, the Rangers went shopping for a goalie. Not finding an easy solution, the team turned to a prospect who most recently played for the Swift Current Indians of the Saskatchewan Amateur Hockey Association: Steve Buzinski. Although modest in size (5-8, 140), Buzinski had a style that caught the attention of the Rangers' brass. Unfortunately, his talent couldn't keep up.

Opening the season with Buzinski in net, the Rangers got pounded by the Leafs, 7-2. Things didn't improve for game two, as he allowed an even dozen goals in a humbling loss to the Red Wings. Buzinski, who displayed a flair for the dramatic, feigning an injury if the mood suited him, did manage to pick up his first win (4-3) on November 7 in overtime against the Canadiens, but then coughed up 10 markers to the same team the next night. Finally, after nine games, the 2-6-1 Rangers mercifully put an end to the Buzinski era, cutting the theatrical netminder loose. His coach Frank Boucher—as reported by Brian McFarlane in "Best of the Original Six"—

had this to say: "I thought I'd seen some lousy goaltending during my career in hockey, but all the sieves I'd seen were aces compared to Buzinski."

Shortly after Buzinski's departure, the NHL made a concession to the needs of the war effort. In order for trains to keep their schedules, overtime was dropped — teams tied after regulation would remain so.

Rebounding from their playoff disaster of the previous season, Detroit (25-14-11, 61) skated to the regular season championship, fending off the Bruins by four points. Toronto and Montreal captured the other playoff spots, while Chicago finished one slim point out of the running. As expected, after their dismal start, the Rangers thumped into the cellar. Individually, Chicago's Doug Bentley (33-40-73) scored the most goals and tied the NHL's record for most points. Boston's Bill Cowley did set a new mark for assists (45), while Jimmy Orlando (Detroit) was whistled for the most penalty minutes (99). In net, Detroit's Johnny Mowers (2.47, 6) dominated, allowing over 30 fewer goals than any other goalie, while shutting out more opponents than all of the other netminders combined.

In the new format of the playoffs, first-place Detroit squared off against the third-place Leafs, while the second-place Bruins hosted the fourth-place Canadiens. In the opening rounds, both of the top seeds won — Detroit in six games over Toronto, Boston in five over Montreal, with both series' clinching games decided in overtime. In the finals, Detroit bruised the Bruins 6–2 in the first game, then pulled out a 4–3 victory in game two. After that, the Bruins didn't score as the Wings whitewashed them, 4–0 and 2–0 to wrap up the Cup. A pair of Red Wings — Carl Liscombe and Joe Carveth — each scored a playoff-leading six goals, with the former also claiming the most points (14). Boston's Art Jackson also earned a share of the leadership with six goals of his own, while his teammate Bill Hollett collected the most assists (9). Detroit netminder Johnny Mowers allowed the fewest playoff goals and posted the most shutouts (1.94, 2).

After his demotion, Buzinski served in the armed forces for the duration of the war. Following hostilities, he returned to his previous team, the Swift Current Indians, serving as their goalie until his retirement in 1951.

To be fair to Buzinski, none of the other three goalies employed by the Rangers in 1942-43 exactly sparkled, so their last place finish can't be put squarely on his shoulders. Still, his 5.89 career GAA remains one of the worst of all-time. So, in time-honored hockey tradition, he was given an appropriate moniker — Steve "the Puck goes Inski" Buzinski. His brief career was summed up best by his coach, Frank Boucher, who continues: "Steve was a beautiful little guy. He was earnest and sincere and we all liked him tremendously. There was just one little problem. He couldn't stop a puck worth a damn."

1942-1943

STANDINGS

TEAM	GP	W	L	T	PTS	GF	GA
DETROIT	50	25	14	11	61	169	124
BOSTON	50	24	17	9	57	195	176
TORONTO	50	22	19	9	53	198	159
MONTREAL	50	19	19	12	50	181	191
CHICAGO	50	17	18	15	49	179	180
NEW YORK	50	11	31	8	30	161	253

LEADERS

PLAYER	TM	GP	G	A	PTS	PIM
Doug Bentley	CHI	50	33	40	73	18
Bill Cowley	BOS	48	27	45	72	10
Max Bentley	CHI	47	26	44	70	2
Lynn Patrick	NY	50	22	39	61	28
Lorne Carr	TOR	50	27	33	60	15
Billy Taylor	TOR	50	18	42	60	2
Bryan Hextall	NY	50	27	32	59	28
Toe Blake	MTL	48	23	36	59	26
Elmer Lach	MTL	45	18	40	58	14
Herb O'Connor	MTL	50	15	43	58	2

GOALS	
D. Bentley, CHI	33
Benoit, MTL	30
Hamill, CHI	28
Three tied with	27

ASSISTS	
Cowley, BOS	45
M. Bentley, CHI	44
O'Connor, MTL	43
Taylor, TOR	42
Two tied with	40

GOALTENDER	TM	GP	MIN	GA	SH	GAA
Johnny Mowers	DET	50	3010	124	6	2.47
Turk Broda	TOR	50	3000	159	1	3.18
Frank Brimsek	BOS	50	3000	176	1	3.52
Bert Gardiner	CHI	50	3020	180	1	3.58
Paul Bibeault	MTL	50	3010	191	1	3.81
Jim Franks	NY	23	1380	103	0	4.48

PENALTY MINUTES	
Orlando, DET	99
Hamilton, TOR	68
Stewart, DET	68
Chamberlain, BOS	67
Myles, NY	57

SHUTOUTS	
Mowers, DET	6
Five tied with	1

DETROIT
Red Wings

25-14-11   61   1st   Jack Adams

		REGULAR SEASON					POSTSEASON				
PLAYER	POS	GP	G	A	PTS	PIM	GP	G	A	PTS	PIM
Syd Howe	C	50	20	35	55	10	7	1	2	3	0
Modere Bruneteau	R	50	23	22	45	2	9	5	4	9	0
Carl Liscombe	L	50	19	23	42	19	10	6	8	14	2
Sid Abel	C	49	18	24	42	33	10	5	8	13	4
Joe Carveth	R	43	18	18	36	6	10	6	2	8	4
Don Grosso	C	50	15	17	32	10	10	4	2	6	10
Harry Watson	L	50	13	18	31	10	7	0	0	0	0
Eddie Wares	D	47	12	18	30	10	10	3	3	6	4
Connie Brown	C	23	5	16	21	6					
Les Douglas	C	21	5	8	13	4	10	3	2	5	2
Jack Stewart	D	44	2	9	11	68	10	1	2	3	35
Alex Motter	C	50	6	4	10	42	5	0	1	1	2

		REGULAR SEASON					POSTSEASON				
PLAYER	POS	GP	G	A	PTS	PIM	GP	G	A	PTS	PIM
Jimmy Orlando	D	40	3	4	7	99	10	0	3	3	14
Bill Jennings	R	8	3	3	6	2					
Ebbie Goodfellow	C	11	1	4	5	4					
Hal Jackson	D	4	0	4	4	6	6	0	1	1	4
John Holota	C	12	2	0	2	0					
Cullen Simon	D	34	1	1	2	34	9	0	1	1	4
Bill Quackenbush	D	10	1	1	2	4					
Dick Behling	D	2	1	0	1	2					
Joe Fisher	R	1	1	0	1	0	1	0	0	0	0
Johnny Mowers	G	50	0	0	0	0	10	0	0	0	0
Jud McAtee	L	1	0	0	0	0					
Adam Brown	L						6	1	1	2	2

	REGULAR SEASON					POSTSEASON				
GOALTENDER	GP	MIN	GA	SH	GAA	GP	MIN	GA	SH	GAA
Johnny Mowers (25-14-11)	50	3010	124	6	2.47	10	679	22	2	1.94

BOSTON 24-17-9 57 2nd Art Ross
Bruins

		REGULAR SEASON					POSTSEASON				
PLAYER	POS	GP	G	A	PTS	PIM	GP	G	A	PTS	PIM
Bill Cowley	C	48	27	45	72	10	9	1	7	8	4
Art Jackson	C	50	22	31	53	20	9	6	3	9	7
Frank Boll	L	43	25	27	52	20					
Bill Hollett	D	50	19	25	44	19	9	0	9	9	4
Herb Cain	L	45	18	18	36	19	7	4	2	6	0
Harvey Jackson	L	44	19	15	34	38	9	1	2	3	10
Don Gallinger	C	48	14	20	34	16	9	3	1	4	10
Murph Chamberlain	C	45	9	24	33	67	6	1	1	2	12
Jack Crawford	D	49	5	18	23	24	6	1	1	2	10
Dit Clapper	R	38	5	18	23	12	9	2	3	5	9
Bep Guidolin	L	42	7	15	22	43	9	0	4	4	12
Jackie Schmidt	L	45	6	7	13	6	5	0	0	0	0
Irwin Boyd	R	20	6	5	11	6	5	0	1	1	4
Jack Shewchuk	D	48	2	6	8	50	9	0	0	0	12
William Shill	R	7	4	1	5	4					
Ab DeMarco (2-2)	C	3	4	1	5	0	9	3	0	3	2
Ossie Aubuchon	L	3	3	0	3	0	6	1	0	1	0
Norm Calladine	C	3	0	1	1	0					
Frank Brimsek	G	50	0	0	0	0	9	0	0	0	0
Dutch Hiller	L	3	0	0	0	0					
Bill Anderson	D						1	0	0	0	0

	REGULAR SEASON					POSTSEASON				
GOALTENDER	GP	MIN	GA	SH	GAA	GP	MIN	GA	SH	GAA
Frank Brimsek (24-17-9)	50	3000	176	1	3.52	9	560	33	0	3.54

TORONTO Maple Leafs

22-19-9   53   3rd   Hap Day

PLAYER	POS	REGULAR SEASON					POSTSEASON				
		GP	G	A	PTS	PIM	GP	G	A	PTS	PIM
Lorne Carr	R	50	27	33	60	15	6	1	2	3	0
Billy Taylor	C	50	18	42	60	2	6	2	2	4	0
Gaye Stewart	L	48	24	23	47	20	4	0	2	2	4
Mel Hill	R	49	17	27	44	47	6	3	0	3	0
Syl Apps	C	29	23	17	40	2					
Babe Pratt (2–2)	D	40	12	25	37	44	6	1	2	3	8
David Schriner	L	37	19	17	36	13	4	2	2	4	0
Bob Davidson	L	50	13	23	36	20	6	1	2	3	7
Bud Poile	R	48	16	19	35	24	6	2	4	6	4
Reg Hamilton	D	48	4	17	21	68	6	1	1	2	9
Jack McLean	C	27	9	8	17	33	6	2	2	4	2
Jack Forsey	R	19	7	9	16	10	3	0	1	1	0
Bucko McDonald	D	40	2	11	13	39	6	1	0	1	4
Bobby Copp	D	38	3	9	12	24					
Hank Goldup (1–2)	L	8	1	7	8	4					
Jack Hamilton	C	13	1	6	7	4	6	1	1	2	0
Shep Mayer	R	12	1	2	3	4					
George Boothman	D	9	1	1	2	4					
Rhys Thompson	D	18	0	2	2	22					
Johnny Ingoldsby	R	8	0	1	1	0					
Ab DeMarco (1–2)	C	4	0	1	1	0					
Ted Kennedy	C	2	0	1	1	0					
Turk Broda	G	50	0	0	0	0	6	0	0	0	0
Alvin Jones	D	16	0	0	0	22	6	0	0	0	8
Joe Klukay	L						1	0	0	0	0

GOALTENDER		REGULAR SEASON					POSTSEASON				
		GP	MIN	GA	SH	GAA	GP	MIN	GA	SH	GAA
Turk Broda	(22-**19**-9)	50	3000	159	1	3.18	6	439	20	0	2.73

MONTREAL Canadiens

19-19-12   50   4th   Dick Irvin

PLAYER	POS	REGULAR SEASON					POSTSEASON				
		GP	G	A	PTS	PIM	GP	G	A	PTS	PIM
Toe Blake	L	48	23	36	59	26	5	4	3	7	0
Elmer Lach	C	45	18	40	58	14	5	2	4	6	6
Herb O'Connor	C	50	15	43	58	2	5	4	5	9	0
Joe Benoit	R	49	30	27	57	23	5	1	3	4	4
Gordie Drillon	R	49	28	22	50	14	5	4	2	6	0
Ray Getliffe	L	50	18	28	46	26	5	0	1	1	8
Leo Lamoureux	D	46	2	16	18	53					
Emile Bouchard	D	45	2	16	18	47	5	0	1	1	4
Jack Portland	D	49	3	14	17	52	5	1	2	3	2
Dutch Hiller	L	39	8	6	14	4	5	1	0	1	4
Glen Harmon	D	27	5	9	14	25	5	0	1	1	2
Terry Reardon	C	13	6	6	12	2					
Charlie Sands	C	31	3	9	12	0	2	0	0	0	0
Maurice Richard	R	16	5	6	11	4					

		REGULAR SEASON					*POSTSEASON*				
PLAYER	*POS*	*GP*	*G*	*A*	*PTS*	*PIM*	*GP*	*G*	*A*	*PTS*	*PIM*
Bill Meronek	C	12	3	6	9	0	1	0	0	0	0
Alex Smart	L	8	5	2	7	0					
Tony Demers	R	9	2	5	7	0					
John Mahaffy	C	9	2	5	7	4					
Marcel Dheere	L	11	1	2	3	2	5	0	0	0	6
Red Goupile	D	6	2	0	2	8					
Tony Graboski	L	9	0	2	2	4					
Paul Bibeault	G	50	0	0	0	0	5	0	0	0	0
Charlie Phillips	D	17	0	0	0	6					
Ernie Laforce	D	1	0	0	0	0					
Bobby Lee	C	1	0	0	0	0					
Frank Mailley	D	1	0	0	0	0					
Irv McGibbon	R	1	0	0	0	2					
Gerry Heffernan	R						2	0	0	0	0
Mike McMahon	D						5	0	0	0	14

		REGULAR SEASON				*POSTSEASON*			
GOALTENDER		*GP*	*MIN*	*GA*	*SH*	*GAA*	*GP*	*MIN*	*GA*	*SH*	*GAA*
Paul Bibeault	(19-19-12)	50	3010	191	1	3.81	5	320	18	1	3.00

CHICAGO 17-18-15 49 5th Paul Thompson
Blackhawks

		REGULAR SEASON					*POSTSEASON*
PLAYER	*POS*	*GP*	*G*	*A*	*PTS*	*PIM*	*no postseason play*
Doug Bentley	L	50	33	40	73	18	
Max Bentley	C	47	26	44	70	2	
Red Hamill	L	50	28	16	44	44	
Bill Thoms	C	47	15	28	43	3	
Harold March	R	50	7	29	36	46	
Bob Carse	L	47	10	22	32	6	
Earl Seibert	D	44	5	27	32	48	
Cliff Purpur	R	50	13	16	29	14	
Cully Dahlstrom	C	38	11	13	24	10	
George Allen	L	47	10	14	24	26	
George Johnston	R	30	10	7	17	0	
Aud Tuten	D	34	3	7	10	38	
Johnny Gottselig	L	10	2	6	8	12	
Art Wiebe	D	33	1	7	8	25	
Phil Hergesheimer	R	9	1	3	4	0	
Reg Bentley	L	11	1	2	3	2	
Bill Mosienko	R	2	2	0	2	0	
Bill Mitchell	D	42	1	1	2	47	
Joe Matte	D	12	0	2	2	8	
Leo Carbol	D	6	0	1	1	4	
Bert Gardiner	G	50	0	0	0	0	

		REGULAR SEASON				*POSTSEASON*
GOALTENDER		*GP*	*MIN*	*GA*	*SH*	*GAA*	*no postseason play*
Bert Gardiner	(17-18-**15**)	50	3020	180	1	3.58	

1942-1943 213

NEW YORK   11-31-8   30   6th   Frank Boucher
Rangers
                          REGULAR SEASON   *POSTSEASON*
PLAYER   POS   GP   G   A   PTS PIM   *no postseason play*
Lynn Patrick   C   50 22 39   61   28
Bryan Hextall   R   50 27 32   59   28
Phil Watson   R   46 14 28   42   44
Grant Warwick   R   50 17 18   35   31
Clint Smith   C   47 12 21   33   4
Hank Goldup (2-2)   L   36 11 20   31   33
Bob Kirkpatrick   C   49 12 12   24   6
Alf Pike   L   41   6 16   22   48
Scotty Cameron   C   35   8 11   19   0
Ott Heller   D   45   4 14   18   14
Vic Myles   D   45   6   9   15   57
Gus Mancuso   R   21   6   8   14   13
Joe Shack   L   20   5   9   14   6
Joe Bell   L   15   2   5   7   6
Hub Macey   L   9   3   3   6   0
Gord Davidson   D   35   2   3   5   4
Lin Bend   C   8   3   1   4   2
Bill Gooden   L   12   0   3   3   0
Dudley Garrett   D   23   1   1   2   18
Babe Pratt (1-2)   D   4   0   2   2   6
Bill Warwick   L   1   0   1   1   4
Jim Franks   G   23   0   0   0   0
Bill Beveridge   G   17   0   0   0   0
Steve Buzinski   G   9   0   0   0   0
Vic Lynn   L   1   0   0   0   0
Spence Tatchell   D   1   0   0   0   0
Lionel Bouvrette   G   1   0   0   0   0

                             REGULAR SEASON   *POSTSEASON*
GOALTENDER   GP   MIN   GA   SH   GAA   *no postseason play*
Jim Franks   (5-14-4) 23 1380 103   0 4.48
Bill Beveridge   (4-10-3) 17 1020   89   1 5.24
Steve Buzinski   (2-6-1)   9   560   55   0 5.89
Lionel Bouvrette   (0-1-0)   1   60   6   0 6.00

TEAM TOTALS

								Per Game			
TEAM	GP	G	A	P	PIM	GA	SH	G	A	PIM	GA
Detroit	50	169	229	398	371	**124**	6	3.38	4.58	7.42	**2.48**
Boston	50	195	277	472	364	176	1	3.90	5.54	7.28	3.52
Toronto	50	**198**	**301**	**499**	431	159	1	**3.96**	**6.02**	**8.62**	3.18
Montreal	50	181	300	481	318	191	1	3.62	6.00	6.36	3.82
Chicago	50	179	285	464	361	180	1	3.58	5.70	7.22	3.60
New York	50	161	256	417	352	253	1	3.22	5.12	7.04	5.06
	300	1083	1648	2731	2197	1083	11	3.61	5.49	7.32	3.61

PLAYOFFS

SERIES "A"
Detroit 4, Toronto 2
Toronto 3, Detroit 2 (OT)
Detroit 4, Toronto 2
Toronto 6, Detroit 3
Detroit 4, Toronto 2
Detroit 3, Toronto 2 (OT)

DETROIT, 4-2

SERIES "C"
Detroit 6, Boston 2
Detroit 4, Boston 3
Detroit 4, Boston 0
Detroit 2, Boston 0

DETROIT WINS STANLEY CUP, 4-0

SERIES "B"
Boston 5, Montreal 4 (OT)
Boston 5, Montreal 3
Boston 3, Montreal 2 (OT)
Montreal 4, Boston 0
Boston 5, Montreal 4 (OT)

BOSTON, 4-1

ALL-STAR TEAMS

First Team
G — Johnny Mowers, TOR
D — Earl Seibert, CHI
D — Jack Stewart, DET
C — Bill Cowley, BOS
R — Lorne Carr, TOR
L — Doug Bentley, CHI

Second Team
G — Frank Brimsek, BOS
D — Jack Crawford, BOS
D — Bill Hollett, BOS
C — Syl Apps, TOR
R — Bryan Hextall, NY
L — Lynn Patrick, NY

INDIVIDUAL TROPHY WINNERS

HART TROPHY (Most Valuable Player): Bill Cowley, BOS
LADY BYNG TROPHY (Gentlemanly Conduct): Max Bentley, CHI
VEZINA TROPHY (Best Goaltender): Johnny Mowers, DET
CALDER MEMORIAL TROPHY (Best Rookie): Gaye Stewart, TOR

1943-1944

Disparity

Through its first 25 years, the NHL had seen its share of good team performances, as clubs like the 1929-30 Bruins shredded the league standings. Conversely, the loop had also seen its share of losers, such as the Hamilton clubs of the early 1920s — teams which couldn't seem to buy a break. However, never before had the NHL witnessed extreme highs and lows in the same campaign. For one luckless club, the cause was to be the continuing depletion of its personnel caused by World War II. On the opposite side of the spectrum, a different team was to prosper because it was able to retain the services of its rising star.

Already thin, the New York Rangers — the previous year's doormat — lost a quintet of players to the war effort, including its top offensive star, Lynn Patrick. Looking at these losses, Ranger GM Lester Patrick wanted to suspend operations for the duration, but was talked out of this plan by the other owners. As the season played out, it became apparent that he should have trusted his own instincts.

Conversely, the Montreal Canadiens had a different scenario unfold. Although the team did lose several key players, its budding superstar was allowed to stay put. The previous season, Maurice Richard suffered an ankle injury, curtailing his campaign. It was the lingering effects of this injury which exempted him from the draft. With this offensive cog in the lineup, Montreal's star was on the rise.

Before the season, NHL governors made a significant rule change, adding a center ice red line. This was done to reduce offside calls, leading to more potential offense. As the league was about to witness, offensive play was about to take a sudden upswing, with the red line certainly contributing. However, other factors would also help spur the change in the game.

Bereft of its stars, New York stumbled out of the gate, going winless in its first 15 games. After winning four of its next five, the Rangers dropped another seven straight. After another pair victories in mid-January, the team went winless (0-17-4) for the rest of the campaign. Blame for this shoddy showing fell squarely on the shoulders of the porous defense, which allowed more than ten goals a game on several occasions. One hapless goaltender — Ken McAuley — played all but 20 minutes of the season, finishing with a 6.24 GAA — the worst seen to date.

On the other end of the spectrum, the Canadiens (38-5-7, 83) didn't lose a game until December (11-0-3), finishing the campaign with a 25-point bulge over Detroit. Toronto and Chicago beat out Boston for the final two playoff berths. Despite missing the postseason, Boston's Herb Cain (36-46-82) set a new points record, leading a parade of 30-goal scorers largely fattening up at the Rangers' expense. Leading the group was Chicago's Doug Bentley (38), while teammate Clint Smith (49) set a new assist mark. Montreal enforcer Mike McMahon (98) corralled the most penalty minutes, while goaltenders Bill Durnan (Montreal) and Paul Bibeault (Toronto) posted the best GAA (2.18) and highest shutout totals (5), respectively.

One of the league's 30-goal scorers — Richard — took command in the playoffs. After his team lost the opener to Toronto, he took charge, scoring all five goals in a 5-1 triumph. Three more victories followed, capped by an 11-0 thrashing, as Montreal easily took the opening round. In the other series, Chicago defeated Detroit, dropping only one of the five games. In the finals, Montreal kept its foot to the floor, burying the Blackhawks in the first three games. After Chicago took a 4-1 lead in the fourth game, Montreal's Toe Blake took matters into his own hands. After assisting on three straight markers to draw the Canadiens even, he scored the winner in overtime, giving Montreal the Cup.

Reflecting the impressive 8-1 playoff run, several record-breaking individual postseason accolades were garnered by Canadiens. Richard (12) set a new mark for most goals, mostly set up by his linemates Blake (11) and Elmer Lach (11), who each also set records for most assists. Blake (18) also accumulated the most points — again a new record. In net, Durnan (1.53) allowed the fewest goals.

In hindsight, it would probably have been kinder to let the Rangers sit out the season. The 310 goals they allowed set a record that was not broken for almost 30 years — and then by a team that played a 78-game schedule. In subsequent years, the team took a long time to recover, as they dwelt in the league's cellar for quite a while.

On a positive note, the Canadiens' campaign remains one of the best on

1943–1944

record. Few have topped the club's .830 winning percentage, before or since. This in the end was a far better memory to take away from the 1943-44 season — a season full of hope for some, counterbalancing a season of despair for others.

STANDINGS

TEAM	GP	W	L	T	PTS	GF	GA
MONTREAL	50	38	5	7	83	234	109
DETROIT	50	26	18	6	58	214	177
TORONTO	50	23	23	4	50	214	174
CHICAGO	50	22	23	5	49	178	187
BOSTON	50	19	26	5	43	223	268
NEW YORK	50	6	39	5	17	162	310

LEADERS

PLAYER	TM	GP	G	A	PTS	PIM
Herb Cain	BOS	48	36	46	82	4
Doug Bentley	CHI	50	38	39	77	22
Lorne Carr	TOR	50	36	38	74	9
Carl Liscombe	DET	50	36	37	73	17
Elmer Lach	MTL	48	24	48	72	23
Clint Smith	CHI	50	23	49	72	4
Bill Cowley	BOS	36	30	41	71	12
Bill Mosienko	CHI	50	32	38	70	10
Art Jackson	BOS	49	28	41	69	8
Gus Bodnar	TOR	50	22	40	62	18

GOALS	
D. Bentley, CHI	38
Carr, TOR	36
Cain, BOS	36
Liscombe, DET	36
Bruneteau, DET	35

ASSISTS	
Smith, CHI	49
Lach, MTL	48
Cain, BOS	46
O'Connor, MTL	42
Two tied with	41

GOALTENDER	TM	GP	MIN	GA	SH	GAA
Bill Durnan	MTL	50	3000	109	2	2.18
Paul Bibeault	TOR	29	1740	87	5	3.00
Mike Karakas	CHI	26	1560	79	3	3.04
Connie Dion	DET	26	1560	80	1	3.08
Jim Franks	B-D	18	1080	75	1	4.17
Benny Grant	T-B	21	1260	93	0	4.43
Hec Highton	CHI	24	1440	108	0	4.50
Bert Gardiner	BOS	41	2460	212	1	5.17
Ken McAuley	NY	50	2980	310	0	6.24

PENALTY MINUTES	
McMahon, MTL	98
Egan, D-B	95
Chamberlain, MTL	85
Jackson, DET	76
Dill, NY	66

SHUTOUTS	
Bibeault, TOR	5
Karakas, CHI	3
Durnan, MTL	2
Three Tied with	1

MONTREAL Canadiens   38-5-7   83   1st   Dick Irvin

			REGULAR SEASON				POSTSEASON				
PLAYER	POS	GP	G	A	PTS	PIM	GP	G	A	PTS	PIM
Elmer Lach	C	48	24	48	72	23	9	2	11	13	4
Toe Blake	L	41	26	33	59	10	9	7	11	18	2
Maurice Richard	R	46	32	22	54	45	9	12	5	17	10
Herb O'Connor	C	44	12	42	54	6	8	1	2	3	2

		REGULAR SEASON				*POSTSEASON*				
PLAYER	*POS*	*GP*	*G*	*A*	*PTS*	*PIM*	*GP*	*G*	*A*	*PTS*	*PIM*
Ray Getliffe	L	44	28	25	53	44	9	5	4	9	16
Phil Watson	R	44	17	32	49	61	9	3	5	8	16
Gerry Heffernan	R	43	28	20	48	12	7	1	2	3	8
Murph Chamberlain	C	47	15	32	47	85	9	5	3	8	12
Fern Majeau	C	44	20	18	38	39	1	0	0	0	0
Leo Lamoureux	D	44	8	23	31	32	9	0	3	3	8
Bob Fillion	L	41	7	23	30	14	3	0	0	0	0
Mike McMahon	D	42	7	17	24	98	8	1	2	3	16
Glen Harmon	D	43	5	16	21	36	9	1	2	3	4
Emile Bouchard	D	39	5	14	19	52	9	1	3	4	4
Bill Durnan	G	50	0	0	0	0	9	0	0	0	0
Bobby Walton	C	4	0	0	0	0					
Jean-Claude Campeau	C	2	0	0	0	0					

		REGULAR SEASON				*POSTSEASON*			
GOALTENDER		*GP*	*MIN*	*GA*	*SH*	*GAA*	*GP*	*MIN*	*GA*	*SH*	*GAA*
Bill Durnan	(38-5-7)	50	3000	109	2	2.18	9	549	14	1	1.53

DETROIT 26-18-6 58 2nd Jack Adams
Red Wings

		REGULAR SEASON				*POSTSEASON*				
PLAYER	*POS*	*GP*	*G*	*A*	*PTS*	*PIM*	*GP*	*G*	*A*	*PTS*	*PIM*
Carl Liscombe	L	50	36	37	73	17	5	1	0	1	2
Syd Howe	C	46	32	28	60	6	5	2	2	4	0
Joe Carveth	R	46	21	35	56	6	5	2	1	3	8
Modere Bruneteau	R	39	35	18	53	4	5	1	2	3	2
Don Grosso	C	42	16	31	47	13	5	1	0	1	0
Adam Brown	L	50	24	18	42	56	5	0	0	0	8
Murray Armstrong	C	28	12	22	34	4	5	0	2	2	0
Hal Jackson	D	50	7	12	19	76	5	0	0	0	11
Pat Egan (1–2)	D	23	4	15	19	40					
Bill Hollett (2–2)	D	*27	6	12	18	34	5	0	0	0	6
Bill Quackenbush	D	43	4	14	18	6	2	1	0	1	0
Bill Jennings	R	33	6	11	17	10	4	0	0	0	0
Cullen Simon	D	46	3	7	10	52	5	0	0	0	2
Bill Thomson	C	5	2	2	4	0	2	0	0	0	0
Ken Kilrea	L	14	1	3	4	0	2	0	0	0	0
Dalton Smith	C	10	1	2	3	0					
Hy Buller	D	7	0	3	3	4					
Billy Reay	C	2	2	0	2	0					
Carl Smith	R	7	1	1	2	2					
Jud McAtee	L	1	0	2	2	0					
Bernie Ruelle	L	2	1	0	1	0					
Frank Bennett	L	7	0	1	1	2					
Tony Bukovich	L	3	0	1	1	0					
Eddie Bruneteau	R	2	0	1	1	0					
Roland Rossignol	R	1	0	1	1	0					
Connie Dion	G	26	0	0	0	0	5	0	0	0	0
Jim Franks (2–2)	G	17	0	0	0	0					
John Sherf	L	8	0	0	0	6					

1943–1944

PLAYER	POS	REGULAR SEASON					POSTSEASON
		GP	G	A	PTS	PIM	no postseason play
Gordon Sherritt	D	8	0	0	0	12	
Norm Smith	G	5	0	0	0	0	
Vic Lynn	L	3	0	0	0	4	
Frank Kane	D	2	0	0	0	0	
Rudy Zunich	D	2	0	0	0	2	
Harry Lumley (1–2)	G	2	0	0	0	0	
Lude Check	L	1	0	0	0	0	

GOALTENDER		REGULAR SEASON					POSTSEASON				
		GP	MIN	GA	SH	GAA	GP	MIN	GA	SH	GAA
Norm Smith	(3-1-1)	5	300	15	0	3.00					
Connie Dion	(17-7-2)	26	1560	80	1	3.08	5	300	17	0	3.40
Jim Franks (2–2)	(6-8-3)	17	1020	69	1	4.06					
Harry Lumley (1–2)	(0-2-0)	2	120	13	0	6.50					

TORONTO 23-23-4   50   3rd   Hap Day
Maple Leafs

PLAYER	POS	REGULAR SEASON					POSTSEASON				
		GP	G	A	PTS	PIM	GP	G	A	PTS	PIM
Lorne Carr	R	50	36	38	74	9	5	0	1	1	0
Gus Bodnar	C	50	22	40	62	18	5	0	0	0	0
Babe Pratt	D	50	17	40	57	30	5	0	3	3	4
Ted Kennedy	C	49	26	23	49	2	5	1	1	2	4
Bob Davidson	L	47	19	28	47	21	5	0	0	0	4
Jack Hamilton	C	49	20	17	37	4	5	1	0	1	0
George Boothman	D	49	16	18	34	14	5	2	1	3	2
Elwyn Morris	D	50	12	21	33	22	5	1	2	3	2
Mel Hill	R	17	9	10	19	6					
Jack McLean	C	32	3	15	18	30	3	0	0	0	6
Reg Hamilton	D	39	4	12	16	32	5	1	0	1	8
Tom O'Neill	R	33	8	7	15	29	4	0	0	0	6
Bud Poile	R	11	6	8	14	9					
Don Webster	L	27	7	6	13	28	5	0	0	0	12
Bucko McDonald (1–2)	D	9	2	4	6	8					
Johnny Ingoldsby	R	21	5	0	5	15					
Ross Johnstone	D	18	2	0	2	6	3	0	0	0	0
Frank Dunlap	F	15	0	1	1	2					
Al Carr	L	5	0	1	1	2					
Paul Bibeault	G	29	0	0	0	0	5	0	0	0	0
Benny Grant (1–2)	G	20	0	0	0	0					
Doc Prentice	L	5	0	0	0	4					
Jean Marois	G	1	0	0	0	0					

GOALTENDER		REGULAR SEASON					POSTSEASON				
		GP	MIN	GA	SH	GAA	GP	MIN	GA	SH	GAA
Paul Bibeault	(13-14-2)	29	1740	87	5	3.00	5	600	23	0	5.00
Jean Marois	(1-0-0)	1	60	4	0	4.00					
Benny Grant (1–2)	(9-9-2)	20	1200	83	0	4.15					

CHICAGO Blackhawks 22-23-5 49 4th Paul Thompson

PLAYER	POS	REGULAR SEASON GP	G	A	PTS	PIM	POSTSEASON GP	G	A	PTS	PIM
Doug Bentley	L	50	**38**	39	77	22	9	8	4	12	4
Clint Smith	C	50	23	**49**	72	4	9	4	8	12	0
Bill Mosienko	R	50	32	38	70	10	8	2	2	4	6
Cully Dahlstrom	C	50	20	22	42	8	9	0	4	4	0
George Allen	L	45	17	24	41	36	9	5	4	9	8
Harold March	R	48	10	27	37	16	4	0	0	0	4
Earl Seibert	D	50	8	25	33	20	9	0	2	2	2
Johnny Gottselig	L	45	8	15	23	6	6	1	1	2	2
Cliff Purpur	R	40	9	10	19	13	9	1	1	2	0
Virgil Johnson	D	48	1	8	9	23	9	0	3	3	4
Bill Thoms	C	7	3	5	8	2					
Art Wiebe	D	21	2	4	6	2	8	0	2	2	4
Vic Heyliger	C	26	2	3	5	2					
Don Campbell	L	17	1	3	4	8					
Jacques Toupin	R	8	1	2	3	0	4	0	0	0	0
Jack Dyte	D	27	1	0	1	31					
Joe Cooper	D	13	1	0	1	17	9	1	1	2	18
George Grigor	C	2	1	0	1	0	1	0	0	0	0
Mike Karakas	G	26	0	0	0	0	9	0	0	0	0
Hec Highton	G	24	0	0	0	0					
Gord Buttrey	L	10	0	0	0	0					
Walt Farrant	R	1	0	0	0	0					
Johnny Harms	R	1	0	0	0	0	4	3	0	3	2

GOALTENDER		REGULAR SEASON GP	MIN	GA	SH	GAA	POSTSEASON GP	MIN	GA	SH	GAA
Mike Karakas	(12-9-5)	26	1560	79	3	3.04	9	**549**	24	**1**	**2.62**
Hec Highton	(10-14-0)	24	1440	108	0	4.50					

BOSTON Bruins 19-26-5 43 5th Art Ross

PLAYER	POS	REGULAR SEASON GP	G	A	PTS	PIM
Herb Cain	L	48	36	46	**82**	4
Bill Cowley	C	36	30	41	71	12
Art Jackson	C	49	28	41	69	8
Frank Boll	L	39	19	25	44	2
Norm Calladine	C	49	16	27	43	8
Bep Guidolin	L	47	17	25	42	58
Harvey Jackson	L	42	11	21	32	25
Dit Clapper	R	50	6	25	31	13
Pat Egan (2–2)	D	25	11	13	24	55
Jack Crawford	D	34	4	16	20	8
Don Gallinger	C	23	13	5	18	6
Bill Hollett (1–2)	D	*25	9	7	16	4
Russ Kopak	C	24	7	9	16	0
Alan Rittinger	R	19	3	7	10	0
Aldo Palazzari (1–2)	R	24	6	3	9	4

POSTSEASON
no postseason play

1943–1944 221

PLAYER	POS	REGULAR SEASON					POSTSEASON
		GP	G	A	PTS	PIM	*no postseason play*
Guy Labrie	D	15	2	7	9	2	
Tom Brennan	R	21	2	1	3	2	
Charles Scherza (1–2)	C	9	1	1	2	6	
Ossie Aubuchon (1–2)	L	9	1	0	1	0	
Clarence Schmidt	R	7	1	0	1	2	
Irwin Boyd	R	5	0	1	1	0	
Bert Gardiner	G	41	0	1	1	0	
John Wilkinson	D	9	0	0	0	6	
Maurice Courteau	G	6	0	0	0	0	
Ab DeMarco (1–2)	C	3	0	0	0	0	
Joe Schmidt	D	2	0	0	0	0	
George Abbott	G	1	0	0	0	0	
Jim Franks (1–2)	G	1	0	0	0	0	
Benny Grant (2–2)	G	1	0	0	0	0	

GOALTENDER		REGULAR SEASON					POSTSEASON
		GP	MIN	GA	SH	GAA	*no postseason play*
Bert Gardiner	(17-19-5)	41	2460	212	1	5.17	
Maurice Courteau	(2-4-0)	6	360	33	0	5.50	
Jim Franks (1–2)	(0-1-0)	1	60	6	0	6.00	
George Abbott	(0-1-0)	1	60	7	0	7.00	
Benny Grant (2–2)	(0-1-0)	1	60	10	0	10.00	

NEW YORK   6-39-5   17   6th   Frank Boucher
Rangers

PLAYER	POS	REGULAR SEASON					POSTSEASON
		GP	G	A	PTS	PIM	*no postseason play*
Bryan Hextall	R	50	21	33	54	41	
Dutch Hiller	L	50	18	22	40	15	
Ott Heller	D	50	8	27	35	29	
Ab DeMarco (2–2)	C	36	14	19	33	2	
John Mahaffy	C	28	9	20	29	0	
Ossie Aubuchon (2–2)	L	38	16	12	28	4	
Fern Gauthier	R	33	14	10	24	0	
Jack McDonald	R	43	10	9	19	6	
Bill Gooden	L	41	9	8	17	15	
Grant Warwick	R	18	8	9	17	14	
Kilby MacDonald	L	24	7	9	16	4	
Bob Dill	D	28	6	10	16	66	
Frank Boucher	C	15	4	10	14	2	
Bucko McDonald (2–2)	D	41	5	6	11	14	
Bill Warwick	L	13	3	2	5	12	
Charles Scherza (2–2)	C	5	3	2	5	11	
Don Raleigh	C	15	2	2	4	2	
Gord Davidson	D	16	1	3	4	4	
Roger Leger	D	7	1	2	3	2	
Aldo Palazzari (2–2)	R	11	2	0	2	0	
Tom Dewar	D	9	0	2	2	4	
Charlie Sands	C	9	0	2	2	0	
Hank Damore	C	4	1	0	1	2	

		REGULAR SEASON					*POSTSEASON*
PLAYER	POS	GP	G	A	PTS	PIM	*no postseason play*
Archie Fraser	C	3	0	1	1	0	
Jim Jamieson	D	1	0	1	1	0	
Ken McAuley	G	50	0	0	0	0	
Art Strobel	L	7	0	0	0	0	
Max Labovitch	R	5	0	0	0	4	
Jack Mann	C	3	0	0	0	0	
Tony Demers	R	1	0	0	0	0	
Henry Dyck	C	1	0	0	0	0	
Robert McDonald	R	1	0	0	0	0	
Lloyd Mohns	D	1	0	0	0	0	
Harry Lumley (2–2)	G	1	0	0	0	0	

		REGULAR SEASON				*POSTSEASON*
GOALTENDER		GP	MIN	GA	SH	GAA	*no postseason play*
Harry Lumley	(2–2)	1	20	0	0	0.00	
Ken McAuley	(6-39-5)	50	2980	310	0	6.24	

TEAM TOTALS

								Per Game			
TEAM	GP	G	A	P	PIM	GA	SH	G	A	PIM	GA
Montreal	50	234	365	599	557	109	2	4.68	7.30	11.14	2.18
Detroit	50	214	277	491	374	177	2	4.28	5.54	7.48	3.54
Toronto	50	214	289	503	303	174	5	4.28	5.78	6.06	3.48
Chicago	50	178	274	452	240	187	3	3.56	5.48	4.80	3.74
Boston	50	223	321	544	207	268	1	4.46	6.42	4.07	5.36
New York	50	162	221	383	253	310	0	3.24	4.42	5.06	6.20
	300	1225	1747	2972	1934	1225	13	4.08	5.82	6.45	4.08

PLAYOFFS

SERIES "A"
Toronto 3, Montreal 1
Montreal 5, Toronto 1
Montreal 2, Toronto 1
Montreal 4, Toronto 1
Montreal 11, Toronto 0

MONTREAL, 4–1

SERIES "B"
Chicago 2, Detroit 1
Detroit 4, Chicago 1
Chicago 2, Detroit 0
Chicago 7, Detroit 1
Chicago 5, Detroit 2

CHICAGO, 4–1

SERIES "C"
Montreal 5, Chicago 1
Montreal 3, Chicago 1
Montreal 3, Chicago 2
Montreal 5, Chicago 4 (OT)

**MONTREAL WINS
STANLEY CUP, 4–0**

ALL-STAR TEAMS

First Team
G — Bill Durnan, MTL
D — Babe Pratt, TOR
First Team
D — Earl Seibert, CHI
C — Bill Cowley, BOS
R — Lorne Carr, TOR
L — Doug Bentley, CHI

Second Team
G — Paul Bibeault, TOR
D — Dit Clapper, BOS
Second Team
D — Emile Bouchard, MTL
C — Elmer Lach, MTL
R — Maurice Richard, MTL
L — Herb Cain, BOS

INDIVIDUAL TROPHY WINNERS

HART TROPHY (Most Valuable Player): Babe Pratt, TOR
LADY BYNG TROPHY (Gentlemanly Conduct): Clint Smith, CHI
VEZINA TROPHY (Best Goaltender): Bill Durnan, MTL
CALDER MEMORIAL TROPHY (Best Rookie): Gus Bodnar, TOR

1944-1945
Maurice Richard

In the NHL's first season — 1917-18 — Montreal's Joe Malone set the gold standard of goal scoring, netting 44 during the course of the season. Since then, only one player — Cooney Weiland with 43 in 1929-30 — had come close to the mark. However, that was soon to change, as another Canadien, who had blazed a goal-scoring trail through the playoffs the year before, was about to come into his own.

Maurice Richard, a Montreal native, joined the Canadiens during the 1942-43 season at the age of 21. In a campaign curtailed by an ankle injury, he netted five goals in 16 games. The following year, Richard joined the NHL's scoring elite, as he connected 32 times to lead his team. In the playoffs, he hit full stride, blasting in a record 12 goals, including five in one game. As it would turn out, this would be a mere tune-up for the barrage to come.

During the course of the 1944-45 season, Richard lit the lamp with startling frequency. For instance, on December 28, he scored five times, while adding three assists to set a single-game record. In early March, Richard passed Malone to claim the single-season record. But, there was one more milestone to conquer. Obsessed with scoring a goal a game, Richard's total stood at 49 entering his team's final — and 50th — game. In typically dramatic fashion, he waited nearly to the final instant to make good. The opposing goaltender that night, Boston's Harvey Bennett — as told by Brian McFarlane — relates the tale: "Elmer [Lach] knocked me on my ass, and when I was down and out, *bang*, Richard whipped it into the net." The time was 17:45 of the third period. Heroics like this, mostly caused by his frenetic mode of play, caused hockey writers to give him a nickname — the Rocket.

With this kind of offensive firepower, Montreal (38-8-4, 80) waltzed to the regular season crown by 13 points over Detroit. Toronto finished in the middle of the pack, well ahead of Boston, which scrambled to the final playoff spot over Chicago and New York. Despite his goal-scoring prowess, Richard finished second in the overall scoring race as his linemate, Lach (26-54-80) claimed the title behind a record-setting assist total. Boston's Pat Egan (86) was whistled for the most infractions, while Montreal goaltender Bill Durnan (2.42) ended with the lowest GAA. In addition, Toronto's Frank McCool and Chicago's Mike Karakas, each posted four shutouts.

In the first round of the playoffs, the Canadiens were surprised by the Leafs, falling behind in the series, three games to one. In the next contest, Richard's four scores spurred Montreal to a 10-3 triumph, but Toronto closed them out two nights later with a 3-2 win. In the other semi-final matchup, it took Detroit a full seven games to outlast the pesky Bruins as the Red Wings prevailed in the deciding game, 5-3.

In the finals, in an eerie mirror-like replay of 1942, Toronto took a commanding lead, shutting out Detroit 1-0, 2-0 and 1-0. Then, the Wings answered with three wins of their own — 5-3, 2-0 and 1-0. However, Detroit couldn't finish the job, as the Leafs rose off the mat in the final game, 2-1, to claim the Cup.

Individually, Toronto's Ted Kennedy (7) scored the most goals, edging Richard by one, though the Montreal star played only one series. The top overall scorer was Detroit's Joe Carveth (11), who also contributed the most assists (6). In net, Detroit's Harry Lumley (2.14) allowed the fewest goals, although McCool (Toronto) earned a league-best four shutouts.

After his record-setting campaign, Richard continued to light a fire under the NHL until the early 1960s. Although he never reached the 50-goal level again, he led the league in goals another four times, and was named to 15 consecutive All-Star teams. According to his contemporaries, Richard was never overly concerned with the "assist" column on the scoring ledger, so he never led the league in overall scoring. Upon his retirement following the 1959-60 season, he had scored 544 goals, the most in history to that date. The next year, he was quickly ushered into Hockey's Hall of Fame.

In more recent years, many other players have notched 50-goal seasons, with a few accomplishing the feat in 50 games or less. However, it is probably safe to say that none have done so with the sheer energy and competitive fire of the Rocket. So, to honor one of hockey's greats, the NHL unveiled a new trophy at the beginning of the 21st century. The league's top goal scorer is now given the Maurice Richard Trophy, memorializing hockey's legendary scoring phenom.

STANDINGS

TEAM	GP	W	L	T	PTS	GF	GA
MONTREAL	50	38	8	4	80	228	121
DETROIT	50	31	14	5	67	218	161
TORONTO	50	24	22	4	52	183	161
BOSTON	50	16	30	4	36	179	219
CHICAGO	50	13	30	7	33	141	194
NEW YORK	50	11	29	10	32	154	247

LEADERS

PLAYER	TM	GP	G	A	PTS	PIM
Elmer Lach	MTL	50	26	54	80	37
Maurice Richard	MTL	50	50	23	73	46
Toe Blake	MTL	49	29	38	67	25
Bill Cowley	BOS	49	25	40	65	12
Ted Kennedy	TOR	49	29	25	54	14
Bill Mosienko	CHI	50	28	26	54	0
Joe Carveth	DET	50	26	28	54	6
Ab DeMarco	NY	50	24	30	54	10
Clint Smith	CHI	50	23	31	54	0
Syd Howe	DET	46	17	36	53	6

GOALS	
Richard, MTL	50
Cain, BOS	32
Blake, MTL	29
Kennedy, TOR	29
Mosienko, CHI	28

ASSISTS	
Lach, MTL	54
Cowley, BOS	40
Blake, MTL	38
Howe, DET	36
Bodnar, TOR	36

GOALTENDER	TM	GP	MIN	GA	SH	GAA
Bill Durnan	MTL	50	3000	121	1	2.42
Frank McCool	TOR	50	3000	161	4	3.22
Harry Lumley	DET	37	2220	119	1	3.22
Mike Karakas	CHI	48	2880	187	4	3.90
Harvey Bennett	BOS	25	1470	103	0	4.20
Paul Bibeault	BOS	26	1530	116	0	4.55
Ken McAuley	NY	46	2660	227	1	4.93

PENALTY MINUTES	
Egan, BOS	86
Dill, NY	69
Lamoureux, MTL	58
Cooper, CHI	50
Davidson, TOR	49

SHUTOUTS	
McCool, TOR	4
Karakas, CHI	4
Durnan, MTL	1
Lumley, DET	1
McAuley, NY	1

MONTREAL Canadiens   38-8-4   80   1st   Dick Irvin

		REGULAR SEASON					POSTSEASON				
PLAYER	POS	GP	G	A	PTS	PIM	GP	G	A	PTS	PIM
Elmer Lach	C	50	26	54	80	37	6	4	4	8	2
Maurice Richard	R	50	50	23	73	46	6	6	2	8	10
Toe Blake	L	49	29	38	67	25	6	0	2	2	5
Herb O'Connor	C	50	21	23	44	2	2	0	0	0	0
Dutch Hiller	L	48	20	16	36	20	6	1	1	2	0
Emile Bouchard	D	50	11	23	34	34	6	3	4	7	4
Fern Gauthier	R	50	18	13	31	23	4	0	0	0	0
Leo Lamoureux	C	49	2	22	24	58	6	1	1	2	2
Ray Getliffe	C	41	16	7	23	34	6	0	1	1	2

1944–1945

		REGULAR SEASON					POSTSEASON				
PLAYER	POS	GP	G	A	PTS	PIM	GP	G	A	PTS	PIM
Kenny Mosdell	C	31	12	6	18	16					
Bob Fillion	R	31	6	8	14	12	1	3	0	3	0
Murph Chamberlain	L	32	2	12	14	38	6	1	1	2	10
Glen Harmon	D	42	5	8	13	41	6	1	0	1	2
Frank Eddolls	D	43	5	8	13	20	3	0	0	0	0
Fern Majeau	C	12	2	6	8	4					
Roland Rossignol	R	5	2	2	4	2	1	0	0	0	2
Wilf Field (1–2)	D	9	1	0	1	10					
Nil Tremblay	C	1	0	1	1	0	2	0	0	0	0
Rosario Joanette	C	2	0	1	1	4					
Bill Durnan	G	50	0	0	0	0	6	0	0	0	0
Eddie Emberg	C						2	1	0	1	0
John Mahaffy	C						1	0	1	1	0
Frank Stahan	D						3	0	1	1	2

		REGULAR SEASON					POSTSEASON				
GOALTENDER		GP	MIN	GA	SH	GAA	GP	MIN	GA	SH	GAA
Bill Durnan	(38-8-4)	50	3000	121	1	2.42	6	373	15	0	2.41

DETROIT   31-14-5   67   2nd   Jack Adams
Red Wings

		REGULAR SEASON					POSTSEASON				
PLAYER	POS	GP	G	A	PTS	PIM	GP	G	A	PTS	PIM
Joe Carveth	R	50	26	28	54	6	14	5	6	11	2
Syd Howe	C	46	17	36	53	6	7	0	0	0	2
Modere Bruneteau	R	43	23	24	47	6	14	3	2	5	2
Bill Hollett	D	50	20	21	41	39	14	3	4	7	6
Steve Wojciechowski	R	49	19	20	39	17	6	0	1	1	0
Murray Armstrong	C	50	15	24	39	11	14	4	2	6	2
Carl Liscombe	L	42	23	9	32	18	14	4	2	6	0
Jud McAtee	L	44	15	11	26	6	14	2	1	3	0
Eddie Bruneteau	R	42	12	13	25	6	14	5	2	7	0
Ted Lindsay	L	45	17	6	23	43	14	2	0	2	6
Bill Quackenbush	D	50	7	14	21	10	14	0	2	2	2
Don Grosso (1–2)	L	20	6	10	16	6					
Earl Seibert (2–2)	D	25	5	9	14	10	14	2	1	3	4
Hal Jackson	D	50	5	6	11	45	14	1	1	2	10
Tony Bukovich	L	14	7	2	9	6	6	0	1	1	0
Byron McDonald (1–2)	F	3	1	1	2	0					
Larry Thibeault	L	4	0	2	2	2					
Cullen Simon (1–2)	D	21	0	2	2	26					
Norm Smith	G	1	0	0	0	0					
Billy Reay	C	2	0	0	0	0					
Hy Buller	D	2	0	0	0	0					
Connie Dion	G	12	0	0	0	0					
Harry Lumley	G	37	0	0	0	0	14	0	0	0	0
Cliff Purpur (2–2)	R						7	0	1	1	4
Gerry Couture	R						2	0	0	0	0

		REGULAR SEASON					POSTSEASON				
GOALTENDER		GP	MIN	GA	SH	GAA	GP	MIN	GA	SH	GAA
Norm Smith	(1-0-0)	1	60	3	0	3.00					
Harry Lumley	(24-10-3)	37	2220	119	1	3.22	14	871	31	2	2.14
Connie Dion	(6-4-2)	12	720	39	0	3.25					

TORONTO 24-22-4 52 3rd Hap Day
Maple Leafs

		REGULAR SEASON					POSTSEASON				
PLAYER	POS	GP	G	A	PTS	PIM	GP	G	A	PTS	PIM
Ted Kennedy	C	49	29	25	54	14	13	7	2	9	2
Lorne Carr	R	47	21	25	46	7	13	2	2	4	5
Gus Bodnar	C	49	8	36	44	18	13	3	1	4	4
Babe Pratt	D	50	18	23	41	39	13	2	4	6	8
David Schriner	L	26	22	15	37	10	13	3	1	4	4
Nick Metz	L	50	22	13	35	26	7	1	1	2	2
Mel Hill	R	45	18	17	35	14	13	2	3	5	6
Bob Davidson	L	50	17	18	35	49	13	1	2	3	2
Art Jackson (2-2)	C	31	9	13	22	6	8	0	0	0	0
Reg Hamilton	D	50	3	12	15	41	13	0	0	0	6
Wally Stanowski	D	34	2	9	11	16	13	0	1	1	5
Pete Backor	D	36	4	5	9	6					
Ross Johnstone	D	24	3	4	7	8					
Tom O'Neill	R	33	2	5	7	24					
John McCreedy	R	17	2	4	6	14	8	0	0	0	0
Bill Ezinicki	D	8	1	4	5	17					
Jack McLean	F	8	2	1	3	13	4	0	0	0	0
Elwyn Morris	D	29	0	2	2	18	13	3	0	3	14
Frank McCool	G	50	0	0	0	0	13	0	0	0	0
Don Metz	R						11	0	1	1	4

		REGULAR SEASON					POSTSEASON				
GOALTENDER		GP	MIN	GA	SH	GAA	GP	MIN	GA	SH	GAA
Frank McCool	(24-22-4)	50	3000	161	4	3.22	13	807	30	4	2.23

BOSTON 16-30-4 36 4th Art Ross
Bruins

		REGULAR SEASON					POSTSEASON				
PLAYER	POS	GP	G	A	PTS	PIM	GP	G	A	PTS	PIM
Bill Cowley	C	49	25	40	65	12	7	3	3	6	0
Herb Cain	L	50	32	13	45	16	7	5	2	7	0
Kenny Smith	L	49	20	14	34	2	7	3	4	7	0
Bill Jennings	R	39	20	13	33	25	7	2	2	4	6
Frank Mario	R	44	8	18	26	24					
Armand Gaudreault	L	44	15	9	24	27	7	0	2	2	8
Bill Cupolo	R	47	11	13	24	10	7	1	2	3	0
Jack Crawford	D	40	5	19	24	10	7	0	5	5	0
Dit Clapper	D	46	8	14	22	16	7	0	0	0	0
Pat Egan	D	48	7	15	22	86	7	2	0	2	6
Paul Gladu	C	40	6	14	20	2	7	2	2	4	0
Gino Rozzini	C	31	5	10	15	20	6	1	2	3	6
Art Jackson (1-2)	C	19	5	8	13	10					

1944-1945

		REGULAR SEASON					POSTSEASON				
PLAYER	POS	GP	G	A	PTS	PIM	GP	G	A	PTS	PIM
Jack Shewchuk	D	47	1	7	8	31					
Jack McGill	C	14	4	2	6	0	7	3	3	6	0
Bill Thoms (2-2)	C	17	4	2	6	0	1	0	0	0	2
Norm Calladine	C	11	3	1	4	0					
Tom Brennan	R	1	0	1	1	0					
Murray Henderson	D	5	0	1	1	4	7	0	1	1	2
Fern Flaman	D	1	0	0	0	0					
Marcel Fillion	L	1	0	0	0	0					
Pete Leswick	F	2	0	0	0	0					
Harvey Bennett	G	24	0	0	0	0					
Paul Bibeault	G	26	0	0	0	0	7	0	0	0	0

		REGULAR SEASON					POSTSEASON				
GOALTENDER		GP	MIN	GA	SH	GAA	GP	MIN	GA	SH	GAA
Harvey Bennett	(10-12-2)	25	1470	103	0	4.20					
Paul Bibeault	(6-18-2)	26	1530	116	0	4.55	7	437	22	0	3.02

CHICAGO 13-30-7 33 5th Paul Thompson
Blackhawks Johnny Gottselig

		REGULAR SEASON					POSTSEASON
PLAYER	POS	GP	G	A	PTS	PIM	*no postseason play*
Bill Mosienko	R	50	28	26	54	0	
Clint Smith	C	50	23	31	54	0	
Pete Horeck	L	50	20	16	36	44	
Joe Cooper	D	50	4	17	21	50	
Byron McDonald (2-2)	C	26	6	13	19	0	
Cully Dahlstrom	C	40	6	13	19	0	
Don Grosso (2-2)	L	21	9	6	15	4	
Earl Seibert (1-2)	D	22	7	8	15	13	
Russ Brayshaw	L	43	5	9	14	14	
Harold March	R	38	5	5	10	12	
Johnny Harms	R	43	5	5	10	21	
Harvey Fraser	C	21	5	4	9	0	
Cliff Purpur (1-2)	R	21	2	7	9	11	
Lude Check	L	26	6	2	8	4	
Bill Thoms (1-2)	C	21	2	6	8	8	
Wilf Field (2-2)	D	39	3	4	7	22	
Bill Mitchell	D	40	3	4	7	16	
Les Ramsay	L	11	2	2	4	2	
Cullen Simon (2-2)	D	*29	0	1	1	9	
Joe Papike	R	2	0	1	1	2	
Virgil Johnson	D	2	0	1	1	2	
Mike Karakas	G	48	0	1	1	0	
Johnny Gottselig	L	1	0	0	0	0	
Martin Zoborosky	D	1	0	0	0	2	
Doug Stevenson (2-2)	G	2	0	0	0	0	
Joe Bretto	D	3	0	0	0	4	

230 The National Hockey League, 1917–1967

		REGULAR SEASON					POSTSEASON
GOALTENDER		GP	MIN	GA	SH	GAA	*no postseason play*
Doug Stevenson (2–2)	(1-1-0)	2	120	7	0	3.50	
Mike Karakas	(12-**29**-7)	48	2880	187	4	3.90	

NEW YORK Rangers 11-29-10 32 6th Frank Boucher

		REGULAR SEASON					POSTSEASON
PLAYER	POS	GP	G	A	PTS	PIM	*no postseason play*
Ab DeMarco	C	**50**	24	30	54	10	
Grant Warwick	R	42	20	22	42	25	
Hank Goldup	L	48	17	25	42	25	
Fred Thurier	C	**50**	16	19	35	14	
Fred Hunt	R	44	13	9	22	6	
Joe Shack	L	**50**	4	18	22	14	
Walt Atanas	R	49	13	8	21	40	
Phil Watson	C	45	11	8	19	24	
Ott Heller	D	45	7	12	19	26	
Kilby MacDonald	C	36	9	6	15	12	
Bob Dill	D	48	9	5	14	69	
Bucko McDonald	D	40	2	9	11	0	
Jack Mann	L	6	3	4	7	0	
Bill Moe	D	35	2	4	6	14	
Charles Scherza	C	22	2	3	5	18	
Guy Labrie	D	27	2	2	4	14	
Neil Colville	C	4	0	1	1	2	
Alex Ritson	C	1	0	0	0	0	
Len Wharton	D	1	0	0	0	0	
Jim Drummond	D	2	0	0	0	0	
Doug Stevenson (1–2)	G	4	0	0	0	0	
Hal Cooper	R	8	0	0	0	2	
Ken McAuley	G	46	0	0	0	0	

		REGULAR SEASON					POSTSEASON
GOALTENDER		GP	MIN	GA	SH	GAA	*no postseason play*
Ken McAuley	(11-25-**10**)	46	2660	**227**	1	4.93	
Doug Stevenson (1–2)	(0-4-0)	4	240	20	0	5.00	

TEAM TOTALS

								Per Game			
TEAM	GP	G	A	P	PIM	GA	SH	G	A	PIM	GA
Montreal	50	**228**	271	**499**	426	121	1	**4.56**	5.42	8.52	2.42
Detroit	50	218	238	456	285	161	1	4.36	4.76	5.70	3.22
Toronto	50	183	231	414	337	161	4	3.66	4.62	6.74	3.22
Boston	50	179	214	393	295	219	0	3.58	4.28	5.90	4.38
Chicago	50	141	181	322	250	194	4	2.82	3.62	5.00	3.88
New York	50	154	185	339	315	247	1	3.08	3.70	6.30	4.94
	300	1103	1320	2423	1908	1103	11	3.68	4.40	6.36	3.68

PLAYOFFS

SERIES "A"
Toronto 1, Montreal 0
Toronto 3, Montreal 2
Montreal 4, Toronto 1
Toronto 4, Montreal 3 (OT)
Montreal 10, Toronto 3
Toronto 3, Montreal 2

TORONTO, 4–2

SERIES "B"
Boston 4, Detroit 3
Boston 4, Detroit 2
Detroit 3, Boston 2
Detroit 3, Boston 2
Detroit 3, Boston 2 (OT)
Boston 5, Detroit 3
Detroit 5, Boston 3

DETROIT, 4–3

SERIES "C"
Toronto 1, Detroit 0
Toronto 2, Detroit 0
Toronto 1, Detroit 0
Detroit 5, Toronto 3
Detroit 2, Toronto 0
Detroit 1, Toronto 0 (OT)
Toronto 2, Detroit 1

TORONTO WINS STANLEY CUP, 4–3

ALL-STAR TEAMS

First Team
G — Bill Durnan, MTL
D — Emile Bouchard, MTL
D — Bill Hollett, DET
C — Elmer Lach, MTL
R — Maurice Richard, MTL
L — Toe Blake, MTL

Second Team
G — Mike Karakas, CHI
D — Glen Harmon, MTL
D — Babe Pratt, TOR
C — Bill Cowley, BOS
R — Bill Mosienko, CHI
L — Syd Howe, DET

INDIVIDUAL TROPHY WINNERS

HART TROPHY (Most Valuable Player): Elmer Lach, MTL
LADY BYNG TROPHY (Gentlemanly Conduct): Bill Mosienko, CHI
VEZINA TROPHY (Best Goaltender): Bill Durnan, MTL
CALDER TROPHY (Best Rookie): Frank McCool, TOR

1945-1946
Nerves

By the end of the 1944-45 season, Toronto netminder Frank McCool was on top of the hockey world. Not only had he just won hockey's prestigious Calder Trophy as the top rookie, he had led his team to the Cup. Yet, by the end of the upcoming season, he would be out of the NHL. In this case, it wasn't an injury that caused McCool's demise. Instead, it was a bad case of nerves.

In all of professional sports, the role of hockey goalie is among the most strenuous. Physically, he is expected to stand in the way of fast-skating players, rifling a rock-hard frozen rubber disk at him from all angles. In addition to the physical dangers assaulting him from all sides, the mental fatigue that goes with the position can exact a price. In the game, he is considered the last line of defense — the final barrier between the opponent and the net. His failure is the team's failure. This would weigh heavily on netminders like McCool.

A native of Calgary, McCool was signed by Toronto in the fall of 1944. He was available because he was released from the Armed Services because of stomach ulcers. Over the course of his first season, he shone, compiling a 3.22 GAA, good for second in the league. McCool also blanked four opponents, which tied him for first. In the playoffs, he stepped it up a notch, shutting out the mighty Canadiens in his first game. In the final round, he accomplished what no other goalie had done, blanking an opponent (Detroit) three straight times. During the seventh game, no doubt caused by the mental pressure of the game, McCool's ulcers acted up. Given a 10-minute timeout, he returned and held off the Red Wings. After this fine rookie campaign, it was no great surprise that he was voted the Calder Trophy.

Before the 1945-46 training camp, thinking himself worth more, McCool stayed home in his native Alberta, holding out for a $5,000 salary. Eventually he settled for $4,500 and reported to camp. But as the season started, it was evident that all was not well. He seemed less than enthusiastic about donning the pads, and talked about quitting, as his ulcers were making his career miserable. Finally, unable to continue, he walked away in January.

Bereft of solid backstop, Toronto floundered, ending fifth, only ahead of the Rangers. Meanwhile, Montreal (28-17-5, 61) wrapped its third straight regular season crown, finishing ahead of Boston, Chicago and Detroit. In the scoring race, Chicago's Max Bentley (61) come out on top, while Toronto's Gaye Stewart (37) scored the most goals and Elmer Lach (Montreal) amassed the most assists (34). Detroit's Jack Stewart (73) spent the most time in the penalty box, while Bill Durnan (2.60, 4) won his third straight GAA title, claiming the most shutouts as well.

In the first round of the playoffs, Montreal waxed the Blackhawks in four straight, outscoring them by a combined 26–7. The other opening round victory was claimed by the Bruins, as they polished off the Red Wings in five games, capped by a 4–3 overtime contest. The finals opened with 4–3 Montreal win, as Maurice Richard potted the winner in the first extra session. Three nights later, Montreal scored another OT victory, followed by a 4–2 victory in the third game. Boston managed to squeak out an overtime (3–2) win to stave off elimination, but the Canadiens put them away, 6–3, earning them the Cup.

Lach, with his 12 assists and 17 points, led all playoff scorers, ceding goal-scoring honors to his linemates Richard and Toe Blake, who netted seven each. In net, Durnan posted a league best 2.07 GAA.

After his truncated season, McCool never returned to the game, retiring at the age of 27. In subsequent years, other goalies have also fell victim to the mental toil of the position. For instance, one Hall-of-Fame netminder — Glenn Hall — would become nauseated before every game. The position was summed up best by another legendary goalie, Jacques Plante: "Say you are working in your office, and you make one tiny mistake. Suddenly, a big red light goes on behind you, and 18,000 people scream at you...." With that as a nightly occurrence, it's amazing that anyone wants to play one of sports most difficult positions.

Though he was in the league for less than two years, McCool still owns a piece of the record book. Although another goalie (Clint Benedict in 1926) had also blanked an opponent thrice in the last round, no other netminder — before or since — has ever strung together three straight shutouts in the mental pressure-cooker of a Stanley Cup finals.

STANDINGS

TEAM	GP	W	L	T	PTS	GF	GA
MONTREAL	50	28	17	5	61	172	134
BOSTON	50	24	18	8	56	167	156
CHICAGO	50	23	20	7	53	200	178
DETROIT	50	20	20	10	50	146	159
TORONTO	50	19	24	7	45	174	185
NEW YORK	50	13	28	9	35	144	191

LEADERS

PLAYER	TM	GP	G	A	PTS	PIM
Max Bentley	CHI	47	31	30	**61**	6
Gaye Stewart	TOR	50	37	15	52	8
Toe Blake	MTL	50	29	21	50	2
Clint Smith	CHI	50	26	24	50	2
Maurice Richard	MTL	50	27	21	48	50
Bill Mosienko	CHI	40	18	30	48	12
Ab DeMarco	NY	50	20	27	47	20
Elmer Lach	MTL	50	13	**34**	47	34
Alex Kaleta	CHI	49	19	27	46	17
Two tied with					41	

GOALS
- Stewart, TOR — 37
- M. Bentley, CHI — 31
- Blake, MTL — 29
- Richard, MTL — 27
- Smith, CHI — 26

ASSISTS
- Lach, MTL — 34
- M. Bentley, CHI — 30
- Mosienko, CHI — 30
- DeMarco, NY — 27
- Kaleta, CHI — 27

GOALTENDER	TM	GP	MIN	GA	SH	GAA
Bill Durnan	MTL	40	2400	104	4	**2.60**
Paul Bibeault	B-M	26	1560	75	2	2.88
Harry Lumley	DET	50	3000	159	2	3.18
Frank Brimsek	BOS	34	2040	111	2	3.26
Mike Karakas	CHI	48	2880	**166**	1	3.46
Frank McCool	TOR	22	1320	81	0	3.68
Charlie Rayner	NY	40	2377	149	1	3.76

PENALTY MINUTES
- Stewart, DET — 73
- Guidolin, BOS — 62
- Mariucci, CHI — 58
- Bouchard, MTL — 52
- Richard, MTL — 50

SHUTOUTS
- Durnan, MTL — 4
- Bibeault, B-M — 2
- Brimsek, BOS — 2
- Lumley, DET — 2
- Three tied with — 1

MONTREAL Canadiens   28-17-5   61   1st   Dick Irvin

		REGULAR SEASON					POSTSEASON				
PLAYER	POS	GP	G	A	PTS	PIM	GP	G	A	PTS	PIM
Toe Blake	L	50	29	21	50	2	9	7	6	13	5
Maurice Richard	R	50	27	21	48	50	9	7	4	11	15
Elmer Lach	C	50	13	34	47	34	9	5	12	17	4
Jimmy Peters	R	47	11	19	30	10	9	3	1	4	6
Billy Reay	C	44	17	12	29	10	9	1	2	3	4
Murph Chamberlain	C	40	12	14	26	42	9	4	2	6	**18**
Herb O'Connor	C	45	11	11	22	2	9	2	3	5	0
Joe Benoit	R	39	9	10	19	8					
Dutch Hiller	L	45	7	11	18	4	9	4	2	6	2

		REGULAR SEASON					POSTSEASON				
PLAYER	POS	GP	G	A	PTS	PIM	GP	G	A	PTS	PIM
Glen Harmon	D	49	7	10	17	28	9	1	4	5	0
Emile Bouchard	D	45	7	10	17	52	9	2	1	3	17
Bob Fillion	L	50	10	6	16	12	9	4	3	7	6
Leo Lamoureux	D	45	5	7	12	18	9	0	2	2	2
Ken Reardon	D	43	5	4	9	45	9	1	1	2	4
Kenny Mosdell	C	13	2	1	3	8	9	4	1	5	6
Gerry Plamondon	L	6	0	2	2	2	1	0	0	0	0
Mike McMahon (1–2)	D	13	0	1	1	2					
Frank Eddolls	D	8	0	1	1	6	8	0	1	1	2
Murdo MacKay	C	5	0	1	1	0					
Moe White	L	4	0	1	1	2					
Bill Durnan	G	40	0	0	0	0	9	0	0	0	0
Paul Bibeault (2–2)	G	10	0	0	0	0					
Vic Lynn	L	2	0	0	0	0					
Nil Tremblay	C	2	0	0	0	0					
Larry Thibeault	L	1	0	0	0	0					

	REGULAR SEASON					POSTSEASON				
GOALTENDER	GP	MIN	GA	SH	GAA	GP	MIN	GA	SH	GAA
Bill Durnan (24-11-5)	40	2400	104	4	2.60	9	581	20	0	2.07
Paul Bibeault (2–2) (4-6-0)	10	600	30	0	3.00					

BOSTON   24-18-8   56   2nd   Dit Clapper
Bruins

		REGULAR SEASON					POSTSEASON				
PLAYER	POS	GP	G	A	PTS	PIM	GP	G	A	PTS	PIM
Don Gallinger	C	50	17	23	40	18	10	2	4	6	2
Woody Dumart	L	50	22	12	34	2	10	4	3	7	0
Bep Guidolin	L	50	15	17	32	62	10	5	2	7	13
Milt Schmidt	C	48	13	18	31	21	10	3	5	8	2
Herb Cain	L	48	17	12	29	4	9	0	2	2	2
William Shill	R	45	15	12	27	12	7	1	2	3	2
Bill Cowley	C	26	12	12	24	6	10	1	3	4	2
Terry Reardon	C	49	12	11	23	21	10	4	0	4	2
Bobby Bauer	R	39	11	10	21	4	10	4	3	7	2
Jack McGill	C	46	6	14	20	21	10	0	0	0	0
Pat Egan	D	41	8	10	18	32	10	3	0	3	8
Jack Crawford	D	48	7	9	16	10	10	1	2	3	4
Murray Henderson	D	48	4	11	15	30	10	1	1	2	4
Jack Church	D	43	2	6	8	28	9	0	0	0	4
Kenny Smith	L	23	2	6	8	0	8	0	4	4	0
Dit Clapper	R	30	2	3	5	0	4	0	0	0	0
Roy Conacher	L	4	2	1	3	0	3	0	0	0	0
Frank Brimsek	G	34	0	0	0	0	10	0	0	0	0
Paul Bibeault (1–2)	G	16	0	0	0	0					
Gordie Bruce	L	5	0	0	0	0					
Mike McMahon (2–2)	D	2	0	0	0	2					
Armand Delmonte	R	1	0	0	0	0					
Fern Flaman	D	1	0	0	0	0					

GOALTENDER		REGULAR SEASON					POSTSEASON				
		GP	MIN	GA	SH	GAA	GP	MIN	GA	SH	GAA
Paul Bibeault	(1–2) (8-4-4)	16	960	45	2	2.81					
Frank Brimsek	(16-14-4)	34	2040	111	2	3.26	**10**	**651**	**29**	**0**	**2.67**

CHICAGO Blackhawks

23-20-7 53 3rd Johnny Gottselig

PLAYER	POS	REGULAR SEASON					POSTSEASON				
		GP	G	A	PTS	PIM	GP	G	A	PTS	PIM
Max Bentley	C	47	31	30	**61**	6	4	1	0	1	4
Clint Smith	C	**50**	26	24	50	2	4	2	1	3	0
Bill Mosienko	R	40	18	30	48	12	4	2	0	2	2
Alex Kaleta	L	49	19	27	46	17	4	0	1	1	2
Pete Horeck	L	**50**	20	21	41	34	4	0	0	0	2
Doug Bentley	L	36	19	21	40	16	4	0	2	2	0
Red Hamill	L	38	20	17	37	23	4	1	0	1	7
George Gee	C	35	14	15	29	12	4	1	1	2	4
George Allen	L	44	11	15	26	16	4	0	0	0	4
Don Grosso	C	47	7	10	17	17	4	0	0	0	17
Eddie Wares	D	45	4	11	15	34	3	0	1	1	0
John Mariucci	D	**50**	3	8	11	58	4	0	1	1	10
George Johnston	R	16	5	4	9	2					
Joe Cooper	D	50	2	7	9	46	4	0	1	1	14
Reg Hamilton	D	48	1	7	8	31	4	0	1	1	2
John Chad	R	13	0	1	1	2	3	0	1	1	0
Mike Karakas	G	48	0	0	0	5	4	0	0	0	0
Leo Reise	D	6	0	0	0	6					
Doug Stevenson	G	2	0	0	0	0					

GOALTENDER		REGULAR SEASON					POSTSEASON				
		GP	MIN	GA	SH	GAA	GP	MIN	GA	SH	GAA
Mike Karakas	(22-19-7)	48	2880	**166**	1	3.46	4	240	26	0	6.50
Doug Stevenson	(1-1-0)	2	120	12	0	6.00					

DETROIT Red Wings

20-20-10 50 4th Jack Adams

PLAYER	POS	REGULAR SEASON					POSTSEASON				
		GP	G	A	PTS	PIM	GP	G	A	PTS	PIM
Joe Carveth	R	48	17	18	35	10	5	0	1	1	0
Adam Brown	L	48	20	11	31	27	5	1	1	2	0
Eddie Bruneteau	R	46	17	12	29	11	4	1	0	1	0
Murray Armstrong	C	40	8	18	26	4	5	0	2	2	0
Harry Watson	L	44	14	10	24	4	5	2	0	2	0
Carl Liscombe	L	44	12	9	21	2	4	1	0	1	0
Bill Quackenbush	D	48	11	10	21	6	5	0	1	1	0
Fern Gauthier	R	30	9	8	17	6	5	3	0	3	2
Ted Lindsay	L	47	7	10	17	14	5	0	1	1	0
Jack Stewart	D	47	4	11	15	73	5	0	0	0	14
Bill Hollett	D	38	4	9	13	16	5	0	2	2	0
Syd Howe	C	26	4	7	11	9					
Modere Bruneteau	R	28	6	4	10	2					

		REGULAR SEASON					*POSTSEASON*				
PLAYER	*POS*	*GP*	*G*	*A*	*PTS*	*PIM*	*GP*	*G*	*A*	*PTS*	*PIM*
Gerry Couture	C	43	3	7	10	18	5	0	2	2	0
Hal Jackson	D	36	3	4	7	36	5	0	0	0	6
Jim Conacher	C	20	1	5	6	10	5	1	1	2	0
Pat Lundy	R	4	3	2	5	2	2	1	0	1	0
Rollie McLenahan	D	9	2	1	3	10	2	0	0	0	0
Roland Rossignol	R	8	1	2	3	4					
Earl Seibert	D	18	0	3	3	18					
Sid Abel	C	7	0	2	2	0	3	0	0	0	0
Gerry Brown	L	10	0	1	1	2					
Doug McCaig	D	6	0	1	1	12					
Harry Lumley	G	50	0	0	0	6	5	0	0	0	0
John Holota	C	3	0	0	0	0					
Les Douglas	C	1	0	0	0	0					

		REGULAR SEASON				*POSTSEASON*			
GOALTENDER		*GP*	*MIN*	*GA*	*SH* *GAA*	*GP*	*MIN*	*GA*	*SH* *GAA*
Harry Lumley	(20-20-10)	50	3000	159	2 3.18	5	310	16	1 3.10

TORONTO 19-24-7 45 5th Hap Day
Maple Leafs

		REGULAR SEASON					*POSTSEASON*
PLAYER	*POS*	*GP*	*G*	*A*	*PTS*	*PIM*	*no postseason play*
Gaye Stewart	L	50	37	15	52	8	
Billy Taylor	C	48	23	18	41	14	
Syl Apps	C	40	24	16	40	2	
Gus Bodnar	C	49	14	23	37	14	
Babe Pratt	D	41	5	20	25	36	
Nick Metz	L	41	11	11	22	4	
Bob Goldham	D	49	7	14	21	44	
David Schriner	L	47	13	6	19	15	
Bob Davidson	L	41	9	9	18	12	
Jack Hamilton	C	40	7	9	16	12	
Lorne Carr	R	42	5	8	13	2	
Wally Stanowski	D	45	3	10	13	10	
Mel Hill	R	35	5	7	12	10	
Bill Ezinicki	R	24	4	8	12	29	
Bud Poile	R	9	1	8	9	0	
Elwyn Morris	D	38	1	5	6	10	
Ted Kennedy	C	21	3	2	5	4	
Ernie Dickens	D	15	1	3	4	6	
Don Metz	L	7	1	0	1	0	
Doug Baldwin	D	15	0	1	1	6	
Jimmy Thomson	D	5	0	1	1	4	
Frank McCool	G	22	0	0	0	5	
Turk Broda	G	15	0	0	0	0	
Gordie Bell	G	8	0	0	0	0	
Aldege Bastien	G	5	0	0	0	0	

GOALTENDER		REGULAR SEASON					POSTSEASON
		GP	MIN	GA	SH	GAA	no postseason play
Turk Broda	(6-6-3)	15	900	53	0	3.53	
Frank McCool	(10-9-3)	22	1320	81	0	3.68	
Gordie Bell	(3-5-0)	8	480	31	0	3.88	
Aldege Bastien	(0-4-1)	5	300	20	0	4.00	

NEW YORK Rangers 13-28-9 35 6th Frank Boucher

PLAYER	POS	REGULAR SEASON				POSTSEASON
		GP	G	A	PTS	PIM	no postseason play
Ab DeMarco	C	50	20	27	47	20
Grant Warwick	R	45	19	18	37	19
Edgar Laprade	C	49	15	19	34	0
Phil Watson	R	49	12	14	26	43
Tony Leswick	L	50	15	9	24	26
Alf Pike	L	33	7	9	16	18
Alex Shibicky	R	33	10	5	15	12
Lynn Patrick	C	38	8	6	14	30
Mac Colville	R	39	7	6	13	8
Cal Gardner	C	16	8	2	10	2
Neil Colville	C	49	5	4	9	25
Bill Moe	D	48	4	4	8	14
Rene Trudell	F	16	3	5	8	4
Hank Goldup	L	19	6	1	7	11
Ott Heller	D	34	2	3	5	14
Church Russell	C	17	0	5	5	2
Bill Juzda	D	32	1	3	4	17
Hal Brown	R	13	2	1	3	2
Muzz Patrick	D	24	0	2	2	4
Hal Laycoe	D	17	0	2	2	6
Alan Kuntz	L	14	0	1	1	2
Bryan Hextall	R	3	0	1	1	0
Charlie Rayner	G	40	0	0	0	6
Jim Henry	G	11	0	0	0	0

GOALTENDER		REGULAR SEASON					POSTSEASON
		GP	MIN	GA	SH	GAA	no postseason play
Charlie Rayner	(12-21-7)	40	2377	149	1	3.76	
Jim Henry	(1-7-2)	11	623	42	1	4.04	

TEAM TOTALS

TEAM	GP	G	A	P	PIM	GA	SH	Per Game			
								G	A	PIM	GA
Montreal	50	172	197	369	337	134	4	3.44	3.94	6.74	2.68
Boston	50	167	187	354	273	156	4	3.34	3.74	5.46	3.12
Chicago	50	200	248	448	339	178	1	4.00	4.96	6.78	3.56
Detroit	50	146	165	311	298	159	2	2.92	3.30	5.96	3.18
Toronto	50	174	194	368	247	185	0	3.48	3.88	4.94	3.70
New York	50	144	147	291	285	191	2	2.88	2.94	5.70	3.82
	300	1003	1138	2141	1779	1003	13	3.34	3.79	5.93	3.34

PLAYOFFS

SERIES "A"
Montreal 6, Chicago 2
Montreal 5, Chicago 1
Montreal 8, Chicago 2
Montreal 7, Chicago 2

MONTREAL, 4-0

SERIES "B"
Boston 3, Detroit 1
Detroit 3, Boston 0
Boston 4, Detroit 2
Boston 4, Detroit 1
Boston 4, Detroit 3 (OT)

BOSTON, 4-1

SERIES "C"
Montreal 4, Boston 3 (OT)
Montreal 3, Boston 2 (OT)
Montreal 4, Boston 2
Boston 3, Montreal 2 (OT)
Montreal 6, Boston 3

MONTREAL WINS
STANLEY CUP, 4-1

ALL-STAR TEAMS

First Team
G — Bill Durnan, MTL
D — Emile Bouchard, MTL
D — Jack Crawford, BOS
C — Max Bentley, CHI
R — Maurice Richard, MTL
L — Gaye Stewart, TOR

Second Team
G — Frank Brimsek, BOS
D — Ken Reardon, MTL
D — Jack Stewart, DET
C — Elmer Lach, MTL
R — Bill Mosienko, CHI
L — Toe Blake, MTL

INDIVIDUAL TROPHY WINNERS

HART TROPHY (Most Valuable Player): Max Bentley, CHI
LADY BYNG TROPHY (Gentlemanly Conduct): Toe Blake, MTL
VEZINA TROPHY (Best Goaltender): Bill Durnan, MTL
CALDER MEMORIAL TROPHY (Best Rookie): Edgar Laprade, NY

1946-1947
Bill Durnan

Like that of most great hockey dynasties, Montreal's success during the 1940s started in its own net. During this period, the club was blessed to have one of the NHL's greats in goal. Interestingly enough, this particular star nearly bypassed the league altogether.

Born in Toronto in 1916, Bill Durnan played his first significant hockey for his native British Crescents in the TMHL, winning a league best 12 games and a circuit-topping 2.04 GAA. Later in the 1930s, he played several seasons with the Kirkland Lake Blue Devils (NOHA), gaining the attention of the Leafs. However, after injuring himself in a pickup football game, Toronto withdrew their offer to Durnan, embittering the young goalie.

Landing with the Montreal Royals of the Quebec Senior Hockey League, Durnan appeared to be content. However, the Canadiens came calling several times, dangling monetary carrots. Finally, Durnan acquiesced, signing a contract before the 1943-44 season. As it turned out, the Canadiens' patience was well placed.

Entering the NHL as a 27-year-old rookie, Durnan paced the league, winning the Vezina Trophy as the top goalie (2.16). Over the next two campaigns, he followed suit, compiling 2.42 and 2.60 marks. During this time, not content to rest on his regular-season laurels, he posted the circuit's best GAA in the playoffs, leading his Canadiens' to the Cup twice. Much to the league's chagrin, Durnan still had plenty of juice left in the tank.

Before the 1946-47 season, the NHL made a schedule adjustment, lengthening the club's slate of games to 60 each. Now, each team would play one another 12 times a season — becoming familiar foes indeed.

Over the course of the season, Montreal (34-16-10, 78) again reigned supreme, for the fourth year in a row. However, this time they did have to weather a serious challenge, as the Maple Leafs finished only six points back. Rounding out the playoff slate were Boston and Detroit, while New York and Chicago finished out of the running. Despite ending in the cellar, the Blackhawks showcased the scoring leader, Max Bentley (72) who edged the goals leader — the Canadiens' Maurice Richard (45) — by a single point. In the assist category, Detroit's Billy Taylor (46) took home honors, helped by a seven-helper game on March 16 in a 10–6 victory over Chicago. In addition, Toronto's Gus Mortson (133) was whistled for the most infractions.

In goal, once more Durnan reigned supreme, this time posting a 2.30 GAA, allowing him to cop the Vezina Trophy once again — his fourth straight. In doing so, he became the first player in twenty years to win four straight GAA titles, coming close to Clint Benedict's five straight from 1919–1923. Durnan also posted four shutouts, tied for second behind New York's Charlie Rayner (5).

In the first round of the playoffs, Durnan's Canadiens ousted the Bruins in five games, with half of the victories coming in overtime. In the other opening series, the Leafs polished off the Wings in similar fashion, their only loss being a 9–1 pasting in the second game. In the first game of the finals, Durnan shut out the Leafs 6–0, but then was on the short end of a 4–0 blanking two nights later. Toronto then took a commanding lead behind 4–2 and 2–1 wins, before Montreal bounced back with a 3–1 win in the fifth game. The series ended two days later, as Toronto finished off the Canadiens, 2–1, claiming their third Cup in six years.

Despite being on the losing end, Durnan still posted the best playoff GAA (1.92) to go with his one shutout. Individual scoring leaders also graced the Montreal roster, as Richard and Billy Reay each scored the most goals (6), with the former garnering the most points (11) as well. In addition, their teammate Toe Blake (7) added the most helpers.

The next season, Durnan's bid for five straight Vezinas fizzled, as he finished third. Undaunted, he returned to form the next two years, winning the coveted trophy both times, while shutting out his opponents 18 times during the two-year span. After the latter season, Durnan abruptly walked away from the NHL, at the age of 34. According to teammates, he had simply had enough of the grind, echoing the sentiments of many other netminders. Following a brief stint as a coach in the QMHL, Durnan left the game for good.

Although Durnan played only a short seven years in the NHL, his legacy remains secure, as over his septet of campaigns, he won the Vezina a record six times. Although that record would eventually be eclipsed by a future Montreal netminder, Durnan should be remembered as the league's best goalie of his time, and after his induction into the Hall of Fame in 1964, as one of the best of all time.

STANDINGS

TEAM	GP	W	L	T	PTS	GF	GA
MONTREAL	60	34	16	10	78	189	138
TORONTO	60	31	19	10	72	209	172
BOSTON	60	26	23	11	63	190	175
DETROIT	60	22	27	11	55	190	193
NEW YORK	60	22	32	6	50	167	186
CHICAGO	60	19	37	4	42	193	274

LEADERS

PLAYER	TM	GP	G	A	PTS	PIM
Max Bentley	CHI	60	29	43	72	12
Maurice Richard	MTL	60	45	26	71	69
Billy Taylor	DET	60	17	46	63	35
Milt Schmidt	BOS	59	27	35	62	40
Ted Kennedy	TOR	60	28	32	60	27
Doug Bentley	CHI	52	21	34	55	18
Bobby Bauer	BOS	58	30	24	54	4
Roy Conacher	DET	60	30	24	54	6
Bill Mosienko	CHI	59	25	27	52	2
Woody Dumart	BOS	60	24	28	52	12

GOALS
Richard, MTL — 45
Conacher, DET — 30
Bauer, BOS — 30
M. Bentley, CHI — 29
Kennedy, TOR — 28

ASSISTS
Taylor, DET — 46
M. Bentley, CHI — 43
Schmidt, BOS — 35
D. Bentley, CHI — 34
Kennedy, TOR — 32

GOALTENDER	TM	GP	MIN	GA	SH	GAA
Bill Durnan	MTL	60	3600	138	4	2.30
Turk Broda	TOR	60	3600	172	4	2.87
Frank Brimsek	BOS	60	3600	175	3	2.92
Charlie Rayner	NY	58	3480	177	5	3.05
Harry Lumley	DET	52	3120	159	3	3.06
Paul Bibeault	CHI	41	2460	170	1	4.15

PENALTY MINUTES
Mortson, TOR — 133
Mariucci, CHI — 110
Chamberlain, MTL — 97
Thomson, TOR — 97
Ezinicki, TOR — 93

SHUTOUTS
Rayner, NY — 5
Durnan, MTL — 4
Broda, TOR — 4
Brimsek, BOS — 3
Lumley, DET — 3

MONTREAL   34-16-10   78   1st   Dick Irvin
Canadiens

		REGULAR SEASON					POSTSEASON				
PLAYER	POS	GP	G	A	PTS	PIM	GP	G	A	PTS	PIM
Maurice Richard	R	60	45	26	71	69	10	6	5	11	44
Toe Blake	L	60	21	29	50	6	11	2	7	9	0
Billy Reay	C	59	22	20	42	17	11	6	1	7	14
Leo Gravelle	R	53	16	14	30	12	6	2	0	2	2
Elmer Lach	C	31	14	16	30	22					
Herb O'Connor	C	46	10	20	30	6	8	3	4	7	0

1946–1947

PLAYER	POS	REGULAR SEASON					POSTSEASON				
		GP	G	A	PTS	PIM	GP	G	A	PTS	PIM
Jimmy Peters	R	60	11	13	24	27	11	1	2	3	10
Ken Reardon	D	52	5	17	22	84	7	1	2	3	20
Roger Leger	D	49	4	18	22	12	11	0	6	6	10
George Allen	L	49	7	14	21	12	11	1	3	4	6
Murph Chamberlain	C	49	10	10	20	97	11	1	3	4	19
Kenny Mosdell	C	54	5	10	15	50	4	2	0	2	4
Glen Harmon	D	57	5	9	14	53	11	1	1	2	4
Leo Lamoureux	D	50	2	11	13	14	4	0	0	0	4
Emile Bouchard	D	60	5	7	12	60	11	0	3	3	21
Bob Fillion	L	57	6	3	9	16	8	0	0	0	0
John Quilty	C	3	1	1	2	0	7	3	2	5	9
Hub Macey	L	12	0	1	1	0	7	0	0	0	0
Bill Durnan	G	60	0	0	0	0	11	0	0	0	0
Joe Benoit	R	6	0	0	0	4					
Frank Eddolls	D	6	0	0	0	0	7	0	0	0	4
George Pargeter	L	4	0	0	0	0					
Doug Lewis	L	3	0	0	0	0					
Murdo MacKay	C						9	0	1	1	0

GOALTENDER		REGULAR SEASON					POSTSEASON				
		GP	MIN	GA	SH	GAA	GP	MIN	GA	SH	GAA
Bill Durnan	(34-16-10)	60	3600	138	4	2.30	11	720	23	1	1.92

TORONTO 31-19-10   72   2nd   Hap Day
Maple Leafs

PLAYER	POS	REGULAR SEASON					POSTSEASON				
		GP	G	A	PTS	PIM	GP	G	A	PTS	PIM
Ted Kennedy	C	60	28	32	60	27	11	4	5	9	4
Syl Apps	C	54	25	24	49	6	11	5	1	6	0
Howie Meeker	R	55	27	18	45	76	11	3	3	6	6
Bill Ezinicki	R	60	17	20	37	93	11	0	2	2	30
Bud Poile	R	59	19	17	36	19	7	2	0	2	2
Harry Watson	L	44	19	15	34	10	11	3	2	5	6
Gaye Stewart	L	60	19	14	33	15	11	2	5	7	8
Joe Klukay	L	55	9	20	29	12	11	1	0	1	0
Nick Metz	L	60	12	16	28	15	6	4	2	6	0
Vic Lynn	L	31	6	14	20	44	11	4	1	5	16
Wally Stanowski	D	51	3	16	19	12	8	0	0	0	0
Gus Mortson	D	60	5	13	18	**133**	11	1	3	4	22
Jimmy Thomson	D	60	2	14	16	97	11	0	1	1	22
Don Metz	L	40	4	9	13	10	11	2	3	5	4
Gus Bodnar	C	39	4	6	10	10	1	0	0	0	0
Bill Barilko	D	18	3	7	10	33	11	0	3	3	18
Garth Boesch	D	35	4	5	9	47	11	0	2	2	6
Sid Smith	L	14	2	1	3	0					
Bob Goldham	D	11	1	1	2	10					
Harry Taylor	C	9	0	2	2	0					
Turk Broda	G	60	0	0	0	0	11	0	0	0	0
Bobby Dawes	D	1	0	0	0	0					

		REGULAR SEASON					POSTSEASON				
GOALTENDER		GP	MIN	GA	SH	GAA	GP	MIN	GA	SH	GAA
Turk Broda	(31-19-10)	**60**	**3600**	172	4	2.87	**11**	680	27	1	2.38

BOSTON 26-23-11 63 3rd Dit Clapper
Bruins

		REGULAR SEASON				POSTSEASON				
PLAYER	POS	GP	G	A	PTS	PIM	GP	G	A	PTS	PIM
Milt Schmidt	C	59	27	35	62	40	5	3	1	4	4
Bobby Bauer	R	58	30	24	54	4	5	1	1	2	0
Woody Dumart	L	60	24	28	52	12	5	1	1	2	8
Bill Cowley	C	51	13	25	38	16	5	0	2	2	0
Joe Carveth	R	51	21	15	36	18	5	2	1	3	0
Don Gallinger	C	47	11	19	30	12	4	0	0	0	7
Pat Egan	D	60	7	18	25	89	5	0	2	2	6
Bep Guidolin	L	56	10	13	23	73	3	0	1	1	6
Kenny Smith	L	60	14	7	21	4	5	3	0	3	2
Terry Reardon	C	60	6	14	20	17	5	0	3	3	2
Jack Crawford	D	58	1	17	18	16	2	1	0	1	0
Murray Henderson	D	57	5	12	17	63	4	0	0	0	4
Jack McGill	C	24	5	9	14	19	5	0	0	0	11
Mark Marquess	R	27	5	4	9	6	4	0	0	0	0
Babe Pratt	D	31	4	4	8	25					
Fern Flaman	D	23	1	4	5	41	5	0	0	0	8
Ed Barry	L	19	1	3	4	2					
Clare Martin	D	6	3	0	3	0	5	0	1	1	0
William Shill	R	27	2	0	2	2					
Don Grasso	C	33	0	2	2	2					
Norm McAtee	C	13	0	1	1	0					
Frank Brimsek	G	60	0	0	0	2	5	0	0	0	0
Dit Clapper	C	6	0	0	0	0					
Johnny Peirson	R	5	0	0	0	0					
Pentti Lund	R						1	0	0	0	0

		REGULAR SEASON					POSTSEASON				
GOALTENDER		GP	MIN	GA	SH	GAA	GP	MIN	GA	SH	GAA
Frank Brimsek	(26-23-**11**)	**60**	**3600**	175	3	2.92	5	343	16	0	2.80

DETROIT 22-27-11 55 4th Jack Adams
Red Wings

		REGULAR SEASON				POSTSEASON				
PLAYER	POS	GP	G	A	PTS	PIM	GP	G	A	PTS	PIM
Billy Taylor	C	60	17	46	63	35	5	1	5	6	4
Roy Conacher	L	60	30	24	54	6	5	4	4	8	2
Sid Abel	C	60	19	29	48	29	3	1	1	2	2
Ted Lindsay	L	59	27	15	42	57	5	2	2	4	10
Pat Lundy	R	59	17	17	34	10	5	0	1	1	2
Jim Conacher	C	33	16	13	29	2	5	2	1	3	2
Pete Horeck (2-2)	L	38	12	13	25	59	5	2	0	2	6
Eddie Bruneteau	R	60	9	14	23	14	4	1	4	5	0
Gordie Howe	R	58	7	15	22	52	5	0	0	0	18
Bill Quackenbush	D	44	5	17	22	6	5	0	0	0	2

1946–1947

PLAYER	POS	REGULAR SEASON					POSTSEASON				
		GP	G	A	PTS	PIM	GP	G	A	PTS	PIM
Gerry Couture	C	30	5	10	15	0	1	0	0	0	0
Jack Stewart	D	55	5	9	14	83	5	0	1	1	12
Adam Brown (1–2)	L	*22	8	5	13	30					
Fern Gauthier	R	40	1	12	13	2	3	1	0	1	0
Leo Reise (2–2)	D	31	4	6	10	14	5	0	1	1	4
Doug McCaig	D	47	2	4	6	62	5	0	1	1	4
Hal Jackson	D	37	1	5	6	39					
Lloyd Doran	C	24	3	2	5	10					
Al Dewsbury	D	23	2	1	3	12	2	0	0	0	4
Les Douglas	C	12	0	2	2	2					
Tony Licari	R	9	0	1	1	0					
Cliff Simpson	C	6	0	1	1	0	1	0	0	0	0
Harry Lumley	G	52	0	0	0	4					
Johnny Mowers	G	7	0	0	0	2	1	0	0	0	0
Calum MacKay	L	5	0	0	0	0					
Steve Wojciechowski	R	5	0	0	0	0					
Doug Baldwin	D	4	0	0	0	0					
Hugh Millar	D	4	0	0	0	0	1	0	0	0	0
Thain Simon	D	3	0	0	0	0					
Red Almas	G	1	0	0	0	0	5	0	0	0	0
Jim McFadden	C						4	0	2	2	0
Enio Sclisizzi	L						1	0	0	0	0

GOALTENDER		REGULAR SEASON					POSTSEASON				
		GP	MIN	GA	SH	GAA	GP	MIN	GA	SH	GAA
Harry Lumley	(22-20-10)	52	3120	159	3	3.06					
Johnny Mowers	(0-6-1)	7	420	29	0	4.14	1	40	5	0	7.50
Red Almas	(0-1-0)	1	60	5	0	5.00	5	263	13	0	2.97

NEW YORK 22-32-6   50   5th   Frank Boucher
Rangers

PLAYER	POS	REGULAR SEASON					POSTSEASON
		GP	G	A	PTS	PIM	no postseason play
Tony Leswick	L	59	27	14	41	51	
Grant Warwick	R	54	20	20	40	24	
Edgar Laprade	C	58	15	25	40	9	
Bryan Hextall	R	60	20	10	30	18	
Cal Gardner	C	52	13	16	29	30	
Church Russell	C	54	20	8	28	8	
Rene Trudell	F	59	8	16	24	38	
Neil Colville	C	60	4	16	20	16	
Ab DeMarco	C	44	9	10	19	4	
Alf Pike	L	31	7	11	18	2	
Phil Watson	R	48	6	12	18	17	
Bill Moe	D	59	4	10	14	44	
Hal Laycoe	D	58	1	12	13	25	
Joe Bell	L	47	6	4	10	12	
Joe Cooper	D	59	2	8	10	38	
Bill Juzda	D	45	3	5	8	60	
J-P Lamirande	D	14	1	1	2	14	

		REGULAR SEASON					*POSTSEASON*
PLAYER	*POS*	*GP*	*G*	*A*	*PTS*	*PIM*	*no postseason play*
Joe Levandoski	R	8	1	1	2	0	
Jean-Paul Denis	R	6	0	1	1	0	
Harry Bell	D	1	0	1	1	0	
Charlie Rayner	G	58	0	0	0	0	
Mac Colville	R	14	0	0	0	8	
Mel Read	C	6	0	0	0	8	
Jim Henry	G	2	0	0	0	0	
Jack Lancien	D	1	0	0	0	0	
Norm Larson	R	1	0	0	0	0	
Sherm White	C	1	0	0	0	0	

		REGULAR SEASON					*POSTSEASON*
GOALTENDER		*GP*	*MIN*	*GA*	*SH*	*GAA*	*no postseason play*
Charlie Rayner	(22-**30**-6)	58	3480	177	5	3.05	
Jim Henry	(0-2-0)	2	120	9	0	4.50	

CHICAGO   19-37-4   42   6th   Johnny Gottselig
Blackhawks

		REGULAR SEASON					*POSTSEASON*
PLAYER	*POS*	*GP*	*G*	*A*	*PTS*	*PIM*	*no postseason play*
Max Bentley	C	60	29	43	72	12	
Doug Bentley	L	52	21	34	55	18	
Bill Mosienko	R	59	25	27	52	2	
Alex Kaleta	L	57	24	20	44	37	
Red Hamill	L	60	21	19	40	12	
George Gee	C	60	20	20	40	26	
Adam Brown (2–2)	L	*42	11	25	36	57	
Clint Smith	C	52	9	17	26	6	
Bill Gadsby	D	48	8	10	18	31	
Eddie Wares	D	60	4	7	11	21	
John Mariucci	D	52	2	9	11	110	
Pete Horeck (1–2)	L	18	4	6	10	12	
Frank Ashworth	C	18	5	4	9	2	
Ralph Nattrass	D	35	4	5	9	34	
Jack Jackson	D	48	2	5	7	38	
George Johnston	R	10	3	1	4	0	
Hank Blade	L	18	1	3	4	2	
Reg Hamilton	D	10	0	3	3	2	
Tom Fowler	C	24	0	1	1	18	
Paul Bibeault	G	41	0	0	0	2	
Emile Francis	G	19	0	0	0	0	
Leo Reise (1–2)	D	17	0	0	0	18	
Harry Dick	D	12	0	0	0	12	

		REGULAR SEASON					*POSTSEASON*
GOALTENDER		*GP*	*MIN*	*GA*	*SH*	*GAA*	*no postseason play*
Paul Bibeault	(13-25-3)	41	2460	170	1	4.15	
Emile Francis	(6-12-1)	19	1140	104	0	5.47	

1946-1947

TEAM TOTALS

TEAM	GP	G	A	P	PIM	GA	SH	Per Game G	A	PIM	GA
Montreal	60	189	239	428	561	138	4	3.15	3.98	9.35	**2.30**
Toronto	60	**209**	**264**	**473**	**669**	172	4	**3.48**	**4.40**	**11.15**	2.87
Boston	60	190	254	444	463	175	3	3.17	4.23	7.72	2.92
Detroit	60	190	261	451	535	193	3	3.17	4.35	8.92	3.22
New York	60	167	201	368	426	186	5	2.78	3.35	7.10	3.10
Chicago	60	193	259	452	467	274	1	3.22	4.32	7.78	4.57
	360	1138	1478	2616	3121	1138	20	3.16	4.11	8.67	3.16

PLAYOFFS

SERIES "A"
Montreal 3, Boston 1
Montreal 2, Boston 1 (OT)
Boston 4, Montreal 2
Montreal 5, Boston 1
Montreal 4, Boston 3 (OT)

MONTREAL, 4-1

SERIES "B"
Toronto 3, Detroit 2 (OT)
Detroit 9, Toronto 1
Toronto 4, Detroit 1
Toronto 4, Detroit 1
Toronto 6, Detroit 1

TORONTO, 4-1

SERIES "C"
Montreal 6, Toronto 0
Toronto 4, Montreal 0
Toronto 4, Montreal 2
Toronto 2, Montreal 1 (OT)
Montreal 3, Toronto 1
Toronto 2, Montreal 1

TORONTO WINS STANLEY CUP, 4-2

ALL-STAR TEAMS

First Team
G — Bill Durnan, MTL
D — Emile Bouchard, MTL
D — Ken Reardon, MTL
C — Milt Schmidt, BOS
R — Maurice Richard, MTL
L — Doug Bentley, CHI

Second Team
G — Frank Brimsek, BOS
D — Bill Quackenbush, BOS
D — Jack Stewart, DET
C — Max Bentley, CHI
R — Bobby Bauer, BOS
L — Woody Dumart, BOS

INDIVIDUAL TROPHY WINNERS

HART TROPHY (Most Valuable Player): Maurice Richard, MTL
LADY BYNG TROPHY (Gentlemanly Conduct): Bobby Bauer, BOS
VEZINA TROPHY (Best Goaltender): Bill Durnan, MTL
CALDER MEMORIAL TROPHY (Best Rookie): Howie Meeker, TOR

1947-1948
Two Men Out

Dating back to its beginning, organized sports has fallen under the influence of gambling interests. Lured by the excitement, bettors long have wagered on the outcome of the different contests. Wanting to control the events to their own liking, some gamblers sought to influence the results of particular games by bribing the contestants — mostly into "laying down" to let their opponents win. Although most famously affecting baseball in the 1919 World Series, hockey fell victim as well. This would sadly come to pass during the upcoming season, costing some players dearly.

Two years previously, in January 1946, it had come to the attention of the NHL that a "bull ring" — that is, a betting circle, was operating freely in Toronto's Maple Leaf Gardens. To stop the action, one of its main instigators, Toronto's Babe Pratt, was suspended for a few games for admitting to wagering on his own team. When the practice failed to stop during the following season, the NHL announced that any more infractions would be dealt with more severely.

Midway through the 1947-48 season, a Detroit newspaper broke a story which stated that two Boston Bruins had been in touch with a gambler named James Tamer. This led to a wiretap on Tamer's phone, which revealed the following conversation, as reported by Corey Bryant in his article "The Gambling Scandal of 1948": "Tamer: How are things going tonight? Voice: Don't worry about the game tonight.... I don't intend to do so good. Bet $500 for me."

After an investigation, it was revealed that the two players involved were Billy Taylor — since traded to the Rangers — and Don Gallinger, both NHL veterans. Taylor had been the in the NHL for seven years, with a handful of top-10 scoring campaigns to his credit, including an assist crown the previous year. Gallinger, though only a 23-year-old, was in his fifth season for the Bruins and had been a double-digit scorer each year.

Right away, Taylor admitted to the infractions, and was expelled from the NHL, while Gallinger, who denied even knowing Tamer, was merely suspended. A few months later, Gallinger finally fessed up and was expelled as well.

While these events were swirling around the league, Toronto (32-15-13, 77) broke Montreal's four-season run at the top. Detroit and Boston finished second and third, while New York grabbed the final playoff rung. The Canadiens' tumble sent them all the way to fifth, only five points ahead of last-place Chicago. In an interesting twist, the Blackhawks were actually the most prolific scoring team in the league, netting 17 more goals than their nearest rival. Unfortunately, they also allowed the most tallies, explaining their sixth-place finish.

Individually, Elmer Lach (31-31-62) won the scoring title by a single point over New York's Herb O'Connor. Detroit's Ted Lindsay (33) scored the most goals, while Chicago's Doug Bentley (37) collected the most assists. Toronto's young defenseman, Bill Barilko, showed toughness, compiling 147 penalty minutes. In goal, the Maple Leaf's Turk Broda (2.38) unseated Bill Durnan as the top netminder, while Detroit's Harry Lumley (7) picked up the most shutouts.

In one opening round series, Toronto excised Boston in five games. Feeling the effects of their missing player and all the hoopla surrounding the scandal, the Bruins only scored 13 goals in the five contests, winning only the fourth game, 3–2. Meanwhile, the other series lasted a bit longer, as Detroit outlasted New York in six. In the latter slate, the Rangers clawed their way back in, posting back-to-back wins (3–1 and 3–2), but the Wings prevailed with two straight wins (3–1 and 4–2) of their own. In the finals, it was all Toronto, as the Leafs swept to their second straight Cup — 5–3, 4–2, 2–0 and 7–2. All of the top playoff scorers were present on the winner's roster: Ted Kennedy for most goals (8) and points (14) and Max Bentley for most assists (14). Between the pipes, Broda posted the lowest GAA (2.15).

As the years passed, Gallinger sought his return to the game, but was repeatedly denied. Finally, 1970, both men were allowed back in. Later, Taylor found work for the Penguins as a scout, but Gallinger never participated in official league activities again.

For both, their youthful mistakes cost them dearly, tarnishing them, as well as the game that employed them. This incident, thankfully never repeated, remains the biggest gambling scandal to have rocked the NHL.

STANDINGS

TEAM	GP	W	L	T	PTS	GF	GA
TORONTO	60	32	15	13	77	182	143
DETROIT	60	30	18	12	72	187	148
BOSTON	60	23	24	13	59	167	168
NEW YORK	60	21	26	13	55	176	201

TEAM	GP	W	L	T	PTS	GF	GA
MONTREAL	60	20	29	11	51	147	169
CHICAGO	60	20	34	6	46	195	225

LEADERS

PLAYER	TM	GP	G	A	PTS	PIM	GOALS	
Elmer Lach	MTL	60	31	31	**61**	72	Lindsay, DET	33
Herb O'Connor	NY	60	24	36	60	8	Lach, MTL	28
Doug Bentley	CHI	60	20	37	57	16	Richard, MTL	28
Gaye Stewart	T-C	**61**	27	29	56	83	Stewart, T-C	27
Max Bentley	C-T	58	26	28	54	14	Two tied with	26
Bud Poile	T-C	58	25	29	54	17		
Maurice Richard	MTL	53	28	25	53	89	ASSISTS	
Syl Apps	TOR	55	26	27	53	12	D. Bentley, CHI	37
Ted Lindsay	DET	60	**33**	19	52	95	O'Connor, NY	36
Roy Conacher	CHI	52	22	27	49	4	Laprade, NY	34
							Lach, MTL	31
							Abel, DET	30

GOALTENDER	TM	GP	MIN	GA	SH	GAA	PENALTY MINUTES	
Turk Broda	TOR	60	**3600**	143	5	**2.38**	Barilko, TOR	147
Harry Lumley	DET	60	3592	147	7	2.46	Reardon, MTL	129
Bill Durnan	MTL	59	3505	162	5	2.77	Mortson, TOR	118
Frank Brimsek	BOS	60	**3600**	168	3	2.89	Ezinicki, TOR	97
Jim Henry	NY	48	2880	153	2	3.19	Lindsay, DET	95
Emile Francis	CHI	54	3240	**183**	1	3.39		

SHUTOUTS
Lumley, DET — 7
Durnan, MTL — 5
Broda, TOR — 5
Brimsek, BOS — 3
Henry, NY — 2

TORONTO 32-15-13 77 1st Hap Day
Maple Leafs

		REGULAR SEASON					POSTSEASON				
PLAYER	POS	GP	G	A	PTS	PIM	GP	G	A	PTS	PIM
Syl Apps	C	55	26	27	53	12	9	4	4	8	0
Max Bentley (2–2)	C	53	23	25	48	10	9	4	7	11	0
Ted Kennedy	C	60	25	21	46	32	9	**8**	6	**14**	0
Harry Watson	L	57	21	20	41	16	9	5	2	7	9
Howie Meeker	R	58	14	20	34	62	9	2	4	6	15
Vic Lynn	L	60	12	22	34	53	9	2	5	7	**20**
Bill Ezinicki	R	60	11	20	31	97	9	3	1	4	6
Joe Klukay	L	59	15	15	30	28	9	1	1	2	2
Jimmy Thomson	D	59	0	29	29	82	9	1	1	2	9
Gus Mortson	D	58	7	11	18	118	5	1	2	3	2
Sid Smith	L	31	7	10	17	10	2	0	0	0	0
Bill Barilko	D	57	5	9	14	**147**	9	1	0	1	17
Wally Stanowski	D	54	2	11	13	12	9	0	2	2	2
Nick Metz	L	60	4	8	12	8	9	2	0	2	2

1947–1948

PLAYER	POS	REGULAR SEASON					POSTSEASON				
		GP	G	A	PTS	PIM	GP	G	A	PTS	PIM
Don Metz	L	26	4	6	10	2	2	0	0	0	2
Garth Boesch	D	45	2	7	9	52	8	2	1	3	2
Cy Thomas (2–2)	L	8	1	2	3	4					
Bud Poile (1–2)	R	4	2	0	2	0					
Gaye Stewart (1–2)	L	*7	1	0	1	0					
John McCormack	C	3	0	1	1	0					
Turk Broda	G	60	0	0	0	2	9	0	0	0	10
Fleming Mackell	C	3	0	0	0	2					
Tod Sloan	R	1	0	0	0	0					
Les Costello	L						5	2	2	4	2
Phil Samis	D						5	0	1	1	2

GOALTENDER		REGULAR SEASON					POSTSEASON				
		GP	MIN	GA	SH	GAA	GP	MIN	GA	SH	GAA
Turk Broda	(32-15-13)	60	3600	143	5	2.38	9	557	20	1	2.15

DETROIT 30-18-12 72 2nd Tommy Ivan
Red Wings

PLAYER	POS	REGULAR SEASON					POSTSEASON				
		GP	G	A	PTS	PIM	GP	G	A	PTS	PIM
Ted Lindsay	L	60	33	19	52	95	10	3	1	4	6
Jim McFadden	C	60	24	24	48	12	10	5	3	8	10
Gordie Howe	R	60	16	28	44	63	10	1	1	2	11
Sid Abel	C	60	14	30	44	69	10	0	3	3	16
Jim Conacher	C	60	17	23	40	2	9	2	0	2	2
Pete Horeck	L	50	12	17	29	44	10	3	7	10	12
Don Morrison	C	40	10	15	25	6	3	0	1	1	0
Bep Guidolin	L	58	12	10	22	78	2	0	0	0	4
Bill Quackenbush	D	58	6	16	22	17	10	0	2	2	0
Red Kelly	D	60	6	14	20	13	10	3	2	5	2
Jack Stewart	D	60	5	14	19	91	9	1	3	4	6
Rod Morrison	R	34	8	7	15	4	3	0	0	0	0
Marty Pavelich	L	41	4	8	12	10	10	2	2	4	6
Leo Reise	D	58	5	4	9	30	10	2	1	3	12
Gerry Couture	C	19	3	6	9	2					
Doug McCaig	D	29	3	3	6	37					
Fern Gauthier	R	35	1	5	6	2	10	1	1	2	5
Pat Lundy	R	11	4	1	5	6	5	1	1	2	0
Max McNab	C	12	2	2	4	2	3	0	0	0	2
Eddie Bruneteau	R	18	1	1	2	2	6	0	0	0	0
Enio Sclisizzi	L	4	1	0	1	0	6	0	0	0	4
Harry Lumley	G	60	0	0	0	8	10	0	0	0	10
Ed Nicholson	D	1	0	0	0	0					
Barry Sullivan	R	1	0	0	0	0					
Tom McGrattan	G	1	0	0	0	0					
Lee Fogolin	D						2	0	1	1	6
Al Dewsbury	D						1	0	0	0	0
Cliff Simpson	C						1	0	0	0	2

		REGULAR SEASON					POSTSEASON				
GOALTENDER		GP	MIN	GA	SH	GAA	GP	MIN	GA	SH	GAA
Harry Lumley (30-18-12)		60	3592	147	7	2.46	10	600	30	0	3.00
Tom McGrattan		1	8	1	0	7.50					

BOSTON   23-24-13   59   3rd   Dit Clapper
Bruins

		REGULAR SEASON				POSTSEASON			
PLAYER	POS	GP	G	A	PTS	PIM	GP	G	A	PTS	PIM
Woody Dumart	L	59	21	16	37	14	5	0	0	0	0
Pete Babando	L	60	23	11	34	52	5	1	1	2	2
Don Gallinger	C	54	10	21	31	37					
Jimmy Peters (2-2)	R	37	12	15	27	38	5	1	2	3	2
Milt Schmidt	C	33	9	17	26	28	5	2	5	7	2
Ed Sandford	L	59	10	15	25	25	5	1	0	1	0
Kenny Smith	L	60	11	12	23	14	5	2	3	5	0
Billy Taylor (1-2)	C	39	4	16	20	25					
Wally Wilson	C	53	11	8	19	18	1	0	0	0	0
Pat Egan	D	60	8	11	19	81	5	1	1	2	2
Clare Martin	D	59	5	13	18	34	5	0	0	0	6
Joe Carveth (1-2)	R	22	8	9	17	2					
Murray Henderson	D	49	6	8	14	50	3	1	0	1	5
Jack Crawford	D	45	3	11	14	10	4	0	1	1	2
Paul Ronty	C	24	3	11	14	0	5	0	4	4	0
Ed Harrison	C	52	6	7	13	8	5	1	0	1	2
Grant Warwick (2-2)	R	18	6	5	11	8	5	0	3	3	4
Fern Flaman	D	56	4	6	10	69	5	0	0	0	12
Johnny Peirson	R	15	4	2	6	0	5	3	2	5	0
John Quilty (2-2)	C	6	3	2	5	2					
Frank Brimsek	G	60	0	0	0	0	5	0	0	0	0
Arnie Kullman	C	1	0	0	0	0					
Ray Manson	L	1	0	0	0	0					
Pentti Lund	R						2	0	0	0	0

		REGULAR SEASON					POSTSEASON				
GOALTENDER		GP	MIN	GA	SH	GAA	GP	MIN	GA	SH	GAA
Frank Brimsek (23-24-13)		60	3600	168	3	2.89	5	317	20	0	3.79

NEW YORK   21-26-13   55   4th   Frank Boucher
Rangers

		REGULAR SEASON				POSTSEASON			
PLAYER	POS	GP	G	A	PTS	PIM	GP	G	A	PTS	PIM
Herb O'Connor	C	60	24	36	60	8	6	1	4	5	0
Edgar Laprade	C	59	13	34	47	7	6	1	4	5	0
Tony Leswick	L	60	24	16	40	76	6	3	2	5	8
Phil Watson	R	54	18	15	33	54	5	2	3	5	2
Don Raleigh	C	52	15	18	33	2	6	2	0	2	2
Eddie Kullman	R	51	15	17	32	32	6	1	0	1	2
Grant Warwick (1-2)	R	40	17	12	29	30					
Cal Gardner	C	58	7	18	25	71	5	0	0	0	0
Bryan Hextall	R	43	8	14	22	18	6	1	3	4	0
Rene Trudell	F	54	13	7	20	30	5	0	0	0	2

1947-1948

PLAYER	POS	REGULAR SEASON					POSTSEASON				
		GP	G	A	PTS	PIM	GP	G	A	PTS	PIM
Frank Eddolls	D	58	6	13	19	16	2	0	0	0	0
Neil Colville	C	55	4	12	16	25	6	1	0	1	6
Bill Moe	D	59	1	15	16	31	1	0	0	0	0
Bill Juzda	D	60	3	9	12	70	6	0	0	0	9
Eddie Slowinski	R	38	6	5	11	2	4	0	0	0	0
Church Russell	C	19	0	3	3	2					
Fred Shero	D	19	1	0	1	2	6	0	1	1	6
Ron Rowe	C	5	1	0	1	0					
J-P Lamirande	D	18	0	1	1	6	6	0	0	0	4
Jim Henry	G	48	0	0	0	0	6	0	0	0	0
Charlie Rayner	G	12	0	0	0	0					
Hub Anslow	C	2	0	0	0	0					
Bing Juckes	L	2	0	0	0	0					
Fern Perreault	L	2	0	0	0	0					
Billy Taylor (2-2)	C	2	0	0	0	0					
Herb Foster	L	1	0	0	0	0					
Larry Kwong	R	1	0	0	0	0					
Bob DeCourcy	G	1	0	0	0	0					
Buck Davies	C						1	0	0	0	0
Dunc Fisher	R						1	0	0	0	0
Jack Lancien	D						2	0	0	0	0
Nick Mickoski	L						2	0	1	1	0

GOALTENDER		REGULAR SEASON					POSTSEASON				
		GP	MIN	GA	SH	GAA	GP	MIN	GA	SH	GAA
Jim Henry	(17-18-**13**)	48	2880	153	2	3.19					
Charlie Rayner	(4-7-0)	12	691	42	0	3.65	6	360	17	0	3.00
Bob DeCourcy	(0-1-0)	1	29	6	0	12.41					

MONTREAL 20-29-11 51 5th Dick Irvin
Canadiens

PLAYER	POS	REGULAR SEASON					POSTSEASON
		GP	G	A	PTS	PIM	no postseason play
Elmer Lach	C	60	31	31	**61**	72	
Maurice Richard	R	53	28	25	53	89	
Toe Blake	L	32	9	15	24	4	
Ken Reardon	D	58	7	15	22	129	
Billy Reay	C	60	6	14	20	24	
Bob Fillion	L	32	9	9	18	8	
Roger Leger	D	48	4	14	18	26	
Jacques Locas	R	56	7	8	15	66	
Norm Dussault	C	28	5	10	15	4	
Glen Harmon	D	56	10	4	14	52	
Joe Carveth (2-2)	R	35	1	10	11	6	
Emile Bouchard	D	60	4	6	10	78	
Murph Chamberlain	C	30	6	3	9	62	
Doug Harvey	D	35	4	4	8	32	
Rip Riopelle	L	55	5	2	7	12	
Bob Carse	L	22	3	3	6	16	
Floyd Curry	R	31	1	5	6	0	

		REGULAR SEASON					*POSTSEASON*
PLAYER	*POS*	*GP*	*G*	*A*	*PTS*	*PIM*	*no postseason play*
John Quilty (1–2)	C	20	2	3	5	4	
Jean-Claude Campeau	C	14	2	2	4	4	
Jimmy Peters (1–2)	R	22	1	3	4	6	
Hal Laycoe	D	14	1	2	3	4	
Gerry Palmondon	L	3	1	1	2	0	
Murdo MacKay	C	14	0	2	2	0	
Kenny Mosdell	C	23	1	0	1	19	
Bill Durnan	G	59	0	0	0	5	
Leo Gravelle	R	15	0	0	0	0	
Gerry McNeil	G	2	0	0	0	0	
Tom Johnson	D	1	0	0	0	0	
George Robertson	C	1	0	0	0	0	

		REGULAR SEASON					*POSTSEASON*
GOALTENDER		*GP*	*MIN*	*GA*	*SH*	*GAA*	*no postseason play*
Bill Durnan	(20-28-10)	59	3505	162	5	2.77	
Gerry McNeil	(0-1-1)	2	95	7	0	4.42	

CHICAGO 20-34-6 46 6th Johnny Gottselig
Blackhawks   Charlie Conacher

		REGULAR SEASON					*POSTSEASON*
PLAYER	*POS*	*GP*	*G*	*A*	*PTS*	*PIM*	*no postseason play*
Doug Bentley	L	60	20	37	57	16	
Gaye Stewart (2–2)	L	*54	26	29	55	83	
Bud Poile (2–2)	R	54	23	29	52	17	
Roy Conacher	L	52	22	27	49	4	
George Gee	C	60	14	25	39	18	
Gus Bodnar	C	46	13	22	35	23	
Alex Kaleta	L	52	10	16	26	40	
Bill Mosienko	R	40	16	9	25	0	
Red Hamill	L	60	11	13	24	18	
Ernie Dickens	D	54	5	15	20	30	
Metro Prystai	C	54	7	11	18	25	
Adam Brown	L	32	7	10	17	41	
Ralph Nattrass	D	60	5	12	17	79	
Bill Gadsby	D	60	6	10	16	66	
Bob Goldham	D	38	2	9	11	38	
Max Bentley (1–2)	C	6	3	3	6	4	
John Mariucci	D	51	1	4	5	63	
Dick Butler	R	7	2	0	2	0	
Hank Blade	L	6	1	0	1	0	
Cy Thomas (1–2)	L	6	1	0	1	8	
Emile Francis	G	54	0	0	0	6	
Doug Jackson	G	6	0	0	0	0	
Doug Baldwin	D	5	0	0	0	2	
Art Michaluk	D	5	0	0	0	0	

		REGULAR SEASON					*POSTSEASON*
GOALTENDER		*GP*	*MIN*	*GA*	*SH*	*GAA*	*no postseason play*
Emile Francis	(18-**31**-5)	54	3240	**183**	1	3.39	
Doug Jackson	(2-3-1)	6	360	42	0	7.00	

1947–1948

TEAM TOTALS

TEAM	GP	G	A	P	PIM	GA	SH	Per Game G	A	PIM	GA
Toronto	60	182	264	446	758	143	5	3.03	4.40	12.63	2.38
Detroit	60	187	247	434	593	148	7	3.12	4.12	9.88	2.47
Boston	60	167	216	383	515	168	3	2.78	3.60	8.58	2.80
New York	60	176	245	421	480	201	2	2.93	4.08	8.00	3.35
Montreal	60	147	191	338	724	169	5	2.45	3.18	12.07	2.82
Chicago	60	**195**	**281**	476	572	225	1	**3.25**	**4.68**	9.53	3.75
	360	1054	1444	2498	3642	1054	23	2.93	4.01	10.12	2.93

PLAYOFFS

SERIES "A"
Toronto 5, Boston 4 (OT)
Toronto 5, Boston 3
Toronto 5, Boston 1
Boston 3, Boston 2
Toronto 3, Boston 2

TORONTO, 4–1

SERIES "B"
Detroit 2, New York 1
Detroit 5, New York 2
New York 3, Detroit 2
New York 3, Detroit 1
Detroit 3, New York 1
Detroit 4, New York 2

DETROIT, 4–2

SERIES "C"
Toronto 5, Detroit 3
Toronto 4, Detroit 2
Toronto 2, Detroit 0
Toronto 7, Detroit 2

**TORONTO WINS
STANLEY CUP, 4–0**

ALL-STAR TEAMS

First Team
G — Turk Broda, TOR
D — Bill Quackenbush, DET
D — Jack Stewart, DET
C — Elmer Lach, MTL
R — Maurice Richard, MTL
L — Ted Lindsay, MTL

Second Team
G — Frank Brimsek, BOS
D — Neil Colville, NY
D — Ken Reardon, MTL
C — Herb O'Connor, NY
R — Bud Poile, T-C
L — Gaye Stewart, T-C

INDIVIDUAL TROPHY WINNERS

HART TROPHY (Most Valuable Player): Herb O'Connor, NY
LADY BYNG TROPHY (Gentlemanly Conduct): Herb O'Connor, NY
VEZINA TROPHY (Best Goaltender): Turk Broda, TOR
CALDER MEMORIAL TROPHY (Best Rookie): Jim McFadden, DET
ART ROSS TROPHY (Scoring Leader): Elmer Lach, MTL

1948-1949
Individual Accolades

During the 1947-48 season, the Chicago Blackhawks had been the most prolific scoring team in the league. Averaging 3.25 goals per game, the club outdistanced its brethren by nearly two dozen markers. Unfortunately for them, this abundance did not have the desired result, as the team finished dead last. In the upcoming campaign, the team would again be an offensive force to reckon with, although in a different way. However, this still would not change the overall team's fortune.

Throughout hockey history, great individual efforts have not necessarily translated into complete team success. For instance, David "Sweeney" Schriner was one of the league's top snipers during the 1930s, winning a pair of scoring titles. Yet his team, the New York Americans did not reap the benefits of this largess, missing the playoffs entirely during one of his title seasons. Also, in an extreme example from a sister league, in 1946-47, Phil Hergesheimer of the American Hockey League's Philadelphia squad won the scoring title (48-44-92), though his team (5-52-7) finished with the worst record in league history.

The reasons for these imbalances are varied, but most revolve a significant weakness in another area. In some cases, these offensive stars have little help, as they rely on supreme individual effort to accomplish their goals. However, most times these offensive superstars are unfortunate enough to play on a team with a shaky defense, shoddy goaltending or both. This was the case with the 1947-48 Blackhawks, as they allowed the most goals by far.

As it would turn out, The NHL was about to witness another case involving a great offensive season by a mediocre team. However, this instance would unfold differently — as it involved not just one, but two players. Not surprisingly, both were seasoned pros who had won several titles between them.

By the end of the of the 1948-49 season, the top scorer, Roy Conacher (26-42-68), who had also led the NHL in goal scoring as a rookie ten years before, graced the roster of the Blackhawks. A slim two points behind him, another Blackhawk — Doug Bentley (23-43-66) — finished second. The latter also ended with the most assists, as he had done the previous two years. Other individual accolades were claimed by Detroit's Sid Abel for most goals (28) and Toronto's Bill Ezinicki for most penalty minutes (144). Goalie Bill Durnan (Montreal) reclaimed his role as the league's best, finishing with a sparkling GAA (2.10) and a league best 10 shutouts, with four of the latter coming in a row to set a new league mark.

Overall, Conacher and Bentley couldn't push the Blackhawks into the playoffs, although the team did finish better than the Rangers. Instead, Detroit (34-19-7, 75) claimed first place, a comfortable nine points ahead of the Bruins. Montreal and Toronto finished third and fourth, the latter only seven points to the better of the Hawks.

In the playoffs, Detroit and Montreal squared off in a memorable battle that wasn't decided until the seventh game. After the Canadiens took a two games to one lead, the remaining four games of the series were decided by 3-1 margins, with the Red Wings winning three of them. In other opening round action, Toronto upset favored Boston in five games, winning the decider by a 3-2 margin. In the finals, the 3-1 score continued to be popular, as three of the four contests ended that way. The other match was decided 3-2. In all four, Toronto was victorious, sweeping to their third straight Stanley Cup, becoming the first team to accomplish the goal.

Despite the lopsided loss, the Red Wings claimed much of the individual playoff glory, as their budding star — Gordie Howe — (8-3-11) scored the most goals and amassed the most points. His teammate, Ted Lindsay (6) added the most helpers, although he was tied by Toronto's Ted Kennedy. In net, Turk Broda (Toronto) finished with the lowest GAA (1.57).

Over the next few seasons, both Conacher and Bentley toiled for the Blackhawks, putting up solid numbers, although neither returned to the upper reaches of the scoring chart. During this time, their team continued to struggle, so neither player took the ice following the conclusion of the regular season.

Though probably proud of their individual accomplishments, most likely Conacher and Bentley would have traded their lofty rankings in 1948-49 for a more satisfying team result. Still, it remains a unique record, though nearly equaled in more recent times by Crosby and Malkin's Penguins. For the time being, Conacher and Bentley remain the only pair to finish one-two in the scoring race in a season while their team finished outside of the playoff hunt.

STANDINGS

TEAM	GP	W	L	T	PTS	GF	GA
DETROIT	60	34	19	7	75	195	145
BOSTON	60	29	23	8	66	178	163
MONTREAL	60	28	23	9	65	152	126
TORONTO	60	22	25	13	57	147	161
CHICAGO	60	21	31	8	50	173	211
NEW YORK	60	18	31	11	47	133	172

LEADERS

PLAYER	TM	GP	G	A	PTS	PIM
Roy Conacher	CHI	60	26	42	68	8
Doug Bentley	CHI	58	23	43	66	38
Sid Abel	DET	60	28	26	54	49
Ted Lindsay	DET	50	26	28	54	97
Jim Conacher	D-C	59	26	23	49	43
Paul Ronty	BOS	60	20	29	49	11
Harry Watson	TOR	60	26	19	45	0
Billy Reay	MTL	60	22	23	45	33
Gus Bodnar	CHI	59	19	26	45	14
Johnny Peirson	BOS	59	22	21	43	45

GOALS	
Abel, DET	28
Watson, TOR	26
R. Conacher, CHI	26
J. Conacher, D-C	26
Lindsay, DET	26

ASSISTS	
D. Bentley, CHI	43
R. Conacher	42
Ronty, BOS	29
Lindsay, DET	28
Bodnar, CHI	26

GOALTENDER	TM	GP	MIN	GA	SH	GAA
Bill Durnan	MTL	60	3600	126	10	2.10
Harry Lumley	DET	60	3600	145	6	2.42
Turk Broda	TOR	60	3600	161	5	2.68
Frank Brimsek	BOS	54	3240	147	1	2.72
Charlie Rayner	NY	58	3480	168	7	2.90
Jim Henry	CHI	60	3600	211	0	3.52

PENALTY MINUTES	
Ezinicki, TOR	145
Guidolin, D-C	116
Chamberlain, MTL	111
Richard, MTL	110
Reardon, MTL	103

SHUTOUTS	
Durnan, MTL	10
Rayner, NY	7
Lumley, DET	6
Broda, TOR	5
Two tied with	1

DETROIT Red Wings — 34-19-7 75 1st Tommy Ivan

		REGULAR SEASON					POSTSEASON				
PLAYER	POS	GP	G	A	PTS	PIM	GP	G	A	PTS	PIM
Sid Abel	C	60	28	26	54	49	11	3	3	6	6
Ted Lindsay	L	50	26	28	54	97	11	2	6	8	31
Bud Poile (2-2)	R	*56	21	21	42	6	10	0	1	1	2
Gordie Howe	R	40	12	25	37	57	11	8	3	11	19
Jim McFadden	C	55	12	20	32	10	8	0	1	1	6
Pete Horeck	L	60	14	16	30	46	11	1	1	2	10
Gerry Couture	C	51	19	10	29	6	10	2	0	2	2
Marty Pavelich	L	60	10	16	26	40	9	0	1	1	8
Max McNab	C	51	10	13	23	14	10	1	0	1	2

1948–1949

PLAYER	POS	REGULAR SEASON GP	G	A	PTS	PIM	POSTSEASON GP	G	A	PTS	PIM
Bill Quackenbush	D	60	6	17	23	0	11	1	1	2	0
George Gee (2–2)	C	47	7	12	19	27	10	1	3	4	22
Enio Sclisizzi	L	50	9	8	17	24	6	0	0	0	2
Red Kelly	D	59	5	11	16	10	11	1	1	2	10
Jack Stewart	D	60	4	11	15	96	11	1	1	2	32
Leo Reise	D	59	3	7	10	60	11	1	0	1	4
Pat Lundy	R	15	4	3	7	4	4	0	0	0	0
Fern Gauthier	R	41	3	2	5	2					
Lee Fogolin	D	43	1	2	3	59	9	0	0	0	4
Jim Conacher (1–2)	C	4	1	0	1	2					
Don Morrison	C	13	0	1	1	0					
Harry Lumley	G	60	0	0	0	0	11	0	0	0	2
Bep Guidolin (1–2)	L	*4	0	0	0	0					
Eddie Bruneteau	R	1	0	0	0	0					
Calum MacKay	L	1	0	0	0	0					
Doug McCaig (1–2)	D	1	0	0	0	0					
Nels Podolsky	L	1	0	0	0	0	7	0	0	0	4
Fred Glover	C						2	0	0	0	0
Gerry Reid	C						2	0	0	0	2

GOALTENDER		REGULAR SEASON GP	MIN	GA	SH	GAA	POSTSEASON GP	MIN	GA	SH	GAA
Harry Lumley	(34-19-7)	60	3600	145	6	2.42	11	726	26	0	2.15

BOSTON 29-23-8 66 2nd Dit Clapper
Bruins

PLAYER	POS	REGULAR SEASON GP	G	A	PTS	PIM	POSTSEASON GP	G	A	PTS	PIM
Paul Ronty	C	60	20	29	49	11	5	1	2	3	2
Johnny Peirson	R	59	22	21	43	45	5	3	1	4	4
Kenny Smith	L	59	20	20	40	6	5	0	2	2	4
Grant Warwick	R	58	22	15	37	14	5	2	0	2	0
Ed Sandford	L	56	16	20	36	57	5	1	3	4	2
Pete Babando	L	58	19	14	33	34	4	0	0	0	2
Milt Schmidt	C	44	10	22	32	25	4	0	2	2	8
Jimmy Peters	R	60	16	15	31	8	4	0	1	1	0
Pat Egan	D	60	6	18	24	92	5	0	0	0	16
Woody Dumart	L	59	11	12	23	6	5	3	0	3	0
Fern Flaman	D	60	4	12	16	62	5	0	1	1	8
Jack Crawford	D	55	2	13	15	14	3	0	0	0	0
Murray Henderson	D	60	2	9	11	28	5	0	1	1	2
Ed Harrison	C	59	5	5	10	20	4	0	0	0	0
Ed Kryzanowski	D	36	1	3	4	10	5	0	1	1	2
Dave Creighton	C	12	1	3	4	0	3	0	0	0	0
Zellio Toppazzini	R	5	1	1	2	0	2	0	0	0	0
Cliff Thompson	D	10	0	1	1	0					
Frank Brimsek	G	54	0	0	0	2	5	0	0	0	0
Jack Gelineau	G	4	0	0	0	0					
Gord Henry	G	1	0	0	0	0					
Les Colvin	G	1	0	0	0	0					

	REGULAR SEASON					*POSTSEASON*				
GOALTENDER		GP	MIN	GA	SH	GAA	GP	MIN	GA	SH	GAA
Gord Henry	(1-0-0)	1	60	0	1	0.00					
Frank Brimsek	(26-20-8)	54	3240	147	1	2.72	5	316	16	0	3.04
Jack Gelineau	(2-2-0)	4	240	12	0	3.00					
Les Colvin	(0-1-0)	1	60	4	0	4.00					

MONTREAL 28-23-9   65   3rd   Dick Irvin
Canadiens

		REGULAR SEASON					*POSTSEASON*				
PLAYER	POS	GP	G	A	PTS	PIM	GP	G	A	PTS	PIM
Billy Reay	C	**60**	22	23	45	33	7	1	5	6	4
Maurice Richard	R	59	20	18	38	110	7	2	1	3	14
Joe Carveth	R	**60**	15	22	37	8	7	0	1	1	8
Elmer Lach	C	36	11	18	29	59	1	0	0	0	4
Kenny Mosdell	C	**60**	17	9	26	50	7	1	1	2	4
Glen Harmon	D	59	8	12	20	44	7	1	1	2	4
Norm Dussault	C	47	9	8	17	6	2	0	0	0	0
Rip Riopelle	L	48	10	6	16	34	7	1	1	2	2
Doug Harvey	D	55	3	13	16	87	7	0	1	1	10
Ken Reardon	D	46	3	13	16	103	7	0	0	0	18
Roger Leger	D	28	6	7	13	10	5	0	1	1	2
Murph Chamberlain	C	54	5	8	13	111	4	0	0	0	8
Bob Fillion	L	59	3	9	12	14	7	0	1	1	4
Gerry Plamandon	L	27	5	5	10	8	7	5	1	6	0
Leo Gravelle	R	36	4	6	10	6	7	2	1	3	0
Jean-Claude Campeau	C	26	3	7	10	12	1	0	0	0	0
Hal Laycoe	D	51	3	5	8	31	7	0	1	1	13
George Robertson	C	30	2	5	7	6					
Emile Bouchard	D	27	3	3	6	42	7	0	0	0	6
Bill Durnan	G	**60**	0	0	0	0	7	0	0	0	0
Eddie Dorohoy	R	16	0	0	0	6					
Jacques Locas	R	3	0	0	0	0					
James MacPherson	D	3	0	0	0	2					
Murdo MacKay	C						6	1	1	2	0
Floyd Curry	R						2	0	0	0	2

	REGULAR SEASON					*POSTSEASON*				
GOALTENDER		GP	MIN	GA	SH	GAA	GP	MIN	GA	SH	GAA
Bill Durnan	(28-23-9)	**60**	**3600**	126	**10**	**2.10**	7	468	17	0	2.18

TORONTO 22-25-13   57   4th   Hap Day
Maple Leafs

		REGULAR SEASON					*POSTSEASON*				
PLAYER	POS	GP	G	A	PTS	PIM	GP	G	A	PTS	PIM
Harry Watson	L	**60**	26	19	45	0	9	4	2	6	2
Max Bentley	C	**60**	19	22	41	18	9	4	3	7	2
Ted Kennedy	C	59	18	21	39	25	9	2	**6**	8	2
Cal Gardner	C	53	13	22	35	35	9	2	5	7	0
Bill Ezinicki	R	52	13	15	28	**145**	9	1	4	5	20
Joe Klukay	L	45	11	10	21	11	9	2	3	5	4
Jimmy Thomson	D	**60**	4	16	20	56	9	1	5	6	10

		REGULAR SEASON					POSTSEASON				
PLAYER	POS	GP	G	A	PTS	PIM	GP	G	A	PTS	PIM
Vic Lynn	L	52	7	9	16	36	8	0	1	1	2
Ray Timgren	L	36	3	12	15	9	9	3	3	6	2
Gus Mortson	D	60	2	13	15	85	9	2	1	3	8
Howie Meeker	R	30	7	7	14	56					
Harry Taylor	C	42	4	7	11	30	1	0	0	0	0
Garth Boesch	D	59	1	10	11	43	9	0	2	2	6
Don Metz	L	33	4	6	10	12	3	0	0	0	0
Bill Barilko	D	60	5	4	9	95	9	0	1	1	20
Tod Sloan	R	29	3	4	7	0					
Les Costello	L	15	2	3	5	11					
Bill Juzda	D	38	1	2	3	23	9	0	2	2	8
Frank Mathers	D	15	1	2	3	2					
Ray Ceresino	R	12	1	1	2	2					
Fleming Mackell	C	11	1	1	2	6	9	2	4	6	4
Bobby Dawes	D	5	1	0	1	0	9	0	0	0	2
Al Buchanan	L	3	0	1	1	2					
Turk Broda	G	60	0	0	0	0	9	0	0	0	2
Ray Hannigan	R	3	0	0	0	2					
Chuck Blair	R	1	0	0	0	0					
Stan Kemp	D	1	0	0	0	2					
John McCormack	C	1	0	0	0	0					
Sid Smith	L	1	0	0	0	0	6	5	2	7	0

		REGULAR SEASON					POSTSEASON				
GOALTENDER		GP	MIN	GA	SH	GAA	GP	MIN	GA	SH	GAA
Turk Broda	(22-25-13)	60	3600	161	5	2.68	9	574	15	1	1.57

CHICAGO 21-31-8 50 5th Charlie Conacher
Blackhawks

		REGULAR SEASON					POSTSEASON
PLAYER	POS	GP	G	A	PTS	PIM	no postseason play
Roy Conacher	L	60	26	42	68	8	
Doug Bentley	L	58	23	43	66	38	
Jim Conacher (2-2)	C	55	25	23	48	41	
Gus Bodnar	C	59	19	26	45	14	
Bill Mosienko	R	60	17	25	42	6	
Gaye Stewart	L	54	20	18	38	57	
Bep Guidolin (2-2)	L	*56	4	17	21	116	
Adam Brown	L	58	8	12	20	69	
Metro Prystai	C	59	12	7	19	19	
Ralph Nattrass	D	60	4	10	14	99	
Bill Gadsby	D	50	3	10	13	85	
Red Hamill	L	57	8	4	12	16	
Bob Goldham	D	60	1	10	11	43	
Ernie Dickens	D	59	2	3	5	14	
Doug McCaig (2-2)	D	55	1	3	4	60	
Bert Olmstead	L	9	0	2	2	4	
George Gee (1-2)	C	4	0	2	2	4	
Jim Henry	G	60	0	0	0	0	
Bud Poile (1-2)	R	*4	0	0	0	2	

		REGULAR SEASON					POSTSEASON
GOALTENDER		GP	MIN	GA	SH	GAA	no postseason play
Jim Henry	(21-**31**-8)	**60**	**3600**	**211**	0	3.52	

NEW YORK   18-31-11   47   6th   Frank Boucher
Rangers

		REGULAR SEASON					POSTSEASON
PLAYER	POS	GP	G	A	PTS	PIM	no postseason play
Herb O'Connor	C	46	11	24	35	0	
Alex Kaleta	L	56	12	19	31	18	
Edgar Laprade	C	56	18	12	30	12	
Pentti Lund	R	59	14	16	30	16	
Tony Leswick	L	**60**	13	14	27	70	
Don Raleigh	C	41	10	16	26	8	
Dunc Fisher	R	**60**	9	16	25	40	
Nick Mickoski	L	54	13	9	22	20	
Clint Albright	C	59	14	5	19	19	
Jackie Gordon	C	31	3	9	12	0	
Allan Stanley	D	40	2	8	10	22	
Eddie Kullman	R	18	4	5	9	14	
Fred Shero	D	59	3	6	9	64	
Wally Stanowski	D	**60**	1	8	9	16	
Bill Moe	D	**60**	0	9	9	60	
Frank Eddolls	D	34	4	2	6	10	
Neil Colville	C	14	0	5	5	2	
Wes Trainor	C	17	1	2	3	6	
Eddie Slowinski	R	20	1	1	2	2	
Elwyn Morris	D	18	0	1	1	8	
Ray Manson	L	1	0	1	1	0	
Al Staley	C	1	0	1	1	0	
Charlie Rayner	G	58	0	0	0	2	
Jack Evans	D	3	0	0	0	4	
Ralph Buchanan	R	2	0	0	0	0	
Emile Francis	G	2	0	0	0	0	
Val Delory	L	1	0	0	0	0	
Dick Kotanen	D	1	0	0	0	0	
Odie Lowe	C	1	0	0	0	0	

		REGULAR SEASON					POSTSEASON
GOALTENDER		GP	MIN	GA	SH	GAA	no postseason play
Emile Francis	(2-0-0)	2	120	4	0	2.00	
Charlie Rayner	(16-**31**-11)	58	3480	168	7	2.90	

TEAM TOTALS

TEAM	GP	G	A	P	PIM	GA	SH	Per Game G	A	PIM	GA
Detroit	60	**195**	249	444	621	145	6	**3.25**	4.15	10.35	2.42
Boston	60	178	233	411	434	163	2	2.97	3.88	7.23	2.72
Montreal	60	152	197	349	**782**	**126**	10	2.53	3.28	**13.03**	**2.10**
Toronto	60	147	207	354	706	161	5	2.45	3.45	11.77	2.68
Chicago	60	173	**257**	430	695	211	0	2.88	**4.28**	11.58	3.52
New York	60	133	189	322	413	174	7	2.22	3.15	6.88	2.90
	360	978	1332	2310	3651	978	30	2.72	3.70	10.14	2.72

PLAYOFFS

SERIES "A"
Detroit 2, Montreal 1 (OT)
Montreal 4, Detroit 3 (OT)
Detroit 3, Montreal 1
Detroit 3, Montreal 1
Montreal 3, Detroit 1
Detroit 3, Montreal 1

DETROIT, 4–3

SERIES "C"
Toronto 3, Detroit 2
Toronto 3, Detroit 1
Toronto 3, Detroit 1
Toronto 3, Detroit 1

**TORONTO WINS
STANLEY CUP, 4–0**

SERIES "B"
Toronto 3, Boston 0
Toronto 3, Boston 2
Boston 5, Toronto 4 (OT)
Toronto 3, Boston 1
Toronto 3, Boston 2

TORONTO, 4–1

ALL-STAR TEAMS

First Team
G — Bill Durnan, MTL
D — Bill Quackenbush, DET
D — Jack Stewart, DET
C — Sid Abel, DET
R — Maurice Richard, MTL
L — Roy Conacher, CHI

Second Team
G — Charlie Rayner, NY
D — Glen Harmon, MTL
D — Ken Reardon, MTL
C — Doug Bentley, CHI
R — Gordie Howe, DET
L — Ted Lindsay, DET

INDIVIDUAL TROPHY WINNERS

HART TROPHY (Most Valuable Player): Sid Abel, DET
LADY BYNG TROPHY (Gentlemanly Conduct): Bill Quackenbush, DET
VEZINA TROPHY (Best Goaltender): Bill Durnan, MTL
CALDER MEMORIAL TROPHY (Best Rookie): Pentti Lund, NY
ART ROSS TROPHY (Scoring Leader): Roy Conacher, CHI

1949-1950

Linemates

In the game of hockey, the forward line is one of its most crucial elements. Consisting of three players — a center, right wing and left wing — this trio most often played as a unit. Staying together sometimes for years, these groupings were often given colorful nicknames, indicative of a characteristic of the players or the region in which they played. As the NHL was about to find out, one of its most famous group of linemates was on the threshold of greatness.

One of the NHL's first lines to be given a nickname played in Toronto in the early 1930s. Dubbed the Kid Line, because of their relatively young age (LW Harvey "Busher" Jackson, C Joe Primeau and RW Charlie Conacher) this group was one of the top scoring trios of the era. For instance, in 1931-32, Jackson and Primeau finished first and second in the scoring race, while Conacher ended fourth. A few years later, a new line in Boston upped the ante. Called the Kraut Line, after the ethnic origins of its members (C Milt Schmidt, LW Woody Dumart and RW Bobby Bauer) this group ended the 1939-40 season in the first three scoring slots. In the late 1940s, a new powerful line was coalescing in the Motor City. Soon, this grouping would lead the Wings to the top of the heap.

During the 1947-48 season, veteran Detroit center, Sid Abel was given a new pair of linemates. The first, was a tough left winger named Ted Lindsay, who had joined the team a few years previously. Joining them was an equally tough newcomer — right winger Gordie Howe, who was in his second season. The line didn't click right away, as only Lindsay managed to crack the top ten in scoring. The following year, both Lindsay and Abel finished in the top five. Soon, the third member of the group would make his presence known.

Over the course of the newly expanded 70-game schedule, the Red Wings

(37-19-14, 88) rolled to a comfortable first place finish. Instrumental to their success was their top line. Now called the Production Line, after Detroit's auto industry, this line outpaced all others, as the trio grabbed the top three scoring slots, duplicating the Kraut Lines' ten-year-old feat. In first was assist leader Lindsay (23-55-78), followed by Abel (34-35-69) and Howe (35-33-68), the latter besting goals leader Montreal's Maurice Richard (43) by three points. Other noteworthy achievements included Bill Ezinicki's (Toronto) second straight tough guy award (144). In goal, Montreal's Bill Durnan (2.20) won his sixth GAA crown, although he ceded the shutout glory to Toronto's Turk Broda (9).

Behind Detroit, the other playoff spots were nabbed by Montreal, Toronto and New York, while Boston and Chicago finished out of the running. In the first round, Toronto shutout the Wings in two of the first three games, before Detroit came back with a 2–1 overtime win to knot the series. After a third shutout victory by the Leafs, Detroit turned the tables — blanking Toronto twice (the latter a 1–0 overtime tilt) to take the hard fought series. In the other slate, the Rangers surprised the Canadiens in five games, the only blemish a 3–2 overtime loss in the fourth game.

Once again in the finals, after many years, the Rangers faced the same quandary that had plagued them before. Ousted from their home by the circus, the team was forced to play their "home" games in a neutral site — this time Toronto. Despite this handicap, New York battled Detroit tooth and nail for the crown. After the Red Wings took a two games to one lead, the Rangers took command, winning a pair of overtime contests (4–3 and 2–1) — both winners coming off the stick of Don Raleigh. Detroit then edged the Rangers, 5–4, setting up a final showdown. In the seventh game, New York took a lead in the third period, only to have the Red Wings tie it up with less than five minutes left. Scoreless in the first extra stanza, Detroit's Pete Babando scored eight minutes into the second overtime, giving Detroit a 4–3 win and the Cup.

The Production Lines' Abel led all playoff scorers with six goals, while his teammate George Gee garnered the most assists (6). The top scorer, Pentii Lund — who also netted six markers — graced the roster of the Rangers (11). In net, semifinal loser — Toronto's Turk Broda — posted the lowest GAA (1.33), courtesy of his three shutouts.

The NHL's habit of nicknaming its lines continued for a while, before falling into disuse today, mostly because of changing strategy which now mixes and matches forward lineups. As for the Production Line, it too continued for many years. Although remaining prolific, this line — or any other for that matter — never again duplicated the difficult feat of placing all three of its members at the top of the league's scoring chart.

STANDINGS

TEAM	GP	W	L	T	PTS	GF	GA
DETROIT	70	37	19	14	88	229	164
MONTREAL	70	29	22	19	77	172	150
TORONTO	70	31	27	12	74	176	173
NEW YORK	70	28	31	11	67	170	189
BOSTON	70	22	32	16	60	198	228
CHICAGO	70	22	38	10	54	203	244

LEADERS

PLAYER	TM	GP	G	A	PTS	PIM
Ted Lindsay	DET	69	23	**55**	78	141
Sid Abel	DET	69	34	35	69	46
Gordie Howe	DET	70	35	33	68	69
Maurice Richard	MTL	70	**43**	22	65	114
Paul Ronty	BOS	70	23	36	59	8
Roy Conacher	CHI	70	25	31	56	16
Doug Bentley	CHI	64	20	33	53	28
Johnny Peirson	BOS	57	27	25	52	49
Metro Prystai	CHI	65	29	22	51	31
Bep Guidolin	CHI	70	17	34	51	42

GOALS	
Richard, MTL	43
Howe, DET	35
Abel, DET	34
Prystai, CHI	29
Peirson, BOS	27

ASSISTS	
Lindsay, DET	55
Ronty, BOS	36
Abel, DET	35
Guidolin, CHI	34
Three tied with	33

GOALTENDER	TM	GP	MIN	GA	SH	GAA
Bill Durnan	MTL	64	3840	141	8	**2.20**
Harry Lumley	DET	63	3780	148	7	2.35
Turk Broda	TOR	68	4040	167	**9**	2.48
Charlie Rayner	NY	69	4140	181	6	2.62
Jack Gelineau	BOS	67	4020	220	3	3.28
Frank Brimsek	CHI	**70**	**4200**	**244**	5	3.49

PENALTY MINUTES	
Ezinicki, TOR	144
Kyle, NY	143
Lindsay, DET	141
Gadsby, CHI	138
Mortson, TOR	125

SHUTOUTS	
Broda, TOR	9
Durnan, MTL	8
Lumley, DET	7
Rayner, NY	6
Brimsek, CHI	5

DETROIT Red Wings   37-19-14   88   1st   Tommy Ivan

		REGULAR SEASON					POSTSEASON				
PLAYER	POS	GP	G	A	PTS	PIM	GP	G	A	PTS	PIM
Ted Lindsay	L	69	23	**55**	78	141	13	4	4	8	16
Sid Abel	C	69	34	35	69	46	**14**	6	2	8	6
Gordie Howe	R	70	35	33	68	69	1	0	0	0	7
Red Kelly	D	70	15	25	40	9	**14**	1	3	4	2
George Gee	C	69	17	21	38	42	**14**	3	6	9	0
Gerry Couture	C	69	24	7	31	21	**14**	5	4	9	2
Jimmy Peters	R	70	14	16	30	20	8	0	2	2	0
Jim McFadden	C	68	14	16	30	8	**14**	2	3	5	8
Joe Carveth (2-2)	R	*60	13	17	30	13	**14**	2	4	6	6

1948–1949   267

		REGULAR SEASON					POSTSEASON				
PLAYER	POS	GP	G	A	PTS	PIM	GP	G	A	PTS	PIM
Marty Pavelich	L	65	8	15	23	58	14	4	2	6	13
Steve Black	L	69	7	14	21	53	13	0	0	0	13
Leo Reise	D	70	4	17	21	46	14	2	0	2	19
Jack Stewart	D	65	3	11	14	86	14	1	4	5	20
Pete Babando	L	56	6	6	12	25	8	2	2	4	2
Lee Fogolin	D	63	4	8	12	63	10	0	0	0	16
Max McNab	C	65	4	4	8	8	10	0	0	0	0
Clare Martin	D	64	2	5	7	14	10	0	1	1	0
Al Dewsbury	D	11	2	2	4	2	4	0	3	3	8
Harry Lumley	G	63	0	0	0	0	14	0	0	0	0
Fred Glover	C	7	0	0	0	0					
Terry Sawchuk	G	7	0	0	0	0					
Enio Sclisizzi	L	4	0	0	0	2					
Glen Skov	L	2	0	0	0	0					
Johnny Wilson	L	1	0	0	0	0	8	0	1	1	0
Larry Wilson	C	1	0	0	0	2	4	0	0	0	0
Marcel Pronovost	D						9	0	1	1	10
Gord Haidy	R						1	0	0	0	0
Doug McKay	L						1	0	0	0	0

		REGULAR SEASON					POSTSEASON				
GOALTENDER		GP	MIN	GA	SH	GAA	GP	MIN	GA	SH	GAA
Terry Sawchuk	(4-3-0)	7	420	16	1	2.29					
Harry Lumley	(33-16-14)	63	3780	148	7	2.35	14	910	28	3	1.85

MONTREAL   29-22-19   77   2nd   Dick Irvin
Canadiens

		REGULAR SEASON					POSTSEASON				
PLAYER	POS	GP	G	A	PTS	PIM	GP	G	A	PTS	PIM
Maurice Richard	R	70	43	22	65	114	5	1	1	2	6
Elmer Lach	C	64	15	33	48	33	5	1	2	3	4
Billy Reay	C	68	19	26	45	48	4	0	1	1	0
Norm Dussault	C	67	13	24	37	22	5	3	1	4	0
Leo Gravelle	R	70	19	10	29	18	4	0	0	0	0
Ken Reardon	D	67	1	27	28	109	2	0	2	2	12
Kenny Mosdell	C	67	15	12	27	42	5	0	0	0	12
Doug Harvey	D	70	4	20	24	76	5	0	2	2	10
Rip Riopelle	L	66	12	8	20	27	1	0	0	0	0
Glen Harmon	D	62	3	16	19	28	5	0	1	1	21
Calum MacKay	L	52	8	10	18	44	5	0	1	1	2
Floyd Curry	R	49	8	8	16	8	5	1	0	1	2
Roger Leger	D	55	3	12	15	21	4	0	0	0	2
Grant Warwick	R	26	2	6	8	19					
Emile Bouchard	D	69	1	7	8	88	5	0	2	2	2
Gerry Plamandon	L	37	1	5	6	0	3	0	1	1	2
Bob Fillion	L	57	1	3	4	8	5	0	0	0	0
Bert Hirschfeld	L	13	1	2	3	2	5	1	0	1	0
Giles Dube	L	12	1	2	3	2					
Joe Carveth (1-2)	R	*11	1	1	2	2					
Hal Laycoe	D	30	0	2	2	21	2	0	0	0	0

		REGULAR SEASON				POSTSEASON				
PLAYER	POS	GP	G	A	PTS	PIM	GP	G	A	PTS	PIM
Bob Fryday	R	2	1	0	1	0					
Bill Durnan	G	64	0	1	1	2	3	0	0	0	0
Lulu Denis	R	2	0	1	1	0					
Gerry McNeil	G	6	0	0	0	0	2	0	0	0	0
Bob Frampton	L	2	0	0	0	0	3	0	0	0	0
Paul Meger	L						2	0	0	0	2
Tom Johnson	D						1	0	0	0	0

		REGULAR SEASON				POSTSEASON				
GOALTENDER		GP	MIN	GA	SH	GAA	GP	MIN	GA	SH	GAA
Gerry McNeil	(3-1-2)	6	360	9	1	1.50	2	135	5	0	2.22
Bill Durnan	(26-21-17)	64	3840	141	8	**2.20**	3	180	10	0	3.33

TORONTO 31-27-12 74 3rd Hap Day
Maple Leafs

		REGULAR SEASON				POSTSEASON				
PLAYER	POS	GP	G	A	PTS	PIM	GP	G	A	PTS	PIM
Sid Smith	L	68	22	23	45	6	7	0	3	3	2
Ted Kennedy	C	53	20	24	44	34	7	1	2	3	8
Max Bentley	C	69	23	18	41	14	7	3	3	6	0
Howie Meeker	R	70	18	22	40	35	7	0	1	1	4
Harry Watson	L	60	19	16	35	11	7	0	0	0	2
Joe Klukay	L	70	15	16	31	19	7	3	0	3	4
Cal Gardner	C	31	7	19	26	12	7	1	0	1	4
Ray Timgren	L	68	7	18	25	22	6	0	4	4	2
Bill Ezinicki	R	67	10	12	22	**144**	5	0	0	0	13
Vic Lynn	L	70	7	13	20	39	7	0	2	2	2
Fleming Mackell	C	36	7	13	20	24	7	1	1	2	11
Bill Barilko	D	59	7	10	17	85	7	1	1	2	18
Gus Mortson	D	68	3	14	17	125	7	0	0	0	18
Bill Juzda	D	62	1	14	15	68	7	0	0	0	16
Jimmy Thomson	D	70	0	13	13	76	7	0	2	2	7
John McCormack	C	34	6	5	11	0	6	1	0	1	0
Garth Boesch	D	58	2	6	8	63	6	0	0	0	4
Rudy Migay	C	18	1	5	6	8					
Bobby Dawes	D	11	1	2	3	2					
Frank Mathers	D	6	0	1	1	2					
Turk Broda	G	68	0	0	0	2	7	0	0	0	0
John Arundel	D	3	0	0	0	9					
George Armstrong	C	2	0	0	0	0					
Hugh Bolton	D	2	0	0	0	0					
Phil Samis	D	2	0	0	0	0					
Al Rollins	G	2	0	0	0	0					
Al Buchanan	L	1	0	0	0	0					
Bob Hassard	C	1	0	0	0	0					
Tim Horton	D	1	0	0	0	2	1	0	0	0	2
Bill Johansen	C	1	0	0	0	0					
Frank Sullivan	D	1	0	0	0	0					
Gil Mayer	G	1	0	0	0	0					
Les Costello	L						1	0	0	0	0

1948-1949 269

GOALTENDER		*REGULAR SEASON*					*POSTSEASON*				
		GP	MIN	GA	SH	GAA					
Gil Mayer	(0-1-0)	1	60	2	0	2.00	*no postseason play*				
Al Rollins	(1-1-0)	2	100	4	1	2.40					
Turk Broda	(30-25-12)	68	4040	167	9	2.48	7	450	10	**3**	**1.33**

NEW YORK 28-31-11 67 4th Lynn Patrick
Rangers

		REGULAR SEASON					*POSTSEASON*				
PLAYER	POS	GP	G	A	PTS	PIM	GP	G	A	PTS	PIM
Edgar Laprade	C	60	22	22	44	2	12	3	5	8	4
Tony Leswick	L	69	19	25	44	85	12	2	4	6	12
Eddie Slowinski	R	63	14	23	37	12	12	2	6	8	6
Don Raleigh	C	70	12	25	37	11	12	4	5	9	4
Dunc Fisher	R	70	12	21	33	42	12	3	3	6	14
Herb O'Connor	C	66	11	22	33	4	12	4	2	6	4
Alex Kaleta	L	67	17	14	31	40	10	0	3	3	0
Pentti Lund	R	64	18	9	27	16	12	**6**	5	**11**	0
Nick Mickoski	L	45	10	10	20	10	12	1	5	6	2
Pat Egan	D	70	5	11	16	50	12	3	1	4	6
Jackie McLeod	R	38	6	9	15	2	7	0	0	0	0
Fred Shero	D	67	2	8	10	71	7	0	1	1	2
Bud Poile (1-2)	R	27	3	6	9	8					
Allan Stanley	D	55	4	4	8	58	12	2	5	7	10
Gus Kyle	D	70	3	5	8	143	12	1	2	3	**30**
Frank Eddolls	D	58	2	6	8	20	11	0	1	1	4
J-P Lamirande	D	16	4	3	7	6	2	0	0	0	0
Jack Lancien	D	43	1	4	5	27	4	0	1	1	0
Bing Juckes	L	14	2	1	3	6					
Wally Stanowoski	D	37	1	1	2	10					
Don Smith	C	11	1	1	2	0	1	0	0	0	0
Odie Lowe	C	3	1	1	2	0					
Sherm White	C	3	0	2	2	0					
Doug Adams	L	4	0	1	1	0					
Jean-Paul Denis	R	4	0	1	1	2					
Charlie Rayner	G	69	0	0	0	6	12	0	0	0	0
Chick Webster	C	14	0	0	0	4					
Bill McDonagh	L	4	0	0	0	2					
Jack Evans	D	2	0	0	0	2					
Bill Kyle	C	2	0	0	0	0					
Jackie Gordon	C	1	0	0	0	0	9	1	1	2	7
Fern Perreault	L	1	0	0	0	0					
Emile Francis	G	1	0	0	0	0					

GOALTENDER		*REGULAR SEASON*					*POSTSEASON*				
		GP	MIN	GA	SH	GAA	GP	MIN	GA	SH	GAA
Charlie Rayner	(28-30-11)	69	4140	181	6	2.62	12	775	29	1	2.00
Emile Francis	(0-1-0)	1	60	8	0	8.00					

BOSTON 22-32-16 60 5th Georges Boucher
Bruins

REGULAR SEASON   *POSTSEASON*

PLAYER	POS	GP	G	A	PTS	PIM
Paul Ronty	C	70	23	36	59	8
Johnny Peirson	R	57	27	25	52	49
Phil Maloney	C	70	15	31	46	6
Milt Schmidt	C	68	19	22	41	41
Kenny Smith	L	66	10	31	41	12
Woody Dumart	L	69	14	25	39	14
Dave Creighton	C	64	18	13	31	13
Bud Poile (2–2)	R	39	16	14	30	6
Ed Harrison	C	70	14	12	26	23
Bill Quackenbush	D	70	8	17	25	4
Sam Bettio	L	44	9	12	21	32
Ed Kryzanowski	D	57	6	10	16	12
Murray Henderson	D	64	3	8	11	42
Zellio Toppazzini	R	36	5	5	10	18
Pete Horeck	L	34	5	5	10	22
Jack Crawford	D	46	2	8	10	8
Fern Flaman	D	69	2	5	7	122
Ed Sandford	L	19	1	4	5	6
Lorne Ferguson	L	3	1	1	2	0
Arnie Kullman	C	12	0	1	1	11
George Sullivan	C	3	0	1	1	0
Gord Byers	D	1	0	1	1	0
Jack McIntyre	L	1	0	1	1	0
Jack Gelineau	G	67	0	0	0	0
Ross Lowe	D	3	0	0	0	0
Gord Henry	G	2	0	0	0	0
Bart Bradley	C	1	0	0	0	0
Norm Corcoran	C	1	0	0	0	0
Dick Bittner	G	1	0	0	0	0

REGULAR SEASON   *POSTSEASON*

GOALTENDER		GP	MIN	GA	SH	GAA
Gord Henry	(0-2-0)	2	120	5	0	2.50
Dick Bittner	(0-0-1)	1	60	3	0	3.00
Jack Gelineau	(22-30-15)	67	4020	220	3	3.28

no postseason play

CHICAGO 22-38-10 54 6th Charlie Conacher
Blackhawks

REGULAR SEASON   *POSTSEASON*

PLAYER	POS	GP	G	A	PTS	PIM
Roy Conacher	L	70	25	31	56	16
Doug Bentley	L	64	20	33	53	28
Metro Prystai	C	65	29	22	51	31
Bep Guidolin	L	70	17	34	51	42
Bert Olmstead	L	70	20	29	49	40
Bill Mosienko	R	69	18	28	46	10
Gaye Stewart	L	70	24	19	43	43
Gus Bodnar	C	70	11	28	39	6

no postseason play

1948–1949

PLAYER	POS	REGULAR SEASON GP	G	A	PTS	PIM	POSTSEASON
							no postseason play
Bill Gadsby	D	70	10	25	35	138	
Jim Conacher	C	66	13	20	33	14	
Ralph Nattrass	D	68	5	11	16	96	
Ernie Dickens	D	70	0	13	13	22	
Bob Goldham	D	67	2	10	12	57	
Red Hamill	L	59	6	2	8	6	
Adam Brown	L	25	2	2	4	16	
Doug McCaig	D	63	0	4	4	49	
Vic Stasiuk	L	17	1	1	2	2	
Ed Leier	C	5	0	1	1	0	
Frank Brimsek	G	70	0	0	0	2	
Jack Miller	C	6	0	0	0	0	
Jim Bedard	D	5	0	0	0	2	

GOALTENDER		REGULAR SEASON GP	MIN	GA	SH	GAA	POSTSEASON
Frank Brimsek	(22-38-10)	70	4200	244	5	3.49	no postseason play

TEAM TOTALS

TEAM	GP	G	A	P	PIM	GA	SH	Per Game G	A	PIM	GA
Detroit	70	**229**	307	**536**	736	164	8	**3.27**	4.39	10.51	2.34
Montreal	70	172	257	429	736	**150**	9	2.46	3.67	10.51	**2.14**
Toronto	70	176	264	440	**804**	173	**10**	2.51	3.77	**11.49**	2.47
New York	70	170	235	405	639	189	6	2.43	3.36	9.13	2.70
Boston	70	198	288	486	449	228	3	2.83	4.11	6.41	3.26
Chicago	70	203	**313**	516	620	244	5	2.90	**4.47**	8.86	3.49
	420	1148	1664	2812	3984	1148	41	2.73	3.96	9.49	2.73

PLAYOFFS

SERIES "A"
Toronto 5, Detroit 0
Detroit 3, Toronto 1
Toronto 2, Detroit 0
Detroit 2, Toronto 1 (OT)
Toronto 2, Detroit 0
Detroit 4, Toronto 0
Detroit 1, Toronto 0 (OT)

DETROIT, 4–3

SERIES "C"
Detroit 4, New York 1
New York 3, Detroit 1
Detroit 4, New York 0
New York 4, Detroit 3 (OT)
New York 2, Detroit 1 (OT)

SERIES "B"
New York 3, Montreal 1
New York 3, Montreal 2
New York 4, Montreal 1
Montreal 3, New York 0 (OT)
New York 3, Montreal 0

NEW YORK, 4–1

Detroit 5, New York 4
Detroit 4, New York 3 (OT)

**DETROIT WINS
STANLEY CUP, 4-3**

ALL-STAR TEAMS

First Team
G — Bill Durnan, MTL
D — Gus Mortson, TOR
D — Ken Reardon, MTL
C — Sid Abel, DET
R — Maurice Richard, MTL
L — Ted Lindsay, MTL

Second Team
G — Charlie Rayner, NY
D — Red Kelly, DET
D — Leo Reise, DET
C — Ted Kennedy, TOR
R — Gordie Howe, DET
L — Tony Leswick, NY

INDIVIDUAL TROPHY WINNERS

HART TROPHY (Most Valuable Player): Charlie Rayner, NY
LADY BYNG TROPHY (Gentlemanly Conduct): Edgar Laprade, NY
VEZINA TROPHY (Best Goaltender): Bill Durnan, MTL
CALDER MEMORIAL TROPHY (Best Rookie): Jack Gelineau, BOS
ART ROSS TROPHY (Scoring Leader): Ted Lindsay, DET

1950-1951

A Moment in Time

In the back of every hockey players mind is a dream — a dream about being a hero — a dream in which you net a crucial goal in a big game. This moment was about to come true for one young defenseman, just rounding into form as one the game's top players. Tragically for him, his moment in the sun was to be brief.

In the late 1940s, a defenseman named Bill Barilko made his debut for the Toronto Maple Leafs. The rugged player debuted in 1946-47, splitting his time between the Leafs and the Hollywood Wolves of the PCHA. Back for good the following year, the 20-year-old Barilko announced his presence, leading the league with 147 penalty minutes. Over the next two seasons, he honed his game, perfecting his signature move, the hip check, which he used with great regularity.

Over the course of the 1950-51 campaign, Barilko and the Leafs put together a 95-point season, a result that shattered the NHL's existing best. Unfortunately for them, the Red Wings (44-13-13, 101) also enjoyed a stupendous campaign, becoming the first team to cross the century threshold in points. Much further behind, Montreal and Boston grabbed the third and fourth playoff spots, just ahead of New York. The moribund Blackhawks, with only 13 wins, finished dead last.

Individually, Detroit's Gordie Howe (43-43-86) dominated the scoring sheet, setting a record for most points, while leading the circuit in goals and assists, though he was tied in the latter category by Toronto's Ted Kennedy. The Leafs also showcased the toughest player, Gus Mortson (144 penalty minutes) and the top goaler, Al Rollins (1.77), the latter sharing time with Turk Broda in one of the league's first goalie platoon systems. Also, Detroit newcomer Terry Sawchuk blanked 11 opponents.

In the first game of the opening round, Boston stunned the favored Leafs, 2–0. Curfew ended the second contest with the combatants tied 1–1. Resuming action the next night, Toronto went on to sweep the next four games, allowing the Bruins only two goals. In the other opening series, Montreal turned the tables on the Red Wings, as Maurice Richard netted a pair of overtime winners to give the Canadiens a quick two game lead. Although Detroit eventually tied the series, Montreal posted 5–2 and 3–2 wins to move into the finals.

In the first game of what was to be a classic series, Toronto edged Montreal 3–2 on Sid Smith's overtime winner. Three nights later, Richard scored his third overtime marker of the postseason, as the Canadiens evened the score. The next two contests also went beyond regulation, with Toronto's Ted Kennedy and Harry Watson giving the Leafs a commanding series lead. With all of the previous contests going to overtime, no one was surprised when the fifth game remained tied after 60 minutes. Less than three minutes into the extra session, Toronto struck. Leaf player Watson, as described in Kevin Shea's *Barilko—Without a Trace* recalls: "Barilko was supposed to stay on the blue line, but he saw the puck coming out, so he just roared in and took a slap at it. He made contact at it and sent it toward the goal. McNeil [Montreal's goalie] had gone down on the ice and Barilko was on his way too.... There have been a lot of great overtime goals in the history of the NHL but to me, Barilko's was one of the best ... a perfect ending to a tremendous series." Overall, in the playoffs, Toronto's Max Bentley and Richard each collected 13 points, with Bentley amassing 11 assists, while Richard scored nine goals. In net, Turk Broda (1.10, 2) reigned supreme.

In August 1951, as summer was winding down, Barilko and a pilot friend—Dr. Henry Hudson—decided to take a fishing trip to northern Ontario in Hudson's aircraft. On one of the return legs, the pair disappeared, vanishing into the wilds. The overdue plane triggered a massive manhunt, as all of Canada waited for news about its hockey hero. Despite thousands of man hours devoted to the search—the largest ever undertaken to that point—no trace of Barilko and Hudson was found—at least not yet.

In May 1962, Gary Fields, on a routine flight, spotted a "glint of yellow" in the swamp below. It was the pontoon of Hudson's plane, missing these eleven years. Fields speculates why it wasn't found during the original search: "When I found the spot ... I saw that you had to be directly over the place before you could see anything.... They must have stalled and gone straight down."

Despite the tragic end to Barilko's story, we can take some comfort in the fact that his shining Cup moment was captured on film. Shot by Nat Turofsky, this photo perfectly captures the flying Barilko just after he releases the game winner, preserving this moment in time — a moment that all can remember with fondness about an individual whose time ended much too soon.

STANDINGS

TEAM	GP	W	L	T	PTS	GF	GA
DETROIT	70	44	13	13	101	236	139
TORONTO	70	41	16	13	95	212	138
MONTREAL	70	25	30	15	65	173	184
BOSTON	70	22	30	18	62	178	197
NEW YORK	70	20	29	21	61	169	201
CHICAGO	70	13	47	10	36	171	280

LEADERS

PLAYER	TM	GP	G	A	PTS	PIM
Gordie Howe	DET	70	43	43	86	74
Maurice Richard	MTL	65	42	24	66	97
Max Bentley	TOR	67	21	41	62	34
Sid Abel	DET	69	23	38	61	30
Milt Schmidt	BOS	62	22	39	61	33
Ted Kennedy	TOR	63	18	43	61	32
Ted Lindsay	DET	67	24	35	59	110
Tod Sloan	TOR	70	31	25	56	105
Red Kelly	DET	70	17	37	54	24
Two tied with					51	

GOALS
Howe, DET	43
Richard, MTL	42
Sloan, TOR	31
Smith, TOR	30
Conacher, CHI	26

ASSISTS
Howe, DET	43
Kennedy, TOR	43
M. Bentley, TOR	41
Schmidt, BOS	39
Abel, DET	38

GOALTENDER	TM	GP	MIN	GA	SH	GAA
Al Rollins	TOR	40	2373	70	5	**1.77**
Terry Sawchuk	DET	70	4200	139	11	1.99
Turk Broda	TOR	31	1827	68	6	2.23
Gerry McNeil	MTL	70	4200	184	6	2.63
Jack Gelineau	BOS	70	4200	197	4	2.81
Charlie Rayner	NY	66	3940	187	2	2.85
Harry Lumley	CHI	64	3785	246	3	3.90

PENALTY MINUTES
Mortson, TOR	142
Johnson, MTL	128
Ezinicki, BOS	119
Leswick, NY	112
Lindsay, DET	110

SHUTOUTS
Sawchuk, DET	11
Broda, TOR	6
McNeil, MTL	6
Rollins, TOR	5
Gelineau, BOS	4

DETROIT 44-13-13 101 1st Tommy Ivan
Red Wings

		REGULAR SEASON					POSTSEASON			
PLAYER	POS	GP	G	A	PTS	PIM	GP	G	A	PTS	PIM
Gordie Howe	R	70	43	43	86	74	6	4	3	7	4
Sid Abel	C	69	23	38	61	30	6	4	3	7	0
Ted Lindsay	L	67	24	35	59	110	6	0	1	1	8
Red Kelly	D	70	17	37	54	24	6	0	1	1	0
Jimmy Peters	R	68	17	21	38	14	6	0	0	0	0
Metro Prystai	C	62	20	17	37	27	3	1	0	1	0

		REGULAR SEASON				*POSTSEASON*				
PLAYER	*POS*	*GP*	*G*	*A*	*PTS*	*PIM*	*GP*	*G*	*A*	*PTS*	*PIM*
George Gee	C	70	17	20	37	19	6	0	1	1	0
Jim McFadden	C	70	14	18	32	10	6	0	0	0	2
Gaye Stewart	L	67	18	13	31	18	6	0	2	2	4
Marty Pavelich	L	67	9	20	29	41	6	0	1	1	2
Bob Goldham	D	61	5	18	23	31	6	0	1	1	2
Leo Reise	D	68	5	16	21	67	6	2	3	5	2
Gerry Couture	C	53	7	6	13	2	6	1	1	2	0
Glen Skov	L	19	7	6	13	13	6	0	0	0	0
Vic Stasiuk (1–2)	L	50	3	10	13	12					
Clare Martin	D	50	1	6	7	12	2	0	0	0	0
Marcel Pronovost	D	37	1	6	7	20	6	0	0	0	0
Joe Carveth	R	30	1	4	5	0					
Clare Raglan	D	33	3	1	4	14					
Leo Gravelle (2–2)	R	18	1	2	3	6					
Lee Fogolin (1–2)	D	19	0	1	1	16					
Lou Jankowski	C	1	0	1	1	0					
Terry Sawchuk	G	70	0	0	0	2	6	0	0	0	0
Steve Black (1–2)	L	5	0	0	0	2					
Benny Woit	R	2	0	0	0	2					
Alex Delvecchio	C	1	0	0	0	0					
Fred Glover	C						6	0	0	0	0
Max McNab	C						2	0	0	0	0
Johnny Wilson	L						1	0	0	0	0

	REGULAR SEASON					*POSTSEASON*				
GOALTENDER	*GP*	*MIN*	*GA*	*SH*	*GAA*	*GP*	*MIN*	*GA*	*SH*	*GAA*
Terry Sawchuk (44-13-13)	70	4200	139	11	1.99	6	463	13	1	1.68

TORONTO 41-16-13 95 2nd Joe Primeau
Maple Leafs

		REGULAR SEASON				*POSTSEASON*				
PLAYER	*POS*	*GP*	*G*	*A*	*PTS*	*PIM*	*GP*	*G*	*A*	*PTS*	*PIM*
Max Bentley	C	67	21	41	62	34	11	2	11	13	4
Ted Kennedy	C	63	18	43	61	32	11	4	5	9	6
Tod Sloan	R	70	31	25	56	105	11	4	5	9	18
Sid Smith	L	70	30	21	51	10	11	7	3	10	0
Cal Gardner	C	66	23	28	51	42	11	1	1	2	4
Harry Watson	L	68	18	19	37	18	5	1	2	3	4
Jimmy Thomson	D	69	3	33	36	76	11	0	1	1	34
Danny Lewicki	L	61	16	18	34	26	9	0	0	0	0
Joe Klukay	L	70	14	16	30	16	11	4	3	7	0
Fleming Mackell	C	70	12	13	25	40	11	2	3	5	9
Howie Meeker	R	49	6	14	20	24	11	1	1	2	14
John McCormack	C	46	6	7	13	2					
Gus Mortson	D	60	3	10	13	142	11	0	1	1	4
Bill Barilko	D	58	6	6	12	96	11	3	2	5	31
Ray Timgren	L	70	1	9	10	20	11	0	1	1	2
Bill Juzda	D	65	0	9	9	64	11	0	0	0	7
Fern Flaman (2–2)	D	39	2	6	8	64	9	1	0	1	8
Hugh Bolton	D	13	1	3	4	4					

		REGULAR SEASON					POSTSEASON				
PLAYER	POS	GP	G	A	PTS	PIM	GP	G	A	PTS	PIM
Phil Maloney (2–2)	C	1	1	0	1	0					
Bob Hassard	C	12	0	1	1	0					
Al Rollins	G	40	0	0	0	0	4	0	0	0	0
Turk Broda	G	31	0	0	0	4	8	0	0	0	0
George Blair	C	2	0	0	0	0					
Bobby Copp	D	2	0	0	0	2					
Andy Barbe	R	1	0	0	0	2					

		REGULAR SEASON					POSTSEASON				
GOALTENDER		GP	MIN	GA	SH	GAA	GP	MIN	GA	SH	GAA
Al Rollins	(27-5-8)	40	2373	70	5	**1.77**	4	210	6	0	2.00
Turk Broda	(14-11-5)	31	1827	68	6	2.23	8	492	9	**2**	**1.10**

MONTREAL   25-30-15   65   3rd   Dick Irvin
Canadiens

		REGULAR SEASON					POSTSEASON				
PLAYER	POS	GP	G	A	PTS	PIM	GP	G	A	PTS	PIM
Maurice Richard	R	65	42	24	66	97	11	9	4	13	13
Elmer Lach	C	65	21	24	45	48	11	2	2	4	2
Bert Olmstead (2–2)	L	39	16	22	38	50	11	2	4	6	9
Kenny Mosdell	C	66	13	18	31	24	11	1	1	2	4
Doug Harvey	D	70	5	24	29	93	11	0	5	5	12
Calum MacKay	L	70	18	10	28	69	11	1	0	1	0
Floyd Curry	R	69	13	14	27	23	11	0	2	2	2
Billy Reay	C	60	6	18	24	24	11	3	3	6	10
Norm Dussault	C	64	4	20	24	15					
James MacPherson	D	62	0	16	16	40	11	0	2	2	8
Bernie Geoffrion	R	18	8	6	14	9	11	1	1	2	6
Glen Harmon	D	57	2	12	14	27	1	0	0	0	0
Emile Bouchard	D	52	3	10	13	80	11	1	1	2	2
Vern Kaiser	L	50	7	5	12	33	2	0	0	0	0
Tom Johnson	D	70	2	8	10	128	11	0	0	0	6
Leo Gravelle (1–2)	R	31	4	2	6	0					
Paul Meger	L	17	2	4	6	6	11	1	3	4	4
Paul Masnick	C	43	4	1	5	14	11	2	1	3	4
Bobby Dawes	D	15	0	5	5	4	1	0	0	0	0
Jean Beliveau	C	2	1	1	2	0					
Hal Laycoe (1–2)	D	38	0	2	2	25					
Bert Hirschfield	L	20	0	2	2	0					
Claude Robert	L	23	1	0	1	9					
Frank King	C	10	1	0	1	2					
Gerry Desaulniers	C	3	0	1	1	2					
Gerry McNeil	G	70	0	0	0	0	11	0	0	0	0
Tom Manastersky	D	6	0	0	0	11					
Ernie Roche	D	4	0	0	0	2					
Dollard St. Laurent	D	3	0	0	0	0					
Fred Burchell	C	2	0	0	0	0					
Hugh Currie	D	1	0	0	0	0					
Lulu Denis	R	1	0	0	0	0					
Dick Gamble	L	1	0	0	0	0					

		REGULAR SEASON					*POSTSEASON*				
PLAYER	*POS*	*GP*	*G*	*A*	*PTS*	*PIM*	\multicolumn{5}{c}{no postseason play}
Gerry Plamandon	L	1	0	0	0	0					
Ross Lowe (2–2)	D						2	0	0	0	0
Eddie Mazur	L						2	0	0	0	0
Sid McNabney	C						5	0	1	1	2

	REGULAR SEASON					*POSTSEASON*			
GOALTENDER	*GP*	*MIN*	*GA*	*SH*	*GAA*	*GP*	*MIN*	*GA*	*SH*	*GAA*
Gerry McNeil (25-30-15)	70	4200	184	6	2.63	11	785	25	1	1.91

BOSTON   22-30-18   62   4th   Lynn Patrick
Bruins

		REGULAR SEASON					*POSTSEASON*				
PLAYER	*POS*	*GP*	*G*	*A*	*PTS*	*PIM*	*GP*	*G*	*A*	*PTS*	*PIM*
Milt Schmidt	C	62	22	39	61	33	6	0	1	1	7
Woody Dumart	L	70	20	21	41	7	6	1	2	3	0
Johnny Peirson	R	70	19	19	38	43	2	1	1	2	2
Bill Ezinicki	R	53	16	19	35	119	6	1	1	2	18
Lorne Ferguson	L	70	16	17	33	31	6	1	0	1	2
Paul Ronty	C	70	10	22	32	20	6	0	1	1	2
Dunc Fisher (2–2)	R	53	9	20	29	20	6	1	0	1	0
Bill Quackenbush	D	70	5	24	29	12	6	0	1	1	0
Pete Horeck	L	66	10	13	23	57	4	0	0	0	13
Ed Sandford	L	51	10	13	23	33	6	0	1	1	4
Vic Lynn	L	56	14	6	20	69	5	0	0	0	2
Murray Henderson	D	66	4	7	11	37	5	0	0	0	2
Max Quackenbush	D	47	4	6	10	26	6	0	0	0	4
Dave Creighton	C	56	5	4	9	4	5	0	1	1	0
Ed Kryzanowski	D	69	3	6	9	10	6	0	0	0	2
Ross Lowe (1–2)	D	43	5	3	8	40					
Kenny Smith	L	14	1	3	4	11					
Phil Maloney (1–2)	C	13	2	0	2	2					
Fern Flaman (1–2)	D	14	1	1	2	37					
Hal Laycoe (2–2)	D	6	1	1	2	4	6	0	1	1	5
Ed Reigle	D	17	0	2	2	25					
Ed Harrison (1–2)	C	9	1	0	1	0					
Zellio Toppazzini (1–2)	R	4	0	1	1	0					
Jack Gelineau	G	70	0	0	0	4	4	0	0	0	0
Steve Kraftcheck	D	22	0	0	0	8	6	0	0	0	7
Bob Armstrong	D	2	0	0	0	2					
Jack McIntyre	L						2	0	0	0	0
George Sullivan	C						2	0	0	0	2
Gord Henry	G						2	0	0	0	0

	REGULAR SEASON					*POSTSEASON*			
GOALTENDER	*GP*	*MIN*	*GA*	*SH*	*GAA*	*GP*	*MIN*	*GA*	*SH*	*GAA*
Jack Gelineau (22-30-18)	70	4200	197	4	2.81	4	260	7	1	1.62
Gord Henry						2	120	10	0	5.00

1950-1951

NEW YORK 20-29-21 61 5th Neil Colville
Rangers

PLAYER	POS	GP	G	A	PTS	PIM
Reg Sinclair	R	70	18	21	39	70
Don Raleigh	C	64	15	24	39	18
Herb O'Connor	C	66	16	20	36	0
Nick Mickoski	L	64	20	15	35	12
Eddie Kullman	R	70	14	18	32	88
Eddie Slowinski	R	69	14	18	32	15
Zellio Toppazzini (2-2)	R	55	14	14	28	27
Tony Leswick	L	70	15	11	26	112
Edgar Laprade	C	42	10	13	23	0
Allan Stanley	D	70	7	14	21	75
Pentti Lund	R	59	4	16	20	6
Pat Egan	D	70	5	10	15	70
Jackie McLeod	R	41	5	10	15	2
Frank Eddolls	D	68	3	8	11	24
Alex Kaleta	L	58	3	4	7	26
Wally Stanowski	D	49	1	5	6	28
Gus Kyle	D	64	2	3	5	92
Bill Kyle	C	1	0	3	3	0
Jack Evans	D	49	1	0	1	95
Ed Harrison (1-2)	C	4	1	0	1	0
Vic Howe	R	3	1	0	1	0
Jack Lancien	D	19	0	1	1	8
Jackie Gordon	C	4	0	1	1	0
Charlie Rayner	G	66	0	0	0	6
Dunc Fisher (1-2)	R	12	0	0	0	0
Emile Francis	G	5	0	0	0	0
Dick Kotanen	D	1	0	0	0	0
Robert Wood	D	1	0	0	0	0
Bill Wylie	C	1	0	0	0	0

POSTSEASON: no postseason play

GOALTENDER		GP	MIN	GA	SH	GAA
Charlie Rayner	(19-28-19)	66	3940	187	2	2.85
Emile Francis	(1-1-2)	5	260	14	0	3.23

POSTSEASON: no postseason play

CHICAGO 13-47-10 36 6th Ebbie Goodfellow
Blackhawks

PLAYER	POS	GP	G	A	PTS	PIM
Roy Conacher	L	70	26	24	50	16
Pete Babando	L	70	18	19	37	36
Jim Conacher	C	52	10	27	37	16
Bill Mosienko	R	65	21	15	36	18
Bep Guidolin	L	69	12	22	34	56
Doug Bentley	L	44	9	23	32	20
Adam Brown	L	53	10	12	22	61
Ray Powell	C	31	7	15	22	2
Don Morrison	C	59	8	12	20	6

POSTSEASON: no postseason play

		REGULAR SEASON					*POSTSEASON*
PLAYER	POS	GP	G	A	PTS	PIM	no postseason play
Gus Bodnar	C	44	8	12	20	8	
Al Dewsbury	D	67	5	14	19	79	
Pat Lundy	R	61	9	9	18	9	
Lee Fogolin (2-2)	D	35	3	10	13	63	
Steve Black (2-2)	L	39	4	6	10	22	
Bill Gadsby	D	25	3	7	10	32	
Ernie Dickens	D	70	2	8	10	20	
Vic Stasiuk (1-2)	L	20	5	3	8	6	
Doug McCaig	D	53	2	5	7	29	
Gordie Fashoway	L	13	3	2	5	14	
Bert Olmstead (1-2)	L	15	2	1	3	0	
Hugh Coflin	D	31	0	3	3	33	
Ed Leier	C	11	2	0	2	2	
Jim Bedard	D	17	1	1	2	6	
Jack Stewart	D	26	0	2	2	49	
Fred Hucul	D	3	1	0	1	2	
Harry Lumley	G	64	0	0	0	4	
Jack Miller	C	11	0	0	0	4	
Marcel Pelletier	G	6	0	0	0	2	
Guyle Fielder	C	3	0	0	0	0	
Red Hamill	L	2	0	0	0	0	
Glen Smith	R	2	0	0	0	0	
John Michaluk	L	1	0	0	0	0	
Red Almas	G	1	0	0	0	0	

		REGULAR SEASON					*POSTSEASON*
GOALTENDER		GP	MIN	GA	SH	GAA	no postseason play
Harry Lumley	(12-41-10)	64	3785	246	3	3.90	
Marcel Pelletier	(1-5-0)	6	355	29	0	4.90	
Red Almas	(0-1-0)	1	60	5	0	5.00	

TEAM TOTALS

								Per Game			
TEAM	GP	G	A	P	PIM	GA	SH	G	A	PIM	GA
Detroit	70	236	339	575	566	139	11	3.37	4.84	8.09	1.99
Toronto	70	212	322	534	823	138	11	3.03	4.60	11.76	**1.97**
Montreal	70	173	249	422	**835**	184	6	2.47	3.56	**11.93**	2.63
Boston	70	178	247	425	656	197	4	2.54	3.53	9.37	2.81
New York	70	169	229	398	774	201	2	2.41	3.27	11.06	2.87
Chicago	70	171	252	423	615	280	3	2.44	3.60	8.79	4.00
	420	1139	1638	2777	4269	1139	37	2.71	3.90	10.16	2.71

PLAYOFFS

SERIES "A"
Montreal 3, Detroit 2 (OT)
Montreal 1, Detroit 0 (OT)
Detroit 2, Montreal 0

SERIES "B"
Boston 2, Toronto 0
Boston 1, Toronto 1 (Curfew)
Toronto 3, Boston 0

1950-1951

Detroit 4, Montreal 1
Montreal 5, Detroit 2
Montreal 3, Detroit 2

MONTREAL, 4-2

SERIES "C"
Toronto 3, Montreal 2 (OT)
Montreal 3, Toronto 2 (OT)
Toronto 2, Montreal 1 (OT)
Toronto 3, Montreal 2 (OT)
Toronto 3, Montreal 2 (OT)

**TORONTO WINS
STANLEY CUP, 4-1**

Toronto 3, Boston 1
Toronto 4, Boston 1
Toronto 6, Boston 0

TORONTO, 4-1

ALL-STAR TEAMS

First Team
G — Terry Sawchuk, DET
D — Bill Quackenbush, BOS
D — Red Kelly, DET
C — Milt Schmidt, BOS

R — Gordie Howe, DET
L — Ted Lindsay, MTL

Second Team
G — Charlie Rayner, NY
D — Leo Reise, DET
D — Jimmy Thomson, TOR
C — Ted Kennedy, TOR
C — Sid Abel, DET
R — Maurice Richard, MTL
L — Sid Smith, BOS

INDIVIDUAL TROPHY WINNERS

HART TROPHY (Most Valuable Player): Milt Schmidt, BOS
LADY BYNG TROPHY (Gentlemanly Conduct): Red Kelly, DET
VEZINA TROPHY (Best Goaltender): Al Rollins, TOR
CALDER MEMORIAL TROPHY (Best Rookie): Terry Sawchuk, DET
ART ROSS TROPHY (Scoring Leader): Gordie Howe, DET

1951-1952
Detroit Red Wings

During the previous campaign, in winning its third straight regular season title, one NHL team had rewritten the record books, becoming the first team to crest the 100-point plateau. Despite this success, the postseason had ended in disappointment, as the club was ousted in the playoffs too early. In the upcoming year, the league was about to be cold-cocked by this team once more, and this time they would finish the deal in style.

In 1926, the city of Detroit, Michigan, placed its first club in the NHL. Called the Cougars, because the original roster consisted of several ex–Victoria Cougars from the newly defunct WHL team, the club finished dead last with 12 wins in 44 games. Rechristened the Falcons in 1930, the team qualified for the playoffs several times, but the ultimate prize eluded them.

In the summer of 1932, the team was purchased by James Norris, who soon put his own stamp on the club. Not satisfied with the Falcons moniker, he gave his a team a new name, based partly on his past association with a club called the "Winged Wheelers." In 1933-34, Norris's "Red Wings" cruised to its first division crown, advancing to the finals for the first time. Although thwarted in their first trip, the team claimed the ultimate prize two years later, repeating the feat the following season.

In 1942, the Wings returned to the finals, losing an epic battle to the Leafs in a series which they had squandered a three games to none lead. In 1945, Detroit nearly reversed these events, coming back from a three-game deficit to tie the Leafs. Alas, the comeback fell short, as Toronto pulled out a victory in the seventh game.

Later, in the latter years of the decade, the team began an impressive streak. Beginning in 1948-49, the team won three regular season titles in a row, claiming the Cup in the middle year of the string. The last year, although Cupless, was particularly satisfying, netting a record 44 wins.

In 1951-52, the Red Wings started hot and stayed that way. The team lost only twice during the first month, and only dropped two in a row once during the campaign. Riding a six-game winning streak in February, the team made a serious run at their 101 point record of a year before. However a 3–3 tie with Montreal in the penultimate game cost them the record (44-14-12, 100), although they tied their record-breaking win total of the previous year. Along the way, Detroit had little company as no team finished within 20 points of the leaders.

Overall, the team had few weaknesses. Gordie Howe (47-39-86) scored the most goals and won the scoring race. His linemates Ted Lindsay (30-39-69) and Sid Abel (17-36-53) also prospered, finishing second and eighth, respectively. Between the pipes, Terry Sawchuk blossomed, posting a league best 1.90 GAA, helped immensely by a dozen shutouts. Other league leaders included Elmer Lach's (Montreal) 50 assists and Gus Kyle's (Boston) 127 penalty minutes.

In the playoffs, Detroit continued full bore, determined to finish what they had started in October. Facing third-place Toronto, the Wings whitewashed the Leafs 3–0 and 1–0 in the first two contests. In the next two, Detroit's Sawchuk did actually allow a few goals, but his team (6–2 and 3–1) easily swept to victory. The other semifinal series, featuring second place Montreal and fourth place Boston, the latter well ahead of New York and Chicago, was a battle royale, which wasn't decided until the final game. After taking a two game lead, the Canadiens ceded the next two to the Bruins. When Boston took the next game, 1–0, Montreal came back strong, winning 3–2 and 3–1 to advance to the finals.

For Detroit, the final stage in the battle for the Cup, was a duplicate of the first. After posting 2–1 and 3–1 wins, the Detroit goalie barred the door, giving Montreal nothing over the final two games — winning both by the score of 3–0. Overall, Sawchuk (0.63, 4) had arguably the best playoffs in the history of the NHL, blanking his opponents in fully half of the games. Three Detroit scorers — Howe, Lindsay and Metro Prystai — each accumulated seven points, with the former and the latter earning five assists each, while the middle man scored five goals.

After their sweep to the Cup, the Red Wings added to their collection of regular season crowns, winning a couple of more Cups by the mid–1950s. In more recent years, the team has once more become a juggernaut, regularly traveling deep into the playoffs. Although it played more than 50 years ago, this particular Red Wing squad remains special. Only one other time in NHL history — before or since — has a team swept to the Cup in eight straight games, forever etching the name of the 1951-52 Red Wings on the tablet of the league's truly great teams.

STANDINGS

TEAM	GP	W	L	T	PTS	GF	GA
DETROIT	70	44	14	12	100	215	133
MONTREAL	70	34	26	10	78	195	164
TORONTO	70	29	25	16	74	168	157
BOSTON	70	25	29	16	66	162	176
NEW YORK	70	23	34	13	59	192	219
CHICAGO	70	17	44	9	43	158	241

LEADERS

PLAYER	TM	GP	G	A	PTS	PIM
Gordie Howe	DET	70	47	39	86	78
Ted Lindsay	DET	70	30	39	69	123
Elmer Lach	MTL	70	15	50	65	36
Don Raleigh	NY	70	19	42	61	14
Sid Smith	TOR	70	27	30	57	6
Bernie Geoffrion	MTL	67	30	24	54	66
Bill Mosienko	CHI	70	31	22	53	10
Sid Abel	DET	62	17	36	53	32
Ted Kennedy	TOR	70	19	33	52	33
Two tied with					50	

GOALS	
Howe, DET	47
Mosienko, CHI	31
Lindsay, DET	30
Geoffrion, MTL	30
Two tied with	27

ASSISTS	
Lach, MTL	50
Raleigh, NY	42
Howe, DET	39
Lindsay, DET	39
Abel, DET	36

GOALTENDER	TM	GP	MIN	GA	SH	GAA
Terry Sawchuk	DET	70	4200	133	12	1.90
Al Rollins	TOR	70	4170	154	5	2.20
Gerry McNeil	MTL	70	4200	164	5	2.34
Jim Henry	BOS	70	4200	176	7	2.51
Charlie Rayner	NY	53	3180	159	2	3.00
Harry Lumley	CHI	70	4180	241	2	3.46

PENALTY MINUTES	
Kyle, BOS	127
Lindsay, DET	123
Flaman, TOR	110
Mortson, TOR	106
Dewsbury, CHI	99

SHUTOUTS	
Sawchuk, DET	12
Henry, BOS	7
McNeil, MTL	5
Rollins, TOR	5
Two tied with	2

DETROIT 44-14-12 100 1st Tommy Ivan
Red Wings

		REGULAR SEASON				POSTSEASON				
PLAYER	POS	GP	G	A	PTS	PIM	GP	G	A	PTS	PIM
Gordie Howe	R	70	47	39	86	78	8	2	5	7	2
Ted Lindsay	L	70	30	39	69	123	8	5	2	7	8
Sid Abel	C	62	17	36	53	32	7	2	2	4	12
Red Kelly	D	67	16	31	47	16	5	1	0	1	0
Metro Prystai	C	69	21	22	43	16	8	2	5	7	0
Alex Delvecchio	C	65	15	22	37	22	8	0	3	3	4
Marty Pavelich	L	68	17	19	36	54	8	2	2	4	2

1951-1952

PLAYER	POS	REGULAR SEASON					POSTSEASON				
		GP	G	A	PTS	PIM	GP	G	A	PTS	PIM
Glen Skov	L	70	12	14	26	48	8	1	4	5	16
Tony Leswick	L	70	9	10	19	93	8	3	1	4	22
Marcel Pronovost	D	69	7	11	18	50	8	0	1	1	10
Fred Glover	C	54	9	9	18	25					
Vic Stasiuk	L	58	5	9	14	19	7	0	2	2	0
Bob Goldham	D	69	0	14	14	24	8	0	1	1	8
Benny Woit	R	58	3	8	11	20	8	1	1	2	2
Leo Reise	D	54	0	11	11	34	6	1	0	1	27
Johnny Wilson	L	28	4	5	9	18	8	4	1	5	5
Enio Sclisizzi	L	9	2	1	3	0					
Larry Zeidel	D	19	1	0	1	14	5	0	0	0	0
Terry Sawchuk	G	70	0	0	0	2	8	0	0	0	0
Larry Wilson	C	5	0	0	0	4					
Bill Folk	D	4	0	0	0	2					

GOALTENDER	REGULAR SEASON					POSTSEASON				
	GP	MIN	GA	SH	GAA	GP	MIN	GA	SH	GAA
Terry Sawchuk (44-14-12)	70	4200	133	12	1.90	8	480	5	4	0.63

MONTREAL 34-26-10 78 2nd Dick Irvin
Canadiens

PLAYER	POS	REGULAR SEASON					POSTSEASON				
		GP	G	A	PTS	PIM	GP	G	A	PTS	PIM
Elmer Lach	C	70	15	50	65	36	11	1	2	3	4
Bernie Geoffrion	R	67	30	24	54	66	11	3	1	4	6
Maurice Richard	R	48	27	17	44	44	11	4	2	6	6
Paul Meger	L	69	24	18	42	44	11	0	3	3	2
Billy Reay	C	68	7	34	41	20	10	2	2	4	7
Dick Gamble	L	64	23	17	40	8	7	0	2	2	0
Floyd Curry	R	64	20	18	38	10	11	4	3	7	6
Bert Olmstead	L	69	7	28	35	49	11	0	1	1	4
Dickie Moore	L	33	18	15	33	44	11	1	1	2	12
Doug Harvey	D	68	6	23	29	82	11	0	3	3	8
Kenny Mosdell	C	44	5	11	16	19	2	1	0	1	0
Dollard St. Laurent	D	40	3	10	13	30	9	0	3	3	6
Emile Bouchard	D	60	3	9	12	45	11	0	2	2	14
John McCormack	C	54	2	10	12	4					
Tom Johnson	D	67	0	7	7	76	11	1	0	1	2
Ross Lowe	D	31	1	5	6	42					
James MacPherson	D	54	2	1	3	24	11	0	0	0	0
Paul Masnick	C	15	1	2	3	2	6	1	0	1	12
Lorne Davis	R	3	1	1	2	2					
Calum MacKay	L	12	0	1	1	8					
Gerry Couture	C	10	0	1	1	4					
Gerry McNeil	G	70	0	0	0	0	11	0	0	0	0
Bob Fryday	R	3	0	0	0	0					
Cliff Malone	R	3	0	0	0	0					
Gene Achtymichuk	C	1	0	0	0	0					
Garry Edmundson	L	1	0	0	0	2	2	0	0	0	4
Don Marshall	L	1	0	0	0	0					

		REGULAR SEASON					POSTSEASON				
PLAYER	POS	GP	G	A	PTS	PIM	GP	G	A	PTS	PIM
Stan Long	D						3	0	0	0	0
Eddie Mazur	L						5	2	0	2	4

		REGULAR SEASON				POSTSEASON				
GOALTENDER		GP	MIN	GA	SH	GAA	GP	MIN	GA	SH	GAA
Gerry McNeil	(34-26-10)	70	4200	164	5	2.34	11	688	23	1	2.01

TORONTO 29-25-16 74 3rd Joe Primeau
Maple Leafs

		REGULAR SEASON					POSTSEASON				
PLAYER	POS	GP	G	A	PTS	PIM	GP	G	A	PTS	PIM
Sid Smith	L	70	27	30	57	6	4	0	0	0	0
Ted Kennedy	C	70	19	33	52	33	4	0	0	0	4
Tod Sloan	R	68	25	23	48	89	4	0	0	0	10
Max Bentley	C	69	24	17	41	40	4	1	0	1	2
Cal Gardner	C	70	15	26	41	40	3	0	0	0	2
Harry Watson	L	70	22	17	39	18	4	1	0	1	2
Jimmy Thomson	D	70	0	25	25	86	4	0	0	0	25
Howie Meeker	R	54	9	14	23	50	4	0	0	0	11
Hugh Bolton	D	60	3	13	16	73	3	0	0	0	4
Danny Lewicki	L	51	4	9	13	26					
Joe Klukay	L	43	4	8	12	6	4	1	1	2	0
Gus Mortson	D	65	1	10	11	106	4	0	0	0	8
Fleming Mackell (1-2)	C	32	2	8	10	16					
Bob Solinger	L	24	5	3	8	4					
Fern Flaman	D	61	0	7	7	110	4	0	2	2	18
George Armstrong	C	20	3	3	6	30	4	0	0	0	2
Ray Timgren	L	50	2	4	6	11	4	0	1	1	0
Bill Juzda	D	46	1	4	5	65	3	0	0	0	2
Rudy Migay	C	19	2	1	3	12					
Jim Morrison (2-2)	D	17	0	1	1	4	2	0	0	0	0
Leo Boivin	D	2	0	1	1	0					
Al Rollins	G	70	0	0	0	4	2	0	0	0	0
Tim Horton	D	4	0	0	0	8					
Earl Balfour	L	3	0	0	0	2	1	0	0	0	0
Frank Mathers	D	2	0	0	0	0					
John McLellan	C	2	0	0	0	0					
Eric Nesterenko	R	1	0	0	0	0					
Bob Sabourin	R	1	0	0	0	2					
Turk Broda	G	1	0	0	0	0	2	0	0	0	0

		REGULAR SEASON				POSTSEASON				
GOALTENDER		GP	MIN	GA	SH	GAA	GP	MIN	GA	SH	GAA
Al Rollins	(29-24-16)	70	4170	154	5	2.20	2	120	6	0	3.00
Turk Broda	(0-1-0)	1	30	3	0	6.00	2	120	7	0	3.50

BOSTON 25-29-16 66 4th Lynn Patrick
Bruins

		REGULAR SEASON					POSTSEASON				
PLAYER	POS	GP	G	A	PTS	PIM	GP	G	A	PTS	PIM
Milt Schmidt	C	69	21	29	50	57	7	2	1	3	0

1951-1952

		REGULAR SEASON					POSTSEASON				
PLAYER	POS	GP	G	A	PTS	PIM	GP	G	A	PTS	PIM
Johnny Peirson	R	68	20	30	50	30	7	0	2	2	4
Dave Creighton	C	49	20	17	37	18	7	2	1	3	2
Jack McIntyre	L	52	12	19	31	18	7	1	2	3	2
Dunc Fisher	R	65	15	12	27	2	2	0	0	0	0
Ed Sandford	L	65	13	12	25	54	7	2	2	4	0
Real Chevrefils	L	33	8	17	25	8	7	1	1	2	6
George Sullivan	C	67	12	12	24	24	7	0	0	0	0
Bill Quackenbush	D	69	2	17	19	6	7	0	3	3	0
Adam Brown	L	33	8	9	17	6					
Woody Dumart	L	39	5	8	13	0	7	0	1	1	0
Gus Kyle	D	69	1	12	13	127	2	0	0	0	4
Hal Laycoe	D	70	5	7	12	61	7	1	1	2	11
Bill Ezinicki	R	28	5	5	10	47					
Fleming Mackell (2-2)	C	30	1	8	9	24	5	2	1	3	12
Ed Kryzanowski	D	70	5	3	8	33	7	0	0	0	0
Lorne Ferguson	L	27	3	4	7	14					
Leo Labine	R	15	2	4	6	9	5	0	1	1	4
Murray Henderson	D	56	0	6	6	51	7	0	0	0	4
Pentti Lund	R	23	0	5	5	0	2	1	0	1	0
Vic Lynn	L	12	2	2	4	4					
Ray Berry	C	18	1	2	3	6					
Bobby Bauer	R	1	1	1	2	0					
Jim Morrison (1-2)	D	14	0	2	2	2					
Jim Henry	G	70	0	0	0	0	7	0	0	0	0
Bob Armstrong	D						5	0	0	0	2

		REGULAR SEASON				POSTSEASON			
GOALTENDER		GP	MIN	GA	SH	GAA	GP	MIN	GA	SH	GAA
Jim Henry	(25-29-16)	70	4200	176	7	2.51	7	448	18	1	2.41

NEW YORK Rangers   23-34-13   59   5th   Neil Colville / Bill Cook

		REGULAR SEASON				POSTSEASON
PLAYER	POS	GP	G	A	PTS	PIM	no postseason play
Don Raleigh	C	70	19	42	61	14
Eddie Slowinski	R	64	21	22	43	18
Paul Ronty	C	65	12	31	43	16
Gaye Stewart	L	69	15	25	40	22
Wally Hergesheimer	R	68	26	12	38	6
Edgar Laprade	C	70	9	29	38	8
Hy Buller	D	68	12	23	35	96
Reg Sinclair	R	69	20	10	30	33
Herb Dickenson	L	37	14	13	27	8
Eddie Kullman	R	64	11	10	21	59
Nick Mickoski	L	43	7	13	20	20
Allan Stanley	D	50	5	14	19	52
Steve Kraftcheck	D	58	8	9	17	30
Jim Ross	D	51	2	9	11	25
Frank Eddolls	D	42	3	5	8	18
Jack Evans	D	52	1	6	7	83

		REGULAR SEASON					*POSTSEASON*
PLAYER	*POS*	*GP*	*G*	*A*	*PTS*	*PIM*	*no postseason play*
Jack Stoddard	R	20	4	2	6	2	
Jackie McLeod	R	13	2	3	5	2	
Zellio Toppazzini	R	16	1	1	2	4	
Jim Conacher (2–2)	C	16	0	1	1	2	
Clare Martin (1–2)	D	14	0	1	1	6	
Charlie Rayner	G	53	0	0	0	4	
Emile Francis	G	14	0	0	0	0	
Lloyd Ailsby	D	3	0	0	0	2	
Lorne Anderson	G	3	0	0	0	0	

		REGULAR SEASON				*POSTSEASON*
GOALTENDER		*GP*	*MIN*	*GA*	*SH*	*GAA*	*no postseason play*
Charlie Rayner	(18-25-10)	53	3180	159	2	3.00	
Emile Francis	(4-7-3)	14	840	42	0	3.00	
Lorne Anderson	(1-2-0)	3	180	18	0	6.00	

CHICAGO Blackhawks 17-44-9 43 6th Ebbie Goodfellow

		REGULAR SEASON					*POSTSEASON*
PLAYER	*POS*	*GP*	*G*	*A*	*PTS*	*PIM*	*no postseason play*
Bill Mosienko	R	70	31	22	53	10	
George Gee	C	70	18	31	49	39	
Gus Bodnar	C	69	14	26	40	26	
Jimmy Peters	R	70	15	21	36	16	
Jim McFadden	C	70	10	24	34	14	
Bep Guidolin	L	67	13	18	31	78	
Pete Babando	L	49	11	14	25	29	
Al Dewsbury	D	69	7	17	24	99	
Bill Gadsby	D	59	7	15	22	87	
Pete Horeck	L	60	9	11	20	22	
Sid Finney	C	35	6	5	11	0	
Steve Witiuk	R	33	3	8	11	14	
Fred Hucul	D	34	3	7	10	37	
Lee Fogolin	D	69	0	9	9	96	
Doug Bentley	L	8	2	3	5	4	
Clare Raglan	D	35	0	5	5	28	
Roy Conacher	L	12	3	1	4	0	
Jack Stewart	D	37	1	3	4	12	
Steve Hrymnak	D	18	2	1	3	4	
Clare Martin (2–2)	D	31	1	2	3	8	
Harry Taylor	C	15	1	1	2	0	
Jim Conacher (1–2)	C	5	1	1	2	0	
Max Quackenbush	D	14	0	1	1	4	
Pete Conacher	L	2	0	1	1	0	
Harry Lumley	G	70	0	0	0	2	
Mike Buchanan	D	1	0	0	0	0	
Tony Poeta	R	1	0	0	0	0	
Jack Price	D	1	0	0	0	0	
Kenny Wharram	R	1	0	0	0	0	
Moe Roberts	G	1	0	0	0	0	

1951-1952

GOALTENDER		REGULAR SEASON					POSTSEASON
		GP	MIN	GA	SH	GAA	*no postseason play*
Moe Roberts		1	20	0	0	0.00	
Harry Lumley	(17-44-9)	70	4180	241	2	3.46	

TEAM TOTALS

									Per Game		
TEAM	GP	G	A	P	PIM	GA	SH	G	A	PIM	GA
Detroit	70	215	300	515	694	133	12	3.07	4.29	9.91	1.90
Montreal	70	195	302	497	661	164	5	2.79	4.31	9.44	2.34
Toronto	70	168	257	425	841	157	5	2.40	3.67	12.01	2.24
Boston	70	162	243	405	601	176	7	2.31	3.47	8.59	2.51
New York	70	192	281	473	532	219	2	2.74	4.01	7.60	3.13
Chicago	70	158	247	405	627	241	2	2.26	3.53	8.96	3.44
	420	1090	1630	2720	3956	1090	33	2.60	3.88	9.42	2.60

PLAYOFFS

SERIES "A"
Detroit 3, Toronto 0
Detroit 1, Toronto 0
Detroit 6, Toronto 2
Detroit 3, Toronto 1

DETROIT, 4-0

SERIES "B"
Montreal 5, Boston 1
Montreal 4, Boston 0
Boston 4, Montreal 1
Boston 3, Montreal 2
Boston 1, Montreal 0
Montreal 3, Boston 2 (OT)
Montreal 3, Boston 1

MONTREAL, 4-3

SERIES "C"
Detroit 3, Montreal 1
Detroit 2, Montreal 1
Detroit 3, Montreal 0
Detroit 3, Montreal 0

**DETROIT WINS
STANLEY CUP, 4-0**

ALL-STAR TEAMS

First Team
G — Terry Sawchuk, DET
D — Doug Harvey, MTL
D — Red Kelly, DET
C — Elmer Lach, MTL
R — Gordie Howe, DET
L — Ted Lindsay, MTL

Second Team
G — Jim Henry, BOS
D — Hy Buller, NY
D — Jimmy Thomson, TOR
C — Milt Schmidt, BOS
R — Maurice Richard, MTL
L — Sid Smith, TOR

INDIVIDUAL TROPHY WINNERS

HART TROPHY (Most Valuable Player): Gordie Howe, DET
LADY BYNG TROPHY (Gentlemanly Conduct): Sid Smith, TOR
VEZINA TROPHY (Best Goaltender): Terry Sawchuk, DET
CALDER MEMORIAL TROPHY (Best Rookie): Bernie Geoffrion, MTL
ART ROSS TROPHY (Scoring Leader): Gordie Howe, DET

1952-1953
Original Seven

Before the 1942-43 season, the NHL entered the era of what is now called the "Original Six." Earlier, the league had embraced as many as ten clubs, but with the demise of the Americans, the roster dropped to a half-dozen. Over the next ten years, though overtures were made by a few applicants, league membership remained at six. However, before the 1952-53 season, a new entity made its bid known.

For ten years, the cozy club of the NHL was quite content to keep its number the same. Even when a city well within the league's sphere of locality — Philadelphia applied for NHL membership in June 1945, league governors still turned them down. However, a more viable candidate emerged in the early 1950s — an applicant difficult to refuse.

For many years, the city of Cleveland, Ohio had featured teams in the top minor hockey league in the land — the American Hockey League. In the late 1940s, the Barons had dominated the circuit, setting a new league mark for points (98) in 1947-48, and winning the championship Calder Cup twice, first in 1948, and again three years later. After the latter win, the team's owner, Jim Hendy, made a strong bid for NHL membership, well-armed with a purported $400,000 deposit. Impressed with his resume, and with his financial plan seemingly strong, NHL governors voted to accept Cleveland as its seventh member in May 1952.

However, as it turned out, the proposed expansion franchise was on shakier ground then first thought. Brian McFarlane in *50 Years of Hockey* described what happened next: "With all the stipulations met, or so he thought, Jim Hendy showed up at the June governors' meeting. He was greeted warmly, but suspiciously, on the grounds that the franchise was in debt for the money he had raked up. The governors felt the amount was too great to pay back ... and suggested the city try again at a later date."

With Cleveland's bid dead in the water, the Original Six marched through the 1952-53 season. Predictably, Detroit (36-16-18, 90) once again finished on top, giving the Wings its fifth straight regular season crown. Montreal, Boston and surprising Chicago ended second through fourth, the latter making an impressive 26-point jump from the previous year. Toronto ended two points out of the running, well ahead of the last place Rangers.

For the second time in three years, Detroit's Gordie Howe (49-46-95) swept the scoring categories, setting a new high mark for points, while nearly equaling Maurice Richard's record of 50 goals. Richard did pick up the most penalty minutes (112), while Detroit goalie Terry Sawchuk allowed the fewest goals (1.90). In addition, Montreal's Gerry McNeil and Toronto's Harry Lumley each posted 10 shutouts.

In the first game of the playoffs, Detroit whacked Boston 7–0, but was then ambushed by Boston in the next three contests by a combined 13–6 mark. The Red Wings then bounced back with a 6–4 decision, but were eliminated 4–2 in the sixth game. In the other opening series, the Blackhawks, enjoying their return to the postseason, gave the Canadiens all they could handle. After Montreal took the first two games, Chicago won the next three in a row to take command of the series. At this point, things looked bleak for the Canadiens, as their starting goalie — McNeil — was unable to continue, suffering as it turned out from a malady that had befallen other netminders — nerves. With their starter unable to continue, Montreal turned to their 24-year-old rookie, Jacques Plante, who led the club to two straight wins — 3–0 and 4–1, enabling the team to advance.

In the finals, the buoyant Canadiens had little trouble dispatching the Bruins, who were without the services of their regular netminder, Jim Henry, who had fallen ill. In his place, minor leaguer Gord Henry couldn't pass muster, allowing 11 goals in his three games, as Montreal took the Cup in five games. Despite being on the short end, two Bruins — Fleming Mackell (2-7-9) and Ed Sandford (8-3-11) — racked up the most goals, assists and points. In net, Plante was the stingiest playoff goalie (1.75).

As it turned out, Cleveland had to wait a while longer for its NHL team, as the Barons did not make their appearance in the league until the late 1970s, and only then as a replacement franchise for the California Golden Seals. Despite being ignored by the circuit, hockey did prosper in the Ohio city, as the team remained in the AHL for many years, before joining the major league WHA in 1972.

Although successfully dodging expansion this time, the NHL was not able to escape in the late 1960s. Then, several locales desired entrance, and the NHL finally broke away from its cozy six locations, in a move that would embrace the whole country.

STANDINGS

TEAM	GP	W	L	T	PTS	GF	GA
DETROIT	70	36	16	18	90	222	133
MONTREAL	70	28	23	19	75	155	148
BOSTON	70	28	29	13	69	152	172
CHICAGO	70	27	28	15	69	169	175
TORONTO	70	27	30	13	67	156	167
NEW YORK	70	17	37	16	50	152	211

LEADERS

PLAYER	TM	GP	G	A	PTS	PIM
Gordie Howe	DET	70	49	46	95	57
Ted Lindsay	DET	70	32	39	71	111
Maurice Richard	MTL	70	28	33	61	112
Wally Hergesheimer	NY	70	30	29	59	10
Alex Delvecchio	DET	70	16	43	59	28
Paul Ronty	NY	70	16	38	54	20
Metro Prystai	DET	70	16	34	50	12
Red Kelly	DET	70	19	27	46	8
Bert Olmstead	MTL	69	17	28	45	83
Two tied with					44	

GOALS	
Howe, DET	49
Lindsay, DET	32
Hergesheimer, NY	30
Richard, MTL	28
Mackell, BOS	27

ASSISTS	
Howe, DET	46
Delvecchio, DET	43
Lindsay, DET	39
Ronty, NY	38
Prystai, DET	34

GOALTENDER	TM	GP	MIN	GA	SH	GAA
Terry Sawchuk	DET	63	3780	120	9	1.90
Gerry McNeil	MTL	66	3960	140	10	2.12
Harry Lumley	TOR	70	4200	167	10	2.39
Jim Henry	BOS	70	4200	172	7	2.46
Al Rollins	CHI	70	4200	175	6	2.50
Lorne Worsley	NY	50	3000	153	2	3.06

PENALTY MINUTES	
Richard, MTL	112
Lindsay, DET	111
Flaman, TOR	110
Gee, CHI	99
Two tied with	97

SHUTOUTS	
McNeil, MTL	10
Lumley, TOR	10
Sawchuk, DET	9
Henry, BOS	7
Rollins, CHI	6

DETROIT 36-16-18 90 1st Tommy Ivan
Red Wings

		REGULAR SEASON					POSTSEASON				
PLAYER	POS	GP	G	A	PTS	PIM	GP	G	A	PTS	PIM
Gordie Howe	R	70	49	46	95	57	6	2	5	7	2
Ted Lindsay	L	70	32	39	71	111	6	4	4	8	6
Alex Delvecchio	C	70	16	43	59	28	6	2	4	6	2
Metro Prystai	C	70	16	34	50	12	6	4	4	8	2
Red Kelly	D	70	19	27	46	8	6	0	4	4	0
Johnny Wilson	L	70	23	19	42	22	6	2	5	7	0
Marty Pavelich	L	64	13	20	33	49	6	2	1	3	7
Tony Leswick	L	70	15	12	27	87	6	1	0	1	11
Glen Skov	L	70	12	15	27	54	6	1	0	1	2

		REGULAR SEASON					POSTSEASON				
PLAYER	POS	GP	G	A	PTS	PIM	GP	G	A	PTS	PIM
Marcel Pronovost	D	68	8	19	27	72	6	0	0	0	6
Reg Sinclair	R	69	11	12	23	36	3	1	0	1	0
Bob Goldham	D	70	1	13	14	32	6	1	1	2	2
Marcel Bonin	L	37	4	9	13	14	5	0	1	1	0
Benny Woit	R	70	1	5	6	40	6	1	3	4	0
Jim Hay	D	42	1	4	5	2	4	0	0	0	2
Larry Wilson	C	15	0	4	4	6					
Lou Jankowski	C	22	1	2	3	0	1	0	0	0	0
Terry Sawchuk	G	63	0	0	0	5	6	0	0	0	10
Larry Zeidel	D	9	0	0	0	8					
Bill Folk	D	8	0	0	0	2					
Glenn Hall	G	6	0	0	0	0					
Vic Stasiuk	L	3	0	0	0	0					
Red Almas	G	1	0	0	0	0					
Guyle Fielder	C						4	0	0	0	0
Steve Hrymnak	D						2	0	0	0	0

		REGULAR SEASON					POSTSEASON				
GOALTENDER		GP	MIN	GA	SH	GAA	GP	MIN	GA	SH	GAA
Glenn Hall	(4-1-1)	6	360	10	1	1.67					
Terry Sawchuk	(32-15-16)	63	3780	120	9	**1.90**	6	372	21	1	3.39
Red Almas	(0-0-1)	1	60	3	0	3.00					

MONTREAL 28-23-19 75 2nd Dick Irvin
Canadiens

		REGULAR SEASON					POSTSEASON				
PLAYER	POS	GP	G	A	PTS	PIM	GP	G	A	PTS	PIM
Maurice Richard	R	70	28	33	61	112	12	7	1	8	2
Bert Olmstead	L	69	17	28	45	83	12	2	2	4	4
Elmer Lach	C	53	16	25	41	56	12	1	6	7	6
Bernie Geoffrion	R	65	22	17	39	37	12	6	4	10	12
Doug Harvey	D	69	4	30	34	67	12	0	5	5	8
Paul Meger	L	69	9	17	26	38	5	1	2	3	4
Dick Gamble	L	69	11	13	24	26	5	1	0	1	2
Floyd Curry	R	68	16	6	22	10	12	2	1	3	2
Kenny Mosdell	C	63	5	14	19	27	7	3	2	5	4
Billy Reay	C	56	4	15	19	26	11	0	2	2	4
Paul Masnick	C	53	5	7	12	44	6	1	0	1	7
Tom Johnson	D	70	3	8	11	63	12	2	3	5	8
Emile Bouchard	D	58	2	8	10	55	12	1	1	2	6
John McCormack	C	59	1	9	10	9	9	0	0	0	0
Dollard St. Laurent	D	54	2	6	8	34	12	0	3	3	4
Dickie Moore	L	18	2	6	8	19	12	3	2	5	13
Jean Beliveau	C	3	5	0	5	0					
James MacPherson	D	59	2	3	5	67	4	0	1	1	9
Gaye Stewart (2-2)	L	5	0	2	2	0					
Ed Litzenberger	R	2	1	0	1	2					
Ivan Irwin	D	4	0	1	1	0					
Gerry Desaulniers	C	2	0	1	1	2					
Gerry McNeil	G	66	0	0	0	0	8	0	0	0	0

		REGULAR SEASON					POSTSEASON				
PLAYER	POS	GP	G	A	PTS	PIM	GP	G	A	PTS	PIM
Reg Abbott	C	3	0	0	0	0					
Jacques Plante	G	3	0	0	0	0	4	0	0	0	0
Rollie Rousseau	D	2	0	0	0	0					
Hal Murphy	G	1	0	0	0	0					
Calum MacKay	L						7	1	3	4	10
Eddie Mazur	L						7	2	2	4	11
Lorne Davis	R						7	1	1	2	6
Doug Anderson	C						2	0	0	0	0

		REGULAR SEASON					POSTSEASON				
GOALTENDER		GP	MIN	GA	SH	GAA	GP	MIN	GA	SH	GAA
Jacques Plante	(2-0-1)	3	180	4	0	1.33	4	240	7	1	**1.75**
Gerry McNeil	(25-23-**18**)	66	3960	140	**10**	2.12	8	486	16	**2**	1.98
Hal Murphy	(1-0-0)	1	60	4	0	4.00					

BOSTON 28-29-13 69 3rd Lynn Patrick
Bruins

		REGULAR SEASON					POSTSEASON				
PLAYER	POS	GP	G	A	PTS	PIM	GP	G	A	PTS	PIM
Fleming Mackell	C	65	27	17	44	63	11	2	7	9	7
Ed Sandford	L	61	14	21	35	44	11	8	3	**11**	11
Milt Schmidt	C	68	11	23	34	30	10	5	1	6	6
Real Chevrefils	L	69	19	14	33	44	7	0	1	1	6
Johnny Peirson	R	49	14	15	29	32	11	3	6	9	2
Joe Klukay	L	70	13	16	29	20	11	1	2	3	9
Jerry Toppazzini	R	69	10	13	23	36	11	0	3	3	9
Leo Labine	R	51	8	15	23	69	7	2	1	3	**19**
Jack McIntyre	L	70	7	15	22	31	10	4	2	6	2
Bill Quackenbush	D	69	2	16	18	6	11	0	4	4	4
Pentti Lund	R	54	8	9	17	2	2	0	0	0	0
Dave Creighton	C	45	8	8	16	14	11	4	5	9	10
Woody Dumart	L	62	5	9	14	2	11	0	2	2	0
Warren Godfrey	D	60	1	13	14	40	11	0	1	1	2
Hal Laycoe	D	54	2	10	12	36	11	0	2	2	10
George Sullivan	C	32	3	8	11	8	3	0	0	0	0
Bob Armstrong	D	55	0	8	8	45	11	1	1	2	10
Frank Martin	D	14	0	2	2	6	6	0	1	1	2
Dunc Fisher	R	7	0	1	1	0					
Jim Henry	G	70	0	0	0	0	9	0	0	0	0
Norm Corcoran	C	1	0	0	0	0					
Gord Henry	G						3	0	0	0	0

		REGULAR SEASON					POSTSEASON				
GOALTENDER		GP	MIN	GA	SH	GAA	GP	MIN	GA	SH	GAA
Jim Henry	(28-29-13)	70	4200	172	7	2.46	9	510	26	0	3.06
Gord Henry							3	163	11	0	4.05

1952-1953

CHICAGO Blackhawks   27-28-15   69   4th   Sid Abel

PLAYER	POS	REGULAR SEASON					POSTSEASON				
		GP	G	A	PTS	PIM	GP	G	A	PTS	PIM
Jim McFadden	C	70	23	21	44	29	7	3	0	3	4
Jimmy Peters	R	69	22	19	41	16	7	0	1	1	4
George Gee	C	67	18	21	39	99	7	1	2	3	6
Gerry Couture	C	70	19	18	37	22	7	1	0	1	0
Bill Mosienko	R	65	17	20	37	8	7	4	2	6	7
Cal Gardner	C	70	11	24	35	60	7	0	2	2	4
Gus Bodnar	C	66	16	13	29	26	7	1	1	2	2
Gus Mortson	D	68	5	18	23	88	7	1	1	2	6
Bill Gadsby	D	68	2	20	22	84	7	0	1	1	4
Al Dewsbury	D	69	5	16	21	97	7	1	2	3	4
Fred Hucul	D	57	5	7	12	25	6	1	0	1	10
Pete Conacher	L	41	5	6	11	7	2	0	0	0	0
Pete Babando (1-2)	L	29	5	5	10	14					
Lee Fogolin	D	70	2	8	10	79	7	0	1	1	4
Vic Lynn	L	29	0	10	10	23	7	1	1	2	4
Sid Abel	C	39	5	4	9	6	1	0	0	0	0
Fred Glover	C	31	4	2	6	37					
Sid Finney	C	18	4	2	6	4	7	0	2	2	0
Clare Raglan	D	32	1	3	4	10	3	0	0	0	0
Enio Sclisizzi	L	14	0	2	2	0					
Jim McBurney	L	1	0	1	1	0					
Al Rollins	G	70	0	0	0	0	7	0	0	0	0
Jack Price	D	10	0	0	0	2	4	0	0	0	0
Ed Kryzanowski	D	5	0	0	0	0					

GOALTENDER		REGULAR SEASON					POSTSEASON				
		GP	MIN	GA	SH	GAA	GP	MIN	GA	SH	GAA
Al Rollins	(27-28-15)	70	4200	175	6	2.50	7	425	18	0	3.00

TORONTO Maple Leafs   27-30-13   67   5th   Joe Primeau

PLAYER	POS	REGULAR SEASON					POSTSEASON
		GP	G	A	PTS	PIM	no postseason play
Sid Smith	L	70	20	19	39	6	
Ted Kennedy	C	43	14	23	37	42	
Gord Hannigan	C	65	17	18	35	51	
Ron Stewart	C	70	13	22	35	29	
Bob Hassard	C	70	8	23	31	14	
Tod Sloan	R	70	15	10	25	76	
George Armstrong	C	52	14	11	25	54	
Harry Watson	L	63	16	8	24	8	
Max Bentley	C	36	12	11	23	16	
Jimmy Thomson	D	69	0	22	22	73	
Eric Nesterenko	R	35	10	6	16	27	
Tim Horton	D	70	2	14	16	85	
Leo Boivin	D	70	2	13	15	97	
Rudy Migay	C	40	5	4	9	22	
Jim Morrison	D	56	1	8	9	36	

		REGULAR SEASON					*POSTSEASON*
PLAYER	POS	GP	G	A	PTS	PIM	*no postseason play*
Fern Flaman	D	66	2	6	8	110	
Phil Maloney	C	29	2	6	8	2	
Howie Meeker	R	25	1	7	8	26	
Danny Lewicki	L	4	1	3	4	2	
Bob Solinger	L	18	1	1	2	2	
Harry Lumley	G	70	0	0	0	18	
Ray Timgren	L	12	0	0	0	4	
Hugh Bolton	D	9	0	0	0	10	
Frank Sullivan	D	5	0	0	0	23	
Willie Marshall	C	2	0	0	0	0	
Wally Maxwell	C	2	0	0	0	0	
Dave Reid	C	2	0	0	0	0	
Parker MacDonald	C	1	0	0	0	0	

	REGULAR SEASON					*POSTSEASON*
GOALTENDER	GP	MIN	GA	SH	GAA	*no postseason play*
Harry Lumley (27-30-13)	70	4200	167	10	2.39	

NEW YORK Rangers   17-37-16   50   6th   Bill Cook

		REGULAR SEASON					*POSTSEASON*
PLAYER	POS	GP	G	A	PTS	PIM	*no postseason play*
Wally Hergesheimer	R	70	30	29	59	10	
Paul Ronty	C	70	16	38	54	20	
Nick Mickoski	L	70	19	16	35	39	
Jack Stoddard	R	60	12	13	25	29	
Hy Buller	D	70	7	18	25	73	
Neil Strain	L	52	11	13	24	12	
Don Raleigh	C	55	4	18	22	2	
Leo Reise	D	61	4	15	19	53	
Eddie Kullman	R	70	8	10	18	61	
Allan Stanley	D	70	5	12	17	52	
Harry Howell	D	67	3	8	11	46	
Steve Kraftcheck	D	69	2	9	11	45	
Dean Prentice	L	55	6	3	9	20	
Aldo Guidolin	D	30	4	4	8	24	
Pete Babando (2–2)	L	29	4	4	8	4	
Herb Dickenson	L	11	4	4	8	2	
Eddie Slowinski	R	37	2	5	7	14	
George Senick	L	13	2	3	5	8	
Jim Conacher	C	17	1	4	5	2	
Ron Murphy	L	15	3	1	4	0	
Edgar Laprade	C	11	2	1	3	2	
Gaye Stewart (1–2)	L	18	1	1	2	8	
Jim Ross	D	11	0	2	2	4	
Kelly Burnett	C	3	1	0	1	0	
Aggie Kukulowicz	C	3	1	0	1	0	
Andy Bathgate	R	18	0	1	1	6	
Gord Haworth	C	2	0	1	1	0	
Lorne Worsley	G	50	0	0	0	2	

1952-1953

PLAYER	POS	REGULAR SEASON					POSTSEASON
		GP	G	A	PTS	PIM	*no postseason play*
Charlie Rayner	G	20	0	0	0	2	
Mickey MacIntosh	R	4	0	0	0	4	
Mike Labadie	R	3	0	0	0	0	
Jackie McLeod	R	3	0	0	0	2	
Frank Bathgate	C	2	0	0	0	2	

GOALTENDER		REGULAR SEASON					POSTSEASON
		GP	MIN	GA	SH	GAA	*no postseason play*
Charlie Rayner	(4-8-8)	20	1200	58	1	2.90	
Lorne Worsley	(13-29-8)	50	3000	153	2	3.06	

TEAM TOTALS

								Per Game			
TEAM	GP	G	A	P	PIM	GA	SH	G	A	PIM	GA
Detroit	70	**222**	**323**	**545**	645	**133**	10	**3.17**	**4.61**	9.21	**1.90**
Montreal	70	155	249	404	777	148	10	2.21	3.56	11.10	2.11
Boston	70	152	233	385	528	172	7	2.17	3.33	7.54	2.46
Chicago	70	169	240	409	736	175	6	2.41	3.43	10.51	2.50
Toronto	70	156	235	391	**812**	167	10	2.23	3.36	**11.60**	2.39
New York	70	152	233	385	548	211	3	2.17	3.33	7.83	3.01
	420	1006	1513	2519	4046	1006	46	2.40	3.60	9.63	2.40

PLAYOFFS

SERIES "A"
Detroit 7, Boston 0
Boston 5, Detroit 3
Boston 2, Detroit 1 (OT)
Boston 6, Detroit 2
Detroit 6, Boston 4
Boston 4, Detroit 2

BOSTON, 4-2

SERIES "C"
Montreal 4, Boston 2
Boston 4, Montreal 1
Montreal 3, Boston 0
Montreal 7, Boston 3
Montreal 1, Boston 0 (OT)

**MONTREAL WINS
STANLEY CUP, 4-1**

SERIES "B"
Montreal 3, Chicago 1
Montreal 4, Chicago 3
Chicago 2, Montreal 1
Chicago 3, Montreal 1
Chicago 4, Montreal 2
Montreal 3, Chicago 0
Montreal 4, Chicago 1

MONTREAL, 4-3

ALL-STAR TEAMS

First Team
G — Terry Sawchuk, DET
D — Doug Harvey, MTL
D — Red Kelly, DET
C — Fleming Mackell, BOS
R — Gordie Howe, DET
L — Ted Lindsay, MTL

Second Team
G — Gerry McNeil, MTL
D — Bill Gadsby, CHI
D — Bill Quackenbush, BOS
C — Alex Delvecchio, DET
R — Maurice Richard, MTL
L — Bert Olmstead, MTL

INDIVIDUAL TROPHY WINNERS

HART TROPHY (Most Valuable Player): Gordie Howe, DET
LADY BYNG TROPHY (Gentlemanly Conduct): Red Kelly, DET
VEZINA TROPHY (Best Goaltender): Terry Sawchuk, DET
CALDER MEMORIAL TROPHY (Best Rookie): Lorne Worsley, NY
ART ROSS TROPHY (Scoring Leader): Gordie Howe, DET

1953-1954

Gordie Howe

One of the main factors behind the Detroit Red Wings' domination of the rest of the NHL in the early 1950s was the rise of a superstar in Gordie Howe. Playing right wing on the famed Production Line, Howe held sway over the rink on both ends of the ice. Having already rewritten the NHL record book by the age of 25, the league was about to find out that he had plenty of good hockey ahead of him.

Gordon "Gordie" Howe, a native of Saskatchewan, had his first taste of the NHL in 1943 as an attendee at the Rangers training camp. A bad case of homesickness curtailed his experience, not to be unexpected since he was only 15 years old. Two years later, the Red Wings gave Howe a try — and this time he stuck. After a year of seasoning with Omaha in the United States Hockey League, he joined Detroit in the fall of 1946. Not a prolific scorer right away, Howe was still a very tough customer, and not afraid to mix it up. One minor league veteran recalled that dealing with Howe was like fending off a "wildcat."

In his rookie season, Howe scored seven goals and accumulated 22 points, doubling the total the next year. He came into his own during the 1949-50 season as part of the famed Production Line, which also featured Sid Abel and Ted Lindsay. That year, he finished third (35-33-68) in the scoring race, right behind his linemates.

Over the next three seasons, Howe dominated the league as few had done before. In each campaign, he led the loop in goals (43, 47 and 49), coming within one tally of tying Maurice Richard's sacred mark of 50 in 1952-53. Howe also paced the NHL in assists (43 and 46) in the first and last years of the string. Predictably, he also won the scoring race (86, 88 and 95) each time as well, raising the NHL record point total in the latter season. Not content just to be a fancy scorer, Howe also defended himself, finishing with over 100 penalty minutes per season on a regular basis.

In 1953-54, Howe (33-48-81) won his fourth straight scoring title, collecting the league's most assists along the way. However, he did drop to second in the goal scoring column, ceding the title to Richard (37). Typically, Howe also finished fifth in penalty minutes, 23 behind Chicago's Gus Mortson (132). In goal, Harry Lumley (Toronto) posted the lowest GAA and blanked the most opponents (1.86, 13).

As a team, Detroit (37-19-14, 88) followed Howe's lead, winning their sixth straight regular season title. Montreal finished seven points back, while Toronto and Boston rounded out the playoff slate, ahead of both New York and Chicago.

In the opening round, Detroit trimmed the Leafs, losing only one of the five contests. In the other set, Montreal humbled the Bruins, shutting out Boston twice while outscoring them 16–4 in the four game sweep. In the finals, Detroit won three of the first four contests, but the Canadiens came back with 1–0 and 4–1 wins to even the series. The seventh and deciding game went into overtime knotted 1–1, before Detroit's Tony Leswick ended matters five minutes into the extra stanza, giving Detroit its third Cup in five years.

In the playoffs, Howe (4-5-9) posted solid numbers, but was still outperformed by a trio of Canadiens. In a game effort, Bernie Geoffrion (6) scored the most goals, while Jean Beliveau and Dickie Moore (8) each amassed the most helpers, with the latter also collecting the most points (13). In the cage, Gerry McNeil (0.95) shone in his three games.

In subsequent years, Howe remained a dominant force in NHL circles. Before the end of the decade, he claimed another scoring crown, with another to follow in the 1960s. Finally, after his 25th season — at age 43 — he called it quits in 1971. Two years later, after his Hall of Fame induction, he returned to pro hockey, playing alongside his sons in the World Hockey Association. Not content to be just a sideshow, Howe enjoyed a solid career in this major league caliber circuit, twice crossing the century mark in points. When his WHA team was merged into the NHL in 1980, he played a full season at the age of 51 before retiring for good. Years later, Howe returned for a cameo appearance at the age of 70, playing a shift for Detroit's IHL Vipers, recording a shot on goal during his time on the ice.

In many facets of the game, Howe's career remains unique. To start, it is unlikely that anyone will equal his 32 years in the majors. Although his NHL total of 801 goals has been eclipsed, his combined (with the WHA) 975 markers remains the benchmark of excellence. In addition, Howe's 21 consecutive top-ten scoring seasons remain a record, as does his 21 All-Star selections. Because of these achievements, many think Howe to have been the greatest player to lace up his skates. If he wasn't, he certainly was close.

STANDINGS

TEAM	GP	W	L	T	PTS	GF	GA
DETROIT	70	37	19	14	88	191	132
MONTREAL	70	35	24	11	81	195	141
TORONTO	70	32	24	14	78	152	131
BOSTON	70	32	28	10	74	177	181
NEW YORK	70	29	31	10	68	161	182
CHICAGO	70	12	51	7	31	133	242

LEADERS

PLAYER	TM	GP	G	A	PTS	PIM
Gordie Howe	DET	70	33	48	81	109
Maurice Richard	MTL	70	37	30	67	112
Ted Lindsay	DET	70	26	36	62	110
Bernie Geoffrion	MTL	54	29	25	54	87
Bert Olmstead	MTL	70	15	37	52	85
Red Kelly	DET	62	16	33	49	18
Earl Reibel	DET	69	15	33	48	18
Ed Sandford	BOS	70	16	31	47	42
Fleming Mackell	BOS	67	15	32	47	60
Two tied with					46	

GOALS	
Richard, MTL	37
Howe, DET	33
Geoffrion, MTL	29
Hergesheimer, NY	27
Lindsay, DET	26

ASSISTS	
Howe, DET	48
Olmstead, MTL	37
Lindsay, DET	36
Four tied with	33

GOALTENDER	TM	GP	MIN	GA	SH	GAA
Harry Lumley	TOR	69	4140	128	13	1.86
Terry Sawchuk	DET	67	4004	129	12	1.93
Gerry McNeil	MTL	53	3180	114	6	2.15
Jim Henry	BOS	70	4200	181	8	2.59
Johnny Bower	NY	70	4200	182	5	2.60
Al Rollins	CHI	66	3960	213	5	3.23

PENALTY MINUTES	
Mortson, CHI	132
Richard, MTL	112
Lindsay, DET	110
Harvey, MTL	110
Two tied with	109

SHUTOUTS	
Lumley, TOR	13
Sawchuk, DET	12
Henry, BOS	8
McNeil, MTL	6
Three tied with	5

DETROIT   37-19-14   88   1st   Tommy Ivan
Red Wings

		REGULAR SEASON					POSTSEASON				
PLAYER	POS	GP	G	A	PTS	PIM	GP	G	A	PTS	PIM
Gordie Howe	R	70	33	48	81	109	12	4	5	9	31
Ted Lindsay	L	70	26	36	62	110	12	4	4	8	14
Red Kelly	D	62	16	33	49	18	12	5	1	6	0
Earl Reibel	C	69	15	33	48	18	9	1	3	4	0
Johnny Wilson	L	70	17	17	34	22	12	3	0	3	0

		REGULAR SEASON				*POSTSEASON*				
PLAYER	*POS*	*GP*	*G*	*A*	*PTS*	*PIM*	*GP*	*G*	*A*	*PTS*	*PIM*
Alex Delvecchio	C	69	11	18	29	34	12	2	7	9	7
Marty Pavelich	L	65	9	20	29	57	12	2	2	4	4
Glen Skov	L	70	17	10	27	95	12	1	2	3	16
Metro Prystai	C	70	12	15	27	26	12	2	3	5	0
Bill Dineen	R	70	17	8	25	34	12	0	0	0	2
Tony Leswick	L	70	6	18	24	90	12	3	1	4	18
Marcel Pronovost	D	57	6	12	18	50	12	2	3	5	12
Bob Goldham	D	69	1	15	16	50	12	0	2	2	2
Vic Stasiuk	L	42	5	2	7	4					
Jimmy Peters (2–2)	R	25	0	4	4	10	10	0	0	0	0
Keith Allen	D	10	0	4	4	2	5	0	0	0	0
Benny Woit	R	70	0	2	2	38	12	0	1	1	8
Terry Sawchuk	G	67	0	1	1	31	12	0	0	0	2
Al Arbour	D	36	0	1	1	18					
Jim Hay	D	12	0	0	0	0					
Dave Gatherum	G	3	0	0	0	0					
Marcel Bonin	L	1	0	0	0	0					
Earl Johnson	L	1	0	0	0	0					
Ed Stankiewicz	L	1	0	0	0	2					
Lefty Wilson	G	1	0	0	0	0					
Gilles Dube	L						2	0	0	0	0

		REGULAR SEASON				*POSTSEASON*			
GOALTENDER		*GP*	*MIN*	*GA*	*SH*	*GAA*	*GP*	*MIN*	*GA*	*SH*	*GAA*
Lefty Wilson		1	16	0	0	0.00					
Dave Gatherum	(2-0-1)	3	180	3	1	1.00					
Terry Sawchuk	(35-19-13)	67	4004	129	12	1.93	12	751	20	2	1.63

MONTREAL   35-24-11   81   2nd   Dick Irvin
Canadiens

		REGULAR SEASON				*POSTSEASON*				
PLAYER	*POS*	*GP*	*G*	*A*	*PTS*	*PIM*	*GP*	*G*	*A*	*PTS*	*PIM*
Maurice Richard	R	70	37	30	67	112	11	3	0	3	22
Bernie Geoffrion	R	54	29	25	54	87	11	6	5	11	18
Bert Olmstead	L	70	15	37	52	85	11	0	1	1	19
Kenny Mosdell	C	67	22	24	46	64	11	1	0	1	4
Doug Harvey	D	68	8	29	37	110	10	0	2	2	12
Jean Beliveau	C	44	13	21	34	22	10	2	8	10	4
Paul Masnick	C	50	5	21	26	57	10	0	4	4	4
Elmer Lach	C	48	5	20	25	28	4	0	2	2	0
Calum MacKay	L	47	10	13	23	54	3	0	1	1	0
Floyd Curry	R	70	13	8	21	22	11	4	0	4	4
Eddie Mazur	L	67	7	14	21	95	11	0	3	3	7
Tom Johnson	D	70	7	11	18	85	11	1	2	3	30
John McCormack	C	51	5	10	15	12	7	0	1	1	0
Dollard St. Laurent	D	53	3	12	15	43	10	1	2	3	8
Paul Meger	L	44	4	9	13	24	6	1	0	1	4
Dick Gamble	L	32	4	8	12	18					
Emile Bouchard	D	70	1	10	11	89	11	2	1	3	4
Lorne Davis	R	37	6	4	10	2	11	2	0	2	8

1953–1954 303

PLAYER	POS	REGULAR SEASON					POSTSEASON				
		GP	G	A	PTS	PIM	GP	G	A	PTS	PIM
Dickie Moore	L	13	1	4	5	12	11	5	8	13	8
James MacPherson	D	41	0	5	5	41	3	0	0	0	4
Andre Corriveau	C	3	0	1	1	0					
Gerry McNeil	G	53	0	0	0	0	3	0	0	0	0
Jacques Plante	G	17	0	0	0	0	8	0	0	0	0
Gerry Desaulniers	C	3	0	0	0	0					
Ed Litzenberger	R	3	0	0	0	0					
Fred Burchell	C	2	0	0	0	2					
Gaye Stewart	L						3	0	0	0	0

GOALTENDER		REGULAR SEASON					POSTSEASON				
		GP	MIN	GA	SH	GAA	GP	MIN	GA	SH	GAA
Jacques Plante	(7-5-5)	17	1020	27	5	1.59	8	480	15	2	1.88
Gerry McNeil	(28-19-6)	53	3180	114	6	2.15	3	190	3	1	**0.95**

TORONTO 32-24-14 78 3rd King Clancy
Maple Leafs

PLAYER	POS	REGULAR SEASON					POSTSEASON				
		GP	G	A	PTS	PIM	GP	G	A	PTS	PIM
Tod Sloan	R	67	11	32	43	100	5	1	1	2	4
Sid Smith	L	70	22	16	38	28	5	1	1	2	0
Ted Kennedy	C	67	15	23	38	78	5	1	1	2	2
George Armstrong	C	63	17	15	32	60	5	1	0	1	2
Tim Horton	D	70	7	24	31	94	5	1	1	2	4
Harry Watson	L	70	21	7	28	30	5	0	1	1	2
Jimmy Thomson	D	61	2	24	26	86	3	0	0	0	2
Ron Stewart	C	70	14	11	25	72	5	0	1	1	10
Eric Nesterenko	R	68	14	9	23	70	5	0	1	1	9
Rudy Migay	C	70	8	15	23	60	5	1	0	1	4
Jim Morrison	D	60	9	11	20	51	5	0	0	0	4
Bob Bailey	R	48	2	7	9	70	5	0	2	2	4
Gord Hannigan	C	35	4	4	8	18	5	2	0	2	4
Fern Flaman	D	62	0	8	8	84	2	0	0	0	0
Leo Boivin	D	58	1	6	7	81	5	0	0	0	2
Bob Solinger	L	39	3	2	5	2					
Bob Hassard	C	26	1	4	5	4					
Howie Meeker	R	5	1	0	1	0					
Earl Balfour	L	17	0	1	1	6					
Danny Lewicki	L	7	0	1	1	12					
Harry Lumley	G	69	0	0	0	6	5	0	0	0	0
Hugh Bolton	D	9	0	0	0	10	5	0	1	1	4
Gil Mayer	G	1	0	0	0	0					

GOALTENDER		REGULAR SEASON					POSTSEASON				
		GP	MIN	GA	SH	GAA	GP	MIN	GA	SH	GAA
Harry Lumley	(32-24-**13**)	69	4140	128	**13**	**1.86**	5	321	15	0	2.80
Gil Mayer	(0-0-1)	1	60	3	0	3.00					

BOSTON 32-28-10 74 4th Lynn Patrick
Bruins

PLAYER	POS	REGULAR SEASON					POSTSEASON				
		GP	G	A	PTS	PIM	GP	G	A	PTS	PIM
Ed Sandford	L	70	16	31	47	42	3	0	1	1	4
Fleming Mackell	C	67	15	32	47	60	4	1	1	2	8
Johnny Peirson	R	68	21	19	40	55	4	0	0	0	2
Dave Creighton	C	69	20	20	40	27	4	0	0	0	0
Joe Klukay	L	70	20	17	37	27	4	0	0	0	0
Leo Labine	R	68	16	19	35	57	4	0	1	1	8
Cal Gardner	C	70	14	20	34	62	4	1	1	2	0
Milt Schmidt	C	62	14	18	32	28	4	1	0	1	20
Doug Mohns	F	70	13	14	27	27	4	1	0	1	4
Frank Martin	D	68	3	17	20	38	4	0	1	1	0
Hal Laycoe	D	58	3	16	19	29	2	0	0	0	0
Bill Quackenbush	D	45	0	17	17	6	4	0	0	0	0
Warren Godfrey	D	70	5	9	14	71	4	0	0	0	4
Bob Armstrong	D	64	2	10	12	81	4	0	1	1	0
Woody Dumart	L	69	4	3	7	6	4	0	0	0	0
Ray Gariepy	D	35	1	6	7	39					
Gus Bodnar	C	14	3	3	6	10	1	0	0	0	0
Real Chevrefils	L	14	4	1	5	2					
Jerry Toppazzini (1–2)	R	37	0	5	5	24					
Jim Henry	G	70	0	0	0	0	4	0	0	0	0
Wayne Brown	R						4	0	0	0	2
Guyle Fielder	C						2	0	0	0	2

GOALTENDER		REGULAR SEASON					POSTSEASON				
		GP	MIN	GA	SH	GAA	GP	MIN	GA	SH	GAA
Jim Henry	(32-28-10)	70	4200	181	8	2.59	4	240	16	0	4.00

NEW YORK 29-31-10 68 5th Frank Boucher
Rangers

PLAYER	POS	REGULAR SEASON					POSTSEASON
		GP	G	A	PTS	PIM	no postseason play
Paul Ronty	C	70	13	33	46	18	
Don Raleigh	C	70	15	30	45	16	
Wally Hergesheimer	R	66	27	16	43	42	
Camille Henry	C	66	24	15	39	10	
Nick Mickoski	L	68	19	16	35	22	
Max Bentley	C	57	14	18	32	15	
Dean Prentice	L	52	4	13	17	18	
Hy Buller	D	41	3	14	17	40	
Harry Howell	D	67	7	9	16	58	
Eddie Kullman	R	70	4	10	14	44	
Ivan Irwin	D	56	2	12	14	109	
Ike Hildebrand (1–2)	R	31	6	7	13	12	
Doug Bentley	L	20	2	10	12	2	
Bob Chrystal	D	64	5	5	10	44	
Jack Evans	D	44	4	4	8	73	
Leo Reise	D	70	3	5	8	71	
Aldo Guidolin	D	68	2	6	8	51	

		REGULAR SEASON					POSTSEASON
PLAYER	POS	GP	G	A	PTS	PIM	no postseason play
Edgar Laprade	C	35	1	6	7	2	
Andy Bathgate	R	20	2	2	4	18	
Ron Murphy	L	27	1	3	4	20	
Glen Sonmor	L	15	2	0	2	17	
Billy Dea	C	14	1	1	2	2	
Allan Stanley	D	10	0	2	2	11	
Johnny Bower	G	70	0	0	0	0	
Bill McCreary	L	2	0	0	0	2	
Bill Chalmers	C	1	0	0	0	0	
Vic Howe	R	1	0	0	0	0	
Aggie Kukulowicz	C	1	0	0	0	0	

		REGULAR SEASON				POSTSEASON
GOALTENDER		GP	MIN	GA	SH	GAA	no postseason play
Johnny Bower	(29-31-10)	70	4200	182	5	2.60	

CHICAGO Blackhawks   12-51-7   31   6th   Sid Abel

		REGULAR SEASON					POSTSEASON
PLAYER	POS	GP	G	A	PTS	PIM	no postseason play
Larry Wilson	C	66	9	33	42	22	
Bill Gadsby	D	70	12	29	41	108	
Bill Mosienko	R	65	15	19	34	17	
Pete Conacher	L	70	19	9	28	23	
Lou Jankowski	C	68	15	13	28	7	
George Gee	C	69	10	16	26	59	
Al Dewsbury	D	69	6	15	21	44	
Gus Bodnar (1-2)	C	45	6	15	21	20	
Gus Mortson	D	68	5	13	18	132	
Jack McIntyre	L	23	8	3	11	4	
Gerry Couture	C	40	6	5	11	14	
Jimmy Peters (1-2)	R	46	6	4	10	21	
Jack Price	D	46	4	6	10	22	
Jerry Toppazzini (2-2)	R	14	5	3	8	18	
Kenny Wharram	R	29	1	7	8	8	
Larry Zeidel	D	64	1	6	7	102	
Jim McFadden	C	19	3	3	6	6	
Murray Costello	C	40	3	2	5	6	
Ike Hildebrand (2-2)	R	7	1	4	5	4	
Fred Hucul	D	27	0	3	3	19	
Vic Lynn	L	11	1	0	1	2	
Lee Fogolin	D	68	0	1	1	95	
Al Rollins	G	66	0	0	0	20	
Fred Sasakamoose	C	11	0	0	0	6	
Sid Finney	C	6	0	0	0	0	
Sid Abel	C	3	0	0	0	0	
Hec Lalande	C	2	0	0	0	0	
Jack Gelineau	G	2	0	0	0	0	
Jean Marois	G	2	0	0	0	0	
Hillary Menard	L	1	0	0	0	0	

PLAYER	POS	*REGULAR SEASON*					*POSTSEASON*
		GP	G	A	PTS	PIM	no postseason play
John Sleaver	C	1	0	0	0	2	
Bob Wilson	D	1	0	0	0	0	

GOALTENDER		*REGULAR SEASON*					*POSTSEASON*
		GP	MIN	GA	SH	GAA	no postseason play
Al Rollins	(12-47-7)	66	3960	213	5	3.23	
Jean Marois	(0-2-0)	2	120	11	0	5.50	
Jack Gelineau	(0-2-0)	2	120	18	0	9.00	

TEAM TOTALS

TEAM	GP	G	A	P	PIM	GA	SH	*Per Game*			
								G	A	PIM	GA
Detroit	70	191	296	487	814	132	13	2.73	4.23	11.63	1.89
Montreal	70	**195**	**316**	**511**	**1064**	141	11	**2.79**	**4.51**	**15.20**	2.01
Toronto	70	152	220	372	1022	**131**	13	2.17	3.14	14.60	**1.87**
Boston	70	174	277	451	685	181	8	2.49	3.96	9.79	2.59
New York	70	161	237	398	717	182	5	2.30	3.39	10.24	2.60
Chicago	70	136	209	345	797	242	5	1.94	2.99	11.39	3.46
	420	1009	1555	2564	5095	1009	55	2.40	3.70	12.14	2.40

PLAYOFFS

SERIES "A"
Detroit 5, Toronto 0
Toronto 3, Detroit 1
Detroit 3, Toronto 1
Detroit 2, Toronto 1
Detroit 4, Toronto 3 (OT)

DETROIT, 4–1

SERIES "B"
Montreal 2, Boston 0
Montreal 8, Boston 1
Montreal 4, Boston 3
Montreal 2, Boston 0

MONTREAL, 4–0

SERIES "C"
Detroit 3, Montreal 1
Montreal 3, Detroit 1
Detroit 5, Montreal 2
Detroit 2, Montreal 0
Montreal 1, Detroit 0 (OT)
Montreal 4, Detroit 1
Detroit 2, Montreal 1 (OT)

DETROIT WINS STANLEY CUP, 4–3

ALL-STAR TEAMS

First Team
G — Harry Lumley, TOR
D — Doug Harvey, MTL

Second Team
G — Terry Sawchuk, DET
D — Bill Gadsby, CHI

1953–1954

First Team
D — Red Kelly, DET
C — Kenny Mosdell, MTL
R — Gordie Howe, DET
L — Ted Lindsay, DET

Second Team
D — Tim Horton, TOR
C — Ted Kennedy, TOR
R — Maurice Richard, MTL
L — Ed Sandford, BOS

INDIVIDUAL TROPHY WINNERS

HART TROPHY (Most Valuable Player): Al Rollins, CHI
LADY BYNG TROPHY (Gentlemanly Conduct): Red Kelly, DET
VEZINA TROPHY (Best Goaltender): Harry Lumley, TOR
CALDER MEMORIAL TROPHY (Best Rookie): Camille Henry, NY
ART ROSS TROPHY (Scoring Leader): Gordie Howe, DET
JAMES NORRIS TROPHY (Best Defenseman): Red Kelly, TOR

1954-1955

Riot

Throughout his career, Montreal's Maurice Richard was known as a fiery, emotional player, frequently at odds with opponents. In addition, league officials also bore the brunt of his temper. Late in the 1954-55 season, it would be one of the latter encounters that would boil over, engulfing a whole city.

Before 1955, Richard's most notorious run-in with NHL officials occurred in March 1951. On the third day of that month, in Montreal, he was given a game misconduct penalty by referee Hugh McLean in a game against the Red Wings — a penalty which resulted in immediate ejection from the contest. Outraged by the call, Richard took it to the next level, confronting the official in a New York hotel the next day. Pouncing on McLean, he had to be restrained by teammates, who luckily intervened before too much damage was done. Because he was restrained before many punches were thrown, no suspension was levied — only a $500 fine. Richard would not be as fortunate the next time.

As the 1954-55 season unfolded, for the first time in many years, the Detroit Red Wings found themselves in a spirited race for the crown, actually trailing the Canadiens late in the season. Leading Montreal's surge was none other than Richard, who was poised to win his first scoring crown. Unfortunately, his temper got the better of him once again. On the night of March 13, in a game against Boston, Richard lost it. Retaliating against Hal Laycoe after a high stick check, he swung his lumber at the Bruin defenseman, striking him in the head. When linesman Cliff Thompson tried to intervene, Richard fought back, giving the arbiter a black eye. The NHL's justice was swift, as league president Clarence Campbell suspended him for the rest of the season — including the playoffs. Montreal's fans were outraged, thinking the sentence too harsh.

Then, in an inexplicable move, Campbell fanned the flames by actually attending a Montreal game in person on March 17. The ugliness started early, as reported in a *Maclean Magazine* article by Sidney Katz: "Throughout the first period the crowd had vented their anger at Campbell ... showering him with rotten fruit, eggs, pickled pig's feet and empty bottles." A few minutes later, someone lobbed a tear gas bomb onto the ice, leading to a prompt evacuation of the building. Spreading outside, the altercation sped through the streets of Montreal. Katz continues: "For 15 blocks they left in their path a swath of destruction. It looked like the aftermath of a wartime blitz in London." In all, dozens of people — both civilians and policemen — were injured, with many thousands of dollars in damage done to area businesses.

In the aftermath of the hoopla, Detroit (42-17-11, 95) caught and bested Montreal by two points, winning their seventh straight title. Well back, Toronto and Boston claimed the other playoff berths, while New York and Chicago finished out of the running. On an individual level, Richard scored the most goals (38), but his suspension also cost him the scoring title, as his teammate Bernie Geoffrion (38-37-75) beat him by a single point. Another Canadien — Bert Olmstead — garnered the most assists (48), while Boston's Fern Flaman (150) served the most time in the sin bin. Toronto's Harry Lumley (1.93) edged Terry Sawchuk (Detroit) for the GAA crown, although the latter blanked the most opponents (12).

Despite the loss of Richard, the Canadiens easily handled the Bruins in the opening round of the playoffs, defeating the fourth-place team in five games. Detroit also had a cake-walk in the opening set, outscoring the Maple Leafs 14–6 in a four game sweep. In the finals, the NHL's two best teams went toe-to-toe in a series that went the limit. After Detroit took the first two contests, 4–2 and 7–1, Montreal returned the favor, evening the series with 4–2 and 5–3 wins. The Wings took the next game, 5–1, but the Canadiens sent the finals to a deciding game with a 6–3 triumph in the sixth game. In the season's final contest, Detroit's Alex Delvecchio scored a pair of goals, sealing a 3–1 win and giving Detroit its fourth Cup in six years. In addition, Red Wing players garnered all the individual glory, as Gordie Howe tallied the most goals (9) and points (20), Ted Lindsay (12) collected the most assists and goaler Sawchuk allowed the fewest scores (2.36).

To be fair, the "Richard Riot," as it became known, cannot be laid solely at the feet of the Montreal player, although in the aftermath of the event, a contrite Richard shouldered his share of the blame. In reality, the flash-point was caused by Campbell, whose foolish choice to attend the game on March 17 actually triggered the unrest. Thankfully, the Richard Riot remains to this day a unique event, gratefully never repeated in the annals of the league.

STANDINGS

TEAM	GP	W	L	T	PTS	GF	GA
DETROIT	70	42	17	11	95	204	134
MONTREAL	70	41	18	11	93	228	157
TORONTO	70	24	24	22	70	147	135
BOSTON	70	23	26	21	67	169	188
NEW YORK	70	17	35	18	52	150	210
CHICAGO	70	13	40	17	43	161	235

LEADERS

PLAYER	TM	GP	G	A	PTS	PIM
Bernie Geoffrion	MTL	70	**38**	37	**75**	57
Maurice Richard	MTL	67	**38**	36	74	125
Jean Beliveau	MTL	70	37	36	73	58
Earl Reibel	DET	70	25	41	66	15
Gordie Howe	DET	64	29	33	62	68
George Sullivan	CHI	70	19	42	61	51
Bert Olmstead	MTL	70	10	**48**	58	103
Sid Smith	TOR	70	33	21	54	14
Kenny Mosdell	MTL	70	22	32	54	82
Danny Lewicki	NY	70	29	24	53	8

GOALS
Richard, MTL 38
Geoffrion, MTL 38
Beliveau, MTL 37
Smith, TOR 33
Two tied with 29

ASSISTS
Olmstead, MTL 48
Harvey, MTL 43
Kennedy, TOR 42
G. Sullivan, CHI 42
Reibel, DET 41

GOALTENDER	TM	GP	MIN	GA	SH	GAA
Harry Lumley	TOR	**69**	**4140**	133 (1)	8	**1.93**
Terry Sawchuk	DET	68	4080	132	**12**	1.94
Jacques Plante	MTL	52	3080	109 (1)	5	2.10
John Henderson	BOS	45	2628	109	5	2.49
Lorne Worsley	NY	65	3900	**195** (2)	4	3.00
Jim Henry	BOS	27	1572	79	1	3.02
Al Rollins	CHI	44	2640	149 (1)	0	3.39

PENALTY MINUTES
Flaman, BOS 150
Leswick, DET 137
Hollingworth, CHI 135
Mortson, CHI 133
Richard, MTL 125

SHUTOUTS
Sawchuk, DET 12
Lumley, TOR 8
Plante, MTL 5
Henderson, BOS 5
Worsley, NY 4

DETROIT 42-17-11 95 1st Jim Skinner
Red Wings

PLAYER	POS	REGULAR SEASON					POSTSEASON				
		GP	G	A	PTS	PIM	GP	G	A	PTS	PIM
Earl Reibel	C	70	25	41	66	15	11	5	7	12	2
Gordie Howe	R	64	29	33	62	68	11	9	11	**20**	24
Alex Delvecchio	C	69	17	31	48	37	11	7	8	15	2
Red Kelly	D	70	15	30	45	28	11	2	4	6	17
Ted Lindsay	L	49	19	19	38	85	11	7	**12**	19	12
Marcel Bonin	L	69	16	20	36	53	11	0	2	2	4
Marcel Pronovost	D	70	9	25	34	90	11	1	2	3	6
Marty Pavelich	L	70	15	15	30	59	11	1	3	4	12
Glen Skov	L	70	14	16	30	53	11	2	0	2	8

		REGULAR SEASON				POSTSEASON				
PLAYER	POS	GP	G	A	PTS	PIM	GP	G	A	PTS	PIM
Johnny Wilson	L	70	12	15	27	14	11	0	1	1	0
Tony Leswick	L	70	10	17	27	137	11	1	2	3	20
Bill Dineen	R	69	10	9	19	36	11	0	1	1	8
Vic Stasiuk	L	59	8	11	19	67	11	5	3	8	6
Bob Goldham	D	69	1	16	17	14	11	0	4	4	4
Benny Woit	R	62	2	3	5	22	11	0	1	1	6
Metro Prystai (1–2)	C	12	2	3	5	9					
Lorne Davis (1–2)	R	22	0	5	5	2					
Terry Sawchuk	G	68	0	1	1	10	11	0	0	0	12
Jim Hay	D	21	0	1	1	20	5	1	0	1	0
Keith Allen	D	18	0	0	0	6					
Larry Hillman	D	6	0	0	0	2	3	0	0	0	0
Don Poile	C	4	0	0	0	0					
Ed Zeniuk	D	2	0	0	0	0					
Glenn Hall	G	2	0	0	0	0					

		REGULAR SEASON				POSTSEASON				
GOALTENDER		GP	MIN	GA	SH	GAA	GP	MIN	GA	SH	GAA
Glenn Hall	(2-0-0)	2	120	2	0	1.00					
Terry Sawchuk	(40-17-11)	68	4080	132	12	1.94	11	660	26	1	2.36

MONTREAL 41-18-11 93 2nd Dick Irvin
Canadiens

		REGULAR SEASON				POSTSEASON				
PLAYER	POS	GP	G	A	PTS	PIM	GP	G	A	PTS	PIM
Bernie Geoffrion	R	70	38	37	75	57	12	8	5	13	8
Maurice Richard	R	67	38	36	74	125					
Jean Beliveau	C	70	37	36	73	58	12	6	7	13	18
Bert Olmstead	L	70	10	48	58	103	12	0	4	4	21
Kenny Mosdell	C	70	22	32	54	82	12	2	7	9	8
Doug Harvey	D	70	6	43	49	58	12	0	8	8	6
Dickie Moore	L	67	16	20	36	32	12	1	5	6	22
Calum MacKay	L	50	14	21	35	39	12	3	8	11	8
Jackie Leclair	C	59	11	22	33	12	12	5	0	5	2
Tom Johnson	D	70	6	19	25	74	12	2	0	2	22
Floyd Curry	R	68	11	10	21	36	12	8	4	12	4
Dollard St. Laurent	D	58	3	14	17	24	12	0	5	5	12
Emile Bouchard	D	70	2	15	17	81	12	0	1	1	37
Ed Litzenberger (1–2)	R	*29	7	4	11	12					
James MacPherson	D	30	1	8	9	55					
Don Marshall	L	39	5	3	8	9	12	1	1	2	2
Eddie Mazur	L	25	1	5	6	21					
Paul Meger	L	13	0	4	4	6					
Paul Masnick (1,3–3)	C	19	0	1	1	0					
Jean-Guy Talbot	D	3	0	1	1	0					
Guy Rousseau	L	2	0	1	1	0					
Jacques Plante	G	52	0	0	0	2	12	0	0	0	0
Charlie Hodge	G	14	0	0	0	0	4	0	0	0	0
Paul Ronty (2–2)	C	4	0	0	0	0	5	0	0	0	2
Orval Tessier	C	4	0	0	0	0					

		REGULAR SEASON					POSTSEASON				
PLAYER	POS	GP	G	A	PTS	PIM	GP	G	A	PTS	PIM
Claude Evans	G	4	0	0	0	0					
Kim Bartlett	L	2	0	0	0	4	2	0	0	0	0
Garry Blaine	R	1	0	0	0	0					
J-P Lamirande	D	1	0	0	0	0					
Andre Binette	G	1	0	0	0	0					
Dick Gamble (2–2)	L						2	0	0	0	0
George McAvoy	D						4	0	0	0	0

		REGULAR SEASON					POSTSEASON				
GOALTENDER		GP	MIN	GA	SH	GAA	GP	MIN	GA	SH	GAA
Jacques Plante	(31-13-7)	52	3080	109 (1)	5	2.10	12	640	30	0	2.82
Charlie Hodge	(7-3-4)	14	840	31	1	2.21	4	83	6	0	4.29
Claude Evans	(2-2-0)	4	220	12	0	3.27					
Andre Binette	(1-0-0)	1	60	4	0	4.00					

TORONTO 24-24-22 70 3rd King Clancy
Maple Leafs

		REGULAR SEASON					POSTSEASON				
PLAYER	POS	GP	G	A	PTS	PIM	GP	G	A	PTS	PIM
Sid Smith	L	70	33	21	54	14	4	3	1	4	0
Ted Kennedy	C	70	10	42	52	74	4	1	3	4	0
Eric Nesterenko	R	62	15	15	30	99	4	0	1	1	6
Tod Sloan	R	63	13	15	28	89	4	0	0	0	2
George Armstrong	C	66	10	18	28	80	4	1	0	1	4
Rudy Migay	C	67	8	16	24	66	3	0	0	0	10
Hugh Bolton	D	69	2	19	21	55	4	0	3	3	6
Ron Stewart	C	53	14	5	19	20	4	0	0	0	2
Jim Morrison	D	70	5	12	17	84	4	0	1	1	4
Joe Klukay (1–2)	L	56	8	8	16	44	4	0	0	0	4
Jimmy Thomson	D	70	4	12	16	63	4	0	0	0	16
Tim Horton	D	67	5	9	14	84					
Parker MacDonald	C	62	8	3	11	36	4	0	0	0	4
Brian Cullen	C	27	3	5	8	6	4	1	0	1	0
Bob Bailey	R	32	4	2	6	52	1	0	0	0	0
Bob Solinger	L	17	1	5	6	11					
Larry Cahan	D	59	0	6	6	64	4	0	0	0	0
Willie Marshall	C	16	1	4	5	0					
Dave Creighton (1–2)	C	14	2	1	3	8					
Harry Watson (2–2)	L	8	1	1	2	0					
Gord Hannigan	C	13	0	2	2	8					
Harry Lumley	G	69	0	0	0	9	4	0	0	0	0
Leo Boivin	D	7	0	0	0	8					
Gerry Foley	R	4	0	0	0	8					
Jack Caffery	C	3	0	0	0	0					
Dick Duff	L	3	0	0	0	2					
Gerry James	R	1	0	0	0	0					
Paul Knox	R	1	0	0	0	0					
Marc Reaume	D	1	0	0	0	4	4	0	0	0	2
Dave Reid	C	1	0	0	0	0					

PLAYER	POS	REGULAR SEASON					POSTSEASON				
		GP	G	A	PTS	PIM	GP	G	A	PTS	PIM
Ray Timgren (1–2)	L	1	0	0	0	2					
Gil Mayer	G	1	0	0	0	0					

GOALTENDER		REGULAR SEASON					POSTSEASON				
		GP	MIN	GA	SH	GAA	GP	MIN	GA	SH	GAA
Gil Mayer	(1-0-0)	1	60	1	0	1.00					
Harry Lumley	(23-24-**22**)	69	4140	133 (1)	8	**1.93**	4	240	14	0	3.50

BOSTON
Bruins

23-26-21   67   4th   Lynn Patrick
                      Milt Schmidt

PLAYER	POS	REGULAR SEASON					POSTSEASON				
		GP	G	A	PTS	PIM	GP	G	A	PTS	PIM
Leo Labine	R	67	24	18	42	75	5	2	1	3	11
Don McKenney	C	69	22	20	42	34	5	1	2	3	4
Real Chevrefils	L	64	18	22	40	30	5	2	1	3	4
Cal Gardner	C	70	16	22	35	70	5	0	0	0	4
Fleming Mackell	C	60	11	24	35	76	4	0	1	1	0
Lorne Ferguson	L	69	20	14	34	24	4	1	0	1	2
Ed Sandford	L	60	14	20	34	38	5	1	1	2	6
Doug Mohns	F	70	14	18	32	82	5	0	0	0	4
Bill Quackenbush	D	68	2	20	22	8	5	0	5	5	0
Fern Flaman	D	70	4	14	18	**150**	4	1	0	1	2
Warren Godfrey	D	62	1	17	18	58	3	0	0	0	0
Leo Boivin (2–2)	D	59	6	11	17	105	5	0	1	1	4
Hal Laycoe	D	70	4	13	17	34	5	1	0	1	0
Murray Costello	C	54	4	11	15	25	1	0	0	0	2
Milt Schmidt	C	23	4	8	12	26					
Gus Bodnar	C	67	4	4	8	14	5	0	1	1	4
Bob Armstrong	D	57	1	3	4	38	5	0	0	0	2
Floyd Smith	R	3	0	1	1	0					
John Henderson	G	45	0	0	0	0	2	0	0	0	0
Jim Henry	G	27	0	0	0	0	3	0	0	0	0
Joe Klukay (2–2)	L	10	0	0	0	4					
Norm Corcoran	C	2	0	0	0	2	4	0	0	0	6
Skip Teal	C	1	0	0	0	0					
Don Cherry	D						1	0	0	0	0
Gord Wilson	L						2	0	0	0	0

GOALTENDER		REGULAR SEASON					POSTSEASON				
		GP	MIN	GA	SH	GAA	GP	MIN	GA	SH	GAA
John Henderson	(15-14-15)	45	2628	109	5	2.49	2	120	8	0	4.00
Jim Henry	(8-12-6)	27	1572	79	1	3.02	3	183	8	0	2.62

NEW YORK
Rangers

17-35-18   52   5th   Muzz Patrick

PLAYER	POS	REGULAR SEASON					POSTSEASON
		GP	G	A	PTS	PIM	*no postseason play*
Danny Lewicki	L	70	29	24	53	8	
Andy Bathgate	R	70	20	20	40	37	
Don Raleigh	C	69	8	32	40	19	

		REGULAR SEASON					*POSTSEASON*
PLAYER	*POS*	*GP*	*G*	*A*	*PTS*	*PIM*	*no postseason play*
Dean Prentice	L	70	16	15	31	20	
Ron Murphy	L	66	14	16	30	36	
Larry Popein	C	70	11	17	28	27	
Pete Conacher (2–2)	L	52	10	7	17	10	
Bill Gadsby (2–2)	D	52	8	8	16	44	
Harry Howell	D	70	2	14	16	87	
Bob Chrystal	D	68	6	9	15	68	
Paul Ronty (1–2)	C	55	4	11	15	8	
Edgar Laprade	C	60	3	11	14	0	
Nick Mickoski (1–2)	L	18	0	14	14	6	
Ivan Irwin	D	60	0	13	13	85	
Camile Henry	C	21	5	2	7	4	
Aldo Guidolin	D	70	2	5	7	34	
Wally Hergesheimer	R	14	4	2	6	4	
Vic Howe	R	29	2	4	6	10	
Jack Evans	D	47	0	5	5	91	
Lou Fontinato	D	27	2	2	4	60	
Bill Ezinicki	R	16	2	2	4	22	
Jackie McLeod	R	11	1	1	2	4	
Bill McCreary	L	8	0	2	2	0	
Allan Stanley (1–2)	D	12	0	1	1	2	
Lorne Worsley	G	65	0	0	0	2	
Glen Sonmor	L	13	0	0	0	4	
Johnny Bower	G	5	0	0	0	0	
Ron Howell	D	3	0	0	0	0	
Dick Bouchard	R	1	0	0	0	0	

	REGULAR SEASON					*POSTSEASON*
GOALTENDER	*GP*	*MIN*	*GA*	*SH*	*GAA*	*no postseason play*
Johnny Bower (2-2-1)	5	300	13	0	2.60	
Lorne Worsley (15-**33**-17)	65	3900	**195**	(2)	4	3.00

CHICAGO 13-40-17 43 6th Frank Eddolls
Blackhawks

		REGULAR SEASON					*POSTSEASON*
PLAYER	*POS*	*GP*	*G*	*A*	*PTS*	*PIM*	*no postseason play*
George Sullivan	C	70	19	42	61	51	
Ed Litzenberger (2–2)	R	*44	16	24	40	38	
Harry Watson (1–2)	L	43	14	16	30	4	
Jack McIntyre	L	65	16	13	29	40	
Nick Mickoski (2–2)	L	52	10	19	29	42	
Bill Mosienko	R	64	12	15	27	24	
Jerry Toppazzini	R	70	9	18	27	59	
Allan Stanley (2–2)	D	52	10	15	25	22	
Metro Prystai (2–2)	C	57	11	13	24	28	
Dave Creighton (2–2)	C	49	7	7	14	6	
Gus Mortson	D	65	2	11	13	133	
John McCormack	C	63	5	7	12	8	
Frank Martin	D	66	4	8	12	35	
Gord Hollingworth	D	70	3	9	12	135	

		REGULAR SEASON					POSTSEASON
PLAYER	POS	GP	G	A	PTS	PIM	no postseason play
Bill Gadsby (1–2)	D	18	3	5	8	17	
Pete Conacher (1–2)	L	18	2	4	6	2	
Lou Jankowski	C	36	3	2	5	8	
Dick Gamble (1–2)	L	14	2	0	2	6	
Ray Timgren (2–2)	L	14	1	1	2	2	
Paul Masnick (2–3)	C	11	1	0	1	8	
Lee Fogolin	D	9	0	1	1	16	
Al Dewsbury	D	2	0	1	1	10	
Al Rollins	G	44	0	0	0	0	
Hank Bassen	G	21	0	0	0	0	
Bob Hassard	C	17	0	0	0	4	
Lorne Davis (2–2)	R	8	0	0	0	4	
Ray Frederick	G	5	0	0	0	0	
Ike Hildebrand	R	3	0	0	0	0	
Frank Sullivan	D	1	0	0	0	0	

		REGULAR SEASON					POSTSEASON
GOALTENDER		GP	MIN	GA	SH	GAA	no postseason play
Hank Bassen	(4-9-8)	21	1260	63	0	3.00	
Al Rollins	(9-27-8)	44	2640	149 (1)	0	3.39	
Ray Frederick	(0-4-1)	5	300	22	0	4.40	

TEAM TOTALS

								Per Game			
TEAM	GP	G	A	P	PIM	GA	SH	G	A	PIM	GA
Detroit	70	204	310	514	827	**134**	12	2.91	4.43	11.81	**1.91**
Montreal	70	**228**	**380**	**608**	890	157	6	**3.26**	**5.43**	12.71	2.24
Toronto	70	147	221	368	**990**	135	8	2.10	3.16	**14.14**	1.93
Boston	70	169	260	429	863	188	6	2.41	3.71	12.33	2.69
New York	70	149	237	386	690	210	4	2.13	3.39	9.86	3.00
Chicago	70	162	242	404	733	235	0	2.31	3.46	10.47	3.36
	420	1059	1650	2709	4993	1059	36	2.52	3.93	11.86	2.52

PLAYOFFS

SERIES "A"
Detroit 7, Toronto 4
Detroit 2, Toronto 1
Detroit 2, Toronto 1
Detroit 3, Toronto 0

DETROIT, 4–0

SERIES "B"
Montreal 2, Boston 0
Montreal 3, Boston 1
Boston 4, Montreal 2
Montreal 4, Boston 3 (OT)
Montreal 5, Boston 1

MONTREAL, 4–1

SERIES "C"
Detroit 4, Montreal 2
Detroit 7, Montreal 1
Montreal 4, Detroit 2

Montreal 5, Detroit 3
Detroit 5, Montreal 1
Montreal 6, Detroit 3
Detroit 3, Montreal 1

**DETROIT WINS
STANLEY CUP, 4-3**

ALL-STAR TEAMS

First Team
G — Harry Lumley, TOR
D — Doug Harvey, MTL
D — Red Kelly, DET
C — Jean Beliveau, MTL
R — Maurice Richard, MTL
L — Sid Smith, TOR

Second Team
G — Terry Sawchuk, DET
D — Bob Goldham, DET
D — Fern Flaman, BOS
C — Kenny Mosdell, MTL
R — Bernie Geoffrion, MTL
L — Danny Lewicki, BOS

INDIVIDUAL TROPHY WINNERS

HART TROPHY (Most Valuable Player): Ted Kennedy, TOR
LADY BYNG TROPHY (Gentlemanly Conduct): Sid Smith, TOR
VEZINA TROPHY (Best Goaltender): Terry Sawchuk, DET
CALDER MEMORIAL TROPHY (Best Rookie): Ed Litzenberger, M-C
ART ROSS TROPHY (Scoring Leader): Bernie Geoffrion, MTL
JAMES NORRIS TROPHY (Best Defenseman): Doug Harvey, MTL

1955-1956

Montreal Canadiens

During the first half of the 1950s, the Detroit Red Wings had run roughshod over the rest of the league, claiming seven consecutive regular titles and winning four Cups. However, there was another club lurking in the wings, ready to go on a streak of its own. In 1954-55, this contender knocked on the first place door, nearly wresting the prize from the Red Wings. The next year, they wouldn't just knock—they would kick it in.

The Montreal Canadiens can trace their roots nearly to the dawn of professional hockey, as the club was one of the founding members of the NHL's direct ancestor, the National Hockey Association. During its nine years in the league (1909–17), the Canadiens won a lone Cup (1916), defeating the PCHA's Portland Rosebuds in a thrilling five-game series.

When the NHL was formed in the fall of 1917, the Canadiens were again one of the charter members. Over the first few years of the league, the club iced a strong club, which regularly contended for the Cup. In its first tilt for Lord Stanley's prize in 1919, the Canadiens didn't win, but they didn't lose either, as an influenza epidemic halted the finals with Seattle. Montreal's first NHL Cup came in 1924, followed by another pair in 1930 and 1931. Their foremost star in these triumphs was sniper Howie Morenz, who deposited pucks into opposing nets with startling frequency.

During the rest of the 1930s, the team made the playoffs most years, but could never elevate itself to the highest level. This era came to a sudden end in 1943-44, as the club broke out of the doldrums and posted a record 83-point season, capped by another Cup. Instrumental in the team's success was the NHL's next big star—Maurice Richard—who shattered the league's goal scoring mark (50) the following season. After other titles in 1946 and 1953, the team treaded water, waiting for the domination of the Red Wings to end. By the mid 1950s, the wait was nearly over.

In 1954-55, the Canadiens posted the highest point total in their history (93), falling just short of Detroit. The following season, Montreal (45-15-10, 100) ratcheted up the effort, leaving the rest of the league far behind. Buoyed by an eight-game winning streak in December and another six-game streak in February, the team became the second club in league annals to cross the century threshold. Slipping badly, second place Detroit managed only 76 points, giving the Canadiens one of the largest margins of victory in league history.

Paving the way for the team's success was one of its youngest players, Jean Beliveau (47-41-86), who captured the scoring title while netting the most markers. He was ably assisted by veterans Richard (38-33-71) and Bert Olmstead (14-56-70), the latter breaking the league record for assists. In goal, Jacques Plante (1.86) was the league's stingiest netminder, though Detroit's Glenn Hall posted the most shutouts (12). In addition, New York's Lou Fontinato set a new record, racking up 202 penalty minutes.

In the first round of the postseason, Montreal eliminated the third-place Rangers in five games. In the other opening series, Detroit bested fourth-place Toronto (which had beaten out Boston and Chicago for the final spot) in five games as well. In the finals, Detroit started out strongly and was leading Montreal 4-2 after two periods of the first game. Invigorated by a rousing speech by their first-year coach, Toe Blake, the Canadiens scored four times in the final stanza, skating off with a 6-4 win. Over the next four games, Detroit managed only four more goals, winning only once. The fifth and final game went to Montreal by a 3-1 score, giving the Canadiens their first Cup in three years.

Following up on their regular season accolades, Beliveau and Olmstead finished as the playoffs' top scorers, with the former collecting the most goals (12) and points (19) and the latter dishing off the most assists (10). In addition, Plante shutout two opponents while posting a 1.80 GAA.

Immediately after its 1956 Cup triumph, the greatness of this Montreal club became apparent, as the NHL changed one of its rules in order to slow down the team. Up through the 1955-56 season, if a player was sent to the penalty box, he remained there for the duration of the infraction. Montreal thrived in these extra-man situations, often scoring multiple times on each penalty. So, beginning in 1956-57, the NHL ruled that once a goal is scored on a power play, the whistled individual could return to action.

Despite this change, Montreal followed up its triumph with several more, finishing off the decade with a singular run. Later in the 1970s, the team crested again — setting new records for wins and points — while capturing another string of Cups. Today, the team remains one of the stalwart members of the league as it celebrates its 100th anniversary.

STANDINGS

TEAM	GP	W	L	T	PTS	GF	GA
MONTREAL	70	45	15	10	100	222	131
DETROIT	70	30	24	16	76	183	148
NEW YORK	70	32	28	10	74	204	203
TORONTO	70	24	33	13	61	153	181
BOSTON	70	23	34	16	59	147	185
CHICAGO	70	19	39	12	50	155	216

LEADERS

PLAYER	TM	GP	G	A	PTS	PIM
Jean Beliveau	MTL	70	47	41	86	143
Gordie Howe	DET	70	38	41	79	100
Maurice Richard	MTL	70	38	33	71	89
Bert Olmstead	MTL	70	14	56	70	94
Tod Sloan	TOR	70	37	29	66	100
Andy Bathgate	NY	70	19	47	66	59
Bernie Geoffrion	MTL	59	29	33	62	66
Earl Reibel	DET	68	17	39	56	10
Three tied with					51	

GOALS
Beliveau, MTL	47
Richard, MTL	38
Howe, DET	38
Sloan, TOR	37
Geoffrion, MTL	29

ASSISTS
Olmstead, MTL	56
Bathgate, NY	47
Gadsby, NY	42
Beliveau, MTL	41
Howe, DET	41

GOALTENDER	TM	GP	MIN	GA	SH	GAA
Jacques Plante	MTL	64	3840	119	7	**1.86**
Glenn Hall	DET	70	4200	147 (1)	**12**	2.10
Terry Sawchuk	BOS	68	4080	177 (4)	9	2.60
Harry Lumley	TOR	59	3527	159	3	2.70
Lorne Worsley	NY	70	4200	199 (4)	4	2.84
Al Rollins	CHI	58	3480	172 (2)	3	2.97

PENALTY MINUTES
Fontinato, NY	202
Lindsay, DET	161
Beliveau, MTL	143
Armstrong, BOS	122
Stasiuk, BOS	118

SHUTOUTS
Hall, DET	12
Sawchuk, BOS	9
Plante, MTL	7
Worsley, NY	4
Two tied with	3

MONTREAL   45-15-10   100   1st   Toe Blake
Canadiens

		REGULAR SEASON					POSTSEASON			
PLAYER	POS	GP	G	A	PTS	PIM	GP	G	A	PTS	PIM
Jean Beliveau	C	70	47	41	86	143	10	12	7	19	22
Maurice Richard	R	70	38	33	71	89	10	5	9	14	24
Bert Olmstead	L	70	14	56	70	94	10	4	10	14	8
Bernie Geoffrion	R	59	29	33	62	66	10	5	9	14	6

		REGULAR SEASON					POSTSEASON				
PLAYER	POS	GP	G	A	PTS	PIM	GP	G	A	PTS	PIM
Dickie Moore	L	70	11	39	50	55	10	3	6	9	12
Doug Harvey	D	62	5	39	44	60	10	2	5	7	10
Henri Richard	C	64	19	21	40	46	10	4	4	8	21
Floyd Curry	R	70	14	18	32	10	10	1	5	6	12
Kenny Mosdell	C	67	13	17	30	48	9	1	1	2	2
Claude Provost	R	60	13	16	29	30	10	3	3	6	12
Jackie Leclair	C	54	6	8	14	30	8	1	1	2	4
Jean-Guy Talbot	D	66	1	13	14	80	9	0	2	2	4
Dollard St. Laurent	D	46	4	9	13	58	4	0	0	0	2
Tom Johnson	D	64	3	10	13	75	10	0	2	2	8
Don Marshall	L	66	4	1	5	10	10	1	0	1	0
Bob Turner	D	33	1	4	5	35	10	0	1	1	10
Dick Gamble	L	12	0	3	3	8					
Jacques Plante	G	64	0	0	0	10	10	0	0	0	2
Emile Bouchard	D	36	0	0	0	22	1	0	0	0	0
Bob Perreault	G	6	0	0	0	0					
Wally Clune	D	5	0	0	0	6					
Connie Broden	C	3	0	0	0	2					
Jacques Deslauriers	D	2	0	0	0	0					

		REGULAR SEASON					POSTSEASON				
GOALTENDER		GP	MIN	GA	SH	GAA	GP	MIN	GA	SH	GAA
Jacques Plante	(42-12-10)	64	3840	119	7	**1.86**	10	600	18	2	**1.80**
Bob Perreault	(3-3-0)	6	360	12	1	2.00					

DETROIT   30-24-16   76   2nd   Jim Skinner
Red Wings

		REGULAR SEASON					POSTSEASON				
PLAYER	POS	GP	G	A	PTS	PIM	GP	G	A	PTS	PIM
Gordie Howe	R	70	38	41	79	100	10	3	9	12	8
Earl Reibel	C	68	17	39	56	10	10	0	2	2	2
Alex Delvecchio	C	70	25	26	51	24	10	7	3	10	2
Ted Lindsay	L	67	27	23	50	161	10	6	3	9	22
Red Kelly	D	70	16	34	50	39	10	2	4	6	2
Metro Prystai (2-2)	C	*63	12	16	28	10	9	1	2	3	6
Bill Dineen	R	70	12	7	19	30	10	1	0	1	8
Bob Goldham	D	68	3	16	19	32	10	0	3	3	4
Norm Ullman	C	66	9	9	18	26	10	1	3	4	13
Marty Pavelich	L	70	5	13	18	38	10	0	1	1	14
Marcel Pronovost	D	68	4	13	17	46	10	0	2	2	8
Lorne Ferguson (2-2)	L	31	8	7	15	12	10	1	2	3	12
John Bucyk	L	38	1	8	9	20	10	1	1	2	8
Warren Godfrey	D	67	2	6	8	86					
Jerry Toppazzini (1-2)	R	40	1	7	8	31					
Real Chevrefils (2-2)	L	38	3	4	7	24					
Larry Hillman	D	47	0	3	3	53	10	0	1	1	6
Gord Hollingworth	D	41	0	2	2	28	3	0	0	0	2
Glenn Hall	G	70	0	0	0	14	10	0	0	0	0
Murray Costello (2-2)	C	24	0	0	0	0	4	0	0	0	0
Ed Stankiewicz	L	5	0	0	0	0					

1955–1956

PLAYER	POS	REGULAR SEASON					POSTSEASON				
		GP	G	A	PTS	PIM	GP	G	A	PTS	PIM
Ed Sandford (1–2)	L	4	0	0	0	0					
Cummy Burton	R	3	0	0	0	0	3	0	0	0	0
Norm Corcoran (2–2)	C	2	0	0	0	0					
Jerry Melnyk	C						6	0	0	0	0
Al Arbour	D						4	0	1	1	0

GOALTENDER	REGULAR SEASON					POSTSEASON				
	GP	MIN	GA	SH	GAA	GP	MIN	GA	SH	GAA
Glenn Hall (30-24-16)	70	4200	147 (1)	12	2.10	10	604	28	0	2.78

NEW YORK Rangers   32-28-10   74   3rd   Phil Watson

PLAYER	POS	REGULAR SEASON					POSTSEASON				
		GP	G	A	PTS	PIM	GP	G	A	PTS	PIM
Andy Bathgate	R	70	19	47	66	59	5	1	2	3	2
Dave Creighton	C	70	20	31	51	43	5	0	0	0	4
Bill Gadsby	D	70	9	42	51	84	5	1	3	4	4
Danny Lewicki	L	70	18	27	45	26	5	0	3	3	0
Ron Murphy	L	66	16	28	44	71	5	0	1	1	2
Dean Prentice	L	70	24	18	42	44	5	1	0	1	2
Wally Hergesheimer	R	70	22	18	40	26	5	1	0	1	0
Larry Popein	C	64	14	25	39	37	5	0	1	1	2
Andy Hebenton	R	70	24	14	38	8	5	1	0	1	2
Bronco Horvath	C	66	12	17	29	40	5	1	2	3	4
Pete Conacher	L	41	11	11	22	10	5	0	0	0	0
Lou Fontinato	D	70	3	15	18	202	4	0	0	0	6
Harry Howell	D	70	3	15	18	77	5	0	1	1	4
Don Raleigh	C	29	1	12	13	4					
Jean-Guy Gendron	L	63	5	7	12	38	5	2	1	3	2
Jack Evans	D	70	2	9	11	104	5	1	0	1	18
Aldo Guidolin	D	14	1	0	1	8					
Ivan Irwin	D	34	0	1	1	20	5	0	0	0	8
Jim Bartlett	L	12	0	1	1	8					
Lorne Worsley	G	70	0	0	0	2	3	0	0	0	2
Ron Howell	D	1	0	0	0	0					
Gordie Bell	G						2	0	0	0	0

GOALTENDER	REGULAR SEASON					POSTSEASON				
	GP	MIN	GA	SH	GAA	GP	MIN	GA	SH	GAA
Lorne Worsley (32-28-10)	70	4200	199 (4)	4	2.84	3	180	14	0	4.67
Gordie Bell						2	120	9	0	4.50

TORONTO Maple Leafs   24-33-13   61   4th   King Clancy

PLAYER	POS	REGULAR SEASON					POSTSEASON				
		GP	G	A	PTS	PIM	GP	G	A	PTS	PIM
Tod Sloan	R	70	37	29	66	100	2	0	0	0	5
George Armstrong	C	67	16	32	48	97	5	4	2	6	0
Dick Duff	L	69	18	19	37	74	5	1	4	5	2
Rudy Migay	C	70	12	16	28	52	5	0	0	0	6

		REGULAR SEASON				POSTSEASON				
PLAYER	POS	GP	G	A	PTS	PIM	GP	G	A	PTS	PIM
Ron Stewart	C	69	13	14	27	35	5	1	1	2	2
Billy Harris	C	70	9	13	22	8	5	1	0	1	4
Sid Smith	L	55	4	17	21	8	5	1	0	1	0
Hugh Bolton	D	67	4	16	20	65	5	0	1	1	0
Earl Balfour	L	59	14	5	19	40	3	0	1	1	2
Jim Morrison	D	63	2	17	19	77	5	0	0	0	4
Gord Hannigan	C	48	8	7	15	40	4	0	0	0	4
Ron Hurst	R	50	7	5	12	62	3	0	2	2	4
Marc Reaume	D	48	0	12	12	50	5	0	2	2	6
Eric Nesterenko	R	40	4	6	10	65					
Brian Cullen	R	21	2	6	8	8	5	1	0	1	2
Jimmy Thomson	D	62	0	7	7	96	5	0	3	3	10
Gerry James	R	46	3	3	6	50	5	1	0	1	8
Tim Horton	D	35	0	5	5	36	2	0	0	0	4
Larry Cahan	D	21	0	2	2	46					
Joe Klukay	L	18	0	1	1	2					
Jack Bionda	D	13	0	1	1	18					
Bill Burega	D	4	0	1	1	4					
Barry Cullen	R	3	0	0	0	4					
Harry Lumley	G	59	0	0	0	2	5	0	0	0	2
Bob Bailey	R	6	0	0	0	6					
Willie Marshall	C	6	0	0	0	0					
Gil Mayer	G	6	0	0	0	0					
Ed Chadwick	G	5	0	0	0	0					
Dave Reid	C	4	0	0	0	0					
Ray Gariepy	D	1	0	0	0	4					
Al MacNeil	D	1	0	0	0	2					
Lefty Wilson	G	1	0	0	0	0					

		REGULAR SEASON					POSTSEASON
GOALTENDER		GP	MIN	GA	SH	GAA	no postseason play
Lefty Wilson		1	13	0	0	0.00	
Ed Chadwick	(2-0-3)	5	300	3	2	0.60	
Harry Lumley	(21-28-10)	59	3527	159	3	2.70	
Gil Mayer	(1-5-0)	6	360	18 (1)	0	3.10	

BOSTON 23-34-13 59 5th Milt Schmidt
Bruins

		REGULAR SEASON				POSTSEASON
PLAYER	POS	GP	G	A	PTS	PIM	no postseason play
Vic Stasiuk	L	59	19	18	37	118
Cal Gardner	C	70	15	21	36	57
Leo Labine	R	68	16	18	34	104
Don McKenney	C	65	10	24	34	20
Johnny Peirson	R	33	11	14	25	10
Bill Quackenbush	D	70	3	22	25	4
Fern Flaman	D	62	4	17	21	70
Leo Boivin	D	68	4	16	20	80
Real Chevrefils (1–2)	L	25	11	8	19	10
Doug Mohns	F	64	10	8	18	48

1955-1956

PLAYER	POS	REGULAR SEASON					POSTSEASON
		GP	G	A	PTS	PIM	no postseason play
Marcel Bonin	L	67	9	9	18	49	
Fleming Mackell	C	52	7	9	16	59	
Jerry Toppazzini (2-2)	R	28	7	7	14	22	
Lorne Ferguson (1-2)	L	32	7	5	12	18	
Murray Costello (1-2)	C	41	6	6	12	19	
Bob Armstrong	D	68	0	12	12	122	
Hal Laycoe	D	65	5	5	10	16	
Orval Tessier	C	23	2	3	5	6	
Ed Panagabko	C	28	0	3	3	38	
Lionel Heinrich	L	35	1	1	2	33	
Lorne Davis	R	15	0	1	1	0	
Terry Sawchuk	G	68	0	0	0	20	
Al Nicholson	L	14	0	0	0	4	
Ellard O'Brien	D	2	0	0	0	0	
Claude Pronovost	G	1	0	0	0	2	
John Henderson	G	1	0	0	0	0	

GOALTENDER		REGULAR SEASON					POSTSEASON
		GP	MIN	GA	SH	GAA	no postseason play
Claude Pronovost	(1-0-0)	1	60	0	1	0.00	
Terry Sawchuk	(22-**33**-13)	68	4080	177 (4)	9	2.60	
John Henderson	(0-1-0)	1	60	1	0	4.00	

CHICAGO 19-39-12 50 6th Dick Irvin
Blackhawks

PLAYER	POS	REGULAR SEASON					POSTSEASON
		GP	G	A	PTS	PIM	no postseason play
George Sullivan	C	63	14	26	40	58	
Nick Mickoski	L	70	19	20	39	52	
Ed Litzenberger	R	70	10	29	39	36	
Johnny Wilson	L	70	24	9	33	12	
Hank Ciesla	C	70	8	23	31	22	
Glen Skov	L	70	7	20	27	26	
Hec Lalande	C	65	8	18	26	70	
Harry Watson	L	55	11	14	25	6	
Tony Leswick	L	70	11	11	22	71	
Ed Sandford (2-2)	L	57	12	9	21	56	
Allan Stanley	D	59	4	14	18	70	
Jack McIntyre	L	46	10	5	15	14	
Gus Mortson	D	52	5	10	15	87	
Al Dewsbury	D	37	3	12	15	22	
Frank Martin	D	61	3	11	14	21	
Benny Woit	R	63	1	8	9	46	
Pierre Pilote	D	20	3	5	8	34	
Lee Fogolin	D	15	0	8	8	88	
Norm Corcoran (1-2)	C	23	1	3	4	19	
Metro Prystai (1-2)	C	*8	1	3	4	8	
Al Rollins	G	58	0	0	0	10	
Hank Bassen	G	12	0	0	0	2	
Kenny Wharram	R	3	0	0	0	0	

PLAYER	POS	REGULAR SEASON GP	G	A	PTS	PIM	POSTSEASON no postseason play
Larry Wilson	C	2	0	0	0	2	
Frank Sullivan	D	1	0	0	0	0	

GOALTENDER		REGULAR SEASON GP	MIN	GA	SH	GAA	POSTSEASON no postseason play
Al Rollins	(17-30-11)	58	3480	172 (2)	3	2.97	
Hank Bassen	(2-9-1)	12	720	41 (1)	1	3.42	

TEAM TOTALS

TEAM	GP	G	A	P	PIM	GA	SH	Per Game G	A	PIM	GA
Montreal	70	**222**	**361**	**583**	977	**131**	8	**3.17**	**5.16**	13.96	**1.87**
Detroit	70	183	274	457	794	148	12	2.61	3.91	11.34	2.11
New York	70	204	338	542	911	203	4	2.91	4.83	13.01	2.90
Toronto	70	153	234	387	**1051**	181	5	2.19	3.34	**15.01**	2.59
Boston	70	147	227	374	929	185	10	2.10	3.24	13.27	2.64
Chicago	70	155	258	413	826	216	4	2.21	3.69	11.80	3.09
	420	1064	1692	2756	5488	1064	43	2.53	4.03	13.07	2.53

PLAYOFFS

SERIES "A"
Montreal 7, New York 1
New York 4, Montreal 2
Montreal 3, New York 1
Montreal 5, New York 3
Montreal 7, New York 0

MONTREAL, 4–1

SERIES "B"
Detroit 3, Toronto 2
Detroit 3, Toronto 1
Detroit 5, Toronto 4 (OT)
Toronto 2, Detroit 0
Detroit 3, Toronto 1

DETROIT, 4–1

SERIES "C"
Montreal 6, Detroit 4
Montreal 5, Detroit 1
Detroit 3, Montreal 1
Montreal 3, Detroit 0
Montreal 3, Detroit 1

MONTREAL WINS STANLEY CUP, 4–1

ALL-STAR TEAMS

First Team
G — Jacques Plante, MTL
D — Doug Harvey, MTL
D — Bill Gadsby, NY
C — Jean Beliveau, MTL
R — Maurice Richard, MTL
L — Ted Lindsay, MTL

Second Team
G — Glenn Hall, CHI
D — Tom Johnson, MTL
D — Red Kelly, DET
C — Tod Sloan, TOR
R — Gordie Howe, DET
L — Bert Olmstead, MTL

INDIVIDUAL TROPHY WINNERS

HART TROPHY (Most Valuable Player): Jean Beliveau, MTL
LADY BYNG TROPHY (Gentlemanly Conduct): Earl Reibel, DET
VEZINA TROPHY (Best Goaltender): Jacques Plante, MTL
CALDER MEMORIAL TROPHY (Best Rookie): Glenn Hall, CHI
ART ROSS TROPHY (Scoring Leader): Jean Beliveau, MTL
JAMES NORRIS TROPHY (Best Defenseman): Doug Harvey, MTL

1956-1957
Jacques Plante

One of the keys to Montreal's success during the latter part of the 1950s was its stingy defense. On the blue line, the team featured a robust defenseman named Doug Harvey, who also quarterbacked the vaunted Canadiens' power play. Further back, in goal, the team was lucky enough to feature one of the best netminders of the era. In addition, this particular goalie stepped beyond his role with Montreal, leading the NHL's puckstoppers into a new era.

Jacques Plante — a native of Shawinigan Falls, Quebec — made a memorable NHL debut in 1952-53. Thrust in the midst of the Stanley Cup playoffs, with only three regular season games under his belt, the 24-year-old goalie sparkled, leading Montreal to the Cup and finishing with the lowest GAA (1.75). After another partial season with the Canadiens, Plante became a full-timer in 1954-55, posting a 2.17 average with five shutouts. Known for his mobility, he frequently strayed from the cage, stopping pucks behind the net and feeding them up the ice — almost like a third defenseman. The following year, Plante (1.86) took home the Vezina — emblematic of the league's best netminder. As it turned out, it wouldn't be his last.

During the regular 1956-57 season, Plante once again posted the NHL's best GAA (2.00), while blanking the most opponents (9). However, it was not enough as Detroit (38-20-12, 88) bested the Canadiens by six points. Boston ended third, while New York snagged fourth — both substantially ahead of Toronto and Chicago. In the offensive end, Detroit's Gordie Howe (45-44-89) scored the most goals, winning the scoring race by a slim point over teammate Ted Lindsay, the latter also amassing the most assists (55). In addition, Chicago toughman Gus Mortson collected the most penalty minutes (147).

In the playoffs, Boston grabbed a quick lead on the favored Red Wings, but Detroit roared back with a 7–2 win in the second game. However it was all Bruins after that, as Boston won the next three games — 4–3, 2–0 and 4–3 — earning themselves a berth in the finals. In the other opening series, Montreal won the opener, 4–1, but the Rangers knotted the set with an overtime win in the second game. The Canadians then buried New York, 8–3, before winning the next two, ending the series in five games.

In the finals, Montreal outscored Boston 10–3 in the first three games — all victories — with Plante posting a shutout in the middle game. The first game of the string was also noteworthy, as Maurice Richard scored four of his team's five goals in the 5–1 win. Trailing three games to nil, the Bruins battled back as Don Simmons posted one of his two playoff shutouts, blanking the Canadiens, 2–0. However, it all ended two nights later, as the Canadiens breezed to a 5–1 win, claiming their second straight Stanley Cup.

As he did during the regular season, Plante led all playoff goalies with a 1.66 GAA, the third time in five years he had accomplished the feat. His teammate Bernie Geoffrion (11-7-18) scored the most goals and accumulated the most points. A fellow Canadien — Bert Olmstead — scored no goals, but did rack up nine assists to best all playoff participants.

After 1956-57, Plante went on to post three more Vezinas in a row, leading his Canadiens to the promised land on each occasion. During the final year of the string, he started a trend which had league-wide ramifications. Injured in the face during a November 1959 game, Plante returned to the ice wearing a mask — a protection which he frequently wore in practice. With the singular headgear in place, he posted a 3–1 win over the Rangers. Within a few years, following in Plante's footsteps, other netminders followed, eventually making masks the norm rather than the exception.

After another pair of GAA titles, Plante was dealt to the Rangers before the 1963-64 season. After a pair of seasons in the Big Apple, he retired, but was lured back into action when the NHL expanded a few years later. Playing for the St. Louis Blues, Plante earned his record seventh Vezina in 1968-69, helping his club to the Cup finals. After a three-year stint in Toronto, followed by a cameo in Boston, he left the NHL for good. Not done yet, Plante resurfaced in the WHA in 1974-75, posting a respectable 3.32 GAA for Edmonton at the age of 45.

Plante's career numbers ensure him a place among the hockey greats. However, his most important contribution to the game occurred in that historic 1959 game, where he took a step towards safety — a step for which every netminder today can be grateful.

STANDINGS

TEAM	GP	W	L	T	PTS	GF	GA
DETROIT	70	38	20	12	88	198	157
MONTREAL	70	35	23	12	82	210	155
BOSTON	70	34	24	12	80	195	174
NEW YORK	70	26	30	14	66	184	227
TORONTO	70	21	34	15	57	174	192
CHICAGO	70	16	39	15	47	169	225

LEADERS

PLAYER	TM	GP	G	A	PTS	PIM
Gordie Howe	DET	70	44	45	89	72
Ted Lindsay	DET	70	30	55	85	103
Jean Beliveau	MTL	69	33	51	84	102
Andy Bathgate	NY	70	27	50	77	60
Ed Litzenberger	CHI	70	32	32	64	48
Maurice Richard	MTL	63	33	29	62	71
Don McKenney	BOS	69	21	39	60	31
Dickie Moore	MTL	70	29	29	58	56
Henri Richard	MTL	63	18	36	54	71
Norm Ullman	DET	64	16	36	52	47

GOALS
Howe, DET	44
Beliveau, MTL	33
Richard, MTL	33
Litzenberger, CHI	32
Chevrefils, BOS	31

ASSISTS
Lindsay, DET	55
Beliveau, MTL	51
Bathgate, NY	50
Howe, DET	45
Harvey, MTL	44

GOALTENDER	TM	GP	MIN	GA	SH	GAA
Jacques Plante	MTL	61	3660	122 (1)	9	2.00
Glenn Hall	DET	70	4200	157 (1)	4	2.23
Terry Sawchuk	BOS	34	2040	81	2	2.38
Don Simmons	BOS	26	1560	63	4	2.42
Ed Chadwick	TOR	70	4200	186 (6)	5	2.66
Al Rollins	CHI	70	4200	222 (3)	3	3.17
Lorne Worsley	NY	68	4080	217 (3)	3	3.19

PENALTY MINUTES
Mortson, CHI	147
Fontinato, NY	139
Labine, BOS	128
Pilote, CHI	117
Evans, NY	110

SHUTOUTS
Plante, MTL	9
Chadwick, TOR	5
Hall, DET	4
Simmons, BOS	4
Two tied with	3

DETROIT 38-20-12   88   1st   Jim Skinner
Red Wings

		REGULAR SEASON					POSTSEASON				
PLAYER	POS	GP	G	A	PTS	PIM	GP	G	A	PTS	PIM
Gordie Howe	R	70	44	45	89	72	5	2	5	7	6
Ted Lindsay	L	70	30	55	85	103	5	2	4	6	8
Norm Ullman	C	64	16	36	52	47	5	1	1	2	6
Alex Delvecchio	C	48	16	25	41	8	5	3	2	5	2
Earl Reibel	C	70	13	23	36	6	5	0	2	2	0
Red Kelly	D	70	10	25	35	18	5	1	0	1	0
Billy Dea	C	69	15	15	30	14	5	2	0	2	2
Lorne Ferguson	L	70	13	10	23	26	5	1	0	1	6
Metro Prystai	C	70	7	15	22	16	5	2	0	2	0

1956–1957

		REGULAR SEASON					POSTSEASON				
PLAYER	POS	GP	G	A	PTS	PIM	GP	G	A	PTS	PIM
John Bucyk	L	66	10	11	21	41	5	0	1	1	0
Marcel Pronovost	D	70	7	9	16	38	5	0	0	0	6
Marty Pavelich	L	64	3	13	16	48	5	0	0	0	6
Billy McNeill	C	64	5	10	15	34					
Bill Dineen	R	51	6	7	13	12	4	0	0	0	0
Warren Godfrey	D	69	1	8	9	103	5	0	0	0	6
Al Arbour	D	44	1	6	7	38	5	0	0	0	6
Larry Hillman	D	16	1	2	3	4					
Gord Hollingworth	D	25	0	1	1	16					
Glenn Hall	G	70	0	0	0	2	5	0	0	0	10
Dale Anderson	D	13	0	0	0	6	2	0	0	0	0
Gord Strate	D	5	0	0	0	4					
Murray Costello	C	3	0	0	0	0					
Tom McCarthy	L	3	0	0	0	0					
Bob Bailey	R						5	0	2	2	2

		REGULAR SEASON					POSTSEASON				
GOALTENDER		GP	MIN	GA	SH	GAA	GP	MIN	GA	SH	GAA
Glenn Hall	(38-20-12)	70	4200	157 (1)	4	2.23	5	300	15	0	3.00

MONTREAL 35-23-12 82 2nd Toe Blake
Canadiens

		REGULAR SEASON					POSTSEASON				
PLAYER	POS	GP	G	A	PTS	PIM	GP	G	A	PTS	PIM
Jean Beliveau	C	69	33	51	84	102	10	6	6	12	15
Maurice Richard	R	63	33	29	62	71	10	8	3	11	8
Dickie Moore	L	70	29	29	58	56	10	3	7	10	4
Henri Richard	C	63	18	36	54	71	10	2	6	8	10
Doug Harvey	D	70	6	44	50	92	10	0	7	7	10
Bert Olmstead	L	64	15	33	48	74	10	0	9	9	13
Bernie Geoffrion	R	41	19	21	40	18	10	11	7	18	2
Claude Pronovost	R	67	16	14	30	24	10	0	1	1	8
Andre Pronovost	L	64	10	11	21	58	8	1	0	1	4
Don Marshall	L	70	12	8	20	2	10	1	3	4	2
Floyd Curry	R	70	7	9	16	20	10	3	2	5	2
Tom Johnson	D	70	4	11	15	59	10	0	2	2	13
Jackie Leclair	C	47	3	10	13	14					
Jean-Guy Talbot	D	59	0	13	13	70	10	0	2	2	10
Dollard St. Laurent	D	64	1	11	12	49	7	0	1	1	13
Phil Goyette	C	14	3	4	7	0	10	2	1	3	4
Bob Turner	D	58	1	4	5	48	6	0	1	1	0
Al Johnson	R	2	0	1	1	2					
Jacques Plante	G	61	0	0	0	16	10	0	0	0	4
James MacPherson	D	10	0	0	0	4					
Gerry McNeil	G	9	0	0	0	2					
Glen Cressman	C	4	0	0	0	2					
Stan Smrke	L	4	0	0	0	0					
Gene Achtymichuk	C	3	0	0	0	0					
Ralph Backstrom	C	3	0	0	0	0					
Jerry Wilson	C	3	0	0	0	2					

		REGULAR SEASON					*POSTSEASON*				
PLAYER	*POS*	*GP*	*G*	*A*	*PTS*	*PIM*	*GP*	*G*	*A*	*PTS*	*PIM*
Murray Balfour	R	2	0	0	0	2					
Guy Rousseau	L	2	0	0	0	0					
Bronco Horvath (2–2)	C	1	0	0	0	0					
Connie Broden	C						6	0	1	1	0

		REGULAR SEASON				*POSTSEASON*			
GOALTENDER		*GP*	*MIN*	*GA*	*SH*	*GAA*	*GP*	*MIN*	*GA*	*SH*	*GAA*
Jacques Plante	(31-18-12)	61	3660	122 (1)	9	**2.00**	10	616	17 (1)	1	**1.66**
Gerry McNeil	(4-5-0)	9	540	31 (1)	0	3.44					

BOSTON   34-24-12   80   3rd   Milt Schmidt
Bruins

		REGULAR SEASON					*POSTSEASON*				
PLAYER	*POS*	*GP*	*G*	*A*	*PTS*	*PIM*	*GP*	*G*	*A*	*PTS*	*PIM*
Don McKenney	C	69	21	39	60	31	10	1	5	6	4
Real Chevrefils	L	70	31	17	48	38	10	2	1	3	4
Leo Labine	R	67	18	29	47	128	10	2	3	5	14
Vic Stasiuk	L	64	24	16	40	69	10	2	1	3	2
Doug Mohns	F	68	6	34	40	89	10	2	3	5	2
Fleming Mackell	C	65	22	17	39	73	10	5	3	8	4
Johnny Peirson	R	68	13	26	39	41	10	0	3	3	12
Jerry Toppazzini	R	55	15	23	38	26	10	0	1	1	2
Larry Regan	R	69	14	19	33	29	8	0	2	2	10
Cal Gardner	C	70	12	20	32	66	10	2	1	3	2
Fern Flaman	D	68	6	25	31	108	10	0	3	3	19
Allan Stanley	D	60	6	25	31	45					
Bob Armstrong	D	57	1	15	16	79	10	0	3	3	10
Leo Boivin	D	55	2	8	10	55	10	2	3	5	12
Jack Bionda	D	35	2	3	5	43	10	0	1	1	14
Jack Caffery	C	47	2	2	4	20	10	1	0	1	4
Bob Beckett	C	18	0	3	3	2					
Al Nicholson	L	5	0	1	1	0					
Terry Sawchuk	G	34	0	0	0	14					
Don Simmons	G	26	0	0	0	0	10	0	0	0	0
Floyd Smith	R	23	0	0	0	6					
Norm Defelice	G	10	0	0	0	2					
Dick Cherry	D	6	0	0	0	4					
Floyd Hillman	D	6	0	0	0	10					
George Ranieri	L	2	0	0	0	0					
Ed Panagabko	C	1	0	0	0	0					
Carl Boone	R						10	1	0	1	12

		REGULAR SEASON				*POSTSEASON*				
GOALTENDER		*GP*	*MIN*	*GA*	*SH*	*GAA*	*GP*	*MIN*	*GA*	*SH*	*GAA*
Terry Sawchuk	(18-10-6)	34	2040	81	2	2.38					
Don Simmons	(13-9-4)	26	1560	63	4	2.42	10	600	29	2	2.90
Norm Defelice	(3-5-2)	10	600	30	0	3.00					

1956–1957

NEW YORK Rangers   26-30-14   66   4th   Phil Watson

		REGULAR SEASON					POSTSEASON				
PLAYER	POS	GP	G	A	PTS	PIM	GP	G	A	PTS	PIM
Andy Bathgate	R	70	27	50	77	60	5	2	0	2	27
Andy Hebenton	R	70	21	23	44	10	5	2	0	2	2
Dean Prentice	L	68	19	23	42	38	5	0	2	2	4
Bill Gadsby	D	70	4	37	41	72	5	1	2	3	2
Dave Creighton	C	70	18	21	39	42	5	2	2	4	2
Danny Lewicki	L	70	18	20	38	47	5	0	1	1	2
Larry Popein	C	67	11	19	30	20	5	0	3	3	0
Camille Henry	C	36	14	15	29	2	5	2	3	5	0
George Sullivan	C	42	6	17	23	36	5	1	2	3	4
Ron Murphy	L	33	7	12	19	14	5	0	0	0	0
Gerry Foley	R	69	7	9	16	48	3	0	0	0	0
Jean-Guy Gendron	L	70	9	6	15	40	5	0	1	1	6
Parker MacDonald	C	45	7	8	15	24	1	1	1	2	0
Lou Fontinato	D	70	3	12	15	139	5	0	0	0	7
Harry Howell	D	65	2	10	12	70	5	1	0	1	6
Larry Cahan	D	61	5	4	9	65	3	0	0	0	2
Jack Evans	D	70	3	6	9	110	5	0	1	1	4
Bruce Cline	R	30	2	3	5	10					
Bronco Horvath (1–2)	C	7	1	2	3	4					
Lorne Worsley	G	68	0	0	0	19	5	0	0	0	0
Johnny Bower	G	2	0	0	0	0					

		REGULAR SEASON					POSTSEASON				
GOALTENDER		GP	MIN	GA	SH	GAA	GP	MIN	GA	SH	GAA
Johnny Bower	(0-2-0)	2	120	6 (1)	0	3.00					
Lorne Worsley	(26-28-14)	68	4080	217 (3)	3	3.19	5	316	21	0	3.99

TORONTO Maple Leafs   21-34-15   57   5th   Howie Meeker

		REGULAR SEASON					POSTSEASON
PLAYER	POS	GP	G	A	PTS	PIM	no postseason play
George Armstrong	C	54	18	26	44	37	
Sid Smith	L	70	17	24	41	4	
Dick Duff	L	70	26	14	40	50	
Rudy Migay	C	66	15	20	35	51	
Ron Stewart	C	65	15	20	35	28	
Tod Sloan	R	52	14	21	35	33	
Tim Horton	D	66	6	19	25	72	
Bob Pulford	L	65	11	11	22	32	
Ted Kennedy	C	30	6	16	22	35	
Brian Cullen	C	46	8	12	20	27	
Marc Reaume	D	63	6	14	20	81	
Jim Morrison	D	63	3	17	20	44	
Barry Cullen	R	51	6	10	16	30	
Gerry James	R	53	4	12	16	90	
Al MacNeil	D	53	4	8	12	84	
Jimmy Thomson	D	62	0	12	12	50	
Billy Harris	C	23	4	6	10	6	

		REGULAR SEASON					*POSTSEASON*
PLAYER	*POS*	*GP*	*G*	*A*	*PTS*	*PIM*	*no postseason play*
Gary Aldcorn	L	22	5	1	6	4	
Bob Baun	D	20	0	5	5	37	
Mike Nykoluk	R	32	3	1	4	20	
Ron Hurst	R	14	2	2	4	8	
Frank Mahovlich	L	3	1	0	1	2	
Kenny Girard	R	3	0	1	1	2	
Ed Chadwick	G	70	0	0	0	0	
Hugh Bolton	D	6	0	0	0	2	

		REGULAR SEASON				*POSTSEASON*
GOALTENDER		*GP*	*MIN*	*GA*	*SH*	*GAA*	*no postseason play*
Ed Chadwick	(21-34-15)	70	4200	186 (6)	5	2.66	

CHICAGO 16-39-15 47 6th Tommy Ivan
Blackhawks

		REGULAR SEASON					*POSTSEASON*
PLAYER	*POS*	*GP*	*G*	*A*	*PTS*	*PIM*	*no postseason play*
Ed Litzenberger	R	70	32	32	64	48	
Johnny Wilson	L	70	18	30	48	24	
Glen Skov	L	67	14	28	42	69	
Nick Mickoski	L	70	16	20	36	24	
Jack McIntyre	L	70	18	14	32	32	
Harry Watson	L	70	11	19	30	9	
Hec Lalande	C	50	11	17	28	38	
Eric Nesterenko	R	24	8	15	23	32	
Gus Mortson	D	70	5	18	23	147	
Forbes Kennedy	C	69	8	13	21	102	
Hank Ciesla	C	70	10	8	18	28	
Pierre Pilote	D	70	3	14	17	117	
Elmer Vasko	D	64	3	12	15	31	
Ed Kachur	R	34	5	7	12	21	
Wally Hergesheimer	R	41	2	8	10	12	
Frank Martin	D	70	1	8	9	12	
Ron Ingram	D	45	1	6	7	21	
Kenny Mosdell	C	25	2	4	6	10	
John Sleaver	C	12	1	0	1	4	
Al Rollins	G	70	0	1	1	9	
Eddie Mazur	L	15	0	1	1	4	
Ian Cushenan	D	11	0	0	0	13	
Benny Woit	R	9	0	0	0	2	
Zellio Toppazzini	R	7	0	0	0	0	

		REGULAR SEASON				*POSTSEASON*
GOALTENDER		*GP*	*MIN*	*GA*	*SH*	*GAA*	*no postseason play*
Al Rollins	(16-**39**-**15**)	70	4200	222 (3)	3	3.17	

TEAM TOTALS

								Per Game		
TEAM	*GP*	*G*	*A*	*P*	*PIM*	*GA*	*SH*	*G*	*A*	*PIM*	*GA*
Detroit	70	198	316	514	656	157	4	2.83	4.51	9.37	2.24
Montreal	70	**210**	**339**	**549**	870	**155**	9	**3.00**	**4.84**	12.43	**2.21**

								Per Game		
TEAM	GP	G	A	P	PIM	GA	SH	G	A	PIM	GA
Boston	70	195	322	517	978	174	6	2.79	4.60	13.97	2.49
New York	70	184	297	481	870	227	3	2.63	4.24	12.43	3.24
Toronto	70	174	272	446	829	192	5	2.49	3.89	11.84	2.74
Chicago	70	169	274	443	809	225	3	2.41	3.91	11.56	3.21
	420	1130	1820	2950	5012	1130	30	2.69	4.33	11.93	2.69

PLAYOFFS

SERIES "A"
Boston 3, Detroit 1
Detroit 7, Boston 2
Boston 4, Detroit 3
Boston 2, Detroit 0
Boston 4, Detroit 3

BOSTON, 4–1

SERIES "B"
Montreal 4, New York 1
New York 4, Montreal 3 (OT)
Montreal 8, New York 3
Montreal 3, New York 1
Montreal 4, New York 3 (OT)

MONTREAL, 4–1

SERIES "C"
Montreal 5, Boston 1
Montreal 1, Boston 0
Montreal 4, Boston 2
Boston 2, Montreal 0
Montreal 5, Boston 1

MONTREAL WINS
STANLEY CUP, 4–1

ALL-STAR TEAMS

First Team
G — Glenn Hall, CHI
D — Doug Harvey, MTL
D — Red Kelly, DET
C — Jean Beliveau, MTL
R — Gordie Howe, DET
L — Ted Lindsay, MTL

Second Team
G — Jacques Plante, MTL
D — Bill Gadsby, NY
D — Fern Flaman, BOS
C — Ed Litzenberger, CHI
R — Maurice Richard, MTL
L — Real Chevrefils, BOS

INDIVIDUAL TROPHY WINNERS

HART TROPHY (Most Valuable Player): Gordie Howe, DET
LADY BYNG TROPHY (Gentlemanly Conduct): Andy Hebenton, NY
VEZINA TROPHY (Best Goaltender): Jacques Plante, MTL
CALDER MEMORIAL TROPHY (Best Rookie): Larry Regan, BOS
ART ROSS TROPHY (Scoring Leader): Gordie Howe, DET
JAMES NORRIS TROPHY (Best Defenseman): Doug Harvey, MTL

1957-1958

Pioneer

Midway through the 1957-58 season, one particular rookie made his debut in the NHL. Called up from the ranks of the Quebec Hockey League, this player was one of many making their first appearance in the NHL that season. However, this was no ordinary rookie, thus making his elevation to the big leagues a ground-breaking event.

Sadly, the permanent integration of the African American player into the limelight of major league sports didn't occur until after World War II. For instance, the National Football League introduced its first two African Americans in many years in 1946, in Los Angeles. Baseball's Jackie Robinson broke the color barrier the same year, reaching the majors the following season with Brooklyn. Over the next decade, baseball's major leagues integrated team by team, with Boston's Red Sox becoming the last club to add an African American to the roster in 1959. Interestingly enough, while this city was the last to embrace equality in one sport, a year earlier it had paved the way in another.

On the night of January 18, 1958, Willie O'Ree suited up for the Bruins in a game played in Montreal, becoming the first African American player to lace up his skates in the NHL. A native of New Brunswick, the speedy 22-year-old winger had been plying his trade for the Quebec Aces of the QHL. Although held scoreless in his two game stint, O'Ree summed up his experience in a positive way, thrilled like any young player to be playing with the best.

Over the course of the season, Montreal (43-17-10, 96) reclaimed the top spot with a juggernaut of a squad, which out-goaled every other team by at least 50 markers. The Rangers—with one of their best clubs of the decade—scrambled into second, while Detroit and Boston rounded out the playoff slate. Chicago finally rose out of the cellar, edging the last place Maple Leafs by two points.

Two Canadiens topped the leaderboard for individual statistics. Dickie Moore lit the lamp the most times (36) on his way to winning the scoring title (84), while Henri Richard — the younger brother of Maurice — amassed the most assists (52). In goal, their teammate Jacques Plante remained dominant, compiling the stingiest GAA (2.11), while whitewashing the most foes (9). New York enforcer Lou Fontinato (152) was whistled for the most penalty minutes.

In the first round of the playoffs, New York and Boston were square after the first four contests, before the Bruins put them away with a 14-goal barrage in the final two matches. In the other opener, Montreal whipped the Wings in straight sets, outscoring Detroit 19–6, which included an 8–1 drubbing in the first game. Montreal continued its success into the finals, winning the first game — 2–1 — but Boston answered with a 5–2 win of its own. After the two clubs split the next two contests, Maurice Richard netted an overtime game-winner in the fifth game, then Bernie Geoffrion added a pair of tallies in the sixth contest, helping the Canadiens to a 3–1 win, which gave them their third Cup in a row.

Individually, Maurice Richard (11) scored the most postseason goals, while Boston's Fleming Mackell recorded the most assists (14), the latter accumulating the most points (19). In the cage, Plante posted the lowest playoff GAA (1.91).

After his tryout with the Bruins, O'Ree played in the minors for the next couple of years, eventually latching on to Kingston's Eastern Pro Hockey League club. In 1960-61, he skated a longer stint in Boston, going 4-10-14 in 49 games. Over the rest of the decade, and into the 1970s, O'Ree enjoyed a solid career in the top-tier Western Hockey League, playing for the Los Angeles Blades and San Diego Gulls. In his 13 years in the WHL, he posted four 30-goal seasons, leading the circuit in 1964-65 with 38. Overall, O'Ree scored over 300 goals in WHL play, earning him a place in the top dozen career leaders. After retiring in the mid–1970s, O'Ree made a brief comeback at the age of 43, scoring 21 goals for the Pacific Coast League's San Diego club. These achievements are even more remarkable since it was later revealed that he was playing with a significant handicap, as he was nearly blind in one eye — the result of an on-ice accident before he made his NHL debut.

Since O'Ree's time, several African Americans have played in the NHL — including notables like Grant Fuhr, who backstopped the Oilers to several Cups in the 1980s. Currently, Jarome Iginla — twice a 50-goal scorer — remains one of the league's top offensive threats. Although only relatively few African Americans have made pro hockey their career, they can all thank Willie O'Ree — a true pioneer who single-handedly integrated a sport.

STANDINGS

TEAM	GP	W	L	T	PTS	GF	GA
MONTREAL	70	43	17	10	96	250	158
NEW YORK	70	32	25	13	77	195	188
DETROIT	70	29	29	12	70	176	207
BOSTON	70	27	28	15	69	199	194
CHICAGO	70	24	39	7	55	163	202
TORONTO	70	21	38	11	53	192	226

LEADERS

PLAYER	TM	GP	G	A	PTS	PIM
Dickie Moore	MTL	70	**36**	48	**84**	65
Henri Richard	MTL	67	28	**52**	80	56
Andy Bathgate	NY	65	30	48	78	42
Gordie Howe	DET	64	33	44	77	40
Bronco Horvath	BOS	67	30	36	66	71
Ed Litzenberger	CHI	70	32	30	62	63
Fleming Mackell	BOS	70	20	40	60	72
Jean Beliveau	MTL	55	27	32	59	93
Alex Delvecchio	DET	70	21	38	59	22
Don McKenney	BOS	70	28	30	58	22

GOALS	
Moore, MTL	36
Howe, DET	33
Litzenberger, CHI	32
Henry, NY	32
Two tied with	30

ASSISTS	
H. Richard, MTL	52
Moore, MTL	48
Bathgate, NY	48
Howe, DET	44
Mackell, BOS	40

GOALTENDER	TM	GP	MIN	GA	SH	GAA
Jacques Plante	MTL	57	3386	119	9	**2.11**
Lorne Worsley	NY	37	2220	86	4	2.32
Don Simmons	BOS	38	2228	92 (1)	5	2.48
Harry Lumley	BOS	25	1500	71	3	2.84
Glenn Hall	CHI	70	**4200**	200 (2)	7	2.86
Terry Sawchuk	DET	70	**4200**	205 (2)	3	2.94
Marcel Paille	NY	33	1980	102	1	3.09
Ed Chadwick	TOR	70	**4200**	223 (3)	4	3.19

PENALTY MINUTES	
Fontinato, NY	152
Kennedy, DET	135
Harvey, MTL	131
Lindsay, CHI	110
Evans, NY	108

SHUTOUTS	
Plante, MTL	9
Hall, CHI	7
Simmons, BOS	5
Worsely, NY	4
Chadwick, TOR	4

MONTREAL Canadiens   43-17-10   96   1st   Toe Blake

		REGULAR SEASON				POSTSEASON			
PLAYER	POS	GP	G	A	PTS	PIM	GP	G	A	PTS	PIM
Dickie Moore	L	70	36	48	84	65	10	4	7	11	4
Henri Richard	C	67	28	**52**	80	56	10	1	7	8	11
Jean Beliveau	C	55	27	32	59	93	10	4	8	12	10
Claude Provost	R	70	19	32	51	71	10	1	3	4	8
Bernie Geoffrion	R	42	27	23	50	51	10	6	5	11	2
Phil Goyette	C	70	9	37	46	8	10	4	1	5	4
Don Marshall	L	68	22	19	41	14	10	0	2	2	4
Doug Harvey	D	68	9	32	41	131	10	2	9	11	16
Marcel Bonin	L	66	15	24	39	37	9	0	1	1	2

1957-1958

		REGULAR SEASON				POSTSEASON				
PLAYER	POS	GP	G	A	PTS	PIM	GP	G	A	PTS	PIM
Bert Olmstead	L	57	9	28	37	71	9	0	3	3	0
Maurice Richard	R	28	15	19	34	28	10	11	4	15	10
Andre Pronovost	L	66	16	12	28	55	10	2	0	2	16
Dollard St. Laurent	D	65	3	20	23	68	5	0	0	0	10
Tom Johnson	D	66	3	18	21	75	2	0	0	0	0
Jean-Guy Talbot	D	55	4	15	19	65	10	0	3	3	12
Gene Achtymichuk	C	16	3	5	8	2					
Floyd Curry	R	42	2	3	5	8	7	0	0	0	2
Connie Broden	C	3	2	1	3	0	1	0	0	0	0
Bob Turner	D	66	0	3	3	30	10	0	0	0	2
Stan Smrke	L	5	0	3	3	0					
Murray Balfour	R	3	1	1	2	4					
Jack Bownass	D	4	0	1	1	0					
Ralph Backstrom	C	2	0	1	1	0					
Kenny Mosdell	C	2	0	1	1	0					
Jacques Plante	G	57	0	0	0	13	10	0	0	0	2
Charlie Hodge	G	12	0	0	0	0					
Claude Laforge	L	5	0	0	0	0					
Billy Carter	C	1	0	0	0	0					
Al Langlois	D	1	0	0	0	0	7	0	0	0	0
John Aiken	G	1	0	0	0	0					
Len Broderick	G	1	0	0	0	0					
Alvin McDonald	L						2	0	0	0	2

		REGULAR SEASON					POSTSEASON				
GOALTENDER		GP	MIN	GA	SH	GAA	GP	MIN	GA	SH	GAA
Len Broderick	(1-0-0)	1	60	2	0	2.00					
Jacques Plante	(34-14-8)	57	3386	119	9	2.11	10	618	20	1	1.94
Charlie Hodge	(8-2-2)	12	720	31	1	2.58					
John Aiken	(0-1-0)	1	34	6	0	10.59					

NEW YORK Rangers — 32-25-13 — 77 — 2nd — Phil Watson

		REGULAR SEASON					POSTSEASON				
PLAYER	POS	GP	G	A	PTS	PIM	GP	G	A	PTS	PIM
Andy Bathgate	R	65	30	48	78	42	6	5	3	8	6
Camille Henry	C	70	32	24	56	2	6	1	4	5	5
Dave Creighton	C	70	17	35	52	40	6	3	3	6	2
Bill Gadsby	D	65	14	32	46	48	6	0	3	3	4
George Sullivan	C	70	11	35	46	61	1	0	0	0	0
Andy Hebenton	R	70	21	24	45	17	6	2	3	5	4
Larry Popein	C	70	12	22	34	22	6	1	0	1	4
Danny Lewicki	L	70	11	19	30	26	6	0	0	0	6
Jean-Guy Gendron	L	70	10	17	27	68	6	1	0	1	11
Dean Prentice	L	38	13	9	22	14	6	1	3	4	4
Parker MacDonald	C	70	8	10	18	30	6	1	2	3	2
Jack Evans	D	70	4	8	12	108	6	0	0	0	17
Harry Howell	D	70	4	7	11	62	6	1	0	1	8
Lou Fontinato	D	70	3	8	11	**152**	6	0	1	1	6
Hank Ciesla	C	60	2	6	8	16	6	0	2	2	0

		REGULAR SEASON					*POSTSEASON*				
PLAYER	*POS*	*GP*	*G*	*A*	*PTS*	*PIM*	*GP*	*G*	*A*	*PTS*	*PIM*
Gerry Foley	R	68	2	5	7	43	6	0	1	1	2
Larry Cahan	D	34	1	1	2	20	5	0	0	0	4
Lorne Worsley	G	37	0	0	0	10	6	0	0	0	0
Marcel Paille	G	33	0	0	0	0					
Ivan Irwin	D	1	0	0	0	0					

		REGULAR SEASON					*POSTSEASON*				
GOALTENDER		*GP*	*MIN*	*GA*	*SH*	*GAA*	*GP*	*MIN*	*GA*	*SH*	*GAA*
Lorne Worsley	(21-10-6)	37	2220	86	4	2.32	6	365	28	0	4.60
Marcel Paille	(11-15-7)	33	1980	102	1	3.09					

DETROIT Red Wings — 29-29-12 — 70 — 3rd — Sid Abel

		REGULAR SEASON					*POSTSEASON*				
PLAYER	*POS*	*GP*	*G*	*A*	*PTS*	*PIM*	*GP*	*G*	*A*	*PTS*	*PIM*
Gordie Howe	R	64	33	44	77	40	4	1	1	2	0
Alex Delvecchio	C	70	21	38	59	22	4	0	1	1	0
Norm Ullman	C	69	23	28	51	38	4	0	2	2	4
Johnny Wilson	L	70	12	27	39	14	4	2	1	3	0
Red Kelly	D	61	13	18	31	26	4	0	1	1	2
Forbes Kennedy	C	70	11	16	27	135	4	1	0	1	12
Jack McIntyre (2-2)	L	41	15	7	22	4	4	1	1	2	0
Nick Mickoski (2-2)	L	37	8	12	20	30	4	0	0	0	4
Marcel Pronovost	D	62	2	18	20	52	4	0	1	1	4
Warren Godfrey	D	67	2	16	18	56	4	0	0	0	0
Don Poile	C	62	7	9	16	12	4	0	0	0	0
Billy McNeill	C	35	5	10	15	29	4	1	1	2	4
Bob Bailey (1-2)	R	36	6	6	12	41	4	0	0	0	16
Earl Reibel (1-2)	C	29	4	5	9	4					
Billy Dea (1-2)	C	29	4	4	8	6					
Al Arbour	D	69	1	6	7	104	4	0	1	1	4
Bill Dineen (1-2)	R	22	2	4	6	2					
Lorne Ferguson (1-2)	L	15	1	3	4	0					
Tom McCarthy	L	18	2	1	3	4					
Gord Hollingworth	D	27	1	2	3	22					
Tony Leswick	L	22	1	2	3	2	4	0	0	0	0
Metro Prystai	C	15	1	1	2	4					
Pete Goegan	D	14	0	2	2	28	4	0	0	0	18
Hec Lalande (1-2)	C	12	0	2	2	2					
Bill McCreary	L	3	1	0	1	2					
Cummy Burton	R	26	0	1	1	12					
Brian Smith	L	4	0	1	1	0					
Murray Oliver	C	1	0	1	1	0					
Terry Sawchuk	G	70	0	0	0	0	4	0	0	0	0
Gord Strate	D	45	0	0	0	24					
Guyle Fielder	C	6	0	0	0	2					
Dennis Olson	C	4	0	0	0	0					
Dave Amadio	D	2	0	0	0	2					
Stu McNeill	C	2	0	0	0	0					

1957–1958

PLAYER	POS	REGULAR SEASON					POSTSEASON				
		GP	G	A	PTS	PIM					
Jake Hendrickson	D	1	0	0	0	0	no postseason play				
Brian Kilrea	C	1	0	0	0	0					

GOALTENDER	REGULAR SEASON					POSTSEASON				
	GP	MIN	GA	SH	GAA	GP	MIN	GA	SH	GAA
Terry Sawchuk (29-29-**12**)	**70**	**4200**	205 (2)	3	2.94	4	252	19	0	4.52

BOSTON   27-28-15   69   4th   Milt Schmidt
Bruins

PLAYER	POS	REGULAR SEASON					POSTSEASON				
		GP	G	A	PTS	PIM	GP	G	A	PTS	PIM
Bronco Horvath	C	67	30	36	66	71	**12**	5	3	8	8
Fleming Mackell	C	**70**	20	40	60	72	**12**	5	**14**	**19**	12
Don McKenney	C	**70**	28	30	58	22	**12**	9	8	17	0
Vic Stasiuk	L	**70**	21	35	56	55	**12**	0	5	5	13
John Bucyk	L	68	21	31	52	57	**12**	0	4	4	16
Jerry Toppazzini	R	64	25	24	49	51	**12**	9	3	12	2
Larry Regan	R	59	11	28	39	22	**12**	3	8	11	6
Allan Stanley	D	69	6	25	31	37	**12**	1	3	4	6
Larry Hillman	D	**70**	3	19	22	60	11	0	2	2	6
Leo Labine	R	62	7	14	21	60	11	0	2	2	10
Doug Mohns	F	54	5	16	21	28	**12**	3	10	13	18
Real Chevrefils	L	44	9	9	18	21	1	0	0	0	0
Fern Flaman	D	66	0	15	15	71	**12**	2	2	4	10
Carl Boone	R	34	5	3	8	28	**12**	1	1	2	13
Norm Johnson	C	15	2	3	5	8	**12**	4	0	4	6
Bob Armstrong	D	47	1	4	5	66					
Jack Bionda	D	42	1	4	5	50					
Johnny Peirson	R	53	2	2	4	10	5	0	1	1	0
Leo Boivin	D	33	0	4	4	54	**12**	0	3	3	21
Jack Caffery	C	7	1	0	1	2					
Gerry Ehman	R	1	1	0	1	0					
Don Simmons	G	38	0	0	0	0	11	0	0	0	0
Harry Lumley	G	25	0	0	0	0	1	0	0	0	0
Bob Beckett	C	9	0	0	0	2					
Al Millar	G	6	0	0	0	0					
Willie O'Ree	R	2	0	0	0	0					
Harry Pidhirny	C	2	0	0	0	0					
Claude Evans	G	1	0	0	0	0					
Lefty Wilson	G	1	0	0	0	0					

GOALTENDER		REGULAR SEASON					POSTSEASON				
		GP	MIN	GA	SH	GAA	GP	MIN	GA	SH	GAA
Lefty Wilson	(0-0-1)	1	52	1	0	1.15					
Don Simmons	(15-14-8)	38	2228	92 (1)	5	2.48	11	671	27	**1**	2.41
Harry Lumley	(11-10-4)	25	1500	71	3	2.84	1	60	5	0	5.00
Claude Evans	(0-0-1)	1	60	4	0	4.00					
Al Millar	(1-4-1)	6	360	25	0	4.17					

CHICAGO Blackhawks

24-39-7   55   5th   Rudy Pilous

PLAYER	POS	GP	G	A	PTS	PIM
Ed Litzenberger	R	70	32	30	62	63
Bobby Hull	L	70	13	34	47	62
Ted Lindsay	L	68	15	24	39	110
Eric Nesterenko	R	70	20	18	38	104
Glen Skov	L	70	17	18	35	35
Pierre Pilote	D	70	6	24	30	91
Ron Murphy	L	69	11	17	28	32
Elmer Vasko	D	59	6	20	26	51
Earl Reibel (2-2)	C	40	4	12	16	6
Lorne Ferguson (2-2)	L	39	6	9	15	24
Billy Dea (2-2)	C	34	5	8	13	4
Bill Dineen (2-2)	R	41	4	9	13	8
Gus Mortson	D	67	3	10	13	62
Ed Kachur	R	62	5	7	12	14
Nick Mickoski (1-2)	L	28	5	6	11	20
Jimmy Thomson	D	70	4	7	11	75
Ian Cushenan	D	61	2	8	10	67
Bob Bailey (2-2)	R	28	3	6	9	38
Hec Lalande (2-2)	C	22	2	2	4	10
Jack McIntyre (1-2)	L	27	0	4	4	10
Glenn Hall	G	70	0	0	0	10
Doug Barkley	D	3	0	0	0	0
Frank Martin	D	3	0	0	0	10
Don Ward	D	3	0	0	0	0

POSTSEASON: no postseason play

GOALTENDER	GP	MIN	GA	SH	GAA
Glenn Hall (24-39-7)	70	4200	200 (2)	7	2.86

POSTSEASON: no postseason play

TORONTO Maple Leafs

21-38-11   53   6th   Billy Reay

PLAYER	POS	GP	G	A	PTS	PIM
Dick Duff	L	65	26	23	49	79
Billy Harris	C	68	16	28	44	32
Brian Cullen	C	67	20	23	43	29
George Armstrong	C	59	17	25	42	93
Barry Cullen	R	70	16	25	41	37
Ron Stewart	C	70	15	24	39	51
Tod Sloan	R	59	13	25	38	58
Frank Mahovlich	L	67	20	16	36	67
Bob Pulford	L	70	14	17	31	48
Tim Horton	D	53	6	20	26	39
Gary Aldcorn	L	59	10	14	24	12
Jim Morrison	D	70	3	21	24	62
Rudy Migay	C	48	7	14	21	18
Paul Masnick	C	41	2	9	11	14
Bob Baun	D	67	1	9	10	91

POSTSEASON: no postseason play

1957–1958

		REGULAR SEASON					*POSTSEASON*
PLAYER	*POS*	*GP*	*G*	*A*	*PTS*	*PIM*	*no postseason play*
Marc Reaume	D	68	1	7	8	49	
Gerry James	R	15	3	2	5	61	
Sid Smith	L	12	2	1	3	2	
Pete Conacher	L	5	0	1	1	5	
Ed Chadwick	G	70	0	0	0	0	
Al MacNeil	D	13	0	0	0	9	
Bob Nevin	R	4	0	0	0	0	
Kenny Girard	R	3	0	0	0	0	
Carl Brewer	D	2	0	0	0	0	
Earl Balfour	L	1	0	0	0	0	
Noel Price	D	1	0	0	0	5	

		REGULAR SEASON					*POSTSEASON*
GOALTENDER		*GP*	*MIN*	*GA*	*SH*	*GAA*	*no postseason play*
Ed Chadwick	(21-**38**-11)	70	4200	**223**	(3)	4	3.19

TEAM TOTALS

								Per Game			
TEAM	*GP*	*G*	*A*	*P*	*PIM*	*GA*	*SH*	*G*	*A*	*PIM*	*GA*
Montreal	70	**250**	**430**	**680**	**945**	158	10	**3.57**	**6.14**	**13.50**	2.26
New York	70	195	310	505	781	188	5	2.79	4.43	11.16	2.69
Detroit	70	176	284	460	758	207	3	2.51	4.06	10.83	2.96
Boston	70	199	342	541	849	194	8	2.84	4.89	12.13	2.77
Chicago	70	163	273	436	906	202	7	2.33	3.90	12.94	2.89
Toronto	70	192	304	496	861	226	4	2.74	4.34	12.30	3.23
	420	1175	1943	3118	5100	1175	37	2.80	4.63	12.14	2.80

PLAYOFFS

SERIES "A"
Montreal 8, Detroit 1
Montreal 5, Detroit 1
Montreal 2, Detroit 1 (OT)
Montreal 4, Detroit 3

MONTREAL, 4-0

SERIES "B"
New York 5, Boston 3
Boston 4, New York 3 (OT)
Boston 5, New York 0
New York 5, Boston 2
Boston 6, New York 1
Boston 8, New York 2

BOSTON, 4-2

SERIES "C"
Montreal 2, Boston 1
Boston 5, Montreal 2
Montreal 3, Boston 0
Boston 3, Montreal 1
Montreal 3, Boston 2
Montreal 5, Boston 3

**MONTREAL WINS
STANLEY CUP, 4-2**

ALL-STAR TEAMS

First Team
G — Glenn Hall, CHI
D — Doug Harvey, MTL
D — Bill Gadsby, NY
C — Henri Richard, MTL
R — Gordie Howe, DET
L — Dickie Moore, MTL

Second Team
G — Jacques Plante, MTL
D — Marcel Pronovost, DET
D — Fern Flaman, BOS
C — Jean Beliveau, MTL
R — Andy Bathgate, NY
L — Camille Henry, NY

INDIVIDUAL TROPHY WINNERS

HART TROPHY (Most Valuable Player): Gordie Howe, DET
LADY BYNG TROPHY (Gentlemanly Conduct): Camille Henry, NY
VEZINA TROPHY (Best Goaltender): Jacques Plante, MTL
CALDER MEMORIAL TROPHY (Best Rookie): Frank Mahovlich, TOR
ART ROSS TROPHY (Scoring Leader): Dickie Moore, MTL
JAMES NORRIS TROPHY (Best Defenseman): Doug Harvey, MTL

1958-1959
Dynamic Duo

As the Montreal Canadiens laid waste to the National Hockey League during the late 1950s, they were led by a bevy of stars. Some — like defenseman Doug Harvey and goaltender Jacques Plante — kept opponents at bay. However, the team was more noteworthy for its scoring stars — two of which were about to enjoy record-breaking seasons.

Jean Beliveau made his professional debut in 1951 with the Canadiens, joining the professional ranks from the roster of the Quebec Aces — a member of the Quebec Major Hockey League. After another two years with the Aces, Beliveau joined the NHL for good in 1953, accumulating 34 points in 34 games. The following season, he netted 37 markers in 1954-55, increasing the total to a league-best 47 the following campaign, firmly establishing himself as the team's top center. After a downward turn in the following two seasons, Beliveau was about to rebound with authority.

Richard "Dickie" Moore began his Montreal career about the same time as Beliveau, but took a different path to excellence. After several middling seasons spent bouncing back and forth between the NHL and the minors, he latched on with the Canadiens full-time in 1955-56. After a pair of decent 50-point seasons, Moore blossomed in 1957-58. Paired with Beliveau as his left-winger, he put a 36-48-84 campaign together, leading the league in goals and points. As it would turn out, this fine season was to be a mere prelude to an even better effort.

Fresh off its third Cup in a row, the Canadiens got off to a pedestrian start in the fall of 1958, giving their NHL brethren at least a faint hope of knocking them off. However, Montreal put any thoughts of faltering to rest, as they went undefeated for the month of December, putting a good amount of distance between them and the pack. By seasons end, the Canadiens (39-

18-13, 91) owned a substantial 18-point bulge over surprising Boston, which showcased its best team in ten years. Chicago claimed third, while Toronto slipped into fourth by a single point, passing the Rangers on the final day. In a big surprise, the Red Wings — despite claiming four slots on the Second All-Star Team — thumped into the cellar, giving Detroit its first last-place team in over 30 years.

While helping the Canadiens eliminate the Rangers, 4–2, on the last night of the regular season, Beliveau and Moore each achieved significant milestones. During the contest, Beliveau earned his 91st point of the campaign, becoming the first NHL center to accomplish the feat. In the same contest, Moore scored a goal and added an assist, claiming his second scoring title (41-55-96). In doing so, the latter eased past Gordie Howe's 1952-53 95-point total, becoming the new single-season record holder. Beliveau's goal (45) and Moore's assist (55) totals also served as league benchmarks, while teammate Jacques Plante (2.15) allowed the fewest goals, while posting the most shutouts (9). Tough guy Ted Lindsay (Chicago) served the most time in the penalty box (184).

In one opening round playoff matchup, Montreal knocked off the Blackhawks in six games. In the other, Toronto had a far harder time with the Bruins. After Boston took a quick two-game lead, the Leafs notched a pair of overtime wins to even the series. After a 4–1 Toronto win in game five, Boston pulled out a 5–4 win in game six, thanks to a late Bronco Horvath tally. In the seventh game, Toronto scored three times in the third to eke out a 3–2 win, earning the right to face the Canadiens in the finals. Once there, the worn out Leafs proved to be no match for Montreal, bowing to the Habs in five games, giving the Canadiens their fourth straight Stanley Cup.

In the postseason, Moore continued his domination of the scoring charts, racking up the most assists (12) and points (17). Complementing him was relative unknown Marcel Bonin, who scored a league best ten playoff markers, nearly equaling his regular season total. In the net, Plante posted the lowest GAA (2.33).

Through the 1960s, Beliveau continued as a Montreal star, eventually retiring in the early 1970s with over 500 career goals — a total which led to his logical inclusion in the Hockey Hall of Fame. His 91-point campaign served as a high-point in his career, as he never again achieved such a lofty total.

On the other hand, Moore's rapid rise to the top was followed by an equally precipitous slide to mediocrity. After his record-breaking campaign, he never again approached that high level and within a few years, had retired from the game.

Though the records set by Beliveau and Moore were eclipsed within 10 years, both achievements remain noteworthy. It was rare enough for a season to witness one record-breaking mark, but to have two linemates earn similar scoring milestones at the same time — in the same game — makes this a nearly singular occurrence.

STANDINGS

TEAM	GP	W	L	T	PTS	GF	GA
MONTREAL	70	39	18	13	91	258	158
BOSTON	70	32	29	9	73	205	215
CHICAGO	70	28	29	13	69	197	208
TORONTO	70	27	32	11	65	189	201
NEW YORK	70	26	32	12	64	201	217
DETROIT	70	25	37	8	58	167	218

LEADERS

PLAYER	TM	GP	G	A	PTS	PIM
Dickie Moore	MTL	70	41	55	96	61
Jean Beliveau	MTL	64	45	46	91	67
Andy Bathgate	NY	70	40	48	88	48
Gordie Howe	DET	70	32	46	78	57
Ed Litzenberger	CHI	70	33	44	77	37
Bernie Geoffrion	MTL	59	22	44	66	30
George Sullivan	NY	70	21	42	63	56
Don McKenney	BOS	70	32	30	62	20
Tod Sloan	CHI	59	27	35	62	79
Andy Hebenton	NY	70	33	29	62	8

GOALS	
Beliveau, MTL	45
Moore, MTL	41
Bathgate, NY	40
Litzenberger, CHI	33
Hebenton, NY	33

ASSISTS	
Moore, MTL	55
Bathgate, NY	48
Howe, DET	46
Beliveau, MTL	46
Gadsby, NY	46

GOALTENDER	TM	GP	MIN	GA	SH	GAA
Jacques Plante	MTL	67	4000	144	9	2.15
Johnny Bower	TOR	39	2340	107	3	2.74
Ed Chadwick	TOR	31	1860	92 (1)	3	2.97
Glenn Hall	CHI	70	4200	208	1	2.97
Lorne Worsley	NY	67	4001	199 (6)	2	2.98
Terry Sawchuk	DET	67	4020	202 (7)	5	3.01
Don Simmons	BOS	58	3480	183 (1)	3	3.16

PENALTY MINUTES	
Lindsay, CHI	184
Fontinato, NY	149
Brewer, TOR	125
Bartlett, NY	118
Two tied with	109

SHUTOUTS	
Plante, MTL	9
Sawchuk, DET	5
Bower, TOR	3
Chadwick, TOR	3
Simmons, BOS	3

MONTREAL 39-18-13 91 1st Toe Blake
Canadiens

		REGULAR SEASON					POSTSEASON			
PLAYER	POS	GP	G	A	PTS	PIM	GP	G	A	PTS	PIM
Dickie Moore	L	70	41	55	96	61	11	5	12	17	8
Jean Beliveau	C	64	45	46	91	67	3	1	4	5	4
Bernie Geoffrion	R	59	22	44	66	30	11	5	8	13	10
Henri Richard	F	63	21	30	51	33	11	3	8	11	13
Marcel Bonin	L	57	13	30	43	38	11	10	5	15	4
Ralph Backstrom	C	64	18	22	40	19	11	3	5	8	12

		REGULAR SEASON				POSTSEASON				
PLAYER	POS	GP	G	A	PTS	PIM	GP	G	A	PTS	PIM
Tom Johnson	D	70	10	29	39	76	11	2	3	5	8
Maurice Richard	R	42	17	21	38	27	4	0	0	0	2
Claude Provost	R	69	16	22	38	37	11	6	2	8	2
Alvin McDonald	L	69	13	23	36	35	11	1	1	2	6
Don Marshall	C	70	10	22	32	12	11	0	2	2	2
Phil Goyette	C	63	10	18	28	8	10	0	4	4	0
Bob Turner	D	68	4	24	28	66	11	0	2	2	20
Andre Pronovost	L	70	9	14	23	48	11	2	1	3	6
Jean-Guy Talbot	D	69	4	17	21	77	11	0	1	1	10
Doug Harvey	D	61	4	16	20	61	11	1	11	12	22
Ian Cushenan	D	35	1	2	3	28					
Al Langlois	D	48	0	3	3	26	7	0	0	0	4
Jacques Plante	G	67	0	1	1	11	11	0	0	0	0
Claude Cyr	G	1	0	0	0	0					
Charlie Hodge	G	2	0	0	0	0					
Claude Pronovost	G	2	0	0	0	0					
Bill Hicke	R						1	0	0	0	0
Kenny Mosdell	C						2	0	0	0	0

		REGULAR SEASON				POSTSEASON			
GOALTENDER		GP	MIN	GA	SH	GAA	GP	MIN	GA	SH	GAA
Jacques Plante	(38-16-13)	67	4000	144	9	2.15	11	670	26	0	2.33
Charlie Hodge	(1-1-0)	2	120	6	0	3.00					
Claude Cyr		1	20	1	0	3.00					
Claude Pronovost	(0-1-0)	2	60	7	0	7.00					

BOSTON 32-29-9   73   2nd   Milt Schmidt
Bruins

		REGULAR SEASON				POSTSEASON				
PLAYER	POS	GP	G	A	PTS	PIM	GP	G	A	PTS	PIM
Don McKenney	C	70	32	30	62	20	7	2	5	7	0
Vic Stasiuk	L	70	27	33	60	63	7	4	2	6	11
John Bucyk	L	69	24	36	60	36	7	2	4	6	6
Jerry Toppazzini	R	70	21	23	44	61	7	4	2	6	0
Fleming Mackell	C	57	17	23	40	28	7	2	6	8	8
Bronco Horvath	C	45	19	20	39	58	7	2	3	5	0
Leo Labine	R	70	9	23	32	74	7	2	1	3	12
Doug Mohns	D	47	6	24	30	40	4	0	2	2	12
Jim Morrison	D	70	8	17	25	42	6	0	6	6	16
Jean-Guy Gendron	L	60	15	9	24	57	7	1	0	1	18
Leo Boivin	D	70	5	16	21	94	7	1	2	3	4
Fern Flaman	D	70	0	21	21	101	7	0	0	0	8
Norm Johnson (2-2)	C	39	2	17	19	25					
Larry Leach	C	29	4	12	16	26	7	1	1	2	8
Earl Reibel	C	63	6	8	14	16	4	0	0	0	0
Larry Hillman	D	55	3	10	13	19	7	0	1	1	0
Larry Regan (1-2)	W	36	5	6	11	10					
Bob Armstrong	D	60	1	9	10	50	7	0	2	2	4
Real Chevrefils	L	30	1	5	6	8					
Jack Bionda	D	3	0	1	1	2	1	0	0	0	0

1958–1959

		REGULAR SEASON					POSTSEASON				
PLAYER	POS	GP	G	A	PTS	PIM	GP	G	A	PTS	PIM
Gord Redahl	F	18	0	1	1	2					
Dan Poliziani	R	1	0	0	0	0	3	0	0	0	0
Don Keenan	G	1	0	0	0	0					
Ken Yackel	R	6	0	0	0	2	2	0	0	0	2
Harry Lumley	G	11	0	0	0	0	7	0	0	0	4
Don Simmons	G	58	0	0	0	4					

		REGULAR SEASON					POSTSEASON				
GOALTENDER		GP	MIN	GA	SH	GAA	GP	MIN	GA	SH	GAA
Harry Lumley	(8-2-1)	11	660	27	1	2.45	7	436	20	0	2.75
Don Simmons	(24-26-8)	58	3480	183 (1)	3	3.16					
Don Keenan	(0-1-0)	1	60	4	0	4.00					

CHICAGO 28-29-13 69 3rd Rudy Pilous
Blackhawks

		REGULAR SEASON					POSTSEASON				
PLAYER	POS	GP	G	A	PTS	PIM	GP	G	A	PTS	PIM
Ed Litzenberger	R	70	33	44	77	37	6	3	5	8	8
Tod Sloan	C	59	27	35	62	79	6	3	5	8	0
Ted Lindsay	L	70	22	36	58	184	6	2	4	6	13
Bobby Hull	L	70	18	32	50	50	6	1	1	2	2
Ron Murphy	L	59	17	30	47	52					
Pierre Pilote	D	70	7	30	37	79	6	0	2	2	10
Eric Nesterenko	C	70	16	18	34	81	6	2	2	4	8
Danny Lewicki	L	58	8	14	22	4	3	0	0	0	0
Kenny Wharram	C	66	10	9	19	14	6	0	2	2	2
Earl Balfour	L	70	10	8	18	10	6	0	2	2	0
Lorne Ferguson	L	67	7	10	17	44	6	2	1	3	2
Elmer Vasko	D	63	6	10	16	52	6	0	1	1	4
Dollard St. Laurent	D	70	4	8	12	28	6	0	1	1	2
Al Arbour	D	70	2	10	12	86	6	1	2	3	26
Jack Evans	D	70	1	8	9	75	6	0	0	0	10
Glen Skov	C	70	3	5	8	4	6	2	1	3	4
John McKenzie	R	32	3	4	7	22	2	0	0	0	2
Phil Maloney	C	24	2	2	4	6	6	0	0	0	0
Norm Johnson (1–2)	C	7	1	0	1	8					
Stan Mikita	F	3	0	1	1	4					
Howie Glover	R	13	0	1	1	2					
Glenn Hall	G	70	0	0	0	0	6	0	0	0	0

		REGULAR SEASON					POSTSEASON				
GOALTENDER		GP	MIN	GA	SH	GAA	GP	MIN	GA	SH	GAA
Glenn Hall	(28-29-13)	70	4200	208	1	2.97	6	360	21	0	3.50

TORONTO 27-32-11 65 4th Billy Reay
Maple Leafs Punch Imlach

		REGULAR SEASON					POSTSEASON				
PLAYER	POS	GP	G	A	PTS	PIM	GP	G	A	PTS	PIM
Dick Duff	L	69	29	24	53	73	12	4	3	7	8
Billy Harris	C	70	22	30	52	29	12	3	4	7	16

		REGULAR SEASON					POSTSEASON				
PLAYER	POS	GP	G	A	PTS	PIM	GP	G	A	PTS	PIM
Frank Mahovlich	L	63	22	27	49	94	12	6	5	11	18
Bert Olmstead	R	70	10	31	41	74	12	4	2	6	13
Bob Pulford	F	70	23	14	37	53	12	4	4	8	8
George Armstrong	C	59	20	16	36	37	12	0	4	4	10
Ron Stewart	C	70	21	13	34	23	12	3	3	6	6
Tim Horton	D	70	5	21	26	76	12	0	3	3	16
Gerry Ehman (2–2)	R	38	12	13	25	12	12	6	7	13	8
Larry Regan (2–2)	W	32	4	21	25	2	8	1	1	2	2
Carl Brewer	D	69	3	21	24	125	12	0	6	6	40
Allan Stanley	D	70	1	22	23	47	12	0	3	3	2
Brian Cullen	C	59	4	14	18	10	10	1	0	1	0
Barry Cullen	R	40	6	8	14	17	2	0	0	0	0
Dave Creighton	C	34	3	9	12	4	5	0	1	1	0
Bob Baun	D	51	1	8	9	87	12	0	0	0	24
Marc Reaume	D	51	1	5	6	67	10	0	0	0	0
Gary Aldcorn	L	5	0	3	3	2					
Rudy Migay	C	19	1	1	2	4	2	0	0	0	0
Steve Kraftcheck	D	8	1	0	1	0					
Willie Marshall	C	9	0	1	1	2					
Bob Nevin	R	2	0	0	0	2					
Noel Price	D	28	0	0	0	4	5	0	0	0	2
Ed Chadwick	G	31	0	0	0	0					
Johnny Bower	G	39	0	0	0	2	12	0	0	0	0
Gary Collins	C						2	0	0	0	0

		REGULAR SEASON					POSTSEASON				
GOALTENDER		GP	MIN	GA	SH	GAA	GP	MIN	GA	SH	GAA
Johnny Bower	(15-17-7)	39	2340	107	3	2.74	12	746	38	0	3.06
Ed Chadwick	(12-15-4)	31	1860	92 (1)	3	2.97					

NEW YORK Rangers   26-32-12   64   5th   Phil Watson

		REGULAR SEASON					POSTSEASON
PLAYER	POS	GP	G	A	PTS	PIM	no postseason play
Andy Bathgate	C	70	40	48	88	48	
George Sullivan	C	70	21	42	63	56	
Andy Hebenton	R	70	33	29	62	8	
Camille Henry	L	70	23	35	58	2	
Bill Gadsby	D	70	5	46	51	56	
Dean Prentice	L	70	17	33	50	11	
Larry Popein	C	61	13	21	34	28	
Eddie Shack	F	67	7	14	21	109	
Jim Bartlett	L	70	11	9	20	118	
Hank Ciesla	C	69	6	14	20	21	
Harry Howell	D	70	4	10	14	101	
Lou Fontinato	D	64	7	6	13	149	
Les Colwill	R	69	7	6	13	16	
Jack Hanna	D	70	1	10	11	83	
Wally Hergesheimer	R	22	3	0	3	6	
Jack Bownass	D	35	1	2	3	20	

		REGULAR SEASON					POSTSEASON
PLAYER	POS	GP	G	A	PTS	PIM	no postseason play
Earl Ingarfield	C	35	1	2	3	10	
Larry Cahan	D	16	1	0	1	8	
Marcel Paille	G	1	0	0	0	0	
Julius Klymkiw	G	1	0	0	0	0	
Bruce Gamble	G	2	0	0	0	0	
Lorne Worsley	G	67	0	0	0	10	

		REGULAR SEASON					POSTSEASON
GOALTENDER		GP	MIN	GA	SH	GAA	no postseason play
Lorne Worsley (26-30-11)		67	4001	199 (6)	2	2.98	
Bruce Gamble	(0-2-0)	2	120	6	0	3.00	
Marcel Paille	(0-0-1)	1	60	4	0	4.00	
Julius Klymkiw		1	19	2	0	6.32	

DETROIT 25-37-8 58 6th Sid Abel
Red Wings

		REGULAR SEASON					POSTSEASON
PLAYER	POS	GP	G	A	PTS	PIM	no postseason play
Gordie Howe	R	70	32	46	78	57	
Norm Ullman	C	69	22	36	58	42	
Alex Delvecchio	C	70	19	35	54	6	
Marcel Pronovost	D	69	11	21	32	44	
Jack McIntyre	L	55	15	14	29	14	
Johnny Wilson	L	70	11	17	28	18	
Len Lunde	L	68	14	12	26	15	
Nick Mickoski	R	66	11	15	26	20	
Red Kelly	C	67	8	13	21	34	
Charlie Burns	C	70	9	11	20	32	
Pete Goegan	D	67	1	11	12	109	
Warren Godfrey	D	69	6	4	10	44	
Billy McNeill	C	54	2	5	7	32	
Claude Laforge	L	57	2	5	7	18	
Tom McCarthy	L	15	2	3	5	4	
Forbes Kennedy	C	67	1	4	5	49	
Chuck Holmes	R	15	0	3	3	6	
Stu McNeill		3	1	1	2	2	
Gerry Ehman (1–2)	R	6	0	1	1	4	
Cummy Burton	R	14	0	1	1	9	
Lou Marcon	D	21	0	1	1	12	
Gus Mortson	D	36	0	1	1	22	
Bob Perreault	G	3	0	0	0	0	
Jake Hendrickson	D	3	0	0	0	2	
Dunc Fisher	R	8	0	0	0	0	
Gord Strate	D	11	0	0	0	6	
Gene Achtymichuk	C	12	0	0	0	0	
Terry Sawchuk	G	67	0	0	0	12	

		REGULAR SEASON					POSTSEASON
GOALTENDER		GP	MIN	GA	SH	GAA	no postseason play
Bob Perreault	(2-1-0)	3	180	9	0	3.00	
Terry Sawchuk	(23-36-8)	67	4020	202 (7)	5	3.01	

TEAM TOTALS

TEAM	GP	G	A	PTS	PIM	GA	SH	Per Game G	A	PIM	GA
Montreal	70	**258**	**438**	**696**	760	**158**	9	**3.69**	**6.26**	10.86	**2.26**
Boston	70	205	344	549	838	215	4	2.93	4.91	11.97	3.07
Chicago	70	197	315	512	921	208	1	2.81	4.50	**13.16**	2.97
Toronto	70	189	302	491	846	201	6	2.70	4.31	12.09	2.87
New York	70	201	327	528	860	217	2	2.87	4.67	12.29	3.10
Detroit	70	167	260	427	613	218	6	2.39	3.71	8.75	3.11
	420	1217	1986	3203	4838	1217	28	2.90	4.73	11.52	2.90

PLAYOFFS

SERIES "A"
Montreal 4, Chicago 2
Montreal 5, Chicago 1
Chicago 4, Montreal 2
Chicago 3, Montreal 1
Montreal 5, Chicago 2
Montreal 5, Chicago 4
Toronto 3, Boston 2

TORONTO, 4–3

SERIES "B"
Boston 5, Toronto 1
Boston 4, Toronto 2
Toronto 3, Boston 2 (OT)
Toronto 3, Boston 2 (OT)
Toronto 4, Boston 1
Boston 5, Toronto 4

MONTREAL, 4–2

SERIES "C"
Montreal 5, Toronto 3
Montreal 3, Toronto 1
Toronto 3, Montreal 2 (OT)
Montreal 3, Toronto 2
Montreal 5, Toronto 3

MONTREAL WINS STANLEY CUP, 4–1

ALL-STAR TEAMS

First Team
G — Jacques Plante, MTL
D — Tom Johnson, MTL
D — Bill Gadsby, NY
C — Jean Beliveau, MTL
R — Andy Bathgate, NY
L — Dickie Moore, MTL

Second Team
G — Terry Sawchuk, DET
D — Marcel Pronovost, DET
D — Doug Harvey, MTL
C — Henri Richard, MTL
R — Gordie Howe, DET
L — Alex Delvecchio, DET

INDIVIDUAL TROPHY WINNERS

ART ROSS TROPHY (Scoring Leader): Dickie Moore, MTL
HART TROPHY (Most Valuable Player): Andy Bathgate, NY
LADY BYNG TROPHY (Gentlemanly Conduct): Alex Delvecchio, DET
VEZINA TROPHY (Best Goaltender): Jacques Plante, MTL
CALDER MEMORIAL TROPHY (Best Rookie): Ralph Backstrom, MTL
JAMES NORRIS TROPHY (Best Defenseman): Tom Johnson, MTL

1959-1960

The Drive for Five

By vanquishing its five brethren in 1958-59, the Montreal Canadiens accomplished a feat that none other before had achieved. Up until that time, no other NHL team had claimed the Stanley Cup four times in a row. With the record in their grasp, the team was not content to rest on its laurels, for there still was another milestone left to achieve.

In other sports, clubs had pieced together championship streaks longer than Montreal's run in the late 1950s. For instance, in the 1920s, two top minor league baseball clubs — the Baltimore Orioles and the Fort Worth Panthers — each won an improbable seven flags in a row. Further up the food chain, baseball's major league Yankees had recently won five consecutive World Series (1949–53). This was the goal on which the Canadiens set their sights.

To accomplish the difficult feat of stringing together championships, these aforementioned teams followed different paths. For example, the minor league baseball clubs — the Orioles and Panthers — were able to keep the nucleus of their rosters intact through the duration of the run, adding new pieces as needed. For the Yankees, a strong farm system and good scouting kept the nine competitive over many years. For the Canadiens, they relied on a different method. As the only NHL team in French-speaking Canada, they were the primary lure for hundreds of budding hockey players in the region. In short, before the era of the amateur draft, Montreal had its pick of the cream of the whole province — an advantage that the team utilized to the utmost.

As the 1959-60 season got underway, Montreal made its presence known in the usual way. Riding an eight-game winning streak in November and a six-match victory set in February, the Canadiens (40-18-12, 92) captured their third straight regular season championship, ending more than a dozen points to the good of Toronto. Further behind, Chicago and Detroit clambered onto the other playoff rungs, as Boston and New York were left out of the running.

Although Montreal's French-Canadian stars enjoyed solid seasons, they were outshone this season by a brash newcomer and a minor league veteran, enjoying his first extended time in the NHL. Boston's Bronco Horvath (39-41-80) led up until the very end, when Chicago's 20-year-old left winger, Bobby Hull (39-42-81) passed him in the last game. No other player surpassed the duo's 39 goals, but both had their assist total eclipsed by Boston's Don McKenney (49). In addition, Toronto's Carl Brewer (150) amassed the most penalty minutes. In net, the newly masked Jacques Plante (2.54) edged Glenn Hall (Chicago) for the GAA title — his fifth in a row — although the latter did earn the most shutouts (6).

In one opening round series, Toronto dispatched Detroit in six games, winning the final two 5-4 and 4-2. In the other group, Montreal slid by Chicago, 4-3, in the opener, to take an early advantage. In the second match, their defenseman Doug Harvey coughed up the puck late in the third, allowing Chicago's Bill Hay to knot the score at three. A few minutes later, Harvey atoned for his miscue, netting the winner eight minutes into overtime. For the Hawks, it was all downhill after that, as the Canadiens didn't allow them a single tally, completing the sweep with 4-0 and 2-0 blankings.

In the finals, Toronto didn't have any better luck, as they were held to five goals in the first four games. In the same time frame, Montreal scored 15 markers of their own, giving them wins in each game of the quartet. After the final win, their 38-year-old captain — Maurice Richard — was presented with the team's fifth straight Stanley Cup. In a quick eight game double-sweep, the major league record for championships in a row had been equaled.

As usual, several Canadiens contributed to the team's success. Henri Richard (3-9-12) and Bernie Geoffrion (2-10-12) finished tied for the most points, with the latter collecting the most assists as well. In addition, Dickie Moore (6) scored the most goals, while Jacques Plante (1.35) sparkled in net, posting three shutouts.

By successfully completing their "drive for five," the Canadiens set the bar high. In the last 50 years, in any of the major sports, no team has managed to equal the mark, giving this set of hockey champions a special niche in the history of sports.

STANDINGS

TEAM	GP	W	L	T	PTS	GF	GA
MONTREAL	70	40	18	12	92	255	178
TORONTO	70	35	26	9	79	199	195
CHICAGO	70	28	29	13	69	191	180

1959-1960

TEAM	GP	W	L	T	PTS	GF	GA
DETROIT	70	26	29	15	67	186	197
BOSTON	70	28	34	8	64	220	241
NEW YORK	70	17	38	15	49	187	247

LEADERS

PLAYER	TM	GP	G	A	PTS	PIM
Bobby Hull	CHI	70	39	42	81	68
Bronco Horvath	BOS	68	39	41	80	60
Jean Beliveau	MTL	60	34	40	74	57
Andy Bathgate	NY	70	26	48	74	28
Henri Richard	MTL	70	30	43	73	66
Gordie Howe	DET	70	28	45	73	46
Bernie Geoffrion	MTL	59	30	41	71	36
Don McKenney	BOS	70	20	49	69	28
Vic Stasiuk	BOS	69	29	39	68	121
Dean Prentice	NY	70	32	34	66	43

GOALS
Hull, CHI	39
Horvath, BOS	39
Beliveau, MTL	34
Prentice, NY	32
Two tied with	30

ASSISTS
McKenney, BOS	49
Bathgate, NY	48
Howe, DET	45
Richard, MTL	43
Two tied with	42

GOALTENDER	TM	GP	MIN	GA	SH	GAA
Jacques Plante	MTL	69	4140	175	3	**2.54**
Glenn Hall	CHI	70	4200	180	6	2.57
Johnny Bower	TOR	66	3960	178 (2)	5	2.68
Terry Sawchuk	DET	58	3480	156	5	2.69
Don Simmons	BOS	28	1680	91 (3)	2	3.25
Harry Lumley	BOS	42	2520	146 (1)	2	3.48
Lorne Worsley	NY	39	2301	135 (2)	0	3.52

PENALTY MINUTES
Brewer, TOR	150
Fontinato, NY	137
Stasiuk, BOS	121
Mikita, CHI	119
Flaman, BOS	112

SHUTOUTS
Hall, CHI	6
Sawchuk, DET	5
Bower, TOR	5
Plante, MTL	3
Two tied with	2

MONTREAL Canadiens
40-18-12   92   1st   Toe Blake

		REGULAR SEASON					POSTSEASON				
PLAYER	POS	GP	G	A	PTS	PIM	GP	G	A	PTS	PIM
Jean Beliveau	C	60	34	40	74	57	8	5	2	7	6
Henri Richard	C	70	30	43	73	66	8	3	9	12	9
Bernie Geoffrion	R	59	30	41	71	36	8	2	10	12	4
Dickie Moore	L	62	22	42	64	54	8	6	4	10	4
Marcel Bonin	L	59	17	34	51	59	8	1	4	5	12
Claude Provost	R	70	17	29	46	42	8	1	1	2	0
Phil Goyette	C	65	21	22	43	4	8	2	1	3	4
Don Marshall	L	70	16	22	38	4	8	2	2	4	0
Maurice Richard	R	51	19	16	35	50	8	1	3	4	2
Andre Pronovost	L	69	12	19	31	61	8	1	2	3	0
Tom Johnson	D	64	4	25	29	59	8	0	1	1	4
Ralph Backstrom	C	64	13	15	28	24	7	0	3	3	2
Doug Harvey	D	66	6	21	27	45	8	3	0	3	6

		REGULAR SEASON					POSTSEASON				
PLAYER	POS	GP	G	A	PTS	PIM	GP	G	A	PTS	PIM
Alvin McDonald	L	68	9	13	22	26					
Jean-Guy Talbot	D	69	1	14	15	60	8	1	1	2	8
Al Langlois	D	67	1	14	15	48	8	0	3	3	18
Bill Hicke	R	43	3	10	13	17	7	1	2	3	0
Bob Turner	D	54	0	9	9	40	8	0	0	0	0
J.C. Tremblay	D	11	0	1	1	0					
Jacques Plante	G	69	0	0	0	2	8	0	0	0	0
Cec Hoekstra	C	4	0	0	0	0					
Reg Fleming	L	3	0	0	0	2					
Charlie Hodge	G	1	0	0	0	0					

		REGULAR SEASON					POSTSEASON				
GOALTENDER		GP	MIN	GA	SH	GAA	GP	MIN	GA	SH	GAA
Jacques Plante	(**40**-17-12)	69	4140	175	3	**2.54**	8	489	11	**3**	**1.35**
Charlie Hodge	(0-1-0)	1	60	3	0	3.00					

TORONTO   35-26-9   79   2nd   Punch Imlach
Maple Leafs

		REGULAR SEASON					POSTSEASON				
PLAYER	POS	GP	G	A	PTS	PIM	GP	G	A	PTS	PIM
Bob Pulford	L	**70**	24	28	52	81	10	4	1	5	10
George Armstrong	C	**70**	23	28	51	60	10	1	4	5	4
Dick Duff	L	67	19	22	41	51	10	2	4	6	6
Frank Mahovlich	L	**70**	18	21	39	61	10	3	1	4	27
Billy Harris	C	**70**	13	25	38	29	9	0	3	3	4
Bert Olmstead	L	53	15	21	36	63	10	3	4	7	0
Ron Stewart	C	67	14	20	34	28	10	0	2	2	2
Allan Stanley	D	64	10	23	33	22	10	2	3	5	2
Tim Horton	D	**70**	3	29	32	69	10	0	1	1	6
Johnny Wilson	L	**70**	15	16	31	8	10	1	2	3	2
Gerry Ehman	R	69	12	16	28	26	9	0	0	0	0
Carl Brewer	D	67	4	19	23	**150**	10	2	3	5	16
Larry Regan	R	47	4	16	20	6	10	3	3	6	0
Bob Baun	D	61	8	9	17	59	10	1	0	1	17
Gerry James	R	34	4	9	13	56	10	0	0	0	0
Red Kelly (2–2)	D	18	6	5	11	8	10	3	8	11	2
Garry Edmundson	L	39	4	6	10	47	9	0	1	1	4
Ted Hampson	C	41	2	8	10	17					
Dave Creighton	C	14	1	5	6	4					
Joe Crozier	D	5	0	3	3	2					
Marc Reaume (1–2)	D	36	0	1	1	6					
Johnny Bower	G	66	0	0	0	0	10	0	0	0	0
Al MacNeil	D	4	0	0	0	2					
Ed Chadwick	G	4	0	0	0	0					
Kenny Girard	R	1	0	0	0	0					
Pat Hannigan	L	1	0	0	0	0					
Rudy Migay	C	1	0	0	0	0					

1959–1960

GOALTENDER		GP	REGULAR SEASON MIN	GA	SH	GAA	GP	POSTSEASON MIN	GA	SH	GAA
Johnny Bower	(34-24-8)	66	3960	178 (2)	5	2.68	10	645	31	0	2.88
Ed Chadwick	(1-2-1)	4	240	15		0	3.75				

CHICAGO 28-29-13   69   3rd   Rudy Pilous
Blackhawks

PLAYER	POS	GP	G	A	PTS	PIM	GP	G	A	PTS	PIM
Bobby Hull	L	70	39	42	81	68	3	1	0	1	2
Bill Hay	C	70	18	37	55	31	4	1	2	3	2
Pierre Pilote	D	70	7	38	45	100	4	0	1	1	8
Tod Sloan	R	70	20	20	40	54	3	0	0	0	0
Ron Murphy	L	63	15	21	36	18	4	1	0	1	0
Eric Nesterenko	R	61	13	23	36	71	4	0	0	0	2
Murray Balfour	R	61	18	12	30	55	4	1	0	1	0
Ed Litzenberger	R	52	12	18	30	15	4	0	1	1	4
Elmer Vasko	D	69	3	27	30	110	4	0	0	0	0
Stan Mikita	C	67	8	18	26	119	3	0	1	1	2
Ted Lindsay	L	68	7	19	26	91	4	1	1	2	0
Kenny Wharram	R	59	14	11	25	16	4	1	1	2	0
Dollard St. Laurent	D	68	4	13	17	60	4	0	1	1	0
Phil Maloney	C	21	6	4	10	0					
Earl Balfour	L	70	3	5	8	16	4	0	0	0	0
Glen Skov	L	69	3	4	7	16	4	0	0	0	2
Al Arbour	D	57	1	5	6	66	4	0	0	0	4
Jack Evans	D	68	0	4	4	60	4	0	0	0	4
Glenn Hall	G	70	0	1	1	2	4	0	0	0	0
Doug Barkley	D	3	0	0	0	2					
Wayne Hicks	R						1	0	1	1	0
Norm Johnson	C						2	0	0	0	0

GOALTENDER		GP	REGULAR SEASON MIN	GA	SH	GAA	GP	POSTSEASON MIN	GA	SH	GAA
Glenn Hall	(28-29-13)	70	4200	180	6	2.57	4	249	14	0	3.37

DETROIT 26-29-15   67   4th   Sid Abel
Red Wings

PLAYER	POS	GP	G	A	PTS	PIM	GP	G	A	PTS	PIM
Gordie Howe	R	70	28	45	73	46	6	1	5	6	4
Norm Ullman	C	70	24	34	58	46	6	2	2	4	0
Gary Aldcorn	L	70	22	29	51	32	6	1	2	3	4
Alex Delvecchio	C	70	19	28	47	8	6	2	6	8	0
Murray Oliver	C	54	20	19	39	16	6	1	0	1	4
Jim Morrison	D	70	3	23	26	62	6	0	2	2	0
Marcel Pronovost	D	69	7	17	24	38	6	1	1	2	2
Len Lunde	L	66	6	17	23	40	6	1	2	3	0
Jerry Melnyk	C	63	10	10	20	12	6	3	0	3	0
John McKenzie	R	59	8	12	20	50	2	0	0	0	0
Red Kelly (1–2)	D	50	6	12	18	10					
Billy McNeill	C	47	5	13	18	33					

		REGULAR SEASON				POSTSEASON				
PLAYER	POS	GP	G	A	PTS	PIM	GP	G	A	PTS	PIM
Jack McIntyre	L	49	8	7	15	6	6	1	1	2	0
Warren Godfrey	D	69	5	9	14	60	6	1	0	1	10
Barry Cullen	R	55	4	9	13	23	4	0	0	0	2
Val Fonteyne	L	69	4	7	11	2	6	0	4	4	0
Brian Smith	L	31	2	5	7	2	5	0	0	0	0
Pete Goegan	D	21	3	0	3	6	6	1	0	1	13
Len Haley	R	27	1	2	3	12	6	1	3	4	6
Forbes Kennedy	C	17	1	2	3	8					
Lou Marcon	D	38	0	3	3	30					
Marc Reaume (1–2)	D	9	0	1	1	2	2	0	0	0	0
Terry Sawchuk	G	58	0	0	0	0	6	0	0	0	0
Dennis Riggin	G	9	0	0	0	0					
Lloyd Haddon	D	8	0	0	0	2	1	0	0	0	0
Stu McNeill	C	5	0	0	0	0					
Gilles Boisvert	G	3	0	0	0	0					
Bob Solinger	L	1	0	0	0	0					

		REGULAR SEASON					POSTSEASON				
GOALTENDER		GP	MIN	GA	SH	GAA	GP	MIN	GA	SH	GAA
Gilles Boisvert	(0-3-0)	3	180	8 (1)	0	2.67					
Terry Sawchuk	(24-20-14)	58	3480	156	5	2.69	6	405	20	0	2.96
Dennis Riggin	(2-6-1)	9	540	31 (1)	1	3.44					

BOSTON 28-34-8 64 5th Milt Schmidt
Bruins

		REGULAR SEASON				POSTSEASON
PLAYER	POS	GP	G	A	PTS	PIM	*no postseason play*
Bronco Horvath	C	68	39	41	80	60
Don McKenney	C	70	20	49	69	28
Vic Stasiuk	L	69	29	39	68	121
John Bucyk	L	56	16	36	52	26
Doug Mohns	F	65	20	25	45	62
Jerry Toppazzini	R	69	12	33	45	26
Leo Labine	R	63	16	28	44	58
Jean-Guy Gendron	L	67	24	11	35	64
Charlie Burns	C	62	10	17	27	46
Leo Boivin	D	70	4	21	25	66
Fleming Mackell	C	47	7	15	22	19
Fern Flaman	D	60	2	18	20	112
Larry Leach	C	69	7	12	19	47
Bob Armstrong	D	69	5	14	19	96
Dick Meissner	R	60	5	6	11	22
Aut Erickson	D	58	1	6	7	29
Lorne Davis	R	10	1	1	2	10
Dallas Smith	D	5	1	1	2	0
Nick Mickoski	L	18	1	0	1	2
Don Ward	D	31	0	1	1	16
Larry Hillman	D	2	0	1	1	2
Harry Lumley	G	42	0	0	0	12
Don Simmons	G	28	0	0	0	4

1959–1960

		REGULAR SEASON					*POSTSEASON*
PLAYER	*POS*	*GP*	*G*	*A*	*PTS*	*PIM*	*no postseason play*
Stan Baluik	C	7	0	0	0	2	
Dale Rolfe	D	3	0	0	0	0	
Pierre Gagne	L	2	0	0	0	0	
Gord Turlick	L	2	0	0	0	2	

		REGULAR SEASON					*POSTSEASON*
GOALTENDER		*GP*	*MIN*	*GA*	*SH*	*GAA*	*no postseason play*
Don Simmons	(12-13-3)	28	1680	91 (3)	2	3.25	
Harry Lumley	(16-21-5)	42	2520	146 (1)	2	3.48	

NEW YORK Rangers   17-38-15   49   6th   Phil Watson / Alf Pike

		REGULAR SEASON					*POSTSEASON*
PLAYER	*POS*	*GP*	*G*	*A*	*PTS*	*PIM*	*no postseason play*
Andy Bathgate	R	70	26	48	74	28	
Dean Prentice	L	70	32	34	66	43	
Andy Hebenton	R	70	19	24	46	4	
George Sullivan	C	70	12	25	37	81	
Larry Popein	C	66	14	22	36	16	
Bill Gadsby	D	65	9	22	31	60	
Ken Schinkel	R	69	13	16	29	27	
Brian Cullen	C	64	8	21	29	6	
Camille Henry	C	49	12	15	27	6	
Eddie Shack	L	62	8	10	18	110	
Bob Kabel	C	44	5	11	16	32	
Harry Howell	D	67	7	6	13	58	
Lou Fontinato	D	64	2	11	13	137	
Jim Bartlett	L	44	8	4	12	48	
Jack Hanna	D	61	4	8	12	87	
Jack Bownass	D	37	2	5	7	34	
Art Stratton	C	18	2	5	7	2	
Mel Pearson	L	23	1	5	6	13	
Irv Spencer	D	32	1	2	3	20	
Earl Ingarfield	C	20	1	2	3	2	
Bill Sweeney	C	4	1	0	1	0	
Ian Cushenan	D	17	0	1	1	22	
Lorne Worsley	G	39	0	0	0	12	
Marcel Paille	G	17	0	0	0	0	
Al Rollins	G	10	0	0	0	0	
Noel Price	D	6	0	0	0	2	
Parker MacDonald	C	4	0	0	0	0	
Jack McCartan	G	4	0	0	0	0	
Dave Balon	L	3	0	0	0	0	
Joe Schaefer	G	1	0	0	0	0	

		REGULAR SEASON					*POSTSEASON*
GOALTENDER		*GP*	*MIN*	*GA*	*SH*	*GAA*	*no postseason play*
Jack McCartan	(1-1-2)	4	240	7	0	1.75	
Al Rollins	(3-4-3)	10	600	31	0	3.10	
Lorne Worsley	(7-23-8)	39	2301	135 (2)	0	3.52	

GOALTENDER		REGULAR SEASON					POSTSEASON
		GP	MIN	GA	SH	GAA	no postseason play
Marcel Paille	(6-9-2)	17	1020	67	1	3.94	
Joe Schaefer	(0-1-0)	1	39	5	0	7.69	

TEAM TOTALS

TEAM	GP	G	A	PTS	PIM	GA	SH	Per Game G	A	PIM	GA
Montreal	70	255	430	685	756	178	3	3.64	6.14	10.80	2.54
Toronto	70	199	330	529	859	195	5	2.84	4.71	12.27	2.79
Chicago	70	191	321	512	970	180	6	2.73	4.59	13.86	2.57
Detroit	70	186	304	490	538	197	6	2.66	4.34	7.69	2.81
Boston	70	220	375	595	932	241	4	3.14	5.36	13.31	3.44
New York	70	187	300	487	850	247	1	2.67	4.29	12.14	3.53
	420	1238	2060	3298	4905	1238	25	2.95	4.90	11.68	2.95

PLAYOFFS

SERIES "A"
Montreal 4, Chicago 3
Montreal 4, Chicago 3 (OT)
Montreal 4, Chicago 0
Montreal 2, Chicago 0

MONTREAL, 4-0

SERIES "B"
Detroit 2, Toronto 1
Toronto 4, Detroit 2
Toronto 5, Detroit 4 (OT)
Detroit 2, Toronto 1 (OT)
Toronto 5, Detroit 4
Toronto 4, Detroit 2

TORONTO, 4-2

SERIES "C"
Montreal 4, Toronto 2
Montreal 2, Toronto 1
Montreal 5, Toronto 2
Montreal 4, Toronto 0

**MONTREAL WINS
STANLEY CUP, 4-0**

ALL-STAR TEAMS

First Team
G — Glenn Hall, CHI
D — Doug Harvey, MTL
D — Marcel Pronovost, DET
C — Jean Beliveau, MTL
R — Gordie Howe, DET
L — Bobby Hull, CHI

Second Team
G — Jacques Plante, MTL
D — Pierre Pilote, CHI
D — Allan Stanley, TOR
C — Bronco Horvath, BOS
R — Bernie Geoffrion, MTL
L — Dean Prentice, NY

INDIVIDUAL TROPHY WINNERS

HART TROPHY (Most Valuable Player): Gordie Howe, DET
LADY BYNG TROPHY (Gentlemanly Conduct): Don McKenney, BOS
VEZINA TROPHY (Best Goaltender): Jacques Plante, MTL
CALDER MEMORIAL TROPHY (Best Rookie): Bill Hay, CHI
ART ROSS TROPHY (Scoring Leader): Bobby Hull, CHI
JAMES NORRIS TROPHY (Best Defenseman): Doug Harvey, MTL

1960-1961
Banana Blade

During the 1940s, Rangers forward Andy Bathgate and his brother made an interesting discovery. As noted by Bruce Dowbiggin in "Hockey Sticks," they noticed that adding a curve to the blade "gave their shot a slingshot quality, a marked increase in speed." The curve was applied to the blade by heating the stick, then bending it using some kind of mold. When cooled, the stick was permanently bent. Although an interesting twist, the idea fizzled, unsupported by management.

A few years later, during a practice in the midst of the 1960-61 season, Chicago forward Stan Mikita accidentally rediscovered Bathgate's secret. As recalled later, he damaged the blade of one of his sticks so it was bent at an angle. Horsing around, Mikita noticed that when he shot the puck with the now curved blade, that the disc seemed to jump off the stick, behaving in an unnatural manner. There was no magic in the air, nor was there a hex on his stick. The puck was simply obeying the law of physics.

During the first half-century of the NHL, hockey sticks were crafted from wood — usually a light-weight wood like birch or ash. This was to give the shaft of the stick flexibility, bending and then straightening when the puck was released. This gave extra snap, translating to more speed to the shot. The blade of the stick, also made of wood, was even thinner and also reacted to the weight of the puck when a shot was made. So, if a blade was curved in the direction of the shot, at the moment of impact it would be forced straight. Continuing this line of thought, as the puck leaves the forcibly straightened blade, the blade reverts back to its naturally curved state, adding extra power to the effort.

Intrigued by the possibilities, Mikita shared this insight with his teammates, most notably Bobby Hull. Both of them copied Bathgate's method, forcing their blades into a curved position. For Hull, in particular, this was a particularly potent weapon. As one of the purveyors of the "slap shot," which involved full extension of the shooting motion with the stick raised high above the head, the force of the stick hitting the puck was tremendous. So, to counter the terrific torque, Hull bent his sticks at an extreme angle, imitating — in some cases — the shape of a banana.

Using their new-fangled toys, Mikita and Hull enjoyed solid seasons in 1960-61, but were both vastly outpointed by Montreal's Bernie Geoffrion (50-45-95) who tied the recently retired Maurice Richard's single season goal record. The most assists were gathered by his teammate, Jean Beliveau (58), while Chicago's Pierre Pilote (165) was whistled for the most infractions. In goal, Montreal's Charlie Hodge (2.47) secured the lowest GAA, while Glenn Hall (Chicago) posted the most shutouts (6).

Overall, Montreal (41-19-10, 92) finished in its accustomed first place position, followed by Toronto, Chicago, Detroit, New York and Boston. However, the Canadiens received a surprise in the first round of the playoffs. In their march to a sixth straight Cup, Chicago upended them in six games, posting back-to-back 3-0 shutouts in the final two contests. In the other opening series, Detroit also upset the higher seeded Maple Leafs, winning four straight after dropping the first match in overtime. In the finals, the Hawks and Wings traded wins for the first four games. Then, Chicago powered its way to the Cup, winning the final two games by a combined 11-4, giving the Windy City its first NHL championship in 23 years.

In the postseason, the bent blade innovator — Mikita — paved the way with six goals, but was overshadowed by his teammate Pilote, who stayed out of the penalty box long enough to register a playoff high 12 assists and 15 points. In net, Hall was especially stingy, allowing only 2.02 goals per game.

Many years before, Bathgate had noted a liability to the curved blade. Later, as the 1960s progressed, this drawback was rediscovered. Although one could unleash a more powerful shot with a bent blade, accuracy suffered, as pucks flew helter-skelter. Afraid of a serious injury to player or spectator, NHL rule makers eventually passed legislation, regulating the size of a blade's curve. Still, even with these rules in place, the straight stick is virtually extinct in today's hockey world. The curved blade, as discovered by Bathgate, and refined by hockey's 1960s innovators, is here to stay.

STANDINGS

TEAM	GP	W	L	T	PTS	GF	GA
MONTREAL	70	41	19	10	92	254	188
TORONTO	70	39	19	12	90	234	176
CHICAGO	70	29	24	17	75	198	180

1960–1961

TEAM	GP	W	L	T	PTS	GF	GA
DETROIT	70	25	29	16	66	195	215
NEW YORK	70	22	38	10	54	204	248
BOSTON	70	15	42	13	43	176	254

LEADERS

PLAYER	TM	GP	G	A	PTS	PIM
Bernie Geoffrion	MTL	64	50	45	95	29
Jean Beliveau	MTL	69	32	58	90	57
Frank Mahovlich	TOR	70	48	36	84	131
Andy Bathgate	NY	70	29	48	77	22
Gordie Howe	DET	64	23	49	72	30
Norm Ullman	DET	70	28	42	70	34
Red Kelly	TOR	64	20	50	70	12
Dickie Moore	MTL	57	35	34	69	62
Henri Richard	MTL	70	24	44	68	91
Alex Delvecchio	DET	70	27	35	62	26

GOALS	
Geoffrion, MTL	50
Mahovlich, TOR	48
Moore, MTL	35
Beliveau, MTL	32
Hull, CHI	31

ASSISTS	
Beliveau, MTL	58
Kelly, TOR	50
Howe, DET	49
Bathgate, NY	48
Hay, CHI	48

GOALTENDER	TM	GP	MIN	GA	SH	GAA
Charlie Hodge	MTL	30	1800	74 (2)	4	2.47
Johnny Bower	TOR	58	3480	145	2	2.50
Glenn Hall	CHI	70	4200	176 (4)	6	2.51
Jacques Plante	MTL	40	2400	112	2	2.80
Hank Bassen	DET	35	2050	98 (4)	0	2.87
Terry Sawchuk	DET	37	2150	112 (1)	2	3.13
Lorne Worsley	NY	59	3473	191 (2)	1	3.30
Bruce Gamble	BOS	52	3120	193 (2)	0	3.71

PENALTY MINUTES	
Pilote, CHI	165
Fleming, CHI	145
Talbot, MTL	143
Mahovlich, TOR	131
Nesterenko, CHI	125

SHUTOUTS	
Hall, CHI	6
Hodge, MTL	4
Bower, TOR	2
Plante, MTL	2
Sawchuk, DET	2

MONTREAL 41-19-10 92 1st Toe Blake
Canadiens

		REGULAR SEASON					POSTSEASON				
PLAYER	POS	GP	G	A	PTS	PIM	GP	G	A	PTS	PIM
Bernie Geoffrion	R	64	50	45	95	29	4	2	1	3	0
Jean Beliveau	C	69	32	58	90	57	6	0	5	5	0
Dickie Moore	L	57	35	34	69	62	6	3	1	4	4
Henri Richard	C	70	24	44	68	91	6	2	4	6	22
Marcel Bonin	L	65	16	35	51	45	6	0	1	1	29
Bill Hicke	R	70	18	27	45	31	5	2	0	2	19
Doug Harvey	D	58	6	33	39	48	6	0	1	1	8
Ralph Backstrom	C	69	12	20	32	44	5	0	0	0	4
Don Marshall	L	70	14	17	31	8	6	0	2	2	0
Jean-Guy Talbot	D	70	5	26	31	143	6	1	1	2	10
J-G Gendron (2–2)	L	53	9	12	21	51	5	0	0	0	2
Gilles Tremblay	L	45	7	11	18	4	6	1	3	4	0
Tom Johnson	D	70	1	15	16	54	6	0	1	1	8

		REGULAR SEASON					*POSTSEASON*				
PLAYER	*POS*	*GP*	*G*	*A*	*PTS*	*PIM*	*GP*	*G*	*A*	*PTS*	*PIM*
Claude Provost	R	49	11	4	15	32	6	1	3	4	4
Al Langlois	D	61	1	12	13	56	5	0	0	0	6
Phil Goyette	C	62	7	4	11	4	6	3	3	6	0
Andre Pronovost (1–2)	L	21	1	5	6	4					
Bob Turner	D	60	2	2	4	16	5	0	0	0	0
J.C. Tremblay	D	29	1	3	4	18	5	0	0	0	2
Bobby Rousseau	R	15	1	2	3	4					
Cliff Pennington	C	4	1	0	1	0					
Jean Gauthier	D	4	0	1	1	8					
Jacques Plante	G	40	0	0	0	2	6	0	0	0	2
Charlie Hodge	G	30	0	0	0	0					
Wayne Connelly	R	3	0	0	0	0					
Glen Skov	L	3	0	0	0	0					

		REGULAR SEASON					*POSTSEASON*				
GOALTENDER		*GP*	*MIN*	*GA*	*SH*	*GAA*	*GP*	*MIN*	*GA*	*SH*	*GAA*
Charlie Hodge	(19-8-3)	30	1800	74 (2)	4	**2.47**					
Jacques Plante	(22-11-7)	40	2400	112	2	2.80	6	412	16	0	2.33

TORONTO 39-19-12 90 2nd Punch Imlach
Maple Leafs

		REGULAR SEASON					*POSTSEASON*				
PLAYER	*POS*	*GP*	*G*	*A*	*PTS*	*PIM*	*GP*	*G*	*A*	*PTS*	*PIM*
Frank Mahovlich	L	70	48	36	84	131	5	1	1	2	6
Red Kelly	D	64	20	50	70	12	2	1	0	1	0
Bob Nevin	R	68	21	37	58	13	5	1	0	1	2
Bert Olmstead	L	67	18	34	52	84	3	1	2	3	10
Dave Keon	C	70	20	25	45	6	5	1	1	2	0
Billy Harris	C	66	12	27	39	30	5	1	0	1	0
Allan Stanley	D	68	9	25	34	42	5	0	3	3	0
Dick Duff	L	67	16	17	33	54	5	0	1	1	2
George Armstrong	C	47	14	19	33	21	5	1	1	2	0
Bob Pulford	L	40	11	18	29	41	5	0	0	0	8
Eddie Shack (2–2)	L	55	14	14	28	90	4	0	0	0	2
Ron Stewart	C	51	13	12	25	8	5	1	0	1	2
Tim Horton	D	57	6	15	21	75	5	0	0	0	0
Bob Baun	D	70	1	14	15	70	3	0	0	0	8
Carl Brewer	D	51	1	14	15	92	5	0	0	0	4
Larry Hillman	D	62	3	10	13	59	5	0	0	0	0
Larry Regan	R	37	3	5	8	2	4	0	0	0	0
John MacMillan	R	31	3	5	8	8	4	0	0	0	0
Gerry Ehman	R	14	1	1	2	2					
Johnny Wilson (2–2)	L	3	0	1	1	0					
Johnny Bower	G	58	0	0	0	0	3	0	0	0	2
Cesare Maniago	G	7	0	0	0	2					
Gerry McNamara	G	5	0	0	0	2					
Garry Edmundson	L	3	0	0	0	0					
Gary Jarrett	L	1	0	0	0	0					
Jack Martin	C	1	0	0	0	0					

1960–1961

GOALTENDER		REGULAR SEASON					POSTSEASON				
		GP	MIN	GA	SH	GAA	GP	MIN	GA	SH	GAA
Gerry McNamara	(2-2-1)	5	300	12 (1)	0	2.40					
Cesare Maniago	(4-2-1)	7	420	17 (1)	0	2.43	2	145	6	0	2.48
Johnny Bower	(33-15-10)	58	3480	145	2	2.50	3	180	8	0	2.67

CHICAGO 29-24-17 75 3rd Rudy Pilous
Blackhawks

		REGULAR SEASON					POSTSEASON				
PLAYER	POS	GP	G	A	PTS	PIM	GP	G	A	PTS	PIM
Bill Hay	C	69	11	49	60	45	12	2	5	7	20
Bobby Hull	L	67	31	25	56	43	12	4	10	14	4
Stan Mikita	C	66	19	34	53	100	12	6	5	11	21
Murray Balfour	R	70	21	27	48	123	11	5	5	10	14
Kenny Wharram	R	64	16	29	45	12	12	3	5	8	12
Ron Murphy	L	70	21	19	40	30	12	2	1	3	0
Eric Nesterenko	R	68	19	19	38	125	11	2	3	5	6
Pierre Pilote	D	70	6	29	35	165	12	3	12	15	8
Tod Sloan	R	67	11	23	34	48	12	1	1	2	8
Alvin McDonald	L	61	17	16	33	22	8	2	2	4	0
Ed Litzenberger	R	62	10	22	32	14	10	1	3	4	2
Elmer Vasko	D	63	4	18	22	40	12	1	1	2	23
Dollard St. Laurent	D	67	2	17	19	58	11	1	2	3	12
Reg Fleming	L	66	4	4	8	145	12	1	0	1	12
Jack Evans	D	69	0	8	8	58	12	1	1	2	14
Earl Balfour	L	68	3	3	6	4	12	0	0	0	2
Al Arbour	D	53	3	2	5	40	7	0	0	0	2
Glenn Hall	G	70	0	1	1	0	12	0	0	0	0
Wayne Hicks	R	1	0	0	0	0	1	0	0	0	0
Wayne Hillman	D						1	0	0	0	0
Ron Maki	R						1	0	0	0	0

GOALTENDER		REGULAR SEASON					POSTSEASON				
		GP	MIN	GA	SH	GAA	GP	MIN	GA	SH	GAA
Glenn Hall	(29-24-17)	70	4200	176 (4)	6	2.51	12	772	27	2	2.02

DETROIT 25-29-16 66 4th Sid Abel
Red Wings

		REGULAR SEASON					POSTSEASON				
PLAYER	POS	GP	G	A	PTS	PIM	GP	G	A	PTS	PIM
Gordie Howe	R	64	23	49	72	30	11	4	11	15	10
Norm Ullman	C	70	28	42	70	34	11	0	4	4	4
Alex Delvecchio	C	70	27	35	62	26	11	4	5	9	0
Al Johnson	R	70	16	21	37	14	11	2	2	4	6
Pete Goegan	D	67	5	29	34	78	11	0	1	1	18
Howie Glover	R	66	21	8	29	46	11	1	2	3	5
Parker MacDonald	C	70	14	12	26	6	9	1	0	1	0
Jerry Melnyk	C	70	9	16	25	2	11	1	0	1	2
Murray Oliver (1–2)	C	*49	11	12	23	8					
Vic Stasiuk (2–2)	L	23	10	13	23	16	11	2	5	7	4
Warren Godfrey	D	63	3	16	19	62	11	0	2	2	18
Len Lunde	L	53	6	12	18	10	10	2	0	2	0

		REGULAR SEASON				POSTSEASON				
PLAYER	POS	GP	G	A	PTS	PIM	GP	G	A	PTS	PIM
Marcel Pronovost	D	70	6	11	17	44	9	2	3	5	0
Val Fonteyne	L	66	6	11	17	4	11	2	3	5	0
Leo Labine (2–2)	R	24	2	9	11	32	11	3	2	5	4
Gary Aldcorn (1–2)	L	*49	2	6	8	16					
Howie Young	D	29	0	8	8	108	11	2	2	4	30
Gerry Odrowski	D	68	1	4	5	45	10	0	0	0	4
John McKenzie	R	16	3	1	4	16					
Brian Smith	L	26	0	2	2	10					
Claude Laforge	L	10	1	0	1	2					
Len Haley	R	3	1	0	1	2					
Marc Reaume	D	38	0	1	1	8					
Terry Sawchuk	G	37	0	1	1	8	8	0	0	0	0
Hank Bassen	G	35	0	1	1	6	4	0	0	0	0
Bruce MacGregor	C	12	0	1	1	0	8	1	2	3	6
Ed Diachuk	L	12	0	0	0	19					
Rich Healey	D	1	0	0	0	2					

		REGULAR SEASON					POSTSEASON				
GOALTENDER		GP	MIN	GA	SH	GAA	GP	MIN	GA	SH	GAA
Hank Bassen	(13-13-8)	35	2050	98 (4)	0	2.87	4	220	9	0	2.45
Terry Sawchuk	(12-16-8)	37	2150	112 (1)	2	3.13	8	465	18	1	2.32

NEW YORK Rangers   22-38-10   54   5th   Alf Pike

		REGULAR SEASON					POSTSEASON
PLAYER	POS	GP	G	A	PTS	PIM	no postseason play
Andy Bathgate	R	70	29	48	77	22	
Andy Hebenton	R	70	26	28	54	10	
Camille Henry	C	53	28	25	53	8	
Dean Prentice	L	56	20	25	45	17	
George Sullivan	C	70	9	31	40	66	
Bill Gadsby	D	65	9	26	35	49	
Earl Ingarfield	C	66	13	21	34	18	
Brian Cullen	C	42	11	19	30	6	
Johnny Wilson (1–2)	L	56	14	12	26	24	
Pat Hannigan	L	53	11	9	20	24	
Ted Hampson	C	69	6	14	20	4	
Harry Howell	D	70	7	10	17	62	
Floyd Smith	R	29	5	9	14	0	
Irv Spencer	D	56	1	8	9	30	
Jack Hanna	D	46	1	8	9	34	
Ken Schinkel	R	38	2	6	8	18	
Don Johns	D	63	1	7	8	34	
Jim Morrison	D	19	1	6	7	6	
Orland Kurtenbach	C	10	0	6	6	2	
Lou Fontinato	D	53	2	3	5	100	
Len Ronson	L	13	2	1	3	10	
Jean Ratelle	C	3	2	1	3	0	
Dave Balon	L	13	1	2	3	8	
Eddie Shack (1–2)	L	12	1	2	3	17	

		REGULAR SEASON					*POSTSEASON*
PLAYER	*POS*	*GP*	*G*	*A*	*PTS*	*PIM*	no postseason play
Danny Belisle	R	4	2	0	2	0	
Bob Kabel	C	4	0	2	2	2	
Al LeBrun	D	4	0	2	2	4	
Larry Popein	C	4	0	1	1	0	
Bob Cunningham	C	3	0	1	1	0	
Rod Gilbert	R	1	0	1	1	2	
Leon Rochefort	R	16	1	0	0	0	
Lorne Worsley	G	59	0	0	0	10	
Ron Hutchinson	C	9	0	0	0	0	
Jack McCartan	G	8	0	0	0	0	
Wayne Hall	L	4	0	0	0	0	
Phil Latreille	R	4	0	0	0	2	
Marcel Paille	G	4	0	0	0	0	
Noel Price	D	1	0	0	0	2	
Joe Schaefer	G	1	0	0	0	0	

		REGULAR SEASON					*POSTSEASON*
GOALTENDER		*GP*	*MIN*	*GA*	*SH*	*GAA*	no postseason play
Lorne Worsley	(20-29-8)	59	3473	191 (2)	1	3.30	
Joe Schaefer	(0-1-0)	1	47	3	0	3.83	
Marcel Paille	(1-2-1)	4	240	16	0	4.00	
Jack McCartan	(1-6-1)	8	440	35 (1)	1	4.77	

BOSTON 15-42-13   43   6th   Milt Schmidt
Bruins

		REGULAR SEASON					*POSTSEASON*
PLAYER	*POS*	*GP*	*G*	*A*	*PTS*	*PIM*	no postseason play
Jerry Toppazzini	R	67	15	35	50	35	
Don McKenney	C	68	26	23	49	22	
Charlie Burns	C	62	15	26	41	16	
John Bucyk	L	70	19	20	39	48	
Doug Mohns	F	65	12	21	33	63	
Bronco Horvath	C	47	15	15	30	15	
Vic Stasiuk (1–2)	L	46	5	25	30	35	
Jim Bartlett	L	63	15	9	24	95	
Leo Boivin	D	57	6	17	23	50	
Andre Pronovost (2–2)	L	47	11	11	22	30	
Leo Labine (1–2)	R	40	7	12	19	34	
Murray Oliver (2–2)	C	*21	6	10	16	8	
Willie O'Ree	R	43	4	10	14	26	
Fern Flaman	D	62	2	9	11	59	
Dallas Smith	D	70	1	9	10	79	
Bob Armstrong	D	54	0	10	10	72	
Gerry Oullette	R	34	5	4	9	0	
Tom McCarthy	L	24	4	5	9	0	
Aut Erickson	D	68	2	6	8	65	
J-G Gendron (1–2)	L	13	1	7	8	24	
Orval Tessier	C	32	3	4	7	0	
Gary Aldcorn (2–2)	L	*21	2	3	5	12	
Dick Meissner	R	9	0	1	1	2	

		REGULAR SEASON					*POSTSEASON*
PLAYER	POS	GP	G	A	PTS	PIM	*no postseason play*
Bruce Gamble	G	52	0	0	0	14	
Don Simmons	G	18	0	0	0	6	
Billy Carter	C	8	0	0	0	2	
Art Chisholm	C	3	0	0	0	0	
Ted Green	D	1	0	0	0	2	

		REGULAR SEASON				*POSTSEASON*
GOALTENDER		GP	MIN	GA	SH	GAA	*no postseason play*
Jerry Toppazzini		1	1	0	0	0.00	
Don Simmons	(3-9-6)	18	1079	58 (1)	1	3.23	
Bruce Gamble	(12-33-7)	52	3120	193 (2)	0	3.71	

TEAM TOTALS

								Per Game			
TEAM	GP	G	A	PTS	PIM	GA	SH	G	A	PIM	GA
Montreal	70	254	410	664	811	188	6	**3.63**	**5.86**	11.59	2.69
Toronto	70	234	379	613	844	**176**	2	3.34	5.41	12.06	**2.51**
Chicago	70	198	344	542	**1072**	180	6	2.83	4.91	**15.31**	2.57
Detroit	70	195	319	514	655	215	2	2.79	4.56	9.36	3.07
New York	70	204	334	538	591	248	2	2.91	4.77	8.44	3.54
Boston	70	176	292	468	810	254	1	2.51	4.17	11.57	3.63
	420	1261	2078	3339	4783	1261	19	3.00	4.95	11.39	3.00

PLAYOFFS

SERIES "A"
Montreal 6, Chicago 2
Chicago 4, Montreal 3
Chicago 2, Montreal 1 (OT)
Montreal 5, Chicago 2
Chicago 3, Montreal 0
Chicago 3, Montreal 0

CHICAGO, 4–2

SERIES "C"
Chicago 3, Detroit 2
Detroit 3, Chicago 1
Chicago 3, Detroit 1
Detroit 2, Chicago 1
Chicago 6, Detroit 3
Chicago 5, Detroit 1

**CHICAGO WINS
STANLEY CUP, 4–2**

SERIES "B"
Toronto 3, Detroit 2 (OT)
Detroit 4, Toronto 2
Detroit 2, Toronto 0
Detroit 4, Toronto 1
Detroit 3, Toronto 2

DETROIT, 4–1

1960-1961

ALL-STAR TEAMS

First Team
G — Johnny Bower, TOR
D — Doug Harvey, MTL

Second Team
G — Glenn Hall, CHI
D — Pierre Pilote, CHI

First Team
D — Marcel Pronovost, DET
C — Jean Beliveau, MTL
R — Bernie Geoffrion, MTL
L — Frank Mahovlich, TOR

Second Team
D — Allan Stanley, TOR
C — Henri Richard, MTL
R — Gordie Howe, DET
L — Dickie Moore, MTL

INDIVIDUAL TROPHY WINNERS

HART TROPHY (Most Valuable Player): Bernie Geoffrion, MTL
LADY BYNG TROPHY (Gentlemanly Conduct): Red Kelly, TOR
VEZINA TROPHY (Best Goaltender): Johnny Bower, TOR
CALDER MEMORIAL TROPHY (Best Rookie): Dave Keon, TOR
ART ROSS TROPHY (Scoring Leader): Bernie Geoffrion, MTL
JAMES NORRIS TROPHY (Best Defenseman): Doug Harvey, MTL

1961-1962
Glenn Hall

By the end of the 1961-62 season, one NHL player was sitting on a streak of nearly 500 consecutive games played. This notable string was made even more remarkable by the fact that this player plied his trade in probably the most nerve-wracking position on the ice.

Born in 1931, goaltender Glenn Hall saw his first professional action at the age of 20 with the Indianapolis Capitals of the American Hockey League. After putting together a solid campaign in which he led the league in minutes played, the Saskatchewan native moved on to the Western Hockey League in 1952. Midway through his first campaign for Edmonton, Hall was called up by the Red Wings, as a substitute for the injured Terry Sawchuk. In six games with Detroit, he posted a stellar 4-1-1 mark, allowing only 10 goals (1.67) and earning a shutout. Back in Edmonton in 1953-54, Hall slipped a bit, finishing last among WHL qualifying netminders. The following year, he rebounded, lowering his GAA to 2.83, which placed him third. In February of 1955, Hall returned to Detroit for a pair of games, winning both while allowing only a single tally in each. While in the minors, he gained a reputation for reliability, frequently appearing in all of his team's contests, a durability which would become his trademark.

In 1954-55, Hall joined the Red Wings for good, playing in each of the club's 70 games. In his first NHL season, he blanked a league-leading 12 opponents, along with a 2.10 GAA and was the recipient of the Calder Trophy, given to the circuit's top rookie. After another 70-game campaign the following year, Hall was traded to Chicago as part of a six-player deal. In Chicago, he continued to play in every game, but never led the league in GAA or shutouts, not surprising considering the Blackhawks perennial cellar dwelling place. As the 1950s merged into the 1960s, Chicago's fortunes rose behind a cluster of new offensive stars. Hall began to reap the dividends of this turnaround, leading the NHL in shutouts in both 1959-60 and 1960-61.

Like many others of his ilk, Hall toiled under a terrific mental strain. His reaction was to vomit before every game. This got to be such a habit that his teammates expected Hall's trip to the men's room, not feeling comfortable about the night's match until their goalie had made an offering to the porcelain god. Despite these upheavals, Hall played game after game, never missing a start. By the end of the 1960-61 season, he had played six consecutive seasons without a break — more than 400 games.

During the 1961-62 campaign, Hall took his customary place between the pipes, again appearing in all 70 games. In nine of them, he shut out his foe, leading the NHL for the third straight time. His rival, Montreal's Jacques Plante (2.37) earned the lowest GAA. On the offensive end, Hall's teammate, Bobby Hull (50-34-84), became the third member of the 50-goal club, sharing the overall points lead with assists leader, the Rangers' Andy Bathgate (56). In addition, Montreal's Lou Fontinato led all NHL toughmen with 167 penalty minutes.

In the team standings, Montreal (42-14-14, 98) finished on the top shelf for the fifth year in a row, well ahead of playoff qualifiers Toronto, Chicago and New York. Detroit and Boston fell out of the running, the latter with a moribund 47-loss season.

In the playoffs, the league leaders once again got blindsided by the Blackhawks, squandering a two game lead. In the other slate, Toronto and New York also played a six game set, with the Leafs prevailing in the end. In the finals, Toronto won the first match, 4–1, then took the next 3–2, giving them a commanding lead. Hall posted a shutout in the next game (3–0), then the Blackhawks forged a tie with a 4–1 triumph. In the fifth game, Toronto buried Hall and the Hawks 8–4, then completed their drive to the Cup with a 2–1 win, giving Toronto its first title in eleven years.

Bobby Hull, with eight goals, led all playoff snipers, while his teammate Stan Mikita (6-15-21) set a new record for assists and points. In goal, Toronto's Johnny Bower (2.07) allowed the fewest goals.

A month into the following season, Hall's fabulous streak came to an end, as he was lifted partway through a match with Montreal because of a back injury. Over the next several seasons, he continued to star for the Blackhawks, finally leading the NHL in GAA (2.38) in 1966-67 at the age of 36. Following this triumph, Hall was claimed by the St. Louis Blues in the Expansion Draft, a locale where he spent the final four years of his career. In the second of those campaigns, he won the Vezina Trophy, sharing it with his former rival Jacques Plante.

Although finishing among the career leaders in games, wins and shutouts, Hall is most remembered for his singular streak. In all likelihood, this barefaced warrior's run of 503 consecutive games in goal will never be surpassed.

STANDINGS

TEAM	GP	W	L	T	PTS	GF	GA
MONTREAL	70	42	14	14	98	259	166
TORONTO	70	37	22	11	85	232	180
CHICAGO	70	31	26	13	75	217	186
NEW YORK	70	26	32	12	64	195	207
DETROIT	70	23	33	14	60	184	219
BOSTON	70	15	47	8	38	177	306

LEADERS

PLAYER	TM	GP	G	A	PTS	PIM
Bobby Hull	CHI	70	50	34	84	35
Andy Bathgate	NY	70	28	56	84	44
Gordie Howe	DET	70	33	44	77	54
Stan Mikita	CHI	70	25	52	77	97
Frank Mahovlich	TOR	70	33	38	71	87
Alex Delvecchio	DET	70	26	43	69	18
Ralph Backstrom	MTL	66	27	38	65	29
Norm Ullman	DET	70	26	38	64	54
Bill Hay	CHI	60	11	52	63	34
Claude Provost	MTL	70	33	29	62	22

GOALS	
Hull, CHI	50
Howe, DET	33
Provost, MTL	33
Mahovlich, TOR	33
Tremblay, MTL	32

ASSISTS	
Bathgate, NY	56
Hay, CHI	52
Mikita, CHI	52
Howe, DET	44
Delvecchio, DET	43

GOALTENDER	TM	GP	MIN	GA	SH	GAA
Jacques Plante	MTL	70	4200	166	4	2.37
Johnny Bower	TOR	59	3540	151 (1)	2	2.56
Glenn Hall	CHI	70	4200	185 (1)	9	2.64
Hank Bassen	DET	27	1620	75 (1)	3	2.78
Lorne Worsley	NY	60	3531	173 (1)	2	2.94
Terry Sawchuk	DET	43	2580	141 (2)	5	3.28
Don Head	BOS	38	2280	161	2	4.24
Bruce Gamble	BOS	28	1680	121 (2)	1	4.32

PENALTY MINUTES	
Fontinato, MTL	167
Green, BOS	116
Pulford, TOR	98
Three tied with	97

SHUTOUTS	
Hall, CHI	9
Sawchuk, DET	5
Plante, MTL	4
Bassen, DET	3
Three tied with	2

MONTREAL   42-14-14   98   1st   Toe Blake
Canadiens

		REGULAR SEASON				POSTSEASON				
PLAYER	POS	GP	G	A	PTS	PIM	GP	G	A	PTS	PIM
Ralph Backstrom	C	66	27	38	65	29	5	0	1	1	6
Claude Provost	R	70	33	29	62	22	6	2	2	4	2
Bernie Geoffrion	R	62	23	36	59	36	5	0	1	1	6
Gilles Tremblay	L	70	32	22	54	28	6	1	0	1	2

1961-1962 371

PLAYER	POS	REGULAR SEASON					POSTSEASON				
		GP	G	A	PTS	PIM	GP	G	A	PTS	PIM
Bill Hicke	R	70	20	31	51	42	6	0	2	2	14
Henri Richard	C	54	21	29	50	48					
Jean-Guy Talbot	D	70	5	42	47	90	6	1	1	2	10
Don Marshall	L	66	18	28	46	12	6	0	1	1	2
Bobby Rousseau	R	70	21	24	45	26	6	0	2	2	0
Dickie Moore	L	57	19	22	41	54	6	4	2	6	8
Jean Beliveau	C	43	18	23	41	36	6	2	1	3	4
Phil Goyette	C	69	7	27	34	18	6	1	4	5	2
Marcel Bonin	L	33	7	14	21	41					
J.C. Tremblay	D	70	3	17	20	18	6	0	2	2	2
Tom Johnson	D	62	1	17	18	45	6	0	1	1	0
Lou Fontinato	D	54	2	13	15	167	6	0	1	1	23
Al MacNeil	D	61	1	7	8	74	5	0	0	0	2
Red Berenson	C	4	1	2	3	4	5	2	0	2	0
Jean Gauthier	D	12	0	1	1	10					
Jacques Plante	G	70	0	0	0	0	6	0	0	0	0
Billy Carter	C	7	0	0	0	4					
Chuck Hamilton	L	1	0	0	0	0					
Keith McCreary	R						1	0	0	0	0

GOALTENDER	REGULAR SEASON					POSTSEASON				
	GP	MIN	GA	SH	GAA	GP	MIN	GA	SH	GAA
Jacques Plante (42-14-14)	70	4200	166	4	2.37	6	360	19	0	3.17

TORONTO 37-22-11 85 2nd Punch Imlach
Maple Leafs

PLAYER	POS	REGULAR SEASON					POSTSEASON				
		GP	G	A	PTS	PIM	GP	G	A	PTS	PIM
Frank Mahovlich	L	70	33	38	71	87	12	6	6	12	29
Dave Keon	C	64	26	35	61	2	12	5	3	8	0
George Armstrong	C	70	21	32	53	27	12	7	5	12	2
Red Kelly	D	58	22	27	49	6	12	4	6	10	0
Bob Nevin	R	69	15	30	45	10	12	2	4	6	6
Bob Pulford	L	70	18	21	39	98	12	7	1	8	24
Tim Horton	D	70	10	28	38	88	12	3	13	16	16
Dick Duff	L	51	17	20	37	37	12	3	10	13	20
Bert Olmstead	L	56	13	23	36	10	4	0	1	1	0
Allan Stanley	D	60	9	26	35	24	12	0	3	3	6
Billy Harris	C	67	15	10	25	14	12	2	1	3	2
Carl Brewer	D	67	1	22	23	89	8	0	2	2	22
Eddie Shack	L	44	7	14	21	62	9	0	0	0	18
Ed Litzenberger (2-2)	R	37	10	10	20	14	10	0	2	2	4
Ron Stewart	C	60	8	9	17	14	11	1	6	7	4
Bob Baun	D	65	4	11	15	94	12	0	3	3	19
Al Arbour	D	52	1	5	6	68	8	0	0	0	6
John MacMillan	R	31	1	0	1	8	3	0	0	0	0
Les Kozak	L	12	1	0	1	2					
Johnny Bower	G	59	0	1	1	4	10	0	0	0	0
Don Simmons	G	9	0	0	0	0	3	0	0	0	0
Larry Hillman	D	5	0	0	0	4					

PLAYER	POS	REGULAR SEASON					POSTSEASON				
		GP	G	A	PTS	PIM	GP	G	A	PTS	PIM
Arnie Brown	D	2	0	0	0	0					
Larry Keenan	L	2	0	0	0	0					
Gerry Cheevers	G	2	0	0	0	0					
Brian Conacher	C	1	0	0	0	0					
Alex Faulkner	C	1	0	0	0	0					

GOALTENDER		REGULAR SEASON					POSTSEASON				
		GP	MIN	GA	SH	GAA	GP	MIN	GA	SH	GAA
Don Simmons	(5-3-1)	9	540	21	1	2.33	3	165	8	0	2.91
Johnny Bower	(31-18-10)	59	3540	151 (1)	2	2.56	10	579	20	0	**2.07**
Gerry Cheevers	(1-1-0)	2	120	6 (1)	0	3.00					

CHICAGO Blackhawks 31-26-13 75 3rd Rudy Pilous

PLAYER	POS	REGULAR SEASON					POSTSEASON				
		GP	G	A	PTS	PIM	GP	G	A	PTS	PIM
Bobby Hull	L	70	50	34	84	35	12	8	6	14	12
Stan Mikita	C	70	25	52	77	97	12	6	15	21	19
Bill Hay	C	60	11	52	63	34	12	3	7	10	18
Bronco Horvath	C	68	17	29	46	21	12	4	1	5	6
Pierre Pilote	D	59	7	35	42	97	12	0	7	7	8
Alvin McDonald	L	65	22	18	40	8	12	6	6	12	0
Kenny Wharram	R	62	14	23	37	24	12	3	4	7	8
Murray Balfour	R	49	15	15	30	72	12	1	1	2	15
Eric Nesterenko	R	68	15	14	29	97	12	0	5	5	22
Ron Murphy	L	60	12	16	28	41					
Elmer Vasko	D	64	2	22	24	87	12	0	0	0	4
Jerry Melnyk	C	63	5	16	21	6	7	0	0	0	2
Jack Evans	D	70	3	14	17	80	12	0	0	0	26
Reg Fleming	L	70	7	9	16	71	12	2	2	4	27
Dollard St. Laurent	D	64	0	13	13	44	12	0	4	4	18
Bob Turner	D	69	8	2	10	52	12	1	0	1	6
Ron Maki	R	16	4	6	10	2					
Wayne Hillman	D	19	0	2	2	14					
Glenn Hall	G	70	0	0	0	12	12	0	0	0	0
Murray Hall	R	2	0	0	0	0					
Merv Kuryluk	L						2	0	0	0	0

GOALTENDER		REGULAR SEASON					POSTSEASON				
		GP	MIN	GA	SH	GAA	GP	MIN	GA	SH	GAA
Glenn Hall	(31-26-13)	70	**4200**	185 (1)	9	2.64	12	720	31	2	2.58

NEW YORK Rangers 26-32-12 64 4th Doug Harvey

PLAYER	POS	REGULAR SEASON					POSTSEASON				
		GP	G	A	PTS	PIM	GP	G	A	PTS	PIM
Andy Bathgate	R	70	28	56	84	44	6	1	2	3	4
Dean Prentice	L	68	22	38	60	20	3	0	2	2	0
Earl Ingarfield	C	70	26	31	57	18	6	3	2	5	2
Andy Hebenton	R	70	18	24	42	10	6	1	2	3	0

1961–1962

PLAYER	POS	REGULAR SEASON					POSTSEASON				
		GP	G	A	PTS	PIM	GP	G	A	PTS	PIM
Camille Henry	C	60	23	15	38	8	5	0	0	0	0
Doug Harvey	D	69	6	24	30	42	6	0	1	1	2
Ken Schinkel	R	65	7	21	28	17	2	1	0	1	0
Ted Hampson	C	68	4	24	28	10	6	0	1	1	0
Jean-Guy Gendron	L	69	14	11	25	71	6	3	1	4	2
Al Langlois	D	69	7	18	25	90	6	0	1	1	2
Pat Hannigan	L	56	8	14	22	34	4	0	0	0	2
Harry Howell	D	66	6	15	21	89	6	0	1	1	8
Dave Balon	L	30	4	11	15	11	6	2	3	5	2
Johnny Wilson	L	40	11	3	14	14	6	2	2	4	4
Jean Ratelle	C	31	4	8	12	4					
Irv Spencer	D	43	2	10	12	31	1	0	0	0	2
Larry Cahan	D	57	2	7	9	85	6	0	0	0	10
Vic Hadfield	L	44	3	1	4	22	4	0	0	0	2
Pete Goegan (2–2)	D	7	0	2	2	6					
Lorne Worsley	G	60	0	0	0	12	6	0	0	0	0
Marcel Paille	G	10	0	0	0	0					
Jack Bownass	D	4	0	0	0	4					
Mel Pearson	L	3	0	0	0	2					
Bob Cunningham	C	1	0	0	0	0					
Rod Gilbert	R	1	0	0	0	0	4	2	3	5	4
Dan Olesevich	G	1	0	0	0	0					
Dave Dryden	G	1	0	0	0	0					

GOALTENDER		REGULAR SEASON					POSTSEASON				
		GP	MIN	GA	SH	GAA	GP	MIN	GA	SH	GAA
Marcel Paille	(4-4-2)	10	600	28	0	2.80					
Lorne Worsley	(22-27-9)	60	3531	173 (1)	2	2.94	6	384	21	0	3.28
Dan Olesevich	(0-0-1)	1	29	2	0	4.14					
Dave Dryden	(0-1-0)	1	40	3	0	4.50					

DETROIT 23-33-14 60 5th Sid Abel
Red Wings

PLAYER	POS	REGULAR SEASON					POSTSEASON
		GP	G	A	PTS	PIM	no postseason play
Gordie Howe	R	70	33	44	77	54	
Alex Delvecchio	C	70	26	43	69	18	
Norm Ullman	C	70	26	38	64	54	
Vic Stasiuk	L	59	15	28	43	45	
Bill Gadsby	D	70	7	30	37	88	
Ed Litzenberger (1–2)	R	32	8	12	20	4	
Claude Laforge	L	38	10	9	19	20	
Bruce MacGregor	C	65	6	12	18	16	
Marcel Pronovost	D	70	4	14	18	38	
Warren Godfrey	D	69	4	13	17	84	
Howie Glover	R	39	7	8	15	44	
Parker MacDonald	C	32	5	7	12	8	
Marc Boileau	C	54	5	6	11	8	
Al Johnson	R	31	5	6	11	14	
Len Lunde	L	23	2	9	11	4	

		REGULAR SEASON					POSTSEASON
PLAYER	POS	GP	G	A	PTS	PIM	no postseason play
Val Fonteyne	L	70	5	5	10	4	
Pete Goegan (1–2)	D	39	5	5	10	24	
Larry Jeffrey	L	18	5	3	8	20	
Leo Labine	R	48	3	4	7	30	
Gerry Odrowski	D	69	1	6	7	24	
Howie Young	D	30	0	2	2	67	
Forbes Kennedy	C	14	1	0	1	8	
Chuck Holmes	R	8	1	0	1	4	
Noel Price	D	20	0	1	1	6	
Hubert Martin	C	1	0	1	1	0	
Terry Sawchuk	G	43	0	0	0	12	
Hank Bassen	G	27	0	0	0	8	
Bob Dillabough	C	5	0	0	0	2	
Wayne Rivers	R	2	0	0	0	0	
Jake Hendrickson	D	1	0	0	0	2	
Lowell MacDonald	L	1	0	0	0	2	

		REGULAR SEASON					POSTSEASON
GOALTENDER		GP	MIN	GA	SH	GAA	no postseason play
Hank Bassen	(9-12-6)	27	1620	75 (1)	3	2.78	
Terry Sawchuk	(14-21-8)	43	2580	141 (2)	5	3.28	

BOSTON 15-47-8 38 6th Phil Watson
Bruins

		REGULAR SEASON					POSTSEASON
PLAYER	POS	GP	G	A	PTS	PIM	no postseason play
John Bucyk	L	67	20	40	60	32	
Don McKenney	C	70	22	33	55	10	
Jerry Toppazzini	R	70	19	31	50	26	
Murray Oliver	C	70	17	29	46	21	
Doug Mohns	F	69	16	29	45	74	
Cliff Pennington	C	70	9	32	41	2	
Charlie Burns	C	70	11	17	28	43	
Andre Pronovost	L	70	15	8	23	74	
Leo Boivin	D	65	5	18	23	70	
Wayne Connelly	R	61	8	12	20	34	
Terry Gray	R	42	8	7	15	15	
Tommy Williams	C	26	6	6	12	2	
Ted Green	D	66	3	8	11	116	
Ed Westfall	R	63	2	9	11	53	
Bob Beckett	C	34	7	2	9	14	
Pat Stapleton	D	69	2	5	7	42	
Larry Leach	C	28	2	5	7	18	
Dick Meissner	R	66	3	3	6	13	
Bob Armstrong	D	9	2	1	3	20	
Don Head	G	38	0	0	0	14	
Bruce Gamble	G	28	0	0	0	4	
Orland Kurtenbach	C	8	0	0	0	6	
Dallas Smith	D	7	0	0	0	10	
Ed Chadwick	G	4	0	0	0	0	

	REGULAR SEASON					POSTSEASON
GOALTENDER	GP	MIN	GA	SH	GAA	no postseason play
Don Head	(9-26-3) 38	2280	161	2	4.24	
Bruce Gamble	(6-18-4) 28	1680	121 (2)	1	4.32	
Ed Chadwick	(0-3-1) 4	240	22	0	5.50	

TEAM TOTALS

TEAM	GP	G	A	PTS	PIM	GA	SH	*Per Game* G	A	PIM	GA
Montreal	70	**259**	422	**681**	818	**166**	4	**3.70**	6.03	11.69	**2.37**
Toronto	70	232	361	593	762	180	3	3.31	5.16	10.89	2.57
Chicago	70	217	372	589	**894**	186	9	3.10	5.31	**12.77**	2.66
New York	70	195	333	528	668	207	2	2.79	4.76	9.54	2.96
Detroit	70	184	306	490	684	219	8	2.63	4.37	9.77	3.13
Boston	70	177	295	472	712	306	3	2.53	4.21	10.17	4.37
	420	1264	2089	3353	4538	1264	29	3.01	4.97	10.80	3.01

PLAYOFFS

SERIES "A"
Montreal 2, Chicago 1
Montreal 4, Chicago 3
Chicago 4, Montreal 1
Chicago 5, Montreal 3
Chicago 4, Montreal 3
Chicago 2, Montreal 0

CHICAGO, 4-2

SERIES "B"
Toronto 4, New York 2
Toronto 2, New York 1
New York 5, Toronto 4
New York 4, Toronto 2
Toronto 3, New York 2 (OT)
Toronto 7, New York 1

TORONTO, 4-2

SERIES "C"
Toronto 4, Chicago 1
Toronto 3, Chicago 2
Chicago 3, Toronto 0
Chicago 4, Toronto 1
Toronto 8, Chicago 4
Toronto 2, Chicago 1

**TORONTO WINS
STANLEY CUP, 4-2**

ALL-STAR TEAMS

First Team
G — Jacques Plante, MTL
D — Doug Harvey, NY
D — Jean-Guy Talbot, MTL
C — Stan Mikita, CHI
R — Andy Bathgate, NY
L — Bobby Hull, CHI

Second Team
G — Glenn Hall, CHI
D — Carl Brewer, TOR
D — Pierre Pilote, CHI
C — Dave Keon, TOR
R — Gordie Howe, DET
L — Frank Mahovlich, TOR

INDIVIDUAL TROPHY WINNERS
HART TROPHY (Most Valuable Player): Jacques Plante, MTL
LADY BYNG TROPHY (Gentlemanly Conduct): Dave Keon, TOR
VEZINA TROPHY (Best Goaltender): Jacques Plante, MTL
CALDER MEMORIAL TROPHY (Best Rookie): Bobby Rousseau, MTL
ART ROSS TROPHY (Scoring Leader): Bobby Hull, CHI
JAMES NORRIS TROPHY (Best Defenseman): Doug Harvey, NY

1962-1963
Toronto Maple Leafs

Finally breaking Montreal's quintet of regular season titles, another NHL club rose to the forefront in 1962-63, copping the flag after a spirited duel. And unlike the Canadiens' champions of the two previous years, this group would finish the job.

Like Montreal, the city of Toronto, Ontario, fielded a variety of teams in the National Hockey Association, the immediate antecedent of the NHL. Clubs named the Tecumsehs and Blueshirts iced teams during most years of the NHA, with the latter winning the Cup in 1914. With the formation of the NHL in 1917, a new Toronto team was formed — the Arenas — which won Lord Stanley's Cup after the league's first season.

The St. Patricks came into being in 1919, but Toronto's NHL entry was finally given the nickname Maple Leafs in 1927 after Conn Smythe purchased the club. During Smythe's era, the team featured some of its strongest entries, most notably the 1931-32 version, which carted home the Cup. Spurring this entry, and the three division winners to follow, was the famed Kid Line — featuring youngsters Harvey Jackson, Joe Primeau and Charlie Conacher.

The 1940s was also a strong decade for the Maple Leafs. In the first half, they won a pair of Cups (1942 and 1945), snatching the former out from under the Red Wings in a singular comeback. Later, the Leafs became the first team to capture three Cups in a row (1947–49), then added another in 1951 courtesy of Bill Barilko's final goal.

Like most of the NHL, the Leafs sat back and watched the Red Wings and Canadiens duke it out during the rest of the 1950s. After the Blackhawks finally broke the stranglehold in 1961, Toronto followed up with a Cup of its own. As the league was about to find out, the team wasn't going to let go of their prize without a fight.

Over the fall of 1962 and into the winter of 1963, the NHL featured its best race, as all but New York and Boston — which would finish fifth and sixth — were in the running for the championship. At the beginning of March, Chicago (74) owned a five-point bulge over Toronto (69), while Montreal (66) and Detroit (63) were still in the picture. Then, over the final ten games of the schedule, Chicago slumped badly, winning only twice. During the same time, Toronto (35-23-12, 82) only lost two, vaulting them into the lead. Montreal also played well, and didn't lose any of their final four contests, although they didn't win any either. On the season's final day, Chicago finally won, pulling them into second, one point behind the Leafs. On the same day, the Canadiens skated to their record 23rd tie, ending two points behind Chicago. The Red Wings also finished with a rush, winning their final four, ending two behind Montreal. In all, only five points separated the top four clubs.

Although the Leafs boasted several fine individual performances, only Frank Mahovlich (36-37-73) cracked the top ten. Instead, Gordie Howe (38-48-86) skated off with the scoring crown, netting the most goals to boot. In addition, Montreal's Henri Richard (50) amassed the most assists, while Detroit enforcer Howie Young (273) obliterated the NHL's single season penalty mark. In net, Jacques Plante (2.49) (Montreal) squeezed out a GAA win over Toronto's Don Simmons (2.50), with the former shutting out the most foes as well (5), a mark he shared with Chicago's Glenn Hall.

In the postseason, Toronto dispatched Montreal in five games in one opening series, while the Red Wings outlasted the Blackhawks in six games in the other. In the finals, Toronto took the first two games, both by 4–2 margins. The Red Wings responded with a 3–2 win in the third match, then the Leafs barred the door. In the fourth contest, Toronto won its third 4–2 game of the series, then finished off Detroit with a 3–1 victory, becoming one of a handful of clubs with more than one set of back-to-back championships.

Like the regular season, the Leafs didn't showcase a single offensive leader in the playoffs. Chicago's Bobby Hull (8) scored the most goals, while Detroit's Gordie Howe and Norm Ullman contributed 16 points, the latter with a league best 12 assists. In net, the Leafs did show their strength, as Johnny Bower (1.60) enjoyed a fine playoff run.

The following season, the Leafs won the ultimate prize yet again, following up with another three years later. Since the latter (1967), the team has fallen short each season, though not for lack of trying. So, it is with great fondness that Toronto hockey fans recall their champions from the 1960s, champions that did not rely on superstars to lead them to glory, but instead relied upon teamwork, showing everyone the way the game is meant to be played.

1962-1963 379

STANDINGS

TEAM	GP	W	L	T	PTS	GF	GA
TORONTO	70	35	23	12	82	221	180
CHICAGO	70	32	21	17	81	194	178
MONTREAL	70	28	19	23	79	225	183
DETROIT	70	32	25	13	77	200	194
NEW YORK	70	22	36	12	56	211	233
BOSTON	70	14	39	17	45	198	281

LEADERS

PLAYER	TM	GP	G	A	PTS	PIM
Gordie Howe	DET	70	38	48	86	100
Andy Bathgate	NY	70	35	46	81	54
Stan Mikita	CHI	65	31	45	76	69
Frank Mahovlich	TOR	67	36	37	73	56
Henri Richard	MTL	67	23	50	73	57
Jean Beliveau	MTL	69	18	49	67	68
John Bucyk	BOS	69	27	39	66	36
Alex Delvecchio	DET	70	20	44	64	8
Bobby Hull	CHI	65	31	31	62	27
Murray Oliver	BOS	65	22	40	62	38

GOALTENDER	TM	GP	MIN	GA	SH	GAA
Jacques Plante	MTL	56	3320	135	5	2.49
Don Simmons	TOR	28	1680	70	1	2.50
Terry Sawchuk	DET	48	2775	117 (2)	3	2.53
Glenn Hall	CHI	66	3910	166	5	2.55
Johnny Bower	TOR	42	2520	109 (1)	1	2.60
Lorne Worsley	NY	67	3980	217 (2)	2	3.27
Eddie Johnston	BOS	50	2913	193 (3)	1	3.97

GOALS
Howe, DET	38
Henry, NY	37
Mahovlich, TOR	36
Bathgate, NY	35
MacDonald, DET	33

ASSISTS
Richard, MTL	50
Beliveau, MTL	49
Howe, DET	48
Bathgate, NY	46
Mikita, CHI	45

PENALTY MINUTES
Young, DET	273
Brewer, TOR	168
Fontinato, MTL	141
Green, BOS	117
Gadsby, DET	116

SHUTOUTS
Hall, CHI	5
Plante, MTL	5
Sawchuk, DET	3
Worsley, NY	2
Four tied with	1

TORONTO   35-23-12   82   1st   Punch Imlach
Maple Leafs

		REGULAR SEASON				POSTSEASON			
PLAYER	POS	GP	G	A	PTS	PIM	GP	G	A	PTS	PIM
Frank Mahovlich	L	67	36	37	73	56	9	0	2	2	8
Red Kelly	D	66	20	40	60	8	10	2	6	8	6
Dave Keon	C	68	28	28	56	2	10	7	5	12	0
Bob Pulford	L	70	19	25	44	49	10	2	5	7	14
George Armstrong	C	70	19	24	43	27	10	3	6	9	4
Dick Duff	L	69	16	19	35	56	10	4	1	5	2
Bob Nevin	R	58	12	21	33	4	10	3	0	3	2
Ron Stewart	C	63	16	16	32	26	10	4	0	4	2
Billy Harris	C	65	8	24	32	22	10	0	1	1	0

380 The National Hockey League, 1917–1967

		REGULAR SEASON				POSTSEASON				
PLAYER	POS	GP	G	A	PTS	PIM	GP	G	A	PTS	PIM
Eddie Shack	L	63	16	9	25	97	10	2	1	3	11
Tim Horton	D	70	6	19	25	69	10	1	3	4	10
Carl Brewer	D	70	2	23	25	168	10	0	1	1	12
Kent Douglas	D	70	7	15	22	105	10	1	1	2	2
Allan Stanley	D	61	4	15	19	22	10	1	6	7	8
Ed Litzenberger	R	58	5	13	18	10	9	1	2	3	6
Bob Baun	D	48	4	8	12	65	10	0	3	3	6
Bronco Horvath (1–2)	C	10	0	4	4	12					
Norm Armstrong	D	7	1	1	2	2					
John MacMillan	R	6	1	1	2	6	1	0	0	0	0
Al Arbour	D	4	1	0	1	4					
Jim Mikol	L	4	0	1	1	2					
Rod Seiling	D	1	0	1	1	0					
Johnny Bower	G	42	0	0	0	2	10	0	1	1	0
Don Simmons	G	28	0	0	0	0					
Larry Hillman	D	5	0	0	0	2					
Andre Champagne	L	2	0	0	0	0					
Bruce Draper	C	1	0	0	0	0					

		REGULAR SEASON					POSTSEASON				
GOALTENDER		GP	MIN	GA	SH	GAA	GP	MIN	GA	SH	GAA
Don Simmons	(15-8-5)	28	1680	70	1	2.50					
Johnny Bower	(20-15-7)	42	2520	109 (1)	1	2.60	10	600	16	2	1.60

CHICAGO 32-21-17   81   2nd   Rudy Pilous
Blackhawks

		REGULAR SEASON				POSTSEASON				
PLAYER	POS	GP	G	A	PTS	PIM	GP	G	A	PTS	PIM
Stan Mikita	C	65	31	45	76	69	6	3	2	5	2
Bobby Hull	L	65	31	31	62	27	5	8	2	10	4
Alvin McDonald	L	69	20	41	61	12	6	2	3	5	9
Bill Hay	C	64	12	33	45	36	6	3	2	5	6
Kenny Wharram	R	55	20	18	38	17	6	1	5	6	0
Ron Murphy	L	68	18	16	34	28	1	0	0	0	0
Murray Balfour	R	65	10	23	33	75	6	0	2	2	12
Len Lunde	L	60	6	22	28	30	4	0	0	0	2
Eric Nesterenko	R	67	12	15	27	106	6	2	3	5	8
Pierre Pilote	D	59	8	18	26	57	6	0	8	8	8
Ron Maki	R	65	7	17	24	35	6	0	1	1	2
Al MacNeil	D	70	2	19	21	100	4	0	1	1	4
Reg Fleming	L	64	7	7	14	99	6	0	0	0	27
Elmer Vasko	D	64	4	9	13	70	6	0	1	1	8
Wayne Hillman	D	67	3	5	8	74	6	0	2	2	2
Jack Evans	D	68	0	8	8	46	6	0	0	0	4
Bob Turner	D	70	3	3	6	20	6	0	0	0	6
Glenn Hall	G	66	0	0	0	0	6	0	0	0	0
Denis DeJordy	G	5	0	0	0	0					
Aut Erickson	D	3	0	0	0	8					
Murray Hall	R						4	0	0	0	0
Ron Ingram	D						2	0	0	0	0

1962–1963

		REGULAR SEASON					POSTSEASON				
GOALTENDER		GP	MIN	GA	SH	GAA	GP	MIN	GA	SH	GAA
Denis DeJordy	(2-1-2)	5	290	12	0	2.48					
Glenn Hall	(30-20-15)	66	3910	166	5	2.55	6	360	25	0	4.17

MONTREAL   28-19-23   79   3rd   Toe Blake
Canadiens

		REGULAR SEASON				POSTSEASON			
PLAYER	POS	GP	G	A	PTS	PIM	GP	G	A	PTS	PIM
Henri Richard	C	67	23	50	73	57	5	1	1	2	2
Jean Beliveau	C	69	18	49	67	68	5	2	1	3	2
Dickie Moore	L	67	24	26	50	61	5	0	1	1	2
Claude Provost	R	67	20	30	50	26	5	0	1	1	2
Gilles Tremblay	L	60	25	24	49	42	5	2	0	2	0
Bernie Geoffrion	R	51	23	18	41	73	5	0	1	1	4
Bill Hicke	R	70	17	22	39	39	5	0	0	0	0
Bobby Rousseau	R	62	19	18	37	15	5	0	1	1	2
Ralph Backstrom	C	70	23	12	35	51	5	0	0	0	2
Don Marshall	L	65	13	20	33	6	5	0	0	0	0
Jean-Guy Talbot	D	70	3	22	25	51	5	0	0	0	8
J.C. Tremblay	D	69	1	17	18	10	5	0	0	0	0
Jean Gauthier	D	65	1	17	18	46	5	0	0	0	12
Phil Goyette	C	32	5	8	13	2	2	0	0	0	0
Lou Fontinato	D	63	2	8	10	141					
Tom Johnson	D	43	3	5	8	28					
Red Berenson	C	37	2	6	8	15	5	0	0	0	0
Bill McCreary	L	14	2	3	5	0					
Terry Harper	D	14	1	1	2	10	5	1	0	1	8
Jacques Laperriere	D	6	0	2	2	2	5	0	1	1	4
Gerry Brisson	R	4	0	2	2	4					
Jacques Plante	G	56	0	1	1	2	5	0	0	0	0
Cesare Maniago	G	14	0	0	0	2					
Claude Larose	R	4	0	0	0	0					
Ernie Wakely	G	1	0	0	0	0					
Bill Sutherland	C						2	0	0	0	0

		REGULAR SEASON					POSTSEASON				
GOALTENDER		GP	MIN	GA	SH	GAA	GP	MIN	GA	SH	GAA
Jacques Plante	(22-14-19)	56	3320	135	5	2.49	5	300	14	0	2.80
Ernie Wakely	(1-0-0)	1	60	3	0	3.00					
Cesare Maniago	(5-5-4)	14	820	42	0	3.07					

DETROIT   32-25-13   77   4th   Sid Abel
Red Wings

		REGULAR SEASON				POSTSEASON			
PLAYER	POS	GP	G	A	PTS	PIM	GP	G	A	PTS	PIM
Gordie Howe	R	70	38	48	86	100	11	7	9	16	22
Alex Delvecchio	C	70	20	44	64	8	11	3	6	9	2
Parker MacDonald	C	69	33	28	61	32	11	3	2	5	2
Norm Ullman	C	70	26	30	56	53	11	4	12	16	14
Bill Gadsby	D	70	4	24	28	116	11	1	4	5	36
Doug Barkley	D	70	3	24	27	78	11	0	3	3	16

		REGULAR SEASON				*POSTSEASON*				
PLAYER	*POS*	*GP*	*G*	*A*	*PTS*	*PIM*	*GP*	*G*	*A*	*PTS*	*PIM*
Floyd Smith	R	51	9	17	26	10	11	2	3	5	4
Bruce MacGregor	C	67	11	11	22	12	10	1	4	5	10
Alex Faulkner	C	70	10	10	20	6	8	5	0	5	2
Val Fonteyne	L	67	6	14	20	2	11	0	0	0	2
Andre Pronovost (2–2)	L	47	13	5	18	18	11	1	4	5	6
Vic Stasiuk	L	36	6	11	17	37	11	3	0	3	4
Larry Jeffrey	L	53	5	11	16	62	9	3	3	6	8
Marcel Pronovost	D	69	4	9	13	48	11	1	4	5	8
Billy McNeill	C	42	3	7	10	12					
Eddie Joyal	C	14	2	8	10	0	11	1	0	1	2
Howie Young	D	64	4	5	9	273	8	0	2	2	16
Pete Goegan	D	62	1	8	9	48	11	0	2	2	12
Lowell MacDonald	L	26	2	1	3	8	1	0	0	0	2
Hank Bassen	G	17	0	1	1	14					
Ron Harris	D	1	0	1	1	0					
Terry Sawchuk	G	48	0	0	0	14	11	0	0	0	0
Dennis Riggin	G	9	0	0	0	0					
Bo Elik	L	3	0	0	0	0					
Roger Lafreniere	L	3	0	0	0	4					
Paul Henderson	R	2	0	0	0	2					
Al Johnson	R	2	0	0	0	0					
Dave Lucas	D	1	0	0	0	0					
Lou Marcon	D	1	0	0	0	0					
Gerry Odrowski	D	1	0	0	0	0	2	0	0	0	2
Bob Dillabough	C						1	0	0	0	0

		REGULAR SEASON					*POSTSEASON*			
GOALTENDER		*GP*	*MIN*	*GA*	*SH*	*GAA*	*GP*	*MIN*	*GA*	*SH*	*GAA*
Terry Sawchuk	(22-16-7)	48	2775	117 (2)	3	2.53	11	660	36	0	3.27
Dennis Riggin	(4-4-1)	9	445	22	0	2.97					
Hank Bassen	(6-5-5)	17	980	52 (1)	0	3.18					

NEW YORK 22-36-12 56 5th Muzz Patrick
Rangers George Sullivan

		REGULAR SEASON				*POSTSEASON*
PLAYER	*POS*	*GP*	*G*	*A*	*PTS*	*PIM*
Andy Bathgate	R	70	35	46	81	54
Camille Henry	C	60	37	23	60	8
Earl Ingarfield	C	69	19	24	43	40
Doug Harvey	D	68	4	35	39	92
Dean Prentice (1–2)	L	49	13	25	38	18
Andy Hebenton	R	70	15	22	37	8
Rod Gilbert	R	70	11	20	31	20
Harry Howell	D	70	5	20	25	55
Dave Balon	L	70	11	13	24	72
Don McKenney (2–2)	C	21	8	16	24	4
Bronco Horvath (1–2)	C	41	7	15	22	34
Jean Ratelle	C	48	11	9	20	8
Larry Cahan	D	56	6	14	20	47
Jim Neilson	D	69	5	11	16	38

no postseason play

1962–1963   383

		REGULAR SEASON					*POSTSEASON*
PLAYER	*POS*	*GP*	*G*	*A*	*PTS*	*PIM*	no postseason play
Al Langlois	D	60	2	14	16	62	
Ken Schinkel	R	69	6	9	15	15	
Vic Hadfield	L	36	5	6	11	32	
Leon Rochefort	R	23	5	4	9	6	
Ted Hampson	C	46	4	2	6	2	
Don Johns	D	6	0	4	4	6	
Bryan Hextall, Jr.	C	21	0	2	2	10	
Mel Pearson	L	5	1	0	1	6	
Ralph Keller	D	3	1	0	1	6	
Lorne Worsley	G	67	0	0	0	14	
Marcel Paille	G	3	0	0	0	0	
Duane Rupp	D	2	0	0	0	0	
Marcel Pelletier	G	2	0	0	0	0	

		REGULAR SEASON					*POSTSEASON*
GOALTENDER		*GP*	*MIN*	*GA*	*SH*	*GAA*	no postseason play
Lorne Worsley	(22-34-10)	67	3980	217	(2) 2	3.27	
Marcel Paille	(0-1-2)	3	180	10	0	3.33	
Marcel Pelletier	(0-1-0)	2	40	3	(1) 0	4.50	

BOSTON 14-39-17 45 6th Phil Watson
Bruins   Milt Schmidt

		REGULAR SEASON					*POSTSEASON*
PLAYER	*POS*	*GP*	*G*	*A*	*PTS*	*PIM*	no postseason play
John Bucyk	L	69	27	39	66	36	
Murray Oliver	C	65	22	40	62	38	
Tommy Williams	C	69	23	20	43	11	
Jean-Guy Gendron	L	66	21	22	43	42	
Jerry Toppazzini	R	65	17	18	35	6	
Don McKenney (1–2)	C	41	14	19	33	2	
Forbes Kennedy	C	49	12	18	30	46	
Doug Mohns	F	68	7	23	30	63	
Leo Boivin	D	62	2	24	26	48	
Charlie Burns	C	68	12	10	22	13	
Bobby Leiter	C	51	9	13	22	34	
Irv Spencer	D	69	5	17	22	34	
Cliff Pennington	C	27	7	10	17	4	
Wayne Hicks	R	65	7	9	16	14	
Dean Prentice (2–2)	L	19	6	9	15	4	
Ted Green	D	70	1	11	12	117	
Ed Westfall	R	48	1	11	12	34	
Warren Godfrey	D	66	2	9	11	56	
Wayne Connelly	R	18	2	6	8	2	
Don Blackburn	L	6	0	5	5	4	
Pat Stapleton	D	21	0	3	3	8	
Andre Pronovost (1–2)	L	21	0	2	2	6	
Matt Ravlich	D	2	1	0	1	0	
Eddie Johnston	G	50	0	0	0	10	
Bob Perreault	G	22	0	0	0	0	
Jeannot Gilbert	C	5	0	0	0	4	

	REGULAR SEASON					POSTSEASON
GOALTENDER	GP	MIN	GA	SH	GAA	no postseason play
Bob Perreault (3-12-6)	22	1287	82 (3)	1	3.82	
Eddie Johnston (11-27-11)	50	2913	193 (3)	1	3.97	

TEAM TOTALS

								Per Game			
TEAM	GP	G	A	PTS	PIM	GA	SH	G	A	PIM	GA
Toronto	70	221	344	565	816	180	2	3.16	4.91	11.66	2.57
Chicago	70	194	330	524	906	**178**	5	2.77	4.71	12.94	**2.54**
Montreal	70	**225**	**360**	**585**	751	183	5	3.21	**5.14**	10.73	2.61
Detroit	70	200	316	516	**964**	194	3	2.86	4.51	**13.77**	2.77
New York	70	211	334	545	657	233	2	3.01	4.77	9.39	3.33
Boston	70	198	338	536	636	281	2	2.83	4.83	9.09	4.01
	420	1249	2022	3271	4730	1249	19	2.97	4.81	11.26	2.97

PLAYOFFS

SERIES "A"
Toronto 3, Montreal 1
Toronto 3, Montreal 2
Toronto 2, Montreal 0
Montreal 3, Toronto 1
Toronto 5, Montreal 0

TORONTO, 4–1

SERIES "B"
Chicago 5, Detroit 4
Chicago 5, Detroit 2
Detroit 4, Chicago 2
Detroit 4, Chicago 1
Detroit 4, Chicago 2
Detroit 7, Chicago 4

DETROIT, 4–2

SERIES "C"
Toronto 4, Detroit 2
Toronto 4, Detroit 2
Detroit 3, Toronto 2
Toronto 4, Detroit 2
Toronto 3, Detroit 1

**TORONTO WINS
STANLEY CUP, 4–1**

ALL-STAR TEAMS

First Team
G — Glenn Hall, CHI
D — Pierre Pilote, CHI
D — Carl Brewer, TOR
C — Stan Mikita, CHI
R — Gordie Howe, DET
L — Frank Mahovlich, TOR

Second Team
G — Terry Sawchuk, DET
D — Tim Horton, TOR
D — Elmer Vasko, CHI
C — Henri Richard, MTL
R — Andy Bathgate, NY
L — Bobby Hull, CHI

INDIVIDUAL TROPHY WINNERS

HART TROPHY (Most Valuable Player): Gordie Howe, DET
LADY BYNG TROPHY (Gentlemanly Conduct): Dave Keon, TOR
VEZINA TROPHY (Best Goaltender): Glenn Hall, CHI
CALDER MEMORIAL TROPHY (Best Rookie): Kent Douglas, TOR
ART ROSS TROPHY (Scoring Leader): Gordie Howe, DET
JAMES NORRIS TROPHY (Best Defenseman): Pierre Pilote, CHI

1963-1964
A League of Their Own

During its first four decades, most of the NHL's players cut their teeth in one of many minor hockey circuits, which sprang up beginning in the 1920s. To refine this process, some NHL clubs either owned outright or participated in working agreements with certain minor league teams, giving a home to their budding players. For instance, in the 1920s and 1930s, the New York Americans stocked the roster of the Canadian-American Hockey League's New Haven Ramblers. Later, the Detroit Red Wings claimed a nascent farm system, sending players to teams in both the American Hockey League (Indianapolis) and the United States Hockey League (Omaha). However, there was no league-wide system that developed skaters for the NHL. This was about to change.

Before the 1963-64 season, the NHL — under the direction of Detroit executive Jack Adams — decided they needed a developmental league. Rather than starting from scratch, an existing minor league circuit — the Eastern Pro Hockey League — was tabbed to be the nucleus of the new project. The four-team EPHL — three in Canada and one in St. Louis, was relocated, expanded and renamed the Central Pro Hockey League.

In its first season, the CPHL retained the St. Louis franchise, adding to it teams in Minneapolis, St. Paul, Indianapolis and Omaha. Each one of the five would serve as a direct link to an NHL franchise, with only Toronto being left out of the mix. Three weeks into its inaugural season, a fire destroyed the Indianapolis rink, necessitating a move to Cincinnati. Montreal's farm team — the Omaha Knights — won the regular season championship, then the playoffs, claiming the first Adams Cup — named after the league's founder and first president. Individually, Blackhawk's farmhand (St. Louis) Alain Caron scored 77 goals, setting a new pro mark. But, it was one of his teammates who netted

80 points in only 43 games, that would go on to leave a lasting mark in the NHL.

Meanwhile, echoing their farm club, Montreal (36-21-13, 85) returned to the top of the pile in 1963-64, edging the Blackhawks by a single point. Toronto and Detroit claimed the other two playoff berths, both double-digit point totals ahead of New York and Boston. Chicago's Stan Mikita (39-50-89) registered the highest point total, edging his teammate, goals leader Bobby Hull (43). Andy Bathgate, who played for both New York and Toronto, corralled the most assists (58), while his half-season teammate — Vic Hadfield — was whistled for the most penalty minutes (151). In net, Toronto's Johnny Bower (2.11) posted the lowest GAA, while Montreal's Charlie Hodge blanked the most foes (5).

Both opening round series featured see-saw battles that weren't decided until the very end. In one group, Detroit took a two games to one edge over the Blackhawks, but Chicago responded with a pair of 3–2 wins, the first coming in overtime. However, helped by Norm Ullman's hat trick, Detroit laced Chicago 7–2 in the sixth game, then finished off the Hawks with a 4–2 triumph. In the other series, Toronto and Montreal exchanged wins over the first six games, with none of the matches decided by more than two goals. With the series on the line, Toronto's Dave Keon took control, scoring all three markers in the Leaf's 3–1 win.

Duplicating the early round efforts, the finals also featured a grouping that went the distance. After losing the first contest, Detroit won the next two by 4–3 scores, the first coming in extra time. The Leafs took the next contest, 4–2, but Detroit took command with a 2–1 win. Needing only one win for the Cup, the Wings took Toronto into overtime in the sixth game. Less than two minutes into the extra stanza, Toronto's Bob Baun took a shot through a maze of players that somehow found its way to the back of the net. The demoralized Detroit squad then dropped the seventh game, 4–0, giving the Leafs their third straight Cup.

In defeat, Detroit's Gordie Howe (9-10-19) was superb, netting the most markers and amassing the most points. For Toronto, Frank Mahovlich (11) collected the most assists, while Johnny Bower (2.12) allowed the fewest goals.

For the next 20 years, the CPHL (renamed CHL in 1969) served as a feeder league to the NHL until its demise in the 1980s. Since then, other leagues — the International Hockey League, and now exclusively the American Hockey League — fulfill the role of the last step before the NHL.

As for the young pro (Phil Esposito) who finished with 80 points in the CPHL's first season, he went on to a "decent" career himself, scoring over 700 goals in a 19-year NHL stay. Though most CPHL alums could not claim the gaudy stats of an Esposito, all that went on to the NHL could thank folks like Jack Adams, whose foresight long ago created a venue for young hockey players to hone their skills.

STANDINGS

TEAM	GP	W	L	T	PTS	GF	GA
MONTREAL	70	36	21	13	85	209	167
CHICAGO	70	36	22	12	84	218	169
TORONTO	70	33	25	12	78	192	172
DETROIT	70	30	29	11	71	191	207
NEW YORK	70	22	38	10	54	186	242
BOSTON	70	18	40	12	48	170	212

LEADERS

PLAYER	TM	GP	G	A	PTS	PIM
Stan Mikita	CHI	70	39	50	89	146
Bobby Hull	CHI	70	43	44	87	50
Jean Beliveau	MTL	68	28	50	78	42
Andy Bathgate	N-T	71	19	58	77	34
Gordie Howe	DET	69	26	47	73	70
Kenny Wharram	CHI	70	39	32	71	18
Murray Oliver	BOS	70	24	44	68	41
Phil Goyette	NY	67	24	41	65	15
Rod Gilbert	NY	70	24	40	64	62
Dave Keon	TOR	70	23	37	60	6

GOALS	
Hull, CHI	43
Wharram, CHI	39
Mikita, CHI	39
Henry, NY	29
Beliveau, MTL	28

ASSISTS	
Bathgate, N-T	58
Mikita, CHI	50
Beliveau, MTL	50
Howe, DET	47
Pilote, CHI	46

GOALTENDER	TM	GP	MIN	GA	SH	GAA
Johnny Bower	TOR	51	3009	106 (1)	5	**2.11**
Charlie Hodge	MTL	62	3720	140 (1)	**8**	2.26
Glenn Hall	CHI	65	3860	148 (2)	7	2.30
Terry Sawchuk	DET	53	3140	138 (2)	5	2.64
Eddie Johnston	BOS	**70**	**4200**	211 (1)	6	3.01
Jacques Plante	NY	65	3900	**220** (4)	3	3.38

PENALTY MINUTES	
Hadfield, NY	151
Harper, MTL	149
Mikita, CHI	146
Green, BOS	145
Fleming, CHI	140

SHUTOUTS	
Hodge, MTL	8
Hall, CHI	7
Johnston, BOS	6
Bower, TOR	5
Sawchuk, DET	5

MONTREAL
Canadiens   36-21-13   85   1st   Toe Blake

		REGULAR SEASON					POSTSEASON				
PLAYER	POS	GP	G	A	PTS	PIM	GP	G	A	PTS	PIM
Jean Beliveau	C	68	28	50	78	42	5	2	0	2	18
Bobby Rousseau	R	70	25	31	56	32	7	1	1	2	2
Henri Richard	C	66	14	39	53	73	7	1	1	2	9
John Ferguson	L	59	18	27	45	125	7	0	1	1	25

		REGULAR SEASON					POSTSEASON				
PLAYER	POS	GP	G	A	PTS	PIM	GP	G	A	PTS	PIM
Dave Balon	L	70	24	18	42	80	7	1	1	2	25
Bernie Geoffrion	R	55	21	18	39	41	7	1	1	2	4
Gilles Tremblay	L	61	22	15	37	21	2	0	0	0	0
Claude Provost	R	68	15	17	32	37	7	2	2	4	22
Jacques Laperriere	D	65	2	28	30	102	7	1	1	2	8
Ralph Backstrom	C	70	8	21	29	41	7	2	1	3	8
J.C. Tremblay	D	70	5	16	21	24	7	2	1	3	9
Bill Hicke	R	48	11	9	20	41	7	0	2	2	2
Terry Harper	D	70	2	15	17	149	7	0	0	0	6
Red Berenson	C	69	7	9	16	12	7	0	0	0	4
Jean-Guy Talbot	D	66	1	13	14	83	7	0	2	2	10
Andre Boudrias	L	4	1	4	5	2					
Yvan Cournoyer	R	5	4	0	4	0					
Claude Larose	R	21	1	1	2	43	2	1	0	1	0
Bryan Watson	D	39	0	2	2	18	6	0	0	0	2
Jimmy Roberts	D	15	0	1	1	2	7	0	1	1	14
Ted Harris	D	4	0	1	1	0					
Charlie Hodge	G	62	0	0	0	2	7	0	0	0	0
Lorne Worsley	G	8	0	0	0	0					
Jack Hanna	D	6	0	0	0	2					
Terry Gray	R	4	0	0	0	6					
Marc Reaume	D	3	0	0	0	2					
Leon Rochefort	R	3	0	0	0	0					
Wayne Hicks	R	2	0	0	0	0					
Jean Gauthier	D	1	0	0	0	2					
Jean-Guy Morissette	G	1	0	0	0	0					

		REGULAR SEASON					POSTSEASON				
GOALTENDER		GP	MIN	GA	SH	GAA	GP	MIN	GA	SH	GAA
Charlie Hodge	(33-18-11)	62	3720	140 (1)	8	2.26	7	420	16	1	2.29
Lorne Worsley	(3-2-2)	8	444	22	1	2.97					
Jean-Guy Morissette	(0-1-0)	1	36	4	0	6.67					

CHICAGO 36-22-12 84 2nd Billy Reay
Blackhawks

		REGULAR SEASON					POSTSEASON				
PLAYER	POS	GP	G	A	PTS	PIM	GP	G	A	PTS	PIM
Stan Mikita	C	70	39	50	89	146	7	3	6	9	8
Bobby Hull	L	70	43	44	87	50	7	2	5	7	2
Kenny Wharram	R	70	39	32	71	18	7	2	2	4	6
Bill Hay	C	70	23	33	56	30	7	3	1	4	4
Pierre Pilote	D	70	7	46	53	84	7	2	6	8	6
Alvin McDonald	L	70	14	32	46	19	7	2	2	4	0
Eric Nesterenko	R	70	7	19	26	93	7	2	1	3	8
Al MacNeil	D	70	5	19	24	91	7	0	2	2	25
Ron Maki	R	68	8	14	22	70	7	0	0	0	15
Elmer Vasko	D	70	2	18	20	65	7	0	0	0	4
Ron Murphy	L	70	11	8	19	32	7	0	1	1	8
John McKenzie	R	45	9	9	18	50	4	0	1	1	6
Murray Balfour	R	41	2	10	12	36	7	2	2	4	4

		REGULAR SEASON					POSTSEASON				
PLAYER	POS	GP	G	A	PTS	PIM	GP	G	A	PTS	PIM
Reg Fleming	L	61	3	6	9	140	7	0	0	0	18
Howie Young	D	39	0	7	7	99					
Phil Esposito	C	27	3	2	5	2	4	0	0	0	0
Wayne Hillman	D	59	1	4	5	51	7	0	1	1	15
Murray Hall	R	23	2	0	2	4					
Glenn Hall	G	65	0	2	2	2	7	0	0	0	0
Aut Erickson	D	31	0	1	1	34	6	0	0	0	0
Denis DeJordy	G	6	0	0	0	0	1	0	0	0	0
Doug Robinson	L						4	0	0	0	0

		REGULAR SEASON					POSTSEASON				
GOALTENDER		GP	MIN	GA	SH	GAA	GP	MIN	GA	SH	GAA
Glenn Hall	(34-19-11)	65	3860	148 (2)	7	2.30	7	408	22	0	3.24
Denis DeJordy	(2-3-1)	6	340	19	0	3.35	1	20	2	0	6.00

TORONTO   33-25-12   78   3rd   Punch Imlach
Maple Leafs

		REGULAR SEASON					POSTSEASON				
PLAYER	POS	GP	G	A	PTS	PIM	GP	G	A	PTS	PIM
Dave Keon	C	70	23	37	60	6	14	7	2	9	2
Frank Mahovlich	L	70	26	29	55	66	14	4	11	15	20
Bob Pulford	L	70	18	30	48	73	14	5	3	8	20
Red Kelly	D	70	11	34	45	16	14	4	9	13	4
George Armstrong	C	66	20	17	37	14	14	5	8	13	10
Tim Horton	D	70	9	20	29	71	14	0	4	4	20
Allan Stanley	D	70	6	21	27	60	14	1	6	7	20
Eddie Shack	L	64	11	10	21	128	13	0	1	1	25
Ron Stewart	C	65	14	5	19	46	14	0	4	4	24
Jim Pappin	R	50	11	8	19	33	11	0	0	0	0
Bob Nevin (1–2)	R	49	7	12	19	26					
Billy Harris	C	63	6	12	18	17	9	1	1	2	4
Bob Baun	D	52	4	14	18	113	14	2	3	5	42
Andy Bathgate (2–2)	R	*15	3	*15	18	8	14	5	4	9	25
Dick Duff (1–2)	L	52	7	10	17	59					
Don McKenney (2–2)	C	15	9	6	15	2	12	4	8	12	0
Carl Brewer	D	57	4	9	13	114	12	0	1	1	30
Larry Hillman	D	33	0	4	4	31	11	0	0	0	2
Ed Litzenberger	R	19	2	0	2	0	1	0	0	0	10
Gerry Ehman	R	4	1	1	2	0	9	1	0	1	4
Kent Douglas	D	43	0	1	1	29					
Al Arbour	D	6	0	1	1	0	1	0	0	0	0
Johnny Bower	G	51	0	0	0	4	14	0	0	0	0
Don Simmons	G	21	0	0	0	0					
John MacMillan (1–2)	R	13	0	0	0	4					
Arnie Brown	D	4	0	0	0	6					
Ron Ellis	R	1	0	0	0	0					
Pete Stemkowski	C	1	0	0	0	2					

		REGULAR SEASON				POSTSEASON				
GOALTENDER		GP	MIN	GA	SH	GAA	GP	MIN	GA	SH	GAA
Johnny Bower (24-16-11)		51	3009	106 (1)	5	**2.11**	14	850	30	2	**2.12**
Don Simmons (9-9-1)		21	1191	63 (2)	3	3.17					

DETROIT 30-29-11 71 4th Sid Abel
Red Wings

		REGULAR SEASON					POSTSEASON				
PLAYER	POS	GP	G	A	PTS	PIM	GP	G	A	PTS	PIM
Gordie Howe	R	69	26	47	73	70	14	9	10	19	16
Alex Delvecchio	C	70	23	30	53	11	14	3	8	11	0
Norm Ullman	C	61	21	30	51	55	14	7	10	17	6
Parker MacDonald	C	68	21	25	46	25	14	3	3	6	2
Doug Barkley	D	67	11	21	32	115	14	0	5	5	33
Bruce MacGregor	C	63	11	21	32	15	14	5	2	7	12
Floyd Smith	R	52	18	13	31	22	14	4	3	7	4
Larry Jeffrey	L	58	10	18	28	87	14	1	6	7	28
Andre Pronovost	L	70	7	16	23	54	14	4	3	7	26
Hubert Martin	C	50	9	12	21	28	14	1	4	5	14
Marcel Pronovost	D	67	3	17	20	42	14	0	2	2	14
Bill Gadsby	D	64	2	16	18	80	14	0	4	4	22
Eddie Joyal	C	47	10	7	17	6	14	2	3	5	10
Alex Faulkner	C	30	5	7	12	9	4	0	0	0	0
Ron Ingram (2–2)	D	50	3	6	9	50					
Al Langlois (2–2)	D	17	1	6	7	13	14	0	0	0	12
Paul Henderson	R	32	3	3	6	14	14	2	3	5	6
Claude Laforge	L	17	2	3	5	4					
Lowell MacDonald	L	10	1	4	5	0					
Irv Spencer	D	25	3	0	3	8	11	0	0	0	0
John MacMillan (2–2)	R	20	0	3	3	6	4	0	1	1	2
Art Stratton	C	5	0	3	3	2					
Billy McNeill	C	15	1	1	2	2					
John Miszuk	D	42	0	2	2	30	3	0	0	0	2
Ted Hampson	C	7	0	1	1	0					
Wayne Muloin	D	3	0	1	1	2					
Terry Sawchuk	G	53	0	0	0	0	13	0	0	0	2
Roger Crozier	G	15	0	0	0	0	3	0	0	0	0
Pete Goegan	D	12	0	0	0	8					
Ian Cushenan	D	5	0	0	0	4					
Warren Godfrey	D	4	0	0	0	2					
Ron Harris	D	3	0	0	0	7					
Howie Menard	C	3	0	0	0	0					
Bill Mitchell	D	1	0	0	0	0					
Jim Watson	D	1	0	0	0	0					
Hank Bassen	G	1	0	0	0	0					
Harrison Gray	G	1	0	0	0	0					
Pat Rupp	G	1	0	0	0	0					
Bob Dillabough	C						1	0	0	0	0
Bob Champoux	G						1	0	0	0	0

392 The National Hockey League, 1917–1967

GOALTENDER		REGULAR SEASON					POSTSEASON				
		GP	MIN	GA	SH	GAA	GP	MIN	GA	SH	GAA
Terry Sawchuk	(25-20-7)	53	3140	138 (2)	5	2.64	13	677	31	1	2.75
Roger Crozier	(5-6-4)	15	900	51	2	3.40	3	126	5	0	2.38
Hank Bassen	(0-1-0)	1	60	4	0	4.00					
Pat Rupp	(0-1-0)	1	60	4	0	4.00					
Harrison Gray	(0-1-0)	1	40	5	0	7.50					
Bob Champoux							1	55	4	0	4.36

NEW YORK Rangers 22-38-10 54 5th George Sullivan

PLAYER	POS	REGULAR SEASON					POSTSEASON
		GP	G	A	PTS	PIM	no postseason play
Phil Goyette	C	67	24	41	65	15	
Rod Gilbert	R	70	24	40	64	62	
Andy Bathgate (1–2)	R	*56	16	*43	59	26	
Camille Henry	C	68	29	26	55	8	
Harry Howell	D	70	5	31	36	75	
Jim Neilson	D	69	5	24	29	93	
Earl Ingarfield	C	63	15	11	26	26	
Don McKenney (1–2)	C	55	9	17	26	6	
Vic Hadfield	L	69	14	11	25	**151**	
Val Fonteyne	L	69	7	18	25	4	
Don Marshall	L	70	11	12	23	8	
Larry Cahan	D	53	4	8	12	80	
Don Johns	D	57	1	9	10	26	
Bob Nevin (2–2)	R	14	5	4	9	9	
Dick Duff (2–2)	L	14	4	4	8	2	
Dick Meissner	R	35	3	5	8	0	
Jean Ratelle	C	15	0	7	7	6	
Al Langlois (1–2)	D	44	4	2	6	32	
Dave Richardson	L	34	3	1	4	21	
Ron Ingram (1–2)	D	16	1	3	4	8	
Doug Harvey	D	14	0	2	2	10	
Howie Glover	R	25	1	0	1	9	
Marc Dufour	R	10	1	0	1	2	
Jacques Plante	G	65	0	1	1	6	
Mike McMahon	D	18	0	1	1	16	
Rod Seiling	D	2	0	1	1	0	
Gord Labossiere	C	15	0	0	0	12	
Gilles Villemure	G	5	0	0	0	0	
Ken Schinkel	R	4	0	0	0	0	
Sandy McGregor	R	2	0	0	0	2	

GOALTENDER		REGULAR SEASON					POSTSEASON
		GP	MIN	GA	SH	GAA	no postseason play
Jacques Plante	(22-36-7)	65	3900	**220** (4)	3	3.38	
Gilles Villemure	(0-2-3)	5	300	18	0	3.60	

1963–1964

BOSTON 18-40-12 48 6th Milt Schmidt
Bruins

PLAYER	POS	GP	G	A	PTS	PIM
Murray Oliver	C	70	24	44	68	41
John Bucyk	L	62	18	36	54	36
Dean Prentice	L	70	23	16	39	37
Orland Kurtenbach	C	70	12	25	37	91
Doug Mohns	F	70	9	17	26	95
Forbes Kennedy	C	70	8	17	25	95
Tom Johnson	D	70	4	21	25	33
Leo Boivin	D	65	10	14	24	42
Andy Hebenton	R	70	12	11	23	8
Tommy Williams	C	37	8	15	23	8
Gary Dornhoefer	R	32	12	10	22	20
Bobby Leiter	C	56	6	13	19	43
Jean-Guy Gendron	L	54	5	13	18	43
Ted Green	D	70	4	10	14	145
Jerry Toppazzini	R	65	7	4	11	15
Bob McCord	D	65	1	9	10	49
Wayne Rivers	R	12	2	7	9	6
Ed Westfall	R	55	1	5	6	35
Wayne Connelly	R	26	2	3	5	12
Ron Schock	C	5	1	2	3	0
Don Awrey	D	16	1	0	1	4
Bob Beckett	C	7	0	1	1	0
Eddie Johnston	G	70	0	0	0	0
Skip Krake	C	2	0	0	0	0
Ted Irvine	L	1	0	0	0	0

POSTSEASON: no postseason play

GOALTENDER	GP	MIN	GA	SH	GAA
Eddie Johnston (18-**40**-12)	70	4200	211	(1) 6	3.01

TEAM TOTALS

TEAM	GP	G	A	PTS	PIM	GA	SH	G	A	PIM	GA
Montreal	70	209	335	544	982	**167**	9	2.99	4.79	14.03	**2.39**
Chicago	70	**218**	**354**	**572**	**1116**	169	7	**3.11**	**5.06**	**15.94**	2.41
Toronto	70	192	296	488	928	172	8	2.74	4.23	13.26	2.46
Detroit	70	191	313	504	771	204	7	2.73	4.47	11.01	2.91
New York	70	186	321	507	715	242	3	2.66	4.58	10.21	3.46
Boston	70	170	293	463	858	212	6	2.43	4.18	12.26	3.03
	420	1166	1912	3078	5370	1166	40	2.78	4.55	12.79	2.78

PLAYOFFS

SERIES "A"
Montreal 2, Toronto 0
Toronto 2, Montreal 1

SERIES "B"
Chicago 4, Detroit 1
Detroit 5, Chicago 4

Montreal 3, Toronto 2
Toronto 5, Montreal 3
Montreal 4, Toronto 2
Toronto 3, Montreal 0
Toronto 3, Montreal 1

TORONTO, 4-3

SERIES "C"
Toronto 3, Detroit 2
Detroit 4, Toronto 3 (OT)
Detroit 4, Toronto 3
Toronto 4, Detroit 2
Detroit 2, Toronto 1
Toronto 4, Detroit 3 (OT)
Toronto 4, Detroit 0

TORONTO WINS
STANLEY CUP, 4-3

Detroit 3, Chicago 0
Chicago 3, Detroit 2 (OT)
Chicago 3, Detroit 2
Detroit 7, Chicago 2
Detroit 4, Chicago 2

DETROIT, 4-3

ALL-STAR TEAMS

First Team
G — Glenn Hall, CHI
D — Tim Horton, TOR
D — Pierre Pilote, CHI
C — Stan Mikita, CHI
R — Kenny Wharram, CHI
L — Bobby Hull, CHI

Second Team
G — Charlie Hodge, MTL
D — Jacques Laperriere, MTL
D — Elmer Vasko, CHI
C — Jean Beliveau, MTL
R — Gordie Howe, DET
L — Frank Mahovlich, TOR

INDIVIDUAL TROPHY WINNERS

HART TROPHY (Most Valuable Player): Jean Beliveau, MTL
LADY BYNG TROPHY (Gentlemanly Conduct): Kenny Wharram, CHI
VEZINA TROPHY (Best Goaltender): Charlie Hodge, MTL
CALDER MEMORIAL TROPHY (Best Rookie): Jacques Laperriere, MTL
ART ROSS TROPHY (Scoring Leader): Stan Mikita, CHI
JAMES NORRIS TROPHY (Best Defenseman): Pierre Pilote, CHI

1964-1965

Unprotected

Following the 1963-64 season, the Detroit Red Wings were in a quandary. For many years, their goalie — Terry Sawchuk — had been one of the best puck stoppers in the league, leading them to glory on several occasions. However, the veteran netminder was now 35 years old, with maybe his best years behind him. Waiting in the wings for Detroit was a hot new prospect, Roger Crozier, who that many were calling a potential All-Star. The problem was that Detroit couldn't have the young and the old — one would have to go. This was because of a peculiar institution unique to the NHL.

Formed in the early 1950s, the Intra-League Draft came into being to help bolster the NHL's weakest clubs — most notably the Chicago Blackhawks. Basically, it called for existing clubs to protect a nucleus of players, leaving others dangling, ripe for the picking. Any player not protected could then be drafted by another club for a low, waiver price. This way, teams like the Blackhawks, Bruins and Rangers — which were frequently on the bottom end of the standings — would be able to get leftovers from their betters — leftovers which were frequently better than their existing rosters.

At the June 1964 Intra-League Draft, the Red Wings left Sawchuk unprotected, exposing him to the rest of the teams. Without hesitation, Toronto snared him for a bargain price. For the Leafs, Sawchuk's arrival immediately paid dividends. Over the course of the season, albeit in a part-time role, he posted a 2.56 GAA with a shutout. Together with Johnny Bower (2.38), the pair allowed the fewest goals in the league, allowing the duo to share the Vezina Trophy. For Bower it was his second goaltending prize, but for Sawchuk it was his fourth, placing him among a select few goalies with that amount.

While Sawchuk earned himself individual accolades, Crozier — in his rookie campaign—led the Red Wings (40-23-7, 87) to the regular season championship, the team's first in eight years. On his way to winning the Calder Trophy as the best first year player, he finished a close second in the GAA race (2.42) and earned the most shutouts (6).

In the offensive end of the ice, Chicago's Stan Mikita (28-59-87)—the NHL's assist leader—claimed his second straight scoring title, fending off goal leader Norm Ullman (Detroit) by four points (42-41-83). In addition, Toronto's Carl Brewer spent the most minutes in the penalty box (177).

In the first round of the playoffs, first-place Detroit faced off against third-place Chicago, while runner-up Montreal squared off against Toronto. For the third straight year, all four of these teams finished well ahead of New York and Boston. In their series against Chicago, the Red Wings spurted out to a two game advantage, winning the first two contests 4–3 and 6–3. Undaunted, the Blackhawks answered with two victories of their own. In the fifth game, Detroit took a three games to two lead, courtesy of a 4–2 win. However, Chicago then shut the door, allowing the Wings only two markers in the last two contests, while scoring eight themselves.

In the other opening set, after Toronto knotted the slate at two games apiece, Montreal took the next two, clinching their berth in the finals with a 4–3 overtime win. In the finals, Montreal continued its streak, defeating Chicago in the first two contests. Then, as they did against Detroit, the Blackhawks responded, evening the series at two games apiece. Montreal then blistered the Blackhawks 6–0 in the fifth game, only to see Chicago respond with a 2–1 win, sending the series to a seventh game. In the last contest, Montreal's Jean Beliveau took command early, scoring 14 seconds into the game. Three more first period tallies soon followed, and the Canadiens cruised to the Cup, 4–0.

Chicago's Bobby Hull (10-7-17) led all playoff participants in goals and points, while his teammate Ron Maki (9) added the most helpers. In net, Montreal's Lorne Worsley (1.68) proved to be the stingiest, shutting out the Hawks twice in the final round.

In the short run, Detroit's gamble with Sawchuk and Crozier appeared to fall its way, as the Red Wing rookie led his team to the top. However, it was Toronto that had the last laugh. For the Maple Leafs, Sawchuk enjoyed three solid seasons, saving his best for last. Although left unprotected by his Detroit club in 1964, Sawchuk in the end showed the NHL there was still some juice left in the tank by leading his Leafs to the Cup in 1967.

STANDINGS

TEAM	GP	W	L	T	PTS	GF	GA
DETROIT	70	40	23	7	87	224	175
MONTREAL	70	36	23	11	83	211	185

1964–1965

TEAM	GP	W	L	T	PTS	GF	GA
CHICAGO	70	34	28	8	76	224	176
TORONTO	70	30	26	14	74	204	173
NEW YORK	70	20	38	12	52	179	246
BOSTON	70	21	43	6	48	166	253

LEADERS

PLAYER	TM	GP	G	A	PTS	PIM
Stan Mikita	CHI	70	28	59	87	154
Norm Ullman	DET	70	42	41	83	70
Gordie Howe	DET	70	29	47	76	104
Bobby Hull	CHI	61	39	32	71	32
Alex Delvecchio	DET	68	25	42	67	16
Claude Provost	MTL	70	27	37	64	28
Rod Gilbert	NY	70	25	36	61	52
Pierre Pilote	CHI	68	14	45	59	162
Three tied with					55	

GOALS
Ullman, DET	42
Hull, CHI	39
Howe, DET	29
Mikita, CHI	28
Provost, MTL	27

ASSISTS
Mikita, CHI	59
Howe, DET	47
Pilote, CHI	45
Delvecchio, DET	42
Ullman, DET	41

GOALTENDER	TM	GP	MIN	GA	SH	GAA
Johnny Bower	TOR	34	2040	81	3	**2.38**
Roger Crozier	DET	70	4168	168 (3)	6	2.42
Glenn Hall	CHI	41	2440	99 (1)	4	2.43
Denis DeJordy	CHI	30	1760	74 (2)	3	2.52
Charlie Hodge	MTL	53	3180	135	3	2.55
Terry Sawchuk	TOR	36	2160	92	1	2.56
Jacques Plante	NY	33	1938	109 (1)	2	3.37
Eddie Johnston	BOS	47	2820	163 (4)	3	3.47
Marcel Paille	NY	39	2262	135 (1)	0	3.58

PENALTY MINUTES
Brewer, TOR	177
Lindsay, DET	173
Pilote, CHI	162
Baun, TOR	160
Two tied with	156

SHUTOUTS
Crozier, DET	6
Hall, CHI	4
Four tied with	3

DETROIT Red Wings

40-23-7   87   1st   Sid Abel

		REGULAR SEASON					POSTSEASON				
PLAYER	POS	GP	G	A	PTS	PIM	GP	G	A	PTS	PIM
Norm Ullman	C	70	42	41	83	70	7	6	4	10	2
Gordie Howe	R	70	29	47	76	104	7	4	2	6	20
Alex Delvecchio	C	68	25	42	67	16	7	2	3	5	4
Parker MacDonald	C	69	13	33	46	38	7	1	1	2	6
Floyd Smith	R	67	16	29	45	44	7	1	3	4	4
Bruce MacGregor	C	66	21	20	41	19	7	0	2	2	2
Ron Murphy	L	58	20	19	39	32	5	0	1	1	4
Ted Lindsay	L	69	14	14	28	173	7	3	0	3	34
Doug Barkley	D	67	5	20	25	122	5	0	1	1	14
Eddie Joyal	C	46	8	14	22	4	7	1	1	2	4
Paul Henderson	R	70	8	13	21	30	7	0	2	2	0
Hubert Martin	C	58	8	9	17	32	3	0	1	1	2
Marcel Pronovost	D	68	1	15	16	45	7	0	3	3	4
Al Langlois	D	65	1	12	13	107	6	1	0	1	4

398   The National Hockey League, 1917–1967

		REGULAR SEASON				POSTSEASON				
PLAYER	POS	GP	G	A	PTS	PIM	GP	G	A	PTS	PIM
Bill Gadsby	D	61	0	12	12	122	7	0	3	3	8
Gary Bergman	D	58	4	7	11	85	5	0	1	1	4
Val Fonteyne (2–2)	L	16	2	5	7	4	5	0	1	1	0
Larry Jeffrey	L	41	4	2	6	48	2	0	0	0	0
Lowell MacDonald	L	9	2	1	3	0					
Pete Goegan	D	4	1	0	1	2					
John MacMillan	R	3	0	1	1	0					
Andre Pronovost	L	3	0	1	1	0					
Roger Crozier	G	70	0	0	0	10	7	0	0	0	2
Warren Godfrey	D	11	0	0	0	8	4	0	1	1	2
Bob Dillabough	C	4	0	0	0	2	4	0	0	0	0
Butch Paul	C	3	0	0	0	0					
Carl Wetzel	G	2	0	0	0	0					
Ted Hampson	C	1	0	0	0	0					
Claude Laforge	L	1	0	0	0	2					
Jimmy Peters	C	1	0	0	0	0					
Bob Wall	D	1	0	0	0	0	1	0	0	0	0
Jim Watson	D	1	0	0	0	2					
Murray Hall	R						1	0	0	0	0
Irv Spencer	D						1	0	0	0	4

		REGULAR SEASON				POSTSEASON				
GOALTENDER		GP	MIN	GA	SH	GAA	GP	MIN	GA	SH	GAA
Roger Crozier	(40-22-7)	70	4168	168	(3) 6	2.42	7	420	23	0	3.29
Carl Wetzel	(0-1-0)	2	32	4	0	7.50					

MONTREAL   36-23-11   83   2nd   Toe Blake
Canadiens

		REGULAR SEASON				POSTSEASON				
PLAYER	POS	GP	G	A	PTS	PIM	GP	G	A	PTS	PIM
Claude Provost	R	70	27	37	64	28	13	2	6	8	12
Ralph Backstrom	C	70	25	30	55	41	13	2	3	5	10
Henri Richard	C	53	23	29	52	43	13	7	4	11	24
Bobby Rousseau	R	66	12	35	47	26	13	5	8	13	24
John Ferguson	L	69	17	27	44	156	13	3	1	4	28
Jean Beliveau	C	58	20	23	43	76	13	8	8	16	34
Dave Balon	L	63	18	23	41	61	10	0	0	0	10
Claude Larose	R	68	21	16	37	82	13	0	1	1	14
Jacques Laperriere	D	67	5	22	27	92	6	1	1	2	16
Jean-Guy Talbot	D	67	8	14	22	64	13	0	1	1	22
J.C. Tremblay	D	68	3	17	20	22	13	1	9	10	18
Yvan Cournoyer	R	55	7	10	17	10	12	3	1	4	0
Dick Duff (2–2)	L	40	9	7	16	16	13	3	6	9	17
Gilles Tremblay	L	26	9	7	16	16					
Ted Harris	D	68	1	14	15	107	13	0	5	5	45
Jimmy Roberts	D	70	3	10	13	40	13	0	0	0	30
Terry Harper	D	62	0	7	7	93	13	0	0	0	19
Noel Picard	D	16	0	7	7	33	3	0	1	1	0
Red Berenson	C	3	1	2	3	0	9	0	1	1	2
Keith McCreary	R	9	0	3	3	4					

1964–1965

		REGULAR SEASON					POSTSEASON				
PLAYER	POS	GP	G	A	PTS	PIM	GP	G	A	PTS	PIM
Leon Rochefort	R	9	2	0	2	0					
Garry Peters	C	13	0	2	2	6					
Bill Hicke (1–2)	R	17	0	1	1	6					
Bryan Watson	D	5	0	1	1	7					
Charlie Hodge	G	53	0	0	0	2	5	0	0	0	0
Lorne Worsley	G	19	0	0	0	0	8	0	0	0	0
Andre Boudrias	L	1	0	0	0	2					
Jean Gauthier	D						2	0	0	0	4

		REGULAR SEASON					POSTSEASON				
GOALTENDER		GP	MIN	GA	SH	GAA	GP	MIN	GA	SH	GAA
Charlie Hodge	(26-16-**10**)	53	3180	135	3	2.55	5	300	10	1	2.00
Lorne Worsley	(10-7-1)	19	1020	50	1	2.94	8	501	14	**2**	**1.68**

CHICAGO   34-28-8   76   3rd   Billy Reay
Blackhawks

		REGULAR SEASON					POSTSEASON				
PLAYER	POS	GP	G	A	PTS	PIM	GP	G	A	PTS	PIM
Stan Mikita	C	**70**	28	**59**	**87**	154	14	3	7	10	**53**
Bobby Hull	L	61	**39**	32	71	32	14	**10**	7	**17**	27
Pierre Pilote	D	68	14	45	59	162	12	0	7	7	22
Phil Esposito	C	**70**	23	32	55	44	13	3	3	6	15
Kenny Wharram	R	68	24	20	44	27	12	2	3	5	4
Ron Maki	R	65	16	24	40	58	14	3	9	12	8
Bill Hay	C	69	11	26	37	36	14	3	1	4	4
Doug Mohns	F	49	13	20	33	84	14	3	4	7	21
Eric Nesterenko	R	56	14	16	30	63	14	2	2	4	16
Matt Ravlich	D	61	3	16	19	80	14	1	4	5	14
John McKenzie	R	51	8	10	18	46	11	0	1	1	6
Fred Stanfield	L	58	7	10	17	14	14	2	1	3	2
Doug Jarrett	D	46	2	15	17	34	11	1	0	1	10
Dennis Hull	L	55	10	4	14	18	6	0	0	0	0
Doug Robinson (1–2)	L	40	2	9	11	8					
Elmer Vasko	D	69	1	10	11	56	14	1	2	3	20
Al MacNeil	D	69	3	7	10	119	14	0	1	1	34
Camille Henry (2–2)	C	22	5	3	8	2	14	1	0	1	2
John Brenneman (1–2)	L	17	1	0	1	2					
Denis DeJordy	G	31	0	1	1	0	2	0	0	0	0
Wayne Hillman (1–2)	D	19	0	1	1	8					
Glenn Hall	G	41	0	0	0	2	13	0	0	0	0
Ken Hodge	R	1	0	0	0	2					
Larry Mickey	R	1	0	0	0	0					
Jerry Melnyk	C						6	0	0	0	0

		REGULAR SEASON					POSTSEASON				
GOALTENDER		GP	MIN	GA	SH	GAA	GP	MIN	GA	SH	GAA
Glenn Hall	(18-17-5)	41	2440	99 (1)	4	2.43	13	760	28	1	2.21
Denis DeJordy	(16-11-3)	30	1760	74 (2)	3	2.52	2	80	9	0	6.75

TORONTO 30-26-14   74   4th   Punch Imlach
Maple Leafs

		REGULAR SEASON				*POSTSEASON*				
PLAYER	*POS*	*GP*	*G*	*A*	*PTS*	*PIM*	*GP*	*G*	*A*	*PTS*	*PIM*
Frank Mahovlich	L	59	23	28	51	76	6	0	3	3	9
Dave Keon	C	65	21	29	50	10	6	2	2	4	2
Red Kelly	D	70	18	28	46	8	6	3	2	5	2
Andy Bathgate	R	55	16	29	45	34	6	1	0	1	6
Ron Ellis	R	62	23	16	39	14	6	3	0	3	2
Bob Pulford	L	65	19	20	39	46	6	1	1	2	16
George Armstrong	C	59	15	22	37	14	6	1	0	1	4
Tim Horton	D	70	12	16	28	95	6	0	2	2	13
Kent Douglas	D	67	5	23	28	129	5	0	1	1	19
Ron Stewart	C	65	16	11	27	33	6	0	1	1	2
Carl Brewer	D	70	4	23	27	177	6	1	2	3	12
Pete Stemkowski	C	36	5	15	20	33	6	0	3	3	7
Don McKenney	C	52	6	13	19	6	6	0	0	0	0
Jim Pappin	R	44	9	9	18	33					
Bob Baun	D	70	0	18	18	160	6	0	1	1	14
Allan Stanley	D	64	2	15	17	30	6	0	1	1	12
Eddie Shack	L	67	5	9	14	68	5	1	0	1	8
Billy Harris	C	48	1	6	7	0					
Dickie Moore	L	38	2	4	6	68	5	1	1	2	6
Brit Selby	L	3	2	0	2	2					
Terry Sawchuk	G	36	0	2	2	24	1	0	0	0	0
Johnny Bower	G	34	0	0	0	6	5	0	0	0	0
Larry Hillman	D	2	0	0	0	2					
Duane Rupp	D	2	0	0	0	0					
Al Arbour	D						1	0	0	0	2

		REGULAR SEASON					*POSTSEASON*				
GOALTENDER		*GP*	*MIN*	*GA*	*SH*	*GAA*	*GP*	*MIN*	*GA*	*SH*	*GAA*
Johnny Bower	(13-13-8)	34	2040	81	3	**2.38**	5	321	13	0	2.43
Terry Sawchuk	(17-13-6)	36	2160	92	1	2.56	1	60	3	0	3.00

NEW YORK 20-38-12   52   5th   George Sullivan
Rangers

		REGULAR SEASON				*POSTSEASON*
PLAYER	*POS*	*GP*	*G*	*A*	*PTS*	*PIM*
						no postseason play
Rod Gilbert	R	70	25	36	61	52
Phil Goyette	C	52	12	34	46	6
Vic Hadfield	L	70	18	20	38	102
Camille Henry (1–2)	C	48	21	15	36	20
Don Marshall	L	69	20	15	35	2
Jean Ratelle	C	54	14	21	35	14
Bob Nevin	R	64	16	14	30	28
Earl Ingarfield	C	69	15	13	28	40
Rod Seiling	D	68	4	22	26	44
Doug Robinson (2–2)	L	21	8	14	22	2
Harry Howell	D	68	2	20	22	63
Lou Angotti	C	70	9	8	17	20
Bill Hicke (2–2)	R	40	6	11	17	26

		REGULAR SEASON				
PLAYER	POS	GP	G	A	PTS	PIM
Jim Neilson	D	62	0	13	13	58
Dick Duff (1–2)	L	29	3	9	12	20
Arnie Brown	D	58	1	11	12	145
Wayne Hillman (2–2)	D	22	1	7	8	26
John Brenneman (2–2)	L	22	3	3	6	6
Larry Cahan	D	26	0	5	5	32
Jim Mikol	L	30	1	3	4	6
Marcel Paille	G	39	0	1	1	2
Jacques Plante	G	33	0	1	1	6
Val Fonteyne (1–2)	L	27	0	1	1	2
Don Johns	D	22	0	1	1	4
Dave Richardson	L	7	0	1	1	4
Bob Plager	D	10	0	0	0	18
Mel Pearson	L	5	0	0	0	4
Sandy Fitzpatrick	C	4	0	0	0	2
Ulf Sterner	L	4	0	0	0	0
Ted Taylor	L	4	0	0	0	4
Ron Ingram	D	3	0	0	0	2
Marc Dufour	R	2	0	0	0	0
Billy Taylor	C	2	0	0	0	0
Trevor Fahey	L	1	0	0	0	0
Jim Johnson	C	1	0	0	0	0
Gord Labossierre	C	1	0	0	0	0
Mike McMahon	D	1	0	0	0	0
Dick Meissner	R	1	0	0	0	0

POSTSEASON
no postseason play

		REGULAR SEASON				
GOALTENDER		GP	MIN	GA	SH	GAA
Jacques Plante	(10-17-5)	33	1938	109 (1)	2	3.37
Marcel Paille	(10-21-7)	39	2262	135 (1)	0	3.58

POSTSEASON
no postseason play

BOSTON
Bruins

21-43-6   48   6th   Milt Schmidt

		REGULAR SEASON				
PLAYER	POS	GP	G	A	PTS	PIM
John Bucyk	L	68	26	29	55	24
Murray Oliver	C	65	20	23	43	30
Reg Fleming	L	67	18	23	41	136
Ted Green	D	70	8	27	35	156
Tommy Williams	C	65	13	21	34	28
Ed Westfall	R	68	12	15	27	65
Orland Kurtenbach	C	64	6	20	26	86
Dean Prentice	L	31	14	9	23	12
Wayne Rivers	R	58	6	17	23	72
Alvin McDonald	L	60	9	9	18	6
Bill Knibbs	C	53	7	10	17	4
Wayne Maxner	L	54	7	6	13	42
Leo Boivin	D	67	3	10	13	68
Bob Woytowich	D	21	2	10	12	16
Ron Schock	C	33	4	7	11	14

POSTSEASON
no postseason play

		REGULAR SEASON					*POSTSEASON*
PLAYER	POS	GP	G	A	PTS	PIM	*no postseason play*
Forbes Kennedy	C	52	6	4	10	41	
Tom Johnson	D	51	0	9	9	30	
Bob McCord	D	43	0	6	6	26	
Don Awrey	D	47	2	3	5	41	
Bobby Leiter	C	18	3	1	4	6	
Murray Balfour	R	15	0	2	2	26	
Gary Dornhoefer	R	20	0	1	1	13	
Jeannot Gilbert	C	4	0	1	1	0	
Joe Watson	D	4	0	1	1	0	
Eddie Johnston	G	47	0	0	0	4	
Jack Norris	G	23	0	0	0	0	
Bill Goldsworthy	R	2	0	0	0	0	
Wayne Cashman	L	1	0	0	0	0	

		REGULAR SEASON					*POSTSEASON*
GOALTENDER		GP	MIN	GA	SH	GAA	*no postseason play*
Eddie Johnston	(11-**32**-4)	47	2820	163 (4)	3	3.47	
Jack Norris	(10-11-2)	32	1380	85 (1)	1	3.70	

TEAM TOTALS

								Per Game			
TEAM	GP	G	A	PTS	PIM	GA	SH	G	A	PIM	GA
Detroit	70	**224**	357	581	**1121**	175	6	**3.20**	5.10	**16.01**	2.50
Montreal	70	211	344	555	1033	185	4	3.01	4.91	14.76	2.64
Chicago	70	**224**	**359**	**583**	1051	176	7	**3.20**	**5.13**	15.01	2.51
Toronto	70	204	334	538	1068	**173**	4	2.91	4.77	15.26	**2.47**
New York	70	179	297	476	760	246	2	2.56	4.24	10.86	3.51
Boston	70	166	264	430	946	253	4	2.37	3.77	13.51	3.61
	420	1208	1955	3163	5979	1208	27	2.88	4.65	14.24	2.88

PLAYOFFS

SERIES "A"
Detroit 4, Chicago 3
Detroit 6, Chicago 3
Chicago 5, Detroit 2
Chicago 2, Detroit 1
Detroit 4, Chicago 2
Chicago 4, Detroit 0
Chicago 4, Detroit 2

CHICAGO, 4–3

SERIES "C"
Montreal 3, Chicago 2
Montreal 2, Chicago 0
Chicago 3, Montreal 1
Chicago 5, Montreal 1

SERIES "B"
Montreal 3, Toronto 2
Montreal 3, Toronto 1
Toronto 3, Montreal 2 (OT)
Toronto 4, Montreal 2
Montreal 3, Toronto 1
Montreal 4, Toronto 3 (OT)

MONTREAL, 4–2

Montreal 6, Chicago 0
Chicago 2, Montreal 1
Montreal 4, Chicago 0

**MONTREAL WINS
STANLEY CUP, 4-3**

ALL-STAR TEAMS

First Team
G — Roger Crozier, DET
D — Jacques Laperriere, MTL
D — Pierre Pilote, CHI
C — Norm Ullman, DET
R — Claude Provost, MTL
L — Bobby Hull, CHI

Second Team
G — Charlie Hodge, MTL
D — Carl Brewer, TOR
D — Bill Gadsby, DET
C — Stan Mikita, CHI
R — Gordie Howe, DET
L — Frank Mahovlich, TOR

INDIVIDUAL TROPHY WINNERS

HART TROPHY (Most Valuable Player): Bobby Hull, CHI
LADY BYNG TROPHY (Gentlemanly Conduct): Bobby Hull, CHI
VEZINA TROPHY (Best Goaltender): Johnny Bower, TOR; Terry Sawchuk, TOR
CALDER MEMORIAL TROPHY (Best Rookie): Roger Crozier, DET
ART ROSS TROPHY (Scoring Leader): Stan Mikita, CHI
JAMES NORRIS TROPHY (Best Defenseman): Pierre Pilote, CHI
CONN SMYTHE TROPHY (Playoff MVP): Jean Beliveau, MTL

1965-1966
Bobby Hull

In the late 1950s, a veritable tornado of a player emerged on the roster of the NHL's westernmost club. Within a few years, this hard-shooting individual shattered several scoring marks, helping to propel his club out of the doldrums.

After torching the Ontario Hockey Association with 33 goals in 52 games, 18-year-old Bobby Hull made his NHL debut for the Chicago Blackhawks in the fall of 1957. In his first campaign, the Ontario native potted 13 goals, increasing the total to 18 the following year. In 1959-60, Hull (39-42-81) reached stardom, leading the league in goals and points, capturing the title on the very last day of the schedule. Two years later, he reached the magical number of 50, again leading the league in points. In 1963-64, Hull (43-44-87) captured his third goal scoring championship in five years, setting a new personal best point total as well. After a brief downward blip the following year, Hull was about to raise the bar even higher.

The chief weapon at Hull's disposal was his famed slap shot, giving him the hardest shot in the league. Combined with his famous "banana blade" stick, he was every goalie's nightmare. One of his unfortunate contemporaries — goaltender Les Binkley — had this to say about Hull, as reported in the pages of *After the Applause*: "When the puck left his stick, it looked like a pea. Then as it picked up speed it looked smaller and smaller. Then you didn't see it anymore." It was no wonder, with such a weapon at its disposal, the Chicago Blackhawks went from a doormat to a contender in a few short years.

In 1965-66, Hull ratcheted up his game, scoring goal after goal. On March 12, in a game against New York, he scored his 51st marker, shattering the 20-year-old record. In the final game of the season, Hull recorded his

43rd assist, which combined with his 54 goals, gave him 97 points on the season — another new record.

Despite Hull's heroics, Montreal (41-21-8, 90) bested his Blackhawks by eight points during the regular season, both ahead of the final two playoff teams, Toronto and Detroit. Once again, New York and Boston brought up the rear. In other individual accolades, three players — Stan Mikita (Chicago), as well as Bobby Rousseau and Jean Beliveau (Montreal) — each collected 48 assists. Reg Fleming, who fought for both New York and Boston, had the highest penalty minutes total (166). In net, Toronto's Johnny Bower (2.25) posted the lowest GAA, while Detroit's Roger Crozier earned the most shutouts (7).

In the postseason, Montreal waxed Toronto in straight sets in one opening series, while Detroit upset Hull's Blackhawks in the other. The latter slate was knotted at two wins each, when the Red Wings took charge — winning the next two contests, 5–3 and 3–2. In the finals, the fourth place Wings surprised Montreal, taking the first two contests, 3–2 and 5–2. Then the Canadiens took charge, emerging victorious in the next four contests, capped by an overtime winner (4–3) by Henri Richard in the deciding game, giving Montreal the Cup. Despite the loss, all of the playoff scoring leaders came from the Detroit squad. Norm Ullman (6-9-15) collected the most goals and points, although he was tied in the former category by Andy Bathgate. In addition, Alex Delvecchio (11) amassed the most assists. In net, Montreal's Lorne Worsley (1.99) was the hardest to beat.

After his record-breaking campaign, Hull went on to register another three 50 goal seasons for the Blackhawks, raising his record (58) in the middle season (1968-69). Following the third 50-goal-year, he balked at the terms of a potential new contract, instead choosing to sign with the fledgling World Hockey Association's Winnipeg club in 1972 for a record-breaking million dollars. Hull's signing gave the upstart rebels instant credibility, and true to his contract he delivered the goods. Over the seven-year history of the WHA, he scored over 300 goals, including a record 77 in 1975-76. While skating for the Jets, Hull played along side two talented Swedes — Ulf Nilsson and Anders Hedberg — helping to usher in a new era to pro hockey. When his Winnipeg club was absorbed by the NHL in 1979-80, he participated in his final NHL campaign. Late in the season, Hull was traded to Hartford, and played his last nine games alongside another legend — Gordie Howe.

Besides being the most fearsome scorer of his generation, Hull's overall legacy stands the test of time. He scored 610 goals in the NHL, and when added to his WHA total, he has over 900 major league tallies. In the history of the game, only two other skaters have reached that lofty total, putting Hull in elite company indeed.

STANDINGS

TEAM	GP	W	L	T	PTS	GF	GA
MONTREAL	70	41	21	8	90	239	179
CHICAGO	70	37	25	8	82	240	187
TORONTO	70	34	25	11	79	208	187
DETROIT	70	31	27	12	74	221	194
BOSTON	70	21	43	6	48	174	275
NEW YORK	70	18	41	11	47	195	261

LEADERS

PLAYER	TM	GP	G	A	PTS	PIM
Bobby Hull	CHI	65	54	43	97	70
Stan Mikita	CHI	68	30	48	78	58
Bobby Rousseau	MTL	70	30	48	78	20
Jean Beliveau	MTL	67	29	48	77	50
Gordie Howe	DET	70	29	46	75	83
Norm Ullman	DET	70	31	41	72	35
Alex Delvecchio	DET	70	31	38	69	16
Bob Nevin	NY	69	29	33	62	10
Henri Richard	MTL	62	22	39	61	47
Murray Oliver	BOS	70	18	42	60	30

GOALS	
Hull, CHI	54
Mahovlich, TOR	32
Delvecchio, DET	31
Ullman, DET	31
Two tied with	30

ASSISTS	
Mikita, CHI	48
Rousseau, MTL	48
Beliveau, MTL	48
Howe, DET	46
Hull, CHI	43

GOALTENDER	TM	GP	MIN	GA	SH	GAA
Johnny Bower	TOR	35	1998	75 (1)	3	2.25
Lorne Worsley	MTL	51	2899	114 (3)	2	2.36
Glenn Hall	CHI	64	3747	164	4	2.63
Roger Crozier	DET	64	3734	173 (2)	7	2.78
Terry Sawchuk	TOR	27	1521	80 (1)	1	3.16
Cesare Maniago	NY	28	1613	94	2	3.50
Ed Giacomin	NY	35	2036	125 (2)	0	3.68
Bernie Parent	BOS	39	2083	128	1	3.69
Eddie Johnston	BOS	33	1744	108 (1)	1	3.72

PENALTY MINUTES	
Fleming, B-N	166
Ferguson, MTL	153
Watson, DET	133
Green, BOS	113
Hadfield, NY	112

SHUTOUTS	
Crozier, DET	7
Hall, CHI	4
Gamble, TOR	4
Bower, TOR	3
Two tied with	2

MONTREAL Canadiens 41-21-8 90 1st Toe Blake

		REGULAR SEASON					POSTSEASON			
PLAYER	POS	GP	G	A	PTS	PIM	GP	G	A	PTS	PIM
Bobby Rousseau	R	70	30	48	78	20	10	4	4	8	6
Jean Beliveau	C	67	29	48	77	50	10	5	5	10	6
Henri Richard	C	62	22	39	61	47	8	1	4	5	2
Claude Provost	R	70	19	36	55	38	10	2	3	5	2
Gilles Tremblay	L	70	27	21	48	24	10	4	5	9	0
Dick Duff	L	63	21	24	45	78	10	2	5	7	2
Ralph Backstrom	C	67	22	20	42	10	10	3	4	7	4
J.C. Tremblay	D	59	6	29	35	8	10	2	9	11	2

1965–1966

		REGULAR SEASON					POSTSEASON				
PLAYER	POS	GP	G	A	PTS	PIM	GP	G	A	PTS	PIM
Claude Larose	R	64	15	18	33	67	6	0	1	1	31
Jacques Laperriere	D	57	6	25	31	85					
Yvan Cournoyer	R	65	18	11	29	8	10	2	3	5	2
John Ferguson	L	65	11	14	25	153	10	2	0	2	44
Jean-Guy Talbot	D	59	1	14	15	50	10	0	2	2	8
Ted Harris	D	53	0	13	13	87	10	0	0	0	38
Terry Harper	D	69	1	11	12	91	10	2	3	5	18
Jimmy Roberts	D	70	5	5	10	20	10	1	1	2	10
Dave Balon	L	45	3	7	10	24	9	2	3	5	16
Red Berenson	C	23	3	4	7	12					
Noel Price	D	15	0	6	6	8	3	0	1	1	0
Lorne Worsley	G	51	0	1	1	4	10	0	0	0	0
Leon Rochefort	R	1	0	1	1	0	4	1	1	2	4
Charlie Hodge	G	26	0	0	0	0					
Jean Gauthier	D	2	0	0	0	0					
Danny Grant	L	1	0	0	0	0					
Don Johns	D	1	0	0	0	0					

		REGULAR SEASON					POSTSEASON				
GOALTENDER		GP	MIN	GA	SH	GAA	GP	MIN	GA	SH	GAA
Lorne Worsley	(29-14-6)	51	2899	114 (3)	2	**2.36**	10	602	20	1	**1.99**
Charlie Hodge	(12-7-2)	26	1301	56	1	2.58					

CHICAGO 37-25-8 82 2nd Billy Reay
Blackhawks

		REGULAR SEASON					POSTSEASON				
PLAYER	POS	GP	G	A	PTS	PIM	GP	G	A	PTS	PIM
Bobby Hull	L	65	54	43	97	70	6	2	2	4	10
Stan Mikita	C	68	30	48	78	58	6	1	2	3	2
Phil Esposito	C	69	27	26	53	49	6	1	1	2	2
Bill Hay	C	68	20	31	51	20	6	0	2	2	4
Doug Mohns	F	70	22	27	49	63	5	1	0	1	4
Ron Maki	R	68	17	31	48	41	3	1	1	2	0
Kenny Wharram	R	69	26	17	43	28	6	1	0	1	4
Eric Nesterenko	R	67	15	25	40	58	6	1	0	1	4
Pierre Pilote	D	51	2	34	36	60	6	0	2	2	10
Pat Stapleton	D	55	4	30	34	52	6	2	3	5	4
Ken Hodge	R	63	6	17	23	47	5	0	0	0	8
Doug Jarrett	D	66	4	12	16	71	5	0	1	1	9
Matt Ravlich	D	62	0	16	16	78	6	0	1	1	2
Lou Angotti (2-2)	C	30	4	10	14	12	6	0	0	0	2
Len Lunde	L	24	4	7	11	4					
Elmer Vasko	D	56	1	7	8	44	3	0	0	0	4
Dennis Hull	L	25	1	5	6	6	3	0	0	0	0
Fred Stanfield	L	39	2	2	4	2	5	0	0	0	2
John Miszuk	D	2	1	1	2	2	3	0	0	0	4
Glenn Hall	G	64	0	2	2	14	6	0	0	0	0
Dave Dryden	G	11	0	1	1	0	1	0	0	0	0
Al MacNeil	D	51	0	1	1	34	3	0	0	0	0
Dave Richardson	L	3	0	0	0	2					

		REGULAR SEASON					*POSTSEASON*				
PLAYER	*POS*	*GP*	*G*	*A*	*PTS*	*PIM*	*GP*	*G*	*A*	*PTS*	*PIM*
Art Stratton	C	2	0	0	0	0					
John Stanfield	L						1	0	0	0	0

		REGULAR SEASON				*POSTSEASON*			
GOALTENDER		*GP*	*MIN*	*GA*	*SH*	*GAA*	*GP*	*MIN*	*GA*	*SH*	*GAA*
Glenn Hall	(34-21-7)	64	3747	164	4	2.63	6	347	22	0	3.80
Dave Dryden	(3-4-1)	11	453	23	0	3.05	1	13	0	0	0.00

TORONTO 34-25-11 79 3rd Punch Imlach
Maple Leafs

		REGULAR SEASON					*POSTSEASON*				
PLAYER	*POS*	*GP*	*G*	*A*	*PTS*	*PIM*	*GP*	*G*	*A*	*PTS*	*PIM*
Frank Mahovlich	L	68	32	24	56	68	4	1	0	1	10
Bob Pulford	L	70	28	28	56	51	4	1	1	2	12
Dave Keon	C	69	24	30	54	4	4	0	2	2	0
George Armstrong	C	70	16	35	51	12	4	0	1	1	4
Eddie Shack	L	63	26	17	43	88	4	2	1	3	33
Ron Ellis	R	70	19	23	42	24	4	0	0	0	2
Red Kelly	D	63	8	24	32	12	4	0	2	2	0
Tim Horton	D	70	6	22	28	76	4	1	0	1	12
Larry Hillman	D	48	3	25	28	34	4	1	1	2	6
Brit Selby	L	61	14	13	27	26	4	0	0	0	0
Wally Boyer	C	46	4	17	21	23	4	0	1	1	0
Kent Douglas	D	64	6	14	20	97	4	0	1	1	12
Allan Stanley	D	59	4	14	18	35	1	0	0	0	0
Pete Stemkowski	C	56	4	12	16	55	4	0	0	0	26
Orland Kurtenbach	C	70	9	6	15	54	4	0	0	0	20
Marcel Pronovost	D	54	2	8	10	34	4	0	0	0	6
Bob Baun	D	44	0	6	6	68	4	0	1	1	8
Mike Walton	C	6	1	3	4	0					
Jim Pappin	R	7	0	3	3	8					
Larry Jeffrey	L	20	1	1	2	22					
Eddie Joyal	C	14	0	2	2	2					
Dick Gamble	L	2	1	0	1	0					
Johnny Bower	G	35	0	1	1	0	2	0	0	0	0
Terry Sawchuk	G	27	0	1	1	12	2	0	0	0	0
Al Arbour	D	4	0	1	1	2					
Wayne Carleton	L	2	0	1	1	0					
Duane Rupp	D	2	0	1	1	0					
Bruce Gamble	G	10	0	0	0	0					
Gary Smith	G	3	0	0	0	0					
Brian Conacher	C	2	0	0	0	2					
Brent Imlach	F	2	0	0	0	0					
Jim McKenny	R	2	0	0	0	2					
Darryl Sly	D	2	0	0	0	0					
Al Smith	G	2	0	0	0	0					

		REGULAR SEASON					*POSTSEASON*				
GOALTENDER		*GP*	*MIN*	*GA*	*SH*	*GAA*	*GP*	*MIN*	*GA*	*SH*	*GAA*
Al Smith	(1-0-0)	2	62	2	0	1.94					
Johnny Bower	(18-10-5)	35	1998	75 (1)	3	**2.25**	2	120	8	0	4.00

1965-1966

GOALTENDER		REGULAR SEASON					POSTSEASON				
		GP	MIN	GA	SH	GAA	GP	MIN	GA	SH	GAA
Bruce Gamble	(5-2-3)	10	501	21	4	2.51					
Terry Sawchuk	(10-11-3)	27	1521	80 (1)	1	3.16	2	120	6	0	3.00
Gary Smith	(0-2-0)	3	118	7	0	3.56					

DETROIT
Red Wings

31-27-12   74   4th   Sid Abel

PLAYER	POS	REGULAR SEASON					POSTSEASON				
		GP	G	A	PTS	PIM	GP	G	A	PTS	PIM
Gordie Howe	R	70	29	46	75	83	12	4	6	10	12
Norm Ullman	C	70	31	41	72	35	12	6	9	15	12
Alex Delvecchio	C	70	31	38	69	16	12	0	11	11	4
Floyd Smith	R	66	21	28	49	20	12	5	2	7	4
Andy Bathgate	R	70	15	32	47	25	12	6	3	9	6
Paul Henderson	R	69	22	24	46	34	12	3	3	6	10
Bruce MacGregor	C	70	20	14	34	28	12	1	4	5	2
Alvin McDonald	L	43	6	16	22	6	10	1	4	5	2
Doug Barkley	D	43	5	15	20	65					
Gary Bergman	D	61	3	16	19	96	12	0	3	3	14
Bert Marshall	D	61	0	19	19	45	12	1	3	4	16
Bill Gadsby	D	58	5	12	17	72	12	1	3	4	12
P. MacDonald (2-2)	C	37	5	12	17	24	9	0	0	0	2
Dean Prentice (2-2)	L	19	6	9	15	8	12	5	5	10	4
Val Fonteyne	L	59	5	10	15	0	12	1	0	1	4
Ron Murphy (1-2)	L	32	10	7	14	10					
Bryan Watson	D	70	2	7	9	133	12	2	0	2	30
Don McKenney	C	24	1	6	7	0					
Billy Harris	C	24	1	4	5	6					
Leo Boivin (2-2)	D	16	0	5	5	16	12	0	1	1	16
Warren Godfrey	D	26	0	4	4	22	4	0	0	0	0
Hubert Martin (1-2)	C	10	1	1	2	0					
Bob Wall	D	8	1	1	2	8	6	0	0	0	2
Jimmy Peters	C	6	1	1	2	2					
Pete Goegan	D	13	0	2	2	14	1	0	0	0	0
Bob McCord	D	9	0	2	2	16					
Pete Mahovlich	C	3	0	1	1	0					
Roger Crozier	G	64	0	0	0	2	12	0	0	0	0
Hank Bassen	G	11	0	0	0	0					
Gary Doak	D	4	0	0	0	12					
Jim Watson	D	2	0	0	0	4					
Gordon Carruthers	D	1	0	0	0	0					
Bart Crashley	D	1	0	0	0	0					
Murray Hall	R	1	0	0	0	0	1	0	0	0	0
Doug Roberts	R	1	0	0	0	0					
George Gardner	G	1	0	0	0	0					
Irv Spencer	D						3	0	0	0	2

GOALTENDER		REGULAR SEASON					POSTSEASON				
		GP	MIN	GA	SH	GAA	GP	MIN	GA	SH	GAA
George Gardner	(1-0-0)	1	60	1	0	1.00					

		REGULAR SEASON					POSTSEASON				
GOALTENDER		GP	MIN	GA	SH	GAA	GP	MIN	GA	SH	GAA
Hank Bassen	(3-3-0)	11	406	17 (1)	0	2.51	1	54	2	0	2.22
Roger Crozier	(27-**24**-12)	64	3734	173 (2)	7	2.78	12	668	26	1	2.34

BOSTON 21-43-6 48 5th Milt Schmidt
Bruins

		REGULAR SEASON					POSTSEASON
PLAYER	POS	GP	G	A	PTS	PIM	no postseason play
Murray Oliver	C	70	18	42	60	30	
John Bucyk	L	63	27	30	57	12	
Tommy Williams	C	70	16	22	38	31	
Ron Stewart	C	70	20	16	36	17	
Ed Westfall	R	59	9	21	30	42	
Dean Prentice (1-2)	L	50	7	22	29	10	
Hubert Martin (2-2)	C	41	16	11	27	10	
John McKenzie (2-2)	R	36	13	9	22	36	
Bob Dillabough	C	53	7	13	20	18	
Gilles Marotte	D	51	3	17	20	52	
Bob Woytowich	D	68	2	17	19	75	
Ted Green	D	27	5	13	18	116	
Al Langlois	D	65	4	10	14	54	
P. MacDonald (1-2)	C	29	6	4	10	6	
Forbes Kennedy	C	50	4	6	10	55	
Reg Fleming (1-2)	L	34	4	6	10	*42	
Gary Doak (2-2)	D	20	0	8	8	28	
Don Awrey	D	70	4	3	7	74	
Leo Boivin (1-2)	D	46	0	5	5	34	
Bill Goldsworthy	R	13	3	1	4	6	
Ron Schock	C	24	2	2	4	6	
Wayne Maxner	L	8	1	3	4	6	
Bobby Leiter	C	9	2	1	3	2	
Barry Ashbee	D	14	0	3	3	14	
Wayne Rivers	R	2	1	1	2	2	
Gary Dornhoefer	R	10	0	1	1	2	
Poul Popiel	D	3	0	1	1	2	
Ron Murphy (2-2)	L	2	0	1	1	0	
Bernie Parent	G	39	0	0	0	4	
Eddie Johnston	G	33	0	0	0	2	
Gerry Cheevers	G	7	0	0	0	0	
Terry Crisp	C	3	0	0	0	0	
J.P. Parise	L	3	0	0	0	0	
John Arbour	D	2	0	0	0	0	
Skip Krake	C	2	0	0	0	0	
Derek Sanderson	C	2	0	0	0	0	
Dallas Smith	D	2	0	0	0	2	
Murray Davison	D	1	0	0	0	0	
Don Marcotte	L	1	0	0	0	0	
Bob Ring	G	1	0	0	0	0	

1965-1966

GOALTENDER		REGULAR SEASON					POSTSEASON
		GP	MIN	GA	SH	GAA	no postseason play
Bernie Parent	(11-20-3)	39	2083	128	1	3.69	
Eddie Johnston	(10-19-2)	33	1744	108 (1)	1	3.72	
Gerry Cheevers	(0-4-1)	7	340	34	0	6.00	
Bob Ring		1	33	4	0	7.27	

NEW YORK Rangers   18-41-11   47   6th   Emile Francis

PLAYER	POS	REGULAR SEASON					POSTSEASON
		GP	G	A	PTS	PIM	no postseason play
Bob Nevin	R	69	29	33	62	10	
Don Marshall	L	69	26	28	54	6	
Jean Ratelle	C	67	21	30	51	10	
Phil Goyette	C	60	11	31	42	6	
Earl Ingarfield	C	68	20	16	36	35	
Vic Hadfield	L	67	16	19	35	112	
Harry Howell	D	70	4	29	33	92	
Bill Hicke	R	49	9	18	27	21	
Rod Gilbert	R	34	10	15	25	20	
Reg Fleming (2-2)	L	35	10	14	24	*124	
Jim Neilson	D	65	4	19	23	84	
Doug Robinson	L	51	8	12	20	8	
Wayne Hillman	D	68	3	17	20	70	
Rod Seiling	D	52	5	10	15	24	
Mike McMahon	D	41	0	12	12	34	
John McKenzie (1-2)	R	35	6	5	11	36	
Garry Peters	C	63	7	3	10	42	
Arnie Brown	D	64	1	7	8	106	
Bob Plager	D	18	0	5	5	22	
Lou Angotti (1-2)	C	21	2	2	4	2	
Ray Cullen	C	8	1	3	4	0	
Paul Andrea	R	4	1	1	2	0	
Cesare Maniago	G	28	0	2	2	2	
Jim Johnson	C	5	1	0	1	0	
Ted Taylor	L	4	0	1	1	2	
Ed Giacomin	G	35	0	0	0	8	
Don Simmons	G	12	0	0	0	0	
John Brenneman	L	11	0	0	0	14	
Larry Mickey	R	7	0	0	0	2	
Al Hamilton	D	4	0	0	0	0	
Al LeBrun	D	2	0	0	0	0	
Dunc McCallum	D	2	0	0	0	2	

GOALTENDER		REGULAR SEASON					POSTSEASON
		GP	MIN	GA	SH	GAA	no postseason play
Cesare Maniago	(9-14-4)	28	1613	94	2	3.50	
Ed Giacomin	(8-20-6)	35	2036	125 (2)	0	3.68	
Don Simmons	(1-7-1)	12	551	40	0	4.36	

TEAM TOTALS

								Per Game			
TEAM	GP	G	A	PTS	PIM	GA	SH	G	A	PIM	GA
Montreal	70	239	**394**	**633**	884	173	3	3.41	**5.63**	12.63	**2.47**
Chicago	70	**240**	390	630	815	187	4	**3.43**	5.57	11.64	2.67
Toronto	70	208	330	538	811	187	8	2.97	4.71	11.59	2.67
Detroit	70	221	373	594	804	194	7	3.16	5.33	11.49	2.77
Boston	70	174	289	463	787	275	2	2.49	4.13	11.24	3.93
New York	70	195	330	525	**894**	261	2	2.79	4.71	**12.77**	3.73
	420	1277	2106	3383	4995	1277	26	3.04	5.01	11.89	3.04

PLAYOFFS

SERIES "A"
Montreal 4, Toronto 3
Montreal 2, Toronto 0
Montreal 5, Toronto 2
Montreal 4, Toronto 1

MONTREAL, 4-0

SERIES "B"
Chicago 2, Detroit 1
Detroit 7, Chicago 0
Chicago 2, Detroit 1
Detroit 5, Chicago 1
Detroit 5, Chicago 3
Detroit 3, Chicago 2

DETROIT, 4-2

SERIES "C"
Detroit 3, Montreal 2
Detroit 5, Montreal 2
Montreal 4, Detroit 2
Montreal 2, Detroit 1
Montreal 5, Detroit 1
Montreal 3, Detroit 2 (OT)

**MONTREAL WINS
STANLEY CUP, 4-2**

ALL-STAR TEAMS

First Team
G — Glenn Hall, CHI
D — Pierre Pilote, CHI
D — Jacques Laperriere, MTL
C — Stan Mikita, CHI
R — Gordie Howe, DET
L — Bobby Hull, CHI

Second Team
G — Lorne Worsely, MTL
D — Allan Stanley, TOR
D — Pat Stapleton, CHI
C — Jean Beliveau, MTL
R — Bobby Rousseau, MTL
L — Frank Mahovlich, TOR

INDIVIDUAL TROPHY WINNERS

HART TROPHY (Most Valuable Player): Bobby Hull, CHI
LADY BYNG TROPHY (Gentlemanly Conduct): Alex Delvecchio, DET
VEZINA TROPHY (Best Goaltender): Lorne Worsely, MTL; Charlie Hodge, MTL
CALDER MEMORIAL TROPHY (Best Rookie): Brit Selby, TOR
ART ROSS TROPHY (Scoring Leader): Bobby Hull, CHI
JAMES NORRIS TROPHY (Best Defenseman): Jacques Laperriere, MTL
CONN SMYTHE TROPHY (Playoff MVP): Roger Crozier, DET

1966-1967

Chicago Blackhawks

During most of the 1940s and 1950s, one particular NHL club usually found itself at the bottom of the standings. Frequently in financial trouble as well, this club was bailed out on several occasions, leading to the Intra-League Draft designed specifically to help prop them up. However, by the 1960s, thanks to an influx of young talent, this team was a doormat no more. Instead, they were one of the most fearsome sextets of the decade.

Created in the wave of American expansion that doubled the NHL in the mid–1920s, the Chicago Blackhawks were born in 1926. Named after the owner's (Frederic McLaughlin) World War I army division, the nucleus of the first club came from the roster of the recently folded Portland Rosebud club of the Western Hockey League. In their first few years, the Blackhawks usually qualified for the playoffs, breaking through to win their first Cup in 1934.

Later in the 1930s, the team tried an interesting experiment. Wanting to put an American stamp on his Blackhawks, McLaughlin "Americanized" the club, from the coach on down. With eight Americans on the squad, Chicago barely qualified for the playoffs in 1938, but then ran the table, winning the Cup with only a 14-win club.

In the 1940s, the Blackhawks reached one Cup final (1944), but by the end of the decade the team was floundering badly. Beginning in 1946-47, the team finished last eight out of the next ten years. In five of these instances, the team even failed to crack the 20-win barrier.

In the late 1950s, the Hawks laid the foundation for a much stronger club. In short order, they acquired a solid goalie — Glenn Hall — and signed two youngsters, Bobby Hull and Stan Mikita. Behind this nucleus, the team finished third in the last two years of the decade, then won the Cup with another third place effort in 1961. Over the next few seasons, Chicago never ended lower than third, while participating in two more Cup finals.

In 1966-67, the Blackhawks (41-17-12, 94) put together their best club to date, winning the regular season crown by a comfortable 17 points over Montreal. As usual, they were led by their star trio. Mikita (35-62-97), in tying Hull's mark of the previous year, set a new NHL record for assists. In finishing second in the scoring race, Hull (52-28-80) became the first NHL player to post back-to-back 50 goal seasons. Though no longer a 70-game stalwart, Glenn Hall still enjoyed his finest campaign (2.38), compiling the lowest GAA, while earning a Vezina Trophy, shared with his teammate Denis DeJordy. In addition, Montreal's John Ferguson (177) had the most penalty minutes.

Despite their regular season success, the Blackhawks went down in flames in the first round of the playoffs, losing to the third-place Maple Leafs. Backed by the veteran Terry Sawchuk, Toronto won the key fifth game 4–2, despite being outshot, 49–31. In the sixth game, the Leaf's Brian Conacher scored twice in the 3–1 win, sending the Hawks packing. In the other opening series, New York — making a rare 1960s playoff appearance thanks to Ed Giacomin's league-best nine shutouts, faced Montreal. Here, the Rangers, who had outpointed Detroit and Boston, were dispatched quickly by the Canadiens in straight sets.

In the finals, Montreal pinned a pair of 6–2 wins on Toronto — one in the first game and the other in the fourth. In between and following, the Leafs won all the others, skating off with their fourth Cup of the decade after a 3–1 win in the sixth game. In this series, Sawchuk also shone, as the Canadiens poured over 30 shots a game on the veteran goaltender. Individually, Toronto's Jim Pappin (7-8-15) lit the lamp the most times while registering the most points. His teammate, Bob Pulford, collected the most assists (11). In net, Toronto's Johnny Bower (1.64) posted the lowest GAA before being injured, allowing Sawchuk to save the day.

In subsequent years, Chicago continued to contend, winning a cluster of divisional championships in the 1970s, reaching the Cup finals on two occasions. Later, in the early 1990s, the team earned a spot in the finals once again, but fell short. Last spring, the nearly 50-year drought was ended, as the 'Hawks took home the Cup.

For Chicago, 1966-67 was a milestone campaign that saw the team capture the regular season crown for the first time. For them and the rest of the "Original Six," the season also served as the end of an era. While the Blackhawks were running away with the title, the NHL was preparing for its first wave of expansion in 40 years — a wave which would end a chapter in the league's history, setting in place a trend which would forever alter the circuit.

1966–1967 415

STANDINGS

TEAM	GP	W	L	T	PTS	GF	GA
CHICAGO	70	41	17	12	94	264	170
MONTREAL	70	32	25	13	77	202	188
TORONTO	70	32	27	11	75	204	211
NEW YORK	70	30	28	12	72	188	189
DETROIT	70	27	39	4	58	212	241
BOSTON	70	17	43	10	44	182	253

LEADERS

PLAYER	TM	GP	G	A	PTS	PIM
Stan Mikita	CHI	70	35	62	97	12
Bobby Hull	CHI	66	52	28	80	52
Norm Ullman	DET	68	26	44	70	26
Kenny Wharram	CHI	70	31	34	65	21
Gordie Howe	DET	69	25	40	65	53
Bobby Rousseau	MTL	68	19	44	63	58
Phil Esposito	CHI	69	21	40	61	40
Phil Goyette	NY	70	12	49	61	6
Doug Mohns	CHI	61	25	35	60	58
Two tied with					55	

GOALS	
Hull, CHI	52
Mikita, CHI	35
Wharram, CHI	31
Gilbert, NY	28
MacGregor, DET	28

ASSISTS	
Mikita, CHI	62
Goyette, NY	49
Pilote, CHI	46
Ullman, DET	44
Rousseau, MTL	44

GOALTENDER	TM	GP	MIN	GA	SH	GAA
Glenn Hall	CHI	32	1664	66	2	**2.38**
Denis DeJordy	CHI	44	2536	104	4	2.46
Charlie Hodge	MTL	37	2055	88	3	2.57
Ed Giacomin	NY	68	3981	173 (2)	9	2.61
Roger Crozier	DET	58	3256	**182** (1)	4	3.35
Eddie Johnston	BOS	34	1880	116 (2)	0	3.70

PENALTY MINUTES	
Ferguson, MTL	177
Fleming, NY	146
Bergman, DET	129
Marotte, BOS	112
Van Impe, CHI	111

SHUTOUTS	
Giacomin, NY	9
DeJordy, CHI	4
Crozier, DET	4
Hodge, MTL	3
Three tied with	2

CHICAGO   41-17-12   94   1st   Billy Reay
Blackhawks

		REGULAR SEASON					POSTSEASON				
PLAYER	POS	GP	G	A	PTS	PIM	GP	G	A	PTS	PIM
Stan Mikita	C	70	35	62	97	12	6	2	2	4	2
Bobby Hull	L	66	52	28	80	52	6	4	2	6	0
Kenny Wharram	R	70	31	34	65	21	6	2	2	4	2
Phil Esposito	C	69	21	40	61	40	6	0	0	0	7
Doug Mohns	F	61	25	35	60	58	5	0	5	5	8
Pierre Pilote	D	70	6	46	52	90	6	2	4	6	6
Dennis Hull	L	70	25	17	42	33	6	0	1	1	12
Ron Maki	R	56	9	29	38	14	6	0	0	0	0
Eric Nesterenko	R	68	14	23	37	38	6	1	2	3	2

		REGULAR SEASON				POSTSEASON				
PLAYER	POS	GP	G	A	PTS	PIM	GP	G	A	PTS	PIM
Ken Hodge	R	69	10	25	35	59	6	0	0	0	4
Pat Stapleton	D	70	3	31	34	54	6	1	1	2	12
Doug Jarrett	D	70	5	21	26	76	6	0	3	3	8
Bill Hay	C	36	7	13	20	12	6	0	1	1	4
Ed Van Impe	D	61	8	11	19	111	6	0	0	0	8
Lou Angotti	C	63	6	12	18	21	6	2	1	3	2
Wally Boyer	C	42	5	6	11	15	1	0	0	0	0
Matt Ravlich	D	62	0	3	3	39					
Wayne Smith	D	2	1	1	2	2	1	0	0	0	0
Fred Stanfield	L	10	1	0	1	0	1	0	0	0	0
Denis DeJordy	G	44	0	0	0	0	4	0	0	0	0
Glenn Hall	G	32	0	0	0	10	3	0	0	0	0
John Miszuk	D	3	0	0	0	0	2	0	0	0	2
Billy Dea	C						2	0	0	0	2

		REGULAR SEASON					POSTSEASON				
GOALTENDER		GP	MIN	GA	SH	GAA	GP	MIN	GA	SH	GAA
Glenn Hall	(19-5-5)	32	1664	66	2	**2.38**	3	176	8	0	2.73
Denis DeJordy	(22-12-7)	44	2536	104	4	2.46	4	184	10	0	3.26

MONTREAL Canadiens   32-25-13   77   2nd   Toe Blake

		REGULAR SEASON					POSTSEASON				
PLAYER	POS	GP	G	A	PTS	PIM	GP	G	A	PTS	PIM
Bobby Rousseau	R	68	19	44	63	58	10	1	7	8	4
Henri Richard	C	65	21	34	55	28	10	4	6	10	2
John Ferguson	L	67	20	22	42	**177**	10	4	2	6	22
Ralph Backstrom	C	69	14	27	41	39	10	5	2	7	6
Yvan Cournoyer	R	69	25	15	40	14	10	2	3	5	6
Jean Beliveau	C	53	12	26	38	22	10	6	5	11	**26**
Claude Larose	R	69	19	16	35	82	10	1	5	6	15
J.C. Tremblay	D	60	8	26	34	14	10	2	4	6	2
Gilles Tremblay	L	62	13	19	32	16	10	0	1	1	0
Claude Provost	R	64	11	13	24	16	7	1	1	2	0
Dick Duff	L	51	12	11	23	23	10	2	3	5	4
Jacques Laperriere	D	61	0	20	20	48	9	0	1	1	9
Dave Balon	L	48	11	8	19	31	9	0	2	2	6
Ted Harris	D	65	2	16	18	86	10	0	1	1	19
Leon Rochefort	R	27	9	7	16	6	10	1	1	2	4
Terry Harper	D	56	0	16	16	99	10	0	1	1	15
Jean-Guy Talbot	D	68	3	5	8	51	10	0	0	0	0
Jimmy Roberts	D	63	3	0	3	16	4	1	0	1	0
Noel Price	D	24	0	3	3	8					
Carol Vadnais	D	11	0	3	3	35	1	0	0	0	2
Rogie Vachon	G	19	0	1	1	0	9	0	0	0	0
Garry Peters	C	4	0	1	1	2					
Andre Boudrias	L	2	0	1	1	2					
Charlie Hodge	G	37	0	0	0	2					
Lorne Worsley	G	18	0	0	0	4					
Jean Gauthier	D	2	0	0	0	2					

		REGULAR SEASON					POSTSEASON				
PLAYER	POS	GP	G	A	PTS	PIM	GP	G	A	PTS	PIM
Serge Savard	D	2	0	0	0	0					
Garry Bauman	G	2	0	0	0	0					

		REGULAR SEASON					POSTSEASON				
GOALTENDER		GP	MIN	GA	SH	GAA	GP	MIN	GA	SH	GAA
Rogie Vachon	(11-3-4)	19	1137	47 (1)	1	2.48	9	555	22	0	2.38
Garry Bauman	(1-1-0)	2	120	5	0	2.50					
Charlie Hodge	(11-15-7)	37	2055	88	3	2.57					
Lorne Worsley	(9-6-2)	18	888	47	1	3.18	2	80	2	0	1.50

TORONTO 32-27-11   75   3rd   Punch Imlach
Maple Leafs

		REGULAR SEASON					POSTSEASON				
PLAYER	POS	GP	G	A	PTS	PIM	GP	G	A	PTS	PIM
Dave Keon	C	66	19	33	52	2	12	3	5	8	0
Frank Mahovlich	L	63	18	28	46	44	12	3	7	10	8
Ron Ellis	R	67	22	23	45	14	12	2	1	3	4
Bob Pulford	L	67	17	28	45	28	12	1	10	11	12
Red Kelly	D	61	14	24	38	4	12	0	5	5	2
Pete Stemkowski	C	68	13	22	35	75	12	5	7	12	20
George Armstrong	C	70	9	24	33	26	9	2	1	3	6
Jim Pappin	R	64	21	11	32	89	12	7	8	15	12
Larry Jeffrey	L	56	11	17	28	27	6	0	1	1	4
Brian Conacher	C	66	14	13	27	47	12	3	2	5	21
Eddie Shack	L	63	11	14	25	58	8	0	0	0	8
Tim Horton	D	70	8	17	25	70	12	3	5	8	25
Larry Hillman	D	55	4	19	23	40	12	1	2	3	0
Mike Walton	C	31	7	10	17	13	12	4	3	7	2
Marcel Pronovost	D	58	2	12	14	28	12	1	0	1	8
Kent Douglas	D	39	2	12	14	48					
Allan Stanley	D	53	1	12	13	20	12	0	2	2	10
John Brenneman	L	41	6	4	10	4					
Bob Baun	D	54	2	8	10	83	10	0	0	0	4
Brit Selby	L	6	1	1	2	0					
Jim McKenny	R	6	1	0	1	0					
Wayne Carleton	L	5	1	0	1	14					
Terry Sawchuk	G	28	0	0	0	2	10	0	0	0	0
Johnny Bower	G	27	0	0	0	0	4	0	0	0	2
Bruce Gamble	G	23	0	0	0	0					
Duane Rupp	D	3	0	0	0	0					
Gary Smith	G	2	0	0	0	0					
Dick Gamble	L	1	0	0	0	0					
Brent Imlach	F	1	0	0	0	0					
Al Smith	G	1	0	0	0	0					
Aut Erickson	D						1	0	0	0	2
Milan Marcetta	C						3	0	0	0	0

		REGULAR SEASON					POSTSEASON				
GOALTENDER		GP	MIN	GA	SH	GAA	GP	MIN	GA	SH	GAA
Johnny Bower	(12-9-3)	27	1431	63 (2)	2	2.64	4	183	5	1	**1.64**
Terry Sawchuk	(15-5-4)	28	1409	66	2	2.81	10	565	25	0	2.65

		REGULAR SEASON					POSTSEASON				
GOALTENDER		GP	MIN	GA	SH	GAA	\multicolumn{5}{l}{no postseason play}
Bruce Gamble	(5-10-4)	23	1185	67 (1)	0	3.39					
Gary Smith	(0-2-0)	2	115	7	0	3.65					
Al Smith	(0-1-0)	1	60	5	0	5.00					

NEW YORK Rangers   30-28-12   72   4th   Emile Francis

		REGULAR SEASON					POSTSEASON				
PLAYER	POS	GP	G	A	PTS	PIM	GP	G	A	PTS	PIM
Phil Goyette	C	70	12	49	61	6	4	1	0	1	0
Rod Gilbert	R	64	28	18	46	12	4	2	2	4	6
Don Marshall	L	70	24	22	46	4	4	0	1	1	2
Bob Nevin	R	67	20	24	44	6	4	0	3	3	2
Bernie Geoffrion	R	58	17	25	42	42	4	2	0	2	0
Harry Howell	D	70	12	28	40	54	4	0	0	0	4
Orland Kurtenbach	C	60	11	25	36	58	3	0	2	2	0
Earl Ingarfield	C	67	12	22	34	12	4	1	0	1	2
Vic Hadfield	L	69	13	20	33	80	4	1	0	1	17
Reg Fleming	L	61	15	16	31	146	4	0	2	2	11
Jim Neilson	D	61	4	11	15	65	4	1	0	1	0
Wayne Hillman	D	67	2	12	14	43	4	0	0	0	2
Arnie Brown	D	69	2	10	12	61	4	0	0	0	6
Jean Ratelle	C	41	6	5	11	4	4	0	0	0	2
Ken Schinkel	R	20	6	3	9	0	4	0	1	1	0
Bill Hicke	R	48	3	4	7	11					
Red Berenson	C	30	0	5	5	2	4	0	1	1	2
Al MacNeil	D	58	0	4	4	44	4	0	0	0	2
Rod Seiling	D	12	1	1	2	6					
Ed Giacomin	G	68	0	0	0	8	4	0	0	0	0
Larry Mickey	R	8	0	0	0	0					
Cesare Maniago	G	6	0	0	0	0					
Jim Johnson	C	2	0	0	0	0					
Bob Plager	D	1	0	0	0	0					
Doug Robinson	L	1	0	0	0	0					

		REGULAR SEASON					POSTSEASON				
GOALTENDER		GP	MIN	GA	SH	GAA	GP	MIN	GA	SH	GAA
Ed Giacomin	(30-27-11)	68	3981	173 (2)	9	2.61	4	246	14	0	3.41
Cesare Maniago	(0-1-1)	6	219	14	0	3.84					

DETROIT Red Wings   27-39-4   58   5th   Sid Abel

		REGULAR SEASON					POSTSEASON
PLAYER	POS	GP	G	A	PTS	PIM	no postseason play
Norm Ullman	C	68	26	44	70	26	
Gordie Howe	R	69	25	40	65	53	
Alex Delvecchio	C	70	17	38	55	10	
Ted Hampson	C	65	13	35	48	4	
Bruce MacGregor	C	70	28	19	47	14	
Dean Prentice	L	68	23	22	45	18	
Paul Henderson	R	46	21	19	40	10	

1966–1967

		REGULAR SEASON					POSTSEASON
PLAYER	POS	GP	G	A	PTS	PIM	no postseason play
Gary Bergman	D	70	5	30	35	129	
Andy Bathgate	R	60	8	23	31	24	
Floyd Smith	R	54	11	14	25	8	
Leo Boivin	D	69	4	17	21	78	
Howie Young	D	44	3	14	17	100	
Ray Cullen	C	27	8	8	16	8	
Bert Marshall	D	57	0	10	10	68	
Parker MacDonald	C	16	3	5	8	2	
Pete Goegan	D	31	2	6	8	12	
Murray Hall	R	12	4	3	7	4	
Doug Roberts	R	13	3	1	4	0	
Bob Wall	D	31	2	2	4	26	
Pete Mahovlich	C	34	1	3	4	16	
Bob McCord	D	14	1	2	3	27	
Alvin McDonald	L	12	2	0	2	2	
Val Fonteyne	L	28	1	1	2	0	
Bob Falkenberg	D	16	1	1	2	10	
Bryan Watson	D	48	0	1	1	66	
Roger Crozier	G	58	0	0	0	2	
George Gardner	G	11	0	0	0	0	
Hank Bassen	G	8	0	0	0	0	
Gary Jarrett	L	4	0	0	0	0	
Bart Crashley	D	2	0	0	0	2	
Warren Godfrey	D	2	0	0	0	0	
Doug Harvey	D	2	0	0	0	0	
Jimmy Peters	C	2	0	0	0	0	
Ted Taylor	L	2	0	0	0	0	
Gerry Abel	L	1	0	0	0	0	
Craig Cameron	R	1	0	0	0	0	
Real Lemieux	L	1	0	0	0	0	
Dave Rochefort	L	1	0	0	0	0	

		REGULAR SEASON					POSTSEASON
GOALTENDER		GP	MIN	GA	SH	GAA	no postseason play
Roger Crozier	(22-**29**-4)	58	3256	**182** (1)	4	3.35	
Hank Bassen	(2-4-0)	8	384	22	0	3.44	
George Gardner	(3-6-0)	11	560	36	0	3.86	

BOSTON 17-43-10 44 6th Harry Sinden
Bruins

		REGULAR SEASON					POSTSEASON
PLAYER	POS	GP	G	A	PTS	PIM	no postseason play
John Bucyk	L	59	18	30	48	12	
Hubert Martin	C	70	20	22	42	40	
Bobby Orr	D	61	13	28	41	102	
John McKenzie	R	69	17	19	36	98	
Ed Westfall	R	70	12	24	36	26	
Murray Oliver	C	65	9	26	35	16	
Wayne Connelly	R	64	13	17	30	12	
Ron Schock	C	66	10	20	30	8	

		REGULAR SEASON					POSTSEASON
PLAYER	POS	GP	G	A	PTS	PIM	no postseason play
Ron Murphy	L	39	11	16	27	6	
Ron Stewart	C	56	14	10	24	31	
Tommy Williams	C	29	8	13	21	2	
Bob Dillabough	C	60	6	12	18	14	
Ted Green	D	47	6	10	16	67	
Gilles Marotte	D	67	7	8	15	112	
Joe Watson	D	69	2	13	15	38	
Bob Woytowich	D	64	2	7	9	43	
Skip Krake	C	15	6	2	8	4	
Bill Goldsworthy	R	18	3	5	8	21	
J.P. Parise	L	18	2	2	4	10	
Wayne Rivers	R	8	2	1	3	6	
Don Awrey	D	4	1	0	1	6	
Eddie Johnston	G	34	0	1	1	0	
Dallas Smith	D	33	0	1	1	24	
Gary Doak	D	29	0	1	1	50	
Ross Lonsberry	L	8	0	1	1	2	
Gerry Cheevers	G	22	0	0	0	12	
Bernie Parent	G	18	0	0	0	2	
Glen Sather	L	5	0	0	0	0	
Ted Hodgson	R	4	0	0	0	0	
Ron Buchanan	C	3	0	0	0	0	
Nick Beverly	D	2	0	0	0	0	
Derek Sanderson	C	2	0	0	0	0	
Barry Wilkins	D	1	0	0	0	0	

		REGULAR SEASON					POSTSEASON
GOALTENDER		GP	MIN	GA	SH	GAA	no postseason play
Gerry Cheevers	(5-10-6)	22	1298	72	1	3.33	
Bernie Parent	(4-12-2)	18	1022	62 (1)	0	3.64	
Eddie Johnston	(8-21-2)	34	1880	116 (2)	0	3.70	

TEAM TOTALS

TEAM	GP	G	A	PTS	PIM	GA	SH	Per Game G	A	PIM	GA
Chicago	70	264	437	701	747	170	6	3.77	6.24	10.67	2.43
Montreal	70	202	333	535	875	188	5	2.89	4.76	12.50	2.69
Toronto	70	204	332	536	734	211	4	2.91	4.74	10.49	3.01
New York	70	188	304	492	656	189	9	2.69	4.34	9.37	2.70
Detroit	70	212	358	570	717	241	4	3.03	5.11	10.24	3.44
Boston	70	182	288	470	750	253	1	2.60	4.11	10.71	3.61
	420	1252	2052	3304	4479	1252	29	2.98	4.89	10.66	2.98

PLAYOFFS

SERIES "A"
Chicago 5, Toronto 2
Toronto 3, Chicago 1

SERIES "B"
Montreal 6, New York 4
Montreal 3, New York 1

1966–1967

Toronto 3, Chicago 1
Chicago 4, Toronto 3
Toronto 4, Chicago 2
Toronto 3, Chicago 1

TORONTO, 4–2

SERIES "C"
Montreal 6, Toronto 2
Toronto 3, Montreal 0
Toronto 3, Montreal 2 (OT)
Montreal 6, Toronto 2
Toronto 4, Montreal 1
Toronto 3, Montreal 1

**TORONTO WINS
STANLEY CUP, 4–2**

Montreal 3, New York 2
Montreal 2, New York 1 (OT)

MONTREAL, 4–0

ALL-STAR TEAMS

First Team
G — Ed Giacomin, NY
D — Harry Howell, NY
D — Pierre Pilote, CHI
C — Stan Mikita, CHI
R — Kenny Wharram, CHI
L — Bobby Hull, CHI

Second Team
G — Glenn Hall, CHI
D — Tim Horton, TOR
D — Bobby Orr, BOS
C — Norm Ullman, DET
R — Gordie Howe, DET
L — Don Marshall, NY

INDIVIDUAL TROPHY WINNERS

HART TROPHY (Most Valuable Player): Stan Mikita, CHI
LADY BYNG TROPHY (Gentlemanly Conduct): Stan Mikita, CHI
VEZINA TROPHY (Best Goaltender): Denis DeJordy, CHI; Glenn Hall, CHI
CALDER MEMORIAL TROPHY (Best Rookie): Bobby Orr, BOS
ART ROSS TROPHY (Scoring Leader): Stan Mikita, CHI
JAMES NORRIS TROPHY (Best Defenseman): Harry Howell, NY
CONN SMYTHE TROPHY (Playoff MVP): Dave Keon, TOR

Epilogue: The Great Expansion

In February 1966, the NHL made a momentous announcement. After years of planning, the league announced it would be expanding before the 1967-68 season, doubling its roster of clubs. In doing so, the loop would be breaking away from its cozy cluster of clubs, forever leaving the era of the "Original Six" behind.

After the league had trimmed down to six teams in the early 1940s, several aborted attempts at expansion had been floated. In the mid–1940s, a group from Philadelphia sought entrance but was turned down. Later, in the early 1950s, a well-heeled businessman — Jim Hendy — was nearly successful in adding a team from Cleveland to the sextet. However, like its pro sports brethren in baseball and football, the NHL was more interested in expanding westward — possibly to the moneyed markets on the West Coast. With that idea in their minds, the NHL governors voted in their June 1960 meeting to look into moving into the Los Angeles and San Francisco markets when the time was right.

Six years later, after much percolation, the NHL acted, awarding six new franchises to a variety of locales. As discussed previously, two would play in Los Angeles and San Francisco, with two more in the Midwest — in St. Louis and Minneapolis. The final two would share the region of the "Original Six"— Pittsburgh and Philadelphia. To join the club, each of the new owners ponied up over two million dollars.

The NHL's choices for the "Expansion Six," as they became known, was made on a sound basis, as each locale in the group had a solid pedigree in the minors. For instance, the Los Angeles Blades and San Francisco Seals had been members of the high-powered Western Hockey League for many years. Also, at the time of expansion St. Louis was holding a place in the NHL's own Central Pro Hockey League, a circuit which also had featured a team from Minneapolis. In addition, both Pittsburgh and Philadelphia had iced teams in the American Hockey League, the former for more than 20 years. In essence, each market was ready for the NHL.

To maintain a competitive balance, the NHL incorporated some changes to the league structure. Firstly, it created a new division for the six clubs, which were stocked by means of an expansion draft. Secondly, the league created an imbalanced schedule. In the expanded 74-game slate, each division rival would face one another 10 times, while facing each opponent in the opposing division four times each.

Even with this handicap, no team in the new expansion West Division crossed the .500 threshold in 1967-68, as the Philadelphia Flyers (31-32-11, 73) finished first, one point ahead of the Los Angeles Kings. Further behind, the rest of the division consisted of the St. Louis Blues, Minnesota North Stars, Pittsburgh Penguins and Oakland Seals. Despite this disparity, the survivor of the West Division playoffs, St. Louis, gave East Division finalist Montreal all it could handle in the Cup finals. Although the Canadiens won four straight over the Blues, each one was by a single goal, and two of the wins came in overtime.

In later years, the NHL continued to expand, adding pairs of teams throughout the early 1970s. In the last year of the decade, another group joined the circuit, as the league added four remnants from the disbanded World Hockey Association. In the 1990s, still more teams were added, eventually giving the league a total of 30—a figure which remains in effect today.

As for the "Original Six," although their unique grouping died in the summer of 1967, individually each club has continued steadfastly in the NHL. Some, like Montreal in the 1970s and Detroit in the 1990s and 2000s, have flourished, with multiple Cups to their credit. Boston, behind the efforts of a high-octane offense and triggered by a magical defenseman, won a pair of Cups in the 1970s as well. In addition, after a 40-year drought, the Rangers broke through in the mid–1990s, winning their lone Cup of the second half of the century. Although dominant in the 1960s, Chicago waited nearly 50 years for its next, but Toronto has not won a Cup since.

In intervening years, many of the hallowed records set in the first 50 years of the NHL have fallen by the wayside. Bobby Hull's goal scoring record was eclipsed in the 1970s by CPHL alum Phil Esposito, who also set a new point record. All single season goal-assist-point records were obliterated by Wayne Gretzky in the 1980s. In the 1970s, thuggism reached new heights in the NHL, as several enforcers, led by Dave Schultz, fought their way into the record book. However, several goaltending records remain intact, as no one has ever approached George Hainsworth's monumental 1928-29 season.

In telling this story of the first 50 years of the NHL, only the surface has been scratched, as only a handful of stories could be told. However, in looking at the numbers, a much more complete picture unfolds. In consulting the stats (summarized in the appendix) one can see the different trends.

For instance, the first few years of the NHL witnessed a true scoring binge, as each year the circuit averaged four goals per team, per game. In no other year (save the wartime season in 1943-44) did the league average much over three per contest, sometimes dropping well below that mark. As for assists, in the early years, the league averaged less than one helper per goal. Later, in the 1930s, assist totals caught and passed goal totals, and by the 1960s, the NHL was averaging nearly two assists per score.

The rise and fall of goal and assist totals were in direct response to the various rule changes implemented by the NHL. For instance, when rules governing forward passes were loosened, goal scoring, and correspondingly assist totals, both increased. Later, during the war years — when the strong clubs preyed on the weak, helped by the introduction of the red line — goal scoring jumped again, pulling the assist level higher as well.

In contrast, penalty minute totals varied widely over the half-century, without really following a pattern. In the early years, teams averaged over 15 minutes per game, a total which dropped significantly in years to come, no doubt caused by events such as the Bailey incident in the 1950s. Later, those totals were nearly reached again — but not consistently.

Mirroring the cumulative scoring, goaltending totals also went through a series of peaks and valleys. Starting embarrassingly high in the first couple years of the league, GAA totals dropped precipitously by the end of the decade. In some seasons, virtually every starting netminder posted totals under 1.50, with double-digit shutout totals the rule. Later, with a few exceptions, league totals remained between 2.50 and 3.00 for the duration of the half-century.

In summary, the first 50 years of the NHL — encompassing the era of the "Original Six" — introduced a fascinating sport to thousands of Canadian, and later American, fans. The physical nature of the game, played by bare-headed and -faced warriors, more fast-paced than any other sport, was unlike any other offering given to the sporting public. Flexible enough to alter its rules when necessary, the NHL continued to evolve throughout its first half-century, always striving to put a competitive, balanced product on the ice.

Building off this strong foundation, the NHL's brand of hockey continues to retain a special place in fans' hearts. Because of this fan base, its niche in North American sports remains strong as the circuit approaches the end of its first century. Strong enough — one can hope — to carry it well into its second 100 years.

Appendix: Year-by-Year Totals

Year	GP	G	A	P	PIM	GA	SH	Per Game G	A	PIM	GA
1917-18	68	342	142	484	1051	342	2	**5.03**	2.09	15.45	5.03
1918-19	54	224	102	326	812	**224**	3	4.15	1.89	15.03	4.15
1919-20	96	460	212	672	980	460	5	4.79	2.21	10.21	4.79
1920-21	96	406	171	577	965	406	4	4.23	1.78	10.05	4.23
1921-22	96	380	228	608	581	380	2	3.96	2.38	6.05	3.96
1922-23	96	313	182	495	827	313	7	3.26	1.89	8.61	3.26
1923-24	96	255	109	364	670	255	8	2.66	1.14	6.98	2.66
1924-25	180	450	235	685	1857	450	23	2.50	1.31	10.31	2.50
1925-26	252	581	215	796	2560	581	38	2.31	0.85	10.16	2.31
1926-27	**440**	879	414	1293	4594	879	85	2.00	0.94	10.44	2.00
1927-28	**440**	836	418	1254	4830	836	99	1.90	0.95	10.98	1.90
1928-29	**440**	642	382	1024	4515	642	**117**	1.46	0.87	10.26	**1.46**
1929-30	**440**	**1298**	1081	2379	5097	1298	26	2.95	2.46	11.58	2.95
1930-31	**440**	1054	973	2027	4930	1054	58	2.40	2.21	11.20	2.40
1931-32	384	955	1001	1956	4027	955	47	2.49	2.61	10.49	2.49
1932-33	432	983	1189	2172	4395	983	59	2.28	2.75	10.17	2.28
1933-34	432	1043	1180	2223	3451	1041	51	2.41	2.73	7.99	2.41
1934-35	432	1087	1420	2507	3155	1087	51	2.52	3.28	7.30	2.52
1935-36	384	831	1162	1993	3365	831	53	2.16	3.03	8.76	2.16
1936-37	384	946	1198	2141	2679	946	36	2.46	3.12	6.98	2.46
1937-38	384	972	1364	2336	2756	972	36	2.53	3.55	7.18	2.53
1938-39	336	851	1320	2170	2191	851	40	2.53	3.92	6.52	2.53
1939-40	336	838	1227	2065	2510	838	34	2.49	3.65	7.47	2.49
1940-41	336	900	1348	2248	2246	900	23	2.68	4.01	6.68	2.68
1941-42	336	1047	1622	2669	2824	1047	20	3.11	4.82	8.40	3.11
1942-43	300	1083	1648	2731	2197	1083	11	3.61	5.49	7.32	3.61
1943-44	300	1225	1747	2972	1934	1225	13	4.08	**5.82**	6.45	4.08
1944-45	300	1103	1320	2423	1908	1103	11	3.68	4.40	6.36	3.68
1945-46	300	1003	1138	2141	1779	1003	13	3.34	3.79	5.93	3.34
1946-47	360	1138	1478	2616	3121	1138	20	3.16	4.11	8.67	3.16
1947-48	360	1054	1444	2498	3642	1054	23	2.93	4.01	10.12	2.93

								Per Game			
Year	GP	G	A	P	PIM	GA	SH	G	A	PIM	GA
1948-49	360	978	1332	2310	3651	978	30	2.72	3.70	10.14	2.72
1949-50	420	1148	1664	2812	3984	1148	41	2.73	3.96	9.49	2.73
1950-51	420	1139	1638	2777	4269	1139	37	2.71	3.90	10.16	2.71
1951-52	420	1090	1630	2720	3956	1090	33	2.60	3.88	9.42	2.60
1952-53	420	1006	1513	2519	4046	1006	46	2.40	3.60	9.63	2.40
1953-54	420	1009	1555	2564	5095	1009	55	2.40	3.70	12.14	2.40
1954-55	420	1059	1650	2709	4993	1059	36	2.52	3.93	11.86	2.52
1955-56	420	1064	1692	2756	5488	1064	43	2.53	4.03	13.07	2.53
1956-57	420	1130	1820	2950	5012	1130	30	2.69	4.33	11.93	2.69
1957-58	420	1175	1943	3118	5100	1175	37	2.80	4.63	12.14	2.80
1958-59	420	1217	1986	3203	4838	1217	28	2.90	4.73	11.52	2.90
1959-60	420	1238	2060	3298	4905	1238	25	2.95	4.90	11.68	2.95
1960-61	420	1261	2078	3339	4783	1261	19	3.00	4.95	11.39	3.00
1961-62	420	1264	2089	3353	4538	1264	29	3.01	4.97	10.80	3.01
1962-63	420	1249	2022	3271	4730	1249	19	2.97	4.81	11.26	2.97
1963-64	420	1166	1912	3078	5370	1166	40	2.78	4.55	12.79	2.78
1964-65	420	1208	1955	3163	5979	1208	27	2.88	4.65	14.24	2.88
1965-66	420	1277	**2106**	**3383**	4995	1277	26	3.04	5.01	11.89	3.04
1966-67	420	1252	2052	3304	4479	1252	29	2.98	4.89	10.66	2.98
Totals	17,250	47,109	62,367	109,476	172,660	47,109	1,648	2.73	3.62	10.01	2.73

Bibliography

Articles

Addis, Fred. "The Year of the Mask: 1959–60 — A Timeline of Goalie Facial Injuries and Facemask Innovators." *The Hockey Research Journal*, 2005. Society for International Hockey Research.
Borgen, Bob, and Bob Duff. "The Complete NHL Timeline." In *Total Hockey: The Official Encyclopedia of the National Hockey League*, edited by Dan Diamond. New York: Total Sports, 1998.
Bryant, Corey. "The Gambling Scandal of 1948." *The Hockey Research Journal*, 2002. Society for International Hockey Research.
Campbell, Ken. "1954 — Canadiens and Detroit." In *Total Hockey: The Official Encyclopedia of the National Hockey League*, 2d edition, edited by Dan Diamond. New York: Total Sports, 2000.
Christman, Paul. "The Ephemeral Quakers — Pursuing Philadelphia's First NHL Franchise." *The Hockey Research Journal*, 2008. Society for International Hockey Research.
Denault, Todd. "The Ghost of Georges Vezina." *The Hockey Research Journal*, 2008. Society for International Hockey Research.
Dowbiggin, Bruce. "Hockey Sticks." *Total Hockey*, 2d ed., 2000.
Duff, Bob. "Detroit Red Wings." *Total Hockey*, 1998.
_____. "1917–26: Setting the Foundation." *Total Hockey*, 1998.
Duplacey, James. "The Changing Rink." *Total Hockey*, 1998.
Fischler, Stan. "Boston Bruins." *Total Hockey*, 1998.
_____. "Chicago Blackhawks." *Total Hockey*, 1998.
_____. "New York Americans and Brooklyn Americans." *Total Hockey*, 1998.
_____. "New York Rangers." *Total Hockey*, 1998.
_____. "1942 — Toronto and Detroit." *Total Hockey*, 2d ed., 2000.
_____. "1939 — Rangers and Boston." *Total Hockey*, 2d ed., 2000.
Fitsell, Bill. "The Rise and Fall of Ice Polo." *Total Hockey*, 2d ed., 2000.
Fitzsimmons, Ernie. "Early Pro Leagues." *Total Hockey*, 2d ed., 2000.
_____. "Minor Pro Hockey in the 1920s, 1930s and 1940s." *Total Hockey*, 1998.
Goyens, Chris. "Montreal Canadiens." *Total Hockey*, 1998.
Halligan, John. "Forward Lines." *Total Hockey*, 1998.
Hunter, Douglas. "1942–67: The Original Six." *Total Hockey*, 1998.
Katz, Sidney. "The Richard Hockey Riot." *Maclean's*, 9/17/1955 (reprinted in *Total Hockey*, 2d ed., 2000).
Kendall, Brian. "Terry Sawchuk: Great and Greatly Troubled." *Total Hockey*, 1998.

McFarlane, Brian. "The Founding of a New League." *Total Hockey*, 1998.
_____. "1917–1934: Ottawa Senators." *Total Hockey*, 1998.
_____. "Toronto Maple Leafs." *Total Hockey*, 1998.
Nieforth, Joseph. "The Penalty Shot: 70 Years of Excitement." *The Hockey Research Journal*, 1995. Society for International Hockey Research.
Owen, Gerald. "The Origins of Hockey." *Total Hockey*, 2d ed., 2000.
Picard, Thomas D. "The Pacific Coast Hockey Association." *Total Hockey*, 1998.
Wind, Herbert Warren. "Fire on the Ice." Sports Illustrated, 12/6/1954. (Reprinted in *Total Hockey*, 2d ed., 2000)
Zweig, Eric. "Hamilton Tigers" *Total Hockey*, 1998.
_____. "Montreal Maroons." *Total Hockey*, 1998.
_____. "Montreal Wanderers." *Total Hockey*, 1998.
_____. "The National Hockey Association." *Total Hockey*, 1998.
_____. "1928: Maroons and Canadiens." *Total Hockey*, 2d ed., 2000.
_____. "1926–42: The Establishment Years." *Total Hockey*, 1998.
_____. "Philadelphia Quakers." *Total Hockey*, 1998.
_____. "Pittsburgh Pirates." *Total Hockey*, 1998.
_____. "Quebec Bulldogs." *Total Hockey*, 1998.
_____. "St. Louis Eagles." *Total Hockey*, 1998.
Zukerman, Earl. "McGill University." *Total Hockey*, 2d ed., 2000.

Books

Diamond, Dan, ed. *Total Hockey: The Official Encyclopedia of the National Hockey League*. New York: Total Sports, 1998.
_____. *Total Hockey: The Official Encyclopedia of the National Hockey League*, 2d edition. Kingston, New York: Total Sports Publishing, 2000.
_____. *Total Stanley Cup*. Toronto: Dan Diamond, 2002.
Fischler, Stan, and Shirley Fischler. *The Hockey Encyclopedia*. New York: Macmillan, 1983.
Howe, Colleen, Gordie Howe, and Charles Wilkins. *After the Applause*. Toronto: McClelland and Stewart, 1989.
Macskimming, Roy. *Gordie: A Hockey Legend*. Vancouver/Toronto: Douglas and McIntyre, 1994.
McFarlane, Brian. *Best of the Original Six*. Bolton: Fenn, 2004.
_____. *50 Years of Hockey*. Toronto: Pagurian Press, 1967.
Mikita, Stan. *I Play to Win*. New York: Pocket Books, 1970.
Shea, Kevin. *Barilko: Without a Trace*. Bolton: Fenn, 2004.
Styer, Robert. *The Encyclopedia of Hockey*. South Brunswick and New York: A.S. Barnes, 1973.
Surgent, Scott Adam. *World Hockey Association, 1972–79*. Tempe: Xaler Press, 2001.
Willes, Ed. *The Rebel League*. Toronto: McClelland and Stewart, 2004.

Guides

American Hockey League Guide, 1993-94.
American Hockey League Guide, 2006-07.
Boston Bruins Media Guide, 2003-04.
Central Hockey League Guide, 1979-80.
Montreal Canadiens Media Guide, 2008-2009.
National Hockey League Guide, 1959-60, 1963-64 to 1968-69.
National Hockey League Official Guide and Record Book, 2009.
Official National Hockey Guide, 1946

Sweet Caporal Major League Hockey Guide, 1939-40.
Toronto Maple Leafs Media Guide, 2001-02.
Western Hockey League Guide, 1972-73.

Newspapers

The Hockey News
The Boston Globe
New York Times
Detroit Free Press

Unpublished Manuscripts

Wright, Marshall D. "American Hockey League, 1936–2008."
_____. "Central Hockey League, 1963–84."
_____. "Western Hockey League, 1948–74."
Websites
Hockeydb.com
Hockey-Reference.com
SIHR.com

Index

Abbott, George 221
Abbott, Reg 294
Abel, Clarence 63, 73, 82, 91, 100, 110, 120, 130
Abel, Gerry 419
Abel, Sid 176, 185, 192, 203, 206, 209, 237, 244, 251, 257, 258, 263, 264, 265, 266, 272, 275, 281, 283, 284, 295, 299, 305, 305, 338, 349, 355, 363, 373, 381, 391, 397, 409, 418
Achtymichuk, Gene 285, 329, 337, 349
Adams, Doug 269
Adams, Jack 12, 17, 35, 37, 42, 47, 56, 61, 73, 82, 92, 101, 110, 119, 129, 140, 148, 157, 169, 176, 185, 192, 194, 203, 209, 218, 227, 236, 244, 386
Adams, Stew 91, 100, 110, 116
Ahlin, Tony 168
Aiken, John 337
Ailsby, Lloyd 288
Aitkenhead, Andy 114, 120, 130, 140
Albright, Clint 262
Aldcorn, Gary 332, 340, 348, 355, 364, 365
Alexandre, Art 107, 117
Allen, George 174, 184, 194, 202, 212, 220, 236, 243
Allen, Keith 302, 311
Allen, Squee 195
Allum, Bill 193
Almas, Red 245, 280, 293
Amadio, Dave 338
Anderson, Bill 210
Anderson, Dale 329
Anderson, Doug 294
Anderson, Lorne 288
Anderson, Tom 141, 147, 156, 165, 175, 186, 195, 204, 206
Andrea, Paul 411
Andrews, Lloyd 32, 37, 42, 47
Angotti, Lou 400, 407, 411, 416
Anslow, Hub 253
Apps, Syl 153, 156, 161, 163, 165, 170, 175, 179, 184, 192, 197, 199, 201, 206, 211, 214, 237, 243, 250
Arbour, Al 302, 321, 329, 338, 347, 355, 363, 371, 380, 390, 400, 408
Arbour, Amos 17, 22, 27, 33, 37, 42
Arbour, Jack 65, 80
Arbour, John 410
Arbour, Ty 65, 73, 74, 83, 91, 100
Armstrong, Bob 278, 287, 294, 304, 313, 323, 330, 339, 346, 356, 365, 374
Armstrong, George 268, 286, 295, 303, 312, 321, 331, 340, 348, 354, 362, 371, 379, 390, 400, 408, 417
Armstrong, Murray 165, 175, 186, 195, 204, 218, 227, 236
Armstrong, Norm 380
Arundel, John 268
Ashbee, Barry 410
Ashworth, Frank 246
Asmundson, Oscar 120, 130, 138, 141, 157, 166
Atanas, Walt 230
Aubuchon, Ossie 210, 221
Aurie, Larry 73, 82, 92, 101, 110, 119, 124, 129, 140, 148, 153, 157, 161, 169, 176
Awrey, Don 393, 402, 410, 420
Ayres, Vern 98, 108, 117, 127, 138, 150

Babando, Pete 252, 259, 265, 267, 279, 295, 296
Backor, Pete 228
Backstrom, Ralph 329, 337, 345, 350, 353, 361, 370, 381, 389, 398, 406, 416
Bailey, Ace 62, 71, 77, 79, 89, 97, 107, 116, 123, 126
Bailey, Bob 303, 312, 322, 329, 338, 340
Baldwin, Doug 237, 245, 254
Balfour, Earl 286, 303, 322, 341, 347, 355, 363
Balfour, Murray 330, 337, 355, 363, 372, 380, 389, 402
Baliuk, Stan 357
Balon, Dave 357, 364, 373, 382, 389, 398, 407, 416

Barbe, Andy 277
Barilko, Bill 243, 249, 250, 261, 268, 273, 274, 276, 377
Barkley, Doug 340, 355, 381, 391, 397, 409
Barry, Ed 244
Barry, Marty 72, 90, 99, 111, 118, 130, 139, 148, 153, 157, 161, 169, 176, 186
Bartlett, Jim 312, 321, 348, 357, 365
Barton, Cliff 92, 102, 183
Bassen, Hank 315, 323, 364, 374, 382, 391, 409, 410, 419
Bastien, Aldege 237
Bathgate, Andy 296, 305, 313, 321, 331, 337, 342, 348, 350, 357, 359, 360, 364, 369, 372, 375, 382, 384, 387, 390, 392, 400, 405, 409, 419
Bathgate, Frank 297
Bauer, Bobby 158, 167, 173, 179, 182, 188, 189, 190, 191, 197, 202, 235, 244, 247, 264, 287
Bauman, Garry 417
Baun, Bob 332, 340, 348, 354, 362, 371, 380, 387, 390, 400, 408, 417
Beattie, John 99, 111, 119, 130, 139, 148, 158, 165, 167, 169, 176
Beckett, Bob 330, 339, 374, 393
Bedard, Jim 271, 280
Behling, Dick 193, 210
Beisler, Frank 157, 186
Belisle, Danny 365
Beliveau, Jean 277, 293, 300, 302, 311, 316, 318, 319, 324, 325, 329, 333, 336, 342, 343, 344, 345, 350, 353, 358, 360, 361, 367, 371, 381, 388, 394, 396, 398, 403, 405, 406, 412, 416
Bell, Billy 11, 13, 17, 27, 31, 32, 37, 42
Bell, Gordie 237, 321
Bell, Harry 246
Bell, Joe 213, 245
Bellefeuille, Pete 56, 63, 65, 82, 92
Bellemer, Andy 116
Bend, Lin 213
Benedict, Clint 12, 15, 16, 20, 21, 25, 27, 30, 31, 35, 36, 39, 41, 48, 51, 52, 54, 59, 62, 68, 70, 81, 88
Bennett, Frank 218
Bennett, Harvey 224, 229
Bennett, Max 148
Benoit, Joe 194, 204, 211, 234, 243
Benson, Bill 195, 204
Benson, Bobby 49
Bentley, Doug 184, 194, 208, 212, 214, 216, 220, 223, 236, 246, 247, 249, 254, 257, 261, 263, 270, 279, 288, 304
Bentley, Max 194, 202, 212, 233, 236, 239, 241, 246, 247, 249, 250, 254, 260, 268, 274, 276, 286, 295, 304
Bentley, Reg 212
Berenson, Red 371, 381, 389, 398, 407, 418
Bergdinon, Fred 55
Bergman, Gary 398, 409, 419
Berlinquette, Louis 11, 17, 22, 27, 32, 37, 48, 54

Berry, Ray 287
Besler, Phil 149, 176, 178
Bessone, Pete 169
Bettio, Sam 270
Beveridge, Bill 92, 99, 118, 128, 138, 146, 155, 167, 213
Beverly, Nick 420
Bibeault, Paul 195, 204, 212, 216, 219, 223, 229, 235, 246
Binette, Andre 312
Binkley, Les 404
Bionda, Jack 322, 330, 339, 346
Bittner, Dick 270
Black, Steve 267, 276, 280
Blackburn, Don 383
Blade, Hank 246, 254
Blaine, Garry 312
Blair, Andy 77, 79, 89, 97, 107, 114, 116, 126, 136, 146, 159
Blair, Chuck 261
Blair, George 277
Blake, Bob 149
Blake, Francis 138, 146
Blake, Toe 136, 147, 155, 166, 170, 172, 177, 179, 186, 188, 194, 204, 211, 216, 217, 226, 231, 233, 234, 239, 242, 253, 318, 319, 329, 336, 345, 353, 361, 370, 381, 388, 398, 406, 416
Blinco, Russ 127, 136, 145, 155, 166, 178
Bodnar, Gus 219, 223, 228, 237, 243, 254, 261, 270, 280, 288, 295, 304, 305, 313
Boesch, Garth 243, 251, 261, 268
Boileau, Marc 373
Boileau, Rene 56
Boisvert, Gilles 356
Boivin, Leo 286, 295, 303, 312, 313, 322, 330, 339, 346, 356, 365, 374, 383, 393, 401, 409, 410, 419
Boll, Frank 126, 136, 144, 146, 156, 165, 175, 186, 195, 205, 210, 220
Bolton, Hugh 268, 276, 286, 296, 303, 312, 322, 332
Bonin, Marcel 293, 302, 310, 323, 336, 344, 345, 353, 361, 371
Boone, Carl 330, 339
Boothman, George 211, 219
Bostrom, Helge 91, 100, 110, 120
Bouchard, Dick 314
Bouchard, Ed 32, 35, 37, 43, 47, 55, 62, 72, 79, 83
Bouchard, Emile 204, 211, 218, 223, 226, 231, 235, 239, 243, 247, 253, 260, 267, 277, 285, 293, 302, 311, 320
Boucher, Billy 32, 36, 41, 47, 56, 61, 64, 72
Boucher, Bobby 42
Boucher, Clarence 62, 72
Boucher, Frank 31, 63, 68, 72, 75, 77, 82, 84, 86, 91, 93, 100, 103, 105, 109, 114, 120, 121, 122, 130, 132, 140, 142, 150, 159, 168, 180, 183, 193, 200, 208, 213, 221, 221, 230, 238, 245, 252, 262, 304

Index

Boucher, Georges 12, 16, 21, 25, 27, 31, 35, 36, 39, 41, 45, 48, 53, 61, 71, 80, 81, 88, 98, 110, 128, 138, 270
Boudrias, Andre 389, 399, 416
Bourcier, Conrad 148
Bourcier, Jean 148
Bourgeault, Leo 63, 73, 82, 91, 99, 101, 117, 118, 126, 137
Bourque, Claude 177, 185, 187
Bouvrette, Lionel 213
Bower, Johnny 199, 305, 314, 331, 348, 354, 362, 367, 371, 378, 380, 387, 390, 395, 400, 403, 405, 408, 414, 417
Bowman, Ralph 128, 138, 141, 148, 158, 169, 176, 185
Bownass, Jack 337, 348, 357, 373
Boyd, Bill 63, 73, 82, 90
Boyd, Irwin 111, 141, 210, 221
Boyer, Wally 408, 416
Brackenborough, John 55
Bradley, Bart 270
Branigan, Andy 196, 205
Brayshaw, Russ 229
Brennan, Doug 109, 120
Brennan, Tom 221, 229
Brenneman, John 399, 401, 411, 417
Bretto, Joe 229
Brewer, Carl 341, 348, 352, 354, 362, 371, 375, 380, 384, 390, 400, 403
Briden, Archie 64, 65, 92
Brimsek, Frank 171, 174, 179, 183, 188, 189, 190, 192, 197, 198, 202, 206, 210, 214, 235, 239, 244, 247, 252, 255, 259, 271
Brink, Milt 160
Brisson, Gerry 381
Broadbent, Harry 16, 21, 27, 29, 31, 35, 36, 41, 48, 54, 61, 71, 79
Broda, Turk 156, 165, 175, 184, 190, 192, 197, 198, 201, 206, 211, 237, 243, 249, 251, 255, 257, 261, 265, 268, 274, 277, 286
Broden, Connie 320, 330, 337
Broderick, Len 337
Brooks, Arthur 12
Brophy, Bernie 54, 82, 92
Brophy, Frank 23
Brown, Adam 203, 210, 218, 236, 245, 246, 254, 261, 271, 279, 287
Brown, Arnie 372, 390, 401, 411, 418
Brown, Connie 176, 185, 193, 203, 209
Brown, Fred 70
Brown, George 155, 166, 177
Brown, Gerry 203, 237
Brown, Hal 238
Brown, Stan 63, 74
Brown, Wayne 304
Browne, Cecil 74
Bruce, Gordie 192, 202, 235
Bruce, Morley 12, 21, 27, 31
Bruneteau, Eddie 193, 218, 227, 236, 244, 251, 259

Bruneteau, Modere 144, 148, 157, 169, 176, 185, 192, 203, 209, 218, 227, 236
Brydge, Bill 63, 82, 90, 98, 108, 117, 127, 137, 147
Brydson, Glenn 98, 108, 116, 127, 138, 149, 150, 159, 168
Brydson, Gord 89
Buchanan, Al 261, 268
Buchanan, Mike 288
Buchanan, Ralph 262
Buchanan, Ron 420
Bucyk, John 320, 329, 339, 346, 356, 365, 374, 383, 393, 401, 410, 419
Bukovich, Tony 218, 227
Buller, Hy 218, 227, 287, 289, 296, 304
Burch, Billy 37, 42, 46, 50, 55, 62, 66, 71, 79, 90, 98, 108, 119, 120
Burchell, Fred 277, 303
Burega, Bill 322
Burke, Eddie 111, 117, 127, 137
Burke, Marty 70, 73, 79, 88, 97, 107, 117, 118, 126, 139, 150, 159, 166, 168
Burmeister, Roy 90, 98, 108
Burnett, Kelly 296
Burns, Bobby 74, 83, 91
Burns, Charlie 349, 356, 365, 374, 383
Burns, Norm 201
Burry, Bert 118
Burton, Cummy 321, 338, 349
Bush, Eddie 176, 203
Buswell, Walt 119, 129, 141, 147, 155, 166, 177, 186
Butler, Dick 254
Buttrey, Gord 220
Buzinski, Steve 207, 213
Byers, Gord 270

Caffery, Jack 312, 330, 339
Cahan, Larry 312, 322, 331, 338, 349, 373, 382, 392, 401
Cahill, Charlie 55, 64
Cain, Francis 48, 54, 56
Cain, Herb 127, 136, 146, 155, 166, 177, 182, 192, 202, 210, 216, 220, 223, 228, 235
Calladine, Norm 210, 220, 229
Callighen, Francis 73
Cameron, Billy 42, 56
Cameron, Craig 419
Cameron, Harry 10, 12, 16, 17, 22, 26, 30, 31, 37
Cameron, Scotty 213
Campbell, Clarence 308, 309
Campbell, Dave 27
Campbell, Don 220
Campbell, Earl 41, 48, 56
Campeau, Jean-Claude 218, 254, 260
Carbol, Leo 212
Carey, George 22, 28, 33, 37, 42
Carleton, Wayne 408, 417
Caron, Alain 386
Carpenter, Ed 23, 28

Carr, Al 219
Carr, Lorne 130, 137, 147, 156, 165, 175, 186, 195, 201, 211, 214, 219, 223, 228, 237
Carrigan, Gene 101, 129, 138
Carroll, Dick 12, 17, 26
Carroll, George 48, 49
Carruthers, Gordon 409
Carse, Bill 174, 184, 194, 202
Carse, Bob 184, 194, 212, 253
Carson, Bill 62, 71, 80, 81, 90
Carson, Frank 54, 62, 70, 98, 110, 119, 129
Carson, Gerry 79, 82, 88, 117, 126, 137, 155
Carter, Billy 337, 366, 371
Carveth, Joe 193, 203, 208, 209, 218, 225, 227, 236, 244, 252, 253, 260, 266, 267, 276
Cashman, Wayne 402
Ceresino, Ray 261
Chabot, Lorne 63, 67, 73, 80, 86, 89, 97, 107, 116, 126, 134, 140, 142, 144, 146, 157
Chad, John 184, 194, 236
Chadwick, Ed 322, 332, 341, 348, 354, 374
Chalmers, Bill 305
Chamberlain, Murph 165, 175, 184, 194, 205, 210, 218, 227, 234, 243, 253, 260
Champagne, Andre 380
Champoux, Bob 391
Chapman, Art 99, 111, 119, 127, 131, 134, 137, 144, 147, 156, 161, 165, 175, 186
Check, Lude 219, 229
Cheevers, Gerry 372, 410, 411, 420
Cherry, Dick 330
Cherry, Don 313
Chevrefils, Real 287, 294, 304, 313, 320, 322, 330, 333, 339, 346
Chisholm, Art 366
Chisholm, Lex 184, 192
Chouinard, Gene 71
Chrystal, Bob 304, 314
Church, Jack 175, 184, 192, 201, 205, 235
Ciesla, Hank 323, 332, 337, 348
Clancy, King 31, 36, 41, 48, 53, 60, 70, 80, 89, 97, 103, 107, 112, 115, 121, 123, 126, 132, 136, 146, 156, 166, 303, 312, 321
Clapper, Dit 72, 81, 86, 90, 99, 103, 110, 119, 131, 139, 142, 149, 158, 167, 173, 179, 182, 188, 191, 197, 202, 210, 220, 223, 228, 235, 244, 252, 259
Clark, Patrick 72
Cleghorn, Odie 15, 17, 22, 27, 32, 37, 42, 47, 54, 65, 73, 83
Cleghorn, Sprague 16, 21, 26, 27, 30, 32, 37, 40, 42, 47, 55, 64, 72, 108
Cline, Bruce 331
Clune, Wally 320
Coflin, Hugh 280
Collings, Norm 137
Collins, Gary 348
Colville, Mac 150, 159, 167, 174, 183, 193, 201, 238, 246
Colville, Neil 150, 159, 167, 174, 179, 181, 183, 188, 193, 201, 230, 238, 245, 253, 255, 262, 279, 287
Colvin, Les 259
Colwill, Les 348
Conacher, Brian 372, 408, 414, 417
Conacher, Charlie 89, 95, 97, 105, 107, 112, 115, 121, 124, 125, 132, 134, 135, 142, 144, 146, 151, 156, 165, 176, 186, 195, 261, 264, 270, 377
Conacher, Jim 237, 244, 251, 259, 261, 271, 279, 288, 296
Conacher, Lionel 54, 62, 65, 71, 79, 90, 98, 108, 116, 121, 129, 132, 136, 146, 155, 161
Conacher, Pete 288, 295, 305, 314, 315, 321, 341
Conacher, Roy 172, 173, 182, 191, 202, 235, 244, 254, 257, 261, 263, 270, 279, 288
Conn, Maitland 127, 137
Connell, Alec 45, 48, 52, 54, 61, 67, 68, 71, 80, 89, 99, 110, 118, 128, 134, 136, 155
Connelly, Bert 140, 150, 168
Connelly, Wayne 362, 374, 383, 393, 419
Connor, Harry 72, 79, 89, 90, 99
Connors, Bob 62, 82, 92
Convey, Eddie 99, 108, 118
Cook, Bill 59, 63, 72, 82, 91, 100, 103, 105, 109, 112, 114, 120, 121, 130, 132, 140, 150, 159, 180, 287, 296
Cook, Bud 111, 128, 138
Cook, Bun 63, 72, 82, 91, 100, 103, 105, 109, 120, 130, 140, 150, 158, 180
Cook, Lloyd 49
Cook, Tommy 91, 100, 109, 120, 129, 139, 149, 159, 166
Cooper, Carson 49, 55, 61, 64, 73, 82, 92, 101, 110
Cooper, Hal 230
Cooper, Joe 150, 159, 168, 178, 184, 194, 202, 220, 229, 236, 245
Copp, Bobby 211, 277
Corbeau, Bert 11, 17, 22, 27, 32, 37, 42, 47, 52, 56, 63
Corcoran, Norm 270, 294, 313, 321, 323
Cormier, Roger 57
Corrigan, Chuck 165, 195
Corriveau, Andre 303
Costello, Les 251, 261, 268
Costello, Murray 305, 313, 320, 323, 329
Cotch, Charlie 47
Cotton, Harold 54, 65, 73, 80, 83, 89, 97, 107, 116, 126, 136, 147, 157
Coughlin, Jack 12, 22, 23, 28
Coulson, D'Arcy 102
Coulter, Art 110, 120, 129, 139, 142, 150, 150, 159, 163, 168, 170, 174, 179, 181, 183, 188, 193, 201
Coulter, Tom 130
Cournoyer, Yvan 389, 398, 407, 416
Courteau, Maurice 221
Coutu, Billy 11, 17, 22, 25, 28, 32, 37, 42, 47, 56, 64

Couture, Gerry 227, 237, 245, 251, 258, 266, 276, 285, 295, 305
Couture, Rosie 83, 91, 100, 109, 120, 129, 139, 148
Cowley, Bill 138, 149, 158, 167, 170, 172, 182, 190, 191, 197, 202, 208, 210, 214, 220, 223, 228, 231, 235, 243
Cox, Abbie 88, 128, 129, 148
Cox, Danny 63, 71, 79, 89, 99, 110, 118, 128, 130
Crashley, Bart 409, 419
Crawford, Jack 167, 174, 183, 192, 202, 210, 214, 220, 228, 235, 239, 244, 252, 259, 270
Crawford, Rusty 12, 17
Creighton, Dave 259, 270, 278, 287, 294, 304, 312, 314, 321, 331, 337, 348, 354
Creighton, Jimmy 101
Cressman, Glen 329
Crisp, Terry 410
Croghan, Moe 167
Crossett, Stan 102
Crozier, Joe 354
Crozier, Roger 391, 395, 396, 398, 403, 405, 409, 410, 419
Crutchfield, Nels 137
Cude, Wilf 102, 110, 111, 124, 126, 129, 137, 148, 151, 155, 161, 166, 177, 187, 195
Cullen, Barry 322, 331, 340, 348, 356
Cullen, Brian 312, 322, 331, 340, 348, 357, 364
Cullen, Ray 411, 419
Cunningham, Bob 365, 373
Cunningham, Les 157, 184
Cupulo, Bill 228
Currie, Hugh 277
Curry, Floyd 253, 260, 267, 277, 285, 293, 302, 311, 320, 329, 337
Cushenan, Ian 332, 340, 346, 357, 391
Cyr, Claude 346

Dahlstrom, Cully 168, 170, 177, 184, 194, 212, 220, 229
Daley, Frank 82
Dame, Bunny 204
Damore, Hank 221
Damore, Nick 202
Dandurand, Leo 27, 32, 36, 41, 47, 137
Darragh, Harold 54, 65, 73, 83, 92, 99, 102, 107, 116
Darragh, Jack 12, 16, 20, 21, 25, 27, 36, 41
Davidson, Bob 136, 146, 156, 165, 175, 184, 192, 201, 211, 219, 228, 237
Davidson, Gord 213, 221
Davie, Bob 131, 139, 149
Davies, Buck 253
Davis, Bob 119
Davis, Lorne 285, 294, 302, 311, 315, 323, 356
Davison, Murray 410
Dawes, Bobby 243, 261, 268, 277

Day, Hap 47, 56, 63, 71, 80, 89, 97, 107, 116, 126, 136, 146, 156, 165, 192, 199, 201, 211, 219, 228, 237, 243, 250, 260, 268
Dea, Billy 305, 328, 338, 340, 416
Deacon, Don 158, 176, 185
DeCourcy, Bob 253
Defelice, Norm 330
DeJordy, Denis 380, 390, 399, 414, 416
Delmonte, Armand 235
Delory, Val 262
Delvecchio, Alex 276, 284, 292, 298, 302, 309, 310, 320, 328, 338, 349, 350, 355, 363, 373, 381, 391, 397, 405, 409, 412, 418
DeMarco, Ab 178, 184, 210, 211, 221, 221, 230, 238, 245
Demers, Tony 166, 186, 194, 204, 212, 222
Denis, Jean-Paul 246, 269
Denis, Lulu 268, 277
Denneny, Corbett 12, 17, 22, 26, 32, 37, 43, 63, 74
Denneny, Cy 10, 12, 16, 21, 27, 31, 35, 36, 39, 41, 45, 48, 53, 59, 60, 71, 81, 118
Denoird, Gerry 37
Desaulniers, Gerry 277, 293, 303
Desilets, Joffre 147, 155, 166, 177, 184
Desjardins, Vic 100, 109
Deslauriers, Jacques 320
Dewar, Tom 221
Dewsbury, Al 245, 251, 267, 280, 288, 295, 305, 315, 323
Dheere, Marcel 212
Diachuk, Ed 364
Dick, Harry 246
Dickens, Ernie 201, 237, 254, 261, 271, 280
Dickenson, Herb 287, 296
Dickie, Bill 203
Dill, Bob 221, 230
Dillabough, Bob 374, 382, 391, 398, 410, 420
Dillon, Cecil 101, 109, 114, 120, 130, 140, 150, 151, 159, 161, 167, 170, 174, 185
Dineen, Bill 302, 311, 320, 329, 338, 340
Dinsmore, Charles 48, 54, 62, 88
Dion, Connie 218, 227
Doak, Gary 409, 410, 420
Doherty, Frank 17
Dolson, Clarence 82, 92, 101
Donnelly, James 62
Doran, John 127, 147, 157, 169, 187
Doran, Lloyd 245
Doraty, Ken 64, 114, 116, 126, 136, 169
Dornhoefer, Gary 393, 402, 410
Dorohoy, Eddie 260
Douglas, Kent 380, 385, 390, 400, 408, 417
Douglas, Les 193, 209, 237, 245
Draper, Bruce 380
Drillon, Gordie 156, 163, 164, 170, 172, 175, 179, 181, 183, 192, 199, 201, 206, 211
Drouillard, Clare 169
Drouin, Polly 137, 147, 155, 166, 177, 186, 194
Drummond, Jim 230
Drury, Herb 54, 65, 73, 83, 92, 102

Dryden, Dave 373, 407
Duachuk, Ed 364
Dube, Giles 267, 302
Duff, Dick 312, 321, 331, 340, 347, 354, 362, 371, 379, 390, 392, 398, 401, 406, 416
Dufour, Marc 392, 401
Dugal, Jules 177
Duggan, Jack 54
Duguid, Lorne 108, 116, 127, 141, 148, 149, 158
Dukowski, Duke 64, 91, 98, 100, 117, 128, 130
Dumart, Woody 149, 158, 167, 173, 182, 188, 189, 191, 197, 202, 235, 243, 247, 252, 259, 264, 270, 278, 287, 294, 304
Duncan, Art 65, 71, 80, 89, 97, 107
Dunlap, Frank 219
Durnan, Bill 216, 218, 223, 225, 227, 231, 233, 235, 239, 240, 241, 243, 247, 254, 257, 260, 263, 265, 268, 272
Dussault, Norm 253, 260, 267, 277
Dutton, Mervyn 62, 70, 77, 81, 88, 98, 105, 108, 118, 127, 137, 147, 156, 165, 175, 186, 195, 204
Dyck, Henry 222
Dye, Babe 22, 25, 26, 28, 30, 31, 35, 37, 42, 44, 47, 56, 64, 74, 79, 97
Dyte, Jack 220

Eddolls, Frank 227, 235, 243, 253, 262, 269, 279, 287, 314
Edmundson, Garry 285, 354, 362
Egan, Pat 186, 195, 198, 204, 206, 218, 220, 225, 228, 235, 244, 252, 259, 269, 279
Ehman, Gerry 339, 348, 349, 354, 362, 390
Elik, Bo 382
Elliott, Fred 80
Ellis, Ron 390, 400, 408, 417
Emberg, Eddie 227
Emms, Hap 62, 70, 98, 108, 110, 119, 129, 138, 139, 147, 156, 165
Erickson, Aut 356, 365, 380, 390, 417
Esposito, Phil 387, 390, 399, 407, 415, 423
Evans, Claude 312, 339
Evans, Jack 262, 269, 279, 287, 304, 314, 321, 331, 337, 347, 355, 363, 372, 380
Evans, Stew 101, 119, 127, 129, 136, 146, 155, 166, 177
Ezinicki, Bill 228, 237, 243, 250, 257, 260, 265, 268, 278, 287, 314

Fahey, Trevor 401
Falkenberg, Bob 419
Farrant, Walt 220
Fashoway, Gordie 280
Faulkner, Alex 372, 382, 391
Ferguson, John 388, 398, 407, 416
Ferguson, Lorne 270, 278, 287, 313, 320, 323, 328, 338, 340, 347
Field, Wilf 157, 175, 186, 195, 205, 227, 229
Fielder, Guyle 280, 293, 304, 338
Fillion, Bob 218, 227, 235, 243, 253, 260, 267

Fillion, Marcel 229
Filmore, Tommy 101, 108, 110, 117, 131
Finney, Sid 288, 295, 305
Finnigan, Eddie 138, 149
Finnigan, Frank 41, 48, 53, 61, 70, 80, 89, 99, 107, 118, 128, 136, 138, 146, 156
Fisher, Alvin 47
Fisher, Dunc 253, 262, 269, 278, 279, 287, 294, 349
Fisher, Joe 185, 193, 203, 210
Fitzpatrick, Sandy 401
Flaman, Fern 229, 235, 244, 252, 259, 270, 276, 278, 286, 296, 303, 309, 313, 316, 322, 330, 333, 339, 342, 346, 356, 365
Fleming, Reg 354, 363, 372, 380, 390, 401, 405, 410, 411, 418
Fogolin, Lee 251, 259, 267, 276, 280, 288, 295, 305, 315, 323
Foley, Gerry 312, 331, 338
Folk, Bill 285, 293
Fonteyne, Val 356, 364, 374, 382, 392, 398, 401, 409, 419
Fontinato, Lou 314, 318, 321, 331, 335, 337, 348, 357, 364, 369, 371, 381
Forbes, Jake 22, 26, 38, 43, 47, 56, 62, 72, 79, 90, 102, 109, 118
Forsey, Jack 211
Forslund, Gus 118
Fortier, Charles 42
Foster, Harry 91, 111, 129, 141
Foster, Herb 193, 253
Fowler, Jimmy 156, 165, 175
Fowler, Norm 49
Fowler, Tom 246
Foyston, Frank 65, 74
Frampton, Bob 268
Francis, Emile 246, 254, 262, 269, 279, 288, 411, 418
Franks, Jim 158, 169, 213, 218, 221
Fraser, Archie 222
Fraser, Charles 43
Fraser, Gord 64, 74, 82, 88, 92, 102
Fraser, Harvey 229
Frederick, Ray 315
Fredrickson, Frank 64, 65, 72, 81, 83, 92, 101
Frew, Irv 127, 138, 147
Frost, Harry 174
Fryday, Bob 268, 285
Fuhr, Grant 335

Gadsby, Bill 246, 254, 261, 271, 280, 288, 295, 298, 305, 306, 314, 315, 321, 324, 331, 333, 337, 342, 348, 350, 357, 364, 373, 381, 391, 398, 403, 409
Gagne, Art 61, 69, 78, 89, 90, 99, 110
Gagne, Pierre 357
Gagnon, Johnny 95, 97, 106, 117, 126, 137, 139, 147, 154, 166, 177, 186
Gainor, Norm 72, 81, 90, 99, 109, 118, 136
Galbraith, Percy 59, 64, 72, 81, 90, 100, 111, 119, 128, 131

Index

Gallagher, John 98, 108, 116, 119, 129, 157, 165, 175
Gallinger, Don 210, 220, 235, 244, 248, 249, 252
Gamble, Bruce 349, 366, 374, 408, 409, 417
Gamble, Dick 277, 285, 293, 302, 312, 315, 320, 408, 417
Gardiner, Bert 150, 174, 195, 204, 212, 221
Gardiner, Chuck 74, 83, 91, 95, 100, 103, 105, 110, 112, 120, 121, 124, 130, 132
Gardiner, Herb 61, 66, 70, 79, 83
Gardner, Cal 238, 245, 252, 260, 268, 276, 286, 295, 304, 313, 322, 330
Gardner, George 409, 419
Gardner, Jimmy 46
Gariepy, Ray 304, 322
Garrett, Dudley 213
Gatherum, Dave 302
Gaudreault, Armand 228
Gaudreault, Leo 70, 79, 117
Gauthier, Art 61
Gauthier, Fern 221, 226, 236, 245, 251, 259
Gauthier, Jean 362, 371, 381, 389, 399, 407, 416
Gauthier, Paul 166
Gee, George 236, 246, 254, 259, 261, 265, 266, 276, 288, 295, 305
Gelineau, Jack 259, 270, 272, 278, 305
Gendron, Jean-Guy 321, 331, 337, 346, 356, 361, 365, 373, 383, 393
Geoffrion, Bernie 277, 285, 289, 293, 300, 302, 309, 311, 316, 319, 327, 329, 336, 345, 352, 353, 358, 360, 361, 367, 370, 381, 389, 418
Geran, Gerry 13, 55
Gerard, Eddie 12, 16, 21, 27, 31, 32, 36, 48, 54, 61, 67, 70, 80, 98, 108, 116, 126, 138
Getliffe, Ray 149, 158, 167, 174, 186, 194, 204, 211, 218, 226
Giacomin, Ed 411, 414, 418, 421
Giesebrecht, Gus 176, 185, 193, 203
Gilbert, Jeannot 383, 402
Gilbert, Rod 365, 373, 382, 392, 400, 411, 418
Gill, David 60, 70, 80
Gillie, Farrand 82
Girard, Kenny 332, 341, 354
Giroux, Art 117, 139, 148
Gladu, Paul 228
Glover, Fred 259, 267, 276, 285, 295
Glover, Howie 347, 363, 373, 392
Godfrey, Warren 294, 304, 313, 320, 329, 338, 349, 356, 363, 373, 383, 391, 398, 409, 419
Godin, Sammy 71, 80, 126
Goegan, Pete 338, 349, 356, 363, 373, 374, 382, 391, 398, 409, 419
Goldham, Bob 199, 201, 237, 243, 254, 261, 271, 276, 285, 293, 302, 311, 316, 320
Goldsworthy, Bill 402, 410, 420
Goldsworthy, Leroy 82, 91, 101, 119, 130, 137, 140, 147, 158, 167, 175

Goldup, Hank 184, 192, 201, 211, 213, 230, 238
Gooden, Bill 213, 221
Goodfellow, Ebbie 92, 101, 110, 119, 129, 140, 148, 151, 157, 161, 169, 176, 185, 188, 193, 203, 210, 279, 288
Goodman, Paul 163, 168, 185, 194
Gordon, Fred 65, 72
Gordon, Jackie 262, 269, 279
Gorman, Ed 48, 53, 61, 71
Gorman, Tommy 55, 79, 120, 129, 136, 145, 155, 166
Gottselig, Johnny 83, 91, 100, 109, 120, 129, 139, 149, 159, 163, 168, 177, 179, 184, 194, 212, 220, 229, 236, 246, 254
Goupile, Red 148, 155, 166, 177, 186, 194, 204, 212
Goyette, Phil 329, 336, 346, 353, 362, 371, 381, 392, 400, 411, 418
Graboski, Tony 195, 204, 212
Gracie, Bob 97, 107, 115, 127, 131, 136, 138, 145, 155, 166, 177, 178
Graham, Leth 27, 31, 37, 41, 48, 54
Graham, Teddy 74, 91, 100, 110, 120, 127, 129, 138, 141, 149, 157, 158
Grant, Benny 80, 89, 90, 97, 107, 128, 219, 221
Grant, Danny 407
Grasso, Don 244
Gravelle, Leo 242, 254, 260, 267, 276, 277
Gray, Alex 73, 80
Gray, Harrison 391
Gray, Terry 374, 389
Green, Pete 21, 27, 31, 36, 41, 48, 53
Green, Red 42, 44, 45, 46, 55, 62, 71, 81
Green, Shorty 42, 46, 55, 62, 71
Green, Ted 366, 374, 383, 393, 401, 410, 420
Gretzky, Wayne 423
Grigor, George 220
Gronsdahl, Lloyd 202
Gross, Lloyd 63, 127, 129, 131, 141
Grosso, Don 176, 185, 193, 199, 203, 209, 218, 227, 229, 236
Grosvenor, Len 71, 80, 89, 99, 109, 117
Guidolin, Aldo 296, 304, 314, 321
Guidolin, Bep 210, 220, 235, 244, 251, 259, 261, 270, 279, 288

Haddon, Lloyd 356
Hadfield, Vic 373, 383, 387, 392, 400, 411, 418
Haggarty, Jimmy 204
Haidy, Gord 267
Hainsworth, George 59, 61, 66, 68, 70, 75, 77, 79, 84, 86, 88, 95, 97, 107, 117, 126, 133, 136, 146, 155, 156, 423
Halderson, Haldor 63, 65
Haley, Len 356, 364
Hall, Bob 56
Hall, Glenn 233, 293, 311, 318, 320, 324, 325, 329, 333, 340, 342, 347, 352, 355,

358, 360, 363, 368, 369, 372, 375, 378, 380, 384, 385, 390, 394, 399, 407, 412, 413, 414, 416, 421
Hall, Joe 10, 11, 15, 17
Hall, Murray 372, 380, 390, 398, 409, 419
Hall, Wayne 365
Halliday, Milt 61, 71, 80
Hamel, Herb 97
Hamill, Red 167, 174, 183, 192, 202, 202, 212, 236, 246, 254, 261, 271, 280
Hamilton, Al 411
Hamilton, Chuck 371
Hamilton, Jack 211, 219, 237
Hamilton, Reg 146, 156, 165, 175, 184, 192, 201, 211, 219, 228, 236, 246
Hampson, Ted 354, 364, 373, 383, 391, 398, 418
Hanna, Jack 348, 357, 364, 389
Hannigan, Gord 295, 303, 312, 322
Hannigan, Pat 354, 364, 373
Hannigan, Ray 261
Hanson, Emil 119
Hanson, Ossie 168
Harmon, Glen 211, 218, 227, 231, 235, 243, 253, 260, 263, 267, 277
Harms, Johnny 220, 229
Harnott, Walt 131
Harper, Terry 381, 389, 398, 407, 416
Harrington, Hago 55, 72, 117
Harris, Billy 322, 331, 340, 347, 354, 362, 371, 379, 390, 400, 409
Harris, Fred 49
Harris, Henry 99
Harris, Ron 382, 391
Harris, Ted 389, 398, 407, 416
Harrison, Ed 252, 259, 270, 278, 279
Hart, Cecil 39, 56, 61, 69, 78, 88, 97, 106, 154, 166, 177
Hart, David 39
Hart, Wilfred 61, 65, 70, 117
Harvey, Doug 253, 260, 267, 277, 285, 289, 293, 298, 302, 306, 311, 316, 320, 324, 325, 326, 329, 333, 336, 342, 343, 346, 350, 353, 358, 361, 367, 372, 373, 375, 376, 382, 392, 419
Hassard, Bob 268, 277, 295, 303, 315
Haworth, Gord 296
Hay, Bill 355, 358, 363, 372, 380, 389, 399, 407, 416
Hay, George 64, 73, 82, 92, 101, 119, 129
Hay, Jim 293, 302, 311
Haynes, Paul 98, 108, 116, 127, 136, 139, 147, 154, 166, 177, 186, 195
Head, Don 374
Headley, Fern 47, 49
Healey, Rich 364
Hebenton, Andy 321, 331, 333, 337, 348, 357, 364, 372, 382, 393
Hebert, Sammy 12, 41
Heffernan, Frank 22
Heffernan, Gerry 204, 212, 218

Heinrich, Lionel 323
Heller, Ott 109, 120, 130, 140, 150, 159, 168, 174, 183, 193, 197, 201, 213, 221, 230, 238
Helman, Harry 36, 41, 48
Hemmerling, Tony 147, 157
Henderson, John 313, 323
Henderson, Murray 229, 235, 244, 252, 259, 270, 278287
Henderson, Paul 382, 391, 397, 409, 418
Hendrickson, Jake 339, 349, 374
Hendy, Jim 290, 423
Henry, Camille 304, 307, 314, 331, 337, 342, 348, 357, 364, 373, 382, 392, 399, 400
Henry, Gord 259, 270, 278, 291, 294
Henry, Jim 201, 238, 246, 253, 261, 287, 289, 291, 294, 304, 313
Herbert, Jimmy 49, 55, 64, 71, 72, 82, 92
Herchenratter, Art 193
Hergert, Fred 138, 147
Hergesheimer, Phil 184, 194, 203, 212, 256
Hergesheimer, Wally 287, 296, 304, 314, 321, 332, 348
Heron, Red 175, 184, 192, 204, 205
Heximer, Obs 91, 119, 137
Hextall, Bryan 159, 167, 174, 181, 183, 188, 190, 193, 197, 198, 200, 206, 207, 213, 214, 221, 238, 245, 252
Hextall, Bryan, Jr. 383
Heyliger, Vic 168, 220
Hicke, Bill 346, 354, 361, 371, 381, 389, 399, 400, 411, 418
Hicks, Henry 81, 92, 101
Hicks, Wayne 355, 363, 383, 389
Highton, Hec 220
Hildebrand, Ike 304, 305, 315
Hill, Mel 167, 172, 174, 183, 192, 204, 211, 219, 228, 237
Hiller, Dutch 168, 174, 183, 193, 202, 203, 210, 211, 221, 226, 234
Hillman, Floyd 330
Hillman, Larry 311, 320, 329, 339, 346, 356, 362, 371, 380, 390, 400, 408, 417
Hillman, Wayne 363, 372, 380, 390, 399, 401, 411, 418
Himes, Norm 62, 71, 79, 90, 98, 108, 117, 127, 137
Hirschfield, Bert 267, 277
Hitchman, Lionel 36, 41, 48, 49, 55, 64, 72, 81, 90, 100, 111, 119, 131
Hodge, Charlie 311, 337, 346, 354, 360, 362, 387, 389, 394, 399, 403, 407, 412, 416
Hodge, Ken 399, 407, 416
Hodgson, Ted 420
Hoekstra, Hec 354
Hoffinger, Val 74, 83
Hollett, Bill 126, 128, 135, 146, 149, 158, 167, 173, 182, 191, 202, 210, 214, 218, 220, 227, 231, 236
Hollingworth, Gord 314, 320, 329, 338
Holmes, Bill 57, 62, 90
Holmes, Chuck 349, 374

Index 441

Holmes, Hap 10, 12, 17, 65, 74
Holmes, Lou 110, 120
Holota, John 210, 237
Holway, Al 42, 47, 54, 56, 62, 83
Horeck, Pete 229, 236, 244, 246, 251, 258, 270, 278, 288
Horne, George 54, 62, 80
Horner, Red 80, 89, 97, 107, 114, 116, 123, 124, 126, 134, 136, 144, 146, 153, 156, 165, 172, 175, 181, 184
Horton, Tim 268, 286, 295, 303, 307, 312, 322, 331, 340, 348, 354, 362, 371, 380, 384, 390, 394, 400, 408, 417, 421
Horvath, Bronco 321, 330, 331, 339, 346, 352, 356, 358, 365, 372, 380, 382
Howard, Jack 156
Howe, Gordie 244, 251, 257, 258, 263, 264, 265, 266, 272, 273, 275, 281, 283, 284, 289, 291, 292, 298, 299, 300, 301, 307, 309, 310, 320, 324, 326, 328, 333, 338, 342, 344, 349, 350, 355, 358, 363, 367, 373, 375, 378, 381, 384, 385, 387, 391, 394, 397, 403, 409, 412, 418, 421
Howe, Syd 89, 102, 107, 118, 128, 138, 141, 148, 157, 169, 176, 185, 192, 203, 209, 218, 227, 231, 236
Howe, Vic 279, 305, 314
Howell, Harry 296, 304, 314, 321, 331, 337, 348, 357, 364, 373, 382, 392, 400, 411, 418, 421
Howell, Ron 314, 321
Hrymnak, Steve 288, 293
Huard, Rolly 97
Hucul, Fred 280, 288, 295, 305
Hudson, Ronnie 169, 185
Huggins, Al 98
Hughes, Al 98, 108
Hughes, James 92
Hull, Bobby 340, 347, 352, 355, 358, 359, 360, 363, 369, 372, 375, 376, 378, 380, 384, 387, 389, 394, 396, 399, 403, 404, 405, 407, 412, 413, 414, 415, 421, 423
Hull, Dennis 399, 407, 415
Hunt, Fred 195, 230
Hurst, Ron 322, 332
Hutchinson, Ron 365
Hutton, Bill 89, 90, 100, 102
Hyland, Harry 12, 13

Iginla, Jarome 335
Imlach, Brent 408, 417
Imlach, Punch 347, 354, 362, 371, 379, 390, 400, 408, 417
Ingarfield, Earl 349, 357, 364, 372, 382, 392, 400, 411, 418
Ingoldsby, Johnny 211, 219
Ingram, Frank 91, 100, 110
Ingram, Jack 149
Ingram, Ron 332, 380, 391, 392, 401
Ironstone, Joe 56, 71
Irvin, Dick 59, 64, 74, 83, 100, 107, 109, 115, 125, 135, 146, 156, 164, 175, 183, 194, 204, 211, 217, 226, 234, 242, 253, 260, 267, 277, 285, 293, 302, 311, 323
Irvine, Ted 393
Irwin, Ivan 293, 304, 314, 321, 338
Ivan, Tommy 251, 258, 266, 275, 284, 292, 301, 332
Iverson, Emil 120

Jackson, Art 136, 146, 156, 167, 175, 183, 191, 202, 208, 210, 220, 228
Jackson, Doug 254
Jackson, Hal 159, 168, 193, 210, 218, 227, 237, 245
Jackson, Harvey 89, 97, 105, 107, 112, 115, 121, 126, 132, 134, 135, 142, 146, 156, 161, 165, 175, 186, 195, 202, 210, 220, 264, 377
Jackson, Jack 246
Jackson, Lloyd 157
Jackson, Percy 111, 128, 140, 149
Jackson, Stan 32, 42, 47, 49, 55, 61
Jackson, Walt 117, 127, 138, 149
Jacobs, Paul 17
James, Gerry 312, 322, 331, 341, 354
Jamieson, Jim 222
Jankowski, Lou 276, 293, 305, 315
Jarrett, Doug 399, 407, 416
Jarrett, Gary 362, 419
Jarvis, Jim 92, 102, 156
Jeffrey, Larry 374, 382, 391, 398, 408417
Jenkins, Roger 97, 100, 120, 130, 137, 149, 155, 155, 157, 163, 168, 175, 178
Jennings, Bill 193, 203, 210, 218, 228
Jeremiah, Ed 109, 111
Jerwa, Frank 111, 119, 131, 138, 139
Jerwa, Joe 101, 111, 131, 147, 156, 158, 165, 175
Joanette, Rosario 227
Johansen, Bill 268
Johns, Don 364, 383, 392, 401, 407
Johnson, Al 329, 363, 373, 382
Johnson, Earl 302
Johnson, Ivan 63, 72, 82, 91, 101, 103, 109, 112, 120, 121, 130, 132, 140, 150, 159, 165
Johnson, Jim 401, 411, 418
Johnson, Norm 339, 346, 355
Johnson, Tom 254, 268, 277, 285, 293, 302, 311, 320, 324, 329, 337, 346, 350, 353, 361, 371, 381, 393, 402
Johnson, Virgil 168, 220, 229
Johnston, Eddie 383, 393, 402, 410, 411, 420
Johnston, George 203, 212, 236, 246
Johnstone, Ross 219, 228
Joliat, Aurel 37, 42, 47, 56, 61, 69, 78, 88, 95, 97, 103, 106, 112, 117, 126, 132, 137, 142, 147, 154, 166
Joliat, Rene 48
Jones, Alvin 176, 185, 203, 211
Joyal, Eddie 382, 391, 397, 408
Juckes, Bing 253, 269
Juzda, Bill 193, 201, 238, 245, 253, 261, 268, 276, 286

Kabel, Bob 357, 365
Kachur, Ed 332, 340
Kaiser, Vern 277
Kalbfleisch, Jeff 128, 138, 147, 157, 158
Kaleta, Alex 202, 236, 246, 254, 262, 269, 279
Kaminsky, Max 128, 138, 139, 149, 155
Kampman, Rudolph 165, 175, 184, 192, 201
Kane, Frank 219
Karakas, Mike 150, 160, 162, 168, 178, 185, 187, 220, 225, 229, 231, 236
Keating, Jack 108, 118, 176, 185
Keats, Duke 64, 65, 74, 83
Keeling, Butch 63, 71, 77, 82, 91, 100, 109, 120, 130, 140, 150, 159, 168
Keenan, Don 347
Keenan, Larry 372
Keller, Ralph 383
Kelly, Pete 138, 148, 157, 169, 176, 195, 205
Kelly, Red 251, 259, 266, 272, 275, 281, 284, 289, 292, 298, 301, 307, 310, 316, 320, 324, 328, 333, 338, 349, 354, 355, 362, 367, 371, 379, 390, 400, 408, 417
Kelly, Regis 136, 146, 156, 159, 165, 175, 184, 194, 205
Kemp, Stan 261
Kendall, Bill 130, 139, 150, 156, 159, 168
Kennedy, Forbes 332, 338, 349, 356, 374, 383, 393, 402, 410
Kennedy, George 9, 11, 17, 22
Kennedy, Ted 211, 219, 225, 228, 237, 243, 249, 250, 257, 260, 268, 272, 273, 274, 276, 281, 286, 295, 303, 307, 312, 316, 331
Kenny, Ernie 101, 140
Keon, Dave 362, 367, 371, 375, 376, 379, 385, 387, 390, 400, 408, 417, 421
Kerr, Dave 98, 109, 116, 127, 140, 150, 153, 159, 163, 168, 170, 174, 181, 183, 188, 190, 193
Kilrea, Brian 339
Kilrea, Hec 53, 60, 70, 80, 89, 99, 110, 118, 126, 136, 148, 157, 169, 176, 185
Kilrea, Ken 176, 185, 203, 218
Kilrea, Wally 89, 102, 108, 116, 118, 127, 141, 148, 157, 169
King, Frank 277
Kinsella, Ray 99
Kirk, Bobby 168
Kirkpatrick, Bob 213
Kitchen, Chapman 54, 65
Klein, Lloyd 81, 111, 117, 127, 137, 147, 157, 165
Klingbeil, Ernest 159
Klukay, Joe 211, 243, 250, 260, 268, 276, 286, 294, 304, 312, 313, 322
Klymkiw, Julius 349
Knibbs, Bill 401
Knott, Nick 205
Knox, Paul 312
Kopak, Russ 220
Kotanen, Dick 262, 279
Kozak, Les 371

Kraftcheck, Steve 278, 287, 296, 348
Krake, Skip 393, 410, 420
Krol, Joe 159, 174, 205
Kryzanowski, Ed 259, 270, 278, 287, 295
Kuhn, Gord 117
Kukulowicz, Aggie 296, 305
Kullman, Arnie 252, 270
Kullman, Eddie 252, 262, 279, 287, 296, 304
Kuntz, Alan 201, 238
Kurtenbach, Orland 364, 374, 393, 401, 408, 418
Kuryluk, Merv 372
Kwong, Larry 253
Kyle, Bill 269, 279
Kyle, Gus 269, 279, 283, 287

Labadie, Mike 297
Labine, Leo 287, 294, 304, 313, 322, 330, 339, 346, 356, 364, 365, 374
Labossiere, Gord 392, 401
Labovitch, Max 222
Labrie, Guy 221, 230
Lach, Elmer 194, 204, 211, 216, 217, 223, 224, 225, 226, 231, 233, 234, 239, 242, 249, 253, 255, 260, 267, 277, 283, 285, 289, 293, 302
Lacroix, Al 57
Lafleur, Roland 48
Laforce, Ernie 212
Laforge, Claude 337, 349, 364, 373, 391, 398
LaFrance, Adie 126
Lafrance, Leo 61, 70, 74
Lafreniere, Roger 382
Lalande, Hec 305, 323, 332, 338, 340
Lalonde, Newsy 11, 15, 17, 22, 25, 27, 29, 32, 62, 89, 99, 117, 126, 137
Lamb, Joe 70, 80, 81, 86, 89, 99, 108, 119, 131, 137, 138, 146, 157, 165, 169
Lamirande, J-P 245, 253, 269, 312
Lamoureux, Leo 204, 211, 218, 226, 235, 243
Lancien, Jack 246, 253, 269, 279
Lane, Myles 81, 82, 90, 131
Langelle, Pete 175, 184, 192, 201
Langlois, Al 337, 346, 354, 362, 373, 383, 391, 392, 397, 410
Langlois, Charlie 47, 55, 62, 65, 70, 73
Laperriere, Jacques 381, 389, 394, 398, 403, 407, 412, 416
Laprade, Edgar 238, 239, 245, 252, 262, 269, 272, 279, 287, 296, 305, 314
LaPrarie, Ben 159
Larochelle, Wildor 57, 61, 70, 79, 88, 95, 97, 106, 117, 126, 137, 147, 149, 159
Larose, Charles 55
Larose, Claude 381, 389, 398, 407, 416
Larson, Norm 195, 205, 246
Latreille, Phil 365
Lauder, Marty 72
Laviolette, Jack 11
Laycoe, Hal 238, 245, 254, 260, 267, 277, 278, 287, 294, 304, 308, 313, 323

Index 443

Leach, Larry 346, 356, 374
LeBrun, Al 365, 411
Leclair, Jackie 311, 320, 329
Leduc, Al 57, 61, 70, 78, 88, 97, 107, 117, 128, 130, 137
Lee, Bobby 212
Leger, Roger 221, 243, 253, 260, 267
Lehman, Hugh 64, 74
Leier, Ed 271, 280
Leiter, Bobby 383, 393, 402, 410
Lemieux, Real 419
Lepine, Alfred 56, 61, 70, 78, 88, 97, 106, 117, 126, 137, 147, 155, 166, 186
Lepine, Hec 56
Leroux, Gus 148
Lesieur, Art 79, 83, 97, 107, 147
LeSueur, Percy 42
Leswick, Jack 129
Leswick, Pete 157, 229
Leswick, Tony 238, 245, 252, 262, 269, 272, 279, 285, 292, 300, 302, 311, 323, 338
Levandoski, Joe 246
Levinsky, Alex 97, 107, 116, 126, 139, 140, 149, 159, 168, 178
Lewicki, Danny 276, 286, 296, 303, 313, 316, 321, 331, 337, 347
Lewis, Doug 243
Lewis, Herbie 82, 92, 101, 110, 119, 124, 129, 140, 148, 153, 157, 169, 176
Licari, Tony 245
Lichtenhein, Sam 10
Lindsay, Bert 13, 17
Lindsay, Ted 227, 236, 244, 249, 251, 255, 257, 258, 263, 264, 265, 266, 272, 275, 281, 283, 284, 289, 292, 298, 299, 301, 307, 309, 310, 320, 324, 326, 328, 333, 340, 344, 347, 355, 397
Liscombe, Carl 169, 176, 185, 193, 203, 208, 209, 218, 227, 236
Litzenberger, Ed 293, 303, 311, 314, 316, 323, 332, 333, 340, 347, 355, 363, 371, 373, 380, 390
Livingstone, Eddie 6, 9
Locas, Jacques 253, 260
Lockhart, Howie 22, 23, 28, 33, 42, 49
Locking, Norm 139, 150
Long, Stan 286
Lonsberry, Ross 420
LoPresti, Sam 194, 199, 203
Lorrain, Rod 148, 155, 166, 177, 186, 204
Loughlin, Clem 65, 74, 83, 139, 149, 159
Loughlin, Wilf 42
Lowe, Odie 262, 269
Lowe, Ross 270, 278, 285
Lowrey, Eddie 12, 16, 28
Lowrey, Fred 48, 54
Lowrey, Gerry 71, 80, 83, 92, 102, 110, 118
Lucas, Dave 382
Lumley, Harry 219, 222, 225, 227, 237, 245, 249, 251, 259, 267, 280, 288, 291, 296, 300, 303, 306, 307, 309, 312, 316, 322, 339, 347, 356
Lund, Pentti 244, 252, 262, 263, 265, 269, 279, 287, 294
Lunde, Len 349, 355, 363, 373, 380, 407
Lundy, Pat 237, 244, 251, 259, 280
Lynn, Vic 213, 219, 235, 243, 250, 261, 268, 278, 287, 295, 305
Lyons, Ron 100, 102

MacDonald, Kilby 183, 188, 193, 221, 230
MacDonald, Lowell 374, 382, 391, 398
MacDonald, Parker 296, 312, 331, 337, 357, 363, 373, 381, 391, 397, 409, 410, 419
Macey, Hub 201, 213, 243
MacGregor, Bruce 364, 373, 382, 391, 397, 409, 418
MacKay, Calum 245, 259, 267, 277, 285, 294, 302, 311
MacKay, Dave 194
MacKay, Dunc 64, 74, 81, 83, 90
MacKay, Murdo 235, 243, 254, 260
Mackell, Fleming 251, 261, 268, 276, 286, 287, 291, 294, 298, 304, 313, 323, 330, 335, 339, 346, 356
MacKell, Jack 21, 27
MacKenzie, Bill 120, 127, 136, 140, 155, 155, 166, 168, 178, 184
Mackey, Reg 63
Mackie, Howie 157, 169
MacMillan, John 362, 371, 380, 390, 391, 398
MacNeil, Al 322, 331, 341, 354, 371, 380, 389, 399, 407, 418
MacPherson, James 260, 277, 285, 293, 303, 311, 329
Mahaffy, John 212, 221, 227
Mahovlich, Frank 332, 340, 342, 348, 354, 362, 367, 371, 375, 378, 384, 387, 390, 394, 400, 403, 408, 412, 417
Mahovlich, Pete 409, 419
Mailley, Frank 212
Majeau, Fern 218, 227
Maki, Ron 363, 372, 380, 389, 396, 399, 407, 415
Malone, Cliff 285
Malone, Joe 10, 11, 17, 19, 22, 28, 29, 32, 37, 42, 224
Maloney, Phil 270, 277, 278, 296, 347, 355
Manastersky, Tom 277
Mancuso, Gus 166, 177, 187, 213
Maniago, Cesare 362, 381, 411, 418
Mann, Jack 222, 230
Mann, Norm 146, 175, 192
Manners, Ren 92, 102
Manson, Ray 252, 262
Mantha, Georges 79, 88, 97, 107, 117, 126, 137, 147, 154, 166, 177, 186, 195
Mantha, Sylvio 42, 47, 56, 61, 69, 78, 88, 97, 103, 107, 112, 117, 126, 137, 147, 158

Maracle, Henry 101
Marcetta, Milan 417
March, Harold 83, 91, 100, 109, 120, 129, 139, 149, 159, 168, 177, 184, 194, 202, 212, 220, 229
Marcon, Lou 349, 356, 382
Marcotte, Don 410
Mario, Frank 202, 228
Mariucci, John 194, 203, 236, 246, 254
Marker, Gus 119, 129, 136, 146, 155, 166, 175, 184, 192, 205
Markle, Jack 146
Marks, Jack 12, 13, 23
Marois, Jean 219, 305
Marotte, Gilles 410, 420
Marquess, Mark 244
Marshall, Bert 409, 419
Marshall, Don 285, 311, 320, 329, 336, 346, 353, 361, 371, 381, 392, 400, 411, 418, 421
Marshall, Willie 296, 312, 322, 348
Martin, Clare 202, 244, 252, 267, 276, 288
Martin, Frank 294, 304, 314, 323, 332, 340
Martin, Hubert 374, 391, 397, 409, 410
Martin, Jack 362
Martin, Ron 117, 127
Masnick, Paul 277, 285, 293, 302, 311, 315, 340
Mason, Charlie 140, 150, 165, 176, 178
Massecar, George 90, 98, 108
Mathers, Frank 261, 268, 286
Matte, Joe 22, 28, 33, 55, 57, 92, 212
Matz, Johnny 47
Maxner, Wayne 401, 410
Maxwell, Wally 296
Mayer, Gil 268, 303, 313, 322
Mayer, Shep 211
Mazur, Eddie 278, 286, 294, 302, 311, 332
McAdam, Sam 101
McAndrew, Hazen 205
McAtee, Jud 210, 218, 227
McAtee, Norm 244
McAuley, Ken 216, 222, 230
McAvoy, George 312
McBride, Cliff 81, 89
McBurney, Jim 295
McCabe, Stan 92, 101, 116, 127
McCaffrey, Bert 47, 56, 63, 71, 73, 83, 88, 92, 97
McCaig, Doug 203, 237, 245, 251, 259, 261, 271, 280
McCallum, Dunc 411
McCalmon, Allison 74, 102
McCartan, Jack 357, 365
McCarthy, Tom 22, 28, 329, 338, 349, 365
McCartney, Walt 117
McCool, Frank 225, 228, 231, 232, 237
McCord, Bob 393, 402, 409, 419
McCormack, John 251, 261, 268, 276, 285, 293, 302, 314
McCormick, Hugh 67
McCreary, Bill 305, 314, 338, 381

McCreary, Keith 371, 398
McCreedy, John 201, 228
McCulley, Bob 137
McCurry, Francis 54, 65, 73, 83
McDonagh, Bill 269
McDonald, Alvin 337, 346, 354, 363, 372, 380, 389, 401, 409, 419
McDonald, Bucko 141, 148, 157, 169, 175, 176, 184, 192, 199, 201, 206, 211, 219, 221, 230
McDonald, Byron 185, 227, 229
McDonald, Jack 11, 13, 15, 17, 23, 26, 27, 32, 221
McDonald, Robert 222
McDonnell, Moylan 28
McFadden, Jim 245, 251, 255, 258, 266, 276, 288, 295, 305
McFadyen, Don 120, 130, 139, 149
McFarlane, Gord 64
McGibbon, Irv 212
McGill, Jack 137, 147, 155, 202, 229, 235, 244
McGrattan, Tom 251
McGregor, Sandy 392
McGuire, Mickey 65, 73
McInenly, Bert 101, 108, 110, 118, 128, 131, 139, 149
McIntyre, Jack 270, 278, 287, 294, 305, 314, 323, 332, 338, 340, 349, 356
McKay, Doug 267
McKenney, Don 313, 322, 330, 339, 346, 352, 356, 358, 365, 374, 382, 383, 390, 392, 400, 409
McKenny, Jim 408, 417
McKenzie, John 347, 355, 364, 389, 399, 410, 411, 419
McKinnon, Alex 46, 55, 62, 72, 83
McKinnon, John 57, 65, 73, 83, 92, 102
McLaughlin, Frederic 162, 413
McLean, Fred 23, 28
McLean, Hugh 308
McLean, Jack 211, 219, 228
McLellan, John 286
McLenahan, Rollie 237
McLeod, Jackie 269, 279, 288, 297, 314
McMahon, Mike 212, 216, 218, 235, 392, 401, 411
McManus, Sammy 136, 158
McNab, Max 251, 258, 267, 276
McNabney, Sid 278
McNamara, Gerry 362
McNamara, Howard 22
McNaughton, George 23
McNeil, Gerry 254, 268, 274, 277, 285, 291, 293, 298, 300, 303, 329
McNeill, Billy 329, 338, 349, 355, 382, 391
McNeill, Stu 338, 349, 356
McReavy, Pat 174, 183, 192, 202, 203
McVeigh, Charley 64, 74, 79, 90, 98, 108, 117, 127, 137
McVicar, Jack 98, 108
Meeker, Howie 243, 247, 250, 261, 268, 276, 286, 296, 303, 331

Meeking, Harry 12, 17, 64, 65
Meger, Paul 268, 277, 285, 293, 302, 311
Meissner, Dick 356, 365, 374, 392, 401
Melnyk, Jerry 321, 355, 363, 372, 399
Menard, Hillary 305
Menard, Howie 391
Meronek, Bill 186, 212
Merrill, Horace 12, 21
Metz, Don 175, 184, 192, 199, 201, 228, 237, 243, 251, 261
Metz, Nick 136, 146, 156, 165, 175, 184, 192, 201, 228, 237, 243, 250
Michaluk, Art 254
Michaluk, John 280
Mickey, Larry 399, 411, 418
Mickoski, Nick 253, 262, 269, 279, 287, 296, 304, 314, 314, 323, 332, 338, 340, 349, 356
Migay, Rudy 268, 286, 295, 303, 312, 321, 331, 340, 348, 354
Mikita, Stan 347, 355, 359, 360, 363, 369, 372, 375, 380, 384, 387, 389, 394, 396, 399, 403, 405, 407, 412, 413, 414, 415, 421
Mikol, Jim 380, 401
Milks, Hib 54, 65, 73, 83, 92, 102, 109, 118
Millar, Al 339
Millar, Hugh 245
Miller, Bill 136, 146, 147, 155
Miller, Earl 74, 83, 91, 100, 107, 110
Miller, Jack 271, 280
Miller, Joe 68, 72, 73, 83, 92, 102
Miszuk, John 391, 407, 416
Mitchell, Bill 203, 212, 229, 391
Mitchell, Herb 49, 55
Mitchell, Ivan 22, 26, 32
Moe, Bill 230, 238, 245, 253, 262
Moffatt, Ron 119, 129, 141
Mohns, Doug 304, 313, 322, 330, 339, 346, 356, 365, 374, 383, 393, 399, 407, 415
Mohns, Lloyd 222
Molyneaux, Larry 168, 174
Mondou, Armand 79, 88, 97, 107, 117, 126, 133, 137, 147, 155, 166, 177, 186
Moore, Alfie 157, 163, 168, 176, 185
Moore, Dickie 285, 293, 300, 303, 311, 320, 329, 335, 336, 342, 343, 344, 345, 350, 352, 353, 361, 367, 371, 381, 400
Moran, Amby 61, 74
Morenz, Howie 40, 42, 45, 47, 56, 61, 68, 69, 75, 78, 88, 94, 95, 97, 103, 106, 112, 112, 117, 121, 126, 139, 149, 150, 155, 317
Morin, Pete 204
Morris, Bernie 49
Morris, Elwyn 219, 228, 237, 262
Morrison, Don 251, 259, 279
Morrison, Jim 286, 287, 295, 303, 312, 322, 331, 340, 346, 355, 364
Morrison, John 56
Morrison, Rod 251
Morrissette, Jean-Guy 389
Mortson, Gus 241, 243, 250, 261, 268, 272, 273, 276, 286, 295, 300, 305, 314, 323, 326, 332, 340, 349
Mosdell, Kenny 205, 227, 235, 243, 254, 260, 267, 277, 285, 293, 302, 307, 311, 316, 320, 332, 337, 346
Mosienko, Bill 203, 212, 220, 229, 231, 236, 239, 246, 254, 261, 270, 279, 288, 295, 305, 314
Motter, Alex 139, 149, 169, 176, 185, 193, 203, 209
Mowers, Johnny 193, 204, 208, 210, 214, 245
Muldoon, Pete 64
Muloin, Wayne 391
Mummery, Harry 10, 12, 17, 23, 27, 33, 38
Munro, Dunc 48, 54, 61, 70, 81, 87, 88, 98, 107
Munro, Gerry 48, 56
Murdoch, Murray 63, 72, 82, 91, 100, 109, 114, 120, 130, 140, 150, 159
Murphy, Hal 294
Murphy, Ron 296, 305, 314, 321, 331, 340, 347, 355, 363, 372, 380, 389, 397, 409, 410, 420
Murray, Allan 127, 138, 147, 157, 165, 176, 186
Murray, Leo 117
Murray, Mickey 88
Murtin, Hubert 419
Myles, Vic 213

Nattrass, Ralph 246, 254, 261, 271
Neilson, Jim 382, 392, 401, 411, 418
Nesterenko, Eric 286, 295, 303, 312, 322, 332, 340, 347, 355, 363, 372, 380, 389, 399, 407, 415
Neville, Mike 47, 56, 98
Nevin, Bob 341, 348, 362, 371, 379, 390, 392, 400, 411, 418
Newman, John 101
Nicholson, Al 323, 330
Nicholson, Ed 251
Nicholson, Ivan 168
Nighbor, Frank 12, 16, 20, 21, 25, 27, 31, 35, 36, 40, 41, 43, 48, 50, 52, 53, 57, 61, 70, 80, 89
Noble, Reg 10, 12, 17, 22, 26, 32, 37, 39, 42, 47, 48, 54, 62, 74, 82, 92, 101, 110, 116, 119
Nolan, Paddy 32
Norris, Jack 402
Norris, James 282
Northcutt, Lorne 81, 88, 98, 108, 112, 116, 121, 127, 134, 136, 145, 155, 166, 178
Nykoluk, Mike 332

Oatman, Russ 61, 65, 70, 81, 82
O'Brien, Ellard 323
O'Connor, Herb 204, 211, 217, 226, 234, 242, 249, 252, 255, 262, 269, 279
Odrowski, Gerry 364, 374, 382
O'Flaherty, Peanuts 195, 205
O'Grady, George 13
Olesevich, Dan 373

Oliver, Harry 59, 63, 72, 81, 90, 99, 111, 119, 131, 137, 147, 157
Oliver, Murray 338, 355, 363, 365, 374, 383, 393, 401, 410, 419
Olmstead, Bert 261, 270, 277, 280, 285, 293, 298, 302, 309, 311, 318, 319, 324, 327, 329, 337, 348, 354, 362, 371
Olson, Dennis 338
O'Neil, Peggy 131, 139, 149, 158, 195, 204
O'Neill, Tom 219, 228
O'Ree, Willie 334, 335, 339, 365
Orlando, Jimmy 158, 169, 185, 190, 193, 203, 208, 210
Orr, Bobby 419, 421
Oulette, Eddie 149
Oulette, Gerry 365
Owen, George 81, 90, 99, 111, 119

Paille, Marcel 338, 349, 357, 365, 373, 383, 401
Palangio, Pete 61, 74, 79, 159, 168
Palazzari, Aldo 220, 221
Palmondon, Gerry 254
Panagabko, Ed 323, 330
Papike, Joe 194, 203, 229
Pappin, Jim 390, 400, 408, 414, 417
Parent, Bernie 410, 411, 420
Pargeter, George 243
Parise, J.P. 410, 420
Parkes, Ernie 48
Parsons, George 156, 165, 175
Patrick, Frank 24, 67, 139, 148
Patrick, Lester 24, 58, 63, 67, 72, 73, 82, 91, 100, 109, 120, 130, 140, 150, 159, 167, 174, 180, 215
Patrick, Lynn 140, 150, 159, 167, 174, 181, 183, 193, 198, 200, 206, 207, 213, 214, 215, 238, 269, 278, 286, 294, 304, 313
Patrick, Muzz 168, 174, 181, 183, 193, 238, 313, 382
Patterson, George 63, 70, 71, 78, 90, 98, 108, 127, 131, 138, 141
Patterson, Pat 117
Paul, Butch 398
Paulhaus, Rollie 57
Pavelich, Marty 251, 258, 267, 276, 284, 292, 302, 310, 320, 329
Payer, Evariste 11
Pearson, Mel 357, 373, 383, 401
Peer, Bert 185
Peirson, Johnny 244, 252, 259, 270, 278, 287, 294, 304, 322, 330, 339
Pelletier, Marcel 280, 383
Pennington, Cliff 362, 374, 383
Perreault, Bob 320, 349, 383
Perreault, Fern 253, 269
Peters, Frank 101
Peters, Garry 399, 411, 416
Peters, Jimmy 234, 243, 252, 254, 259, 266, 275, 288, 295, 302, 305, 398, 409, 419
Pettinger, Eric 80, 81, 89, 99

Pettinger, Gord 120, 129, 141, 148, 157, 167, 169, 173, 183
Phillips, Bill 88
Phillips, Charlie 212
Phillips, Merlyn 54, 61, 70, 81, 88, 98, 108, 116, 117
Picard, Noel 398
Piche, Clement 32
Picketts, Hal 127
Pidhirny, Harry 339
Pike, Alf 183, 193, 201, 213, 238, 245, 357, 364
Pilote, Pierre 323, 332, 340, 347, 355, 358, 360, 363, 372, 375, 380, 384, 385, 389, 394, 399, 403, 407, 412, 415, 421
Pilous, Rudy 340, 347, 355, 363, 372, 380
Pitre, Didier 11, 15, 17, 22, 27, 32, 37
Plager, Bob 401, 411, 418
Plamandon, Gerry 260, 267, 278, 235
Plante, Jacques 233, 291, 294, 303, 311, 318, 320, 324, 325, 326, 327, 329, 333, 335, 337, 342, 343, 344, 346, 350, 352, 354, 358, 362, 369, 371, 375, 376, 378, 381, 392, 401
Plaxton, Hugh 116
Pletsch, Charles 28
Podolsky, Nels 259
Poeta, Tony 288
Poile, Bud 211, 219, 237, 243, 251, 254, 255, 258, 261, 269, 270
Poile, Don 311, 338
Poirier, Gordie 187
Polich, John 183, 193
Poliziani, Dan 347
Popein, Larry 314, 321, 331, 337, 348, 357, 365
Popiel, Poul 410
Portland, Jack 126, 137, 139, 149, 158, 167, 174, 183, 184, 194, 194, 204, 211
Powell, Ray 279
Powers, Eddie 31, 42, 47, 56
Pratt, Babe 150, 159, 168, 174, 183, 193, 201, 211, 213, 219, 223, 228, 231, 237, 244
Pratt, Jack 99, 111
Prentice, Dean 296, 304, 314, 321, 331, 337, 348, 357, 358, 364, 372, 382, 383, 393, 401, 409, 410, 418
Prentice, Doc 219
Price, Jack 288, 295, 305
Price, Noel 341, 348, 357, 365, 374, 407, 416
Primeau, Joe 71, 80, 89, 95, 97, 105, 107, 112, 115, 124, 126, 132, 135, 146, 264, 276, 286, 295, 377
Pringle, Ellie 98
Prodgers, Goldie 22, 28, 32, 37, 42, 47
Pronovost, Andre 329, 337, 346, 353, 362, 365, 374, 382, 383, 391, 398
Pronovost, Claude 323, 329, 346
Pronovost, Marcel 267, 276, 285, 293, 302, 310, 320, 329, 338, 342, 349, 350, 355, 358, 364, 367, 373, 382, 391, 397, 408, 417

Provost, Claude 320, 336, 346, 353, 362, 370, 381, 389, 398, 403, 406, 416
Prystai, Metro 254, 261, 270, 275, 283, 284, 292, 302, 311, 314, 320, 323, 328, 338
Pudas, Al 63
Pulford, Bob 331, 340, 348, 354, 362, 371, 379, 390, 400, 408, 414, 417
Purpur, Cliff 138, 203, 212, 220, 227, 229
Pusie, Jean 97, 107, 130, 139, 147

Quackenbush, Bill 210, 218, 227, 236, 244, 247, 251, 255, 259, 263, 270, 278, 281, 287, 294, 298, 304, 313, 322
Quackenbush, Max 278, 288
Quenneville, Leo 91
Querrie, Charles 37
Quilty, John 194, 197, 204, 243, 252, 254
Quinn, Mike 22

Radley, Yip 99, 155
Raglan, Clare 276, 288, 295
Raleigh, Don 221, 252, 262, 265, 269, 279, 287, 296, 304, 313, 321
Ramsay, Beattie 71
Ramsay, Les 229
Randall, Ken 10, 12, 17, 22, 26, 32, 37, 43, 46, 55, 62
Ranieri, George 330
Ratelle, Jean 364, 373, 382, 392, 400, 411, 418
Ravlich, Matt 383, 399, 407, 416
Raymond, Armand 166, 187
Raymond, Paul 126, 137, 177
Rayner, Charlie 195, 205, 238, 241, 246, 253, 262, 263, 269, 272, 279, 281, 288, 297
Read, Mel 246
Reardon, Ken 194, 204, 235, 239, 243, 247, 253, 255, 260, 263, 267, 272
Reardon, Terry 174, 183, 192, 204, 211, 235, 244
Reaume, Marc 312, 322, 331, 341, 348, 354, 356, 364, 389
Reay, Billy 218, 227, 234, 241, 242, 253, 260, 267, 277, 285, 293, 340, 347, 389, 399, 407, 415
Redahl, Gord 347
Redding, George 49, 55
Regan, Bill 91, 101, 117
Regan, Larry 330, 333, 339, 346, 348, 354, 362
Reibel, Earl 301, 310, 320, 325, 328, 338, 340, 346
Reid, Dave 296, 312, 322
Reid, Gerry 259
Reid, Gord 157
Reid, Reg 47, 56
Reigle, Ed 278
Reinikka, Ollie 63
Reise, Leo 28, 32, 37, 43, 62, 71, 79, 90, 91, 236, 245, 246, 251, 259, 267, 272, 276, 281, 285, 296, 304

Rheaume, Herb 52, 57
Richard, Henri 320, 329, 335, 336, 342, 345, 350, 352, 353, 361, 367, 371, 378, 381, 384, 388, 398, 405, 406, 416
Richard, Maurice 211, 215, 216, 217, 223, 224, 225, 226, 231, 233, 234, 239, 241, 242, 247, 253, 255, 260, 263, 265, 267, 272, 274, 277, 281, 285, 289, 291, 293, 298, 300, 302, 307, 308, 309, 311, 316, 317, 318, 319, 324, 327, 329, 333, 335, 337, 346, 353
Richardson, Dave 392, 401, 407
Riggin, Dennis 356, 382
Riley, Jack 119, 126, 137, 149
Riley, Jim 64, 65
Ring, Bob 410, 411
Riopelle, Rip 253, 260, 267
Ripley, Vic 83, 91, 100, 109, 119, 120, 130, 131, 138, 140
Ritchie, Dave 12, 13, 17, 23, 27, 48, 57
Ritson, Alex 230
Rittinger, Alan 220
Rivers, Gus 88, 97, 107
Rivers, Wayne 374, 393, 401, 410, 420
Roach, John 30, 32, 37, 42, 45, 47, 56, 63, 71, 77, 82, 91, 101, 105, 109, 119, 121, 129, 141
Roach, Mickey 22, 26, 28, 32, 37, 43, 46, 56, 62
Robert, Claude 277
Roberts, Doug 409, 419
Roberts, Jimmy 389, 398, 407, 416
Roberts, Moe 55, 109, 128, 288
Robertson, Earl 158, 165, 175, 179, 186, 195, 205
Robertson, Fred 107, 126, 129
Robertson, George 254, 260
Robinson, Doug 390, 399, 400, 411, 418
Robinson, Earl 81, 88, 108, 116, 127, 136, 146, 155, 166, 178, 186
Roche, Des 98, 116, 118, 128, 137, 138, 141
Roche, Earl 98, 116, 118, 119, 128, 138, 141
Roche, Ernie 277
Rochefort, Dave 419
Rochefort, Leon 365, 383, 389, 399, 407, 416
Rockburn, Harvey 92, 95, 101, 118
Rodden, Eddie 64, 71, 74, 81, 101
Rolfe, Dale 357
Rollins, Al 268, 273, 277, 281, 286, 295, 305, 307, 315, 323, 332, 357
Romnes, Elwin 100, 110, 120, 129, 139, 149, 151, 159, 162, 168, 175, 178, 186
Ronan, Skene 16
Ronson, Len 364
Ronty, Paul 252, 259, 270, 278, 287, 296, 304, 311, 314
Ross, Art 13, 37, 49, 55, 63, 72, 90, 99, 110, 118, 130, 158, 167, 173, 202, 210, 220, 228
Ross, Jim 287, 296
Rossignol, Roland 218, 227, 237
Rothschild, Sam 48, 54, 62, 72, 73
Roulston, Rolly 148, 157, 169

Rousseau, Bobby 362, 371, 376, 381, 388, 398, 405, 406, 412, 416
Rousseau, Guy 311, 330
Rousseau, Rollie 294
Rowe, Bobby 49
Rowe, Ron 253
Rozzini, Gino 228
Ruelle, Bernie 218
Runge, Paul 100, 111, 127, 137, 147, 149, 155, 166
Rupp, Duane 383, 400, 408, 417
Rupp, Pat 391
Russell, Church 238, 245, 253

Sabourin, bob 286
St. Laurent, Dollard 277, 285, 293, 302, 311, 320, 329, 337, 347, 355, 363, 372
Samis, Phil 251, 268
Sanderson, Derek 410, 420
Sandford, Ed 252, 259, 270, 278, 287, 291, 294, 304, 307, 313, 321, 323
Sands, Charlie 116, 126, 139, 149, 158, 167, 174, 186, 194, 204, 211, 221
Sasakamoose, Fred 305
Sather, Glen 420
Saunders, Ted 128
Savage, Tony 137, 139
Savard, Serge 417
Sawchuk, Terry 267, 273, 276, 281, 283, 285, 289, 291, 293, 298, 302, 306, 309, 311, 316, 323, 330, 338, 349, 350, 356, 364, 368, 374, 382, 384, 391, 395, 400, 403, 408, 409, 414, 417
Schaefer, Joe 357, 365
Schaefer, Paul 160
Scherza, Charles 221, 230
Schinkel, Ken 357, 364, 373, 383, 392, 418
Schmidt, Clarence 221
Schmidt, Jackie 210
Schmidt, Joe 221
Schmidt, Milt 158, 167, 173, 181, 182, 188, 189, 190, 191, 202, 235, 244, 247, 252, 259, 264, 270, 278, 281, 286, 289, 294, 304, 313, 322, 330, 339, 346, 356, 365, 383, 393, 401, 410
Schnarr, Werner 49, 55
Schock, Ron 393, 401, 410, 419
Schriner, David 137, 144, 147, 151, 153, 156, 161, 165, 175, 184, 192, 197, 199, 201, 211, 228, 237, 256
Schultz, Dave 423
Sclisizzi, Enio 245, 251, 259, 267, 285, 295
Scott, Ganton 37, 42, 43, 48
Scott, Laurie 65, 73
Seibert, Earl 109, 120, 130, 140, 142, 149, 150, 151, 159, 161, 168, 170, 178, 179, 184, 188, 194, 197, 202, 206, 212, 214, 220, 223, 227, 229, 237
Seiling, Rod 380, 392, 400, 411, 418
Selby, Brit 400, 408, 412, 417
Selke, Frank 104

Senick, George 296
Shack, Eddie 348, 357, 362, 364, 371, 380, 390, 400, 408, 417
Shack, Joe 213, 230
Shannon, Chuck 186
Shannon, Gerry 128, 138, 139, 149, 155, 167
Shaughnessy, Tom 91
Shay, Norm 49, 55, 56
Shea, Pat 110
Sheppard, Frank 74
Sheppard, Johnny 65, 73, 79, 90, 98, 108, 117, 130, 131
Sherf, John 148, 158, 169, 176, 218
Shero, Fred 253, 262, 269
Sherritt, Gordon 219
Shewchuk, Jack 174, 183, 192, 202, 210, 229
Shibicky, Alex 150, 159, 167, 174, 183, 193, 200, 238
Shields, Al 71, 80, 89, 102, 108, 118, 128, 136, 146, 157, 158, 166
Shill, Jack 126, 139, 146, 156, 165, 168, 178
Shill, William 210, 235, 244
Shore, Eddie 64, 68, 72, 81, 90, 99, 103, 111, 112, 114, 119, 121, 122, 123, 131, 132, 139, 142, 149, 151, 158, 167, 170, 174, 179, 183, 186
Shore, Hamby 12
Shores, Aubrey 102
Siebert, Al 54, 61, 70, 81, 87, 98, 108, 120, 130, 131, 139, 149, 151, 154, 161, 166, 170, 177
Simmons, Don 326, 330, 339, 347, 356, 366, 371, 378, 380, 390, 411
Simon, Cullen 210, 218, 227, 229
Simon, Thain 245
Simpson, Cliff 245, 251
Simpson, Joe 55, 62, 72, 79, 90, 98, 117, 127, 137
Sinclair, Reg 279, 287, 293
Sinden, Harry 419
Singbush, Alex 195
Skilton, Raymond 13
Skinner, Alf 12, 17, 48, 49, 55
Skinner, Jim 310, 320, 328
Skov, Glen 267, 276, 285, 292, 302, 310, 323, 332, 340, 347, 355, 362
Sleaver, John 306, 332
Sloan, Tod 251, 261, 276, 286, 295, 303, 312, 321, 324, 331, 340, 347, 355, 363
Slobodian, Peter 195
Slowinski, Eddie 253, 262, 269, 279, 287, 296
Sly, Darryl 408
Smart, Alex 212
Smeaton, Cooper 102
Smilie, Don 131
Smith, Al 408, 417
Smith, Alex 48, 54, 61, 70, 80, 89, 99, 110, 118, 119, 131, 137
Smith, Alf 16
Smith, Art 71, 80, 89, 99
Smith, Brian 338, 356, 364
Smith, Carl 218

Smith, Clint 159, 167, 174, 179, 183, 193, 200, 213, 216, 220, 223, 229, 236, 246
Smith, Dallas 356, 365, 374, 410, 420
Smith, Dalton 218
Smith, Des 167, 177, 183, 184, 192, 202
Smith, Don 22, 269
Smith, Floyd 313, 330, 364, 382, 391, 397, 409, 419
Smith, Gary 408, 409, 417
Smith, Glen 280
Smith, Kenny 228, 235, 244, 252, 259, 270, 278
Smith, Norm 108, 141, 144, 148, 153, 158, 161, 169, 176, 219, 227
Smith, Reg 48, 53, 61, 70, 81, 87, 98, 108, 116, 127, 136, 145, 151, 158, 165, 175, 186, 195
Smith, Rodger 54, 65, 73, 83, 92, 102
Smith, Sid 243, 250, 261, 268, 274, 276, 281, 286, 289, 295, 303, 312, 316, 322, 331, 341
Smith, Stan 183, 193
Smith, Stu 195, 204
Smith, Tom 23
Smith, Wayne 416
Smrke, Stan 329, 337
Smylie, Rod 26, 32, 37, 41, 47, 56
Smythe, Art 97
Smythe, Conn 62, 71, 79, 89, 104, 377
Solinger, Bob 286, 296, 303, 312, 356
Somers, Art 91, 100, 109, 114, 120, 130, 140
Sonmor, Glen 305, 314
Sorrell, John 101, 110, 119, 129, 140, 148, 157, 165, 169, 175, 186, 195
Sparrow, Emory 49
Spence, Gordon 56
Spencer, Irv 357, 364, 373, 383, 391, 398, 409
Speyer, Chris 42, 47, 128
Spooner, Andrew 92
Spring, Jesse 43, 47, 54, 63, 79, 83, 90, 92
Sproule, Harry 22
Stackhouse, Ted 32
Stahan, Frank 227
Staley, Al 262
Stanfield, Fred 399, 407, 416
Stanfield, John 408
Stankiewicz, Ed 302, 320
Stanley, Allan 262, 269, 279, 287, 296, 305, 314, 314, 323, 330, 339, 348, 354, 358, 362, 367, 371, 380, 390, 400, 408, 412, 417
Stanley, Barney 74
Stanowski, Wally 184, 192, 197, 201, 228, 237, 243, 250, 262, 269, 279
Stapleton, Pat 374, 383, 407, 412, 416
Starr, Harold 89, 99, 108, 117, 118, 127, 140, 150
Starr, Wilf 117, 129, 141, 148
Stasiuk, Vic 271, 276, 280, 285, 293, 302, 311, 322, 330, 339, 346, 356, 363, 365, 373, 382
Steele, Frank 101
Stein, Phil 184

Stemkowski, Pete 390, 400, 408, 417
Sterner, Ulf 401
Stevens, Phil 13, 32, 55
Stevenson, Doug 229, 230, 236
Stewart, Bill 162, 168, 177
Stewart, Charles 49, 55, 64
Stewart, Gaye 201, 211, 214, 233, 237, 239, 243, 251, 254, 255, 261, 270, 276, 287, 293, 296, 303
Stewart, Jack 176, 185, 193, 203, 209, 214, 233, 236, 239, 245, 247, 251, 255, 259, 263, 267, 280, 288
Stewart, Ken 203
Stewart, Nels 52, 54, 57, 59, 61, 70, 80, 87, 93, 98, 108, 119, 130, 139, 147, 153, 156, 158, 165, 175, 186
Stewart, Ron 295, 303, 312, 322, 331, 340, 348, 354, 362, 371, 379, 390, 400, 410, 420
Stoddard, Jack 288, 296
Strain, Neil 296
Strate, Gord 329, 338, 349
Stratton, Art 357, 391, 408
Strobel, Art 222
Stuart, Billy 26, 32, 37, 42, 47, 49, 55, 64
Stuart, Herb 65
Sullivan, Barry 251
Sullivan, Frank 268, 296, 315, 324
Sullivan, George 270, 278, 287, 294, 314, 323, 331, 337, 348, 357, 364, 382, 392, 400
Summerhill, Bill 166, 177, 186, 205
Suomi, Al 160
Sutherland, Bill 381
Sutherland, Max 111
Sweeney, Bill 357

Talbot, Jean-Guy 311, 320, 329, 337, 346, 354, 361, 371, 375, 381, 389, 398, 407, 416
Tamer, James 248
Tatchell, Spence 213
Taylor, Billy 184, 192, 201, 211, 237, 241, 244, 248, 249, 252, 253, 401
Taylor, Bob 90
Taylor, Cyclone 6, 25
Taylor, Harry 243, 261, 288
Taylor, Ralph 74, 82, 83, 91
Taylor, Ted 401, 411, 419
Teal, Skip 313
Teno, Harvie 176
Tessier, Orval 311, 323, 365
Thibeault, Larry 227, 235
Thomas, Cy 251, 254
Thompson, Cliff 202, 259, 308
Thompson, Ken 13
Thompson, Paul 63, 72, 82, 91, 101, 109, 120, 129, 139, 149, 151, 159, 168, 170, 178, 184, 194, 202, 212, 220, 229
Thompson, Percy 28, 32
Thompson, Rhys 187, 211
Thompson, Tiny 77, 81, 90, 93, 100, 103, 105, 111, 114, 119, 122, 131, 139, 142, 144, 149,

151, 153, 158, 163, 167, 170, 171, 174, 177, 185, 189
Thoms, Bill 116, 126, 136, 144, 146, 151, 156, 165, 175, 177, 184, 202, 212, 220, 229
Thomson, Bill 176, 218
Thomson, Jimmy 237, 243, 250, 260, 268, 276, 281, 286, 289, 295, 303, 312, 322, 331, 340
Thorsteinson, Joe 118
Thurier, Fred 195, 205, 230
Timgren, Ray 261, 268, 276, 286, 296, 313, 315
Tobin, Bill 91, 109
Tomson, Jack 176, 186, 195
Toppazzini, Jerry 294, 304, 305, 314, 320, 323, 330, 339, 346, 356, 365, 374, 383, 393
Toppazzini, Zellio 259, 270, 278, 279, 288, 332
Touhey, Bill 70, 80, 89, 99, 111, 118, 128
Toupin, Jacques 220
Townsend, Art 64
Trainor, Wes 262
Trapp, Bob 64, 74
Traub, Percy 64, 74, 82
Tremblay, Gilles 361, 370, 381, 389, 398, 406
Tremblay, J.C. 354, 362, 371, 389, 398, 406, 416
Tremblay, Marcel 177
Tremblay, Nil 227, 235
Trottier, Dave 81, 88, 98, 108, 116, 127, 136, 146, 155, 166, 176
Trudel, Louis 130, 139, 149, 159, 162, 168, 177, 186, 195
Trudell, Rene 238, 245, 252
Tudin, Connie 204
Turlick, Gord 357
Turner, Bob 320, 329, 337, 346, 354, 362, 372, 380
Turner, Joe 204
Tustin, Norm 201
Tuten, Aud 203, 212

Ullman, Norm 320, 328, 338, 349, 355, 363, 373, 378, 381, 387, 391, 396, 397, 403, 405, 409, 418, 421

Vachon, Rogie 416
Vadnais, Carol 416
Vail, Melville 82, 91
Van Impe, Ed 416
Vasko, Elmer 332, 340, 347, 355, 363, 372, 380, 384, 389, 394, 399, 407
Vezina, Georges 10, 11, 15, 17, 22, 27, 32, 37, 39, 40, 42, 45, 48, 51, 57
Villemure, Gilles 392
Vokes, Eddie 100
Voss, Carl 63, 80, 119, 120, 128, 129, 138, 147, 155, 167, 168

Waite, Frank 101
Wakely, Ernie 381

Walker, Jack 65, 74
Wall, Bob 398, 409, 419
Walsh, James 62, 70, 79, 81, 88, 98, 105, 108, 116
Walton, Bobby 218
Walton, Mike 408, 417
Ward, Don 340, 356
Ward, Jimmy 70, 80, 98, 88, 108, 116, 127, 136, 145, 155, 166, 177
Wares, Eddie 159, 169, 176, 185, 193, 203, 209, 236, 246
Warwick, Bill 213, 221
Warwick, Grant 201, 206, 213, 221, 230, 238, 245, 252, 259, 267
Wasnie, Nick 74, 88, 97, 107, 117, 128, 138
Watson, Bryan 389, 399, 409, 419
Watson, Harry 205, 209, 236, 243, 250, 260, 268, 274, 276, 286, 295, 303, 312, 314, 323, 332
Watson, Jim 391, 398, 409
Watson, Joe 402, 420
Watson, Phil 150, 159, 167, 174, 181, 183, 193, 198, 200, 206, 207, 213, 218, 230, 238, 245, 252, 321, 331, 337, 348, 357, 374, 383
Webster, Aubrey 102, 136
Webster, Chick 269
Webster, Don 219
Weiland, Cooney 81, 86, 90, 99, 111, 118, 128, 129, 140, 142, 149, 158, 167, 174, 182
Wentworth, Cy 74, 83, 91, 100, 109, 116, 127, 136, 142, 146, 155, 166, 177, 187
Westfall, Ed 374, 383, 393, 401, 410, 419
Wetzel, Carl 398
Wharram, Kenny 288, 305, 323, 347, 355, 363, 372, 380, 389, 394, 399, 407, 415, 421
Wharton, Len 230
White, Moe 235
White, Sherm 246, 269
White, Tex 54, 65, 73, 79, 83, 92, 102
Whitelaw, Bob 193, 203
Wiebe, Art 120, 139, 150, 159, 168, 178, 184, 194, 203, 212, 220
Wilcox, Archie 88, 98, 108, 116, 127, 131, 138
Wilder, Archie 193
Wilkins, Barry 420
Wilkinson, John 221
Williams, Andy 393
Williams, Burr 129, 138, 139, 158
Williams, Tommy 374, 383, 401, 410, 420
Wilson, Bob 306
Wilson, Cully 20, 22, 26, 27, 32, 37, 64
Wilson, Don 166, 177
Wilson, Gord 313
Wilson, Hub 109
Wilson, Jerry 329
Wilson, Johnny 267, 276, 285, 292, 301, 311, 323, 332, 338, 349, 354, 362, 364, 373
Wilson, Larry 267, 285, 293, 305, 324
Wilson, Lefty 302, 322, 339
Wilson, Wally 252
Winkler, Hal 63, 64, 68, 72

Index

Wiseman, Eddie 119, 129, 140, 147, 148, 156, 165, 175, 183, 186, 190, 191, 202
Witiuk, Steve 288
Woit, Benny 276, 285, 293, 302, 311, 323, 332
Wojciechowski, Steve 227, 245
Wood, Alex 157
Wood, Robert 279
Worsely, Lorne 321, 331, 365, 389, 405, 296, 298, 314, 338, 349, 357, 373, 383, 396, 399, 407, 412, 416
Worters, Roy 55, 65, 73, 79, 84, 88, 90, 95, 99, 103, 109, 112, 118, 128, 132, 138, 147, 157

Woytowich, Bob 401, 410, 420
Wycherly, Ralph 195, 205
Wylie, Bill 279

Yackel, Ken 347
Young, Doug 110, 119, 129, 141, 148, 158, 169, 176, 186, 195
Young, Howie 364, 374, 378, 382, 390, 419

Zeidel, Larry 285, 293, 305
Zeniuk, Ed 311
Zoborosky, Martin 229
Zunich, Rudy 219

www.ingramcontent.com/pod-product-compliance
Lightning Source LLC
Chambersburg PA
CBHW051202300426
44116CB00006B/413